BESIDE THE OCEAN

BESIDE THE OCEAN

Coastal Landscapes at the Bay of Skaill, Marwick, and Birsay Bay, Orkney

Archaeological Research 2003–2018

DAVID GRIFFITHS, JANE HARRISON AND MICHAEL ATHANSON

With contributions by

Diane Alldritt, Steven P. Ashby, Colleen E. Batey, Justine Bayley, Roger C. Doonan, James Graham-Campbell, Vicki Ewens, Amanda K. Forster, Derek Hall, Derek Hamilton, Birgitta Hoffmann, Michael J. Hughes, Anthony M. Krus, Richard Jones, Helen Lewis, Alexandre Lucquin, Ingrid Mainland, Dawn McLaren, Fiona McGibbon, Tom Muir, Rebecca A. Nicholson, Susan Ovenden, Caroline Paterson, Jean-Luc Schwenninger, and Cecily Webster

Foreword by

Andrew Greig

OXBOW | books
Oxford & Philadelphia

Published in the United Kingdom in 2019 by
OXBOW BOOKS
The Old Music Hall, 106–108 Cowley Road, Oxford, OX4 1JE

and in the United States by
OXBOW BOOKS
1950 Lawrence Road, Havertown, PA 19083

Hardcover Edition: ISBN 978-1-78925-096-1
Digital Edition: ISBN 978-1-78925-097-8 (epub)

A CIP record for this book is available from the British Library

Library of Congress Control Number: 2019931261

Typeset in India by Versatile PreMedia Services. www.versatilepremedia.com

For a complete list of Oxbow titles, please contact:

UNITED KINGDOM
Oxbow Books
Telephone (01865) 241249
Email: oxbow@oxbowbooks.com
www.oxbowbooks.com

UNITED STATES OF AMERICA
Oxbow Books
Telephone (800) 791-9354, Fax (610) 853-9146
Email: queries@casemateacademic.com
www.casemateacademic.com/oxbow

Oxbow Books is part of the Casemate Group

*Front cover: The Bay of Skaill, from north, August 2010; showing East Mound excavation to left/centre;
Snusgar Mound (centre); St Peter's Kirk (right) © University of Oxford.*
Back cover: The East Mound longhouse, from north, 2010 © University of Oxford.

Contents

Online archive: DOI 10.5287/bodleian:w4AYn24wk

Foreword

In another life I would have been an archaeologist, drawn to immersion in the land, trying to make the past present that we might understand both better. It is a pursuit at once imaginative and evidence-based. It is good life-work and heart-work and brain-work.

A long time ago I did two digs, at Strathallan in Perthshire and Mavis Grind in Shetland. Both deeply memorable – sore knees, companionship and solitude; above all, spending hours, days, weeks outdoors in one place, entering into it. I first went to Orkney straight from that summer digging in Shetland, and as a result I still think of it as green, kindly and *Sooth*. Within a day I knew I wanted to be involved in Orkney for the rest of my life.

For nearly thirty years I have spent some months of each year on Orkney Mainland. From the start I have been drawn by that sharp northern light, the sky-reflecting water around and within, the unexpected greenness and fertility of a largely treeless landscape, the resulting sense of openness and release, the healing context of living surrounded by elementals.

And of course the archaeology, so ever-present and visible. Standing stones, stone circles, chambered tombs, Skara Brae, Norse longhouses and the Viking cathedral in Kirkwall, the still-emerging wonders of Ness of Brodgar, the remnants and markers of two World Wars. Nowhere else is the past so present.

Some of my dearest friends live there. I proposed to my partner in sight of Skara Brae. We married in Stromness. Our ashes are to be scattered over the beach at Skaill. There is something particular and universal about that curving, windy, sandy bay, the sea in front and the signs of ancient and present human habitation behind, as though right here is where human time and deep time intersect.

The study reported upon here is like none other I know of. It pulls together many excavations, a multiplicity of sites, markers and human stories, landscape, deep time and folk history. It is the science of archaeology raised to a humanist level. In attending to detail within a wider vision, it arouses wonder at what we know and what we don't, what we have been and what we are, and our all-encompassing context of history lived among sea and land and sky.

Andrew Greig

With thanks to Margaret and Paul

This publication is affectionately and respectfully dedicated to two people who sadly are no longer with us, but who in their own generous ways contributed more perhaps than they knew, and whose loss is deeply felt:

Edna Brass (1923–2007), farmer, of Midstove, Sandwick, Orkney.

G. Knight Boyer, MSc (Oxon) (Lt. Col. USAF rtd.) (1937–2009), archaeologist, of Great Chesterton, Oxfordshire.

We are most grateful to the renowned poet, musician, novelist and landscape writer Andrew Greig for contributing the foreword, a homage to his own Orkney. It says all that need be said.

Preface

I have picked up a few curious things from the shore of the great ocean of time (G. Mackay Brown)

The title of this monograph recalls two inspiring but very different contributions to imagining and understanding the past. One was written in Orkney, the other in Oxford. The first of these, from which the quotation above is taken, is George Mackay Brown's *Beside the Ocean of Time*. Published in 1994, it is in part a fictional story of an Orkney island community facing great and terrible change during the middle decades of the 20th century. A gentle, poor, but balanced and happy community on the isle of 'Norday' is largely swept away in a few short years by the transient but irresistible imperatives of war, and by the intrusions of outside political events seemingly well beyond the daily concerns of the islanders. Ironically it was Norday's greatest natural advantage – its coastal plain of soft, fertile cultivable land – which proved to be its downfall, when it was requisitioned and cleared for airfield construction. A few human and physical remnants survived the sudden and brutal onslaught of change, and these serve to remind the reader that we only truly know the value of what we possess when we have lost it.

The second work of inspiration referenced in the title is Barry Cunliffe's *Facing the Ocean*, an archaeological text published by Oxford University Press in 2001. In it, Cunliffe raises his perspective above the myriad of individual site reports and articles, many dominated by geographical and period particularism, to set out a narrative about the peoples of early Western Europe and their relationship with the Atlantic Ocean: the vast, connecting (and to them, unbounded) sea that lay to the west of everything. The common heritage of Oceanic Europe is a fascinating and far-reaching theme. Undermined and marginalised by the territorial historical narratives of Britain, France, Spain and other countries, it deserves to be rehabilitated as a way of understanding patterns of long-term contact and long-distance change – the *longue durée* with which scholars of the Mediterranean have long been familiar. Orkney is positioned at the meeting of the eastern, northern and western sea-roads. The Atlantic, a factor common to the North Africans, Iberians, Bretons, Britons and Irish as also to the Scandinavians, was and remains the bringer of weather, danger, beauty, wealth, strangers and new ideas.

George Mackay Brown's writing is widely acknowledged as a peerless rendition of the magical beauty of the Orkney islands and their characterful tapestry of everyday life. He was born in, lived in, and wrote about, the small West Mainland town and ferry port of Stromness. Arriving at its natural harbour of Hamnavoe provided for me, as with so many other visitors and incomers, my first experience of Orkney. I first came to Orkney at Easter, 1985, as a trainee archaeologist, participating in a three-week excavation at the Earl's Bu, Orphir, one of the great earldom sites mentioned in *Orkneyinga Saga*. When I stepped off the car-ferry 'St Ola' onto Stromness Pier as a fresh-faced and inexperienced young student archaeologist, I did not imagine that Orkney would become such an important and recurrent part of my life. The Orphir excavation was a life-changer in many ways for me, not least because we broke up our days of digging with field-trips. I was astonished by the wonderfully-preserved and dramatically-situated ancient monuments I saw then for the first time in Orkney: the wonders of Rousay and Hoy, and on Mainland, the spectacular cluster of monuments in the Stenness/Brodgar complex including the stalled cairn by the water's edge at Unstan; the spectacular chambered cairn of Maeshowe, and the dramatic stone circles of Stenness and Brodgar.

The road which leads from Brodgar westwards towards the Bay of Skaill is unforgettable. A winding single-track follows the outline of the northern edge of the Loch of Skaill, with clumps of cotton grass growing along its banks. Starkly outlined between loch, sea and sky are the pointed roofs and crow-step gables of Skaill House, the historic residence of the Lairds of Breckness. Close by Skaill House is the Neolithic settlement and World Heritage Site of Skara Brae. In 1985 the modern visitor centre had not yet been built, and visitors were still allowed to climb down into the structures and explore the passages between them. Seen from the tops of their walls, the almost unbelievable clarity and preservation of this tight cluster of stone-age houses, with walls, doorways, furniture and hearths intact, set a young would-be archaeologist's mind racing. How big is this settlement? Are there any others undiscovered nearby? How (incredibly!) do you get to become the person responsible for researching and excavating a place like this? Another wild, stormy afternoon on the Brough of Birsay, the small tidal island at Orkney's north-western extremity, revealed complexities of Pictish and Norse archaeology such as I had never previously imagined. Buildings were built on top of, out of, within and conjoined to each other, forming a vast three-dimensional puzzle, half-eaten by the sea. The distinctive outlines of Norse longhouses, with central passageways and side-benches, lie on the slope of the Brough with their lower ends pointing towards the sea. The knowledge and insight required to make sense of such three-dimensional complexities seemed privileged and remote to me at that time, but is something I have striven for since then.

My own regular participation in excavations in Orkney ceased for a period in the 1990s due to the exigencies of finishing a PhD thesis and getting a job. A period in commercial professional archaeology kept me away from the Northern Isles, but a move back into academia at the end of that decade opened up new possibilities, and indeed responsibilities, for instigating funded research. Part of my new role included teaching and developing courses in Landscape Archaeology, and this was easily and happily combined with an interest in landscape methods and prospection, continuing from my commercial career experiences. A week's holiday in Orkney in glorious early summer weather in 2002 brought these factors unexpectedly together. Walking along Birsay Links, which was at that moment a green, tussocky sea of wild flowers, the question arose – how much is there yet to know about the hidden archaeology of this landscape? And how easily could that knowledge be procured with relatively easily-available geophysical survey techniques which, at that time, had been little practised on a large scale in Orkney? Could the results of such an endeavour, concentrating in particular on the soft, sandy landscapes surrounding the bays, help archaeologists and conservationists better to respond to the ever-present forces of coastal and marine erosion? The following day, a similar walk around the Bay of Skaill rapidly took on the guise of a field recce – which areas could be surveyed? Which doors needed to be knocked upon and landowners spoken to? A seed had been planted.

Yet these landscapes should not be described as if they are purely the arena and plaything of the distant, scientifically-minded researcher, arriving with a van-load of computers and forensic equipment in order to test complex and abstruse hypotheses. These are inhabited, deep, old landscapes, full of folklore, history and the everyday life of many generations. Warfare, sand quarrying, fishing, ploughing and livestock husbandry have all left, and in some cases continue to leave, their mark. Getting to know the local communities of Sandwick and Birsay has been integral to forming this narrative, and little could have been achieved without their consent and help, which was given freely and with the best of humour. The project which resulted from that initial welter of thoughts in 2002 is laid out here. It is not the final answer to understanding the past of these landscapes by any means, but I think undeniably it is an important contribution. Inevitably, new research will come along in future and enhance, probably change, indeed possibly contradict, the conclusions presented here. However I will welcome that. If future researchers derive as much inspiration, stimulation and absorption from knowing and studying these landscapes as I have done, they will be happy people.

David Griffiths
September 2018

Acknowledgments

The Birsay-Skaill Landscape Archaeology Project began in 2003. Throughout it has been hosted and supported in-kind by the University of Oxford (Department for Continuing Education) to which is due immense gratitude for its contributions to working space, staff time and financial administration.

The field and analytical work that form the basis of this monograph were made possible by the funds, hard work and personal commitment of a large number of institutions, organisations and individuals:

The initial grant that allowed the 2003 field season to take place was provided by Orkney Islands Council Reserve Fund (now the Archaeology Fund), which continued to award grants to the project throughout its fieldwork seasons. It is a matter of great pride to us that the research presented here was directly supported by the citizens of Orkney. The Orkney Archaeologist, Julie Gibson, has been a source of advice, encouragement and information throughout.

The project was also supported throughout by Historic Scotland (now Historic Environment Scotland), including annual grants from its archaeology fund, support for scientific dating through SUERC (funding all of the radiocarbon dates) and a generous publication grant towards this monograph. A number of Historic Scotland personnel have helped with advice and assistance along the way since 2003, notably Allan Rutherford and Olwyn Owen, NW Area Team Monuments Inspectors; Rona Walker, Collections Manager; Noel Fojut, formerly Senior Inspector; Richard Welander, Head of Conservation; and Lisa Brown, Manager for Archaeology and World Heritage. Above all, the support, constructive criticism and sound advice of Rod McCullagh, Head of Archaeology until 2016, has been critical to the success of this project.

The Orkney Museum (Tankerness House) contributed advice on finds, assisting with their accession and transport to Edinburgh, and helped with public outreach. The friendly jovial presence of the late Anne Brundle, a frequent visitor to the excavations, is noted with appreciation and sadness at her untimely passing in 2011. Subsequently, help and assistance has been given by Gail Drinkall. We are also grateful to the staff of AOC at Loanhead for conserving and facilitating specialist access to the finds.

We were privileged to receive numerous site visits from experienced specialists in Northern Isles archaeology: Beverley Ballin-Smith, Professor Chris Morris, Dr Alex Sanmark, Dr James Barrett, Dr Caroline Wickham-Jones, and Dr Barbara E. Crawford, who keeps a home in Birsay and who also took part in the digging. The late William P. L. Thomson, Sarah-Jane Gibbon and James Irvine provided welcome advice on medieval and local history.

David Griffiths wishes to record his thanks to the British Academy and Leverhulme Trust, which jointly awarded him a Senior Research Fellowship in 2014–15 in order to work on completing this project. This fellowship year enabled a great deal of vital progress to be made. In addition, a substantial amount of the cost of artefact illustration was met by an award from the Strathmartine Trust, to which gratitude is due. The Hunter Trust made a generous grant to the production costs of this monograph.

The scope and potential of the project have been immeasurably enhanced through the support and generosity of a number of private individuals, most of whom are, or were, participants in the Oxford University International Summer School for Michigan State and Northwestern universities, USA. Pre-eminent amongst these are Margaret Hight and Paul Thompson, who themselves love Orkney and visited the project several times. Bruce and Carol Hallenbeck and Susan and Bruce Lessien donated generously to project funds and also made the trip north to join us on site. Nick Kelne, Cyndi and Al Milano, Caroline Markham, Alvin Shulman, Helen Cunningham, Gail and Sandra Grove, and Kay Gribble also deserve great thanks for their contributions. Their donations were handled by the US Office of Oxford University in New York. In addition, the project received most generous personal donations from Dr Donald Adamson of Edinburgh and Mr Graeme Ferrero of Surrey.

No landscape archaeology project would be viable without access to land for fieldwork. The project wishes to record its thanks to the following landowners and farmers: Bruce Moar, Jack Fraser and Hamish Flett (Birsay Bay); Sheena Hay (Marwick); Tom Stevenson and Barbara Lawrence with their late father Willie Stevenson, Stanley Garson, Major Malcolm Macrae, Stewart Davidson, Ann and Tony Poke, and Charlie Irvine (Bay of Skaill). Most of all, the generosity, friendship and support of Edna, Freddie, Pauline and Michael Brass, upon whose land most of the excavations took place, is acknowledged with lasting gratitude. We are also very grateful to the late Robert Meldrum and his wife Liz, of Seaview, who provided us with the use of their garage perched above the Bay as a comfortable and electrically-equipped site hut.

Many local people helped the project. Nick and Barbara Morrison of Smoogro, Orphir, have been constant supporters in every way. Laraine Jones, warden of the Birsay School Hostel, was a great help in managing accommodation for field teams. Davie and Ann Davidson, proprietors of the Barony Hotel, Birsay, gave an unfailing welcome to our appreciative (and only occasionally boisterously behaved) students, and looked after our visitors with true Orcadian hospitality. The late Freddie Isbister, proprietor of the shop in Quoyloo, was a good-humoured daily provider of cakes, drinks and sundries to the teams, as well as food, boxes, pallets, petrol and storage bags to the project. Every field season we were delighted to make a group visit to the Orkney Brewery in Quoyloo at the invitation of Andrew Fulton, Head Brewer. The logo of this award-winning business adorns the official project T-shirt, and we were made most hospitably welcome by the makers of 'Dark Island', 'Raven Ale', 'Red McGregor', and 'Skull Splitter'. William Shearer of Kirkwall generously provided loan of equipment. The staff of the Skara Brae Visitor Centre, and the caretakers of the public toilet block at the Bay of Skaill, which provided an essential facility to our field teams, are also valued friends of the project.

The teams that undertook the fieldwork and post-excavation work were composed of local and non-local volunteers, specialists, and students from several universities (Oxford, Glasgow, Bradford, Aberdeen, Cambridge, University College London, University College Dublin, and the University of the Highlands and Islands). Some of these were on official placements, including three participants from Bradford, whereas others were volunteers seeking to build up their field experience.

From its inception the project was directed by David Griffiths, assisted by Matthew Edgeworth (2004 season) and Jane Harrison (2005–11 seasons). Jane Harrison has also co-managed the post-excavation campaign and provided essential support and input to every area of the project. Survey control and geomatic support was provided by Tony Johnson (2003 season); Susan Ovenden (2004–2007 seasons); and by Michael Athanson (2008 season onwards). The soil flotation and wet-sieving systems were set up by Neil Wigfield, continued by Susan Hanshaw, and taken over for the crucial 2010 season by Diane Alldritt. Finds supervision was undertaken throughout by Katherine Hamilton and Fay Pendell was in charge of daily site photography.

The field teams were:

(2003) David Griffiths, Tony Johnson, Sean Johnson.

(2004) David Griffiths, Margaret Andrews, Andrew Beverton, Knight Boyer, Jon Cluett, Debbie Day, Matthew Edgeworth, Andrew Ferrero, Katherine Hamilton, Susan Hanshaw, Jane Harrison, Chris Hornig, Alex Johnson, Patsy Jones, Helen Lewis, Lorraine Lindsay-Gale, Fay Pendell, Karen Selway-Richards, Neil Wigfield, Robert Sims, Ruth Garner and Nicola Adams.

(2005) David Griffiths, Jane Harrison, Margaret Andrews, Andrew Beverton, Knight Boyer, Andrew Ferrero, Katherine Hamilton, Susan Hanshaw, Chris Hornig, Helen Lewis, Fay Pendell, Robin Newsome, Julie and Richard Morrey.

(2006) David Griffiths, Jane Harrison, Donald Adamson, Margaret Andrews, Andrew Beverton, Knight Boyer, Marijke de Haas, Andrew Ferrero, Katherine Hamilton, Susan Hanshaw, Chris Hornig, Helen Lewis, Fay Pendell, Tereza Rejskova and Ondrej Tichy.

(2007) David Griffiths, Jane Harrison, Donald Adamson, Margaret Andrews, Andrew Beverton, Knight Boyer, Marijke de Haas, Andrew Ferrero, Katherine Hamilton, Susan Hanshaw, Gill Hey, Chris Hornig, Vix Hughes, James Irvine, Helen Lewis, Fay Pendell, Susan Stalinski, Matt Ginnever, Ben Morton and Geoff Morley.

(2008) David Griffiths, Jane Harrison, Donald Adamson, Lynn Amadio, Margaret Andrews, Mike Athanson, Ruth Barber, Andrew Beverton, Knight Boyer, Katy Chalmers, Barbara Crawford, Andrew Ferrero, Wayne Easton, Marijke de Haas, Katherine Hamilton, Susan Hanshaw, Gill Hey, Chris Hornig, Vix Hughes, Helen Lewis, Kenny Macrae, Fay Pendell, Susan Stalinski, Vanessa Robinson, Kym Thornhurst and Ellen Røyrvik.

(2009) David Griffiths, Jane Harrison, Mike Athanson, Andrew Ferrero and Katherine Hamilton.

(2010) David Griffiths, Jane Harrison, Donald Adamson, Diane Alldritt, Lynn Amadio, Åsmund Asberg, Margaret Andrews, Mike Athanson, Ruth Barber, Andrew Beverton, Pauline Brass, Katy Chalmers, Carmen Guenca-Garcia, Barbara Crawford, Andrew Ferrero, Wayne Easton, Charlene Geddes, Kenneth Green, Tricia Hallam, Katherine Hamilton, Jane Kershaw, Helen Lewis, Kenny Macrae, Eileen O'Donovan, Fay Pendell, Roelie Reed, Tricia Ryan, Hilary Wallner, Neil Wigfield, Mags Williams, Andy Walsh and Conny Wylie.

(2011) David Griffiths, Jane Harrison, Mike Athanson, Katherine Hamilton, Tristan Johnston.

In terms of recording, analysis and illustration, the project could not have been completed without the expertise of the contributors. Site survey, together with the maps, GIS and spatial plots are the work of Michael Athanson. Artefact illustration was undertaken by Alan Braby, the production of site plans by Alison (Floss) Wilkins, and the artefact photography is the work of Ian Cartwright of the Institute of Archaeology, University of Oxford. The soil micromorphology slides were made by Julie Boreham of Earthslides, Cambridge. Derek Hall and Michael J. Hughes (Chapter 20) record their thanks to George Haggarty, Koen de Groote, the late Alan Vince, Cormac McSparron, Ann Bouquet-Lienard, Elisabeth Leclerc and Fabienne Ravoire (INRAP) for discussions regarding the provenance of the glazed and coarse ware pottery.

We are profoundly grateful to Rachel Barrowman for helping edit this volume and prepare it for publication, and to its academic reviewer, a senior academic specialist within North Atlantic Viking Archaeology.

List of contributors

David Griffiths, Jane Harrison, Michael Athanson, Jean-Luc Schwenninger (University of Oxford)

Steven P. Ashby, Alexandre Lucquin (University of York)

Colleen E. Batey, Derek Hamilton, Richard Jones, Anthony M. Krus (University of Glasgow)

Roger C. Doonan (University of Sheffield)

Vicki Ewens (Museum of London Archaeology)

Amanda K. Forster (Dig Ventures)

James Graham-Campbell (University College London)

Helen Lewis (University College Dublin)

Ingrid Mainland, Cecily Webster (University of the Highlands and Islands, Orkney College)

Fiona McGibbon (University of Edinburgh)

Dawn McLaren (AOC Scotland)

Tom Muir (Orkney Museum)

Rebecca A. Nicholson (Oxford Archaeology)

Susan Ovenden (Rose Geophysics, Orkney)

Diane Alldritt, Justine Bayley, Derek Hall, Birgitta Hoffmann, Michael J. Hughes, Caroline Paterson (Independent researchers or contractors)

List of figures

List of tables

Abbreviations used in text

GIS	Geographic Information System
GPR	Ground-Penetrating Radar
GPS	Global Positioning System
GUARD	Glasgow University Archaeological Research Division
HF	Hydrogen Fluoride
ICPS	Inductively-Coupled Plasma Spectrometry
OCGU/ORCA	Orkney College Geophysics Unit, later part of Orkney Research Centre for Archaeology
ON	Old Norse
OS	Ordnance Survey
OSL	Optically-Stimulated Luminescence
NISP	Number of Identified Specimens
NLS	National Library of Scotland
NMS	National Museums of Scotland
PVC	Polyvinyl Carbonate
RCAHMS/RCAMS	Royal Commission on the Ancient [and Historical] Monuments of Scotland
SM	Scheduled (Ancient) Monument
SUERC	Scottish Universities Environmental Research Centre
XRF	X-ray fluorescence

1

Introduction

David Griffiths

Orkney: Landscape and history

Orkney (or the Orkney Isles) is an archipelago off the north coast of Scotland (Fig. 1.1), with a population of *c.* 21,000 inhabiting 20 of around 70 islands and skerries. The topography of the central and largest island, Mainland (ON *Hrossey*, probably 'Horse Island'), together with many of the outlying isles, is predominantly agricultural and rolling. The upper slopes of the hills and some inland bogs remain the province of heather and gorse, with peaty soils conferring a brownish, purplish hue contrasting with the lush green of the lower-lying farmland. On Orkney's west-facing coasts, towering sandstone sea-cliffs meet the Atlantic, their wall interrupted by bays and inlets backed by areas of windblown sand, wetland and links. Towns and villages are few, and are mostly clustered around harbours, whereas farms and crofts are predominantly dispersed in the landscape.

Orkney has been inhabited since Mesolithic peoples moved north after the end of the last Ice Age. The remarkable *floruit* of Neolithic Orkney is seen in its exceptionally well-preserved ritual and funerary monuments, which are distributed throughout the islands, but occur in their greatest concentration along the spine of land between the inland Mainland lochs of Stenness and Harray, including the megalithic rings of Brodgar and Stenness, the spectacular chambered cairn of Maeshowe, and the complex of buildings and other structures on the Ness of Brodgar. Across the archipelago, Neolithic and Bronze Age cairns, brochs of the Iron Age, together with settlements of the Pictish, Viking and medieval periods, may be seen dotting the landscape, either as fenced, gated and signposted guardianship monuments, or (more numerously) as sandy, stony or grassy mounds and hummocks in fields, or perched above beaches. Some

ancient sites underlie later buildings. Orcadian farmhouses and steadings are often replicated on much the same spot from generation to generation. It is not uncommon to pass by a farm where a modern double-glazed house stands next to an older stone one with cracked and cobwebbed windows, now in use as a shed or byre. Beside these might be a yet earlier tumbledown roofless drystone-built structure, once a dwelling, which serves today as an animal pen or is merely overgrown with nettles. In some cases, a cluster of farm buildings will appear to rise up out of the landscape upon a hillock, where the natural topography has been modified by centuries of human activity and the disposal of human and animal refuse. Settlement mounds (known in some accounts as 'Farm Mounds') are found throughout Orkney, most notably on Sanday and North Ronaldsay where the flat natural topography enhances their visual presence. Elsewhere, the patterns of deposition and surface creation which give rise to them are also present, but blend more invisibly into a naturally undulating landscape. Not all such mound sites remain inhabited. Centuries of climatic, economic and population change have seen the depopulation, settlement shift, abandonment, and in some cases reuse of earlier sites.

Dominated by 'improved' farmland delineated by ruler-straight roads and rectilinear fields divided by drystone dykes (walls), much of Orkney's countryside is well-ordered and intensively-farmed. Orcadian agriculture is prodigiously productive, and its dairying, beef and whisky in particular are widely celebrated well beyond the isles. The primacy of these products confers a particular visual signature on the Orkney landscape, characterised by pasture, grass cropping, and barley fields with some continuing peat workings on the hillsides. The roots of improvement go back two

David Griffiths

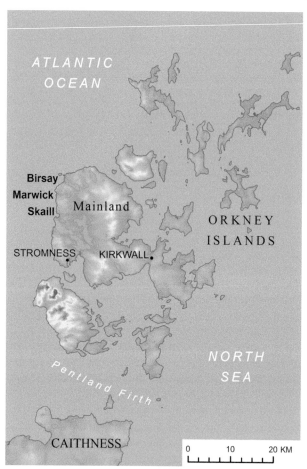

ATLANTIC
OCEAN

Birsay
Marwick
Skaill   Mainland

STROMNESS   KIRKWALL

ORKNEY
ISLANDS

NORTH
SEA

Pentland Firth

CAITHNESS

0   10   20 KM

Fig. 1.1 Orkney, location of project area © Crown Copyright 2018. An Ordnance Survey/EDINA supplied service

centuries and more to the desire of the Lairds to harness a better return on their land, reaching its zenith when the industrial revolution transformed production, technology and society across Britain. The social and economic crisis caused by the price crash and sharp decline of kelp-making from around 1830 (Thomson 1983) prompted the most widespread and systematic re-drawing of the Orkney farming landscape, connecting settlements to new roads, mills, harbours and telegraphs. Two hundred years ago, there was considerable rural poverty. For poorer Orcadian folk, kelp-making provided a precarious and unenviable living; a grim, polluting, arduous process undertaken on and around the shoreline, the presence of which is yet marked by round, shallow, stone-lined pits about a metre in diameter. Inside these modest features, large quantities of wind-dried seaweed were burnt to create a residue of soda and iodine for export to industrial centres in Scotland and England. Kelping continued at the Bay of Skaill in 1858, given its role in the discovery of the Skaill Hoard (Chapter 21). Thereafter it waned yet further in importance as a source of income, although some small-scale sporadic kelp-burning continued into the first decades of the 20th century.

Large-scale improvement got under way between the first and second productions of a nationwide inventory known as the 'Statistical Account of Scotland', a parish-by-parish survey written by kirk ministers in response to standard questions about geography, population and agriculture. These subsequently became widely known as the 'Old' Statistical Account or *OSA* of 1790–95, and the 'New' Statistical Account or *NSA* of 1834–45. The 'improvement' period of the 1830s saw the first systematic measured maps made in order to plan the Orkney landscape (*e.g.* Fig. 2.6). Prior to this, sea charts, beginning with the Dutch surveyor Joannes Blaeu's 1654 map of Orkney and Shetland, Murdoch Mackenzie's charts of the mid-18th century, and antiquarian artistic depictions, gave but a glimpse of the landscape (*e.g.* Figs 2.1 and 2.2). The first Ordnance Survey map editions covering the area at 25 and 6 inches to 1 mile were published in 1882, only after which we have a more consistent cartographic record.

The pre-improvement landscape remains to some extent visible in those areas that preserve a pattern of smaller, less obviously planned and re-drawn infields and landholdings. Its legacy is also preserved in the place-names of the islands. Orkney's geography and everyday language are freighted with Old Norse-derived terms, many of which refer to topographical features, such as –a, –ay or –ey (øy – 'island'), –wick (*–vik* –'bay'), –ness (*–nes* – 'headland') or Howe (*haugr* – 'mound'). From the earldom farms named in Bu (*bý*), and the significant district head farms named in Skaill (*skáli*), to the medium-ranking ones in Garth (*garðr*); Stove (*stofa*); –bister (*bólstaðr*); and –ston or –sta (*staðir*), and the comparatively minor or outlying –quoy (*–kví*) and –setter (*sætr*), Orkney place-names convey a complex picture of past settlement hierarchy, land-use and expansion, the chronology and extent of which continues to be fiercely debated. The majority of Orkney's Scandinavian place-names have survived and been adapted throughout the last five centuries of Scots and English linguistic influence. As such, they provide a link to the Norse or Norn-speaking centuries of the Earldom of Orkney, although the precise date of their origin is in most cases hard to prove. An identification of the imprint of Scandinavian place-names on the Orkney landscape with the earliest Viking presence (often almost uncritically termed the 'Viking take-over') is becoming harder and harder to sustain. Favoured by the historians of the early to mid-20th century, the extent of early Viking cultural dominance is now being questioned in many different ways. A more recent generation of historical writers, exemplified by William Thomson, have stressed the long timescales and nuanced local patterns of naming and landscape development, seeing many apparently 'Viking' innovations in the landscape not as the direct result of violent conquest in the 8th or 9th centuries, but as products of ongoing cultural influence, within and outwith Orkney, in the 10th, 11th and 12th centuries, and even later (*e.g.* Thomson 1995a).

A major problem in attempting to assert the chronology and extent of early historic influences on the landscape is that few surviving documentary sources for Orkney pre-date the impignoration or transfer of sovereignty of the Northern Isles from the Danish to the Scottish Crowns in 1468–71. The Earldom of Orkney, which at its height in the 13th century encompassed Shetland and Caithness as well as the Orkney archipelago itself, was a semi-independent fiefdom originally associated with Norway (and after the Kalmar Union of 1397, Denmark). Linguistic and historical sources for the history of the earldom have been described in many recent publications, which it would be superfluous to repeat here (*e.g.* Crawford 1987; Thomson 2008; Crawford 2013). The pre-Scottish historical record for Orkney is dominated by one source above all, which has influenced every aspect of historical thinking about the islands beyond measure. *Orkneyinga Saga*, a conflation of writings originally known as *Jarl's Saga* which were composed in Iceland around 1200, contains a history and genealogy of the earls of Orkney, and much colourful and spectacular detail on the struggles for power in the Northern Isles. It purports to record that the earldom began in the mid-9th century AD, with a legendary voyage and visit of Harald Fairhair of Norway who gifted the islands to Earl Rognvald of Møre who then passed them on to his brother Sigurd, whom the Saga names as the first Earl of Orkney. Coinciding with the age of Viking attacks across the Irish and North seas, this date is superficially an attractive one for those who would see the Orkney earldom as a straightforward 'colonial' expression of early Scandinavian westward territorial expansion. Some Viking presence in the Northern Isles at this time undoubtedly there was. However, much of *Orkneyinga Saga*'s most detailed and praise-laden coverage is concerned with the lives and exploits of leading personalities, notably in the period 975–1065, which Barbara Crawford calls 'The Age of the Earls'. Two key figures dominated this period: Sigurd II 'The Stout' (*c.* 985–1014) who fought and died at the Battle of Clontarf in Ireland, and his son Thorfinn 'The Mighty' (d. 1064), who oversaw the Christianisation of the islands, founded the bishopric and Christ Church at Birsay, and consolidated the earldom as a powerful and durable political entity. Given the propensity of Icelandic saga-writers to 'rewrite history' to embellish the achievements of the ancestors of their own patrons, it is possible to caution that the accepted chronology of the achievements of the earldom prior to AD 985 is a mixture of fact and fantasy resting on the sparsest of historical foundations. The full impact of Scandinavian culture in Orkney cannot be comprehensively documented for prior to the mid-10th century. By converting claim and legend into historical reality, and therefore artificially 'back-dating' a picture

of full established control by the Norwegian earls by at least a century, 'Saga-History' has made it more difficult to envisage a subtler, intermediate phase involving a limited Scandinavian presence with locally-based leaders who oversaw interaction with existing populations, but perhaps did not exercise overall dominance, between the later 8th and mid-10th centuries.

The last Norwegian earl died in 1231, when the earldom title passed by inheritance into a succession of Scottish lineages: Angus, Stratherne, Sinclair and Stewart, ending with the execution of the last of the Stewart earls, Patrick, in 1615. The Sinclair and Stewart periods provided one of the most important historical groups of sources for later medieval and early post-medieval Orkney in the form of the rental assessments of 1492 (Thomson 1996), 1500 and 1595 (Peterkin 1820). The compiler of the 1492 and 1500 rentals, Lord Henry Sinclair, had inherited the lease or 'tack' of the earldom estates from his grandfather William Sinclair, who was earl from 1434 to 1470. Given the degree of continuity of landed authority at a local level, and the apparent lack of any dispute or hostility surrounding the transfer from Denmark to Scotland, it is hardly surprising that the institutions and conventions of later Scandinavian landholding passed almost unchanged into the period of Scottish sovereignty. The taxes or 'skats' maintained their earlier character – butter skat (which did not merely include butter); malt skat; 'forecop'; and 'wattle' which derived from the Old Norse *viezla* or obligation to provide hospitality to the lord. 'Ley' referred to skat, which continued to be levied on untenanted or abandoned land. Orkney remained divided into Earldom, Bishopric and Udal or freehold taxable land. Bishopric land, which included Birsay, was not included in the 1492 or 1500 rentals. Pennylands, which approximated to one farm, formed the basic unit of taxable land assessment, eighteen of which counted as an Ounceland (or 'Urisland'). Townships were sub-parish units, fundamental to the distribution of agricultural land types between households, which occurred with varying multiples of pennyland values. As with the majority of place-names, it is less than clear how far back in time prior to their occurrence in written record that these land apportionments may be taken chronologically. The view popular amongst an earlier generation of historians, that they represent an unchanged inheritance from the Viking period, has been refuted in recent years.

Thomson's most recent account preferred the 12th century as the period when this system crystallised across Orkney (Thomson 2008). In his preface to his translation of the 1492 rental, Thomson cautions: 'rentals ought not to be regarded as describing a system which stretched back virtually unchanged to the days of King Harald Fairhair, as was at one time supposed' (Thomson 1996, vii). The documented form of 15th-century Orkney landholding is clearly later medieval in character, and the boundaries may have been revised numerous times before 1492, in particular through subdivision. However, there are hints in the values of different townships of older, simpler, land divisions that may help us to interpret patterns of landholding and settlement in earlier times (below, Chapter 25).

With a relative dearth of pre-15th century accurate historical information to hand, runic inscriptions can assist in the search for location, status and power amongst the settlements of Norse Orkney. With the exception of the splendid series of thirty inscriptions in the interior of Maeshowe (Barnes 1994), few of these express more than a few letters of words of relatively abstruse personal (or in some cases purely devotional) meaning. Moreover, many which were carved on stone are no longer in their original positions, having been built into later structures. Folklore in Orkney has a long and prestigious lineage, its connection to the old world or oral tradition being preserved for modern times by the researches and transcriptions of experts such as George Marwick (1836–12) and Ernest Marwick (1915–77). Folk tales, although essentially undated, contain much incidental detail about past perceptions of landscape and society. One traditional Orcadian tale in particular, The Death of the Fin King, is detailed here (Chapter 24, below). In the Orkney folk-tales we see imagination, stories, and unverifiable events intersect with the physical character and history of the landscape. To explore the history and prehistory of the landscape further we must turn to archaeological investigation, which itself requires questions to be posed and choices to be made as to location, technique and focus.

North-west Mainland: Geology and the formation of the landscape

The study area covered selectively by the research published in this monograph covers the coast and coastal hinterland up to *c.* 2 km inland, between the Bay of Skaill and Birsay Bay, a distance of *c.* 10 km. At Birsay, the north-west corner of Mainland forms a shoulder of land jutting into the North Atlantic. At its apex is the Brough of Birsay, a tidal island of considerable and enduring historical significance, which has been excavated many times over the past century. The Brough forms the outermost northern enclosing arm of Birsay Bay, a wide erosive west-facing opening backed by extensive dunes and links. The centre of Birsay Bay is separated into two sub-bays by the Point of Snusan, and its southern limit is formed by a rising line of cliffs leading out to the 87.5 m high vertical sea-cliff at Marwick Head. Immediately south of Marwick Head is the tiny bay of Marwick (or more properly Mar Wick), the stony shore of which forms another window in the line of cliffs which stretch down

the West Mainland coast. Four and a half kilometres south of Marwick is the Bay of Skaill, a deep, near-perfectly circular bay (800 m wide at its mouth). Skaill, Marwick and Birsay Bay are separated by two masses of higher ground, the east–west ridge of Ravie Hill between Birsay and Marwick (which extends with a minor intervening dip to Marwick Head on the coast), and Vestra Fiold between Marwick and Skaill. All three bays have opened up where lower topography and weaker entry points in the Atlantic cliff wall have allowed the relentless force of the ocean, driven by prevailing westerly winds, to eat away at the softer landforms of the bay frontages. Skaill and Birsay, and to a lesser extent Marwick, present soft, pliable edges to the sea, where the waves meet, not sheer rock as along the cliffs, but soft glacial tills, clays, silts and grassed stabilised dune sand. The power of wind, tide and wave, which batter Orkney's western coast, become concentrated as their combined force converges upon the gaps in the wall. Yet for human inhabitants, the access which the bays provide to the sea, combined with their fertile, sheltered and comparatively sunny hinterlands, and their low-lying positions forming a natural collecting-point for freshwater streams, has meant that they also represent convergences of vital environmental advantages and have thus been preferred settlement locations for millennia. This has produced an exceptionally rich archaeological record in these loci, with sites, deposits and structures abounding along the bay frontages, yet one which is acutely vulnerable to the ongoing and near-irresistible forces of marine erosion.

The solid geology of the north-west Mainland (Fig. 1.2) is predominantly composed of Upper and Lower Stromness Red Sandstone Flags, part of the Caithness Sandstone Series, the most characteristic rock of northern Scotland and the Northern Isles. These rocks were laid down as the bed of a shallow, warm lake in the Devonian Period (*c.* 420–360 million years BP). Sandstone outcrops extensively on wave-cut platforms in flat, slab-like laminated beds of approximately 2.5 m thickness, which are relatively easily won from the bedrock, and Orkney's beaches are strewn with flattish boulders eroded from the sandstone base. Stromness Flag forms an ideal constructional material for monoliths, walls, partitions, paved floors and even furniture as seen in building traditions throughout five millennia from the Stones of Stenness and Brodgar, Skara Brae and Maeshowe, through to many 19th century steadings and byres; its closely-related counterpart from quarries mostly in Caithness paved the streets of Victorian Britain. Threading through cracks in the sandstone beds of the west Mainland are thin, linear 'swarms' or 'dykes' of igneous rock (mainly trending south-west to north-east in direction) of dark lamprophyric camptonite rocks which represent the intrusion or swarm of magma through faults in the (older) sandstone beds at a slightly more recent time

Elevation (m)

120   120

0   0

Contour interval = 10 m

Superficial geology

Blown sand   Alluvium

Devensian till   Peat

Marine beach
deposits

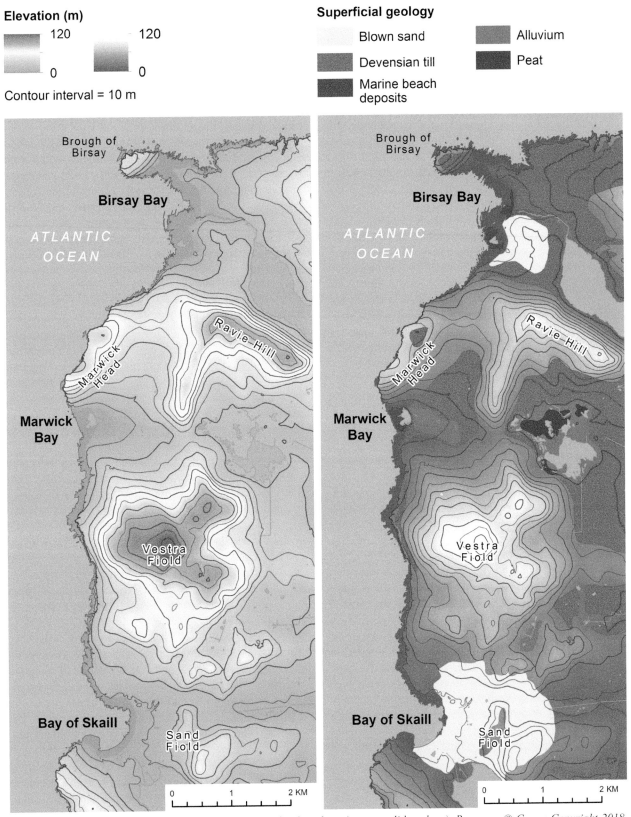

Fig. 1.2 West Mainland, topography and extent of superficial geology (grey = solid geology). Base map © Crown Copyright 2018. An Ordnance Survey/EDINA supplied service

around 283 ± 9 million years BP (Mykura 1976, 96–7). These are generally invisible on land but outcrop on the wave-cut platforms along the coast, a notable exposure of an igneous dyke is visible as an olive-greenish extrusive narrow line contrasting with the yellow and red of the sandstone flags along the north edge of the Buckquoy Peninsula and across the inter-tidal gap between Buckquoy and the Brough of Birsay. As the products of extreme heat resulting from volcanic action beneath the earth's crust, the dykes have a disproportionately strong local effect on magnetic geophysics, and (probably coincidentally) underlie some of the major archaeological sites of the area (Chapter 3, below).

The shapes and positions of the coastlines of the islands represent merely the current, often transient, state of play between the sea and the ability of the land (with occasional, rarely effective, human-made reinforcement) to withstand its relentless power to erode, flood and silt. Overall sea level in the North Atlantic Ocean has been rising (with some shorter-term variations) since the last Ice Age, meaning that much of what was once the lowest-lying coastal and inland land in Orkney, which would have been inhabited and exploited extensively by peoples in the Mesolithic and Neolithic periods, is now underwater. Woodland was more widespread than in the present near-treeless terrain, and resource exploitation by early societies extended well beyond the limits of the present landscape.

The Bay of Skaill (front cover) owes its remarkable sub-circular shape to the marine inundation of what was once a low-lying, sandy and grassy coastal basin of semi-dry land with freshwater ponds or lochs. Peat deposits with tree stumps were identified as long ago as 1820 under the marine silts in the margins of the bay (Watt 1820), and the presence of *phragmities* fresh-water peats under the marine bay silts confirmed by more recent core-sampling. Pollen cores and sediment sampling for multi-disciplinary analyses (including identifying species of microfauna characteristic of lacustrine environments), taken from inter-tidal deposits at two locations at the north side of the Bay, showed that freshwater ponds developed on top of the glacial tills between 5590–5305 cal BC, some of which were later infilled by sand-blows (De la Vega Leinert *et al.* 2000). At this time the coastline probably extended north–south across the present mouth of the bay, and the low-lying, partly-ponded area of land now under the centre of the bay (at that time rich in wildlife and wetland resources) was separated from the sea by a rock and/or dune barrier, possibly by a raised beach. Keatinge and Dickson's palaeoenvironmental studies of the bay environs and the freshwater Loch of Skaill, published in 1979, charted the decline of hazel and birch woodland to around 5000 BP (*c.* 3000 cal BC), possibly partly as a result of early agriculture, although the four-decades old

radiocarbon dates upon which these chronologies were based would now be subject to revision.

The date of the breaching and submergence of the barrier and the resultant flooding of the bay basin by the sea was suggested by Keatinge and Dickson as having been between 5700 and 5000 BP, possibly resulting from a single catastrophic storm-driven salt water incursion, although De la Vega Leinert *et al.*, in their more recent study, implied instead that the incursion of salt water had been gradual. However it is certainly the case that once the sea had opened up the bay, the soft coastal landforms around its periphery were subject to much higher erosive energy as oceanic tides and waves were introduced, and the degree of shelter against westerly storms once afforded by the barrier was lost. The instigation of large-scale sand deposition has been charted both by Keatinge and Dickson at the Loch of Skaill, and by De la Vega Leinert *et al.* at the Bay of Skaill, within the period 5235–3540 cal BC (De la Vega Leinert *et al.* 2000, 525). The influence of Aeolian sand-blow accelerated as a consequence of the ingress of sea into the bay basin and the irruption of high-energy wind and water turbulence on the resulting blow-outs and deflations of raised beaches and other coastal landforms. The process has not been an even one, and there have been periods where stabilising processes have temporarily held the upper hand, but the long-term influence of windblown sand on the bay landscape has been profound.

The succession of events which produced the sandy links across the hinterland of the centre of Birsay Bay must have been similar, although perhaps not so clearly related to a major inundation event; we as yet lack dating evidence such as that gained from the types of palaeoenvironmental studies undertaken at Skaill. At Birsay, the sand is less extensive in depth and inland spread, but nonetheless is a pronounced feature of the coastal plain. Sand deposition is a direct product of erosion. Much of it comes from the exposure of inter-tidal silts, which were particularly extensive and vulnerable to wind-transport at times of atmospheric cooling and climatic downturn when ice formation in the North Atlantic may have led to temporary decreases in sea level, coupled with a period of increased storminess that exaggerated wave action to rip and gnaw at the relatively soft sandstone cliffs. Erosion of solid and drift geology, particularly of the storm beaches, low cliffs and glacial tills forming the flanks of the bays, also contributes tremendous amounts of mobile sediment, which is rolled, blown and washed over other surfaces. Along Birsay Bay (both on the low cliffs and glacial tills of the Brough and the Buckquoy peninsula and on the Links), at the front of Marwick, and in several places around the Bay of Skaill, eroded ancient settlements, structures and deposits present themselves in (often collapsing) sections against the sea.

The striking topography of the Bay of Skaill has given its name to the surrounding parish of Sandwick (ON *Sand-víkr* – 'sandy bay or inlet'). Sandy land 'links' now covers the entire hinterland of the bay, up to 2 km inland, where the higher ground at Kierfiold has provided a topographic barrier. Sand infests the lower-lying central hinterland of the bay, extending to the Loch of Skaill in the south and into the lower-lying gap between Kierfiold and Quoyloo to the north, lapping up like a body of liquid against the rising slopes of improved farmland on the northern and southern limits of the bay. This landscape has evolved over millennia into a grassed machair. It encompasses stabilised sand-dune formations and cultivated areas, where humans have introduced organic matter such as midden, dung and seaweed to produce agriculturally-viable topsoils and create surfaces upon which they can live whilst staving off the twin forces of aeolian erosion and inundation. Aeolian sediment has been an ever-present feature of the landscape throughout almost the entire human timescale, increasing from the Neolithic Period onwards. Particle-size analyses from cores by Keatinge and Dickson taken as far east as Pow, a farm on the extreme north-eastern margins of the Bay hinterland (just over 2 km from the coast), gave clear indications that the sand they observed there was wind-borne, and De la Vega Leinert *et al.*(2000) noted a gradual increase and coarsening of particle-size in their samples from the northern bay margin during and after the Neolithic period, suggesting either (as seems likely) that aeolian processes were increasing in intensity (or as seems equally likely) the eroding or deflating source of the wind-blown sand (likely to have been the shore frontage itself) was working its way closer to the position of the samples (and hence towards the present position of the shoreline). Sand quarrying continued on the higher ground behind the centre of the bay at Sandfield until the early 1990s and its associated trackways and abandoned machinery are still visible amidst the grassy pastures. Archaeological observations at Skara Brae (see below) confirm that the Neolithic settlement was not only built in an already sandy landscape, but experienced repeated and probably increasing problems from sand storms throughout its existence. Early agriculture probably exacerbated these by removing stabilising vegetation, and after numerous attempts to mitigate the effects of windblown sand on the settlement by constructing physical barriers against its ingress, after abandonment the fate of Skara Brae settlement was to disappear under blanketing sand, although the mound was reused for burial in the Pictish period (Chapter 2, below), and there may have been other traces of later activity above the Neolithic settlement that were not recorded when the site was cleared and excavated in the 1920s.

Most of the archaeological excavations that have taken place have resulted from exposure by the sea. Many ancient and early historic settlements are to be found in close proximity to the sea, but most, if not all, of the later historic farms avoid the west-facing bay frontages in favour of higher ground further inland. At Birsay Bay, the houses and steadings of working farms today predominantly occupy land along the Burn of Boardhouse and around the Loch of Boardhouse, and in two noticeable clusters: the North Side, on the north-facing coast 1–1.5 km east of the Point of Buckquoy, and the 'Be-South Quoylands', a line of farms and smallholdings stretching east–west along the north slopes of Ravie Hill. Quoy (ON *kví* -, a common Orkney field-name, often applied to farms), implies this is probably a secondary grouping of habitations. The Barony of Birsay was divided into two portions, Be-North and Be-South, and these separate clusters reflect the two different territorial foci formed in the medieval period (Thomson 1995b). In Marwick, the principal farms of Langskaill and Netherskaill sit well back from the sea, with only the abandoned remnants of an early medieval chapel and the exposed and eroded façade of an earlier settlement mound located close to the shore.

The Bay of Skaill presents a similar picture, with the established households that currently farm the majority of the land clustering away from the beach on the rising ground and the sides of the hills, notably in Scarwell and in the hamlet of Quoyloo to the north of the bay. On the lower-lying land closer to the sea are to be found the historic Skaill House (formerly with its mill, its site now destroyed by the sea) on the south side, and the kirk of St Peter on the north side, close to a group of mounds but away from housing. Both of these historic buildings represent locations of importance and continuity from more ancient times (Chapter 2, below), but are today isolated from modern clusters of inhabitation. The houses that exist near the bay frontage are all relatively modern structures, in most cases from the mid-20th century. A key question that arises in the mind of the landscape archaeologist and historian when exploring the area is how and to what extent do the settlement patterns of earlier times differ from those of the present and more recent past? Do the apparently 'deserted' coastal areas of sand, tussocky grass, and empty shorelines, conceal a story of human endeavour and settlement now all-but lost from history?

The Birsay-Skaill Landscape Archaeology Project

The high-energy coastal environment of Orkney's Atlantic façade is a tempting yet challenging arena for new archaeological research. The project that is reported upon here began in June 2003, with the encouragement of the Orkney Islands Council Archaeologist, Julie Gibson, and a grant from the Council's reserve fund, as an attempt to widen and refresh the data capture from an area already known to have high archaeological potential, initially using extensive landscape survey techniques and later extending to excavation. The project idea attracted the support of Historic Scotland (now Historic Environment Scotland) because it promised to offer new, active, approaches to the perennial problem of assessing and managing the archaeological potential of landscapes vulnerable to coastal erosion. The threat to archaeological sites from sea-level change and storm damage is an ever-present one, and is especially problematic for a country such as Scotland, with an extremely long, exposed and complex shoreline in relation to its relatively low population and resources available for funding excavation. Attempts to arrest coastal erosion with physical barriers, such as concrete-filled sand bags, are in many cases now seen as not only environmentally and aesthetically undesirable, but are in some cases counter-productive as they can *increase* erosion at their margins. Rather than trying to confront the threat of erosion head-on with solid barriers, since the 1980s the response of curatorial management has moved towards understanding the process and likely forward trajectory of coastal change in its broad environmental context, and to develop a strategic, evidence-based approach to focusing future resources on the problem. Instead of responding to the problem of erosion as, or after, it occurred, part of the basis of this project was therefore directed at helping to research and model the archaeological potential of the entire coastal zone, not just the erosive frontage.

The landscape hinterlands of the three bays at Birsay, Marwick and Skaill represented the project's landscape focus. Even then, the areas covered had to be selective. The higher ground between the bays was not subjected to fieldwork, which was concentrated on lower coastal land. Areas closest to archaeological discoveries in the past, such as the Point of Buckquoy, were amongst the initial targets for new fieldwork. At the Bay of Skaill (Fig. 1.3), its northern side was seen as the most promising for entirely new investigations. Skara Brae with its World Heritage buffer zone had hitherto attracted most archaeological and curatorial attention, whereas the group of mounds across the northern rim of the bay were, in 2003, not yet known to be of archaeological origin. The most prominent of the mounds in this location, known as the 'Castle of Snusgar' (or just 'Snusgar'), had received sporadic but inconclusive archaeological comment (mentioned in *e.g.* Morris 1985) (Chapter 2, below). A preparatory visit in 2003 confirmed that at least three other similar mounds exist in its close proximity. The large mound next to the shore (through the flank of which the road cuts), and the lower, less obvious mound in the field immediately north-west of Snusgar, we termed Mounds A and B. Another large sandy mound on the northern bank of the burn, 200 m east of Snusgar, we named 'East Mound', for no

other reason than its juxtaposition to Snusgar. A further possible mound, 200 m east of East Mound (Mound C – informally dubbed the 'Far East Mound'), was shown by geophysics in 2011 to be a probable natural sand feature enhanced by modern activity.

The most significant (but frustratingly the least well-located) single instance of archaeological discovery on the north side of the Bay in the vicinity of Snusgar was the 'Skaill Hoard' found in March 1858 in a sandy rabbit burrow by a boy engaged in kelping activity. A major Viking-Age hoard dated to *c.* AD 970, the circumstances of its discovery are reappraised below by James Graham-Campbell (Chapter 21). 'Chasing' more of the hoard, in the unlikelihood that any of it remained in the ground, was never an objective for this archaeological research project, and no treasure-hunting using metal detectors took place, despite many suggestions made by visitors to that effect. However, the broadly-understood location of the hoard does have significant archaeological implications, summed up by Anna Ritchie in her book *Viking Scotland* when outlining the hoard's discovery: 'There ought to be an important Norse settlement in the vicinity, but none has yet been found...' (Ritchie 1993, 73).

North of the Bay of Skaill is the small bay known as Marwick (Fig. 1.4). The rocky foreshore reveals the face of a badly-eroded settlement mound, which is scheduled as an ancient monument and termed 'Viking Houses' yet little more was known about it. Just inland from the mound is the site of a chapel, also scheduled, but the full extent of which, and its relationship to the settlement, were little explored. Several other relatively minor archaeological features lie nearby. The green bowl of the Marwick hinterland is remarkably fertile, and, as at the Bay of Skaill, most of the historic farms remaining in occupation (including Langskaill and Netherskaill) lie upslope, away from the shore (see above).

Further north, at the much larger and more prominent Birsay Bay (Fig. 1.5), a great deal of previous archaeo-logical research has taken place, much of which has been undertaken relatively recently (*e.g.* Morris 1989; 1996). It may have been thought therefore that few if any questions remained to be answered. Yet considerable scope remained to use geophysical surveying methods to 'infill' between the known concentrations of archaeology and therefore to re-contextualise past discoveries. As described above, most existing archaeology from all three bays is known from the shoreline, having been exposed by the relentless force of the sea and (in some cases) excavated. As described above, Orkney's coast has undoubtedly moved quite considerably even within the human timescale. Its presence and position has dictated in very large part what we currently know about the prehistory and early history of the landscape. Much of the past archaeological endeavour across the project area (Chapter 2, below) has focused all

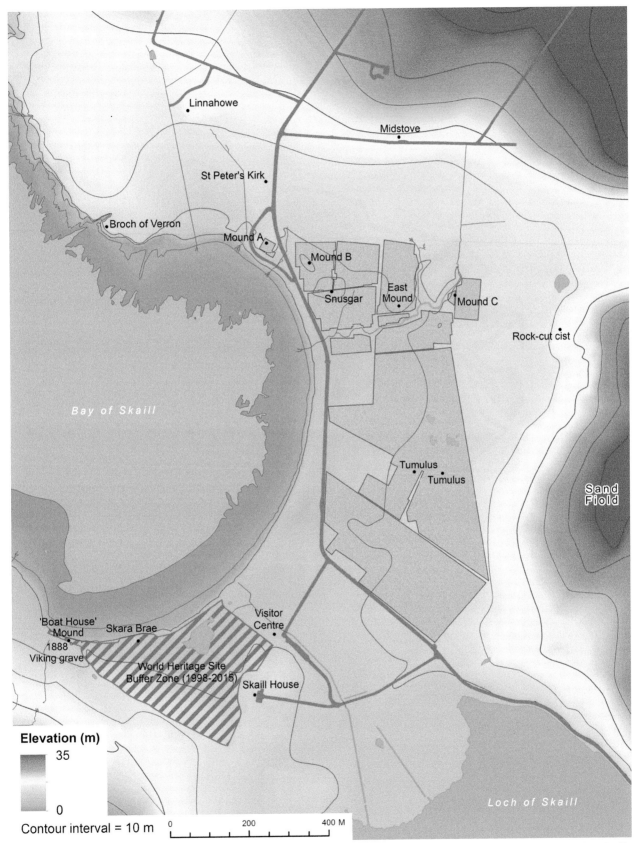

Fig. 1.3 Bay of Skaill, extent of geophysical surveys (in pink) undertaken by this project, in relation to World Heritage Site Buffer Zone. Base map © Crown Copyright 2018. An Ordnance Survey/EDINA supplied service

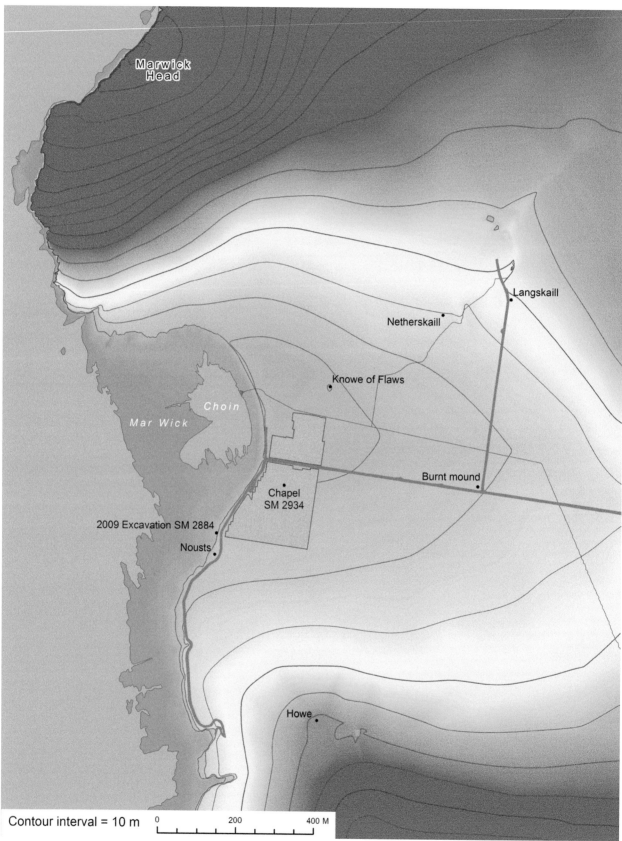

Contour interval = 10 m

0   200   400 M

Fig. 1.4 Marwick, extent of geophysical surveys (in pink) undertaken by this project. Base map © Crown Copyright 2018. An Ordnance Survey/EDINA supplied service

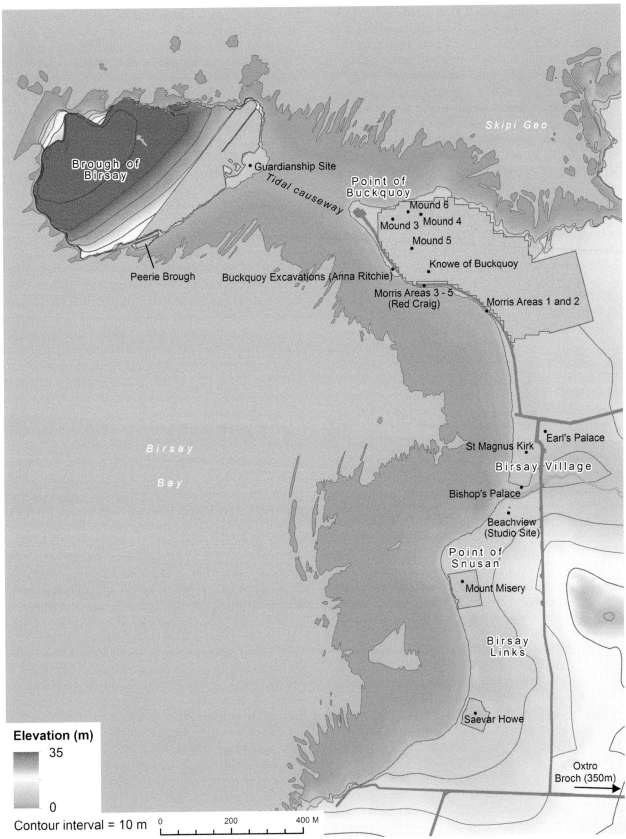

Fig. 1.5 Birsay Bay, extent of geophysical surveys (in pink) undertaken by this project. Base map © Crown Copyright 2018. An Ordnance Survey/EDINA supplied service

or in part on exploring sites already damaged by marine erosion. This has consisted of rescuing evidence from features and deposits already in the process of destruction, or tidying up and making sense of concentrations of archaeological structures that have been protected by the construction of sea defences. Exposure meant recognition, and there was little need to delve into archaeology that was not immediately threatened. This is hardly a matter for criticism: those responsible for administering hard-pressed budgets inevitably concentrated on problems that merited the most urgent response. Less obvious was the research potential within the wider landscape to contextualise the coastal deposits most immediately at risk. If a settlement or burial was appearing in the cliff edge, was it unique, or merely a small part of a bigger systematic deposit? If a midden, or stones indicating part of a house, parts of a burial, or a ditch, was noticed in section, shedding some of its contents onto the beach, how representative was the visible feature of what might lie untouched behind the exposure?

Thirty years ago it was almost impossible to answer these questions. Surface survey was available, which allowed upstanding features to be drawn, measured and recorded, but early attempts at geophysical prospection tended to be too small to gain an effective overview of deposits and to produce generally inconclusive results, often in the form of crude hand-plotted diagrams. Throughout the 1990s there was a transformation in the ability of non-intrusive landscape prospection to make a difference to these questions, operating within an accurate survey framework underpinned by computer-based databases and digital mapping, and at a reasonably affordable cost. In Orkney, surveys at Tofts Ness and Pool on Sanday showed their potential (Dockrill *et al.* 2007; Hunter *et al.* 2007). The three allied techniques of gradiometry, magnetic susceptibility topsoil mapping, and earth resistance survey, offered a combination of newly-available, increasingly extensive, affordable and reliable possibilities for coastal areas, including those particularly affected by windblown sand. No longer were they seen as 'experimental' and usable only by their individual makers, but, based on regular commercial production had become part of the mainstream of British archaeology. Combined with rapid advances in the accuracy of topographic survey now increasingly reliant on Global Positioning Systems, and (where available) Lidar and other remote-sensing data, by the early 2000s a new battery of approaches was available to researchers, allowing a landscape-scale approach to field investigation.

Of course, surface and geophysical survey, whilst increasingly capable and adaptable to landscape research, cannot tell us everything we might wish to know. In most cases they produce more questions than answers. Few traces of past activity can be conclusively identified

and dated by the interpretation of survey data alone. It is impossible to tell in many cases whether a line or cluster of higher magnetic susceptibility, or a point of higher than normal earth resistance, represents a coherent structure of archaeological origin or a conflation of natural or relatively modern effects. Still less is it easy, or even possible, to tell whether an anomaly noticed in geophysical data dates to any particular period. From its beginning, this project sought to add to the stock of known data in these archaeologically-rich coastal environments by taking advantage of the applications of techniques not available to the previous generation of fieldworkers. Combined with antiquarian and 20th century information, the record of existing excavations could therefore be reinterpreted or seen afresh in the light of the new data these newer techniques could produce.

The instigators of the project reported upon here were, however, not content merely to stop at gathering field survey data. In areas where earlier excavations did not exist, or were inadequate, and where survey data revealed particularly intriguing indications of archaeological potential, the door was left open to undertaking a fresh programme of investigation (or 'ground-truthing', an inelegant term that refers to the practice of testing and evaluating physical deposits detected during field survey using targeted excavation, on a selective and/or representative basis). This was aimed at characterising the sub-surface deposits producing the geophysical responses. In some cases, such as small-scale work at Buckquoy, Birsay, in 2004 and at Marwick in 2009, this took the form of limited interventions aimed only at rapidly recording aspects of structural definition and gathering what was technically possible in terms of material for radiocarbon dating. However, the project saw one particular focus of excavation, the cluster of mounds on the sandy northern hinterland of the Bay of Skaill, develop well beyond the initial purpose of testing the first set of geophysical survey results. In an area of high archaeological potential, and virtually no previous archaeological investigation, a series of cumulative decisions led to a more sustained excavation campaign of eight trench areas spread across two mounded foci with test-pits and auger transects between (Fig. 1.6, see also Fig. 3.3). Combined with using additional survey methods such as ground penetrating radar, the two mound sites at Snusgar and East Mound were developed as a detailed case-study in the archaeology of sand landscapes. The creation of deep sections and open area trenches, and harnessing environmental sampling techniques, radiocarbon and optically-stimulated luminescence dating, gave an opportunity to practice the art and science of excavation in sand to an extent comparable to other significant archaeological research projects in Scotland and elsewhere. When it became clear that in East Mound we were dealing with a substantially-preserved

Viking-Late Norse domestic structure, a longhouse and its outbuildings (Fig. 1.7), a sense of responsibility grew that we should finish what had been started, to a proper and meaningful extent (even though the decision was taken not to excavate the longhouse fully, leaving one area of its internal deposits intact towards its western end for future investigation). The excavation of the longhouse at East Mound, which took place in six short summer seasons between 2005 and 2011, inevitably took a large share of the time, energy and resources available for more widespread and selective interventions elsewhere across this landscape. Nevertheless, extensive geophysical and topographic survey, having started in 2003, continued throughout the project. Many pointers to further archaeological potential have been produced by this continued extensive survey campaign, but the need to hold back human and financial resources for post-excavation and publication means it has not been possible to excavate more than a tiny sample of them (a return to these for future fieldwork remains an enticing possibility). It is hoped nevertheless that their potential archaeological significance will be noted and ultimately either protected or realised through excavation. The results of the project, as they currently stand, are presented in the following chapters.

Fig. 1.6 Excavations at East Mound (foreground) with Snusgar, 2010, from E

Fig. 1.7 The eastern (byre) end of the East Mound longhouse emerges from the sand, 2008, showing main entrance and central passageway, from SE

Note on chronology and period terminology

The archaeological chronology of Orkney is well-understood in broad terms, but there is little standardised or universal agreement among archaeologists on the terminologies and precise boundaries of successive periods and their cultural attributions. Several period definitions overlap, yet are not incompatible with each other. We aim to echo mainstream practice, and where the Viking Age and its neighbouring periods are concerned, we adapt the usage described by James Graham-Campbell and Colleen Batey in the introduction to their book *Vikings in Scotland, An Archaeological Survey* (Edinburgh, 1998). 'Viking-Late Norse' is used here as a combined term forming a convenient shorthand covering the entire occupation period of the settlements excavated at the Bay of Skaill, as described in this monograph. The phases of excavation at Snusgar and East Mound, as set out below in Chapter 4, are in the right-hand column in Table 1.1.

Table 1.1 Chronological terms used in this volume

Period/cultural attribution	Date range (c.)	Phase
Mesolithic	9000–3500 BC	
Neolithic	3500–2000 BC	
Bronze Age	2000–800 BC	
Iron Age	800 BC–AD 400	
Late Iron Age/Pictish	400–800	1
Early Viking Age (transitional)	800–900	2
Viking Age	900–1050	3
Viking–Late Norse (combined)	900–1250	3–6
Late Norse or medieval	1050–1500	7
Post-medieval	1500–1800	8
Modern	1800–present	9

2

Past archaeological research

David Griffiths

The Bay of Skaill, Marwick and Birsay Bay have received a patchwork of archaeological attention in the past, mainly focused on the two internationally-known sites of archaeological importance: Skara Brae and the Brough of Birsay. Archaeological activity prior to the mid-19th century appears to have been minimal, with one important exception, the excavation in 1772 by George Low and Sir Joseph Banks on the Links of Skaill (see below). In the mid-19th century a number of individuals undertook excavations (of varying quality) on prominent sites: William Watt at Skara Brae, James Farrer also at Skara Brae and at Saevar Howe, and Sir Henry Dryden on the Brough of Birsay. George Petrie's accounts of the 1858 Skaill Hoard (which unfortunately for our purposes were not definitive as to its precise location), and of Birsay and Skara Brae, remain important antiquarian sources of information. The early 20th century saw a limited continuation of the Victorian tradition of individual initiative, with a brief and inconclusive excavation at Skara Brae in 1913. In the inter-war period, the move towards state guardianship for Skara Brae and the Brough of Birsay led to significant new excavation work supervised by V. Gordon Childe at Skara Brae in 1928–30, and at the Brough of Birsay, by J. S. Richardson in 1934–9, and post-war by C. A. R. Radford and S. Cruden in 1956–64 (Curle 1982, 15). In a parallel development, the 1920s and 1930s also saw important advances in historical and place-name scholarship by J. Storer Clouston and Hugh Marwick, who co-founded the Orkney Antiquarian Society in 1922. The RCAHMS undertook an inventory of Orkney and Shetland, published in 1946 but mainly based on pre-war observations, and the Ordnance Survey re-visited and in some cases re-surveyed a number of sites and scheduled monuments during mapping revisions in the 1960s. In the 1970s and 1980s, the advent of greater funding and curatorial oversight, coupled with the rise in university-based archaeological research, led to an increase in excavation and field survey activity, although as noted above (Chapter 1) this was still focused on rescue work, with excavation funding targeted at sites in the process of erosion-driven disintegration (Ritchie 1977; Hunter 1986; Morris 1989; 1996). In some cases, lengthy delays to publication followed. Excavations at Skara Brae in 1972–3, concentrating on two areas of Neolithic midden, and on the Brough of Birsay (in 1974–82 and 1993) are only now on the verge of publication (Clarke forthcoming; Morris forthcoming). The inclusion of Skara Brae within the 'Heart of Neolithic Orkney' World Heritage Area from its inception in 1999 has led to a further strengthening of the case for extensive archaeological fieldwork within the WHS 'buffer zone' (covering parts of the southern half of the Bay of Skaill hinterland).

The Bay of Skaill
The excavation by George Low and Sir Joseph Banks in 1772

Despite its lack of upstanding megalithic monuments comparable to those of the Brodgar-Stenness complex, the Bay of Skaill was amongst the first areas of Orkney to attract antiquarian attention. Volume III of the journal *Archaeologia* published a letter dated November 27, 1772, from the Revd. George Low, to Mr George Paton of Edinburgh, which had been read out at a meeting of the Society of Antiquaries of London in March 1773. Low (1747–95), then resident and working as a private tutor in Stromness, and who was later to become the parish

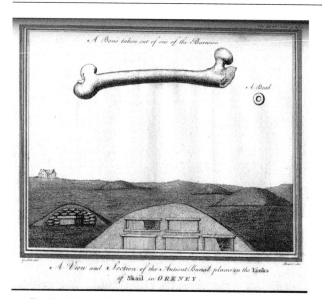

Fig. 2.1 George Low's drawing from Archaeologia 1773

minister of Birsay, was a significant scholar and naturalist, who wrote a history of the Orkney Islands (Cuthbert 2001). In his letter to Paton, Low described accompanying a 'Mr Banks', in fact the renowned naturalist and explorer and later President of the Royal Society (Sir) Joseph Banks (1743–1820), to the Bay of Skaill. Banks, who had recently taken part in James Cook's circumnavigation of the globe aboard *Endeavour*, undertook a tour of Iceland and the Scottish isles aboard the brig *Sir Lawrence* in the summer and early autumn of 1772, visiting Orkney on the return journey. In October 1772, Low and Banks went barrow-digging on the Links of Skaill 'where there are great numbers of tumuli, containing coffins in rows, one above the other'. The opening of one tumulus was illustrated in an accompanying engraving (Fig. 2.1), along with an annular bead and a human femur. The standpoint of this engraving appears to be facing westward across the Links of Skaill, with Skaill House to the left and higher ground rising to the right, although the sea itself is not visible (perhaps hidden from sight by dunes close to the shore). In one tumulus, described by Low as having a flattish conical shape, at least one crouched male inhumation was exposed, together with a 'bag of bones', which he suggested were those of the man's wife, surrounded by 'blackish fibres'. A stone bead and a piece of 'lithanthrax' (a type of coal) were found inside the 'coffin' (evidently a flagstone cist) under a great depth of sand (Low 1773, 277).

Accompanying Low and Banks were several other members of the *Sir Lawrence* party, including the Swedish naturalist Daniel Solander, the surveyor and artist Frederick H. Walden, and twenty-year-old crew member James Roberts. Roberts's own account of the excavation states that two tumuli were opened, and other details corroborate

those in Low's description (quoted by Lysaght 1974, 286); the bones of a man with those of a woman at his feet were found upon a 'coarse mat which was entirely rotten' inside a tomb of flagstones. The male was described as of unusual height and laid in a crouched position 'with his feet nearly up to his chin'. Walden's 'Plan of the Links of Skaill', which was drawn up from sketches made at the time of the excavation (Fig. 2.2), points towards the location of the two tumuli. In the centre are two prominent mounds which are undergoing excavation (stippled areas show the parts of the mounds that have been cut away), and between them is a tiny depiction of a tent used by the barrow-digging party (Fig. 2.3). The higher ground of Kierfiold and Sandfiold hills is in the foreground, below which are numerous mounds, hummocks and dunes. Skaill House is depicted close to the burn connecting the Loch of Skaill with the bay. The OS and RCAHMS recorded four tumuli or barrows in the central area of the Links. Two of these, at HY 2379 1912 and HY 2382 1915 (both now in the garden of Mill Croft) are paired closely together in a north–south orientation and would have presented an appearance to Walden's vantage point very much like those depicted. The other two, at HY 2389 1915 and HY 2394 1915, are 70–100 m east of the others and would have appeared in line with each other. The latter of these two locations coincides with a record by OS in 1967 of a report by Mrs Linklater, a resident of Mill Croft, of a mechanical excavator working on the western edge of a small sand quarry in around 1945 having disturbed a capstone, below which a human skull was found (further consideration is given to the survival of these tumuli in Chapter 3, below).

The curious elongated shape of the Bay of Skaill as depicted by Walden, with a pronounced inlet on its southern side, reflects to some extent its appearance at that time, although it is apparently exaggerated. An area of relatively quiet water used as an anchorage, being sheltered by the southern curve of the bay, was known as the 'Haap', probably from ON *hóp* (bay). Small boats still come and go from the slipway in this area, which is still the most sheltered part of the bay, but the distinctive inlet-shape of the Haap as a topographic feature has evidently reduced somewhat since the 18th century as the result of erosion of the southern margins of the bay. Murdoch Mackenzie's chart of the west Mainland, drawn in 1750, also indicates that the southern extent of the Bay of Skaill perhaps was indeed perceived to have a deeper, narrower shape than is visible today (Irvine 2009, 14), with the current tidal rocky platform at the south-west limit of the bay possibly then having been dry land. The extreme indentation seen in Walden's version, together with the unrealistic shapes of Kierfiold and Sandfiold hills, also appears to result in part from a distorted perspective formed by the situation of the artist. The plan has been

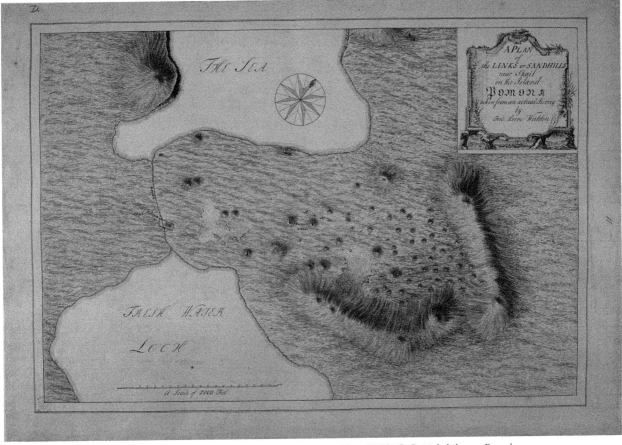

Fig. 2.2 Plan of the Links of Skaill by F. H. Walden (1772) © British Library Board

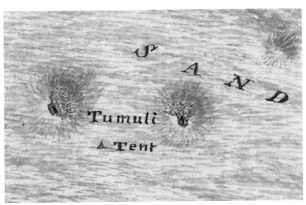

Fig. 2.3 Detail from Fig. 2.2 showing Low and Banks's excavation

Fig. 2.4 The Bay of Skaill in 2015, taken from Sandfiold (vantage point estimated as equivalent to Walden's)

drawn from a vantage point near the top of Sandfiold at *c.* 40 m height OD. From an oblique perspective, the play of light on the apparent tongue of water at the southern end of the bay as visible between exposed rocks at certain low states of tide, especially in strong afternoon sunlight, could easily have led Walden to exaggerate the shape of the 'Haap' (Fig. 2.4).

The 'Castle of Snusgar'

In 1795, the Stromness and Sandwick entry in ('Old') *Statistical Account of Scotland* (OSA), written by the Revd. Charles Clouston (*OSA* 16, 1795, 458–9), describes the barrow-digging exploits of Banks's party, referring to three 'chests' (stone cists), with other details evidently based closely on Low's account (Low was the minister of

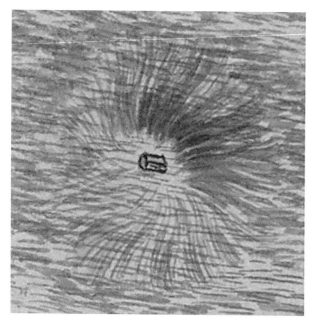

Fig. 2.5 Detail from Fig. 2.2 showing mound and building identifiable as 'Castle of Snusgar' (left) and St Peter's Kirk (right). The name 'Snusgar' is attested in 1795 and is probably from ON Snus 'prominent' + garth 'enclosure'

Birsay Parish, and was the author of its entry in the *OSA*, so may well have supplied these details to his neighbour directly). The *OSA* also states: 'On the west coast of the parish of Sandwick, close by the sea shore, is to be seen the ruins or remains of a large building, which yet bears the name of the Castle of Snusgar.' This is the first documented mention of the name 'Castle of Snusgar'. The most prominent mound visible on Walden's plan lies *c.* 1000 ft/300 m to the north-west of the two tumuli under excavation, and atop it is depicted a building, apparently a house with gables and a roof. Apart from drystone field dykes, no upstanding building or structure is visible in this position or any nearby position today, although the large mound now known as Snusgar is situated at approximately the position depicted by Walden. Furthest to the north-west on Walden's plan at an outscale distance can be seen the small outline of a church with a tower or small spire, apparently St Peter's Kirk in its pre-1836 guise (Fig. 2.5).

A map entitled *Plan of the Township of Scarwell* dated 1834 (Fig. 2.6) (Orkney Archive SC11/58/68) does not show any mounded topography but shows a number of straight land divisions, typical of 'Improvement', which were evidently either recently constructed, or about to be so. One of these still lies east–west across the centre of the Snusgar mound, but not yet the dyke which bisects the field to the north and forms a T-junction with the east–west dyke at the summit, which was constructed between the publication of the 1882 and 1902 OS map editions. Towards the bottom (south) of the 1834 Scarwell Plan, at either end of a line demarcating the boundary between Crown Lands and the property of W. G. Watt

(which is today a boundary marked by a stone dyke), are the annotations 'Castle of Snousgar' (by the shore) and 'Castle of Sandfiold' (inland). No further explanation is given of these. The 'Castle of Snousgar' is put at a point immediately south of the burn (equivalent to HY 2361 1945), in an area of wet and flattish ground on the extreme edge of the land, wholly unsuitable for any form of castle. Equally intriguingly, at the opposite end of this line, at a location that corresponds with HY 2440 1949, is the annotation 'Castle of Sandfiold', which is very close to the location of a prehistoric rock-cut cist grave found accidentally during quarrying in 1989 and subsequently excavated (see below).

The next historic map moving forward in the sequence, the 1849 *Map of Crown Lands* (NAS RHP 2890) is more or less identical to the 1834 plan, and repeats the 1834 annotations. Neither the OSA (1795) nor the 'New' Statistical Account (NSA) of 1845, nor these two mid-19th century maps, explicitly associate the 'Castle of Snusgar' with the most prominent of the mounds at the north-east margin of the bay, but this association subsequently did become a fixture on Ordnance Survey Maps. From the earliest edition of these at 6 inch/1 mile in 1878, and later the 25 inch/1 mile edition of 1882 (revised 1902), put the location of the Castle of Snusgar in its (now) commonly-accepted position on the mound (Fig. 2.7). The OS Name Book (1891–7, but containing earlier material and observations), records: '1/8 mile [201.168 m, or one furlong] south of the Parish Church, is what is said to have been a large building, and well known by the name *Castel of Snusgar*. Mr Smith, feuar of Quoyloo, and others some

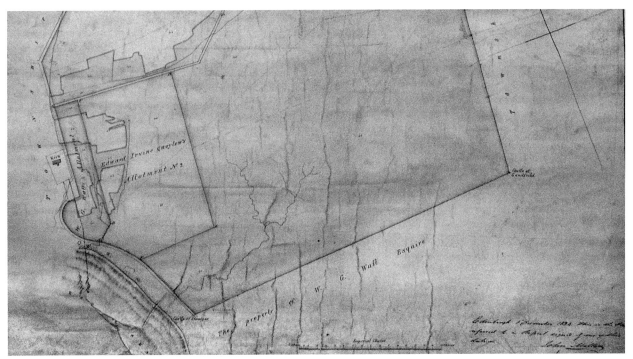

Fig. 2.6 Extract from Plan of Township of Scarwell (1834) © Orkney Library and Archive

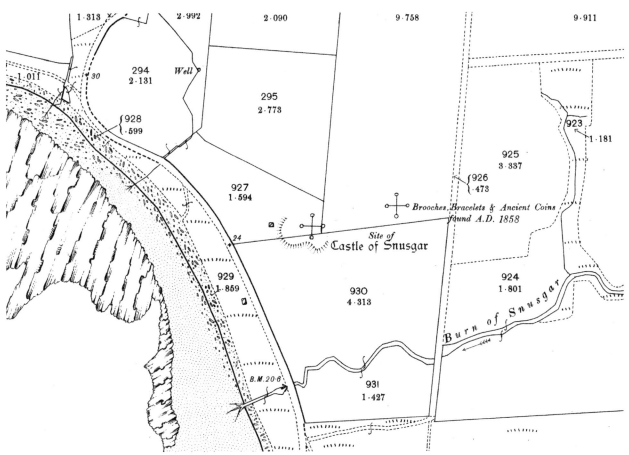

Fig. 2.7 Extract from OS 2nd Edition 25-inch (1902) showing 'Castle of Snusgar' and the Skaill Hoard © Crown Copyright 2018.
An Ordnance Survey/EDINA supplied service

time ago near the site found several silver articles' (this refers to the 1858 Skaill Hoard, see below, Chapter 21).

The establishment of the site of the 'Castle of Snusgar' in OS maps and records is evident in all later versions and speculations. Any upstanding traces of a stone building had evidently disappeared by the early 20th century. A possible conclusion to be drawn from these records (see also Chapter 4) is that upstanding traces of a building on top of the mound of Snusgar possibly did exist in the 18th century, it was almost certainly ruinous, and was probably dismantled and robbed to provide stone for the new improvement dykes, and possibly also for steadings in the district. An examination of the drystone masonry of the dykes confirms that, whilst they are largely composed of small flat sandstone slabs which are easily won and carried by hand from quarries or the nearby beach, there are a number of larger, smoother and less regularly-laid rectilinear blocks of stone included. In 1923, John Fraser in his article 'Antiquities of Sandwick Parish' (Fraser 1923, 24) stated that nothing then remained to indicate the building, and this is confirmed in a note of a Royal Commission inspector's visit in July 1928 (RCAHMS 1946 ii, 271). An OS visit in May 1967 recorded that 'The site is a grassy knoll. Mr Peter Sinclair of Upper Quoys stated that he dug into the W[est] side of the knoll about 33 years ago [i.e. 1934] and discovered traces of walling, but his excavation was of a minor nature and he filled it in. Nothing can now be seen although the name was verified locally'.

Other mounds and archaeological sites on the northern side of the Bay of Skaill

It is possible that Peter Sinclair's account of digging and finding traces of walling at Snusgar could have been confused in some way with the discovery of stone structures and burials during road-works in an adjacent mound in 1934. The road skirts the north shore of the bay and splits; its old route (which is still intact as an unmetalled track) takes a distinctive looping diversion, bending around the western side of a large flat-topped mound ('Mound A', see Fig. 3.2), which stands closest to the shore. The straighter and wider section of tarmac road that omits the older loop was constructed employing local labour during a period of high unemployment in the early 1930s. It slices a north–south cutting through the easterly side of Mound A, with a small portion of the mound remaining untouched on its eastern side. During the digging for the cutting, at HY 2341 1971, 'four unenclosed skeletons, one of which was crouched, were discovered, without grave goods, under ten feet of sand in a double layer of midden deposit', and structural remains and midden deposits were also observed in the mound slope adjacent to the burials (report from Mr Ritch, one of the roadmen, to RCAHMS, 1946, see also Chapter 23).

Mr Sinclair of Upper Quoys (see above), reported that a section of walling was exposed and covered up again, and that there had been many 'old bones, various teeth and fish bones' and at least one bone pin 'similar to one found at Skara Brae' (OS, 19 May 1967). The skeletons were reinterred, shortly after their discovery, with great sensitivity at a spot on the seaward verge of the old road marked by a small monolith with a simple Greek-style cross carved by one of the roadmen. It is still there, almost covered with tussocky grass, but its position is now dangerously close to the eroding cliff edge; the ancient inhumations will almost certainly be disturbed yet again before long, this time by the sea.

Perched above the cliff and a small geo at the north-western extremity of the Bay (HY 2305 1976) is an eroding mound site known as the Knowe of Verron (Fig. 2.8). This has been scheduled (SM 1475) as an Iron Age broch, along with a small area of (medieval or post-medieval) cultivation rigs in the adjacent field. 'Underneath the south side of the mound was a kitchen-midden deposit of cockle-shells and other food refuse, from which a large quantity of coarse broch-type pottery was re-covered by the Commission investigator' (RCAHMS 1946, 254), and nodules of melted iron were found by the OS visitor in 1967. Rescue archaeological work in 2001 consisted of limited excavation and section recording, which indicated that two structures are probably present in the

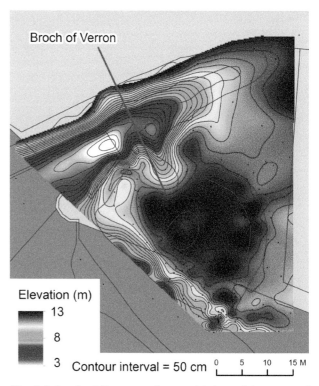

Fig. 2.8 Broch of Verron, surface model derived from ground survey

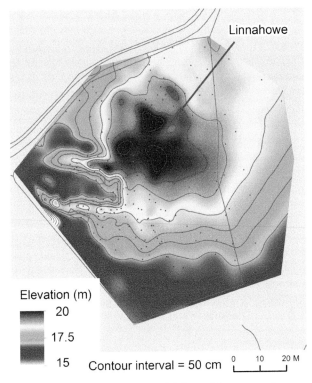

Elevation (m)

20

17.5

15   Contour interval = 50 cm   0   10   20 M

Fig. 2.9 Linnahowe, surface model derived from ground survey

coastal exposure. The earliest structure was noted as sub-rectangular or oval in plan. It had a flagged floor, internal fittings and a large hearth. The later building is more poorly preserved but remnants were noted of a paved floor and a probable flue. Deposits within this building contained quantities of peat ash and metalworking debris (MacKie 2002, 222; Canmore HY21NW22). These could be Iron Age in date, or somewhat later.

Nearby, a short distance inland from the Broch of Verron, is the farm of Linnahowe, the suffix of which (from ON *haugr*) implies a mound (Fig. 2.9). At HY 2327 2006 is a very spread-out, overgrown and degraded stony mound, which was apparently once known as 'The Castle' (RCAHMS 1946, 271). The western side of the mound has been extensively damaged by the construction of a concrete silage pit, and the general accumulation of modern metal refuse at the site made geophysical survey impossible. The OS visit in 1967 recorded that the farmer at Linnahowe had stated that when the silage pit was constructed (apparently in the 1930s/40s), much stone, ashes and old bones were found, but no walls.

The upper, eastern parts of the Links of Skaill on the flanks of Sandfiold, where the wind-blown sand is deepest, saw sporadic sand quarrying, as recently as the 1980s. A small area of past quarrying is still visible as a dished crater, with the remains of rusting metal quarrying equipment lying around its edge. In 1989, towards the western edge of this area, at HY 242 195, the wheel

of a vehicle sank into a deep hole which had appeared unexpectedly. This was revealed to be the result of a partial collapse into a very finely-constructed sandstone cist grave, which was subsequently excavated by Headland Archaeology (Dalland 1999). The cist had a single capstone supported on fine orthostatic flagstone monoliths on three sides, the fourth (with a removable slab) fronting a narrow 'passage' with an opposing drystone wall, all of which was set into a sub-rectangular pit or chamber cut through the natural glacial till into the underlying bedrock. Inside the cist were several cremations, one of which was situated centrally in the cist, and another of which had been placed in an urn standing in one corner. There were fragments of disarticulated unburnt bone from several adults and an (apparently secondary) foetal inhumation. Between the cist and the chamber wall was a deposit of vitrified material containing fuel ash slag and numerous bone fragments, which may have been a funeral pyre deposit. In a remarkable echo of Low's account of 1773, matted organic fibrous material was also found in some quantity in the cist, some of which was interpreted as the remains of basketry. Radiocarbon dating produced three possible scenarios of construction, use and reuse, with the published interpretation favouring a construction date for the chamber in the Neolithic Period with the cist and its contents dating to a long period of reuse in the Bronze Age. The Sandfiold cist was a chance discovery, but its presence confirms the general account of prehistoric burials and barrows on the Links of Skaill as conveyed by the accounts of Low and Roberts, and in the depiction by Walden. The extreme depth of windblown overburden above the Sandfiold cist, reported anecdotally by the tenant farmer of the land as over 16 feet or around 5 m prior to quarrying (P. Davidson pers. comm.), reminds us that upstanding archaeological remains on the Links, perhaps including those visible as relatively recently as the 18th century, are liable to be totally subsumed by sand and entirely lost to sight and memory.

Skara Brae

The power of wave and wind erosion on the soft shoreline has altered the frontage of the Bay of Skaill in the distant past and also within recent times. The large stone building housing the Mill of Skaill, which stood at the mouth of the Burn of Skaill near Skaill House, appears on photographs of the bay taken as recently as the 1970s. It was largely demolished in 1983 after it became undermined by the sea, and its site was subsequently dismantled. Skara Brae, which as we have seen (Chapter 1), was probably several hundred metres away from the shore in prehistory, now stands proud of the shoreline almost as a peninsula, sheltering behind its increasingly vulnerable-looking stone and concrete sea wall. The sea is now eating away at the landward ends of the wall and it will not be long before it gets in behind it, with potentially disastrous implications for the site. Skara Brae (the place-name comes from ON *Skarfa* and Scots *Brae* – 'cormorant hill') was initially explored after a great storm in the winter of 1850 ripped away grass and covering material, exposing parts of its structures and middens from under a large sandy mound, itself evidently the 'Brae'. This, however may not have been the first modern sight of the archaeological remains, as in 1833 the medical doctor and antiquarian Thomas Stewart Traill (1781–1862) noted: 'Below the House of Skaill on the shore is a green tumulus of large size, which consists of burnt earth abounding the bones of various animals & shells chiefly of limpets. In it were found several bone bodkins seeming of the fibula of deer. Fragments of one of their horns were also found' (NLS, Ms 19396, 23 v, quoted in Irvine 2009, 182n). Following the great storm in 1850, the Laird at Skaill House, William Watt, who had earlier discovered peat beds in the bay, opened up the mound and began excavating material from the stone structures and passageways, evidently with great care and attention to detail (Petrie 1868) although only a roughly hand-drawn plan survives as a primary record of his discoveries (Orkney Archive D8/4/12). The tightly-clustered nature of the houses and passages, packed in amongst a dense and complex series of midden deposits full of artefactual and environmental material, was already evident.

Subsequent to Watt's initial excavation, the sandy mound at Skara Brae remained as a truncated and unstable remnant overburden, with the partially-exposed voids and structures of the settlement beneath it, open to (evidently somewhat dangerous) exploration by anyone who chose to do so. In 1861, James Farrer (see Saevar Howe, below), described by V. Gordon Childe as a 'notorious but sadly unmethodical antiquary' (Childe 1931, 4), opened up 'some chambers and passages' but left no record of these beyond a letter to *The Orcadian*. Watt subsequently continued work at the site, which was reported upon by Petrie (1868). Another attempt to excavate occurred in 1913, by a house-party from Skaill House including Balfour Stewart and the eminent palaeolithic archaeologist William Boyd-Dawkins, but the scale of the task seems to have defeated these transitory summer visitors and they left but little useful record of their observations (Stewart 1914). The key moment in the modern history of Skara Brae occurred in 1924, when it came under the guardianship of HM Commissioners of Works. Further storm damage that year prompted the Office of Works to undertake remedial protection measures including building a breakwater, and to begin clearing and making good the network of stone buildings and passages. Initially this was done without archaeological supervision, but from 1928–30 Childe, then recently appointed to the Abercromby Chair of Prehistoric Archaeology at Edinburgh University, was brought in as overseeing archaeologist, with local workmen continuing

to do the digging. Childe's work at Skara Brae has since become seen as one of the greatest investigations of British prehistory, and laid the groundwork for all subsequent interpretations of the site. It was promptly published as an article in *PSAS* and as a monograph in 1931, the latter anachronistically entitled *Skara Brae, A Pictish Village in Orkney.*

Childe's observations were acutely perceptive in many ways, including that the midden material was not simply cast-out refuse, but that its use as a stabilising agent was integral to the constructional life of the settlement, being repeatedly interleaved with layers of windblown sand. He was wrong about the Pictish cultural attribution he gave to the main phases of the site, but was working only with a relative chronology and made some flawed judgements about the dates of certain artefacts based on the diffusionist ideas prevalent at the time. It took until the advent of radiocarbon dating, applied to material from two areas of midden excavated by David V. Clarke and Anna Ritchie in 1972–73 (Clarke 1976 and forthcoming), to confirm what some commentators (such as Stuart Piggott) had already anticipated in the 1930s, that the majority of the site, including the buildings and middens, is in fact Neolithic, dating to between *c.* 3200 and 2200 BC. Nevertheless there was also some later occupation or activity at Skara Brae. Recent radiocarbon dating work on two skulls recovered (with other human remains) from within the settlement in 1884 (Garson 1884; Schulting *et al.* forthcoming) indicated that one of these (346A) is Bronze Age, whereas the other (346B) dates to cal AD 541–635 (95.4% probability) (OxA-26686, 14387 ± 24 BP), putting it within what is now understood to be the Pictish period. Unfortunately, its location cannot be accurately pinpointed from Garson's account beyond 'likely to derive from a group of human bones found in the passageway'. Childe also described two intrusive cist burials found in 1928–30, suggesting they were probably of Viking-Age date (Childe 1931, 143). They were inserted into the windblown sand overlying the prehistoric layers. One of these, an inhumation from a cist south of House 7, has recently been dated to cal AD 420–610 (SUERC-24240) (Tucker and Armit 2009, 215), indicating that it is broadly contemporary with burial 346B above. It is quite possible that traces of Iron Age, Pictish or even Viking occupation were once present in the upper layers of Skara Brae, but were missed or destroyed during its long history of erosion, disturbance and antiquarian activity focusing on the more obvious and substantive Neolithic structures at the heart of the former mound.

Other mounds and archaeological sites on the southern side of the Bay

Given the enduring fame of the Skara Brae discoveries, it is perhaps surprising that other archaeological sites in the near vicinity, which have the potential to include remains of a similar character, have received remarkably little attention or protection from the elements. A small mound or cairn of around 7 m marked as a 'tumulus' on OS maps stands at HY 2340 1870, 60 m to the north-west of Skaill House, which the RCAHMS recorded as having been dug into on its western side (RCHAMS 1946, 268, no. 719). Another, larger mound which lies 150 m west of Skara Brae at HY 2294 1874, divided from it by a sharp indentation where a boat-slip enters the bay from due south. This western mound, sometimes referred to as the 'Boat House Mound' (included in SM 90276) is in a deleterious state of erosion, with a raw and collapsing full-height section of *c.* 45 degrees slope facing the sea, within which can be observed protruding drystone walling at various levels, laminated between reddish and grey midden materials and layers of windblown sand. It may be estimated that less than half of the original mound survives. Its eroded state, coupled with its proximity to Skara Brae and the obvious signs of archaeological deposits in the cliff section, were causing serious concern as long ago as 1978, when a survey was undertaken by C. D. Morris and a team from Durham University. This was extended in 1982 and included a resistivity survey on the grassed top of the remaining part of the mound. No dating evidence or soil samples were taken at that stage, and a hoped-for full rescue excavation never took place subsequently, due to lack of funding (Morris 1985), although some soil samples were taken somewhat more recently for a Stirling soil science PhD project (Cluett 2007).

A cist grave from the 'Boat House' mound was discovered as a result of coastal erosion in 1994 and fully excavated in 1996 (James 1999, 771–5). It was sealed by a sterile layer of sand and topped with a small cairn of stones. The grave was cut into sand layers and older deposits, lined and floored with sandstone slabs, and orientated in a north–south direction. Inside was a single extended skeleton in a prone position with its head turned to the right, which was interpreted as a young adult male. Some congenital abnormalities of the sternum were noted by the osteologist. The cist was in a state of collapse due to erosion but was of good-quality stone. A radiocarbon date was obtained from the right ulna of the skeleton of cal AD 550–680 (GU-7245), putting it within the Pictish period, broadly the same time-frame as Skara Brae 346B (above). The excavators were unsure as to whether the 1994–96 cist burial was pagan or Christian. Some disarticulated bone was found in eroding layers nearby but has not been dated. A furnished Viking grave was found in this same mound in 1888 (Watt 1888). This was also in a 1.8 m long stone cist, aligned north-west to south-east, and affected by erosion and collapse, but had extensive grave goods, including an iron spearhead (15.5 inches long), iron knife blade, an arrowhead, and a nail or rivet, a bone comb and comb case, a whetstone and some fragments of animal

bone. The human remains from the cist found by Watt consisted of a skull and some hand or limb bones, but these were not sent to the NMS along with the finds and their location is currently unknown (see below, Chapter 22). Its date, initially thought to be 8th or 9th century AD, has been revised forwards on artefactual grounds to the 10th century, in line with a number of comparable pagan Viking graves from Orkney and elsewhere.

Skaill House, the residence of the Lairds of Breckness, stands a short distance inland from Skara Brae and is the most prominent building at the Bay of Skaill. The earliest portion of Skaill House dates to 1628. It may however stand on the site of a medieval predecessor. At the eastern and northern sides of Skaill House, part of a medieval cemetery was found in 1996 as a result of drainage works being undertaken (James 1999). Initially six uncisted skeletons (one with its head in a stone box) were retrieved from a pipe trench; part of a cist was also noted but not excavated. GUARD undertook a further excavation in two areas, finding that the initial six graves formed part of a cemetery, from which a total of 27 inhumations were identified, including 12 adults of both sexes with an unusually high proportion (15) of infants and juveniles, but which may be attributed to the excavation area exposing an unrepresentative sample of the overall cemetery. Other discoveries of human bones in the vicinity have been noted in the past, suggesting the cemetery may be considerably larger than the area excavated. The graves were aligned east–west, sealed under *c.* 1.3 m of windblown sand and several had stone markers and head-boxes made of flat stones. Five radiocarbon dates were taken from human bone, dating the group to between the mid-11th and late 14th centuries AD, clearly within the Christian period. Most cemeteries of this date in Orkney are attached to chapels or churches. J. Storer Clouston stated that a chapel existed near Skaill House and was still visible in 1679 (1918, 101), although no structural evidence for it has been proven. Two runic-inscribed stones have been discovered in recent times in the vicinity, both of which are now in the Orkney Museum. In 1963, a sandstone slab measuring 132 × 89 × 5 cm, which was amongst piles of rubble intended for restoration work at Skara Brae, was found to have several runic characters carved on its face. Contemporary accounts are vague; it was apparently found either amid stone quarried from the beach area, from rubble in the sea wall (so may already have been re-deposited earlier in the 20th century), or it possibly came from somewhere near or on the 'Boat House' mound site to the west (Barnes and Page 2006, 194). Only a cursory record was made of the discovery, before it was split longitudinally and used facedown as a paving slab at Skara Brae. After a search in 1982, the slab was re-identified and removed, and the carvings were properly examined. There are five

Fig. 2.10 Skaill Home Farm runestone, in Orkney Museum

characters in two rows; the upper three are 'twig runes' apparently reading 'i b a', and the lower row probably reads 'r k r'. The runes are poorly executed, and given the uncertainties as to the provenance of the slab, Barnes and Page reserved judgement on their authenticity, leaving open the possibility that they might be of modern origin.

A more convincingly authentic runic inscription was found during demolition of a derelict building at Skaill Home Farm in August 1996 (the stone from which was intended to be reused in the construction of drystone facing at the Skara Brae visitor centre), a flat piece of sandstone measuring 96 × 25 × 7.5 cm (Fig. 2.10, now in Orkney Museum) was found to have two partially-surviving runic inscriptions on its edges (Barnes and Page 2006, 206). Despite damage caused by delamination of the stone, the better-preserved and more boldly-cut inscription (Edge A) can be translated as:

þurfinr-r... ... ...:..n.:..

'thorfinnr r[eisti]' (raised) or 'r[aist]' (carved)...n...

(the 'raised' element being a recognisable convention for runic inscriptions). Edge B consists of a short row of weakly-cut vertical strokes, 95 mm long, of which only þ, r, k and a possible æ can be made out, and which were described by Barnes and Page as graffiti, possibly imitative of proper runes. The slab, having been built into the wall of a farm steading long after the Norse period, was clearly out of its original context, and no further information has been obtained as to where it may have come from, although given its size and weight, a very local provenance seems likely.

From Skaill to Marwick
The higher ground north of the Bay of Skaill

North of St Peter's Kirk, the straight road, historically known as the 'Dees gate' or 'well road' (Marwick 1952, 147) heads uphill in a straight line dividing the townships of

Northdyke and Scarwell, towards the dispersed settlement of Quoyloo (a loose agglomeration of mostly later 19th and 20th century houses), which straggles across the northern shoulder of land overlooking the Bay of Skaill. At the heart of Quoyloo is the house of Stove (from ON *stufa* – 'heated room'), which is almost certainly in origin a medieval farmstead, although the current house is a typical single-storied long dwelling of the 18th to 19th centuries. To the west of Quoyloo, on the upper slopes of Vestra Fiold (HY 2390 2176), sandstone outcrops from the peaty turf, and here a probable Neolithic stone quarry was noted in 1946 (RCAHMS 1946, 269). Massive sandstone slabs were found in two groups, one of which had been roughly wedged with stone, evidently being prepared for transport, and the suggestion was made that this was the source of the Brodgar and Maeshowe monoliths. Excavation in 2002–3 has cast further light on the complex, and nearby is evidence of a megalithic cairn, apparently related to the quarrying activity (Richards 2002).

Marwick

Over the watershed to the north that is marked by the Sandwick–Birsay parish boundary, the strikingly fertile Atlantic-facing valley of Marwick (see Fig. 1.4) has received less archaeological attention than the larger bays to its north and south. There is some evidence of possible prehistoric occupation, notably the burnt mound or tumulus known as the Knowe of Flaws (HY 2313 2434). This very disturbed-looking mound has some sandstone protruding from rough turf on its surface; it is approximately 27 m diameter and 1.5 m height and lies in a boggy area behind the shore, which makes geophysical survey difficult, although topographical survey is unproblematic. The *Orkney Herald* carried a brief report on 11 November 1891 that a double cist with an urn had been exposed 'on a natural mound' during an excavation in July 1890, suggesting the Knowe of Flaws is a burial cairn, but other subsequent field observations have suggested it is probably a burnt mound. A more certain identification of a burnt mound has been applied to a very reduced and near-invisible trace of a structure further inland, known as the Knowe of Netherskaill, at HY 2431 2422 beside the turning off the main Marwick Bay road to Netherskaill Farm. Burnt stone was visible on the surface when the OS visited the site in 1967, but little apparently remains of it *in situ*, and Orkney SMR carries a note stating that much of it was removed for road repairs.

The principal concentration of known archaeological potential at Marwick lies upon, and just behind the bay frontage. A series of eroded deposits visible in section between HY 228 239 and HY 229 241 occupying up to 200 m of coastline, expressed behind the coastline in a low mounded form, was scheduled as Ancient Monument 2884 in 1970. This has suffered ongoing erosion by the sea and disturbance by burrowing animals to the extent that its archaeological integrity is now severely compromised, so a survey and partial excavation was undertaken in July 2009 (Chapter 4).

On cultivated farmland 50–75 m inland of the Marwick settlement mound is a low stone structure scheduled as a chapel (SM 2934), the walls and foundations of which remain visible, overgrown with weeds and isolated in the centre of a large field. The stone structure, which is probably of early medieval origin, is surrounded by a very low rectilinear earthen bank forming an enclosure, which is possibly a burial ground, although human remains have yet been identified. A pattern of slight but still-visible cultivation rigs cover much of the field, but these appear to respect the site and do not cross into the chapel enclosure area (Chapter 3). The building foundation measures *c.* 5.2 by 3.8 m internally, and is built of sandstone slabs and rubble with clay mortar. The interior is sharply rectilinear, with a narrow entrance near the south-west corner with a step and stone door-check, but its exterior shape is more bulbous and apparently damaged. The chapel was excavated by J. Storer Clouston in the 1920s. C. A. R. Radford published a plan and description of the site in *The Northern Isles* (Wainwright 1962, 180) (Fig. 2.11) stating that: 'the masonry with traces of mortar and the checked jambs of the door recently exposed...are unlikely to be earlier than the twelfth century', further arguing that the chapel was probably founded newly in the Norse period as it did not encompass the site of any earlier structure.

A cluster of six small stone-lined boat nousts is located on the low cliff edge 55 m to the south of SM 2884. These are probably of relatively recent date, perhaps from the 18th or early 19th century, although earlier origins cannot be ruled out. No other building or structure of pre-20th century date occupies the shore area. At Marwick, as also

at Skaill and Birsay, the principal farmsteads stand well back from the coast, occupying land around the inland rim of the bay hinterland, each at a noticeable elevation from the coastline. Two 'paired' farm names in –*skáli* (Langskaill and Netherskaill) and in –*howe* (East and West Howe), probably reflecting divisions of earlier larger single farms (Thomson 1995a, 49), are situated on the north and south slopes of the Marwick valley respectively. Prompted by survey data in the Soils Survey of Scotland (1981), indicating the presence of discrete areas of deep anthropogenic topsoils on the flanks of the Marwick valley, covering an estimated 150 ha, a team of soil scientists led by Ian Simpson of the University of Stirling investigated their origin and date (Simpson 1997). Topsoil sampling with a hand auger took place at fourteen locations, mainly concentrated on the north-facing slope at West Howe, but with some further survey points on the hillside to the south, in the centre of the bay, between Langskaill and Netherskaill on the north side of the burn, and between Muce and Skorn on the easterly fringes of Marwick township. Simpson's analysis, using soil chemistry and micromorphology, showed that the relict properties of these soils indicated a past regime of infield management involving the enhancement of soil fertility using turf (removed from hill land), manuring, and some seaweed admixture, resulting in a 'plaggen' soil. This type of soil is found across several cultivated infield farm landscapes in the Northern Isles, and Simpson dated its build-up at Marwick to the 12th to 19th centuries. Whilst this is a very broad dating framework, it may suggest that the origins of these important farms on the upper and inland flanks of the Marwick valley occurred in the Late Norse/High Medieval period, thus post-dating the settlement mound on the foreshore (for dating see below, Chapter 5) and probably also the chapel site.

Birsay Bay

Birsay Bay is dominated by the Brough of Birsay and the Point of Buckquoy, on the Orkney Mainland's north-western extremity, south of which is the 'Palace' village and the sweeping dune-backed landscape of Birsay Links (Fig. 2.12). The first terrestrial map of Birsay was Alexander Aberdeen's map of the Barony of Birsay made in 1760 (see Fig. 3.18), so slightly pre-dates Walden's map of Skaill. Birsay's past political status as an early centre of island power has attracted unusual and early historical attentions. Ritchie and Morris have argued that it was significant in the Pictish period (Morris 1989, 12). *Orkneyinga Saga* describes Earl Thorfinn's 'permanent residence' and his foundation of Christ Church at Birsay in the mid-11th century (Pálsson and Edwards 1978, 71). Jo Ben (1529) described Birsay as 'an excellent palace, where in times past the King of Orkney reigned' (Barry 1808, 446). The description also mentions an inscribed

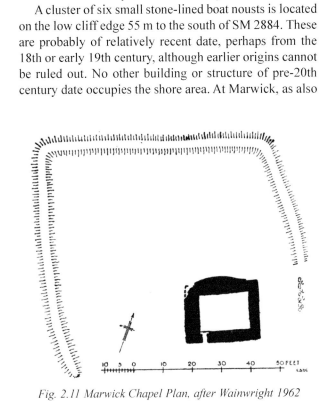

Fig. 2.11 Marwick Chapel Plan, after Wainwright 1962

Fig. 2.12 Birsay Bay from south; Brough of Birsay upper left

Fig. 2.13 Brough of Birsay from air, from NE

stone found at Birsay in the name of Gavus or Ganus (unknown from any other description) that he attributed to Orkney's subjection to the Romans under Julius Caesar (Sandwick received no comparable historical distinction, merely in that it abounded with rabbits and was exceedingly fertile). Jo Ben was referring to the former Bishop's Palace, the site of which is probably under parts of the village, south of St Magnus's Church at approx. HY 248 277 (Morris 1996, 3). This church (Barber, in Morris 1996, 12–13) is now commonly preferred by historians as the most probable location of Earl Thorfinn's Christ Church to the site of the (somewhat later) church on the Brough of Birsay (below). The grandiose but now ruined palace of the Stewart Earls, which was constructed after Jo Ben's observation, was placed at Birsay, not just to administer the large earldom estate in the parish, but clearly to recapture the location's lingering historical prestige. Despite its prominent reputation as a political centre of the earldom, antiquarian activity came rather later to Birsay than to the Bay of Skaill. The first site to be excavated in any spirit of archaeological inquiry was the Broch of Oxtro (otherwise known as Haughster), located on the landward side of Birsay overlooking the Loch of Boardhouse (HY 2537 2678). In 1847, Mr Leask of Boardhouse Farm dug into its grassy, stony knoll, exposing part of a stone cist cemetery with burnt bone and ashes, which was stratified above the remains of the Iron Age broch below. One of the cist slabs was described by George Petrie as having a 'figure of an eagle' carved on it (Petrie 1872, 76–8), although this was built into a farm building at Boardhouse before it could be recorded (no trace of it has since been found). Morris (1989, 24) speculated that the 'eagle' was a Pictish symbol. Also found were stone and clay vessels, Roman Samian pottery, bone or antler combs, a penannular brooch, a cylindrical piece of silver, and a Viking-Age ringed pin, all of which emphasise the probable multi-period nature of the site. The next

excavation in the area was Dryden's exploration on the Brough of Birsay (below).

The Brough of Birsay

The Brough of Birsay (Fig. 2.13) has attracted historical and antiquarian interest across the centuries, not least because its dramatic island site and access via a tidal causeway prompts a sense of detachment and semi-isolation redolent of early Christianity. The majority of visible archaeological remains on the Brough are located on its more sheltered, landward-facing side, stretching for 750 m along its eastern and south-eastern coastline of low sandstone cliffs of around 4 m in height OD. The fenced, grassed guardianship area presents a complex palimpsest of drystone-walled buildings and passages clustering immediately along the cliff line. Immediately to the west of the central group is the modestly-sized but finely-constructed stone shell of the early 12th century Romanesque church with its small claustral range and square graveyard. Beside the church stands a concrete replica of a Pictish symbol stone that was found in July 1935 (Curle 1982, 91). Further to the west and south are several groups of Viking-Norse longhouses, with their long axes aligned to the slope.

The present lawn-girt neatness of the walls and surfaces within the Brough of Birsay guardianship area belies the neglected condition that the site was in a century and a half ago, when what was an amorphous spread of overgrown weed-infested rubble began to yield to clearance and initial investigation. The first serious attempt to expose the church on the Brough was mounted by the English ecclesiastical scholar Sir Henry Dryden in 1866 (reproduced in Morris 1996, 267–8), although parts of it were still partly visible prior to this (*NSA* 1845, 98). Dryden's work revealed its internal plan, which was recorded in a number of sketches, although its date and surrounding context remained obscure. A further excavation by Mr Leask of Boardhouse in 1867 shed little further light on the structures. Greater clarity was achieved during the extensive clearance and restoration work in 1934–39, undertaken by the Office of Works following adoption of part of the Brough into state guardianship, and supervised by J. S. Richardson assisted by Miss Cecil L. Mowbray, later Mrs Curle. Although it took until the 1980s and 1990s for the majority of its findings to be published, as with the similar activity at Skara Brae only a few years before, the 1930s work on the Brough did succeed in making a relatively clear, stable and practical presentation of the archaeology, suitable for visitors to experience without too much danger or confusion.

Richardson and Mowbray's excavations succeeded in disentangling three Norse layers or phases (referred to as horizons in Morris 1996), Upper, Middle and Lower, from a fleeting Pictish phase, for which limited structural evidence survived. The pre-Viking archaeology was however emphasised by an impressive assemblage of finds, not least the symbol stone, but also including combs and beads, and important metalworking remains with clay moulds evidencing the manufacture of penannular brooches, pins and other dress accessories. Dating these phases or horizons was based on relative juxtaposition in broad stratigraphic relationships, coupled with a sense that the predominant style of rectilinear buildings was Norse in origin, whereas underlying smaller, sub-circular or cellular-shaped structures were Pictish (this separation of house types is a product of an enduring belief in a binary cultural distinctiveness which has more recently become open to question). A later generation of archaeologists active on the Brough of Birsay in the 1970s and 1980s, led by C. D. Morris and J. R. Hunter, were able to bring to bear greater stratigraphic precision and modern recording techniques, coupled with radiocarbon dating, and indeed Mrs Curle's account of the finds from the 1930s, together with the field notes of the works foreman William Henderson, were published with their active assistance (Curle 1982; Morris 1996, 269–91). Radford and Cruden's various excavations on the Brough in the 1950s and 1960s were little or no more advanced in terms of technique than the 1930s work, and left a confusing and fragmentary record (summarised in Morris, forthcoming). The excavations undertaken by Morris and Hunter between 1973 and 1982, which were funded by the Scottish Office Development Department following concerns at the eroded state of the site, extended the coverage of rescue excavation from the central site along the cliff edge to the north-east, where Hunter found important Norse metalworking remains at Site VII (Hunter 1986), and to the south-west where discoveries occurred at several sub-sites extending as far as the 'Peerie Brough', an attached stack at the southern end of the complex (Morris forthcoming).

The Point of Buckquoy and the Brough Road

The Point of Buckquoy reaches out towards the Brough of Birsay; at its terminus is a car park above the landward end of the tidal causeway. The surface of the Buckquoy Peninsula is relatively flat, with cliffs between 4 m and 6 m high standing vertically over the beaches and wave-cut platforms on either side. The Brough Road follows its southern edge, beside stone-dyked fields owned by the farms of Walkerhouse and Feaval. Six upstanding mounds of varying height and shape are visible in the westernmost two fields. The largest of these, the Knowe of Buckquoy (HY 2448 2820) is thought to be a possible Neolithic or Bronze burial cairn, and was subjected to an inconclusive excavation by the local antiquarian John Fraser prior to 1935 (RCAHMS 1946, 19), who found several courses of walling, peat ash and animal bones. The mounds attracted the attention of the archaeologist and historian F. T. Wainwright who was looking for a location to investigate Viking remains in Scotland, at the time when Radford and Cruden were working on the adjacent Brough; Cruden drew his attention to them on the assumption that they might be Viking burials. Wainwright made some field notes and conducted an excavation on the apex of the Point in July 1960, finding parts of two Iron Age sub-circular huts, before his premature death the following year, leaving the interpretation and publication of his findings to others (Morris 1989, 71–80).

The southern shore of the Buckquoy Peninsula is exposed to south-westerly gales and high tides, and is particularly prone to erosion. It was very badly affected by storms in the 1970s. Remedial works consisting of piled concrete 'sandbags' were undertaken at this time, although these appear to have been relatively ineffective. Numerous archaeological deposits along the upper cliff-edge may be seen exposed in section (Morris 1989, 36–43). One of the mounds on the cliff-edge noted by Wainwright in 1960 lay across the line of the Brough Road (then an unmetalled track), upon the Peninsula's eroding south-western cliff edge at HY 2436 2823. The seaward portion of this mound was fully excavated as a rescue project in 1970–71 by Anna Ritchie, who discovered a rich sequence of deposits including house structures, middens and burials (Ritchie 1977). Ritchie defined six phases; the first two consisted of small, cellular buildings, and a house structure with both cellular and longhouse-style features, such as side benches and a long central hearth (House 4); Phases III, IV and V consisted of rectilinear buildings interpreted as a byre, a barn and a dwelling, and Phase VI was a furnished, crouched inhumation grave inserted into by-then ruinous walls of House 3, part of the Phase III farmstead. The Phase VI burial included objects characteristic of pagan Viking graves: a ringed pin, an iron knife, a bone mount, a whetstone, and a halved silver penny of Edmund of

Wessex (AD 939–46). A detached long-cist burial in the northern area of the excavation could not be attributed to a particular phase. In the debate about the Pictish to Viking transition, 'Buckquoy' (as this particular excavation is referred to, despite numerous others having taken place on the Peninsula) has become a classic case study. The rich assemblage of artefacts from the site, most of which were interpreted as Pictish, included pins, brooches, combs, an ogham inscription on a spindle whorl, and a painted pebble. Many of these were associated with occupation deposits in (ostensibly Norse) Phases III–V. Apart from the Phase VI grave, there was very little diagnostically Scandinavian material culture at the site; stone gaming boards suggestive of the Viking game *hnefatafl* could feasibly have been insular as much as Scandinavian in derivation, and no steatite was found (*ibid.*, 187). Ritchie took the view that the phases were distinct, beginning with Phase I in the 7th century, with the three Norse occupation phases III–V being 9th century in date, with Phase VI as a closing deposit. The distinctiveness of the phasing and the cultural attribution of the buildings, and the overall chronology, must surely now be subject to revision and reinterpretation in the light of comparable evidence from more recent excavations for an 'intermediate' stage of Pictish/Viking interaction in the Northern Isles, which took place prior to the imposition of more pronounced Scandinavian cultural forms, from *e.g.* Pool (Sanday, Orkney) and Old Scatness, Shetland (Hunter *et al.* 2007; Dockrill *et al.* 2010).

Buckquoy was the first major example of the 'rescue' excavation ethos applied to the problem of coastal erosion in Orkney. Later, in 1976–82, a Durham University project team led by Morris recorded 25 exposures of archaeological deposits, including buildings, middens and stone cists, in the cliff edge between a location just north of the Point of Buckquoy at HY 2434 2839, to a position near the 'Planticru' (a small walled kitchen garden) at the southern end of the peninsula at HY 2469 2803 (Morris 1989). Morris's team also contributed a plane-table plan and topographic description of the Buckquoy mounds (*ibid.*, 34–6), and environmental samples were taken from cuttings and cleaned sections at several locations. Small rescue excavations were mounted in six areas, developing Ritchie's method of excavating top-down through deposits already exposed in section by erosion, within confined trenches clinging precipitously to the cliff edges. These uncovered several cist graves and associated stone cairns dating to the Pictish and Viking periods (Areas 1 and 2, HY 2467 2806 – HY 2466 2807); and a complete elliptical bi-cellular or 'Figure of Eight' type building, east–west aligned, measuring 6.6 m internally on its long axis, with the larger 'room' measuring 4.5 m north–south (Area 3, also known as 'Red Craig' HY 2448 2816). Further fragments of buildings and middens were recorded in

adjacent Areas 4 and 5, HY 2448 2816 – HY 2448 2818), and Area 6 was a re-opening of Wainwright's trench on the Point of Buckquoy at HY 2429 2840. Observations of deposits and structures exposed in section along the coastline were supplemented with an early (if fairly inconclusive) application of resistivity, although one area of high resistance was roughly equated with the building at Area 3/Red Craig (the low resistance was perhaps prompted by voids in the internal rubble deposits, although this was not explained by the report's authors).

Burnside, Beachview and Birsay Links

In order to expand its coverage of sites threatened by erosion around Birsay Bay, the Durham project under Morris undertook another cluster of field survey and trial cuttings along the Boardhouse Burn as it passes south of the village, and at several locations on the eroding foreshore of Birsay Links (Morris 1996, 33–191). South of the burn and immediately across from the probable location of the Bishop's Palace, a significant cluster of archaeological remains was detected by sample cuttings, section cleaning, redevelopment work, coupled with a resistivity survey which produced less-than clear results due to the depth of windblown sand. A substantial (but undated) section of stone walling was discovered alongside the burn at Cutting 2 (Morris 1996, 41–3), and fragments of iron, steatite, antler combs, mortar, industrial waste and a bronze finger ring were discovered at Areas 2 and 3, also excavated close to the banks of the burn (*ibid.*, 45–76). These interventions suggest that the steeply sloping ground on the south side of the burn, as indeed on its north side, represents a large mounded spread of multi-period archaeological deposits. The largest and most productive excavation undertaken in this group of interventions took place in 1978–80 on land next to the property then known as Beachview, which lies south-west of the small bridge carrying the road over the burn, south of the village.

Area 1 or the 'Studio Site' (the name refers to a small outbuilding at Beachview, the redevelopment of which led to the initial discovery in 1976 of archaeological deposits) was situated away from the burn edge in the sandy, hummocky grassland of the Links (HY 2478 2755). The 1978–80 excavation seasons revealed a series of 16 phases of substantial stone-built building remains, although in no case was their full extent demonstrated. The earliest of these (Phase K) was a sub-rectangular building oriented east–west, measuring at least 10 m long and 5 m wide internally, the western end of which remained unexcavated. The walls were reconfigured several times to accommodate the addition of a large slab-built corn-drying hearth in a circular walled extension on its north-east corner (Phase N), before the building was part-abandoned and a western extension built with a central drain (Phases W and X), taking the total internal length of the complex to at least 16 m. The finds, including antler combs, a carved ivory piece, iron nails and rivets, copper alloy brooch parts and a dagger chape, together with a small amount of pottery and an even smaller amount of steatite, suggested a Late Norse date between the 11th to 13th centuries. The small number of pre-AMS radiocarbon dates published by Morris and Gordon Cook (in Morris 1996, 292) did not disagree with this broad date range, but all were taken from bone so would have to be recalibrated in relation to the marine reservoir effect to become a reliable comparison to current examples. The subtleties of taphonomy were carefully considered, and a large amount of the material inside the building was interpreted as redeposited midden infill, possibly displaced from somewhere else nearby, which could mean that the construction of the building itself was somewhat earlier than most of its contents (*ibid.*, 145–7). The Beachview Studio Site excavation was also distinguished by the extent to which environmental analytical techniques were used, with animal and bird bone, marine molluscs, fish remains and botanical remains forming a major focus of the research, in line with sampling strategies developed by the same team on Viking-period projects elsewhere in coastal Scotland, such as at Freswick Links, Caithness (Morris, Batey and Rackham 1995).

The Beachview Studio Site emerged from a mound of midden and sand in the centre of the spread of Links land south of the Boardhouse Burn. As we have seen with the tumuli excavated at the Bay of Skaill, the surface profile of links land or machair is only an approximate guide to the presence of archaeological foci. Mounds of archaeological origin are sometimes expressed very clearly as topographic eminences, whereas in other cases they can be obscured by build-ups of Aeolian sand, or become confused with similarly-shaped sand dunes. Even in an erosive environment, the shifting nature of topography serves to obscure as much as reveal. This has meant that some of the observations made in the 1970s or early 1980s, including earthwork traces of a possible chapel site on Birsay Links at approximately HY 246 274 (Morris 1996, 258) have proved impossible to identify conclusively in the course of more recent fieldwork. Other observations, especially those of middens, kelping pits and stone scatters along the eroding shoreline (*ibid.*, 33) have been easier to re-locate. One relatively prominent sandy mound feature near the Point of Snusan is known as 'Mount Misery' (Fig. 3.19). Marwick described this as a 'relatively modern name for which no explanation can be given' although he did draw attention to another instance of the name, on Sanday, which is a prehistoric chambered tomb (Marwick 1970, 35). Mount Misery was part-excavated by John Fraser in 1931, who found 'a few crude stone implements' but no structures or

burning (RCAHMS 1946, 36). A neighbouring, unnamed, somewhat lower sandy mound was noted by RCAHMS (1946, 24) but was not confirmed as of any archaeological interest.

Saevar Howe

At the southern end of Birsay Links, close to the shore (HY 2460 2700), is a large, prominent, grassed sandy mound (Fig. 2.14) known as Saevar Howe or the Knowe of Saverough (ON *Sævar Haugr*), which Hugh Marwick translated as 'Sea Mound' (Marwick 1970, 35). It was excavated in July 1862 by James Farrer (Marwick wrote dismissively that it was 'howked into by the Englishman Farrer'), the standard of whose work at Skara Brae the previous year was criticised as unmethodical by Childe (see above). Farrer's account of his intervention at Saevar Howe was published as a letter to the editor in the *Gentleman's Magazine* and as a note the following year in *PSAS* (Farrer 1862; 1863). Farrer stated that he found 11 long-cists, in a poor state of preservation, in sand between 0.6 and 3.25 m below the surface. These were orientated with their heads facing the north-west although some faced north. Three more cists were found close to structural remains, which he described as a 'large building'. During a second excavation in 1867, Farrer discovered more walling, a flagged yard and a shell midden (Farrer 1868). The human remains found in 1862 are mostly lost (one skull remains in the collection of the Society of Antiquaries of Scotland), but the finds, more of which survive, indicate that the deposits he encountered were mostly early medieval in date. A bronze-covered iron bell of Early Christian type came from one of the cists, and other unstratified objects included worked bone, querns, a whetstone, a steatite cup, part of a composite comb and an iron knife.

Saevar Howe stands at the head of the beach only a few metres above the high-tide line, and is wholly exposed to the battering of Atlantic westerlies. It is

Fig. 2.14 Saevar Howe, from E

also badly affected by rabbit burrowing, trampling by cattle, and has been used at times for rubbish dumping and motorcycle scrambling. Farrer's excavation created a crater in the top of the mound which has been the source of further deflation, and the limited protective stability of its rough grassed surface is weakened by several large scars of exposed sand. The fragile and eroded condition of the mound (SM 1373) has been of concern to archaeologists and inspectors of ancient monuments since the hey-day of 'rescue' archaeology in the 1970s. In an attempt to assess its remaining archaeological potential, and with a view to clarifying details of Farrer's interventions, an exploratory test excavation took place in 1977 directed by John Hedges (Hedges 1983). This was intended to be the precursor of a fully-fledged excavation which never happened due to funding being diverted to other priorities. Hedges placed four small trenches in a cruciform pattern on the central part of the mound, two of which were 8 × 6 m and the other two 4 × 4 m. These picked up the traces of Farrer's trench, which, even allowing for over a century of deflation and collapse, can only be described as an amorphous and unsystematic shape with numerous offshoots following walls and other features, which had the effect of separating areas of surviving deposits into small islands and severely compromising the ability of Hedges's excavation to make coherent sense of them. Hedges identified two main phases of activity, and re-identified some of the structures in Farrer's account (although not the cist graves). Occupation layers were laminated between intervening episodes of wind-blown sand. Phase I was described as pre-Viking, and was divided into three sub-phases, encompassing limited traces of earlier (presumably Iron Age) activity which was not explored further, and a discontinuous group of

building remains, which were interpreted on the basis of radiocarbon dates as probably being Pictish. Phase II produced a slightly clearer picture, with a fragmentary sequence of three successive 'hall houses' (perhaps a rather too-grandiose description in retrospect), these being rectilinear structures estimated to be up to 11 or 12 m long, although none of them were represented in their entirety. Associated with the earliest of the Phase II structures was a silver penny of Burgred of Mercia (struck between AD 866–868). The other finds from 1977: iron, glass, steatite, worked bone and ceramics (including numerous objects excavated from Farrer's spoil heaps), together with archaeozoological and archaeobotanical evidence, broadly accord with the view that the occupation at the site was predominantly Norse in character. Only nine finds could be associated with Phase I, and although some of the comb fragments and pins represent Pictish types, as with other sites such as Buckquoy (above), their use to reinforce a traditionally-accepted distinction between Pictish and Viking *occupations* would need to be revisited. Similarly, three radiocarbon dates on charcoal and shells, which gave a range between approximately 1200 and 1395 carbon years BP, would need to be recalibrated in any future reappraisal. The true nature of the cist-grave cemetery allegedly found in 1862 and 1867 remains enigmatic. Farrer's account left no doubt that it overlaid the structures that Hedges assigned to (Norse) Phase II, so it could only be later than those. However, cist graves more commonly pre-date the Viking or early Norse period in Orkney, and this style of burial (especially considering the mixed orientations of the Saevar Howe cists) did not continue into the Christian period. Hedges planned to answer these questions in a more complete excavation, which as described above, never took place.

3

Landscape surveys 2003–2015

David Griffiths, Michael Athanson and Susan Ovenden

Methods

As described above in the introduction, by the early 2000s, the utility and extensive capabilities of geophysical and topographical survey had improved to the extent that they became viable as a means of characterising an archaeological landscape hitherto only accessible by chance discoveries and excavation. They also provide a potential means of contextualising coastal exposures driven by marine erosion (the principal driver behind most previous excavation) against a wider landscape picture. The basis for selecting areas and targets for survey could best be described as 'working from the known to the unknown'. Where archaeology (of any period) had been noted in the past (see above, Chapter 2), its presence (even if its known location was less than exact) was a prompt towards survey being implemented in its vicinity. Where upstanding archaeology existed, especially if it had not been recorded previously, topographic surveys were undertaken. In every case an effort was made, within finite resources, to extend the extent of data capture around the chosen area to produce an extent which could be interpreted on a landscape scale. Areas beside, between and around scheduled ancient monuments and older excavations were chosen for geophysical survey, as were the broad environs of past chance discoveries, such as the 1858 Skaill hoard. Within areas covered by more extensive but less detailed survey methods, such as magnetic susceptibility topsoil mapping (Griffiths 2006), more intensive methods (and ultimately in some cases, excavation) were targeted on the most promising responses. Overall survey control covering all techniques allowed a straightforward complementary positioning of survey grids and trenches directly over what presented itself graphically as the clearest priority for further

investigation. The result was the completion of a series of small, medium and in one case, at the Bay of Skaill, a large-scale landscape survey area. Apart from the Links of Skaill, few of the survey areas were contiguous with each other. This is explained by the impossibility of total blanket survey with the time and resources available, the presence of buildings, fencing, car parks, quarrying and other obstacles to uninterrupted survey.

Topographic survey was based on traditional observation – the presence of upstanding or exposed archaeological remains, which were recorded in three dimensions using a total station for which locational control was taken from a series of metal ground-anchors, the positions of which were calculated using intersections taken from fixed, mapped reference objects such as buildings. Later on in the project, a GPS (GNSS) Smartstation was acquired by the host department, and all ground anchors and other survey positions were checked and re-surveyed using this facility. Lidar, where available, was used as an adjunct to ground observation. Lidar data for Orkney is freely available at 5 m-interval resolution and there has so far been some intermittent coverage at higher resolution. These data-sets were run up into a series of working plots, which broadly confirmed the knowledge gained from ground observation as to the presence of large, macro-topographic features such as settlement mounds that have archaeological implications.

In terms of geophysical survey, a key challenge for the project was to produce a consistent body of data from the coastal environment. Areas such as the Point of Buckquoy (surveyed in 2003–4), the Brough of Birsay and Marwick have cultivated farm soils stratified directly above the glacial till. Elsewhere, notably on Birsay Links and the Links of Skaill, areas are dominated by windblown sand, characterising the archaeological potential of which was a major methodological theme of the project. It was anticipated from the start that techniques needed to be varied and adapted to ground conditions. Magnetic susceptibility topsoil mapping is quick to survey using a hand-operated ground-contact coil, and gives a broad indication of areas where ploughing has brought burning and past settlement activity to the surface, the traces which have raised the potential in the upper *c.* 100 mm soil to be magnetised when a weak electric current is passed through it (hence its 'susceptibility'). It was successful on the cultivated farm soils (forming a broad indicative plot within which other techniques could be targeted) but is virtually useless in sandy environments, where the topsoil is mostly separated stratigraphically from the archaeology by depths of sand overburden. Gradiometry, a more intensive and detailed technique than magnetic susceptibility topsoil mapping, based on sensing and mapping magnetic variation in the subsoil, offered the hope of a deeper reach (it is reliable to up to 1.5 m depth) and so formed the most widespread geophysical landscape survey method for the project. Nonetheless, it was understood from the beginning that even though it produced archaeologically-recognisable results, these might not reveal the full picture of buried deposits. The depth reach of conventional gradiometry was not adequate to detect deposits deeply buried (over 1.5 m) within the core of large settlement mounds such as Snusgar, East Mound and Saevar Howe. Because this method can only be deployed from above the ground surface, it is also vulnerable to producing a picture of the archaeology that was to a great extent drowned out by later surface activity of a magnetically-intense character, such as burning and refuse disposal.

To supplement the utility of magnetic susceptibility topsoil mapping and gradiometry in surveying locations of archaeological interest, earth resistance survey was used. This detects a different property in the soil, namely differential patterns of conductivity and resistance, which reflect and map the presence of vectors (moisture) and barriers (often stone walls or voids). This was most successful on relatively stable, non-sand influenced sites with stone buildings, such as at the Marwick Chapel (see below). Its utility on sandier areas was more qualified, with the dry, loose nature of windblown sand (found in particular on the flanks of the mound sites) working against its efficacy. It did, however, produce results that were consonant with those of the gradiometry and thus a recognisable reflection of some aspects of the archaeology. Earth resistance survey is a near-surface-focused technique and did not offer any hope of tackling the difficult question of what, if anything, might lie deeply buried at the heart of the larger sandier mound formations under examination. At Snusgar and East Mound, Ground Penetrating Radar

was used. At the time this was such an intensive technique that it was only practically and financially feasible in very small areas. Of the two frequencies used (400 and 270 MHz), the 270 MHz antenna in particular is capable of producing results to several metres' depth, and indeed was successful in producing not only a representative profile of the more complex, upper archaeological deposits but contributed some useful information on the position and depth of buried soils, including the ground level upon which the mounds originally formed, and some intriguing (if inconclusive) hints of deeper, earlier archaeology. In supplement to these techniques, in 2010 a Glasgow University Archaeology PhD student, Carmen Cuenca-Garcia, used a combination of ground-penetrating radar and electro-magnetic conductivity survey in a sample area on East Mound covering Trench 7 in order to research chemical properties in the soil producing geophysical responses. The results of this work are presented in her thesis (Cuenca-Garcia 2012)

Technology

The equipment and technology available within the realm of technical landscape survey vary from the mainstream to the more unusual and experimental (Gaffney and Gater 2003). Mainstream geophysical techniques such as gradiometry, magnetic susceptibility topsoil mapping, earth resistance survey, ground-penetrating radar, together with three-dimensional surface modelling, are available through reasonably-priced commercially-produced equipment and software which is in widespread academic and professional use. These require care, consistency and accuracy in their operation, but not advanced electronic or computing expertise. In the period 2003 to 2015, the mainstream techniques have seen some updating and refining but fewer basic innovative changes. The gradiometers used in the project's first season in 2003, Geoscan FM36 single sensor machines, were replaced with Bartington Grad 601 dual sensors for the rest of the project. The Bartington Grad 601 is a more efficient machine, covering twice the ground per transect, but does not produce qualitatively different data. Gradiometry is now increasingly available in multi-array carts which speed up the rate of data collection, or through the use of Caesium Vapour machines which are capable of sensing finer magnetic variations. Due to the generally small and tricky areas and fields being surveyed here (which are best covered by hand-carried sensors), and the increasingly-held view that it was the *bigger* rather than the *finer* picture that worked best in this environment, the use of neither of these (far more expensive) techniques was sought. Magnetic susceptibility topsoil mapping is available as a technique using soil samples processed in laboratories (a normal method for excavation spot sampling, see below, Chapter 7) or using a ground-contact coil coupled to a meter such as a Bartington MS2 meter, a much faster if less sensitive method. As a method for landscape prospection, the latter was by far the most practical choice.

The project operated a standard 30 × 30 m grid survey unit in 2003–4 with a sampling interval of 0.25 m, this was changed to a 20 × 20 m unit from 2005 onwards, which was the preference of Orkney College Geophysics Unit which henceforth undertook the majority of the survey work. Earth resistance survey was carried out using a Geoscan RM15 four-array resistance meter with an MPX15 multiplexer, and the majority of Ground Penetrating Radar was done with a GSSSI SIR 3000 GPR System with 270 MHz antennas at 0.02 m intervals along traverses 0.5 m apart. The results were downloaded using a range of system-based download softwares. The geophysical results were processed using Geoplot™ and then combined with topographic survey results in the GIS package ArcGIS™.

One dimension of the project where magnetic prospection technology could potentially have been used more intensively is within the excavation trenches. The confined spaces afforded within trenches, baulks, vertical sections and fragile structures, make intra-site conventional gradiometry virtually impossible. When the last major excavation took place on East Mound in 2010, it was still conventional archaeological practice to test occupation deposits for magnetic susceptibility by removing small soil samples to be processed in a laboratory, the results of which are covered below in Chapter 7. Techniques have, inevitably, moved on since then and taking *in situ* readings, which enable spatial plots to be created as the excavation progresses, would now be preferred.

The Bay of Skaill

The Bay of Skaill has been subjected to two recent campaigns of extensive geophysical survey, by the same contracting organisation (OCGU, now part of the UHI Archaeology Institute), totalling 57.92 hectares of gradiometry, making it one of the largest contiguous areas of coverage to date in Scotland (and the second-largest in Orkney after the Brodgar/Maeshowe section of the World Heritage Area). Almost the entire agricultural landscape of the bay's coastal hinterland has now been surveyed, leaving out only a few areas, which were deemed to be technically problematic due to the presence of buildings, quarrying disturbance, hard surfaces or metallic dumping. The areas north and east of the central road were surveyed between 2003 and 2009 by this project.

The southern half of the bay, south and west of the road, was surveyed by OCGU on behalf of Orkney College in 2007. The latter survey was grant-aided by Historic Scotland as a means of characterising the World Heritage Area buffer zone around Skara Brae. Figure 3.1 is based on a compilation of both sets of results, and has been prepared jointly for publication in the monographs that serve the two projects. Detailed interpretation of the results from the southern area survey will follow in Brend *et al.*(forthcoming). These indicate that the Neolithic settlement at Skara Brae may well be more extensive than hitherto suspected, with dense clusters of positive/negative anomalies occurring on the slope immediately south and south-west of the guardianship site. The fences around the guardianship site have occluded the magnetic signal to some extent, compounded by the presence under the southern extent of the guardianship site of an igneous dyke approximately 5 m in width. Indeed, the large scale of coverage achieved by the two surveys reveals a pattern of parallel igneous dykes or 'swarms' crossing the landscape. Most, including the igneous dyke which underlies the southern edge of the Skara Brae guardianship site, trend north-east to south-west, whereas one (in the centre of the bay perpendicular to the coastline) trends north-west to south-east, crossing the other igneous dykes at an oblique angle. The WHA survey also reveals a strong and extensive pattern of linear contrast representing past agricultural land-use in the form of patterns of field cultivation rigs. These are concentrated on the rising slope of land on the southernmost part of the bay landscape around Skaill Home Farm and the neighbouring (now abandoned) farmstead to its west, Garricott. Concealed within these relict field patterns are a number of discordant curvilinear and sub-circular anomalies that may represent earlier sites and boundaries. The most emphatic of these is a pronounced pattern of two concentric rings, coincident with a slight mounded rise in topography 180 m overlooking the Loch of Skaill, south-east of Skaill House at HY 238 183, which is clearly suggestive of an [Iron Age] broch. The rig cultivation pattern stops at the boundary between the sloping field ploughsoils and the Links. Skaill House stands upon this boundary, and its buildings and services (and those of Skara Brae visitor centre and neighbouring houses) can clearly be seen in the geophysical data, with lines of strongly magnetic character (which are probably old domestic waste pipelines) heading for the bay frontage.

Skara Brae survey 2003

In June 2003, prior to the more extensive survey of the Skara Brae WHA carried out by Orkney College, a small-scale gradiometer survey was undertaken to test the environs of Skara Brae for wider magnetic survey feasibility. A 90 × 30 m area of gradiometry was surveyed in the field immediately south-west of the Skara Brae guardianship area (centred on HY 2308 1870), and a 60 × 30 m area on the surface of the remaining portion of the 'Boat House' mound 150 m west of Skara Brae (centred

Fig. 3.1 Bay of Skaill: full extent of geophysical survey. Data south of central road reproduced by courtesy of UHI Archaeology Institute. Base map © Crown Copyright 2018. An Ordnance Survey/EDINA supplied service

on HY 2293 1874). The results of this survey were published in 2006 (Griffiths 2006, 224 and Fig. 19.8) and were largely superseded by the later and more extensive OCGU/ORCA fieldwork covering most of the same area. The eastern of the two areas, beside Skara Brae, was located in a field sloping downwards towards the bay, with evidence of some slight surface disturbance and modern metallic contamination, especially at its upper, southern boundary bordering the track to Garricott. The lower, northern part of this area was occluded by metal fencing. Nevertheless, a pronounced highly positive linear anomaly trending north-west to south-east across the survey area was noted, unmistakably caused by an igneous dyke deep under the topsoil, which also apparently underlies the southern boundary of the Skara Brae guardianship area. This was detected in the 1973 Clark and Bartlett survey (see Chapter 2) and was subsequently confirmed by the WHA Survey as part of a much more extensive pattern. Two 30 × 30 m gradiometry grids undertaken on the 'Boat House' mound show a curving line of discrete points of raised magnetic potential, roughly according with the extent and shape of the remaining part of the mound. There is a faint hint of a pattern of cultivation rigs trending across the mound surface from north-west to south-east. The south-eastern portion of the survey area, where the track to Garricott crosses it, is subject to modern metallic disturbance from spreads of hardcore in the road surface.

Northern Bay area, mound surveys 2003–2006

It was clear from initial reconnaissance in 2002–3 that a series of large sandy mounds, then as yet of unconfirmed archaeological status, lay in a broadly east–west line stretching inland from the north-easternmost part of the bay frontage (Fig. 3.2). These were termed, from west to east: Mound A (nearest to the shore, see Chapter 2), Mound B (a nearby lower mound in the field just east of the road and north-west of Snusgar), [Castle of] Snusgar, 'East Mound', and slightly later was added Mound C (below), a formation some distance to the east of the other mounds which bears a superficial resemblance (Fig. 3.3). Investigations of the most prominent of these mounds, known as [the Castle of] Snusgar (see Chapter 2), began in June 2003 with topographic survey and with gradiometry covering 0.45 ha (seven 30 × 30 grids). The area of gradiometry was substantially extended in 2004–6 to encompass the north-western field of Snusgar (covering Mound B and the western fringes of Snusgar not surveyed in 2003), together with areas of 40 × 40 m on Mound A, and 40 × 20 m on top of 'East Mound'. Subsequently, in July–August 2006 these areas were joined together and extended to a full landscape gradiometer survey of the surrounding area (Fig. 3.4).

Topographically, Snusgar is by no means a simple mounded structure, nor even can it be truly described as a single mound. The north-west sector plateau, where the clearest structural evidence was detected using geophysics, is noticeably flatter with a more regular and rectilinear surrounding slope morphology than the rest of the mound. This may reflect past modification of the upper mound topography as a building platform and grading of its slopes, and appears to support antiquarian and historical accounts of a stone structure having once stood upon the mound (above, Chapter 2). The northern extension to the pattern of geophysical anomalies on Snusgar is represented topographically by a domed protrusion from the main mound, giving the surface plateau an almost pear-shaped appearance in plan. This may possibly have originated as another, smaller, mound that has gradually become subsumed into the main bulk of Snusgar by infill, build-ups of windblown sand, and by ploughing.

The geophysical survey was split into three fields divided by the inverted T-shape of the stone field dykes. The dykes, which are substantial structures, support wire fencing on top, which despite a survey stand-off of *c.* 2 m, had a mild adverse effect on the clarity and quality of the data within their immediate vicinity. The gradiometer survey of Snusgar (Fig. 3.5) showed a strong cluster of magnetic contrast, indicative of burning and occupation deposits. This is visible as a sub-circular area on top of the mound, showing up against a generally quiet background with only a few isolated ferrous deposits. The high level of magnetic response on top of the mound was encouraging, suggesting probable spreads of midden and settlement-related deposition, but with the caveat that relatively modern activity such as burning and refuse disposal may substantially have overwritten the signal coming from any earlier deposits. From these initial results it was clearly understood that the magnetic character of this and other neighbouring mounds is highly complex and reflective of many superimposed episodes of activity.

Archaeologically, the clearest area within the survey results is an east–west linear trend in the north-western sector, principally but not exclusively confined to the field north-west of the field dykes. This could reasonably result from past ploughing patterns, or it could betray the presence of sub-surface building remains. Represented in white on the greyscale plot, two relatively coherent east–west semi-parallel negative anomalies suggest the possible presence of walls. These appear to cluster in two patterns, the overall shapes of which appear to indicate longhouse type structures.

The northern and most complete anomaly of this type is perceptibly somewhat bow-sided in plan, implying a possible longhouse, the eastern end of which is probably occluded within the much stronger concentration of magnetic contrast resulting from more recent burning activity in the north-eastern sector (the area examined in Trench 1, see below, Chapter 4, which confirmed this was

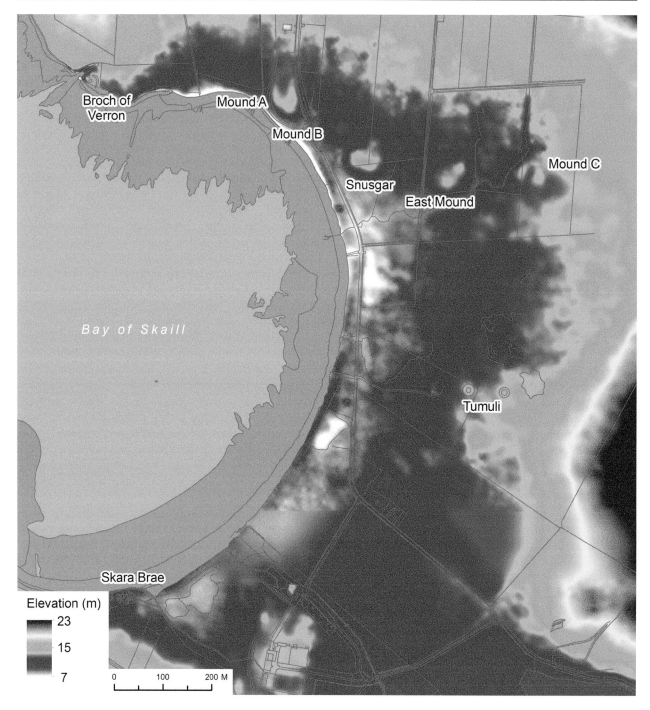

Fig. 3.2 Bay of Skaill: mound sites, surface model derived from ground survey and Lidar Base map © Crown Copyright 2018. An Ordnance Survey/EDINA supplied service; and Lidar data © 2018 Intermap Technologies

substantial, is a very poorly-preserved and fragmentary wall, the finds and deposits associated with which determined a Viking/Norse date). Hints of an opposing south wall on a similar alignment 4.9 m to its south were also picked up in excavation, but this was even less well-defined. The density of magnetic 'noise' resulting from later disturbance made it difficult to be certain of

identifying subtler internal sub-divisions or other features, which may well exist, but would require further excavation across the wall in the north-west sector to explore. Also in the north-west sector, nearer the western/central area of the summit, is another apparent long sub-rectilinear pattern suggesting a possible longhouse anomaly. This is somewhat less clear than the one to the north of the

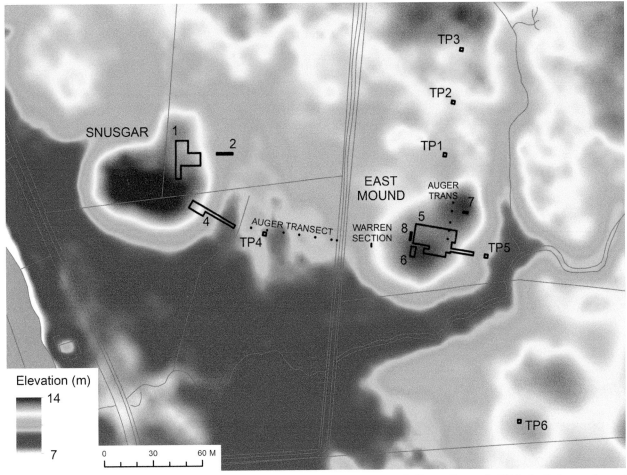

Fig. 3.3 Bay of Skaill: excavation trenches, test pits and auger transects. Base map © Crown Copyright 2018. An Ordnance Survey/ EDINA supplied service; and Lidar data © 2018 Intermap Technologies

mound, and due to problems with securing permission from the landowner, was not subjected to excavation.

In 2004, 0.8 ha of earth resistance survey was undertaken on Snusgar, in the area subjected to gradiometer survey in 2003. This succeeded in confirming the central cluster of highly-magnetised deposits (already identified in gradiometry) as a pear-shaped area of relatively lower resistance. The resistance pattern suggested that the deposits in this area were more coherent, and slightly moister than those in the surrounding area, which would accord with an interpretation of settlement deposits and midden deposits. The resistance data also showed a faint recognition of the east–west linear pattern of negative anomalies in the north-west sector of Snusgar, which gradiometry more strongly indicated were stone walls. On the flanks of the mound was a surrounding band of markedly higher resistance. It was initially thought prior to excavation that this band could relate to a possible defensive bank and ditch around the mound that might have formed part of the 'castle', following a suggestion by Morris (1985, 85) that such a feature may have existed.

However, this suggestion was not borne out during excavation, where no such defensive feature was detected, and the higher resistance effect may merely be attributed to a gravity-induced moisture deficit in the sandy slopes of the mound (Fig. 3.6).

The sub-surface structure and character of Snusgar were further tested with a sample area of Ground Penetrating Radar survey, measuring 80 × 30 m in the southern sector of the mound but aligned to the central east–west boundary dyke. This area therefore included part of the relatively flat top of the mound, a full width sector of its slope, and an area of flat ground beyond the slope. Both a 400 MHz and a 270 MHz antenna were used, with a range of up to 5 m depth (covering the upstanding height of the mound), gathering data at 0.02 m intervals along traverses 0.5 m apart. The data was used to create radargrams and time-slices. The (vertically displayed) 270 MHz radargrams, which have been topographically corrected and show their results in vertical section, show several general responses (Fig. 3.7). Well-defined horizontal reflections are visible throughout, with the highest density at the top. These may

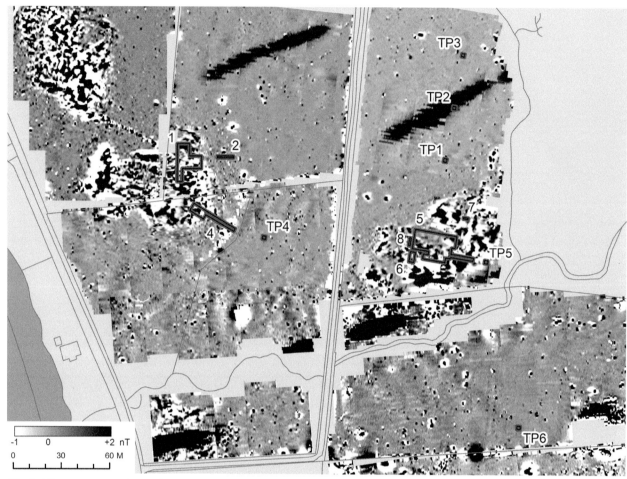

Fig. 3.4 Excavation trenches and test pits superimposed on gradiometry. Base map © Crown Copyright 2018. An Ordnance Survey/ EDINA supplied service

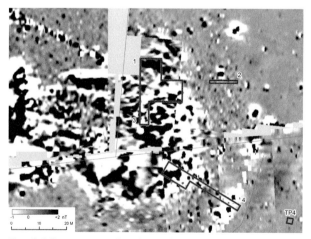

Fig. 3.5 Snusgar, trenches 1-4 and Test Pit 4 superimposed on gradiometry. Base Map © Crown Copyright 2018. An Ordnance Survey/EDINA supplied service

be compared to excavated sections from Trench 4, a long and deep trench on the south-east flank of Snusgar, which broadly followed the same trajectory as the GPR survey. The horizontal reflections clearly relate to buried ground

surfaces that were enriched with midden and stabilised with stone. These are laid horizontally, the most practical plane for occupation, as opposed to in a mounded gradient, which would normally be the case for mound layers that formed around a central, lower focus such as a burial. It is clear from the GPR survey, as well as excavation, that the mounded shape of Snusgar is a product of the forces of erosion and deposition upon an essentially flat, if locally concentrated, stacked sequence of deposits. It therefore more accurately resembles a 'tell' of occupation layers interleaved with windblown sand, as opposed to a heaped mound reminiscent of a barrow or tumulus.

The time-slice maps provide a horizontal counterpart to the radargrams, showing responses in plan at half-metre intervals from 0 to 4 m depth. These are not topographically corrected. The 0–0.5 time slice shows surface variations, together with a north-west to south-east diagonal anomaly, which is the upper part of Trench 4 (this had already begun at the time of the radar survey). Below this, between 0.5 and 2.5 m depth is an area of high amplitude response that agrees well with the sub-oval pattern visible in this area on the gradiometry. This gradually fades out towards 4 m depth.

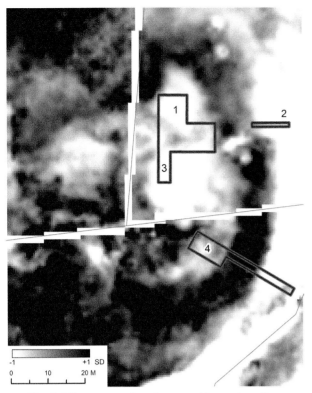

Fig. 3.6 Snusgar, earth resistance with trench outlines

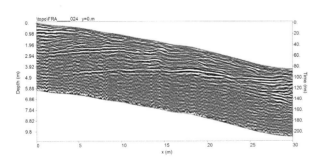

Fig. 3.7 Snusgar, radargram of southern half of mound, summit to left (N), adjusted to topography with surface at top, natural ground level c. 4.5 m below 0

Mounds 'A' and 'B'

Mound 'A' is the large circular flat-topped mound which stands closest to the shore, around which the old road loops, and within which burials and structures were found in the mid-1930s during the creation of the new, straighter road line north of the bay (above, Chapter 2). The new road disrupted the eastern third of the mound (a small portion of the original shape of which still lies east of the road), and the rest of the mound is surrounded by steel and barbed-wire fencing, which has heavily compromised the possibilities for gradiometry. Nonetheless, an area

measuring 40 × 40 m with a small 20 × 10 m extension to the south-west was surveyed in 2004 (Fig. 3.1). Numerous strong discrete anomalies of probable archaeological interest are visible, but this survey was too small to characterise them in anything approaching their full juxtaposition or extent.

Mound 'B' is a smaller, lower mound which is located in the field immediately north-west of Snusgar. It is separated from the north-west flank of Snusgar by a small 'valley' so is clearly a separate landscape formation. A 1.2 ha area of gradiometry was undertaken in 2004, in the north-western field, including all of Mound B and re-surveying a small part of Snusgar which had been covered in 2003. The latter showed a very strong anomaly at the western end of the summit plateau of Snusgar, which is consistent with the steep slope and is not an accurate reflection of the archaeology. Mound B exhibits a compilation of strong signals that are similar to those encountered on Snusgar and suggest an archaeological origin. A well-defined quieter area exists on the north-east flank of this concentration, which appears to be enclosed in a possible ditch-type shape. Crossing the gap between Snusgar and Mound B is a linear anomaly – this is almost certainly an old field boundary, as a similarly-aligned field dyke is visible in this position on the OS 25 inch map edition of 1902 (Fig. 2.7).

Neither Mound A or B nor the north-west sector of Snusgar itself were able to be subjected to any form of excavation or ground-truthing, as they all lie in fields owned by a landowner who allowed geophysical survey to take place in 2003–4, but subsequently withheld permission for excavation.

East Mound

The large mound which became known during the project as 'East Mound' (because it lies to the east of Snusgar) was initially thought not to offer particularly promising archaeological potential. A prominent deflation scar on its west-facing side revealed nothing of its internal structure but layers of slumped and windblown sand, which have been heavily turbated by rabbits and trampled by cattle. It has a broadly flat-topped, oval shape aligned east–west with a smaller, higher mounded extension on the north-east; its southern side stands above a steep slope down to the burn. The only metal fence in its environs is located well down on the southern slope. The possibility that this mound is merely a sand-dune was considered initially likely, given that no archaeological or historical evidence had ever previously been associated with it and it had been missed out entirely as a feature from previous reports covering this area of the bay, from Fraser (1923), to RCAHMS (1946), to Morris (1985). Nonetheless, as with Mounds A and B, to test this, a small area of gradiometry measuring 40 × 20 m was undertaken on its surface in 2004, which was subsequently extended to encompass the whole mound and its landscape surrounds. The initial 2004 gradiometer survey on East Mound showed a similar dense, amorphous cluster of positive and negative magnetic contrast to those exhibited by Snusgar and Mounds A and B. Discerning patterns within this that might be closely indicative of archaeological structures was difficult, although an apparent rectangular area of negative contrast did present itself, aligned east–west across the middle of the two 20 × 20 m survey grids. The similarity between these initial results and the emergent characteristic patterns of response on the other mounds led to a decision to begin a test excavation within the surveyed area on East Mound in 2005, although it was considered likely that the pattern of anomalies could reflect relatively modern activity. (After five seasons of excavation on East Mound, the 'rectangular' anomaly never resolved itself into a detectable feature, and may therefore have been either a response to conditions in the upper topsoil, or was possibly an artifice of data-processing.)

Only when gradiometer survey had been extended in 2006 to encompass the full extent of Snusgar and East Mound (Figs 3.4; 3.8), together with much of the rest of the fields in which they stand (Fig. 3.4), did their character as settlement mounds become clearer. Their shapes are very clearly picked out against a fairly quiet background, in the case of East Mound with dense clusters of positive and negative response in its central, eastern and northern extent. These coincide well with the extent of the archaeological structures and deposits revealed during excavation.

It was felt that the chances of earth resistance working well on East Mound were low, given the dryness and depth of sand observed in the western scar area. However, a 40 × 40 m area was surveyed in 2005. This added little to the picture observed in gradiometry, other than to cast doubt upon the 'rectilinear' anomaly, which failed to show up at all in this technique. A dense cluster of contrast suggested a generalised amorphous possibility of archaeological potential, whereas a localised area of lower resistance on the north-east flank of this area could be due to the depth of dry, windblown sand. To supplement the gradiometer and resistance surveys, GPR surveys were carried out over an area of 15 × 13 m (400 MHz) and 30 × 20 m (270 MHz) on the flat top of East Mound. Of these, the 270 MHz was most successful in characterising traces of sub-surface archaeological potential. Radargrams picked up a spread of possible archaeological interest across the area between 1 and 3 m depth, with a more coherent pattern of reflective anomalies which suggested possible structures, buried land surfaces or stabilised middens, between 2 and 3.5 m below surface, according well with the depth of structures excavated (Chapter 4). The time-slice maps for this area confirm the concentration of reflective deposits towards

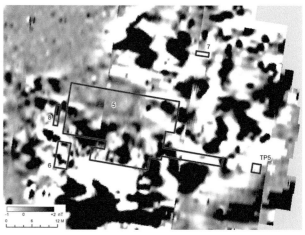

Fig. 3.8 East Mound, trenches 5–8 and Test Pit 5 superimposed on gradiometry. Base Map © Crown Copyright 2018. An Ordnance Survey/EDINA supplied service

the east of the survey area, which show their greatest resolution between 2.5 and 3.5 m depth.

Mound 'C' (the 'Far East Mound'), and an apparent mounded formation south of the burn

Throughout the survey work concentrated on Snusgar and East Mound, attention was given to finding and identifying other mounded sites of possible archaeological interest in their environs. The difficulty of distinguishing settlement mounds from sand dunes by appearance alone has been described above. Two possible mounded formations were identified by walkover survey.

A possible settlement mound was identified 120 m to the east of East Mound at HY 2394 1962, now termed 'Mound C', but which during the survey was informally dubbed the 'Far East Mound'. It is a modest rise on topography along the steep eastern bank of the Burn of Snusgar. Topographically, it appears as a low, regular sandy mounded formation with a substantial depression in its centre. Magnetic survey was complicated by the fact that a metal wire fence and stone field dyke crosses the centre of the feature north–south, and its western extent has been eroded and compromised by its position on the steep edge of the burn. An area of 80 × 40 m together with a smaller area of approximately 20 × 10 m on the western side of the central fence were surveyed using a gradiometer in 2011. The results (Fig. 3.9, north-easternmost area) were neither coherent nor particularly similar to those from East Mound, Snusgar, or Mounds A or B. There was significant ferrous contamination, focusing on the central topographic depression, which appeared largely modern in origin. A 60 × 20 m (east of fence) and 40 × 20 m (west of fence) area of earth resistance was similarly unproductive; an oval area of high resistance, suggesting a possible stone structure or void, was found bridging the two survey areas, but the

Fig. 3.9 Bay of Skaill northern area, gradiometry: mound sites and interpretation points 1–4 referred to in text. Base map © Crown Copyright 2018. An Ordnance Survey/EDINA supplied service

extensive rabbit burrowing across the mound is a probable explanation. Given the dissimilarity of this data to that obtained from the other, demonstrably archaeological, mounds in the vicinity, it must be assumed on the basis of what is currently known that this feature is a natural or semi-natural sand formation that has coincidentally taken on the surface attributes of a mound, and which has been modified by general agricultural activity, rabbit burrowing and the random scattering of piecemeal metallic refuse.

A further small humped mound was identified south of the Burn of Snusgar at HY 2385 1948, with an apparent dimpled excavation scar on top (which gave rise to a provisional thought that it may have been opened by barrow diggers). A 20 × 20 m trial area of gradiometry, supplemented by earth resistance and eventually a 2 × 2 m machine-excavated test-pit (TP6, Fig. 3.4) all proved negative in terms of results, revealing only deeply laminated clean sands, indicating that this feature is a true dune. The apparent excavation scar may simply have been the result of a small episode of superficial sand extraction.

The central Skaill Bay landscape

The northern area of landscape gradiometer survey, to the north of the Burn of Snusgar, was largely completed in 2006. Its extent clearly shows the discrete, dense concentrations of magnetic contrast represented by the group of mounds including Snusgar and East Mound, together with neighbouring mounds A and B. The upstanding portions of the mounds were the initial focus, with survey later being extended to their surrounding contexts and eventually covering the landscape areas between them. An extensive gradiometer survey comprising 21 ha (Fig. 3.9) was carried out across the central Links of Skaill in summer 2009, extending the area surveyed around the northern mound group in 2003–6. The central part of the links is generally flat, low-lying, and is subject to waterlogging in winter. The sand overburden is deep and extensive enough to pose a generalised potential problem to magnetic survey, so expectations of gaining results of dramatically clear archaeological resolution were not high. There are several disused sand quarries on the Links of Skaill, one of which lies at the front centre of the bay, and is now partly used as a public car-park, and debris and disturbance from former sand-quarrying activity is widespread, producing numerous isolated points of ferrous interference. Apart from Skaill House at the southern edge of the Links and the remaining traces of the demolished mill on the shoreline, there are no historic properties in central portion of the bay; the cottages Sea View, Grahamsha', Morven, Skerravoe and Millhouse (now known as Mill Croft), all date to between the later 19th and mid-20th centuries (Irvine 2009, 227–8). There are no earlier stone steadings on these sites, and no evidence

that their positions consciously repeat or respect those of earlier settlements.

From the Burn of Snusgar, for up to 250 m southwards towards the centre of the bay, there is very little in the gradiometer data to indicate any archaeological potential, although responses could have been masked by sand. This area is flat, and two areas bordering the road, the field north-west of the house known as Mill Croft and the car park between Mill Croft and Sea View, are so disturbed by quarrying and introduced hard-core that they were judged not to be worth surveying. A pronounced igneous dyke trending north-east to south-west crosses the northern part of the central links, and there are weaker traces of another to its north, the geophysical signal of which is occluded by alluvial deposits along the Burn, and the northern part of which touches the southern fringe of East Mound. Further to the north, on a similar alignment north-east of Snusgar, are two more.

The central part of the 21 ha survey area covers the locations of the tumuli within which cist burials were excavated by Low and Banks in October 1772 (above, Chapter 2). One of these is almost certainly represented by a diffuse, low sandy mound in the back garden of Mill Croft at HY 2382 1915 (Fig. 3.9 (1)). There is a strong ferrous anomaly in the geophysics at this point – it is unclear whether this effect is produced directly by archaeological deposits, but in view of its strength it is more likely that it represents dumping of metallic materials either in a modern hole, or possibly within the hole left by the Low/Banks excavation. The other three tumuli noted by RCAHMS and OS, if they still exist in any tangible form, are invisible magnetically against the background of widespread ferrous contamination, and topographically it is hard to distinguish diagnostic evidence for their presence, given the ability of windblown sand to obfuscate as well as accentuate minor rises and falls in the topography. Prehistoric burial mounds, unless burnt or containing significant amounts of burnt material, are unlikely to show up in gradiometry as distinctive features against a background of some magnetic complexity. However, the area surrounding the probable locations of the tumuli does exhibit a discrete trace of east–west cultivation pattern, unseen elsewhere on the central links. This may merely be an isolated and faint echo of a short-lived presence of rig cultivation in this unpromising soil, however if it represents conditional magnetic visibility of a more widespread system, this effect could also indicate a slight magnetic enhancement of the soil in this area due to the presence of archaeological deposits.

Immediately north of Morven at HY 2370 1892 (Fig. 3.9 (2)) is a discrete cluster of anomalies that appear to be unrelated to the house (which was built in 1952). A linear patch of high magnetic response immediately north of its garden fence could be explained by modern dumping together with a skew in the data caused by a slight slope. Underlying the neighbouring cottage Grahamsha' is part of an igneous dyke, also visible south of the road, the signal from which peters out within 25 m north of the garden fence. But between the igneous dyke and the fence behind Morven is a bow-sided rectilinear anomaly with straight ends, 30 m long, with an alignment of three circular pits in its interior. These are positive on the scale of nT, indicating that they include material magnetised above the relative zero in the area (walls with midden cores could produce this effect, as well as pits). On its south-east side is a more general, and magnetically slightly weaker, spread of responses. This cluster was not investigated further, but morphologically it bears the suggestive hallmarks of a possible longhouse of Viking or Late Norse date (Fig. 3.10), with spreads of midden in its immediate environs. Further investigatory work, which lay beyond the means of the current project, would be required to confirm this.

On the south-eastern edge of the survey area (Fig. 3.9 (3)) is a diffuse spread of magnetic responses, which are generally ephemeral in form and may relate to modern ground disturbance, although at HY 2390 1882 is a more coherent curvilinear anomaly, which may (on the basis of comparison with more pronounced clusters of a similar type found in the WHA survey) indicate the presence of possible prehistoric domestic structures. To the north of this area, at HY 2391 1905 is a weak but coherent square anomaly measuring 20 × 20 m (Fig. 3.9 (4)) with a (possibly unrelated) more strongly magnetised point at its north-west corner which may be a pit. The very low magnetic contrast between the 'square' and the general

background imply that it lacks occupation deposits, so may be a transient feature possibly related to agriculture, such as the site of an old animal fold.

Marwick

In 2009, consent was obtained to undertake geophysical and topographic survey on the two scheduled ancient monuments at the front of the bay, namely the eroding settlement mound on the foreshore (SM 2884) and chapel (SM 2934) (Chapter 2) (Fig. 3.11). The aim of these surveys, undertaken in June 2009, was to characterise the two sites in more detail, in the case of SM 2884 pending a small rescue excavation which took place in August 2009 (Chapter 4). In order to build a landscape context for the two scheduled areas, a landscape-scale gradiometer survey was undertaken over an area of c. 5 ha measuring 320 m (north–south, interrupted by the road) and 210 m (east–west, max) (Fig. 1.4). Subsequently, resistance survey was concentrated on the scheduled areas. Plans to extend the geophysical survey northwards to include the mound 'Knowe of Flaws' (SM 1296) (Chapter 2) were prevented by a report that a corncrake was allegedly nesting in the vicinity, although topographic survey was undertaken later in 2009.

The gradiometer survey at Marwick (Fig. 3.12) not only revealed distinctive traces of archaeological potential associated with the scheduled monuments but contributed significant information on wider relict patterns of land-use. The field north of the road was the least productive area; although the survey was conducted in dry weather conditions, the ground in this area is often waterlogged

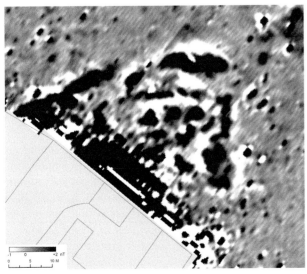

Fig. 3.10 Bay of Skaill northern area, gradiometry: point 2 referred to in text ('longhouse' anomaly, centre). Base map © Crown Copyright 2018. An Ordnance Survey/EDINA supplied service

Fig. 3.11 Extract from 1902 OS 2nd Edition 25-inch (1902) showing Scheduled Monuments and 2009 excavation area © Crown Copyright 2018. An Ordnance Survey/EDINA supplied service

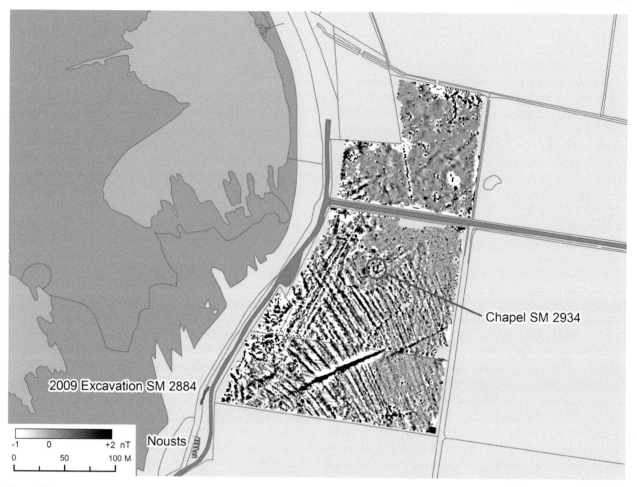

Fig. 3.12 Marwick, gradiometry with known archaeological sites, showing Scheduled monuments and 2009 excavation area. Base map © Crown Copyright 2018. An Ordnance Survey/EDINA supplied service

in winter and early spring. An amorphous group of responses in the north-west corner of this field may have archaeological origins, especially as they are located only 80 m south of the Knowe of Flaws. The rest of the field north of the road was relatively unproductive, producing only a series of weak linear marks, mainly orientated north-east to south-west, which are almost certainly derived from former cultivation rigs (which were much more strongly evident in the southern area of the Marwick gradiometer survey). The clearest responses were found in the south-west corner of the northern field, which appear to relate to the system dominating the southern field and hence pre-date the road. A more distinctive north–south linear mark is an old field boundary, the continuation of which to the north still exists.

The southern, larger sector of the Marwick gradiometer survey shows widespread traces of features of archaeological origin. The most extensive and pronounced of these, which have the effect almost of drowning out other features magnetically and visually, is an extensive multi-phase cultivation rig system, mainly aligned north-

west to south-east but with (perhaps more recent) elements aligned to the field boundaries and against the shore track. This system is still in fact visible on the ground as a very slight but regular undulation to the pasture surface. It does not, however, cover all of the area surveyed, and it appears to avoid the site of the chapel (SM 2934). At the north-west corner of the southern field is a group of amorphous anomalies, one of which is a curve of negative character that may represent a stone wall, possibly associated with the chapel to the south.

The chapel site is clearly visible in the gradiometer data. A positive group of linear marks surrounds the positions of the stone walls, but the chapel enclosure is almost entirely lost magnetically within the cultivation rigs and can only be fully identified by other techniques (see resistance survey, below). Set in a regular square-like pattern around the chapel are four pronounced ferrous anomalies. These would probably be dismissed as random ferrous contamination if it were not for their apparent regularity of placing. Their identity remains unknown, they may possibly be the iron bases of stanchions from an old fence, or of regularly-placed animal feeders.

The mound represented by SM 2884 is most clearly seen in section along the foreshore (Chapter 4). However, its eastern flank extends into the field to the east, across the shore track. Gradiometry shows a dense cluster of responses across SM 2884, such as would normally be interpreted as indicative of settlement (walls and middens), and which are not dissimilar to those found on the settlement mounds on the northern side of the Bay of Skaill. As with the Skaill examples, it is difficult to disentangle individual phases and structures from the cumulative magnetic effect of a deep, focal concentration of deposits. However, in the centre of the settlement cluster is a slightly more distinctive curved anomaly presented in both positive and negative contrast, which could be a midden-filled wall, and on the south-eastern periphery of the cluster, in a magnetically slightly quieter area, is an L-shaped feature that may be the remains of an enclosure. North-east of its apex is an indistinct, slighter feature that may be part of a building. The pronounced positive line that crosses the southern field south-west to north-east is almost certainly an igneous dyke, with the cultivation rigs system crossing it.

Two smaller areas of earth resistance survey, amounting to *c.* 0.32 ha and 0.48 ha, were carried out on SMs 2884 and 2934 respectively. The survey of the coastal settlement mound was compromised by its eroded and disturbed state, but several areas of high resistance were encountered, notably a strong mass of high resistance at the centre of the survey area, together with discrete features with apparent perpendicular elements to its north and south which may represent walls. The resistance survey over SM 2884 did little to advance the interpretation beyond the gradiometer results, but confirms that there are unusually complex, and hence probably archaeological, deposits within its central and western extent. Two 20 × 20 m survey grids on its eastern flank succeeded in picking up the grain of the cultivation rigs field system.

The survey undertaken over the remains of the chapel (SM 2934) was considerably more successful in outlining the extent of archaeological deposits (Fig. 3.13). The rectangular shape of the upstanding chapel walls shows up strongly as a pattern of high resistance, with three further linear marks of high resistance at a stand off of 2–3 m orthogonal to its outline, which are visible as low banks in the field. These may be part of the chapel itself or represent elements of an earlier structure. The chapel enclosure shows up very clearly as a trapezoidal shape measuring *c.* 30 × 25 m, and apparently located to the north-west of the chapel (Radford's plan, reproduced in Chapter 2 as Fig. 2.11 is shown to be quite accurate). Despite a slight unevenness in the data, there is little in the resistance survey to confirm the presence of grave cuts

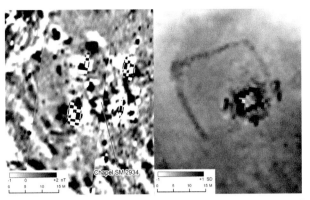

Fig. 3.13 Marwick chapel (SM 2934), gradiometry (left) and earth resistance (right). Base map © Crown Copyright 2018. An Ordnance Survey/EDINA supplied service

within the chapel enclosure, although it remains highly likely that they do exist. It is also possible that a much fainter larger enclosure surrounds the chapel site. As noted above in the interpretation of the gradiometer survey, the pattern of cultivation rigs stops short of entering the chapel area, which seems to be shadowed by a curvilinear outer area or 'buffer zone' between the chapel and the rest of the field. Without excavation, it remains a moot point as to whether this is a genuine boundary, or just a product of differential soil conditions outwith the area coverage of the cultivation rig system.

Birsay Bay

As described above in Chapter 2, Birsay Bay has seen considerable amounts of archaeological survey and excavation in the past, notably of deposits which were suffering erosion and collapse at the coastal margin. Small-scale earth resistance surveys were undertaken in the 1970s and early 1980s on the Brough of Birsay, along the Brough Road and at Beachview (Morris 1989, 61–3; Morris 1996, 37–8). These were innovative for their time, but their limited extent contributed little broader information beyond the extents of the excavated sites. Geophysical surveys were undertaken on three areas of Birsay Bay between 2003 and 2011 as a means not just to cover areas as yet unsurveyed with new coverage, but also for characterising the landscape contexts of the sites that were already known about and excavated. These areas were the Brough of Birsay, the Buckquoy Peninsula at the north of the bay, and a series of mound targets on Birsay Links, the grassy sand-dune landscape south of the 'Palace' village (Fig. 1.5).

The Brough of Birsay

A geophysical survey was undertaken by Oxford University and Orkney College Geophysics Unit on the Brough of Birsay in August 2007, funded by Historic Scotland, and intended to enhance the data from previous excavations undertaken by teams led by C. D. Morris (then of Durham University) in the late 1970s and early 1980s. The full results and interpretation of this survey are being published in conjunction with Morris's third Birsay monograph (Griffiths and Ovenden, in Morris, forthcoming) and to avoid repetition, only a brief summary is offered here.

The Brough of Birsay is approximately 21 ha in extent and the geophysical survey undertaken in August 2007 covered an area of approximately 4.3 ha using both gradiometry and resistance survey. This covered both some of the surveyed and excavated areas of the Guardianship Area (north and east of the churchyard) and the south-western area culminating in the small peninsula known as the 'Little' or 'Peerie' Brough, as well as the ground between them (Fig. 3.14). It was not possible on practical grounds, or even desirable, to survey over most of the dense complex of upstanding preserved structures in the Guardianship Area, not least because there are numerous modern metal objects amongst. A primary aim of the geophysical survey was to determine the extent of the archaeological deposits around and outwith the central Guardianship complex and towards the south side of the Brough. It was hoped to reveal the extent to which the areas previously excavated cover the full archaeological potential in the Brough landscape, whether archaeological

remains are contiguous between the Guardianship group and the Peerie Brough, and how far non-upstanding remains might extend beyond the Guardianship Area.

The data from the gradiometer survey indicates a generally high level of magnetic response across the survey area with isolated pit type responses being evident throughout the survey area. Although an archaeological origin for these isolated responses is very uncertain, with a natural origin being more likely, several clusters of well-defined anomalies suggesting an archaeological origin have been detected, with the strongest response being recorded within the Guardianship Area. The data collected immediately to the north and west of the Guardianship Area suggests that the built-up area of the settlement does not extend significantly beyond the current fenced boundary.

The earth resistance data from the Brough (Fig. 3.15) shows marked variations in background resistance across the site, with the north-eastern portion of the site recording a noticeably lower background resistance. The change appears to be generally associated with a spring-line running north-west to south-east through the centre of the survey area. Most of the Guardianship Area to the north and north-west of the Custodian's hut and the churchyard was surveyed. Wherever possible, the surface archaeology was surveyed. However, in some parts this was impossible

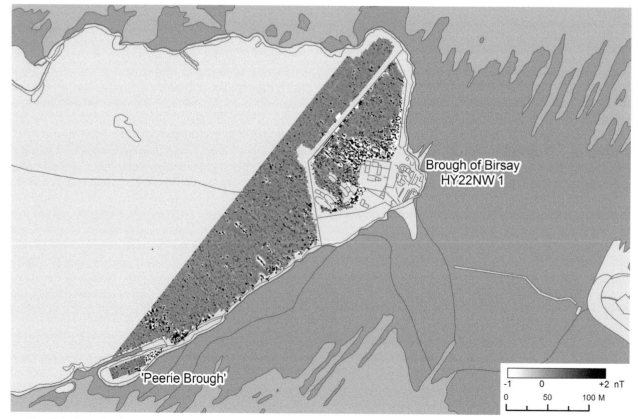

Fig. 3.14 Brough of Birsay, gradiometry. Base map © Crown Copyright 2018. An Ordnance Survey/EDINA supplied service

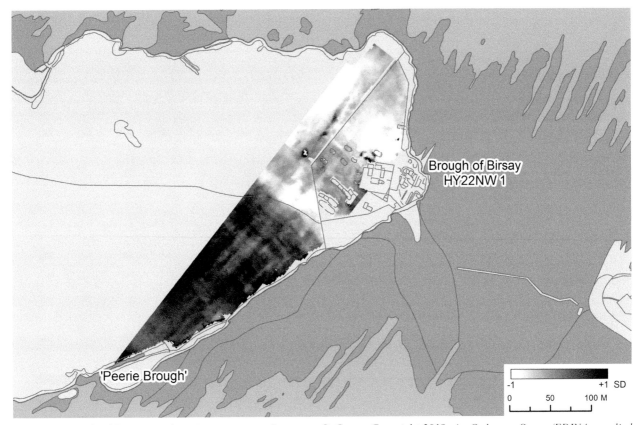

Fig. 3.15 Brough of Birsay, earth resistance survey. Base map © Crown Copyright 2018. An Ordnance Survey/EDINA supplied service

due to topographic constraints or hard surfaces, with some structures having to be omitted in their entirety.

Geophysical investigations on the Brough of Birsay have identified a variety of anomalies of archaeological interest, although the survey results indicate that buried archaeological remains are largely concentrated within and around the previously excavated sites. Both the Guardianship Area and the 'Peerie Brough' show evidence of some archaeological potential beyond those areas which have been excavated, but there does not seem to be strong evidence of contiguous spreads of settlement remains in the area between the Guardianship Area to the 'Peerie Brough' on the same scale as within these two focal areas. The current southern cliff edge between Guardianship Area and the Peerie Brough is characterised by the greatest remaining number and most concentrated clusters of anomalies and structures, however, it is unknown how much archaeology has been lost to coastal erosion over the centuries, or indeed since the archaeological work undertaken on the Brough in the 1970s–1980s.

The Buckquoy Peninsula

The Buckquoy Peninsula reaches westward from the north-west apex of the Mainland towards the Brough of Birsay. It is a generally flat-topped non-sandy landmass of glacial till over sandstone. Its surface is divided into fields by drystone dykes, and there are six mounds upstanding as topographic features in the western two fields. The 2003 survey work began with the creation of a topographic contour map with topsoil magnetic susceptibility mapping survey (Fig. 3.16). The magnetic susceptibility plot showed some interesting and, in some cases, unexpected results. Firstly, it showed a marked contrast amongst the six mounds. Three, the north-west mound in the west field (3), the north mound in the central field (4) and the south mound in the central field (the 'Knowe of Buckquoy'), together with the remaining section of the 'Buckquoy' mound excavated by Anna Ritchie on the south-west boundary of the west field, showed enhanced magnetic susceptibility (indicated by darker shading on the plot). The central mound (5), which is bisected by the dyke between the west and central field showed, if anything, a reduced magnetic susceptibility over the background level, whereas the smallest mound, in the north-east corner of the west field (6), did not provide a conclusive result either way. This suggests that the six mounds represent divergent types of archaeological structure, with at least three showing some evidence for settlement activity.

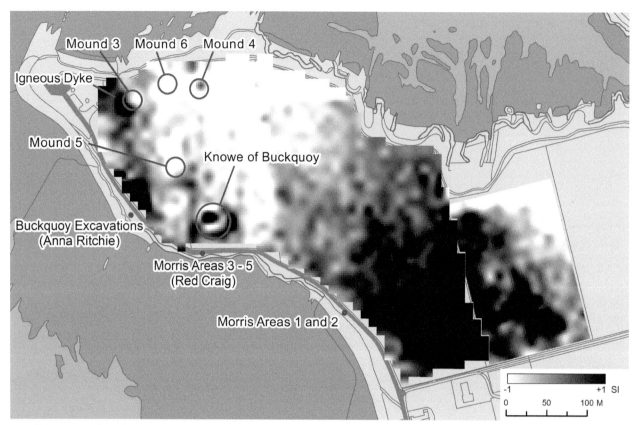

Fig. 3.16 Point of Buckquoy, topsoil magnetic susceptibility. Base map © Crown Copyright 2018. An Ordnance Survey/EDINA supplied service

Apart from the six mounds, magnetic susceptibility topsoil mapping showed a wider enhanced zone in the east of the survey area, which appeared to be trending eastwards into the next field (for which time constraints and a slightly later hay harvest did not permit survey in 2003). This area was more of a surprise, and suggested itself as a target for the more intensive survey method planned, namely gradiometer survey using two separate Geoscan FM36 fluxgate gradiometers in 30 × 30 m squares, with 1 m wide traverses taking readings every 0.25 m, laid out by total station within the overall survey grid. In just under three days approximately thirty-one 30 × 30 m squares were completed.

In the western two fields, gradiometer survey was concentrated on the mounds and their immediate environs (Fig. 3.17). The two mounds in the north of the westernmost field are located in close proximity to the igneous dyke, which is clearly visible as a thick black line on the greyscale plot, and appears to be congruous with the north coast of the Peninsula in this area. The small mound (3) in the north-west corner of the field is visible but surrounded by a *penumbra* of higher readings. These may be a result of archaeological activity connected to the mound spreading into its immediate surroundings – or they may be explained by geological material from the igneous dyke

being upcast and spread by natural and/or archaeological agency. The harder texture of the igneous rock (which is exposed on the wave cut platform a short distance to the north-east) suggests the former explanation is the more likely, but there can be no certainty prior to further investigation. The central mound showed no coherent structural pattern, but on its south-east side very close to the field boundary is a faint indication of a possible rectilinear structure. The two mounds in the central field showed complex internal structural indications – which in both cases appears rectilinear in basis. The larger of the two, the 'Knowe of Buckquoy' is yet more complex, with evidence of disruption probably caused by Fraser's excavation. Survey of the five mounds' environs produced more subtle readings generally in the range ± 1nt over 0, but careful study of the results suggests that a range of archaeological features is represented. A short distance south of the north-east corner of the western field is an interesting anomaly of tri-lobal shape, suggesting stone walls surrounding magnetised deposits in a cloverleaf-type pattern.

In the second field from the Point, a former field boundary is suggested by a transverse east–west line between the two mounds, and a curvilinear ditch shadows the southern edge of the peninsula before terminating

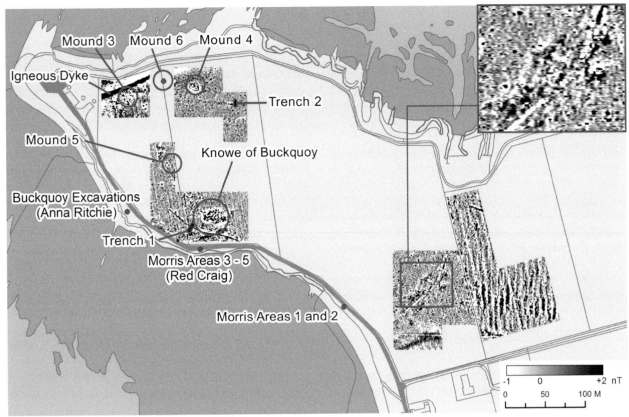

Fig. 3.17 Point of Buckquoy, gradiometry with inset detail and trenches 1 and 2 (with mounds and previous excavation sites). Base map © Crown Copyright 2018. An Ordnance Survey/EDINA supplied service

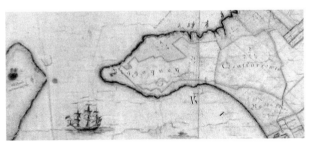

Fig. 3.18 Point of Buckquoy, extract from Alexander Aberdeen's Map of the Barony of Birsay (1760) © 2018 Orkney Library and Archive

in the westernmost field (these two anomalies were investigated using small-scale targeted excavation in 2004, see below, Chapter 4). The east–west linear anomaly across the mid-northern part of the field was revealed to be a substantial boulder-built wall foundation at variance with the current pattern of late 19th to early 20th century field dykes. This feature may possibly be part of the now-superseded irregular rectilinear field boundary system depicted on the 1760 Alexander Aberdeen Map (Fig. 3.18) although its date of origin remains uncertain.

The principal result of the other group of gradiometer survey squares to the east of the survey area was a

linear anomaly of compound positive and negative readings, apparently resulting from a composite of ditch and stone features. This seems to be crossing the neck of the peninsula in a roughly north–south direction, slightly convex towards the east, and dividing it from the mainland hinterland (Fig. 3.17). A field boundary roughly in this position, although slightly convex towards the west, is visible on the 1760 'Aberdeen' Map dividing 'Biggaquoy' land on the western portion of the peninsula from a large field 'Cleatfurrowes' occupying the majority of the landscape north of the Palace. If this feature was last depicted as a pre-modern field boundary, it may yet possibly have more ancient origins as a defensive work delineating the point from the mainland. Earthwork-delineated or defended lowland promontories are known elsewhere in Orkney, such as the Point of Unstan, Stenness (HY 21 SE22) and Grunavi Point on Sanday (HY63 NW74) but in this case the internal area is large and could have included numerous settlements. The Dyke of Sean which crosses the Brodgar Peninsula between the lochs of Stenness and Harray, and encloses the cluster of major Neolithic monuments, is a possible parallel.

The line of the putative linear boundary crossing the neck of the Point of Buckquoy is angled rather than straight, and the angle appears to be respecting the internal position of a group of anomalies immediately to its west which may represent a pre-existing settlement. Rectilinear elements are visible within this group, including a north-east/south-west angled 'building' with a square 'yard' on its eastern side, which appears to be surrounded by a shadow of higher readings suggesting midden deposits may be present. A more pronounced isolated pit-like anomaly exists to the east of the 'defensive' feature, and on the east boundary of the survey area close to its south-east corner is a possible lobed structure. All of these provisional descriptions have yet to be tested and confirmed by further survey and excavation work. An extension of this geophysical survey area into the field immediately to the east (the fourth field east of the Point of Buckquoy) in February 2005 showed that the spread of magnetic susceptibility is broad but discrete and likely to represent *in situ* archaeological material being turned within the topsoil by later medieval to modern ploughing. The 2005 survey revealed particularly strong patterning caused by cultivation rigs, a factor which is in accord with the obsolete field name mentioned on the 1760 map: 'Cleatfurrowes'.

Birsay Links

As described above in Chapter 2, the sand-dune area known as Birsay Links to the south of the 'Palace' village,

has been subject to previous survey and excavation, notably by Durham University in the late 1970s (Morris 1996, 257 ff). Numerous small traces of archaeological deposits were noted exposed on the seaward edge of the dunes, and there are several possible sites within the dune area, not least the well-preserved structures and occupation at the Beachview 'Studio' site. Further south within the Links at HY 246 274, Morris's team noted a possible chapel site, marked by low earthworks and some protruding stone orthostats (Morris 1996, 258). Despite numerous walkovers over several seasons, we were unable to re-locate this in the course of the project reported upon here, and it must be assumed that over the last three decades the sand has reclaimed it from having any surface expression.

Geophysical and topographic survey on the Links took place in August 2006. Contained within the 2006 survey area are two sandy mounds, 'Mount Misery' (NMRS HY22NW4), and a second mound immediately to the south with 'no obvious sign of antiquity' (HY 22 NW3). Mount Misery was examined by John Fraser in 1931. Although a few crude stone implements were discovered, there were no definite traces of buildings (above, Chapter 2; Morris 1989, 26; 1996, 33–4). Gradiometer survey was undertaken over approximately 0.75 ha and coupled with

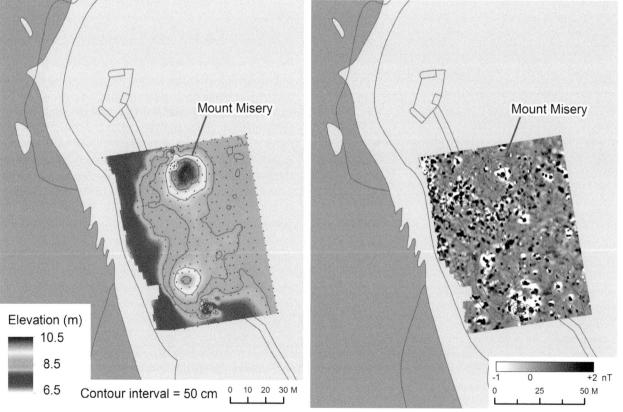

Fig. 3.19 Birsay Links, 'Mount Misery', surface model derived from ground survey (left) and gradiometry (right). Base map © Crown Copyright 2018. An Ordnance Survey/EDINA supplied service

topographic survey (Fig. 3.19). Although the internal structure of the mounds did not reveal coherent patterns of definite archaeological potential, numerous pit-type anomalies and a possible platform area on the southern flank of 'Mount Misery' were identified.

A faint trace of a rectilinear structure was identified south-east of 'Mount Misery', but the area was heavily disturbed and contaminated with ferrous metals by the presence of a derelict 20th-century rifle range with stone footings. The patterns of magnetic responses were clearly shown by the topographic survey to underlie overburdens of windblown sand, which had added to the 'mounded' profile of the sites and partially occluded the strength of the geophysical signal in areas of deeper surface sand deposits.

Saevar Howe

The large (almost certainly multi-period) settlement known as Saevar Howe (HY 22 NW5), on the seaward southern edge of Birsay Links, is expressed topographically as a prominent sandy mound site. Test excavations by John W Hedges in 1977 (Hedges 1983) showed this site had, and probably still has, considerable archaeological potential, for the Pictish and early Viking periods in particular (Chapter 2). Saevar Howe is a highly vulnerable landscape feature. It is located at the head of the beach and exposed to the full force of the Atlantic Ocean. Its seaward-facing flanks in particular are showing evidence of severe erosion, cattle trampling has affected its stability, and rabbit burrows have undermined the sandy overburden. Extensive metallic surface contamination represents a potential problem for magnetic geophysical survey (the hollow created by Hedges's excavation has attracted dumping of rusty metal and tractor parts, and lengths of rusty barbed wire protrude from the sand).

A topographic survey was undertaken of Saevar Howe in 2011, and a gradiometer survey area measuring 80 m (north–south) by 70 m (east–west) was laid out over the mound (Fig. 3.20). The results of the gradiometer survey were, as anticipated, compromised by the amount of ferrous debris lying around, not all of which could easily be cleared by hand. In the northern half of the survey area are a series of strong, discrete magnetic anomalies. With the benefit of experience gained from survey and excavation at Snusgar and East Mound at the Bay of Skaill, these may be interpreted as indications of midden and possible stone structures beneath the surface. In the

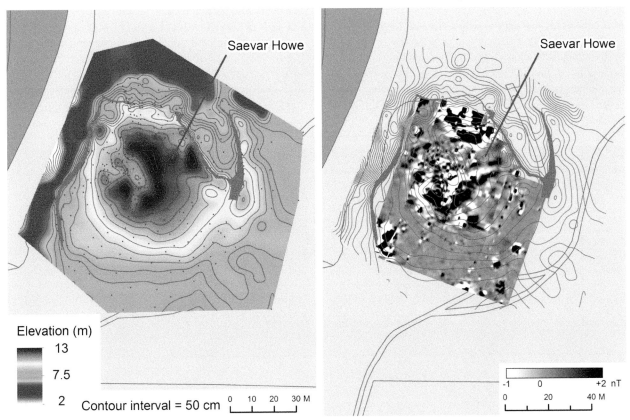

Fig. 3.20 Birsay Links, Saevar Howe surface model derived from ground survey (left) and gradiometry (right). Base map © Crown Copyright 2018. An Ordnance Survey/EDINA supplied service

centre of the survey area, there is a well-defined anomaly with a semi-rectilinear outline. This is coincident with the top of the mound and may imply a structure with midden (or highly magnetised material) retained within it. North of this are more subtle areas of magnetic contrast, which may be a reflection of material filling some of Hedges's excavation trenches. However, this interpretation is highly speculative and the damaged state of the upper mound precludes too neat an explanation. Other magnetic responses on the mound evident in the greyscale plot are intrusive ferrous material.

Summary

The mounds on Birsay Links are to be seen as complex products of archaeological and natural accumulation processes, a phenomenon that is also visible on a number of mound sites at the Bay of Skaill (Griffiths 2006), and also at Marwick. The coastal zone exposures of archaeology have been contextualised and can now be seen as part of a wider pattern of mounded settlement traces within a palimpsest of settlement of varying antiquity. At Birsay, the Point of Buckquoy itself may have been delineated from the Mainland by a north–south linear feature, the position of which appears to respect the position of an as yet unexcavated settlement cluster. Within the area of the promontory, mounded settlement and possibly funerary sites reflect discrete concentrations of archaeological potential within the landscape.

At Marwick, the structure and extent of two scheduled monuments (the chapel and settlement mound) have been defined, and their relationships to the surrounding landscape clarified. Even for a small survey area, these results have confirmed the purpose and value of the wider research project.

At Skaill, the group of mounds on the north side of the Bay has been conclusively identified as a cluster of strong archaeological potential, and several other smaller sites have been discovered on the links. Sand has already been noted as an obfuscating influence on geophysical survey, albeit one which can be compensated for in interpretation. Early in the project, it became clear that it is too simplistic to look at gradiometry plots produced in sand-influenced areas and interpret those in the same detailed small-scale way as might be done, for instance, on hard-ground sites. What appear to be coherent buildings, structures, pits or ditches may well be effects produced by a combination of different overlying responses, with modern burning and intrusions having an overly dominant effect. Individual, subtle features of archaeological interest tend to be lost in the magnetic 'noise' of multiple overlaid responses. However, one key result of the surveys presented in this chapter is that an extensive data capture is a more productive means of characterising archaeological potential in sand landscapes than an intensive one. The initial, small-area gradiometer plots produced of Snusgar, East Mound and their neighbouring mounds showed vivid contrast, expressed in greyscale terms as a mass of black and white anomalies, only some of which took on the guise of possible archaeological features. What made them stand out far more convincingly as concentrations of archaeological potential was much more extensive survey of their environs and the areas between and beyond their grouping. This produced not only a clearly defined limit to their extent, which accorded very closely with their topographic presence, but the vividness of their magnetic character created a visual 'signature' for this type of site. This, for instance, helped with the elimination of other, apparently similar, topographically-mounded features which, despite some surface metallic contamination, lacked the similarly intense magnetic character, and were therefore identified as natural sand features.

4

Excavations

Jane Harrison and David Griffiths

Introduction

Excavation retains an essential place within the range of investigative techniques available to the landscape researcher. Physical intervention and the extraction of dating, environmental and artefactual material is critical in verifying hypotheses suggested by survey data, establishing chronology, cultural attribution and phases of activity, as well as environmental context and the conditions of sub-surface preservation. Inevitably, finite resources and time dictate that excavation should be targeted at precise points of interest where any surface features converge with survey responses.

The excavation practice adopted by the Birsay-Skaill Landscape Archaeology Project consisted of opening trenches over areas of particular interest in the geophysical results (Chapter 3). These were initially of relatively limited size and undertaken to confirm and characterise the presence of subsoil archaeological deposits. The exception to top-down trenching was the vertical excavation of deposits in section at Marwick in 2009, which had already been exposed by coastal erosion. Where archaeological layers were encountered, excavation took place at least to the point where a record could be made in the form of plans, descriptions and photographs. Deeper and more complex investigations of such deposits demanded a more intensive and detailed research strategy. The creation of running vertical sections and open-area plans became essential to understanding, and trenches were extended incrementally in order to encompass a viable overview of the structures and deposits under excavation, and to permit the stepping and battering of trench sides, essential for safety in such an unstable medium as windblown sand. Some of

the excavation undertaken by the project conformed to the initial, 'ground-truthing' purpose described above (Chapter 1), and simply verified the subsoil presence of structures or patterns of deposits (for example at Birsay). However most of these, notably Trench 4 (Snusgar) and Trench 5 (East Mound), became much more complex and in-depth investigations, developing, deepening and extending over several seasons.

The presence of sandy deposits influenced much of the excavation strategy of this project. With the exception of the limited interventions at Birsay in 2004 and Marwick in 2009, all of the trenches and test-pits undertaken were in areas of the Bay of Skaill landscape dominated by windblown sand surface and drift geology. Archaeological layers and deposits were laminated within a complex environmental history of sand accumulation, which affected them in every way. Topsoils had formed over layers of relatively-recent aeolian sand. Beneath topsoil, archaeological deposits and former ground-surfaces were often separated by further episodes of windblown sand going back in time. Indeed, the entirety of Snusgar and East Mound rest upon deep deposits of sand, which as detailed above in Chapter 1, has been a significant environmental factor in the Bay of Skaill landscape for millennia. As recognised in excavations elsewhere in Atlantic Scotland (Barber 2011; Griffiths and Ashmore 2011), aeolian sand formations are subject to ongoing modification by processes such as deflation and post-depositional shifting, which provide a significant challenge in interpreting archaeological sequences during excavation. Animal burrowing (particularly by rabbits) is also widespread, especially on machair links with a superficially stable grass surface. Rabbit burrowing often runs alongside hard sub-surface features such as walls, destroying or compromising their relationships with surrounding layers and deposits (Parker Pearson *et al.* 2011). A rabbit warren in too-close juxtaposition to archaeology mixes *in situ* contexts, introduces external materials and can lead to the wholescale collapse of layers. Predominantly sandy soils also equate to poor-quality agricultural land, and unlike currently cultivated areas, have rarely been kept tidy and free from dumping and disturbance. Intrusive human activity such as aggregates quarrying, stone robbing from archaeological structures, the construction and use of kelping pits, and the sporadic burial of rubbish and dead farm animals are all complicating factors in sand archaeology.

At the Bay of Skaill, the positioning of trenches was determined by the topography of the mounds, the avoidance of obvious areas of recent disturbance, and by aiming at investigating a sample of the most promising parts of the geophysical results. It rapidly became clear that in such windblown sand environments, a great deal of caution must be exercised in predicting exactly how the geophysical traces reflected archaeological features discovered through excavation. The gradiometer plot was perhaps most clearly interpretable in the only area covered by the geophysical survey for which permission to excavate was withheld by the landowner: the field forming the north-western sector of Snusgar. This area shows the parallel east–west walls, about 6 to 7 m apart, of a probable large longhouse, the severely truncated eastern end of which was excavated in Trench 1 (see Fig. 4.10).

Schedule of excavations (Table 4.1)

Jane Harrison

Bay of Skaill: Castle of Snusgar and East Mound (Site code SG04-SG11) (Fig. 3.3)

SNUSGAR

TRENCH 1 (ENCOMPASSING TRENCH 3) (CONTEXTS 1000–1061)

This was a large area (15 m by 15 m) positioned across part of the initial 2003 gradiometer plot on Snusgar (Fig. 4.1). It was located on the generally flat plateau of the mound summit and intended initially to characterise and sample buried deposits. Trench 3 (contexts included within the Trench 1 sequence) was a small southern extension from the south-west edge of Trench 1 (8 m north–south by 3 m), opened to explore a sequence of deposits along the southern section of Trench 1 that could not be interpreted in section.

TRENCH 2 (CONTEXTS 500–508; 1 M BY 10 M)

This trench was undertaken by geoarchaeologists, Helen Lewis and Jon Cluett, on the north-eastern flank of Snusgar (Fig. 6.3). It was deliberately sited to extend from the topographic limit of the mound into the flat sandy plain beyond to test field soils and examine the tail-off of deposits on the periphery of Snusgar.

Table 4.1: Schedule of excavations

Year	Location	Trench number(s)
2004	Buckquoy, Birsay Bay	Trenches 1 and 2
2004	Snusgar mound, Bay of Skaill: north-eastern sector	Trench 1 (with southern extension, Trench 3); Trench 2
2005	Snusgar mound, Bay of Skaill: south-eastern sector	Trench 4
	East Mound, Bay of Skaill	Trench 5 (with southern extension)
2006	Snusgar mound, Bay of Skaill: south-eastern sector	Trench 4
	East Mound, Bay of Skaill	Trench 5 (with southern extension, 5A) Trench 6
2007	East Mound, Bay of Skaill	Trench 5 (with extensions) Trench 7
2008	East Mound, Bay of Skaill	Trench 5 (with extensions) Trench 7
	Environs of Snusgar and East Mound, Bay of Skaill	Machine test pits 1–3
2009	Shore-edge excavation, SAM 2884, Marwick	Vertical excavation
2010	East Mound, Bay of Skaill	Trench 5 (with extensions) Trench 8 (west end of Trench 5)
2011	East Mound, Bay of Skaill	Trench 5, eastern extension and Machine test pits 4–6

A full list of contexts with trench matrices is available in the online archive.

TRENCH 4 (CONTEXTS 1500–1583)

This was located on the south-eastern flank of Snusgar to provide a contrasting methodological approach to Trench 1 by exposing deep mound-flank deposits in section, achieving enough depth and length to see the upper mound-forming deposits in full profile (Figs 4.2 and 4.3). It was also intended as a means of testing the GPR radargram results, which showed a sequence of apparent buried surfaces (see Chapter 3, above). Trench 4 was first opened as a 30 m by 2 m strip running south-east down the mound but the up-slope 10 m of the trench was widened to create a 10 m by 5 m rectangle with a 20 m by 2 m down-slope tail descending the mound to the small seasonal tributary burn surrounding its base in this area (Fig. 4.4). A long 30 m section was recorded from the top to the bottom of this 2005 trench (Figs 4.2 and 4.3). In 2006 only the upper, wider area was reopened and excavated to deep windblown sand deposits through further complex midden layers, across a 2 m by 5 m sector. To achieve

SG 04 Trenches 1 and 3
Plan 6

Fig. 4.1: Trenches 1 & 3, overall plan (colour code Fig. 4.43)

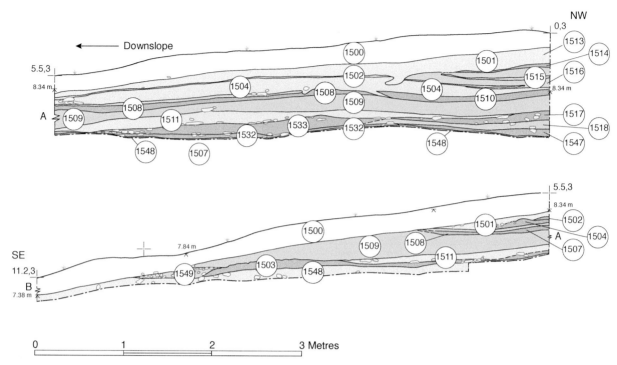

Fig. 4.2: Trench 4, final section, NE facing, part 1 (colour code Fig. 4.43)

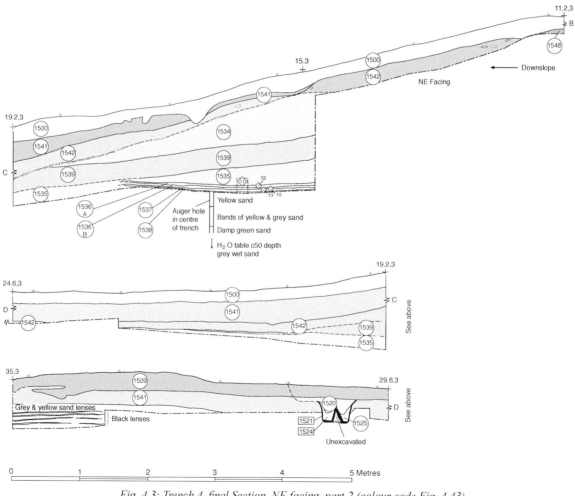

Fig. 4.3: Trench 4, final Section, NE facing, part 2 (colour code Fig. 4.43)

Fig. 4.4: Trench 4 in 2005, from SE

Fig. 4.5: Trench 5 in 2005, from N

this safely, a 1 m batter had to be excavated to the west and a 1 m strip to the north was left as excavated in 2005.

East Mound

Trench 5 (Contexts 2000–2310)

This trench was first excavated as an 8 m by 5 m area on top of East Mound in 2005 (Fig. 4.5), aiming to clarify the gradiometer survey undertaken in 2004. A near-rectangular area of lower magnetic response had been noticed in the survey but this could not be identified at all in excavation, so must have been a superficial magnetic effect, exaggerated by interpolation. However, standing stone walls, vertical stone orthostats and midden deposits were discovered beneath deep windblown sand layers. As a result Trench 5 was gradually extended and deepened through the succeeding seasons, to its largest extent in 2010: maximum 26 m west–east by maximum 17 m north–south (including a 1 m batter to the north; see Fig. 4.18). Two single-season extensions to the south of the main trench were excavated to test the area around the rectangular geophysics anomaly mentioned above. These were a 5 by 5 m area immediately to the south-east in 2005 and a 3 by 5 m area to the south-west in 2006. In 2006 the main trench was also extended 4 m to the west and 2 m north, with a small exploratory extension to the east to test midden layers outside the buildings (Fig. 4.6). The northern extension at that stage was primarily created to step the trench to allow for safe, deep excavation through less stable collapse layers to the buried building complex beneath.

Excavation in the area of East Mound was dominated by stone-built structural remains concentrated in the north and south of the main trench, with a small open paved area between the buildings and other yards to the west (Fig. 4.7). The main structure or longhouse building was aligned west–east, with a sequence of smaller ancillary

Fig. 4.6: Trench 5 in 2006, from N, the latest 'square' building (Phase 6)

buildings to the south of it, separated from the longhouse by the paved central yard. The earliest structure (Phase 3, see below) in the main building sequence was identified in the field by stratigraphy, and broadly by form and associated artefacts, as a Viking-Late Norse hall-building and the later, longer extended building in the same area as a (Phase 5) longhouse. The buildings to the south of it were a succession of smaller buildings belonging to the same complex. The extent and sequence of the structures were revealed gradually as the excavation area was extended and deepened each season.

In the 2007 season, Trench 5 was extended a further 4 m north to explore what turned out to be the central yard area and to allow a 2 m batter to cope with the increasingly depth. A 3 by 5 m extension west from the south-west corner was also excavated to establish the limit of the archaeology in that direction. Then in 2008, the Trench 5 was again extended, this time by 5 m to the north, to allow excavation of the full width of the longhouse. The

Fig. 4.7: Trench 5 (Trench 8 lowest in picture, showing W wall of longhouse) in 2010, N to left (Trench 7 (backfilled) may be seen at top left)

size of the trench was now 17 m north–south by 11 m west–east, with a 3 m by 7.5 m eastern extension. The 2008 extension explored midden deposits south-east of the buildings. In 2010 the trench was extended 10 m west and 2 m east, once again with metre-wide battering around the deep sectors. These extensions were intended to capture the full length and width of the longhouse, based on reasonable doubt that it could exceed 20 m in overall length. The eastern end was exposed, but even so, the western end of the longhouse lay outside Trench 5. Trench 8, 1 m by 5 m, was therefore excavated close to the western end of Trench 5 to identify the position of the western end-wall of the longhouse, which fortunately it did, confirming an overall length of 26.3 m (see Fig. 4.18). An intervening unexcavated strip of the internal longhouse deposits was therefore left *in situ*, allowing for the possibility of further excavation in the future. Finally, in 2011, a long, narrow extension 2 by 15 m long was undertaken on the south-eastern slope of East Mound above the burn, for the same purpose as Trench 4 had been excavated on Snusgar in earlier seasons (see Trench 4, above), namely to test the mound deposits in deep section down to the natural substrate. This extension was extended down the east downslope from the eastern

edge of Trench 5 from a point 4 m north of the southern edge, towards the burn.

Trench 6 (Contexts 3000–3010)

This was a small trench 6 by 3 m placed 10 m west of Trench 5 to investigate a contrasting area of the surface of East Mound nearer to the apparently sand-dominated western edge of the mound (Chapter 6). It produced remarkably little structural archaeology, given its proximity to the complex of structures excavated in Trench 5, revealing only some flat stone slabs, which may have been a pathway.

Trench 7 (Contexts 4000–4032)

This was an 8 by 3 m trench placed on the highest and most prominent north-east crest of East Mound, 10.5 m north of Trench 5, and over a north–south geophysical anomaly suggestive of a stone wall, which was confirmed in excavation (see Fig. 3.8).

Test-pits (TPs)

Six 2 m by 2 m test pits were rapidly machine-excavated in order to test for the presence of archaeological deposits over a wider area than was possible with hand-excavation (see Fig. 3.4). They were recorded using field-notes and photography. In most cases, they reached below the water table, causing slippage and collapse, which made further detailed sampling or recording too dangerous. TPs1–3 were aligned due north of Trench 5 at 30 m intervals. TP4 was situated on the flat ground between Snusgar and East Mound, TP5 was dug on the margins of the Burn of Snusgar 5 m east of the eastern end of the extension to Trench 5 excavated in 2011, and TP6 was located on an apparently 'mounded' rise in the topography in the field south of the Burn about 100 m south-east of Trench 5. The location of TP6 had previously been subjected to gradiometer survey, which showed no results indicative of archaeology. TP6 demonstrated beyond doubt that the topographic rise is a natural dune.

Marwick *(site code MW09, see Figs 4.39–4.41; also see Fig. 3.12)*

A series of exposed deposits, walls, drains, middens and occupation surfaces was identified, cleaned, sampled and recorded using vertical 'tapestry' excavation of the eroding cliff-section of SM 2884, over a distance of 17.5 m. This involved vertical cleaning and investigation of sections like hanging tapestries, with excavation usually limited to minimal cleaning back to clarify stratigraphy and enable the taking of samples (Barber *et al.* 2003; see Sampling Strategy, below). No area excavation was undertaken at Marwick.

Birsay *(site code BS04, see Fig. 3.16)*

Two small trenches were excavated in 2004. The southern trench was intended to sample a ditch feature noticed in the gradiometer results, immediately south-east of the Knowe of Buckquoy, but little diagnostic and no datable material was retrieved, and the feature is probably natural. The northern trench crossed a small east–west linear anomaly visible in the gradiometer survey, which may equate to a former field boundary at the edge of cultivated ground, depicted on the 'Aberdeen' Map of 1760 (Fig. 3.18). This feature proved to be a well-constructed wall footing (Fig. 4.42), confirming the presence of a former boundary, although no dating evidence was associated with it. No further excavation was undertaken at Birsay.

Excavation methodology

Jane Harrison

Introduction

The overwhelming majority of excavation was concentrated on two large mounds near the Bay of Skaill, [The Castle of] Snusgar and East Mound, both located on the northern flanks of the Links of Skaill.

The demands of safe working in sand constrained and shaped our archaeological approach. Although sections composed mainly of organic and silt-rich middens or surfaces proved to be very stable, sections with deep windblown sand layers, or with stones contained within or alternating with sandy deposits, were vulnerable to collapse. The latter type, for example, could slip outward as the weight of stones shifted underlying sand. This type of collapse frequently accelerates the erosion of exposed coastal archaeological sections, as seen at Marwick. Wide 'batters' had to be cut back from deep sandy sections to enable safe working to continue, and backfilled areas were held firmly in place with swathes of Terram geotextile.

As seen from the discussion later in this chapter, most of the trenches, except Trenches 1, 2 and 6, presented deep and complex stratigraphy, usually combining structures, floors, surfaces and a range of middens – archaeological sequences often over 2 m deep. Our excavation approach therefore combined area excavation, to establish plan layouts, with the use of strategic sections to explore vertical relationships and the deep archaeology. Sometimes sections were running sections, each element being recorded on a continuing drawing before being removed; whilst others were left *in situ* for some time before being excavated. Retaining sections from season to season was not always possible, as sandy sections of any depth (and especially those backed by, or containing, quantities of stone) were liable to partial over-winter collapse despite full back-filling at the end of each year of excavation.

Long sections were excavated down the full-lengths of slope on both Snusgar and East Mound – Trench 4 on Snusgar (see Figs 4.2 and 4.3) and the eastern extension to Trench 5 on East Mound (Fig. 4.8) – and these were invaluable in exploring the nature of the mounds' construction, profile and the taphonomy of their archaeological deposits. Sections were also recorded running north–south across the interior of the longhouse area on East Mound: from south of the ancillary buildings, across the central yard and the longhouse interior; across the south-east midden and central yard, and from the metal-working yard to the longhouse interiors. These were either running sections, trench-edge sections or sections created by establishing cross-trench baulks that were subsequently removed (*e.g.* Fig. 4.6). The sections were crucial to understanding the complex processes of repeated rebuilding and alteration; the build-up of yards, middens and surfaces; and the effects of collapse, quarrying and rabbit-burrowing on the deeply stratified, diverse archaeological layers (see below). Micro-sections were created with narrow baulks across floors in the longhouse, ancillary buildings and metal working yards to examine the delicate and finely laminated surfaces (see Fig. 4.24). Successive floors had also been thinned by use and repeated clearing, so complete sequences were in the vast majority of places not deep enough, and too fragile and friable because of underlying and overlying

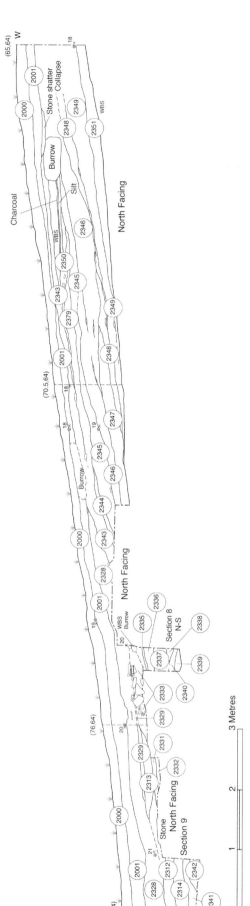

Fig. 4.8: Trench 5, extension down mound to SE in 2011, full section

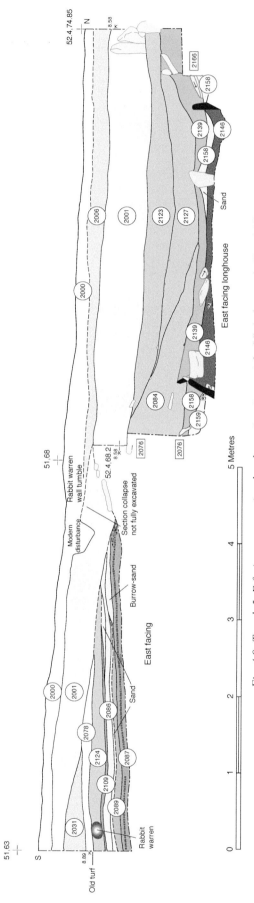

Fig. 4.9: Trench 5, E facing cross-section, longhouse interior to right (N) (colour code Fig. 4.43)

sand, to take many effective Kubiena Tin samples for soil micromorphology. Within the western end of the longhouse and the metal-working yard, in particular, it was evident that ashy-clay floors had been deliberately laid, cleared and renewed many times: their complexity could only be appreciated through these fragile mini-sections.

Site recording and sampling strategy

The project followed a single context recording system with single context drawings made on context sheets and more complex phase, pre-, mid- and after-excavation exposures recorded on detailed scale drawings. All metalwork, worked bone and stone, glass, pottery and steatite were recorded in three dimensions in a site-wide running catalogue of small finds. As well as formal site photographs, many working shots were taken and a site-wide photographic record made at the end of each working day. This latter approach was taken to ensure that sand-section collapse did not lead to the loss of important images, but also as a very helpful post-excavation aid. Contexts were sieved where it was practically possible (some clayey contexts were better broken up by hand), initially every bucket of spoil was sieved, and then if nothing was being recovered in the sieve, we reverted to one bucket in three or five depending on the extent and significance of the context. Major structural elements were also recorded using a total station and/or survey grade GPS.

The importance of understanding the origin, accumulation and possible purposes of midden deposits, layers and spreads, prompted an addition to the standard recording of bulk finds in all contexts (that is everything other than the 'small' or special finds, and mostly bone and shell). Thus, these bulk finds, as well as being identified, described and quantified as far as possible in the field on context sheets, were also recorded in more detail by context in immediate post-excavation and before being sent out to specialists. The work became part of the preparation of each season's *Data Structure Report* and of the finds for specialist analysis, that is when the bulk finds were cleaned, sorted and weighed and divided into animal bone, fish bone, marine shell and other (including bird bone, egg shell and land snails). This extra stage of thorough recording logged the proportions of the different elements relative to each other, and to other components of the context. Abrasion, fragmentation, cut-marks and burning were also recorded in more detail. This was in addition to the subsequent detailed interpretation of ecofactual evidence by the individual specialists working within the project.

All that bulk finds data contributed to the post-excavation characterisation and differentiation of a variety of middens and layers, and helped to distinguish between surfaces enriched and stabilised with midden, spread midden layers, surfaces on which work took place, and midden deposits. The developing database also meant the project team entered each season with an improved understanding of the pre- and post-depositional processes that had created and shaped the mound archaeology. Field recording of context composition was also appropriately detailed, with careful emphasis, especially for midden contexts, on noting the size and sorting of stones and their overall proportion of the context, on sediment grain-size and relative proportion of sediment elements. The role of windblown sand in shaping the archaeology meant that even small lenses and drifts of sand needed to be noted. Although midden-including layers could look dramatically different in the field – compare pink-orange peat ash contexts with dark brown organic contexts for example – it was also the case that many such contexts were variants on mid brown sandy silt with differing stone content: only detailed recording of bulk finds, stone and composition could distinguish the different archaeological histories of these layers. This approach made it much more possible to disentangle the interleaved collapse layers, the reverse stratigraphy and the slumped middens, as well as contributing to the interpretation of contexts. Context types and descriptions are detailed in Table 4.3, and colours of these represented on plans and sections are shown in Fig. 4.43.

All contexts were sampled as part of the standard project-wide environmental sampling programme, unless they were rendered completely unsuitable by large-scale rabbit-burrowing, other major post-depositional disturbance or modern contamination, or were sterile windblown sand (some of the latter deposits were sampled at random and put through the flotation system during the 2010 season to act as a control on field identification). These were bulk environmental samples, or samples for general biological analysis or GBA (Dobney *et al.* 1992; Chapter 8). An approximate centre of collection area was recorded spatially for each sample. Samples were usually 10 litres in size, but many contexts were sampled more than once, either because they were especially significant (floors, pit fills) or particularly extensive or deep (in particular the larger midden contexts); hearths, floor tanks and post-holes were sampled in their entirety. Only small finds were removed from the samples to be recorded in three dimensions, although a number of small finds were subsequently identified in soil sample processing. As well as carbonised cereal grain, chaff, flax and weeds; charcoal and burnt peat; and charred wild economic resources such as heather and nuts, the sampling programme also detected hammerscale and slag. Finally, micro-fragments of bone and shell were retrieved from the flotation process. Insect remains were notable by their relative absence. The overall approach enabled not only the archaeobotanical analysis but also provided the range of choices of material necessary for the radiocarbon dating programme (Chapter 5). In all seasons the samples were processed close to the site, and as excavation progressed, so that results informed both the digging and sampling strategy, meaning more interesting or informative samples could be further targeted.

Small bagged samples for soil chemistry analysis were collected from Trench 5, on a grid within the longhouse – both domestic and byre 'ends', and from locations within the ancillary building and the yards as contrasts and comparisons (Chapter 7). Soil micromorphology samples were collected in columns and Kubiena Tins where practicable (Chapter 6).

Taphonomic factors

As indicated above, site sections revealed the impact on archaeological layers and deposits of both subsequent human activity and the processes inevitable on abandonment and collapse. The following paragraphs explore some of these effects, which frequently worked together.

Windblown sand

All human and post-depositional impacts were modified by the constant movement of windblown sand. On the East Mound in the Trench 5 metal-working yard – an area that was probably roofed, but also partly open-sided – the laminated floors demonstrated how thin drifts of windblown sand blew across the ash-clay floor and adhered to the sticky surface – sand may also have been blown *off* and thus scoured and thinned the surface. The drifting effect was even more noticeable in the open central yard where layers representing phases of activity were interspersed with slightly thicker sand-blow layers (Fig. 4.9). The removal of debris and cleaning of floors in the metal-working yard and longhouse also seemed to have thinned the floors and left them relatively clear of finds; in contrast the open yard was characterised by episodes of debris-dumping. Deflation has often been observed in windblown sand landscapes (Barber 2011). On much of this site horizontal deflation seemed not to have affected the surfaces, probably because the process requires longer exposure to wind and other erosion drivers to scour the sand from *under* layers. Most of the deposits on site were held together too effectively with organic-rich material and then too deeply buried to be vulnerable to these actions. However, on Snusgar it is likely that the dismantling of the longhouse structure in Trench 1 – probably to reuse the stone and clear agricultural land – led to deflation of the internal floors and to a lesser extent of the more organic external middens to the north. The archaeology there was also very much closer to the surface in a field that had been regularly ploughed (remains of cultivation rigs can be seen in Trench 1 sections: see Fig. 4.12).

Working in windblown sand does, however, have one great benefit: everything that is not sand has to have been brought to the site by either natural or human agency, and because of the contrast between shell-sand and all other components of the archaeological or geomorphological layers the presence of added material is easy to see. Colours are vibrant and sequence changes not as hard to discern as on a site where textural variations are slight.

Wall-collapse and abandonment

The partial collapse of stone walls had a considerable effect on the archaeology. The impact and weight of stones up to a metre in length falling onto both interior surfaces and exterior yards had the potential to drive artefacts (especially from the organic wall-fill) into earlier layers. Some of the thin layers were conflated and mixed with wall-fill by sequences of stone collapse, so that artefact residuality became a significant feature (that is the mixing of objects from an earlier phase contained within the wall-fill, with the floor layers and deposits of a later phase). After wall-collapses, sand also tended to infill gaps between stones so artefacts were also able to work their way down into earlier deposits, in particular alongside the courses of still-standing walls. For example, a few sherds of pottery dispersed across the site around the beginning of Phase 6 followed this route to become intrusive finds.

The dismantling and robbing of abandoned buildings in later times particularly affected the archaeology on Snusgar; the building complex on East Mound was differently impacted by slower processes of decay. On East Mound the collapse of stone onto the longhouse floors was captured vividly in both plan and section. After the longhouse ceased to be inhabited and the roof collapsed, the shell of the building was used intermittently as an animal-byre (most of the roof timbers were probably removed, with only shorter or poor-condition timbers being left behind, some of which were probably burnt in a Phase 7 fire-pit (Chapter 8)). Cattle hoof-prints from the final penning were pushed into the rotting organic debris from the roof and were preserved in places by sand blowing into the structure and infilling them. The trampling of the cattle had also effectively truncated the upper sequence of the floors below by mashing the roof debris, cattle fodder and dung into those top layers (see Fig. 4.33).

The effects of slope

One of the main factors requiring careful observation in the mounds' archaeological layers was that of slope. The inherent tendency of sand to shift and move – its character somewhere between fluid and solid – had a significant impact on the archaeology. In Trench 4 (Snusgar) sand mobility combined with slope erosion created reverse stratigraphy. Many of the layers examined in this trench were laid near-horizontal and many met the surface of the sloping sides of the mound at their outward edge. As cattle moved across the field, disturbing the ground, and as sand and heavier materials such as stone followed their natural inclination to travel downwards, so tails of deposits from exposed archaeological layers slid down the slope of the mound bringing sections of a younger layer down below the older intervening deposits originally beneath them. This effect was also recorded in Trench 5, although with slightly different results, in the middens to the east of the ancillary buildings. Here layers had slipped northwards across the central yard bringing with them some earlier deposits. These then settled on top of already accumulated collapse-layers in the central yard so that once again older deposits were found over more recently created ones.

The effects of slope were observed in Trench 5 more often in relation to the direction of collapse of walls and the accumulation of windblown sand deposits. In the Viking-Late Norse periods the natural southward slope downwards from behind the metalworking yard and ancillary buildings was more severe. (The large southern wall of the longhouse was partly dug into the sand of this mound slope.) Thus when the walls collapsed most of the stones fell northwards and interleaved with lesser infill collapses from the south to produce a complex stratigraphy of post-abandonment layers. Within these sequences it was also necessary to be aware that the material used as wall-fill – a combination of midden, sand and stone shatter – was contemporary with or older than the walls, or sections of walls being built or rebuilt. The long sections north–south across Trench 5 also recorded the deep windblown sand layers that collected above the archaeology, deepening to the north (Fig. 4.9). Within these could be detected potential storm or stronger wind episodes, which had moved bigger grains of material.

Linking walls and internal deposits

The difficult task of marrying internal deposits to superimposed phases of wall construction – and reconstruction – was complicated by both Viking-Late Norse building techniques and post-depositional processes. For example, two approaches were taken by the builders who created the southern rectangular ancillary structure in Trench 5. Firstly, existing walls of the preceding building had been refaced, strengthened and realigned by digging down into and disturbing already laid floors (see Fig. 4.21). Subsequently, considerable building-up of the structure's interior and adjoining external areas had been necessary to produce new level surfaces for laying flagging and erecting internal stone orthostatic kerbs and dividers. This build-up of internal surfaces was accomplished using a mixture of sand and organic midden deposits: any materials within this infill – artefacts, faunal and archaeobotanical remains – were to a greater or lesser extent residual. Finally and across the site, as so often

in sand, rabbits – probably as early as in Phase 7 – had burrowed alongside some stretches of wall rendering the task of matching them to structural phases and floors even more difficult. Fortunately, the rabbit burrowing was relatively restricted and strategic sections enabled many sequences to be reconstructed.

The characteristics of middens

Midden is soil characterised by a mixture of organic material and burnt domestic refuse. Midden layers were very varied in extent, colour, depth and composition – from peat-ash dumps to silty, stony spreads. Some comprised many thin layers and small deposits, while others were much more homogenous; some contained a high proportion of bone or shell, others were highly organic or sandier. Sand layers of varying extent and depth indicated intervals when the middens were not being added to in a particular area, and the intensity, location and type of activity had altered for a period. It is impossible to gauge from the sand deposits how long any one hiatus might have been, as windblown sand accumulates at different rates on different topographies and surfaces – for example sticking more to clayey layers, heaping more deeply against any barrier and drifting into hollows. Sand can also blow away from as well as onto an open area, and the rate at which it might be deposited varies enormously with the strength, duration and direction of the wind.

The build-up of midden layers and deposits was not haphazard. The variety of composition and finds suggested in some cases that the by-products of a range of activities had been collected and deposited separately: for example, on Snusgar in particular, shells from bait preparation, or bones resulting from butchery (Chapter 9). The Snusgar layers were also constructed in an architectural manner to ensure a steady increase in the size of the mound. Stony arcs and spreads were laid to hold deposits in place, while some of the organic material seemed to have been spread – and mixed with sand – to stabilise or level an area. Trench 4 demonstrated that much of the bulk of the mound was built up with these midden sequences, interleaved with windblown sand. As excavation progressed downwards, the deposits contracted towards the centre and became less sloped, indicating how the extent and height of Snusgar had increased as middens were laid down.

Preservational factors

Shell-sand – in contrast to mineral-rich sand – has an alkaline pH as a consequence of the calcium carbonate-rich shell fragments, and provides an environment sympathetic to the survival of shell, bone and eggshell. This environment beneficial to preservation was further enhanced by the mostly well-drained nature of the sites. The downward percolation through, rather than pooling of water upon, layers, already evident in the relative dryness of contexts, could also be charted in the incidence of iron-panning. The soils and therefore the groundwater in the Bay of Skaill are quite ferruginous. While water trickles steadily through the well-draining sandy deposits, it moves more slowly through the less porous surfaces – for example, peat ash or very organic midden layers – and deposits thin crusts of iron panning. However, no waterlogged or even particularly damp layers were encountered and the dry deposits within the sand-based soakaways cut in the Viking-Late Norse period testified to the efficacy of windblown sand as a drainage medium. After heavy storms, even relatively organic-rich midden and floor layers exposed during excavation were quick to dry out. As a consequence there was excellent preservation of shell, bone (including fine fish bones) and eggshell, carbonised plant remains and charcoal (providing excellent targets for radiocarbon dating), and of metal, bone and ceramic artefacts in all trenches. However, the absence of any long-term water-logging meant there was poor survival of organics such as unburnt wood, leather, hair, fabric, textile, soft tissue and insect remains.

Excavation narratives
Jane Harrison

Establishing and dating the phases (Table 4.2)
The characterisation of contexts resulting from the excavation strategy, as described above, ensured a detailed set of stratigraphical matrices could be constructed, and relative phasing determined, before any absolute dating, provided initially and broadly by artefacts and finally by the radiocarbon dates, was available to provide chronological anchors for the nine phases. Many artefacts – and in particular many of those discovered in middens and wall-fills – were effectively residual, as their often worn and damaged condition further testified. This artefact residuality has been noted at other sites and highlights the exigency for relative chronologies that are not finds-driven, and the difficulties of formulating relative phasing with too heavy a reliance on finds (*e.g.* Hunter *et al.* 2007).

Table 4.2: Archaeological phases on Snusgar and East Mound

Bay of Skaill: Phase	Date range
Phase 1	pre-Viking
Phase 2	late 9th– early 10th century
Phase 3	10th–early 11th century
Phase 4 (Trench 5 only)	mid-11th century
Phase 5	11th–early 12th century
Phase 6	later 11th–12th century
Phase 7	mid-12th–13th century
Phase 8	*c.* 13th–17th century
Phase 9	*c.* 18th century onwards

Thus initial phasing and relative chronological sequences were determined using stratigraphic relationships informed by the character of the individual contexts; finds were used only to recognise the broad Viking-Late Norse characteristics of the assemblage. The sequence was then anchored chronologically in post-excavation analysis using radiocarbon and OSL-dating. The finds were then examined as chronological entities, within an evidenced dating framework including consideration of factors of redeposition and residuality. Although there were no conflicts between artefacts and chronology at this final stage, the process served further to underline the residual nature of the majority of the finds, usually across one or two phases at most. Finally, the dating of phases was refined using Bayesian analysis (Chapter 5).

Nine phases of activity were established as an overall framework for the Snusgar and the East Mound excavations, encompassing all eight of the trenches excavated (Table 4.3). These range from Phase 1,

Table 4.3: Types of deposits on Snusgar and East Mound

Post use	Post-Late Norse occupation and use of the buildings
Disturbed	Collapse/demolition/robbing/infill and general disturbance
External	General external layer
Deposit (external)	General external deposit (small and deposited in one action)
External surface	External surface used for activity
Layer (internal)	General internal layer
Deposit (internal)	General internal deposit (small and deposited in one action)
Wall fill	Material used as wall core fill between stone facing/courses
Fill	Pit, post-hole, ditch/gully or drain fill
Metal-working yard floor	Floor layer in open-sided and semi-roofed metal-working area
Byre floor (animal)	Floor layer on animal stalling side of byre
Byre floor (workshop)	Floor layer on workshop side of byre
Byre floor	General byre floor
Longhouse floor	Floors in domestic central area of hall building/longhouse
Annex floor	Floors in western annex/cooking area of Phase 5 longhouse
Ancillary building floor	Floors in N–S and W–E rectangular and square ancillary buildings
Midden deposit	Deposit of midden material (internal or external)
Midden layer	Midden layer external to buildings

pre-Viking activity, in this case no earlier than Later Iron Age/Pictish in date; to Phase 2, early Viking to Viking Age; and Phases 3, 4 and 5, which covered the main occupation in the Viking-Norse period of the 10th to 12th centuries. In terms of architecture and complexity of occupation, Phases 3 and 5 dominated. Phase 4 was a transitional phase found only in part of the East Mound complex and falling towards the end of the Viking Age. Phase 6 embraced the Later Norse structural elements, the final ones recorded on these sites; Phase 7 covered the initial structural collapse as well as evidence for localised agricultural activity after the Trench 5 structures were finally abandoned. Phase 8, from the 13th century onwards, incorporated later field-wall construction and the ongoing process of collapse, robbing and disturbance. Finally, Phase 9 comprised more recent/modern evidence for kelp burning work, field drains and animal burials. The differences between these broad phases were evident in the character of the archaeology before they were confirmed by the more refined relative phasing and absolute dating accomplished in post-excavation.

Trenches 1 and 3: Snusgar (see Fig. 4.1)

EXCAVATION STRATEGY

Trenches 1 and 3 were excavated in 2004 on the eastern summit of Snusgar. The archaeology in these trenches was heavily truncated and relatively shallow, so excavation focused on area coverage with vertical sections where preservation allowed. The upper layers revealed a large spread of sand, and relatively recent deposits including metallic dumping, animal burials and kelping activity, which had affected the magnetic responses (Chapter 3). Fragmentary walls and deposits indicating the former presence of a significant building were discovered, with west–east wall alignments which matched patterns visible in the geophysics (Fig. 4.10). The length and form of the building, and the artefacts found in surviving, undisturbed internal layers and middens, confirmed this had been a Viking-Late Norse longhouse. In the area examined, the walls were highly degraded by collapse, stone robbing and other later agricultural disturbance. Only fragments of *in situ* masonry remained. However, a series of rich, laminated middens survived outside the walls. These middens, and an area of later kelp burning activity in the south-east, were investigated and sampled in long metre-wide sondages along the western, southern and eastern trench edges, while the truncated interior of the building was excavated to just above deep windblown sand layers. The north-eastern 7.5 m² quadrant was left unexcavated below topsoil and subsoil 1002 as it was evident that archaeological traces were decreasing to the east and north in the area excavated (Fig. 4.1, Fig. 4.10).

The west–east aligned structural remains on Snusgar, belonging to Phases 2–5, had been severely truncated, disturbed and robbed, whereas the ashy middens to the north and south were somewhat better preserved. Some final elements of Phase 5 domestic occupation in Trench 1 may have been completely lost to truncation, although the lack of significant Phase 5 archaeology in Trench 4 suggested a more general diminishing of activity in this phase (see below). In excavation, Phases 2–5 appeared as two linear spreads of stone and silty wall-fill delineating the remains of the building, with the middens to north and south, and mixed sandy layers between (Fig. 4.11). The east end of the building had been completely lost to erosion and kelp-burning activity, and only a short stretch of the northern wall 1054 survived as coherent foundation courses. Fragile internal floors had been almost obliterated by animal burrowing and the later removal of much structural stone. What remained were patches of organic sand and wall-fill containing some artefacts. Although they were less disturbed by later actions, the dark silty midden layers to the north of the longhouse had been truncated, while the deeper, ashier middens to the south, investigated in Trench 3, had been affected by ploughing and erosion. Auger probing indicated a considerable depth of sterile windblown sand below the wall-lines and midden in Trench 1 suggesting the longhouse structure was erected where sand had accumulated to some depth, masking any previous habitation or activity on the mound. These building remains, which seem better preserved in the north-west field on the mound (in which we were not given landowner permission to excavate) appear to be those which gave rise to the identification of the 'Castle' of Snusgar in the 18th century (Chapter 2).

PHASE 1: NOT PRESENT

PHASE 2: CONSTRUCTION OF THE LONGHOUSE AND CREATION OF FIRST MIDDENS (FIGS 4.10 AND 4.11)

This phase witnessed the building of the Snusgar longhouse, although probably towards the end of the phase. The geophysics had suggested the building could be up to 28 m long if the responses reflected a single structure. Excavation revealed the longhouse was probably about 6.5 m wide in the area investigated, with walls up to 1.3 m thick (see Fig. 4.1). The lowest four courses of the northern wall 1054 survived undisturbed, built onto a clay foundation, 1055. There remained sufficient of the fabric to establish that the wall was double-faced with a core of stone and sand held together by organic additions 1022. Two artefacts were found in the tumble 1023 of the wall and these most likely belonged to this phase: a bone pin (SF 4025) and bone spindle whorl (SF 4031) probably came from the midden additions to the wall-fill. The southern wall 1025 had fared less well, traceable only by a spread of wall facing

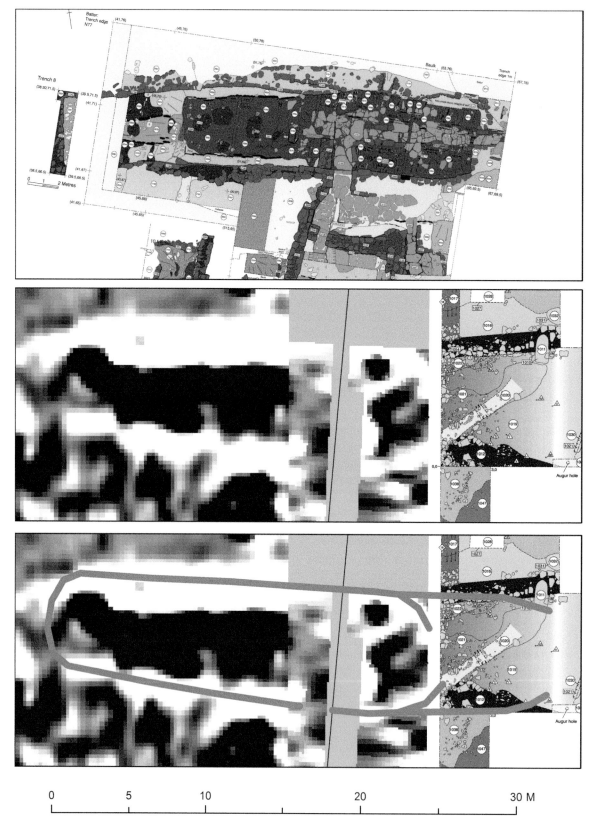

Fig. 4.10: Trenches 1 & 3 (in ascending order), suggested outline of Snusgar longhouse; excavation plan in relation to gradiometry; East Mound longhouse (Trench 5) for comparison (colour code Fig. 4.43)

Fig. 4.11: Trenches 1 & 3 from NE, wall spreads interrupted by later animal burial pits

stone and distinctive wall-core material, with occasional fragments of coherent coursing.

In the south-eastern quadrant of the trench, a small area of midden from Phase 2 had escaped demolition in Phase 9. The location of this charcoal-rich, dark silty sand 1051 probably indicated the eastern end of the longhouse, but may have formed before the building's construction. The midden contained charred grain, but no bone or shell, and returned a radiocarbon date of cal AD 770–1020 (SUERC-17849). In Trench 3 the earliest midden, 1041, excavated to the south of the longhouse, may also have belonged to this phase; unlike the silty spread 1051 to the east, this sandy and very variable layer also produced some mammal bone. To the north of the longhouse, more extensive midden areas were investigated: these layers indicated how the topography of the mound had altered. In the Viking-Late Norse period, the ground had sloped away downwards slightly and then gently upwards north from the house. This dip had been masked by later windblown and accumulations (Fig. 4.12).

The first archaeological layer 1045 immediately north of the northern longhouse wall, and above the lower deep windblown sands, had the characteristics of a trampled external surface, perhaps created around the time the house was being built. Dated to cal AD 880–1020 (SUERC-17848), this extensive silty sand layer produced more organic material, fish and mammal bone closer to the wall, but became increasingly sandy away from the longhouse. Also discovered were two fragments of bone pin, SFs 4029 and 4032. Overlying this surface were smaller peat-ash dominated deposits followed by the final midden of this phase 1017 – another varied midden spread encountered across the full length of the slot north of the wall (dated to cal AD 880–1030: SUERC-17847). The composition of this midden was more influenced by domestic activity: organic, charcoal-rich, with a considerable assemblage of charred grain and animal bone (including red deer), bone pin fragments and part of a bone comb (SFs 4004, 4007, 4022 and 4026).

The lenses and drifts of coarse windblown sand within this midden suggested it accumulated over a relatively long period.

PHASE 3: INTERNAL DEPOSITS WITHIN THE LONGHOUSE

The remnants of internal floors within the longhouse may have been composed principally of Phase 3 elements, although this cannot be confirmed, as they were too disturbed and patchy to qualify for radiocarbon dating. These thin layers, 1019, 1021 and 1059 across the interior of the building were mixed, slightly organic sands producing background amounts of charred grain and larger amounts of mostly very fragmentary bone (Fig. 4.12). However, closer to the walls, where the disturbance was minimal, a number of artefacts were discovered, including bone pin fragments (SFs 4021, 4035), a bone needle (SF 4023) and iron items (Chapter 12). Some of the midden deposits south of the longhouse may have belonged to this phase, but it was impossible to be certain.

PHASE 4: NOT PRESENT

PHASE 5: LATER MIDDENS AND FLOOR LAYERS

A later layer of internal deposits within the longhouse, 1012, focused more towards the southern wall, was a similar bone-rich, silty sand to the earlier layers but contained more ash. This floor spread was notable for the number of artefacts it produced, including the fine green-banded pendant whetstone (SF 4030), a bone needle case (SF 4024) and bone comb and pin fragments. Two pieces of worked antler debitage (SFs 4003 and 4006) from 1012 suggest comb-working (Chapter 14). Above this layer was a Phase 8 buried soil 1016 that had developed over much of the archaeology in the trench.

Two midden layers to the north of the longhouse belonged to Phase 5. Concentrated in a patch by the wall, deposit 1037 was dominated by peat ash, while spread midden 1013 was encountered across the whole of the north-west quadrant. This midden comprised dark sandy silt with lenses of peat ash, much charcoal and fragments of shell and bone, but was especially notable as the first context to produce flax as well as oat and barley. These middens were also sealed by buried soil 1016 as it formed over the truncated, extensively robbed and ploughed remains of the longhouse and its environs. Two bone needles were also found within the midden deposits (dated to cal AD 990–1160: SUERC-17846; SFs 4016 and 4017). As with early midden spread 1017 this layer was clearly the product of domestic activity.

It is probable that several of the hard-to-distinguish midden deposits south of the longhouse in Trench 3 were laid in Phase 5. Some of these deposits were stony

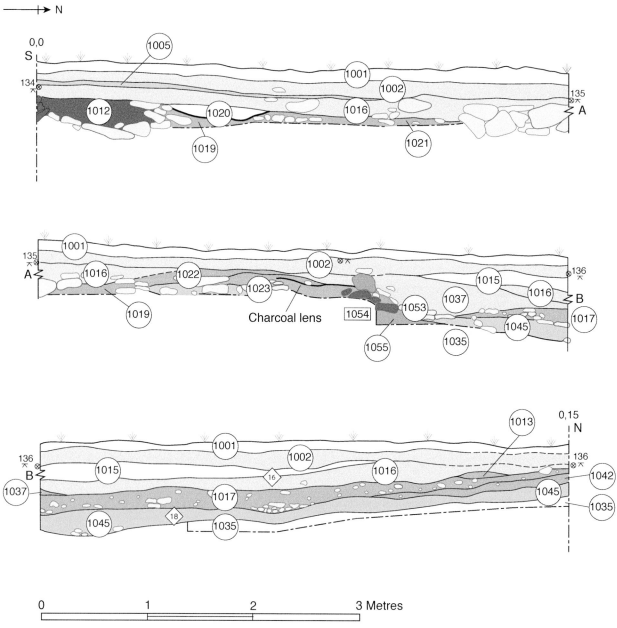

Fig. 4.12: Trenches 1 & 3, sections, E facing (colour code Fig. 4.43)

(1040), some contained much peat-ash (1039, 1047, and 1049), all were more or less sandy silts characterised by their lack of homogeneity. Only one diagnostic artefact was found in this phase of midden formation – a bone needle (SF 4034). The marked difference between the Phase 5 middens south and north of the building suggests either a chronological variance, with those south of the building possibly being later, or the contrast between a 'spread' midden to the north designed also to act as a useable surface, and an accumulation to the south of ash-dominated curated midden for reuse elsewhere. The middens to the south were also overlain by the partially developed Phase 8 soil 1016.

Phases 6–7

Any identifiable archaeological traces of these later medieval phases, if they existed here, were truncated, disturbed or removed. However, dumps of limpet shells discarded in the process of preparing fishing bait may have been deposited in this period (contexts 1002 and 1005).

PHASE 8

This period was represented by the disturbed, patchy and partially developed buried soil 1016, and associated windblown sand layers, which covered the archaeology below.

PHASE 9

Trench 1 produced the most extensive and varied Phase 9 activity. Immediately underlying topsoil, and cut into windblown sand layers, across the south-east quadrant of the trench, was a large spread of kelp burning pits, and associated burnt stone and ash (Fig. 4.13). This area had also been disturbed by a very large rabbit warren. Three of the kelping pits were excavated: 1031, 1033 and 1040. A similar Phase 9 pit was also discovered in Trench 2, one in Trench 4 and a further two in Trench 5. In the north-west quadrant of Trench 1, two recent animal burials had cut into the Viking-Late Norse middens below and further disturbed the truncated line of the northern longhouse wall (see Fig. 4.1: cuts 1010 and 1027).

Trench 2

This small trench was opened to provide geoarchaeological contrast to the main trenches within the sampling strategy (see Fig. 6.3). A Phase 9 kelp-burning pit was uncovered (reported upon in Chapter 6).

Trench 4: Snusgar

EXCAVATION STRATEGY

Trench 4, dug in 2005 and 2006, sloped near south-east down the southern flank of the Snusgar mound (Fig. 4.14). Trenches 1 and 3 were close and to the north-west of Trench 4, but on the other side of a stone wall or dyke. No formal structures were discovered in Trench 4 but long, deep sections were established to investigate the structure and composition of the mound itself. A section running the full 30 m length of the trench was excavated in 2005, when the narrow tail of the trench was also dug down to deep sterile, windblown sand layers and a slot excavated

Fig. 4.13: Trench 1, kelp-burning pit in W facing section

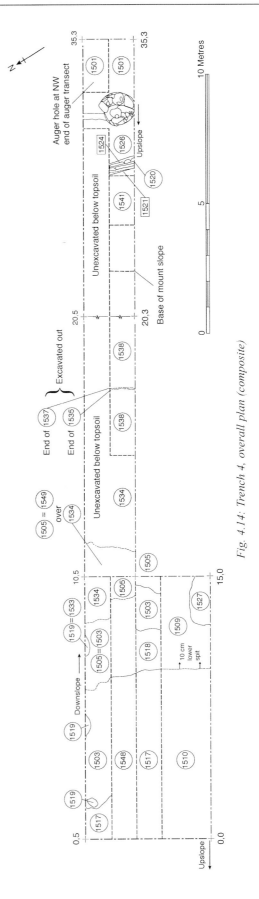

Fig. 4.14: Trench 4, overall plan (composite)

SG 06 Trench 4
Composite final plan: upper 10m

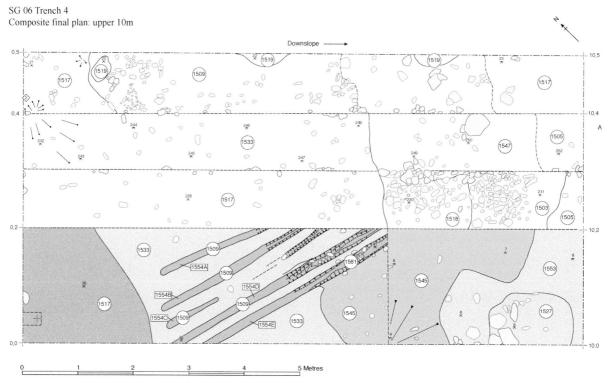

Fig. 4.15: Trench 4, detail plan of upper 10m (colour code Fig. 4.43; photograph Fig. 6.6)

down a further 1.5 m into those layers to investigate the composition of those sands (see Figs 4.2 and 4.3). The up-slope part of the trench was re-opened in 2006 to continue investigation of the midden layers first encountered the previous year (Fig. 4.15). To enable downward excavation and battering, the trench was extended up-slope; this extension was only excavated as far as was necessary to ensure safe working, removing some thin, patchy layers of upper Phase 5 midden and a complex of underlying sand-blows and lenses above the more developed midden sequences. A slot 2 m by 10 m was excavated within the trench, continuing the 2005 sections in that area, down to deep sterile windblown sand, to permit the characterisation and sampling of the lower midden sequences, all of which were laid down in the Phases 2 and 3.

The archaeology of Phases 2–5 had been little disturbed by intrusive actions (the effects of post-depositional, taphonomic factors are discussed above). Below subsoil and windblown sand were varied and organised spreads, layers and deposits of midden to a maximum depth of *c.* 2 m. On excavation some of those deposits were thin, artefact-free and composed of dark silty material or clayey peat ash; others were extensive, stonier and mixed with sand (Figs 4.3 and 4.16). Several were rich in shell and animal, fish and bird bone; others contained artefacts, in particular fragments of identifiably Viking-Late Norse

worked bone. The deposits and spreads were interleaved with and sometimes separated by lenses or layers of windblown sand indicating changes in the intensity and location of activity and midden deposition. The midden layers excavated had mostly been created in Phases 2–3 with the most extensive, richest midden 1504 amassing mainly in Phase 3. The later Phase 5 midden components were relatively thin and patchy: the focus of midden-building may have been elsewhere on the mound – perhaps closer to the Trench 1 building – in this phase.

Phase 1: Buried land surface

The deep slot excavated in the 'tail' of Trench 4 revealed the earliest archaeological layer discovered anywhere on site: a thin sandy buried soil developed over deep and increasingly water-logged windblown sand (see Fig. 4.3; Chapter 6). A cormorant bone found in the fine, otherwise finds-free layer dated the surface to the Later Iron Age or Pictish period: Phase 1 (cal AD 470–680: SUERC-17851; see Table 5.1) and remains the only dateable layer of this period demonstrated to exist on either Snusgar or East Mound. The thin buried soils (1536 and 1537; Fig. 4.3) extended horizontally into the core of the mound, at a level only a little above the height of the surrounding modern land surface. This indicated that the mound was taking shape in this phase, but that people were probably not

Fig. 4.16: Trench 4, middens and windblown sand, SE facing (see also Fig. 4.17)

working regularly in the immediate vicinity. The surface had then been submerged beneath *c.* 1.75 m of sterile windblown sand before the Phase 2 middens began to develop, suggesting a considerable hiatus in soil formation in that area of the mound.

THE SEQUENCE OF VIKING-LATE NORSE MIDDENS: PHASES 2–5

Trench 4 revealed a sequence of middens within which five main episodes of accumulation were recorded. Three of those episodes occurred within Phase 2 of the site chronology (mainly 10th century AD); one within Phase 3 (10th to mid-11th century AD) with the final, and most extensive, deposition towards the end of Phase 3. The Bayesian modelling of radiocarbon dates (Chapter 5) estimates the transition from Phase 2 to 3 probably occurred in cal AD 950–1000 and that Phase 5-related activity on the mound probably ended in cal AD 1020–1090 (68% probability). Thus the midden sequence, as recorded in Trench 4, may have been deposited over a span of up to 200 years, ending in the mid-late 11th century AD. Some of the last of the Viking-Late Norse midden layers appear to have been laid closer to the longhouse and the crown of the mound, and, as in Trench 1, reduced by erosion. No direct stratigraphic link could be established between these Trench 4 middens and those in Trenches 1 and 3 because of the west–east field dyke crossing the mound, but there were many similarities in the composition and content of the deposits.

PHASE 2: VIKING PITS AND MIDDEN SEQUENCE (FIG. 4.16)

The first Phase 2 midden sequence began with the spreading of an extensive stone layer 1567 directly over deep windblown sand, and the digging of a pit 1568, which was quickly filled with organic peaty material. The stone layer, with its mix of sand and organic material, probably intended to stabilise the mound surface and may

have been spread just before, or at the time, the Snusgar longhouse was built. After the deposition of small amounts of midden-type material this sequence was sealed by a large spread of shell-rich ashy silt 1561, within which was found a siltstone whetstone (SF 123), and plentiful burnt grain deposits from which a radiocarbon date was obtained (cal AD 890–1030: SUERC-17856; a second date was taken on willow charcoal, cal AD 880–1030: SUERC-17857). This spread was followed by a complex sequence of peat-ash rich deposits, without animal bone or artefacts, interleaved with sand lenses (*e.g.* 1562, 1563 and 1583). Only one of these peat-ash layers 1560 was stony and produced a small assemblage of bone and shell. Most of these peat-ash deposits were clearly originating from areas where other activity was contributing little detritus to the ashy mix. These layers were finally sealed and stabilised by a second stony silty spread 1556.

The third and structurally most complex midden sequence began with two more extensive and ecofact-rich midden layers (1547, cal AD 900–1040: SUERC-17852; and 1548; Fig. 4.17). The silty clay of 1547 contained both stabilising stones and the first iron artefact: a nail (SF 38). These layers were followed by smaller and varied deposits (*e.g.* 1518 and 1533), held in place by arcs and spreads of stones (*e.g.* 1505; a radiocarbon date of cal AD 900–1040 was obtained from 1518: SUERC-18265). This sequence also included more lenses and thin layers of sand and was the first sequence to produce more than one artefact. 1533 contained an iron rivet (found in flot) and a bone pin (SF 42). The last layer in this sequence, comprising a number of different peat-ash and charcoal rich sandy organic deposits (1517, 1519 and 1546) had been spread and levelled using a plough. The eroded remains of a buried subsoil were just visible in the plough marks, suggesting a soil had begun to form over the archaeological deposits before the levelling was undertaken (Chapter 6; Fig. 4.15). A complete bone pin (SF 12) was found in 1519 along with an iron knife-blade (SF 15). Another bone pin (SF 37) came from an associated sand lens. The use of stone to structure the midden (such as arc or low wall of stone 1549), and the levelling of the area using a plough demonstrates the attention given to the way in which midden-type materials were deposited.

PHASE 3: FINAL MIDDEN SEQUENCES

A windblown sand layer 1509 up to a third of a metre deep then accumulated over the area before the deposition of two ash- and shell-rich midden layers 1508 and 1510 interspersed with lenses and relatively deep layers of sand (*e.g.* 1507). There was also evidence for weathering and water movement with mineral staining and crusts of iron pan, indicating that the laying of midden was more sporadic during this period. Only one artefact was discovered in the midden material: a steatite weight (SF 5) in 1510, but one of the slightly organic sandy

SG 05 & SG 06 Trench 4
Section 14
SE facing

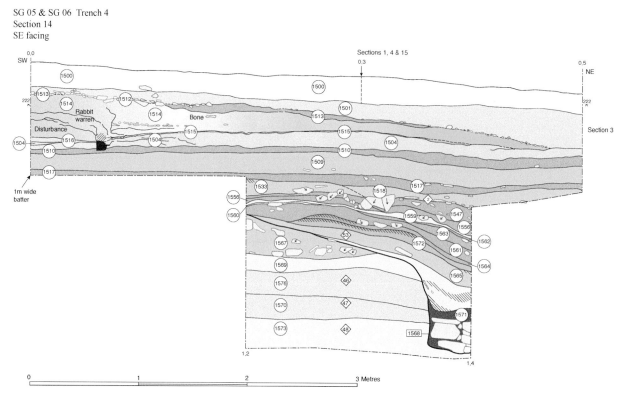

Fig. 4.17: Trench 4, section as Fig. 4.16 (colour code Fig. 4.43)

layers 1506 produced a copper-alloy finger-ring (SF 1). However, the most extensive and richest midden was the final layer in this fourth sequence (1504; cal AD 970–1040: SUERC-17847). The vast majority of the artefacts from Trench 4, including bone needles/pins (SFs 8, 9 and 13), several bone comb fragments (SFs 8, 19, 20, 21, 22 and 139), a bone toggle (SF 36), and iron objects, came from this deep silty, ashy midden, as well as a great deal of limpet shell and bone. In this last major phase of deposition the domestic character of the midden contents was most marked, suggesting the proximity of an inhabited and busy longhouse.

PHASE 5: LESSENING OF ACTIVITY

The final archaeological layers were much more disturbed by animal burrowing and probably belonged to this phase. They comprised small dumps of stone 1503 and 1512 and thin layers of slightly organic and mineral-stained sands (*e.g.* 1515 and 1516) with occasional thin more silty layers with faunal remains 1502 and 1513. The focus of midden accumulation may have moved closer to the longhouse, some at least of which was discovered in Trench 3.

MIDDEN COMPOSITION AND THE FORMATION OF THE SNUSGAR MOUND

Although most of the Trench 4 layers with midden-type material included some burnt grain and peat/

turf (used as fuel) these were in smaller amounts than in midden layers in Trench 1. However, the range of grain was similar – mostly oat with some barley – and contexts 1017 and 1045 from Phase 2 in Trench 1, were of comparable composition to significant midden layers in Phase 2 in Trench 4 (1547, 1548 and 1561; Chapter 8). Interestingly, the lowest midden 1045 in Trench 1 was laid down at a very similar height above sea-level as the sequence around midden 1547 in Trench 4 (*c.* 7.75 m OD). These sequences also returned similar radiocarbon date ranges (from Trench 1: 1045, cal AD 880–1020: SUERC-17848 and 1017, cal AD 880–1030: SUERC-17847; and from Trench 4: 1547, cal AD 900–1040: SUERC-18265 and 1518, cal AD 900–1040). The midden layers most productive of burnt grain and fuel ash residues in Trench 4 were in the Phase 2 sequence between layer 1547 and the levelling episode (*e.g.* 1519, 1547 and 1533). Contexts 1511 and 1533, in the same sequence in Phase 2, also generated two of the largest faunal assemblages (Chapter 9). Later Phase 3 midden 1504, although producing the largest faunal assemblage, generated relatively little evidence for burnt grain.

Although the bone in Trench 4 was dominated, as elsewhere, by cattle, sheep/goat and pig, the middens were distinguished from those on East Mound by the presence of wild species such as red deer, whale and seal; they also produced bones belonging to 20 species of bird and proportionately more sheep/goat than elsewhere. No horse or dog bones were found in Trench 4. More of the bone was burnt; cut marks indicated the primary butchery of cattle and sheep. Layer 1504 at the end of Phase 3 contained the largest mammal and avian assemblage and was notable for the collection of gannet bone, which suggested people had travelled a considerable distance from the site to carry out systematic trapping of the birds then prepared for eating near the longhouse (Chapter 9). Several of the midden-type contexts on the Snusgar mound had small amounts of vitrified material suggesting that iron smithing had been carried out in the vicinity: this contrasted with the *in situ* iron smithing hearths and considerable quantity of iron-working debris found in Trench 5 on East Mound (Chapter 11).

PHASES 6–8

These phases were represented by a thick (*c.* 0.3–0.5 m) windblown sand layer encountered below topsoil and above the surviving Viking-Late Norse archaeology; it is also possible that aspects of later archaeology on the upper mound were lost to slope-erosion and truncation by later animal trampling.

PHASE 9

Phase 9 features were mostly found cut into the deep sandy subsoil and underlying windblown sand accumulations, rather than archaeological layers. These features included a well-preserved kelp-burning pit 1523 and stone field drain 1521 found at the base of the mound, and patches of modern burnt material and a more recent sheep burial 1544 in the upper sector of the trench (see Fig. 4.3: cut 1521).

Trenches 5 and 8: East Mound (Figs 4.7 and 4.18)

EXCAVATION STRATEGY

Trench 5 was excavated over six seasons from 2005 to 2011 on the mound which we named 'East Mound', above the Burn of Snusgar. The structural archaeology revealed was well-preserved and complex. Factors shaping the overall excavation strategy are described above (Phase 1 was not present), but the approach in Trench 5 was defined by the presence of sequences of both buildings and middens under deep sand. The investigation of relationships between structural phases, and between structures and internal floors, external yards and middens, demanded the use of strategic and running sections. Approaches were also constrained by the need to maintain safe working and defined by the aim of limiting the destruction of surviving walls and features. A wide batter had to be maintained to the west and to the south, where the sand deposits were especially extensive, having accumulated in a dip in the surface of the mound.

PHASE 2: CONSTRUCTION OF EARLY BUILDINGS AND CREATION OF FIRST MIDDENS AND YARD

In the earlier Viking Age the shape and size of the mound were notably different to today. The mound summit was just to the south of the main area of the trench and up to 2 m lower than today, and the ground sloped down more steeply towards the burn and the north and west. Archaeology of this early phase was deeply buried and difficult to access and interpret amidst the network of walls and features of later phases. Further information could have been collected only by wholesale demolition of later, well-preserved Viking-Late Norse buildings. However, there were indications of a focus of early activity in the south-east of the trench, and that the first northern building (the hall-building) may have been constructed either at the very end this phase, or early in Phase 3. Thus, a small settlement was founded, partly built into the slope, but not as far as could be determined, over or incorporating any earlier buildings or layers.

THE EASTERN BOUNDARY TO THE SETTLEMENT COMPLEX, SOUTH-EAST BUILDINGS AND MIDDEN

In the small area excavated in the south-east corner of Trench 5 and east of the ancillary building sequence, a short 0.3 m high stretch of the west face of a wall 2289, curving gently to the north-west, was revealed in the trench-edge (Fig. 4.19). When a Phase 3 north–south wall 2207 was constructed to the west, a short linking stretch joined the walls to create a sinuous whole. In 2011, the east face and foundations 2373 of the Phase 2 wall 2289 were exposed at the top of the long eastward mound-slope extension (see Fig. 4.8). A maximum of seven courses of the wall survived, of double-faced dry stone construction, using beach flags and cobbles. The wall clearly demarcated the edge of the focal settlement area to the west, as deposits to the east were quite different and indicated a much more peripheral area. There was some evidence on the east slope (at the top of the long extension) for Phase 2 activity preceding the building of the wall: a v-shaped north–south ditch 2375 had been cut, perhaps as an initial boundary-marker, into sand-stabilising clay and silty sand layers lightly affected by human activity (*e.g.* 2367). The ditch and surrounding area had then been sealed and levelled to prepare a stable surface for wall 2373-2289. A large pit 2738, dug into the incline about 9 m to the south-east, may have been created at the same time as the early ditch, and its fills of ashy and silty sand further testified to human activity nearby (see Fig. 4.8).

Whether wall 2373-2289 was simply a boundary-marker, or part of a Phase 2 building to the west could not

SG 10 Trench 5

Trench 8

Fig. 4.18: Trenches 5 & 8, overall final plan in 2010 (colour code Fig. 4.43) (see inside back cover for A3 version)

Fig. 4.19: Trench 5, wall 2289 and flagging 2287, from S

be conclusively determined. However, within the southern ancillary building area there were other slight structural indications of possible Phase 2 features. Structural stones – wall coursing or small flagstones – were beginning to show up in excavation beneath the earliest floor layer 2245 of the earliest excavated north–south southern building. These could not be investigated further and were relatively ephemeral. Also, midden 2152 had begun to accumulate just to the south of curved wall 2289 in this phase (dated to cal AD 900–1040: SUERC-24713). After its deposition, much of this midden had slipped downslope over later midden and features. It had almost certainly been added to during Phase 3, its finds and rich composition attesting to daily life and work around the hall-building complex during that period. The building and later reconstruction of ancillary buildings west of this midden had also disturbed the layers, adding a further degree of uncertainty about its phasing.

The midden was composed of dumps of highly silty material containing varying amounts of peat ash, burnt clay and turf, charcoal, shell and animal bone, with considerable amounts of burnt grain and seaweed: a mixed midden of general domestic and agricultural waste (Chapter 8). Several sherds of steatite were found (SFs 158, 162, 217 and 219: Chapter 19); iron objects (SFs 155, 275) and bone comb and pin fragments (SFs 265, 266).

Yards west of the midden/possible building

To the west of the midden and possible structural remains a Phase 2 surface 2183-2187 linked that area across to the first yard in the south-west (to be the metal-working yard in Phase 3). The immediately succeeding, initial layers of grey clay-like metal-working yard floor 2234 may have been laid in this phase, composed of sandy ash compacted with greasy cooking residues to create a firm surface. Some charred grain was found within the floor, but also well-preserved willow charcoal suggesting fires had been burning within the first yard. The contrast to the ecofacts from the midden hints at spatial distinctions in activity

areas and in the deposition of waste, which became more obvious in later phases (Chapter 8).

The first hall-building

The first major building – the Phase 2 to Phase 3 hall – was a bow-sided structure nearly 5 m wide and about 10 m long. It was constructed possibly towards the end of Phase 2 or early in Phase 3 and in use in Phase 3. Early walls could clearly be distinguished from those of the Phase 5 configuration of the longhouse both in the northern wall 2166 and parts of wall 2076 in the south; a blocked up entrance was visible in the southern wall just west of the later Phase 5 internal dividing wall (Fig. 4.20). The recut post-hole 2310 at the western end of the hall-building may have supported the roof in Phase 3. An area of primary floor 2146, protected by the laying of the Phase 5 dividing wall 2135, probably belonged to this phase (cal AD 900–1040: SUERC-24714). Some of the finds on the very edge of the floors by the walls and in small lenses of windblown sand were undoubtedly intrusive and belonged to later phases: for example pottery (SF 262) and perhaps some of the iron artefacts. However, those embedded within the dark silty sand compacted with peat-ash were not, and included other iron artefacts (SFs 168, 176, 205, 215, 251, 355, 367, 370 and 371), a fine stone burnisher (SF 264) and whalebone (SF 178). One find was particularly unusual: quarter of a well-worn, decorated rotary quern with a distinctive handle-setting (SF 200; Chapter 18) was discovered sunk into the floor close to the east end of the hall-building. The quern is Iron Age in origin and may have been kept, reused and laid as a deliberate deposit, at some significant point in the early history of the building, probably dug into the earlier floors when the Phase 5 longhouse was constructed.

Phase 3: The hall-building; north–south ancillary building, drains and yard; and metal-working yard (see Fig. 4.18)

The initial settlement complex was in use throughout this phase, and comprised the west–east aligned, bow-sided hall-building in the north and a second smaller and probably also domestic building to the south, lying north–south and across a paved yard from the main building. To the west of the latter structure, the metal-working yard was used intermittently for iron-smithing. The archaeological traces of Phase 3, buried beneath the extensive Phase 5 structures and yards, were encountered only as fragmentary remains and on the whole more difficult to interpret.

The north–south ancillary building, drain system and central yard

Preserved within and below the walls of the later Phase 5 sub-rectangular west–east building were the structural remains of a Phase 3 north–south ancillary building

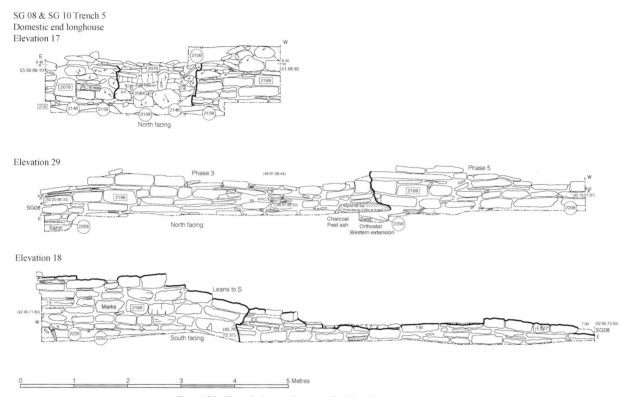

Fig. 4.20: Trench 5, southern wall of longhouse, elevations

about 2.5 m wide and at least 4 m long. Its southern extent could not be precisely determined but sufficient elements of the structure's eastern wall and north-western corner were recovered in deeper sections to recreate the plan of the northern end of the building. Stretches of the slightly bowed eastern 2122 and northern 2177 walls were revealed; although the southern wall could not be detected with certainty, a change in infill-deposits recorded in section marked where the western wall had been removed. Around six courses of the walls remained, up to 0.7 m in height and of drystone construction including rounded beach-cobbles. Wall 2177 was visible as a spur protruding from under the Phase 4–5 walling and in the north where later courses sagged over the curve of the Phase 3 wall. Eastern wall 2122 emerged from behind a later re-facing of its west side and beneath later midden to its east (Fig. 4.21). The inside of the building was investigated by half-sectioning the interior deposits, but not enough diagnostic material was found fully to interpret the uses of the building. It is possible it may have been slightly sunken. The internal layers had been much disturbed by subsequent rebuilding in this area, in particular by the later realignment of the eastern wall, which had involved digging down through the Phase 3 floors. The earliest floor layers were sandy with very few inclusions, but some ashy hearth-deposits were worked into them (*e.g.* 2045 and 2162 which contained an iron object SF 290). A discrete peat-ash deposit returned a

date of cal AD 1010–1160 (2231: SUERC-33722). The upper floors 2155 and 2080 were more disturbed but had originally been clayey and firmer surfaces. Floor 2155 included trample of hearth-related deposits, animal and fish bone and shell. A range of small flags 2151 suggested areas of the floor had been roughly paved. Related and finely laminated floor 2080 contained more bone and shell fragments and areas had been reinforced with yellow clay (cal AD 990–1160: SUERC-24705). The assemblages of charred cereal grain and chaff, peat fuel remains and flax from these floors were similar to the composition of ecofacts from the domestic area of the main longhouse and suggested some crop-related activity was carried out in the building, perhaps drying before storage (Chapter 8). During this phase, the 'ancillary' building may well have been primarily domestic, serving as a second and smaller hall-building, rather than a shed or workspace.

The building was surrounded on the west, east and northern sides by a well-constructed, sand-bottomed drainage system. With stone-lined sides, up to 0.3 m wide, these drains were cut into windblown sand to act as soakaways. Constructed as both drains and pathways they were also neatly flagged with flat paving. Drain 2191-2192 to the west of the building had been concealed by later steps, but north of the steps was incorporated into the soakaway system under the central paved yard. It ran north outside the building towards the yard to merge, at a small circular sump area, with drain 2147, which continued, still

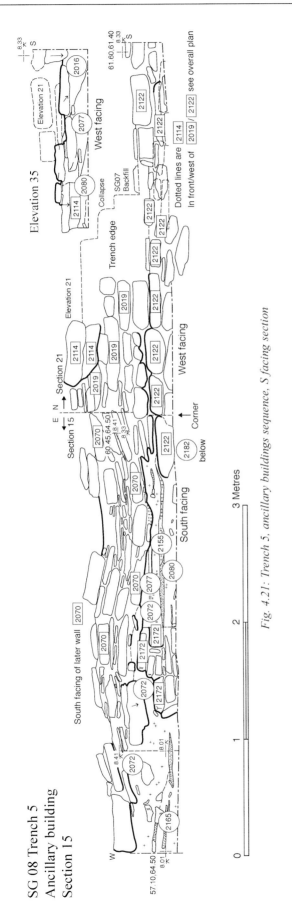

SG 08 Trench 5
Ancillary building
Section 15

Fig. 4.21: Trench 5, ancillary buildings sequence, S facing section

flagged, across the yard towards what may have been the eastern entrance into the Phase 3 hall-building. Here its course was masked by the later Phase 5 byre but may have been preserved in the central west–east drain/pathway of the later byre. The silty fills (*e.g.* 2148-2149) of drain 2147 contained only a little burnt material and fragmentary bone that had trickled down from surfaces above, but included a fragment of hearth bottom (SF 292). The drain fills were dry, testifying to the continued efficacy of a sand-based soakaway. Soil chemistry analysis of those fills revealed high cholesterol levels, linked to the presence of animals, and also of lithocholic or bile acid indicating the presence of both herbivore and omnivore faeces (Chapter 7).

An eastern arm 2287 of the drainage system ran north behind wall 2122 of the ancillary building. It was also flagged with large well-cut 0.8 m wide flags to double as a pathway, and bordered to the east by a narrow wall 2207. This wall turned away from the drain/pathway in the south and had been constructed over and incorporated the earlier curved wall 2289 discussed above. The drain's northern end fed into a narrow arm running west across the yard into the central sump and drain 2147 (see Fig. 4.18).

A working surface 2143-2242 spread to the east of the central yard between the northern and southern building areas and was utilised as bedding for the large flags of the central yard 2132 when that was fully paved, probably in Phase 4, to incorporate the existing drain flagging. Immediately east of the paved area the surface was gradually covered with midden deposits. These deposits accumulated less steadily than those midden layers to the south nearer the Phase 3 ancillary building, and were less rich in bone and shell, but included steatite and iron.

THE SOUTH-EAST MIDDEN AND WALLS

The area immediately to the east of the various ancillary buildings remained a focus for midden deposition through Phases 3–5, and produced some of the most organic and finds-rich deposits external to the buildings on East Mound. In Phase 3 midden began to accumulate in a funnel-shaped space between the eastern wall of the building 2212 and the sinuous wall created by joining new wall 2207 to Phase 2 wall 2289 (see Fig. 4.19). Turf-backed, single-faced wall 2207 ran parallel to the building for a short stretch, and may have been intended originally to shelter the flagged drain/passageway running alongside the outside of the house wall. However, this route clearly fell out of use and midden deposits built up in the space between the walls. The first two layers over the path were a rough stony layer with dumps of peat-ash and cooking waste, indicating the time of the path's neglect (2236, cal AD 980–1160: SUERC-47151) and a peat-ash midden with some charred barley (2288, cal AD 1010–1160: SUERC-33721). More substantial middens accumulated above those, 2254 and 2204, and included general domestic waste, such as fire-cracked

SG 10 Trench 5
Section 4
Metal working area

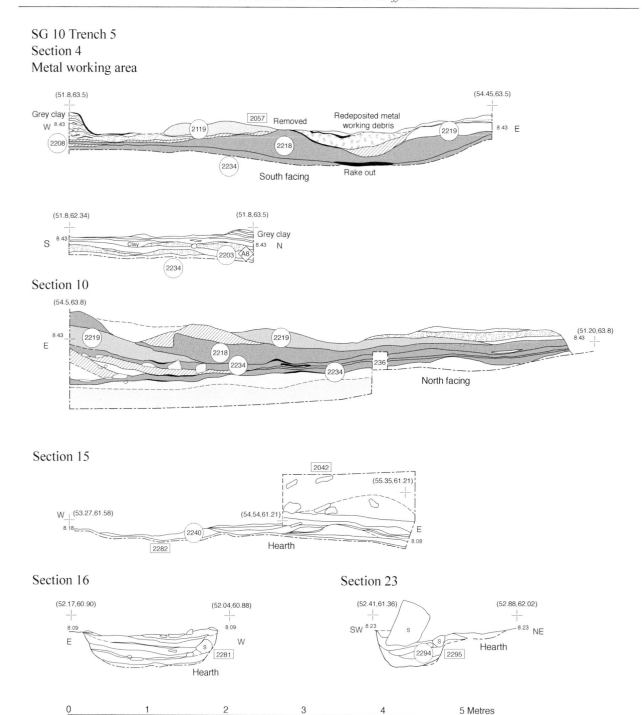

Fig. 4.22: Trench 5, metalworking hearths, sections (colour code Fig. 4.43)

stones, bone and shell as well as bone comb (SF 310) and steatite (SFs 315 and 477). These layers produced charred cereal and flax seeds (flax first appears in Phase 3); weeds of fertilised sandy arable land, and burnt peat used as fuel for fires and cooking hearths or for drying cereal. Charcoal fragments, as well as vitrified waste, present in these midden deposits, could have originated

from the metalworking hearths in the Phase 3 yard to the east (Chapter 8).

THE METAL-WORKING YARD (SEE FIGS 4.22, 4.23)

Just over 2 m west of the southern 'ancillary' north–south building, a metal-working yard was established and in use during Phase 3. Discovered under a small

Fig. 4.23: Trench 5, metalworking yard, from S

Phase 5 unfurnished yard, it was excavated in plan using running sections. Although the hearth superstructures were dismantled during Phase 4 to allow for new wall-building and the laying of a new clay yard-floor, the cuts for the hearth bowls, and some ash rake-outs, hearth bottoms and slag survived to be excavated. Four small, clay-lined bowl-shaped hearths were used successively, and spread from south-east to north across the small, ashy-floored yard (2.5 m by 3 m), shielded by walls 2065 and 2018 to the south and west (see Figs 4.18 and 4.23). The walls were single-stone width and relatively insubstantial, suggesting the area may have been open or perhaps more likely, sheltered by half-height walls and a light timber roof. There was some evidence in Phase 5 that dismantled wooden structural elements with iron fittings were dumped to the north of the former metal-working yard and structure. The range of both diagnostic and non-diagnostic vitrified materials discovered in the area demonstrated that iron smithing was undertaken within the building, probably on a seasonal basis (Chapter 11). Neither the soil chemistry analysis nor the vitrified material produced any evidence for non-ferrous metal-working (see Chapter 7).

Construction of new hearths, and their subsequent dismantling, had considerably disturbed the yard floors 2234-2105, but where they survived best fine laminations of ash, silt, clay and sand could be observed. Radiocarbon dates for 2105 were cal AD 970–1150: SUERC-24715 and cal AD 890–1030: SUERC-24716, both taken on roundwood willow charcoal with bark, and the range reflects the depositional character of the floors. These firm, clay-like floors were formed from a mixture of ash and cooking residues, probably carefully saved from around the domestic fires for their particular properties. As each layer wore thin, another was laid, creating laminations of repeated spreading and possibly also clearing. These laminations, although they were too thin and fragile to be excavated as individual layers, assisted in the phasing of the four hearths. The presence of large quantities of micro-debris in the form of hammerscale flakes and smithing pan, as well as a fragment of hearth bottom,

demonstrated that debris from around an anvil, as well as from the hearths, was worked into the surfaces (see Chapter 11). The hearths, and especially the floor layers, produced large amounts of extremely well-preserved charcoal, including roundwood willow with bark. This concentration of charcoal as fuel for the smithing contrasted with the peat and turf which formed the bulk of fuel for cereal drying, cooking and heating within the buildings (Chapter 8). Inorganic chemistry analysis also suggested the use of heartwood as fuel in the hearths (Chapter 7). Iron objects and fragments were found trampled into the floors (Chapter 12). Some of the many iron artefacts found in the turfed yard 2087 to the south may be linked to the Phase 3 metal-working – perhaps thrown out of the yard during cleaning or when an artefact failed.

Each hearth was bowl-shaped and accompanied by a silty, charcoal and ash-rich tail resulting from the repeated rake-out of material before relighting the hearth; each would originally have had a stone superstructure (Figs 4.22 and 4.23). The earliest hearth 2282 was the best preserved: found in the eastern area of the yard, and cut into floor layers laid over the first, probably Phase 2 yard surface. The hearth's structure had been partially protected by the corner of the western wall 2042 of later buildings. The surviving bowl of hearth 2282 was 0.5 m in diameter and its fill 2240, like all the hearth fills and surviving rake-outs, contained hammerscale flakes from iron-smithing (2240, cal AD 1010–1160: SUERC-33700). The second hearth 2281, 0.5 m to the west, had been partly destroyed by the third hearth 2295. The bowl of 2281 was a similar size but a small amount of the clay lining survived in the fill (2269, cal AD 1010–1160: SUERC-33701); the location of a tuyère was preserved on the north side as an impression in the ground (Chapter 11). Hearth 2295 was differently orientated (north-west–south-east, rather than west–east) and produced more hearth-lining as well as hammerscale and smithing pan (fill 2294, cal AD 980–11160: SUERC-47148). The fourth and final hearth 2293 slightly to the north had been heavily truncated and only the rake-out 2292 survived.

Outside the metal-working yard to the west lay a turfed area, which had been very badly damaged by a modern rabbit warren. This area seemed to remain as a relatively little-used patch of ground through Phases 3–5 (2111-2112, 2078-2109; cal AD 980–1150: SUERC-17868 and SUERC-24704). The metalworking yard was presumably protected on its western side by a shelter or wind-break, which would have made access difficult from that direction.

THE STRUCTURE OF THE FIRST HALL-BUILDING

The archaeology of the first hall-building was more difficult to interpret than the developed Phase 5 longhouse, but sufficient to propose a plan of the building. Elements of the walls could be traced in the standing architecture, in particular in the north where its bow-sided shape was preserved, and in the lower courses of the southern wall where a Phase 3 doorway close to the original east end had been blocked. In the west, a large stone curving out from the surviving southern wall indicated the turn into the western end wall of the original building (see Fig. 4.18; the junction between Phase 3 hall and Phase 5 western annex is also visible in Fig. 4.30).

Phase 3 was the major occupation phase of the first hall-building, but only small areas of its floors survived the later longhouse use of the internal area. At the western end, behind the central posthole for the roof support 2310, a small area of floor 2273 probably belonging to this phase was preserved beneath Phase 5 flagstones (cal AD 970–1040: SUERC-33718). This flooring was dark sandy silt mixed with hearth deposits. The layer could probably be linked to an adjacent area disturbed by wall collapse in Phase 6 (2219, cal AD 970–1150: SUERC-47149), in which were combined residual finds from the floors and floor deposits and the midden from within the collapsed longhouse walls central fill. The wall-fills can only have comprised midden from at the latest Phase 3, as those collapsed stretches at the western end were from walls rebuilt at the beginning of Phase 5. The finds included steatite (SFs 311, 323, 324, 326, 327), worked bone objects (SFs 319, 341, 374) and iron (SF 320). Collapse layer 2221, into which 2219 merged just to the east, also comprised windblown sand, and large wall stones with patches of original wall-fill material, but had not impacted on floor deposits in the same way (cal AD 900–1040: SUERC-47147).

The other small areas of floor that may have originated in Phase 3 were at the eastern end (2283 and 2284) and related to floor 2146 discussed above. Floor area 2283 was at most 0.5 m wide but spread across the width of the east end and had been protected by the later dividing wall and passageway features. Most of the floor was compact dark ash-rich sandy silt with pink peat-ash lenses; it was sandier to the south, where drifts of sand had blown in through the original door in the southern side. A smaller floor area 2284 had been disturbed by the insertion of a three-sided box feature 2188 made of orthostatic flagstones through the Phase 3 floor into the underlying sand (see Fig. 4.18). The main central area of the hall/longhouse was excavated in four quadrants to assist in creating a sampling grid, and to retain more control over the location of the bulk finds of bone and shell (2262 to 2264). Although the lowest laminations in the two quadrants closest to the east end – less disturbed by collapse and animal trample – may have been first been laid in Phase 3 (2262 and 2264), all four quadrants will be discussed together in the Phase 5 section. However, the finely laminated but firm sandy silts

of 2262 and 2264 (cal AD 980–1120: SUERC-33707), compacted with patches of peat ash, grey ash and charcoal, are an indication of the character of at least parts of the Phase 3 floors.

PHASE 4: REALIGNMENT OF THE ANCILLARY BUILDING TO CREATE A WEST–EAST RECTANGULAR STRUCTURE; CLOSING OF THE METAL-WORKING YARD, AND PAVING AND ENCLOSING OF THE CENTRAL YARD

In Phase 4 a major reorganisation was undertaken of the building and yards to the south of the longhouse. This process could be archaeologically attested in the work undertaken completely to rebuild the ancillary building, to close down the metalworking yard to its immediate south-west and create a new walled enclosure (see Fig. 4.18: see overlay to left). This process may also have encompassed the alterations made to the hall-building, but that work could not be documented in the same way – its outcome was seen in the elongated Phase 5 longhouse.

THE ALTERATION OF ANCILLARY BUILDINGS IN THE SOUTH OF THE TRENCH

In this phase the building in the south was completely reconfigured to create a rectangular structure 5.5 m long by 2.5 m wide aligned west–east with double-faced drystone walls averaging 0.7 m thick (walls 2018-2027 south, 2019-2114 east, 2070-2069 north and 2042 west; Fig. 4.24). The northern wall of the new building was built over and beyond the lower courses of the northern wall 2172 of the Phase 3 building; and the eastern wall over the Phase 3 building's eastern wall 2122 (Fig. 4.21). The eastern wall of the earlier structure was slightly bowed outwards so the Phase 4 builders had dug down into the floors that had accumulated within the building, to nearly 0.5 m in depth, and straightened the original wall by adding facing stones 2114 on the inside. Wall 2019 for the new building was then built onto foundations comprising both the new facing and older wall. On excavation of the interior, the facing stones 2114 collapsed outward as they were not bonded into the old wall, but simply held in place by redeposited internal floors. A similar re-facing probably should have been repeated inside the bowed original northern wall, as the Phase 5 wall 2070 constructed over it sagged along the stretch founded on floor deposits rather than the original northern wall 2172 (Fig. 4.21). The western wall of the Phase 3 building was at least partially removed, and the area beyond its floors infilled to make a level surface for the new walls to the west and south. The sand that predominated in these deep infill layers 2072-2077 and 2165 was held together by the addition of midden material – hence the assemblage of animal bone and shell, antler and worked bone artefacts (SFs 177 and 242) – but also consolidated by fragments of the clayey floor surfaces from the Phase 3 building.

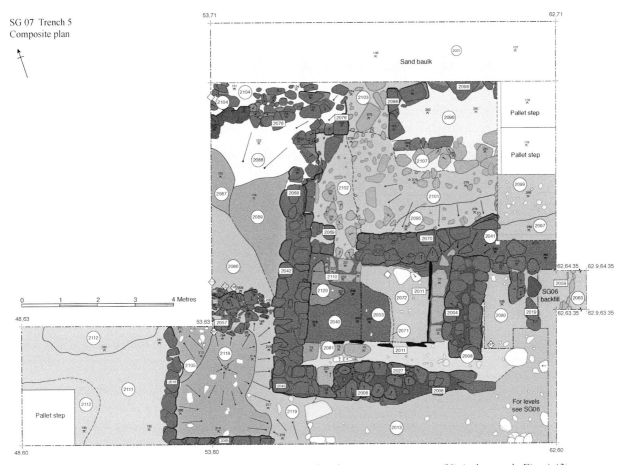

Fig. 4.24: Trench 5, ancillary buildings in 2007, main longhouse entrance at top (N) (colour code Fig. 4.43)

As a result 2077 returned a radiocarbon date of cal AD 770–980 (SUERC-24701). This date may reflect Phase 3 deposition, or even material residual in Phase 3, possibly from the earlier structures hinted at in this area. Layer 2165 infilled the area west of the Phase 3 building; layer 2072-2077 infilled the building itself. The dismantling and levelling of the metal-working yard just to the west, discussed below, was also required to create a long enough foundation surface for the western wall of the Phase 5 building. Thus it was that remains of one of the hearths were preserved below the corner of the structure 2042.

The rectangular ancillary building may at the outset only have been accessed from its south-east corner but soon after its construction a flight of six stone steps 2136 was inserted into the western end of the northern wall 2070, and the gap between them and western wall 2042 filled with a short stretch of wall 2069, which was not keyed into the north–south wall (Figs 4.25 and 4.26). The steps were soundly founded on the flags over the Phase 3 paved soakaway and allowed people to cross easily from the ancillary building across the central yard to the longhouse entrance. Their route passed over the large flags 2132 by then laid across the central yard and was

also soon shielded from the west by the wall 2068, built to join the north-west corner of the ancillary building to the southern longhouse wall just by the entrance (see Fig. 4.18). Initially, there was an entrance through that wall into the open yard to the west, but that was blocked up during Phase 5.

THE SOUTH-EAST MIDDEN

During Phase 4 a pit was dug into the already accumulated Phase 3 middens 2204 and 2254, which had amassed east of the Phase 3 building. Although only a limited area around the pit could be investigated, as the eastern section of the trench was very unstable, the pit fill itself was recovered in half-section. The sub-rectangular pit 2222 was 1.5 m long and nearly 0.5 m deep (see Fig. 4.27). Its sandy silt fill (2205; cal AD 1010–1190: SUERC-47146), rich in stones, peat-ash and deposits of yellow clay had been tipped over a central heap. This pile consisted of angular stones covering a large lump of burnt clay, articulated cow leg bones, bird bone and shell (Chapter 9). The fill also contained one of the largest concentrations of vitrified material and heat-affected debris found on the site, mixed with shell and fish bone. This seemed to be

Fig. 4.25: Trench 5, detail from 2008 from N, showing main longhouse entrance, central flagged yard with drains beneath, and steps up into ancillary building

SG 08 Trench 5
Area 2: steps
Section 25

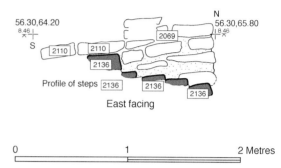

Fig. 4.26: Trench 5, profile of steps, E facing

the remains of an outside hearth that had burnt for some time (Chapter 11) and may have originated with one of the dismantled iron-working hearths. Taken together, the unusual contents of this pit might suggest a deliberate deposit made, perhaps, to mark the major architectural changes occurring in the settlement. The midden 2170-2201 sealing the pit also covered the earlier walls 2207 and 2289, and in later taphonomic processes slipped down north over later midden layers. Although the ash, turf and peat content of this midden was not high it contained a large assemblage of bone including dog, cat and articulated pig bone (Chapter 9) and a considerable collection of artefacts such as steatite sherds (SFs 269, 270 and 272), and a well-used pendant whetstone (SF 260). Rather than a rich organic midden store, this layer was mixed with sand to consolidate an outside surface.

CLOSURE OF THE METALWORKING YARD

The process of dismantling the last hearth structure, any remains of earlier hearths, and removing the anvil, resulted in complex stratigraphy and considerable disturbance of the previous Phase 3 yard floor layers. Phase 4 deposits within the yard clearly showed the effects of the closure process, but also provided further valuable evidence on the nature of the iron smithing undertaken in the yard. Layer 2202-2203 was spread across the yard over the *in situ* remains of the four Phase 3 bowl-hearths (cal AD 1020–1190: SUERC-33699; Fig. 4.18, see overlay to left). This destruction layer included some stones that may have come from hearth superstructures, burnt clay and thin fragments of ash- and charcoal-rich yellow and grey clay floor surface: concentrations of charcoal and ash in the surface indicated the location of the hearth remains beneath. Large amounts of willow charcoal were mixed in with hammerscale, fragments of hearth

bottoms or plan-convex cakes (Chapter 11) and general metal-working debris as well as iron (SFs 316 and 334). Amidst 2202, a discrete dump just over 0.5 m² of peat ash and burnt clay contained fragmentary bone and shell, iron objects (2178; cal AD 1020–1190: SUERC-24720; SFs 283 and 284) and a similar mix of industrial waste to 2203.

The outside area to the north 2087, which sloped down towards the now-blocked southern entrance to the longhouse was composed of multiple thin layers, characterised by degraded turf. Either grassy surfaces had been able to develop over successive spreads of silty sand and waste material or the area had been stabilised with the addition of turf (Chapter 6). The lower laminations contained industrial debris – presumably cleared from the yard to the south – layers became less rich in these inclusions away from the yard. However, the upper laminations were distinctive for holding a collection of nails, rivets and roves which may have marked where timbers of the roof structure over the yard were discarded (Chapter 12; Fig. 4.9). After the blocking of the Phase 3 door into the longhouse to the north, and the building of a north–south wall 2068, running from the ancillary building to the longhouse, which impeded access into the central yard from where both buildings could now be entered, this area seems to have been relatively little used.

PHASE 5: THE RECTANGULAR ANCILLARY BUILDING, PAVED CENTRAL YARD; THE LONGHOUSE WITH ADDED BYRE/WORKSHOP AND COOK-HOUSE ANNEX; EXTERNAL MIDDEN; YARDS AND OTHER AREAS

The Phase 5 archaeology (see Fig. 4.18) was wonderfully preserved and included much standing structural detail, and internal surfaces and stone-built furniture within the buildings. Most of the disturbance to the upper occupation layers of this phase had been caused by immediately

SG 10 Trench 5
Plan 2
SE Midden

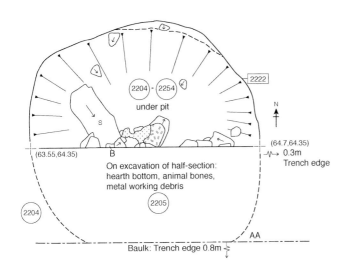

Section 14

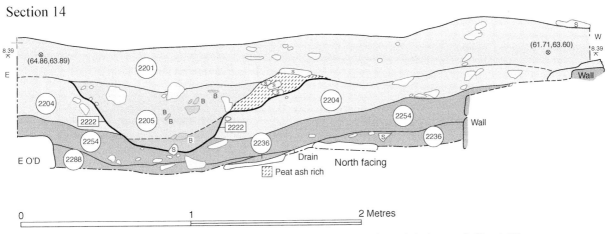

Fig. 4.27: Trench 5, pit 2222 and other middens in SE area of trench (colour code Fig. 4.43)

subsequent activity or collapse. The complete plan of a west–east aligned longhouse 26.3 m long was uncovered and just to the south – across the paved yard and up the flight of steps – a smaller and parallel Phase 5 ancillary building. During this phase, most likely towards the beginning, the longhouse was extended around the core of the preceding hall-building: to the east with a byre and workshop, and to the west with a cookhouse. The ancillary building in the south was reconfigured and then altered again. Thus the longhouse in its most extensive, developed Phase 5 layout comprised a central domestic area with stone side benches and a western extension, joined by a central passageway to a longer eastern section. The central

area of the longhouse was excavated first, revealing part of the eastern extension and the dividing wall 2135 erected to separate the new byre and workshop from the focal domestic area, which encompassed the original Phase 3 hall-building. The western annex and the full length of the eastern extension were explored in 2010.

An imposing entrance into the centre of the longhouse was fashioned by widening the southern walls either side of a substantial flagged path from the central yard, and creating an impressive flagged threshold just over 1 m wide (Fig. 4.28), similar to the entrance to 'Room VII' on the Brough of Birsay (Morris 1996, 235, Illus. 183) This entrance was situated just east of the new internal

Fig. 4.28: Trench 5, main longhouse entrance from interior, from N

transverse dividing wall of the longhouse: north of that wall, internal access to the domestic side was by means of a short north–south passageway with a door at the end and a cupboard or dresser to the north. In the eastern extension, vertical chock-stones indicated the location of a wooden framework for small animal stalls to the south and work-benches in the north. The western annex to the central hall was constructed with wide platforms arranged either side of a central corridor of cooking pits. Soil chemistry analysis underlined the western annex's use for food preparation and cooking. Within the main domestic space orthostatic features were well-preserved: the stone fronts of narrow benches against the walls faced a small metal-working hearth, a floor-fast stone storage/quenching box (see Chapter 11) and a series of other peripatetic hearths. There was no long, permanent central hearth.

THE LONGHOUSE: THE EASTERN BYRE AND WORKSHOP END

A byre and workshop end, *c.* 11.5 m long and 4.75 m wide, was added to the longhouse in this phase. Although later dismantling and disturbance made it impossible to be sure of the configuration of the furthest east end of the building, lower floors elsewhere had survived, despite truncation by Phase 6 activity. A central paved path/soakaway drain 2190-2280 ran gently downslope west–east through the byre, joined in the west to the passageway into the domestic end of the longhouse and the paved entrance into the byre from the south (see Fig. 4.18); charcoal-rich silt 2276 accumulated in the cracks of the flags returned a radiocarbon date of cal AD 900–1120 (SUERC-47156). The passageway probably reused the Phase 3 paved soakaway: it sagged in areas and had been partially re-flagged. The soakaway would have been useful as animals were stalled in the area south of the passageway. Chunky orthostats 2174 edged the passageway, with socketing on the southern run of

stones for a wooden superstructure. The passageway then continued beyond the eastern end of the byre. That route out from the byre probably took people and animals down to the burn where rough surfaces and layers influenced by human activity were found in the burn-side end of the long extension to Trench 5 (see Fig. 4.8). Those surfaces and layers suggested that people were working down by the burn, taking animals to drink and collecting water upstream of them.

The byre area north of the passageway was used as a workshop. Peat ash and other hearth debris had been mixed with sand to create floors 2272-2268-2274-2173: the ash was more concentrated around settings of small orthostats, which probably supported work-benches, cupboards and shelves. Small patches of rough paving in these areas indicted where work had been focused. The surfaces were also more worn and trampled, and finds were concentrated, around the margins of these settings. Floor 2268 was the most extensive and well-preserved in the workshop. Like the floors in the ancillary building and the hall end of the longhouse the floor was worn unevenly and finely laminated with trapped thin drifts of sand blown in through the door. The finds included steatite (SF 473), an iron knife (SF 412) and a stapled hasp, probably a box fitting (SF 436). The overlying floor 2173 was of similar composition, reinforced with patches of clay, but the surface had been more compacted by Phase 6 animal trample. There were a number of finds including iron objects (SFs 280 and 390); worked antler boat fitting (SF 247); and a glass bead (SF 249). More finds were discovered trapped in the ashy silt 2156 that had accumulated over and around the edges of the flags in the southern entrance: iron artefacts (SFs 179 and 184), worked bone (SF 188) and a fine quartzite burnisher (SF 236). Other chock stones indicated a wattle or wooden partition had been erected against the dividing wall to the west.

To the south of the passageway were four stalls for animals: wooden stalling would have been supported by the small orthostats dividing up the area and the notches cut into the blocky stones lining the central passageway. Four north–south aligned dips were visible in the silty floors 2277-2267 marking individual stalls (each 0.8 m wide and 1.2 m long); the higher ridges between them lined up with the socketing on the path edging and held the small orthostatic settings for the dividing panels. The floors themselves contained small amounts of carbonised grain as well as burnt dung mixed with straw; faunal remains although fragmentary included a wide range of shells, crab, fish and mammal bone. The only artefact was iron object SF 434 – a nail. Peat ash and organic material was concentrated in the dips in the floors. Nearest to the door was a sandier, stony area 2271 with different settings of orthostatic supporting stones, perhaps related to another working area. Radiocarbon dates were obtained from floor areas 2271 and 2277: cal AD 1010–1160 (SUERC-33712) and cal AD 1020–1170 (SUERC-33716) respectively. The soil chemistry analyses suggested the byre area was dedicated to a greater range of activities than elsewhere in the longhouse, although excluding the regular cooking and eating of food. The relatively high concentration of lipids and cholesterol in the floors of the animal stalls also supported that interpretation of the use of the southern half of the byre (Chapter 7).

The longhouse: The passageway between the byre and the domestic end of the longhouse

The byre was separated from the living quarters by a new dividing wall 2135 in the south and a cupboard or storage area to the north. Between them was a short flagged passageway 1.5 m long, secured by an orthostatic edging stone flush with its surface at the byre end, and shielded by a large orthostat beyond the edge of the wall within the longhouse. By the end of the passage a triangular paving slab with a central circular jamb socket was sunk into the house floor in just the right location for a door structure (Fig. 4.29). The surface by the slab had been worn down into a hollow as people stepped off the flags and onto the beaten floors. The deposits in the area where the cupboard had been were different from those in the byre: the dark sandy silt 2265 was also notable for its many iron finds most of which were identified as nails or roves, which may have come from the structure of the wooden cupboard/storage area. However, iron artefact (SF 418) was a mount decorated with other metals (Chapter 12). The radiocarbon date for this floor was in the same range as the surviving lower floors of the byre: cal AD 1010–1160 (SUERC-33708).

The longhouse living quarters/hall area

The area of the original hall-building continued to be used as living quarters in this phase: undisturbed floor layers were discovered beneath those trampled by animals in Phase 6.

The side benches:

In front of the long walls, narrow upright/orthostatic flags marked the front of benches 0.5 m wide (see Fig. 4.18). These sitting and sleeping benches had been filled with sand and may have been covered with furs, cloth or plant material, much of which would probably have been removed at abandonment. The upper spits of the layers above the sand infill (2208-S; 2209-N) had been disturbed by episodic falls of large stones from the walls, but a number of finds in the silty sand of the lower layers were probably articles lost when the benches were in use. Infill 2208/2009 contained worked bone (SFs 300,

Fig. 4.29: Trench 5, door socket beside internal doorway to domestic area of longhouse, N to right

306, and SF 322) – a pin. The infill of the north bench was richer in domestic finds, and included steatite and bone working fragments, suggesting the benches may have been used in slightly different ways: the range of finds included iron knife blade (SF 335); steatite sherds and a spindle whorl (SF 302), and worked bone (SFs 301 and 304): a pin and toggle, and worked fragments (Chapter 15).

The floors, hearths and stone furniture in the floors:

The undisturbed floors were excavated in quadrants (2261-NW, 2262-SW, 2263-NE and 2264-SE; see Fig. 4.18); these floors were variegated, finely laminated relatively thin and complex, dipping and deepening towards the long axis of the longhouse and to the east. The dark sandy silts were dominated by the black, pink, orange and grey concentrations of peat ash and hearth deposits spread repeatedly to create the surface (Fig. 4.30), but only at most 5 cm deep. The environmental samples taken from the floors produced carbonised cereal grains and significant quantities of flax seeds, demonstrating cooking and crop processing were being undertaken and that retted flax was being hung to dry above fires in the longhouse roof (Chapter 8). Hearth fuel residues were also present in the form of burnt peat, along with a burnt organic material, possibly burnt straw mixed with dung. Faunal assemblages were mostly fragmentary (Chapter 9).

Several features were cut into the floors. At the west end on the central axis was a large, recut posthole 2310–2308, 0.4 m wide, which had held the original end roof-support post for the Phase 3 building. It was difficult to be certain, because of truncation of deposits, whether this post arrangement had survived into Phase 5, and the recut had also been rapidly backfilled with deposits identical to the surrounding floors when the post was withdrawn. Just north-east of the post-hole was a recut pit 2297-2299, 1 m wide and relatively shallow (0.1 m). The greasy clayey fills 2296-2298 contained charred grain and flax seeds but

Fig. 4.30: Trench 5, interior of longhouse from W showing junction between western annex and central hall, with floors exposed

comparatively little fuel remains, suggesting a dump of material rather than *in situ* burning. This pit may originally have been a cooking hearth or barrel stand, later cleared out and levelled with domestic waste. The valuable ashy waste may have been dug out for spreading elsewhere before the recut pit was re-filled with floor-sweepings and cooking debris.

To the south of pit 2297-2299 and close to the southern bench-line was another cut feature 2300, around which more domestic finds were discovered in the floor layers 2263: iron objects – SFs 397 a rove, SF 399 a plate and SF 466; steatite (SF 395) and two copper alloy fragments (SFs 296 and 446) – a stud. (Only two iron fragments had been found in the north-eastern quadrant (SFs 402 and 410).) This area also produced a higher concentration of charred grain and peat. The metre-long oval cut feature itself had been used as a hearth for cooking and drying grain: burnt stones were also found in the fill, while the windblown sand beneath was discoloured. A radiocarbon date of cal AD 1010–1160 (SUERC-33706) was obtained from floor 2263.

Central to the domestic space was another hearth 2303, which was covered by a thin but extremely large flagstone at the beginning of Phase 6. The flagstone came from the central yard to the south of the main entrance: there was an exactly matching gap in the yard flagging on its eastern edge. This hearth was distinct in being sub-square, about 1 m², with a central burnt stone. Its fill 2304 of crumbly burnt clay, fuel ash waste, peat ash and charcoal, contained a large amount of flax seeds and burnt grain; the edges were delineated by greasy dark deposits and there were rake-out areas to the north-east

and south-west. (The fill gave a radiocarbon date of cal AD 1020–1170: SUERC-33711.) Environmental samples from the floors around the hearth 2262 and 2264 produced smaller quantities of charred grain and flax seeds that in the west, except around the hearth suggesting the area was swept out more frequently. The faunal fragments were relatively few, and only a few iron objects were found.

In the strip of floor-width 2275 nearest the internal doorway were two further cut features: a floor-fast orthostatic stone tank 2281 (Fig. 4.31) and a small metalworking hearth 2301 just to the west of the tank. This floor overlays the possible Phase 3 floors discussed above and was similar in composition to the Phase 5 floors just to the west, although the environmental evidence suggested more plant elements were being blown or walked in. The finds in this floor were dominated by iron objects, many probably intrusive from the collapse or dismantling of the wooden structures of the passageway, but there were also a few sherds of steatite (SFs 379, 383 and 432). Charred barley in this floor returned a date of cal AD 1010–1170 (SUERC-47155). The small hearth 2301 was sub-square, 0.8 m wide at most, with two central stacked stones. It was slightly deeper than the other hearths/cooking pits and running south-west from the stones was a sharp V cut feature lined with burnt clay that may have been a tuyère. The fill was also completely different from the other hearths in the longhouse containing iron objects (SFs 467 and 471) as well as a fragment of hearth bottom, other metal-working waste and hammerscale (Chapter 11). Environmental samples produced no flax or burnt peat but a good deal

Fig. 4.31: Trench 5, stone tank 2281 in centre of longhouse, from S

Fig. 4.32: Trench 5, cooking hearth 2291 in centre of floor of western annex, from S,with E facing section to left

of charcoal along with some cereal grain. The hearth must have been used at least once for metal-working, perhaps more for demonstrative or symbolic reasons, although there was some metal-working waste mixed with the byre floors. The fill gave a radiocarbon date of cal AD 1010–1160 (SUERC-33702). The tank 2281 just next to the hearth was formed of four orthostatic stones to create a box measuring 0.4 square metres. The environmental sample from the silty fill 2285 was dominated by wood charcoal, free of peat ash, and included hammerscale. The fill was dated to cal AD 1020–1170 (SUERC-33709). Found in it were iron nail (SF 452) and a fragment of copper alloy (SF 451). This indicates the box was used at least once in conjunction with the metal-working hearth, perhaps as a quenching tank (Chapter 11). The organic soils chemistry analysis discovered a very high concentration of lipids in the tank fill suggesting it had also been used to store food (Chapter 7).

THE LONGHOUSE WESTERN ANNEX

During Phase 5 a western annex *c.* 7.5 m long was added to the longhouse. In this part of the longhouse the side

benches widened to platforms (up to 1.5 m deep) probably used as working areas. The infill of the northern side was a mixture of windblown sand 2252, residual material from the habitation in Phase 5 (2232; including steatite and bone pin SF 359) and dumped debris from the following phase 2226 with residual finds. On the southern side, the original silty sand bench-packing 2244 had been less disturbed; as on the north, it may have supported a wooden floor. The layer above that, 2225, had been more affected by the collapse of the longhouse wall and belonged to Phase 6, but produced finds that may have been residual from the Phase 5 use of the cooking annex. These included worked bone SF 344, a pin and SF 364, a comb fragment. Between the platforms was a narrow area into which two cooking hearths had been dug. One 2291 was truncated, having been roughly paved over later in Phase 5. The hearth was 1 m in diameter with a burnt stone set in the centre to support pots and fragments of the burnt clay lining still visible (Fig. 4.32). The fill 2290 was a mixture of greasy cooking residues, peat ash, ashy silt and burnt clay, producing abundant charred grain, mostly oats, and flax seeds as well as sherds of steatite (grouped as SF 457). Oats in particular were being dried before storage, given the high chaff and weed content, and in considerable quantities, but cooking also took place. Carbonised oat gave a date of cal AD 1020–1210 (SUERC-33719). The high levels of phosphorus detected in analysis of the floors and fills of the western annex only emphasised the focus on heating and cooking (Chapter 7). The second more ruinous hearth 2306, perhaps a precursor to 2291, was of similar size. The shallow fill 2305 of laminated peat ash and dark sandy silt produced a more varied environmental sample dominated by barley and including flax – missing from the other hearth – and was dated to cal AD 990–1160 (SUERC-33720). Most of the small areas of floor within the annex had been laid before the first hearth was cut and then repaired around both hearths. However, a small patch belonging to the eastern end of the Phase 3 longhouse had been preserved under small stepping-stone flags, and was where the radiocarbon date for 2273 was obtained (SUERC-33718). The finds in the dark silty clay annex floor, rich in peat-ash, belonged to Phase 5 and many were found trapped next to and sheltered by the platform-front orthostats: they included iron (SF 417, 438); steatite sherds (SFs 418, 420, 422–5, Chapter 19); and sherds of coarse ceramic (SF 419 and 454, Chapter 20).

Finally, both the hearths were roughly paved over with small flags, which were interspersed with silty areas rich in peat ash where several sequential temporary hearths may have been established (layer 2241). A relatively large faunal assemblage was recovered of burnt and fragmentary bone as well as domestic artefacts, mostly located next to the orthostats. The finds included steatite (SFs 401, 407), sherds of coarse ceramic (SFs 403, 411) and a glass linen smoother (SF 425).

THE USE OF THE RECTANGULAR ANCILLARY BUILDING AND ITS SHORTENING TO FORM A SQUARE BUILDING

In order to excavate and understand structural and internal sequences earlier than Phase 6 and late Phase 5 in this small area, the eastern wall of the last square building 2004 had to be removed, as it had been constructed across earlier internal deposits and walls (see Fig. 4.25). A series of half- and running-sections within the walls of the rectangular building helped elucidate the complex history of this part of the site. The rectangular ancillary building created during Phase 4 (see above), and aligned parallel to the longhouse, was in use throughout most of this phase, and was shortened to a square plan only towards the very end of the period. The reworking of the internal floors and deposits of all but the final building in this lengthy southern structural sequence meant it was difficult to be certain of the uses to which the buildings were put. However, there was some evidence in the floor deposits for small corner hearths and small-scale crop-drying, suggesting the rectangular building was a flexible, general-purpose storage and working space. Access to the building was still up the existing flight of six steps opposite the southern entrance to the longhouse and across the well-paved central yard. Immediately to the south-east and east of this building rich midden-layers were deposited. Their spread had been partially contained by a wall to the east and no trace was encountered in the long extension down the eastern flank of the mound (see Fig. 4.8). These Phase 5 accumulations had built-up over Phase 3 drains, middens and minor external walls and, in the immediate post-use period, midden layers had slumped down-slope across the central yard. To the south-west, a small, walled and clay-floored yard had been created off the corner of the building and over the previous metal-working yard.

Phase 5 saw the build-up of floors within the rectangular ancillary building (c. 5.5 m long by 2.5 m). These internal floor layers were truncated by the reconfiguration of the structure towards the end of the phase but survived better in the west under the later paving. The earliest floors were 2071 and 2113; both silty sands reinforced with yellow clay and grey ash deposits, including fragments of animal and fish bone and shell. 2113 had been partially preserved beneath a later wall 2004, which truncated subsequent floor layers in that area; layer 2071 dipped and thinned towards the centre of the building indicting how surfaces were worn by the passage of feet. The ecofactual assemblages of carbonised grain from these first floors were small suggesting cooking, or even small-scale crop drying or processing, had not regularly taken place inside during that period. The next floor laid 2120 was more substantial, compacted with peat ash to form silty clay and trampled thin in the centre, but the finds content was similar: fragmentary faunal remains, a little grain and no artefacts. The surviving evidence and ecofactual signature suggests the structure may have been an out-building, used for a range of purposes. The final more sandy layer associated with this building 2053 was probably a make-up layer, levelling the old floors before the new structure was used.

Around the beginning of Phase 6 the rectangular building was shortened to produce a small, near-square structure (3.25 m by 2.75 m; walls 2004-2018-2042-2070; Figs 4.6 and 4.25). This was achieved by demolishing the existing eastern wall 2019 down to the level of the internal floors and capping it with flagstones. A new wall 2004 was built running north–south to the west of the capped courses joining wall 2018 to the south with wall 2070 to the north, and opposite the existing western wall 2042. It was probably at this stage that the south-east corner of wall 2042 was rebuilt to incorporate a small floor-level gap just 0.5 m square; this may have been for ventilation, or to allow small animals or poultry to get in. These features, usually entrances for chickens, can still be seen in older barns in the Northern Isles (Fenton 1978). A paved path 2082, just less than 1 m wide was laid running inside the southern and eastern walls, flanked by thin orthostatic (upright) flagstones 2011. The four low west–east orthostats in the south were separated by gaps of up to 1 m and were no more than 0.5 m long. The two large orthostats in the east were set close together to create a narrow corridor next to the wall: the stones were only a few centimetres wide, both c. 1 m long and 0.8 m high and supported by chock stones. The building was still accessed up the flight of steps from the central yard: there may have been a second, narrow entrance in the south-east corner, but the robbing of this corner during later boundary ditch construction obscured the evidence. Within the central part of the square building, 3 m long by *c.* 2 m wide, floors were established: 2040-2116 and 2115. These were compact, trampled dark silty deposits combined with peat ash, all dipping slightly towards the centre of the internal area, up to 0.1 m thick and composed of laminations built up as surfaces were repeatedly worn down and replaced.

A special deposit:

In the north-west corner of the room one patch of firm clayey floor 1.7 m west–east by north–south by 0.95 (2115) had been particularly well-preserved, having been sealed by the Phase 6 flagging 2182. Pressed into this surface, all under flags and in close proximity (within a square metre), to one another was a striking collection of artefacts: a complete bone comb (SF 108; Chapter 14), an iron candlestick unusual in Orkney (SF 109; Chapter 12) and three sherds of glazed whiteware pottery (SFs 107, 110 and 111), as well as articulated dog bone (Chapter 9). Of the 25 fragments of mammal bone found in the context half were dog bones, with most of the remainder being fragmentary and not identifiable to species, and thus more like the faunal remains usually found in general floor trample. Three dates were obtained relating to this group of floors: one on the articulated bone deposited with the artefact collection, cal AD 990–1210 (SUERC-59189); one from carbonised grain within floor 2115, cal AD 1020–1220 (SUERC-17867); and one from the related floor area 2040 cal AD 1010–1170 (SUERC-17859). The objects had been pushed into the top of the floor and the flags laid down immediately: the comb had been complete when it was laid down and clearly had not been trampled on directly, but simply crushed subsequently by the weight of the flag; the other objects in the group were pressed into the floor and not combined into it. The assemblage appears to have been deposited deliberately when the square building was reflagged at the beginning of Phase 6. During that phase, the structure was only used intermittently and no-one was living in the longhouse: the objects may have been a closing deposit marking the end of habitation in the longhouse complex. Other fragments of the same whiteware were either in Phase 6 layers (SFs 331 and 339), residual (SF 297), or intrusive in sand lenses down the side of walls and benches features (SFs 248 and 262): in sand by wall in 2146; SF 408 in sand by bench orthostat in 2261; SF 430 in sand by wall in 2265; SF 443 in sand by orthostats in 2275, the whiteware sherds seem to have been scattered across the eastern end of the domestic end of the longhouse as it was abandoned as a dwelling, making them possibly the latest artefacts to be deposited in the structure.

YARDS AND SURFACES AROUND THE PHASE 5 ANCILLARY BUILDING

Outside the building extensive sandy sheet middens were fashioned to the east and south, and over the rich middens of previous phases, creating working surfaces around the structures of this phase: these were much disturbed by building work, but continued to accumulate in Phase 6 and are described below.

THE CENTRAL FLAGGED YARD 2132 (SEE FIG. 4.25)

An area of *c.* 3 m north–south by 6 m east–west between the longhouse and the ancillary building was largely kept clear of accumulating deposits in this phase, but areas were reflagged and changes were made to the surrounding walls. There appear to have been structural problems with the north–south wall 2068 on the west side of the yard. After the entrance through wall 2068 to the grassy, open area to the west had been closed, the blocking required reinforcing with a large orthostatic flag. Then a short 2 m stretch of wall 2138 was built over the flags 2132, and in front of the original wall 2068 between the new orthostat to the south and the longhouse entrance to the north. Probably at the same time, the opposing corner of the longhouse entrance was widened and reinforced with a new corner 2137, again built over the large flags on the edge of the yard. The south-western corner of the yard at the bottom of the steps would have seen heavy foot-traffic and was also built over the junction of the Phase 3 soakaway drains, most of which had been incorporated in the later yard and linked to the byre to the north. Inevitably, the flags had sagged, and after the changes had been made to wall 2068 small area of less well-cut, well-fitting paving 2154 was laid to repair and level the yard. The southern wall of the yard – the outside face of the northern wall of the rectangular building – was already a patchwork of phases of walling: then in Phase 5, orthostatic yard furniture was built against the outside face of the wall east of the steps including a stone shelf 2142 and a bench supported on orthostatic stones 2144, which reused the line of the eastern Phase 3 soakaway.

THE SOUTH-WESTERN YARD AND SURROUNDING OUTSIDE AREAS

The former metal-working yard south-west of the rectangular building was maintained unroofed as a floored yard in this period. The yard was now accessed from the east, just by the corner of the ancillary building, and the open side to the north was closed off with a short and shoddily-built single face drystone wall 2057 (see Fig. 4.18). Yard floor 2118 had been much damaged by stones collapsing from the wall to the south; however, the spread effectively sealed the uneven and stony layers below. It presented a compact clayey surface with some evidence for degraded turf and still containing residual willow charcoal and fuel ash slag, characteristic of the metal-working yard sequence below. In contrast, the floor also included more domestic debris: shell and fragmentary animal bone, including cat, (Chapter 8), although little charred grain. At the end of the phase, a silty sand levelling layer 2119 was spread to form a foundation for the minor reconfiguration of the corner of wall 2042, which included creating the chicken run. Layer 2119 also included considerable amounts of willow charcoal.

The area immediately to the north, between the yard and the longhouse, was not intensively used in this phase. Turfy layer 2089 did contain a sherd of steatite (SF 132) and a bone needle (SF 161) and saw some episodic dumping of domestic waste before being covered with windblown sand 2086-2088. Thin layers of turf 2109 were able to develop over the sand (Chapter 6). To the west of the enclosed yard, the ground was also grassed over 2078: both these turf areas returned radiocarbon dates of cal AD 980–1150 (SUERC-17868 and SUERC-24704), but these were layers that had accumulated over long periods.

PHASE 6

In this phase the longhouse was abandoned as an inhabited space and its roof collapsed or more likely was dismantled, after which its open shell served intermittently as an animal fold or pen. The southern square ancillary building was used as a shelter or shed, and the central yard filled in; the south-western yard and the area to the north of it was covered over by sandy spread midden-influenced surfaces.

It is possible that the roof at least partially burned down (Chapter 7). The former longhouse complex was being subsumed into the field system of a farm based elsewhere.

A ROOFLESS ANIMAL PEN

In Phase 6, people moved out of the longhouse. The roof was dismantled, presumably to reuse the timbers elsewhere, and the stone shell used occasionally to pen animals. Some of the dismantling of the eastern end of the byre may have occurred at this point to make access easier for larger groups of animal. A distinctive, quite deep (up to 0.2 m) 'trample layer' developed across the byre composed of the organic remains of the roof and animal dung trampled together by the cattle/sheep into the fine upper floor layers 2259-2164 and 2169 of the lived-in longhouse. There were fine drifts of sand caught in the laminated dark sandy silt, but also windblown sand was trapped by and preserved the little pockets left by the hoof prints of the last animals penned in the structure (Fig. 4.33). The little pockets in the silt were crescent-shaped with a bulb in the centre and 7–10 cm long.

A considerable number of domestic finds came from areas 2164 and 2169 in the byre/workshop, a few of which may have been lost during Phase 6 but many of

Fig. 4.33: Trench 5, byre end of longhouse from E, hoof prints in Phase 6 layers

which were residual from the Phase 5 byre floors. These included from 2164, a flaked stone tethering peg and a rough cobble tool (SF 213), steatite (SF 256) and copper-alloy fragments (SF 218); and from 2169, iron objects (SFs 210, 214, 239); a shell pendant (SF 273) and worked bone (SF 211). Over and into the trample layer, patches of rough paving were established, presumably in areas of heavy traffic or as temporary work surfaces. These were by the southern entrance – a double layer 2141 and 2130 – and in the east of the byre 2230, where work seemed to continue for some time as a more extensive sandy surface developed over the paving 2239.

In the western half of the longhouse very similar layers were encountered. Across the central hall and part of the western annex a thick, mixed silty layer 2224 stretched across the whole area composed of the same elements as the 'trample layer' over the byre, with preserved hoof prints and areas of rough flagging. Again there were many finds: numerous steatite sherds from the western annex area; a copper alloy brooch fragment (SF 375) and many iron objects – some nails and roves possibly from structural remains, with one buckle tongue (SF 346). Over the rest of the annex a rough stone surface 2227 was laid and the silty matrix produced a similar range of residual finds: more steatite, some coarse ceramic sherds and a copper-alloy fragment (SF 416). More residual finds were recovered from collapse layer 2219 above the flagged surface: steatite, rough ceramic and worked bone. That layer indicated when the longhouse was completely abandoned.

THE SQUARE ANCILLARY BUILDING

For at least the first part of Phase 6 the square building (see Fig. 4.6) remained in use as a shed or temporary shelter. A rough stone floor 2183 was constructed over the neat paving laid at the beginning of the phase 2181, and trampled interior deposits 2066 and 2034 developed over that paving within the building: both were silty with peat ash lenses but very few faunal remains and almost no archaeobotanical traces, supporting the idea that this was more of a storage area and was not used for cereal-related activity (Chapter 7). A reasonably thick windblown sand layer blown in through the chicken-run over these floors indicated a period of abandonment of the building.

YARDS AND EXTERNAL SURFACES AROUND THE PHASE 6 BUILDING

Extensive sandy midden-influenced surfaces continued to be spread outside, and to the east and south 2008, of the square building. These were not the highly organic and bone- and finds-rich middens that had accumulated to the east of the buildings in previous phases, although 2008 contained steatite sherds and comb fragments (SFs 61 and 64). Some of these finds may have been residual from earlier phases. The wall-core of the collapsed upper

courses of wall 2018, combined in taphonomic processes with richer midden, originally piled closer to the square building, but mostly redeposited in a later Phase 7 ditch, and producing steatite and iron finds. The radiocarbon date from 2016 probably reflects the midden content of the wall-fill of wall 2018 which could be as early as Phase 3 as the wall was originally constructed during Phase 4: cal AD 980–1150 (SUERC-24710).

To the west of the ancillary building extensive sandy midden-influenced surfaces also developed, related to final activity in the square building: the first layers such as 2062 and 2051 were more varied and interspersed with midden-rich smaller discrete dumps of material (*e.g.* 2061 and 2056: which gave a radiocarbon date of cal AD 1010–1160: SUERC-17861). The final Phase 6 layer 2031 was more homogenous across the whole area, contained peat ash and was badly disturbed by a recent rabbit warren. The finds from this layer were probably mostly residual and brought up from Phase 5 layers and longhouse wall-core from the crumbling walls. Amongst a range of iron artefacts were found a copper-alloy ringed pin (SF 39) and glass bead (SF 44). The layers above this were linked to Phase 7 agricultural activity on the crest of the mound just to the south.

PHASE 7

Within the remains of earlier structures and over the open central yard area, Phase 7 was dominated by the lower layers of post-occupation wall collapse and subsequent infill of the buildings, defined in this phase by the surviving wall-lines. The evidence for wall collapse was dynamic and the effects on archaeology below more obvious. Larger areas of sandy tumble were excavated and there was little evidence for these areas having been exploited by people during this phase. However, the remaining walls of the square building may have been reused as a shelter for field-related work – possibly crop-processing or as a type of shieling for summer grazing on the sandy links. Meanwhile, to the south of those structural remains, a midden dominated by fish-remains accumulated, perhaps to store fertiliser for in-fields or garden plots, as there was some evidence that the contiguous area had been ploughed (see 2006 on Fig. 4.34). Meanwhile, the derelict eastern end of the longhouse, around and over its entrance, was utilised for some temporary purpose in Phase 7, perhaps reusing rough surfaces established in the preceding phase, and exploiting any remaining walls as shelter: this work left evidence for burning and slight occupation deposits, along with a small pit 2227.

WALL COLLAPSE, WALL FILLS AND TUMBLE INFILL OF STRUCTURES

A large group of the Phase 7 contexts reflected the collapse, and partial robbing for building stone, of many

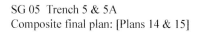

SG 05 Trench 5 & 5A
Composite final plan: [Plans 14 & 15]

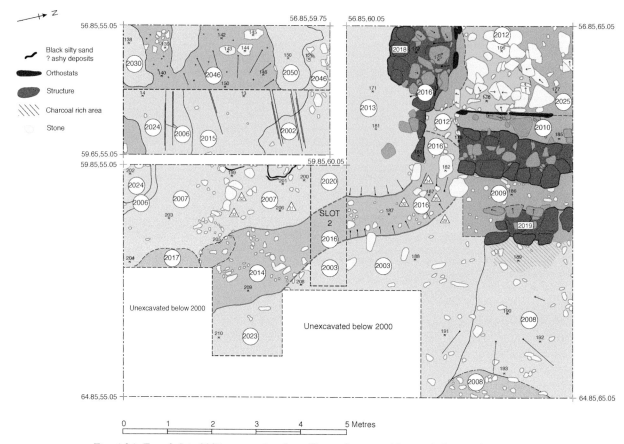

Fig. 4.34: Trench 5 in 2005, composite plan of later phases and layers (colour code Fig. 4.43)

of the walls. The interleaved layers excavated within and around the central yard were extremely complex. Stones, sand and organic wall-fill from ancillary building walls to the south 2070-2069 and 2042, the yard wall 2068 and walling of long building to the north 2098-2137 had all tumbled down into the yard (*e.g.* contexts 2067, 2084, 2102, 2104, 2107, 2117). In some areas, and particularly where larger facing stones had been robbed, the surviving organic material used in the wall core could be examined. From these contexts residual steatite was collected from midden in the fill 2041: SF 91; 2084: SF 143; 2095: SF 103; and 2171: SFs 243, 250. Two radiocarbon dates were obtained, providing possible date ranges for the original midden rather than for the processes of collapse (2095 from wall 2070, cal AD 890–1030: SUERC-24703; 2106, from wall 2137, cal AD 1020–1220: SUERC-17862).

Fig. 4.35: Trench 5, western area of longhouse, showing wall collapse prior to removal

LAYERS DISTURBED BY WALL-COLLAPSE WITHIN THE LONGHOUSE

The longhouse was infilled with deep sandy, stony wall-collapse layers (*e.g.* 2210, 2216 and 2220). In the west and centre the walls had suffered little robbing before or in this phase, and the consequent crashing of large facing stones

onto features and floors below as those walls collapsed in Phase 7 produced mixed layers with residual finds, and pockets of blown-in sand. This was especially marked in layers 2208 and 2209 over the northern and southern wall-benches in the western end of the building (Fig. 4.35). As well as residual and much abraded charred grain a number of residual worked bone artefacts, including pins, toggles and needles (SFs 300, 301, 304, 306 and 322), several iron artefacts, steatite (SFs 302, 305 and 309) and whalebone (SFs 314 and 328) were found in these areas. These may have originated in either wall-fill or been lost along the sides of the benches when they were in use.

FARMING ACTIVITY AND MIDDEN

The earliest activity in Phase 7 was linked to people using stone-free areas around the old buildings for agricultural work and any standing wall-lengths as temporary shelters. To the west of the final ancillary building a surface was established which produced sufficient charred oat and barley to suggest some form of crop processing was being undertaken (2035; Chapter 8). This surface was dated to cal AD 1030–1220 (SUERC-17858). To the south of the stony areas associated with the building, a peat-ash midden rich in fish-bone 2105-2017 had been created next to ground that may have been ploughed 2006 (see Fig. 4.34). This midden also included some animal bone, dominated by large ungulate/cattle. Finally, another work surface 2217 and 2223 was found over the eastern end of the longhouse, sheltered within still surviving walls and rich in charred grain, again with some bone, and clearly generated during farm work. A fire-pit 2237 in this area had been fuelled by both oak and pine, suggesting remnants of structural wood were being reused (Chapter 8).

PHASE 8

WALL COLLAPSE, INFILL IN STRUCTURES AND DISTURBED AREAS

Sealed below the sand and above the Phase 2–6 sequence of smaller southern buildings, the central yard area and much of the larger Phase 2–5 northern structure, Phase 8 was encountered in excavation in the form of the upper layers of post-occupation structural collapse and infill of those structures. These layers were complex and often deep sequences of large quantities of stone from collapsed walls, mixed with sand and organic wall-fill, out of the lower levels of which the lines of surviving walls began to emerge (*e.g.* 2032, 2033, 2052, 2124 and 2249; Fig. 4.5). In one deposit 2032, above and encroaching on a Phase 3–6 wall, a fragment of a sandstone whetstone (SF 78: Chapter 18) was found; the Phase 8 finds in this groups of contexts were otherwise a few iron nails (Chapter 12). There was no evidence that the buildings were being used other than being plundered for building stone, and most of the rubble and stone work only became more deeply buried as Phase 8 went on. However, the ruinous walls of the Phase 5–6 small building to the south must still have been visible, as was much of the northern wall of the large Phase 5 northern building, as that had been integrated into a new field dyke system constructed in Phase 8

(Fig. 4.36). The western stretch of that wall survived to be reused in Phase 9.

DITCHES, AGRICULTURAL LAYERS AND FIELD DYKES

On the margins of the excavated area, around and above the remains of the structural archaeology, Phase 8 features demonstrated that the land, although no longer lived on, was still actively managed. In this phase the ground around the eastern end of the longhouse and immediately south of the whole complex was most readily turned to other purposes as stone was either less prevalent or building remains were already greatly reduced or deeply-buried by windblown sand.

To the south of the area of earlier buildings were a series of shallow U-shaped ditches: 2022, 2026 and 2037, probably boundary features. To the west of the building remains, above the Phase 5 yards, a surface had developed, perhaps a field-related working area 2074. This produced a relatively large quantity of charred grain. In the north-east of the excavated area was further evidence for Phase 8 land management and agricultural activity. There a thin, amended field soil 2213 was discovered sloping down north and east behind the substantial west–east field dyke 2126 (Fig. 4.36). The dyke was constructed during this phase over, disturbing and reusing stones from the northern wall 2166 of the longhouse and probably linked with north–south dykes found in Trench 7 and in the 2011 extension to Trench 5 (indicated by structural stones in context 2333; Fig. 4.8). The field soil 2213 was rich in charred oats. Tumbled wall-fill from the dyke 2126 contained a residual bone gaming piece, probably brought in with midden material (2131; SF 148). The south-eastern wall of longhouse 2098 was the only stretch of structural wall in the longhouse to have been substantially depleted by the removal of stones, some of which may have been taken in this phase to incorporate into the field dykes (see Fig. 4.18).

BURIED SOILS AND WINDBLOWN SANDS

The remaining groups of Phase 8 contexts excavated related to periods of abandonment or lessening activity: pockets of windblown sand such as 2012, 2047 and 2048, and areas where soils had time to begin to develop over buried structural remains and yards such as 2002, 2024 and 2100 (Chapter 6).

PHASE 9

On East Mound, even Phase 8 features were found under considerable depths of sterile windblown sand. Apart from the gradual build-up of this sand, Phase 9 was indicated only by kelp burning pits 2195 and 2248. One of these 2195 was constructed within the remains of a temporary structure 2194, which incorporated a short stretch of the

SG 08 & SG 10 Trench 5
Area 3: Byre end

Elevation 37
Walls & baulk

East end of North facing wall
Wall curves from East to North East in this section

West end of North facing wall

North facing

Elevation 31: SG10

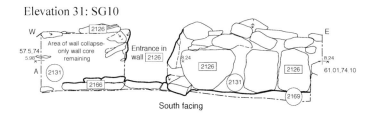

South facing

Elevation 12: SG08

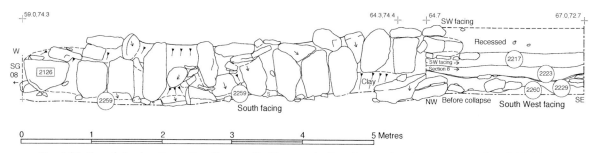

South facing

Fig. 4.36: Trench 5, elevations of northern wall of byre end of longhouse, showing stone reused as field dyke

still-standing western end of the northern wall 2196 of the, by then, mainly buried and long-disused longhouse. In Phase 9, of all the structures only the upper courses of that section of the wall would have been visible protruding through the sand. There was also evidence in the deep windblown sand layer above the eastern end of the structure of a modern instance of sand removal for low-level quarrying purposes, which had disturbed the walls below and especially wall 2098. As Phase 9 progressed into more recent times the entire longhouse complex remained hidden beneath windblown sand, so much so that its existence, as revealed by these excavations, was a complete surprise to those who had owned and worked the land for their entire lives.

Trench 6: East Mound [Location: Fig. 3.4]

This trench was almost impossible to phase with complete confidence, and indeed no material suitable for radiocarbon dating was retrieved. Such archaeology as was encountered seemed to reflect a very peripheral area on the mound. The laminated windblown sand layers had

also been considerably disturbed in relatively recent times by rabbit burrowing.

PHASES 5–7

There were some thin horizontal layers of slightly organic and stained windblown sands found at lower levels in sondages that may have been as early as Phase 7, possibly even Phases 5–6. These layers were probably affected by the human activity focused around the structures to the east; they were separated from possible Phase 8–9 layers by sterile windblown sand.

PHASE 8

This phase may have been represented by a rough pathway of flat slabs found running west–east across the trench towards the almost entirely buried remains of the longhouse and associated with finely laminated and slightly organic sands. There was no evidence for local cultivation or any other activity: the organic material discovered in the sand layers probably blew in from areas in the vicinity, where people were living and working.

PHASE 9

A burnt deposit found in the accumulating windblown sand, similar to ones found elsewhere on site and possibly related to kelp burning, seemed best placed in Phase 9.

Trench 7: East Mound [Location: Fig. 3.4]

This small trench, despite being badly disturbed by a rabbit warren, revealed some substantial archaeology including middens, a stone-built field dyke running west–east across the eastern edge of East Mound, and a Phase 9 layer related to kelp burning activity (Fig. 4.37).

PHASE 7

In the west of Trench 7, below sandy layers associated with the field wall 4009, were discovered middens that may have belonged to this phase of agricultural activity on the mound (Fig. 4.37). These were ashy not silty middens with very few finds – probably material being stored for field fertilising. The midden sequence that best survived the extensive rabbit-warren running through the trench was sealed by a clay capping layer 4015, and, in one of the very ash-rich lower midden layers 4023, were preserved the marks of a spade used to remove midden for uses elsewhere. Again, because of the disturbance of layers, no material suitable for radiocarbon dating was discovered.

PHASE 8

A stretch of stone-built field dyke 4009, also identified in the long eastern extension downslope from Trench 5, was encountered in the east of the trench protruding from overlying windblown sand. This wall was probably contemporary with the field dyke 2126 built above the Trench 5 longhouse's northern wall and running at right angles to the Trench 7 dyke (Fig. 4.38).

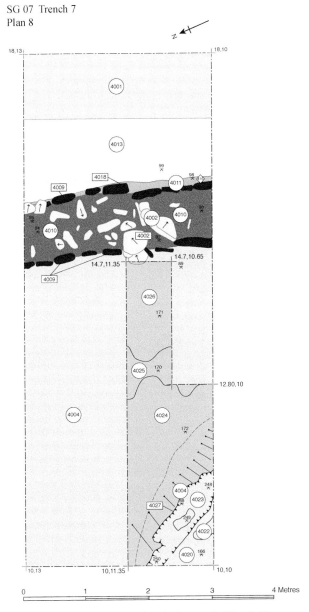

Fig. 4.37: Trench 7, plan (colour code Fig. 4.43)

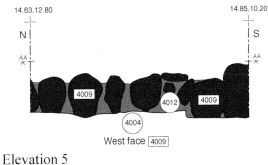

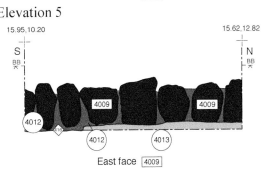

Fig. 4.38: Trench 7, wall elevations (colour code Fig. 4.43)

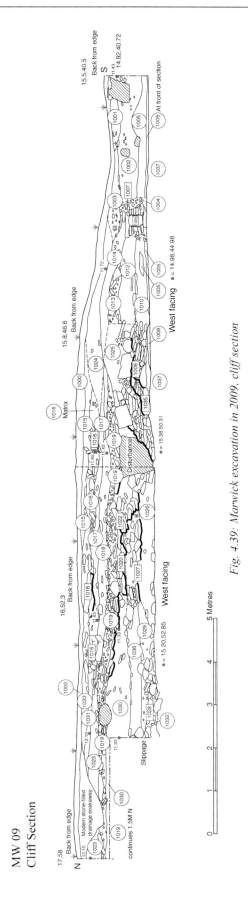

Fig. 4.39: Marwick excavation in 2009, cliff section

MW09: Marwick, Scheduled Ancient Monument 2884 [Location: Fig. 1.4]

EXCAVATION SUMMARY

An 18 m long beach-cliff section was excavated as a vertical section (Fig. 4.39; for geophysics see Chapter 3) across the eroding frontage of Scheduled Ancient Monument (SM 2884), scheduled as 'Viking Houses'. The eroding section rose up to 2 m above a 1 m high slope of natural boulder clay. No diagnostic finds were made but building styles were consistent with both prehistoric and Viking-Late Norse periods. Several structural phases were revealed, together with occupation surfaces and layers indicating levelling and abandonment episodes, demonstrating that the eroding mound held a multi-phase settlement of some complexity. There were at least four phases of building/ re-building. The limited nature of the excavation, and the extensive damage caused by erosion and burrows, inevitably constrained the development of a stratigraphical sequence for the whole section, but the northern stretch showed a number of superimposed surfaces and walls (Fig. 4.40). The sequence in the south was less complex, but a more complete wall and drain discovered there better demonstrated the nature of construction in that phase. The drain (Fig. 4.41) has similarities to Viking-Late Norse constructions on the Brough of Birsay (Hunter 1986).

DATING

Two radiocarbon dates were retrieved from carbonised grain from soil samples (Table 5.1), one from levelling layer 1019 and one from a highly organic internal working surface 1018 packed above. Those two layers marked a major structural reorganisation in that part of the mound, sealing a sequence of walls below. The dates were 1018; cal AD 770–970 (SUERC-33697) and 1019; cal AD 770–980 (SUERC-33698).

THE STRUCTURAL SEQUENCE

Many relationships were rendered uncertain due to slippage and burrows. However, the earliest visible structural sequence in the south was dominated by substantial wall 1009 (Fig. 4.40), built reusing the cobble foundations of an earlier structure. After being partially dismantled this wall was sealed by deposits that suggested the centre of settlement activity moved elsewhere before levelling layer 1019 opened the next major phase in this area.

The beautifully constructed stone drain 1006 in the south was probably built at a similar time to that levelling activity (Fig. 4.41). Over 3 m of its length could be probed as the drain rose at an angle eastwards. It was probably related to structural remains detected to the east by geophysics (Chapter 3). The section in the southern area ended with a final sequence of shell-dominated layers (*e.g.* 1014), which suggested that some unknown length of time after about the 10th century this area reverted to a peripheral activity zone.

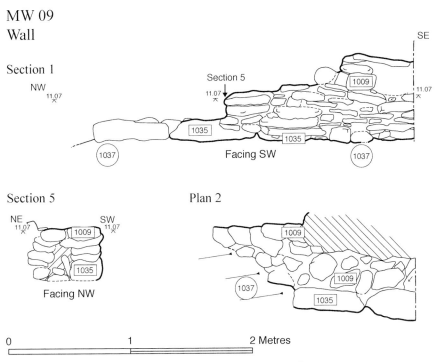

MW 09
Wall

Section 1

NW

Section 5

1009

SE

1035

1035

Facing SW

1037

1037

Section 5

NE   SW

1009

1035

Facing NW

Plan 2

1009

1009

1037

1035

0   1   2 Metres

Fig. 4.40: Marwick excavation in 2009, wall sections

Fig. 4.41: Marwick excavation in 2009, drain 1006 (working shot, see Fig. 4.39 for position and dimensions)

BS04: Buckquoy, Birsay 2004

EXCAVATION SUMMARY

Two small test-trenches were excavated in the penultimate field from the end of the Point of Buckquoy in July 2004, as a means of quickly testing and verifying ('ground-truthing') the geophysical results obtained in 2003 (Chapter 3). In both trenches, turf and topsoil were removed only to a depth of under 0.3 m to expose the surface of the glacial till subsoil. The focus of the project's excavation capacity moved thereafter to the Bay of Skaill from 2005, following promising results at Snusgar and East Mound in 2004, although surface survey continued in the Birsay Bay area. There remains potential to investigate a range of other geophysical anomalies described above in Chapter 3 using targeted excavation.

Trench 1 (centred on HY 2446 2819) was 10 × 1 m and located over a ditch-type feature which showed up in the gradiometer results near SAM 1290 'Knowe of Buckquoy', a prominent mound thought to be a prehistoric chambered cairn (Chapter 2). The shallow ditch feature 103, was cut into the glacial till trending north-west to south-east, but proved disappointing in terms of content, no artefacts were retrieved and no securely-stratified dating material was recovered. It may well be a natural feature.

Trench 2, located to the north-east of the same field (centred on HY 2465 2833), was 6 × 1 m and positioned over an east–west linear anomaly detected in the 2003 gradiometer survey, which appears to continue westwards on the line of a former field boundary, a line which

Fig. 4.42: Buckquoy, Birsay, 2004, Trench 2 from S

Fig. 4.44: Trench 5, marked stones in longhouse walls

■ Stones

■ Kerbs and orthostats

■ Walls

■ Paving

■ Hearths/burnt deposits

■ Midden: darker = higher organic content

■ Floors, internal surfaces and wall-fills:
darker = higher organic content

■ Organic sands: darker = higher organic content

■ Windblown sands: darker = slight organic content

■ External/work surfaces

Fig. 4.43: Colour and context description code for plans and sections

remains to the east of this field as a relict feature on Ordnance Survey maps. Excavation revealed this to be a substantial stone wall foundation 203, in line with the anomaly (Fig. 4.42). No dating or artefactual material was recovered; the date of the wall foundation is suggested to be post-medieval, but we were unable to verify this.

Marked stones in the East Mound (Trench 5) longhouse walls (Fig. 4.44)

David Griffiths

During excavation of Trench 5 in 2008 and 2010 it was noticed that three of the sandstone slabs making up the walls had been deliberately marked or scratched during the life of the building. In all three cases, the marks were extremely faint, only visible in raking light, and virtually impossible to convey adequately in a photograph, despite numerous attempts in different light conditions. The most effective way of recording them was found to be by tracing them using a clear plastic sheet and fine marker pen. The first to be discovered, in 2008, and the clearest and most convincing example (Fig. 4.44, 1), is situated behind the side bench near the south-eastern corner of the central hall, on the north-facing interior wall very close to the Phase 3 southern entrance, which was blocked up in Phase 5. The stone slab bearing the carvings is rectangular with a flat exposed face, upon which are nine thin, somewhat curving vertical strokes at slightly irregular intervals, with a sinuous horizontal line crossing and linking them. Thus ten marks are visible, representing a 'tally mark'. It is impossible to say what was being counted. The presence of such a feature, at shoulder height just behind the seating area, is a poignant indication of the past human presence in the building. Tally marks are also visible inside Maeshowe, although in comparison to the spectacular runes there they are not given prominence in publications or public discourse. Nevertheless they may, by association with the runes, be attributed to the Viking-Late Norse period.

In the 2010 season, two further marked stones were observed in upper courses of the north-western, south-facing interior wall of the longhouse's western annex, which would date them to Phase 5 or later. Unlike the 'tally mark' found in 2008, these were both somewhat hard to interpret, and consist of faint scratches superimposed in a 'palimpsest' manner. The eastern one of the two (Fig. 4.4, 2), found near the junction of the Phase 3 hall and western annex, has more pronounced 'tally' elements than the other (Fig. 4.44, 3) but these are more complex and less clear than in (1). One or two elements of (2) were observed to present a slightly 'runic' appearance, but the leading runologist Professor M. P. Barnes, when shown these illustrations, did not reach the conclusion that any part of them should qualify as genuinely runic, even if only of a very rough and informal kind. Instead, beyond the 'tally' marks, the rest of the two palimpsests must be seen merely as an amorphous and informal series of scratches, compiled for a reason or reasons which we cannot now know.

All three marked stones are integral to the structure of the longhouse walls, and to avoid serious damage to the integrity of the building, they were left *in situ*.

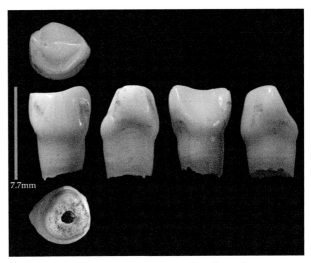

Fig. 4.45: Trench 5, human milk tooth

Human milk-tooth from the East Mound (Trench 5) longhouse (Fig. 4.45)

David Griffiths

A human deciduous canine (a child's milk-tooth) was retrieved in 2010 from soil sample processing (identification confirmed after laboratory examination by Dr Louise Loe of Oxford Archaeology). It came from context 2225 (Phase 6), in the infill of the northern side bench in the longhouse. It may have been redeposited during infilling of the side bench so itself may pre-date the context. Dimensions: L 7.7 mm, W 5 mm, D of root 4 mm.

From a site where no other human bodily remains have been detected, a child's milk-tooth is an unusual and rather poignant find. It represents the start of life, rather than its end, and is possibly the only unambiguous confirmation in the biological evidence of what must have been obvious and unremarkable in the Viking-Late Norse period, namely of children being part of the community at the settlement.

5

Dating and chronology

Derek Hamilton, Anthony M. Krus, Jean-Luc Schwenninger,
Jane Harrison and David Griffiths

Introduction

The overall aim of the dating strategy for the two excavated mound sites at the Bay of Skaill – Snusgar and East Mound – was to develop a chronology that could shed light on: (1) the beginning and end of activity on each mound; (2) the beginning and end of activity associated with each of the archaeological phases; and (3) the temporality of the use of the structures. This was accomplished through the combination of 60 radiocarbon dates with a series of optically stimulated luminescence (OSL) dates and several strong stratigraphical sequences into a Bayesian statistical framework.

The scientific dating strategy was established from the outset with the support of Historic Environment Scotland (see below) and the Luminescence Dating Laboratory at the Research Laboratory for Archaeology and the History of Art (RLAHA), Oxford University. All radiocarbon dates were funded by Historic Environment Scotland and undertaken by the Scottish Universities Environmental Research Centre (SUERC), East Kilbride. From 2010 onwards, the involvement in analysis and interpretation of Derek Hamilton and Tony Krus enabled a Bayesian modelling dimension to be developed, and the record supplemented in post-excavation by further samples for dating, which were selected explicitly within a Bayesian framework. While this has perhaps led to more samples being dated than might otherwise have been necessary, the dating of Snusgar and East Mound was presented with challenges when it came time to integrate the pre- and post-Bayesian dating approaches; however, these could all be surmounted.

The on-site sampling strategy has been driven throughout by the standards set and advice given by Historic Scotland based on longstanding practice (Ashmore 1999): by the character of the deposit, the quality of the sample, and the taphonomic and stratigraphic security of the sample to date the context. Samples selected for radiocarbon dating were single-entities and identified short-lived species and/or fragments of charcoal (i.e. roundwood), grains that represented a single growing season, or animal bones that would have radiocarbon ages averaged over the short lifetime of the animal. This methodology continued when the Bayesian approach was introduced. Dates were submitted after each excavation season. However, once the Bayesian modelling was implemented, the dating evidence was used to re-investigate specific site-formation processes, and further dates were taken from targeted materials and samples. This was beneficial for the Bayesian work as it highlighted the mixed nature of some deposits, while underlining the security attached to others in the context of the dating programme.

In fact, the results from the selected samples suffered from only three misfits – radiocarbon ages that simply disagree with their stratigraphic position – and demonstrated a strong agreement between the dates of the samples and the ordering of the deposits. However, the modelling does have some limitations, inevitable when working with sand-mound deposits and frequently rebuilt structures. Notably the transitions between different phases were the most likely to be either disturbed or truncated by rebuilding work. This was especially true of the earliest phases that suffered most from later disturbance and the final phases that were most vulnerable to the impact of robbing and collapse. This was particularly the case when dating the start and end of the Viking-Late Norse activity in Trench 5 on East Mound.

As the excavation progressed, nine phases were established for the site through careful observation and recording of the stratigraphy, on site and post-excavation studies of taphonomy, analysis of the context composition and the finds assemblage (Table 4.2). The scientific dates were then introduced to provide absolute control on this relative dating framework. The radiocarbon dating of multiple samples from single contexts, sometimes referred to as duplicates or replicates, was used alongside the vertical sequencing on samples/contexts in some areas of the site as a check on the overall security of deposits. Following the rigorous sampling methodology described above, meant not every phase could be dated at both sites. For Snusgar (Trenches 1–4), it was possible to date Phases 1 and 2, as well as the end of activity in Phase 5. The lack of suitably secure material from the Phase 2/3 transition and the end of activity, which occurred at some point during Phase 5, meant these phases could not be dated through the Bayesian modelling. The un-modelled radiocarbon dates provide date ranges for these phases. For the East Mound (Trench 5), the deposits from the earliest and latest identified phases of Viking-Late Norse activity were not amenable to dating through modelling, with the earliest archaeologically discernible activity having a combination of highly disturbed contexts in any case devoid of any suitable material. The complexities of the stratigraphy, and the subsequent effect on the Bayesian modelling, are discussed in further detail in the next section and again in the discussion section.

Results and calibration

Fifty-nine radiocarbon measurements on samples from 58 individual archaeological contexts are available from Snusgar and East Mound in the Bay of Skaill. Single-entity samples of grain, wood charcoal and articulated and disarticulated animal bone (bird, mouse, pig and cow) were submitted to the Scottish Universities Environmental Research Centre (SUERC).

All the samples were processed following methods outlined in Dunbar et al. (2016), and were graphitised and measured following Naysmith et al. (2010). SUERC maintains rigorous internal quality assurance procedures, and participation in international inter-comparisons (Scott 2003) indicates no laboratory offsets; thus validating the measurement precision quoted for the radiocarbon ages.

Conventional radiocarbon ages (Stuiver and Polach 1977) are presented in Table 5.1, where they are quoted in accordance with the Trondheim convention (Stuiver and Kra 1986). Calibrated date ranges were calculated using the calibration curves of Reimer et al. (2013) and OxCal v4.2 (Bronk Ramsey 1995; 1998; 2001; 2009). The date ranges in Table 5.1 have been calculated using the maximum intercept method (Stuiver and Reimer 1986), and quoted with the endpoints rounded outward to ten years. Ranges quoted in italics are posterior density estimates derived from mathematical modelling

of archaeological problems. Ranges in plain type were calculated according to the maximum intercept method (Stuiver and Reimer 1986). All other ranges (i.e. those in *italics*) were derived from the probability method (Stuiver and Reimer 1993).

Optically stimulated luminescence

Twenty-seven samples were collected for dating by optically stimulated luminescence (for principles see Aitken 1998). A selection of ten of these samples were processed at the Research Laboratory for Archaeology and the History of Art (RLAHA) at Oxford University (Table 5.2). Further details regarding individual samples and dating results are provided in Table 5.2 and a technical summary of the OSL analysis presented in Table 5.3.

Samples were collected in black PVC tubing and *in situ* radioactivity measurements were made with a portable gamma-ray spectrometer calibrated against the Oxford blocks (Rhodes and Schwenninger 2007). The age estimates presented in Table 5.2 are based on luminescence measurements of sand-sized quartz (180–255 µm) extracted from the samples using standard preparation techniques including: wet sieving; HCl (10%) treatment to remove carbonates; HF treatment (48%) to dissolve feldspathic minerals and heavy mineral separation with sodium polytungstate. Measurements were performed in an automated luminescence reader made by Risø (Bøtter-Jensen 1988; 1997; 2000) using a SAR post-IR blue OSL measurement protocol (Banerjee et al. 2001; Murray and Wintle 2000; Wintle and Murray 2006). A single saturating exponential function was used to describe the dose response of individual aliquots and a weighted mean value with a weighted standard error was calculated for each sample. Dose rate calculations are based on Aitken (1985) and are derived from the on-site radioactivity measurements. The OSL age estimates include an additional 4% systematic error to account for uncertainties in source calibration and measurement reproducibility. Dose rate calculations are based on beta attenuation factors (Mejdahl 1979), dose rate conversion factors (Adamiec and Aitken 1998) and an absorption coefficient for the water content. The contribution of cosmic radiation to the total dose rate was calculated as a function of latitude, altitude, burial depth and average over-burden density based on data by Prescott and Hutton (1994).

Methodological approach

A Bayesian approach has been applied to the interpretation of the Bay of Skaill chronology (Buck et al. 1996). Although simple calibrated dates are accurate estimates of the age of samples, this is not, usually, what archaeologists really wish to know. It is the dates of the archaeological events represented by those samples that are of interest.

Table 5.1: Radiocarbon dates from East Mound and Snusgar (Bay of Skaill) and Marwick

Lab ID	Context	Context description	Material dated	$\delta^{13}C$ (‰)	$\delta^{15}N$ (‰)	C:N	Radiocarbon age (BP)	Calibrated date cal AD (95% confidence)
East Mound								
SUERC-17858	2035	Trench 5: Dump of stones and domestic debris. Silty sand.	carbonised grain: barley	–23.4	–	–	895±35	1030–1220
SUERC-17859	2040	Trench 5: Domestic refuse within hearth deposit in corner of square structure. Ash and charcoal rich – hearth deposits/rakings (sandy silt with clay).	carbonised grain: barley	–23.2	–	–	950±35	1010–1170
SUERC-17860	2043	Trench 5: Small, single, primary dump of domestic debris.	branch charcoal with bark: *Salix* sp.	–27.0	–	–	915±35	1020–1220
SUERC-17861	2056	Trench 5: Deposit of domestic refuse. Firm clayey silt.	charcoal: *Corylus* sp.	–27.3	–	–	965±35	1010–1160
SUERC-17862	2106	Trench 5: Deposit of domestic refuse. Dark organic silty sand. Overlying levelling of earlier wall and covered by windblown sand.	charcoal: *Betula* sp.	–26.3	–	–	920±35	1020–1220
SUERC-17866	2111	Trench 5: Dump of domestic refuse.	carbonised grain: barley	–29.7	–	–	885±35	1030–1230
SUERC-17867	2115	Trench 5: Floor deposit in corner of square structure. Brown silty sand with charcoal inclusions. bone and shell. Includes hearth debris and general trample. Contained near complete Viking bone comb SF 108 and other significant finds.	carbonised grain: barley	–24.7	–	–	905±35	1020–1220
SUERC-17868	2078	Trench 5: Dumped domestic refuse. Manganese stained silty sand.	carbonised grain: barley	–22.5	–	–	1000±35	980–1150
SUERC-17869	2092	Trench 5: Domestic refuse within yard surface deposit. Silty sand with ash lenses. Contains bone, shell and several artefacts.	carbonised grain: barley	–22.9	–	–	900±35	1020–1220
SUERC-24701	2077	Trench 5: Domestic refuse deposit. Silty sand with yellow clay lenses. Rich in shell, animal and fish bone.	carbonised grain: barley	–21.5	–	–	1160±35	770–980
SUERC-24702	2016	Trench 5: Internal domestic refuse deposit in Structure 1, concentrated in SE corner. Dark, highly organic sandy silt, rich in ash and charcoal (hearth debris), fishbone and shell. Contained Viking/Late Norse steatite sherds and iron objects.	charcoal: *Salix* sp.	–24.6	–	–	990±35	980–1160
SUERC-24703	2095	Trench 5: Domestic dump. Dark charcoal-rich silty sand, containing shell, animal and fish bone and steatite sherds.	carbonised grain: barley	–24.3	–	–	1065±30	890–1030
SUERC-24704	2109	Trench 5: Turf/organic material in secondary working area. Thin, distinct manganese-stained sandy clay rich in carbonised grain.	carbonised grain: barley	–22.9	–	–	1000±35	980–1150

Table 5.1: (Continued)

Lab ID	Context	Context description	Material dated	δ¹³C (‰)	δ¹⁵N (‰)	C:N	Radiocarbon age (BP)	Calibrated date cal AD (95% confidence)
SUERC-24705	2080	Trench 5: Domestic refuse debris in floor trample. Silty sand with yellow clay spreads and lenses. Rich in domestic debris.	carbonised grain: barley	−22.4	–	–	975±35	990–1160
SUERC-24706	2148	Trench 5: Upper fill of drain. Sandy silt with occasional charcoal. Sealed by flagging [2132] and above windblown sand layer (2149) indicating time when drain out of use.	charcoal: *Salix* sp.	−25.9	–	–	1015±35	970–1120
SUERC-24710	2156	Trench 5: Ash and charcoal concentration in dump in byre end of Area 3 long hall structure. Rich in charcoal, ash, shell, animal and fish bone. Also contains iron objects, a fine whetstone, worked bone, and a whalebone gaming piece.	charcoal: *Salix* sp.	−24.5	–	–	1000±35	980–1150
SUERC-24711	2160	Trench 5: Bedding/levelling layer for floor surface in N-S structure in Area 1. Charcoal-rich silty sand.	charcoal: *Salix* sp.	−25.3	–	–	915±35	1020–1220
SUERC-24712	2164	Trench 5: Domestic refuse deposit in byre within organic layer with ash spread as antiseptic and pitted with hoof-marks. Dark very silty sand rich in charcoal, peat ash lenses and Fuel Ash Slag. Context contained worked stone, quern fragment, steatite and copper alloy fragments as well as much shell, animal and fish bone.	carbonised grain: barley	−24.5	–	–	1000±35	980–1150
SUERC-24713	2152	Trench 5: Layer in a dump of shells, charcoal, burnt clay and peat ash. Dark silty sand with charcoal and patches of burnt turf and peat ash. Rich in shell, animal and fish bone; contained steatite, iron objects and worked bone objects including comb pieces.	charcoal: *Salix* sp.	−26.5	–	–	1035±35	900–1040
SUERC-24714	2146	Trench 5. Organic occupation deposit in domestic end of long structure. Dark sandy silt with clay, charcoal and peat-ash lenses. Contained many iron objects and Viking-Norse domestic artefacts including a fine whetstone, quern and whalebone object.	carbonised grain: barley	−24.3	–	–	1035±35	900–1040
SUERC-24715	2105	Trench 5: Metal working deposit. Yellow clay with patches of heavily burnt material and ash: at least 10% charcoal and high content of fuel ash slag, clinker and slag. Contained many iron objects/fragments and worked bone artefacts.	roundwood charcoal with bark: *Salix* sp.	−25.4	–	–	1010±35	970–1150

Table 5.1: Radiocarbon dates from East Mound and Snusgar (Bay of Skaill) and Marwick (Continued)

Lab ID	Context	Context description	Material dated	$\delta^{13}C$ (‰)	$\delta^{15}N$ (‰)	C:N	Radiocarbon age (BP)	Calibrated date cal AD (95% confidence)
SUERC-24716	2105	Trench 5: Metal working deposit. Yellow clay with patches of heavily burnt material and ash: at least 10% charcoal and high content of fuel ash slag, clinker and slag. Contained many iron objects/fragments and worked bone artefacts.	roundwood charcoal with bark: *Salix* sp.	−25.9	–	–	1050±35	890–1030
SUERC-24720	2178	Trench 5: Discrete dump compressed into surface of metalworking area. Possibly a dump from cleaning or refurbishment of hearth. Heat-affected red, sandy clay rich in charcoal.	charcoal: *Salix* sp.	−26.4	–	–	940±35	1020–1190
SUERC-33699	2202	Trench 5: Metalworking hearth.	roundwood charcoal with bark: *Salix* sp.	−28.5	–	–	925±30	1020–1190
SUERC-33700	2240	Trench 5: Rake-out from bowl hearth in metalworking area. Friable black silt with lenses of silty sand; extremely charcoal rich with occasional small pieces of burnt clay. The bowl had been clay lined, surrounded and partly lined with stones.	roundwood charcoal with bark: *Salix* sp.	−25.9	–	–	955±30	1010–1160
SUERC-33701	2269	Trench 5: Fill of small metalworking hearth [2281] in metal working area. Black silty clay, with very abundant visible charcoal. burnt clay and fuel ash slag.	charcoal with bark and outer rings: *Salix* sp.	−24.9	–	–	970±30	1010–1160
SUERC-33702	2301	Trench 5: Square hearth in longhouse. Rich in fuel ash slag, peat ash, charcoal and burnt clay. Possible tuyere in base, hammerscale, slag and small furnace bottom.	carbonised grain: barley	−26.1	–	–	975±30	1010–1160
SUERC-33706	2263	Trench 5: Domestic refuse debris in longhouse floor. Compact dark blackish brown sandy clay with clear areas orangey pink peat ash: patches of black and grey greasy clay; frequent charcoal.	carbonised grain: barley	−25.7	–	–	965±30	1010–1160
SUERC-33707	2264	Trench 5: Domestic refuse debris in longhouse floor. Dark blackish brown slightly sandy silt with patches of orangey pinkish black sandy clay and abundant charcoal.	carbonised grain: barley	−25.2	–	–	1005±30	980–1120
SUERC-33708	2265	Trench 5: Domestic refuse debris in longhouse floor. Friable dark greyish brown sandy (20%) silt – silty clay; concentrations of charcoal: lenses white-orange peat ash.	carbonised grain: barley	−22.4	–	–	975±30	1010–1160
SUERC-33709	2285	Trench 5: Hearth fill in longhouse.	carbonised grain: barley	−24.3	–	–	950±30	1020–1170

Table 5.1: (Continued)

Lab ID	Context	Context description	Material dated	$\delta^{13}C$ (‰)	$\delta^{15}N$ (‰)	C:N	Radiocarbon age (BP)	Calibrated date cal AD (95% confidence)
SUERC-33710	2300	Trench 5: Cooking pit in longhouse floor. Ashy, humic sandy clay with peat-ash concentrations and flecks and concentrations of charcoal.	carbonised grain: barley	−22.7	–	–	985±30	990–1160
SUERC-33711	2304	Trench 5: Main sub-square hearth in longhouse. Crumbly ashy deposits, red burnt clay, black silty clay and sticky grey clay, with firm peat ash lenses, charcoal concentrations and abundant FAS.	carbonised grain: barley	−23.6	–	–	940±30	1020–1170
SUERC-33712	2271	Trench 5: Dark sandy silt deposit with peat ash lenses in corner of 'stalling area'.	carbonised grain: barley	−25.2	–	–	960±30	1010–1160
SUERC-33716	2277	Trench 5: Concentration of charcoal in sub-circular depression in the stalling area of longhouse. Highly organic sandy silt.	carbonised grain: barley	−23.0	–	–	940±30	1020–1170
SUERC-33717	2225	Trench 5: Compact dark brown organic deposit in domestic end of longhouse. Sandy silt with large lenses of peat ash, concentrations of charcoal, grey 'kitchen grease' clay and yellow clay.	roundwood charcoal: *Salix* sp.	−26.1	–	–	940±30	1020–1170
SUERC-33718	2273	Trench 5: Layer built up of hearth rakings in byre. Compact, dark brownish slightly sandy silt – slightly sandy clay; large peat ash lenses; abundant charcoal concentrations and burnt clay.	carbonised grain: barley	−26.5	–	–	1025±30	970–1040
SUERC-33719	2290	Trench 5: Fill of circular cooking pit. Burnt stone around centre; possible lining clay and greasy grey cooking residues. Contains well-preserved oat grains used in cooking activity/grain drying. Friable-compact, burnt orangey clay, pinkish orange peat ash, dark brownish black silt and greasy greyish black silty clay, with abundant charcoal concentrations.	carbonised grain: oat	−24.0	–	–	920±30	1020–1210
SUERC-33720	2305	Trench 5: Peat ash and charcoal rich sandy silt deposit in longhouse.	carbonised grain: barley	−23.1	–	–	990±30	990–1160
SUERC-33721	2288	Trench 5: Single peat ash midden dump. Compact, dark brownish black clayey silt with nearly 50% context pinkish orange lenses of peat ash and abundant charcoal concentrations.	roundwood charcoal: *Salix* sp.	−27.0	–	–	975±30	1010–1160

Table 5.1: Radiocarbon dates from East Mound and Snusgar (Bay of Skaill) and Marwick (Continued)

Lab ID	Context	Context description	Material dated	δ¹³C (‰)	δ¹⁵N (‰)	C:N	Radiocarbon age (BP)	Calibrated date cal AD (95% confidence)
SUERC-33722	2231	Trench 5: Peat ash hearth in early structure. Compact light brownish pink clayey silt; with abundant charcoal concentrations.	carbonised grain: barley	−24.6	–	–	965±30	1010–1160
SUERC-47146	2205	Trench 5: Fill of pit with the remains of a dismantled metal working hearth. Sandy silt with burnt clay, mammal and fish bones, shells and fuel ash slag. Includes an articulated cow element.	articulated animal bone: cow phalange	−22.2	5.3	3.3	941±39	1010–1190
SUERC-47147	2221	Trench 5: Small deposit above western longhouse roof tumble. Silty sand with very occasional charcoal and small collection of animal bone.	articulated animal bone: pig calcaneum	−21.9	8.3	3.2	1033±39	900–1040
SUERC-47148	2294	Trench 5: Fill of metal working hearth. Very finely-laminated. Clay and ash-rich silty sand with abundant charcoal.	articulated animal bone: mouse	−21.3	–	–	999±39	980–1160
SUERC-47149	2219	Trench 5: Deposit in post-abandonment layers over byre. Silty sand with concentrations of charcoal.	roundwood charcoal with bark: *Salix* sp.	−27.6	–	–	1013±39	970–1150
SUERC-47150	2229	Trench 5: Matrix in rough stone surface. Silty sand with concentrations of charcoal.	carbonised grain: barley	−24.7	–	–	887±39	1030–1250
SUERC-47151	2236	Trench 5:Midden deposit. Sandy silt with abundant peat ash and many concentrations of charcoal; fish and animal bone.	charcoal: *Salix* sp.	−26.3	–	–	990±39	980–1160
SUERC-47155	2275	Trench 5: Hearth-related deposit. Sandy silt with frequent charcoal concentrations and clay.	carbonised grain: barley	−24.1	–	–	957±39	1010–1170
SUERC-47156	2276	Trench 5: Silt with concentrations of charcoal covering flagstone path in longhouse.	charcoal: *Corylus*	−27.4	–	–	1024±39	900–1120
SUERC-59189	2115	Trench 5: Floor deposit in corner of square structure.Brown silty sand with charcoal inclusions, bone and shell. Includes hearth debris and general trample. Contained near complete Viking bone comb SF 108 and other significant finds.	Bone: dog tarsal IV	−17.0	13.0	3.3	1124±31	990–1210

Table 5.1: (Continued)

Lab ID	Context	Context description	Material dated	δ13C (‰)	δ15N (‰)	C:N	Radiocarbon age (BP)	Calibrated date cal AD (95% confidence)
Snusgar								
SUERC-17846	1013	Trench 1: Domestic refuse deposit. Ash, charcoal and shell rich silty sand and clay. Viking and Late Norse artefacts found in the deposit.	carbonised grain: barley	−24.2	–	–	975±35	990–1160
SUERC-17847	1017	Trench 1: Domestic refuse deposit. Silty sand with rich organic lenses. Includes Viking and Late Norse artefacts.	carbonised grain: barley	−23.6	–	–	1085±35	880–1030
SUERC-17848	1045	Trench 1: Construction or occupation deposit. Organic sand with fish bones and charcoal. Also includes Viking and Late Norse artefacts.	roundwood charcoal: Salix sp.	−25.9	–	–	1090±35	880–1020
SUERC-17849	1051	Trench 1: Domestic deposit. Compact dark sandy silt with notable charcoal inclusions.	carbonised grain: barley	−23.3	–	–	1115±35	770–1020
SUERC-17850	1504	Trench 4: Domestic occupation deposit. Compact sandy silt with ash-rich layer. Includes several fragments of Viking/Late Norse comb.	carbonised grain: barley	−23.3	–	–	1025±35	970–1040
SUERC-17851	1536	Trench 4: Buried anthropogenic soil. Covered by and overlying very deep windblown sands. Fine yellowish grey sandy silt. Only organic material in the context is a disarticulated bird bone.	animal bone: Cormorant	−15.2	15.1	3.3	1710±35*	470–680
SUERC-17852	1547	Trench 4: Highly organic area in a primary deposit of domestic occupation debris. Compact greyish black silty sand with clay lenses. Contained a bone pin.	carbonised grain: barley	−23.8	–	–	1040±35	900–1040
SUERC-17856	1561	Trench 4: Shell and ash-rich organic deposit of domestic refuse.	carbonised grain: barley	−22.7	–	–	1070±30	890–1030
SUERC-17857	1561	Trench 4: Shell and ash-rich organic deposit of domestic refuse.	charcoal: Salix sp.	−25.7	–	–	1080±35	880–1030
SUERC-18265	1518	Trench 4: Primary deposit of burnt domestic occupation debris. Animal bone and ash-rich organic deposit with burnt stone component. Stabilised by stone layer and contained bone pin fragment.	carbonised grain: barley	−23.2	–	–	1040±35	900–1040
Marwick								
SUERC-33697	1018	MW09: clayey, highly organic occupation surface with metal-working evidence.	carbonised grain	−25.9	–	–	1165±30	770–970
SUERC-33698	1019	MW09: gravelly levelling layer	carbonised grain	−21.9	–	–	1150±30	770–980

*The date for SUERC-17851 is from a seabird and has been calibrated using the Marine13 curve of Reimer et al. (2013), an interpolated marine diet percentage of 72±9, and the local marine reservoir offset of 51±29 years for medieval Scotland calculated by Russell (2011) for Scotland. All other dates have been calibrated using the terrestrial curve, IntCal13, of Reimer et al. (2013)

At Snusgar and East Mound, for example, it is the dating and duration of use of particular features/structures, along with the start and end of the use of these sites in general, that are of most interest, rather than the dates of individual samples. The chronology of this activity can be estimated not only by using the absolute dating derived from the radiocarbon measurements, but also by using the stratigraphic relationships between samples and the relative dating information provided by the archaeological phasing.

Methodology is now available which allows the combination of these different types of information

Table 5.2: Optically stimulated luminescence (OSL) dates from Snusgar and East Mound

Field code	Lab. code	Context	OSL age est. (years before 2007)	OSL date (AD)
SG06-18	X3097	1539	1410±160	435–755
SG06-19	X3098	1538	2015±210	220 BC–AD 430
SG06-20	X3099	2001	185±130	1690–1820
SG06-21	X3100	2001	170±45	1790–1835
SG06-22	X3101	2032	620±125	1260–1385
SG06-23	X3102	2047	1065±95	845–940
SG06-06	X3103	1504	1070±55	880–935
SG06-09	X3104	1533	1315±75	615–690
SG06-11	X3105	1561	1120±130	755–885
SG06-12	X3106	1569	1270±200	535–735

The samples were collected in August 2006 and analysed later in the same year

explicitly, to produce realistic estimates of the dates of archaeological interest. It should be emphasised that the posterior density estimates produced by this modelling are not absolute. They are interpretative estimates, which can and will change as further data become available and as other researchers choose to model the existing data from different perspectives. The technique used is a form of Markov Chain Monte Carlo sampling, and has been applied using the program OxCal v4.2 (http://c14.arch. ox.ac.uk/). Details of the algorithms employed by this program are available in Bronk Ramsey (1995; 1998; 2001; 2009) or from the online manual. The algorithm used in the models can be derived from the OxCal keywords and bracket structure shown in Figs 5.1 and 5.2.

Samples and the model

The site Bayesian model was made up of stratigraphically disparate elements. Thus, for example, the samples from Snusgar (Trenches 1–4) could not be directly related stratigraphically to the samples from East Mound (Trenches 5–8); similarly, samples from the East Mound longhouse and byre could not be directly related to each other in a way conformable to Bayesian modelling. Therefore, because it is impossible to 'know' how any two pieces the site unconnected in this way are related temporally, the modelling has been organised so that feature groups, or selections of the sequence that can be assumed to hold together temporally based on spatial association (*e.g.* the interior of the longhouse), are grouped together visually.

The model is separated by the overall mound groups, into two spatially distinct components. It is not certain whether the two mounds were lived on as part of a continuous occupation of the larger site. The model,

Table 5.3: Summary of the optically stimulated luminescence (OSL) analysis

Sample code	Depth (cm)	Radioisotopes*			Field water %	External γ-dose rate(Gy/ka)	Total dose rate (Gy/ka)	De(Gy)	Age estimate (years before 2007)
		K %	Th ppm	U ppm					
X3097	100	0.80	2.5	1.3	5.4	0.48±0.02	1.42±0.06	2.00±0.21	1410±160
X3098	135	0.75	2.4	1.2	10.0	0.45±0.02	1.28±0.06	2.57±0.24	2015±210
X3099	30	–	–	–	2.3	–	(1.58±0.09)	0.29±0.21	185±130
X3100	54	–	–	–	4.8	–	(1.55±0.08)	0.26±0.06	170±45
X3101	91	0.91	3.2	2.0	6.6	0.64±0.03	1.72±0.07	1.06±0.20	620±125
X3102	85	0.93	3.2	1.8	7.2	0.61±0.03	1.65±0.07	1.76±0.10	1065±95
X3103	61	0.88	2.7	1.3	8.0	0.51±0.03	1.48±0.07	1.59±0.03	1070±55
X3104	85	0.69	3.5	1.6	29.7	0.67±0.03	1.60±0.08	2.10±0.08	1315±75
X3105	110	0.82	3.6	1.9	34.1	0.70±0.03	1.59±0.07	1.78±0.19	1120±130
X3106	170	0.54	2.9	1.5	6.8	0.52±0.03	1.46±0.06	1.86±0.28	1270±200

*Based on *in situ* measurements using a portable γ-ray spectrometer (Ortec micronomad) equipped with a 3×3 inch NaI (Tl) scintillator crystal and calibrated against the Oxford blocks (Rhodes and Schwenninger 2007). No field spectroscopy measurements could be made for samples X3099 and X3100. For both these samples we based our dose rate calculations on the mean concentrations obtained from the other sediment samples in the series. Dose rates were adjusted for the measured field water content expressed as a percentage of the mass of the sample. A systematic error of ±5% was applied to the measured moisture content.

therefore, stipulates that the features associated with the two mounds are not temporally related, thus freeing them to overlap in real time.

Snusgar (Trenches 1–4)

A total of ten radiocarbon dates are available from nine contexts in Trenches 1 and 4. The dated samples comprise roundwood charcoal, single grains of carbonised seeds, and a seabird bone. The dates have been used within a Bayesian model to provide probability estimates for the start and end of occupation activity at this location, and to also estimate the timing of specific events for which there is no direct dating evidence available (*e.g.* transition from Phase 1 to Phase 2).

Trench 1

There were four samples submitted for radiocarbon dating from an equal number of contexts in a sequence from Trench 1. The lowest dated layer 1051 in Trench 1 was a domestic midden deposit that produced one result (SUERC-17849) on a carbonised barley grain. Sometime after the East Mound longhouse was constructed a fragment of willow, roundwood charcoal provided a date (SUERC-17848) from an organic occupation deposit just outside the northern longhouse wall 1045. Above this, a single grain of charred barley was dated (SUERC-17847) from a rich organic lens of domestic debris in the same midden 1017. The Trench 1 sequence was capped off by a result (SUERC-17846) on another single charred barley grain from a domestic refuse deposit 1013.

Trench 4

From Trench 4 there were five radiocarbon dates from contexts in a sequence of midden deposits. Additionally, there are three optically stimulated luminescence (OSL) dates from the sequence (Table 5.2). There is a further radiocarbon date that is not stratigraphically related to the other samples, also from within this trench.

At the base of the sequence there was an OSL result (X3106) on wind-blown sand 1569 that signified the end of Phase 1 in this trench. There were three results from a shell and ash-rich organic deposit 1561 associated with Phase 2. From this there were two radiocarbon results (SUERC-17856 and -17857) on a single charred barley grain and fragment of roundwood willow charcoal, respectively. In addition, there was an OSL result (X3105) from this deposit. Above 1561 there was a complex of highly organic midden layers within with a primary deposit of domestic debris 1547, was associated with Phase 3 activity. A radiocarbon result (SUERC-17852) was available from a single carbonised grain of barley from this deposit. Above 1547 there were two contexts not directly related by stratigraphy. From 1533 there was an OSL result (X3104), while SUERC-18265

comes from a single carbonised barley grain from a charcoal-rich midden deposit 1518. The entire sequence is capped by an OSL result (X3103) and a radiocarbon date (SUERC-17850) on a charred barley grain, from a highly organic midden 1504 within a complex of sand lenses and blows.

There is dating information available from a context that cannot be tied into the main modelling sequence. A disarticulated seabird bone was dated (SUERC-17851) from a buried anthropogenic soil 1536, and this provides a *terminus post quem* for the overlying sand deposits. The marine reservoir effect on the seabird has been corrected for using linear interpolation of the $\delta^{13}C$ values to estimate the percent marine diet. An end member of $-12.0‰$ was used for the fully marine diet (Arneborg *et al.* 1999), with the value of $-22.2‰$ from the cattle bone measured from the site (SUERC-47146) used for fully terrestrial. This indicates a marine input of approximately 72%, to which an error of $±9\%$ was added (Arneborg *et al.* 1999). The correction has been made using the Mix_Curves function in OxCal and applying a local reservoir correction of $-29 ±51$ years (Russell 2011).

East Mound

Trench 5B: 2006 season, west of ancillary buildings

There are three results from an area west of the ancillary buildings. These were from a series of external occupation layers and later midden-like dumps of occupation debris. From a lower small, midden deposit 2056, there was a result (SUERC-17861) on a fragment of hazel roundwood charcoal. There was quite a bit of disturbance recorded within the upper occupation/midden layers in this area, so these were not dated. There were two identified and discrete dumps of midden-like material above these occupation layers. From the lower one 2043 there was a date (SUERC-17860) on charcoal from a small branch of willow; above this there was a result (SUERC-17858) from a charred cereal grain in a stony dump of domestic debris 2035.

Trench 5: 2007, 2008, 2010 seasons, ancillary buildings

A total of seven radiocarbon dates are available from as many contexts. These include deposits from the interior of both the north–south and subsequent west–east buildings. Three contexts were dated from within the Phase 3 north–south building. They overlay structural stones related to the early structure and provided good dating evidence for activity associated with that structure. The first result (SUERC-24711) was on a fragment of willow roundwood charcoal from a charcoal-rich floor surface 2160, while the second (SUERC-33722) was on a charred barley grain from a peat ash hearth 2231 within the structure. These two deposits were overlain by a later clay floor, and a grain of charred barley trampled into that floor surface 2080 produced SUERC-24706.

Above the clay floor there was a deposit related to infilling and levelling in preparation for the construction of the west–east building. From one context in this deposit 2077 a charred barley grain was dated (SUERC-24701). The result is the earliest from the site, and significantly earlier than nearly every other sample dated. The nature of the context would suggest that the sample is residual, and so it has been included in the model as providing a *terminus post quem* for the context.

Three contexts associated with the use of the west–east building were dated. While all of these contexts are definitely later than 2077, there were no sufficiently secure direct stratigraphic relationships between the three for Bayesian purposes. From a deposit of domestic debris 2016 on the floor, in the south-east corner, of the west–east building, a fragment of willow roundwood charcoal was dated (SUERC-24702). Another discrete or special deposit (above, Chapter 4) of domestic material 2115, containing ashy hearth debris, a near complete bone comb (SF 108) and other placed artefacts, produced a measurement (SUERC-17867) on a charred barley grain, and from a dog bone (SUERC-59189), while another charred barley grain from a hearth deposit 2040 produced SUERC-17859.

TRENCH 5: 2007, 2008, 2010 SEASONS, CENTRAL YARD AREA

There are four results from four contexts from the central yard area. Three of these form a sequence. At the bottom of the sequence, there was a result (SUERC-24706) on a fragment of willow charcoal from the fill of a drain 2148. Above this there was a date on a fragment of birch charcoal (SUERC-17862) from a domestic refuse deposit 2106, overlying the partial dismantling of an earlier wall and covered by clean windblown sand.

A charred barley grain was dated (SUERC-24703) from a domestic dump 2095 of material that could not be modelled, stratigraphically, with the other dates in this area. The context is in an area with a high degree of slumping, and, while there is little reason to believe the slumping caused the deposits to be mixed, the slipping can result in areas where there are inversions in the horizontal stratigraphy. The result is earlier than expected, given the other dating from the site, and has been excluded from the modelling.

TRENCH 5: 2008, 2010 SEASONS, SOUTH-EASTERN MIDDEN

There are four radiocarbon results from a series of deposits near the south-east midden. One result (SUERC-47151) was from a fragment of roundwood willow charcoal in a lower dump of midden material 2236. Overlying this there was another discrete dump of peat ash material 2288 from which a fragment of willow roundwood

charcoal was dated (SUERC-33721). Cut into the midden deposits was a pit containing metal-working debris and other midden material. An articulated cow phalange was dated (SUERC-47146) from the fill, which included a dismantled metal-working hearth 2205. Within the surrounding midden deposits, but not stratigraphically connectable for Bayesian dating purposes to the other two midden contexts, there is a result (SUERC-24713) from 2152 on a fragment of willow roundwood charcoal.

TRENCH 5: 2006, 2007, 2008, 2010 SEASONS, METAL-WORKING YARD

Eleven results are available from nine contexts in an area of Trench 5 around and within a metal-working yard. Here there were two sequences of contexts with no direct stratigraphy to be modelled between the two.

The first sequence comes from a grassy area external to the (west of) the yard: at the base, there was a result (SUERC-17866) on a charred barley grain from a dump of domestic refuse 2111. It was noted there was a rabbit warren in this area. The result is too recent when compared to the overlying results from clearly undisturbed deposits, and has been excluded from the model as it is likely an intrusive sample. From an overlying context that was rich in charred grain 2109 there was a result (SUERC-24704) on a barley grain, and a second (SUERC-17868) on a barley grain from an overlying dump of domestic debris 2078.

The second sequence is from the metal-working yard itself, and includes both working floors and hearths. At the base of the sequence there were two results (SUERC-24715 and -24716) on fragments of willow roundwood charcoal from the laminated floor 2105 that was heavily burnt and contained much metal-working debris and charcoal. Above the floor, there was a result (SUERC-33700) from a fragment of willow roundwood charcoal that came from the rake-out 2240 of a bowl hearth cut into the floor. Further up the sequence, one piece of willow roundwood charcoal in a small hearth 2269 produced SUERC-33701. The result (SUERC-47148) from hearth 2294 was from an articulated mouse in the fill (the earliest directly dated house mouse in the Northern Isles). A final hearth 2202 had a fragment of willow charcoal dated (SUERC-33699), while another fragment of willow charcoal from a dump on the surrounding floor 2178 produced SUERC-24720. The two contexts were not directly related through physical proximity. After the area was dismantled, it was levelled and a new yard was laid. A result (SUERC-17869) is available from a charred barley grain in a domestic deposit 2092 on the yard surface.

TRENCH 5: 2007, 2008, 2010 SEASONS, LONGHOUSE

A total of 21 radiocarbon dates are available from deposits associated with various phases of the longhouse occupation. A single result comes from a deposit that can be securely placed to a period before the Phase 5 longhouse use. Eighteen of the dates come from contexts from throughout the longhouse, early and late and from the house end to the byre end. Although many of these 18 samples had archaeologically valid stratigraphy, these were primarily from layers that had a high potential for mixing, especially in the byre end. As a result, these samples were modelled with no stratigraphy. Furthermore, since there was an abundance of results from samples that could potentially represent a short period of the overall use of the site, this period of longhouse activity has been constrained in OxCal to counteract the influence by reducing the 18 independent parameters to only two.

A charred barley grain was dated (SUERC-24714) from an organic occupation deposit 2146 in the first longhouse, which had been sealed by wall 2135. This is the only sample that securely predates the occupation deposits within the Phase 5 longhouse, as the Phase 3 longhouse floor had been protected in this area. From the occupation deposits a large amount of charred cereals were dated. These included charred barley grains that produced: SUERC-33707, from an organic occupation deposit 2264 within the longhouse floor; SUERC-33718, from an ash-rich hearth deposit 2273 in the byre end; SUERC-47150, from the charcoal-rich matrix 2229 in a rough stone surface; SUERC-33716, from a concentration of charcoal 2277 in the byre end; SUERC-33712, from a peat ash lens 2271 in the byre end; SUERC-33708, from a dump of domestic debris 2265 incorporated into the longhouse floor; SUERC-47155, from a hearth-related deposit 2275; SUERC-24712 from a domestic refuse dump 2164 in the byre end; SUERC-33709, from the fill 2285 of a hearth in the longhouse; SUERC-33711, charcoal and ash deposit 2304 in the largest sub-square hearth of the longhouse; SUERC-33702, from the fill 2301 of another small hearth in the longhouse; SUERC-33706, domestic refuse dump 2263 that was incorporated into the longhouse floor; and SUERC-33710; charcoal-rich fill 2300 of a cooking pit in the longhouse floor. There were also two charred oat grains dated: SUERC-33719, from the fill 2290 of a cooking pit; and SUERC-33720, from a charcoal-rich scoop fill 2305 in the longhouse floor. Finally, there were three fragments of charcoal submitted for dating: a fragment of hazel charcoal was dated (SUERC-47156) from a charcoal concentration 2276 that covered flagging in the byre end; a fragment of willow charcoal was dated (SUERC-24710) from a dump of charcoal 2156 in the byre; and a fragment of willow roundwood charcoal was dated (SUERC-33717) from a greasy organic deposit 2225 in the western cooking annex of the longhouse.

There were two dated deposits that formed after the building was out of use. An articulated pig calcaneum was dated (SUERC-47147) from a discrete deposit 2221 above the western longhouse roof tumble. While a fragment

of willow charcoal produced a date (SUERC-47149) for a deposit 2219 in the post-abandonment layers over the byre end. Both dates appear to be too early given their stratigraphic position and have very low individual agreements within the model. SUERC-47147 is from part of an articulated animal, and it is believed that it should accurately reflect the date of this deposit. The pig has a slightly elevated δ^{15}N of 8.3‰ indicating the likely presence of a marine input to the diet, and therefore a marine reservoir offset to the age. This has been corrected for using linear interpolation of the δ^{13}C values to estimate the percent marine diet. An end member of -12.0‰ was used for the fully marine diet (Arneborg *et al.* 1999), with the value of -22.2‰ from the cattle bone measured from the site (SUERC-47146) used for fully terrestrial. This indicates a marine input of approximately 3%, to which an error of ±9% was added (Arneborg *et al.* 1999). The correction has been made using the Mix_Curves function in OxCal and applying a local reservoir correction of -29 ±51 years (Russell 2011). After applying the correction, the radiocarbon date is in good agreement with the stratigraphy.

Results

The modelling shows good agreement between the radiocarbon dates and the archaeology (A_{model}=147).

The model estimates that the dated activity for Phase 1 at Snusgar began in *cal AD 870–995 (95% probability*; Fig. 5.1; *start: Snusgar Mound*), and probably in *cal AD 930–985 (68% probability)*. The transition from Phase 1 to 2 occurred in *cal AD 890–995 (95% probability*; Fig. 5.3; *transition P1/2*), and probably in *cal AD 945–990 (68% probability)*. The transition from Phase 2 to 3 occurred in *cal AD 960–1015 (95% probability*; Fig. 5.1; *transition P2/3*), and probably in *cal AD 975–1005 (68% probability)*. The activity in this mound ended in *cal AD 990–1060 (95% probability*; Fig. 5.1; *end: Snusgar Mound*), and probably in *cal AD 1000–1040 (68% probability)*. The overall span of dated activity was *1–170 years (95% probability*; Fig. 5.4; *use: Snusgar Mound*), and probably *25–105 years (68% probability)*.

The cormorant bone in the buried anthropogenic soil 1536 provided a *tpq* for the overlying windblown sand of *cal AD 555–730 (91% probability*; Fig. 5.1; *SUERC-17851: 1536*) or *cal AD 740–775 (4% probability)*, and probably *cal AD 595–680 (68% probability*: calibrated using the Marine 13 curve).

The earliest dating of activity at East Mound is in *cal AD 995–1025 (95% probability*; Fig. 5.2; *start: East Mound*), and probably in *cal AD 1010–1020 (68% probability)*. This activity persisted for *10–70 years (95% probability*; Fig. 5.4; *use: East Mound*), and probably for *25–50 years (68% probability)*. The dated activity ended in *cal AD 1035–1075 (95% probability*; Figure 2;

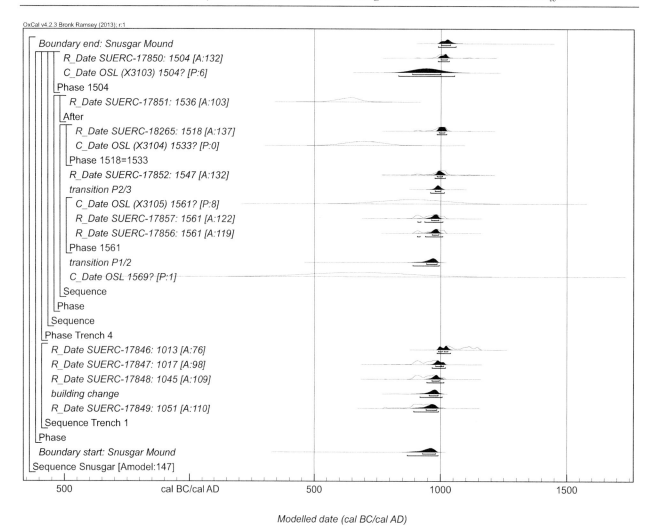

Fig. 5.1: Chronological model for the dated activity at Snusgar (Trenches 1–4). Each distribution represents the relative probability that an event occurred at some particular time. For each of the radiocarbon measurements two distributions have been plotted, one in outline, the result of simple radiocarbon calibration, and a solid one based on the chronological model use. The other distributions correspond to aspects if the model. For example, 'start: Snusgar' is the estimated date that the activity on the site began, based on the radiocarbon dating results. The large square 'brackets' along with the OxCal keywords define the overall model exactly

end: East Mound), and probably in *cal AD 1040–1060 (68% probability)*. It should be emphasised that it was not possible to use Bayesian modelling to date either the earliest or the latest activity on East Mound before the buildings were abandoned.

Discussion

As discussed above, it was not possible using the Bayesian model to provide a date estimate for every phase transition in both the Snusgar and East Mound. This was the result of deposits and layers, which in their stratigraphical location and archaeological character clearly represented the earliest found Viking-Late Norse activity, often being truncated or disturbed by succeeding activity, including the repeated reconfiguration of structures. The layer and deposits representing the final occupation activity were

also often disturbed – by structural collapse or animal trampling. Thus for the East Mound complex, modelling identified date ranges for the earliest dating that could be modelled, within Phase 3; and latest dated activity that could be modelled, towards the end of Phase 5. Thus, activity within Phase 3 and, probably towards the end of, Phase 5 provided the only points for which there was appropriate material, suitable taphonomy and deposits, and applicable stratigraphical relationships.

Excluded dates, such as SUERC-24701 from context 2077 of East Mound, that are too early and thought to represent reworked material, might provide some glimpse at the date of the earliest activity on that mound (cal AD 770–980). That the dated material was in later deposits made them not amenable to modelling. As a result, the modelled date ranges provide a solid core for dating the

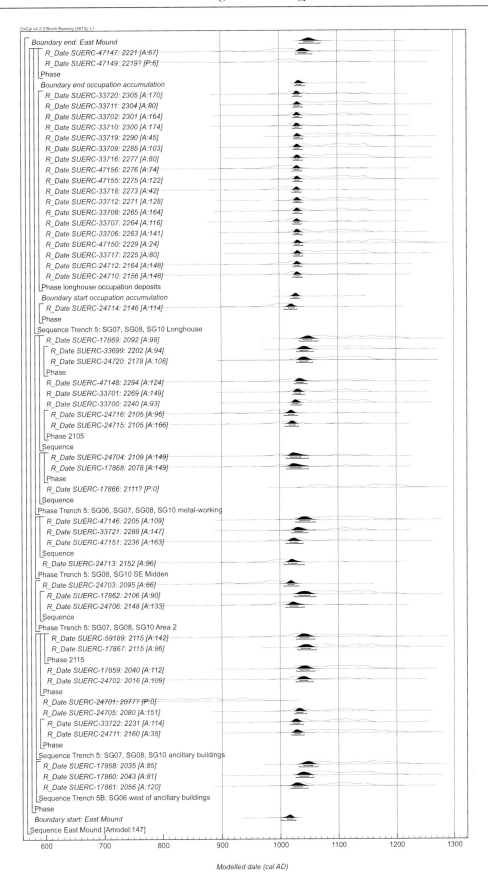

Modelled date (cal AD)

Fig. 5.2: Chronological model for East Mound (Trenches 5-8). The model structure is as described in Fig. 5.1

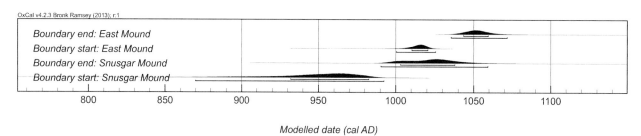

Fig. 5.3: Start and end date probability estimates for Snusgar and East Mound, as derived from the modelling in Figs 5.1 and 5.2

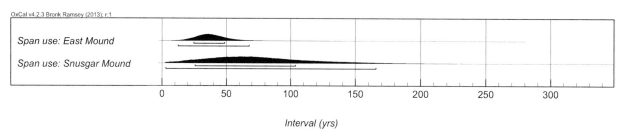

Fig. 5.4: Spans of overall dated activity for Snusgar and East Mound, as modelled in Figs 5.1 and 5.2

site, and a range of other evidence is used elsewhere to extend the chronology into other periods.

The radiocarbon dating programme highlighted just how difficult deep, complex, sandy, mound archaeology can be when sample selection needs to follow the rigours associated with both Historic Environment Scotland standards and Bayesian modelling. Samples had to be chosen with particular care to meet the demands of the sampling criteria and, inevitably, samples came from more

secure, undisturbed deposits in the middle phases of the archaeological 'sandwich'. The tendency of mounded layers in sand to create reverse and slipped stratigraphy added further difficulties. While post-depositional processes could be understood in the field, and thus the actions that originally created the archaeology identified, such processes are extremely difficult to express in stratigraphical matrices and in a way adaptable to the purposes of *a priori* modelling.

6

Geoarchaeology

Helen Lewis

Introduction

Geoarchaeological research at Snusgar and East Mound and in the surrounding landscape aimed to explore buried soils and settlement deposits, and to assess the potential for multi-period landscape history information. Previous regional geoarchaeological studies have focused on land-use history (*e.g.* Simpson 1997; Simpson *et al.* 1998; 1999a; 1999b; Adderley *et al.* 2000; Guttmann 2001; Guttmann *et al.* 2006), on the relationship between environment and settlement, and use-of-space within ancient villages and individual structures (*e.g.* French 1991; 1994; Milek 2001; Simpson *et al.* 2005; Jones *et al.* 2010). This background provided a good basis for targeting sampling, with the aim of developing a detailed geoarchaeological understanding of the history of sites in the region associated with sand mounds. The two excavated mounds revealed industrial and settlement activity on dunes formed partly against structural boundaries created by Viking-Late Norse buildings, along with earlier but currently unknown barriers. The Snusgar mound also revealed a prehistoric buried soil profile. The sites produced evidence for farming, domestic and industrial activities, including seaweed processing and metalworking, along with repeated deposition of blown sand, interrupted by units of 'floor' layers and occasional dune stabilisation under soils. Samples were taken for soil micromorphology study of a variety of deposits and soils, including buried soils, ancillary structure deposits, middens and land use features. A series of samples from the occupation layers supports field and archaeobotanical interpretations of use of peat and/or turf as fuel, and variations in use of space. Some samples were taken but not processed as thin sections, and remain in the project archive (Table 6.1). Those from which thin sections were made

are discussed in the related sections, which summarise aspects of the geoarchaeological work undertaken to date.

Background

Whilst no bedrock was uncovered in the excavations, the area is known to have a geology of siltstones, mudstones, breccias and conglomerates, and sandstones (*e.g.* Upper Stromness Flags, Old Red Sandstone), exposures and dykes of granite and gneiss, surficial glacial till and drift deposits of all of these materials, along with frequent covering aeolian and coastal shell sand, and peat deposits (*e.g.* Reed 1989; Maté 1996). The sites discussed here were mostly located on and within shell sand mounds (dunes) and aeolian shell sand layers in the landscape. Where bedrock was recorded in cliffs during this work, this was mainly sandstone or conglomerates (after Mykura 1975, 1996). Topographically, the Bay of Skaill is a gently undulating landscape adjacent to sea cliffs and beaches, with low hills inland, and the groundcover at the sites discussed here was grazed grassland, arable farmland, and scrub vegetation. Most of the soils discussed here developed on shell sands, with relatively thin A horizons, and are calcareous brown earths in a machair environment (after Maté 1996). Soils on the till have been described previously, including a prehistoric buried brown forest soil at St Magnus Kirk in Birsay (*ibid.*). Past woodland or scrubland vegetation has also been indicated in other buried soils based on molluscan fauna, including from the nearby site of Skara Brae (Spencer 1975; Evans and Vaughan 1983). These models appear to refer to a much earlier landscape than the evidence discussed below, based on pollen evidence

Table 6.1: Soil micromorphology samples from Snusgar and East Mound, Bay of Skaill

Samples	Contexts	Descriptions
2004 14/1-3	506-507-508-510-502	Base of spade marks (506) (pink sand layer); top of (507) greyish brown sandy pit fill (14/1); base of (507) over layers of red sand (508) & yellow sand (502) (14/2); layer (510) (black silty sand layer) over (502) yellow sand (14/3); Snusgar, TR 2
2004 15/1-2	501-509-502	(501) topsoil over greyish brown sand layer (509) (Ea/bA) (15/1), base of (509) over yellow sand (502) (15/2); Snusgar, TR 2
2004 16/1-2	1015-1016-1017	Yellow sand (1015), greyish brown sand, possible buried topsoil (1016), midden (1017); Snusgar
2004 18	1017-1045-1035	Midden (1017), greyish brown with iron panning, brown sand, possible midden or amended soil (1045), yellow sand (1035); Snusgar, TR1
2004 no #	no #	Buried grey silty sand in field uphill inland
2004 no #	no #	Soil layer under structural remains Birsay Bay (John Cluett)
2005 10	2002-2003	Buried soil in upper East Mound, TR 5
2005 11	1535-1536-1537	Buried soil horizons under base of Snusgar mound, TR 4
2005 no #	2005-2007	Possible buried soil in upper East Mound
2006 44	1570-1576	Buried soil layers (grey (1570); pink (1576) under & cut through by pit (1568); Snusgar, TR 4
2006 45	1508-1509-1581	Plough marks (midden layer (1508), plough marks cut midden-influenced sand layer (1509), windblown sand layer (1581) Snusgar, TR 4
2006	1510-1547	(1510) midden; (1547) midden layer stabilised and structured by stones; Snusgar, TR 4
2006 17, 18	2040-2053-2071-2072	Hearth rake-out (2040), yellow-brown sand (2053), clay (2071), yellow sand (2072); East Mound, TR 5
2007 167	2077-2080	Yellow sand (2077), clay (2080), yellow sand; East Mound, TR 5
2007 168	2086-2087	Series of clay & sand layers in 10cm unit (2087); East Mound, TR 5
2007 169	2001-2104	Yellow sand (2001), possible buried soil (2104); East Mound, TR 5
2007 177, 178	2080a & b	Clay layer, sand, clay layer; East Mound, TR 5
2007 416	4011	Grey-brown soil wall footing packing (4011); fine clay layer (no #); East Mound, TR 7
2008 236	2086-2087	Buried cultural deposit; grey ashy clay, charcoal, burnt sediment, rich brown clay & windblown sand layers; East Mound, TR 5
2008 237	2086	Buried cultural deposit, dark brown & grey clay with windblown sand layers; animal bone inclusions; overlies iron pan, under wall (2057), East Mound, TR 5
2008 238	2087	See 2008 236
2008 241	2139-2164	Organic silty sand layer; hoof marks in surface, East Mound, TR 5
2008 247	2105	Spot sample of deposit of burning, yellow clay floor over charcoal layers (2022) related to metal working, East Mound
2010 A8	2119-2202-2203	(2119) tumble; disturbed wall material; (2202) dismantling debris, surface after metal-working area out of use; (2203) lower layer of dismantling debris/surface after metal-working area out of use, East Mound

Samples processed and discussed are indicated by being unshaded; the rest (shaded) remain unprocessed in archive. All descriptions are based on the context record from the project and the author's field notes upon sampling

of early woodland clearance in the area (Keatinge and Dickson 1979; Rackham *et al.* 1989).

The local machair dune landforms have been discussed by de la Vega Leinert *et al.* (2000), who found pre-dune sediments of blue-grey gritty clay under sequences of minerogenic peat and organic marl, and sandy silt and silty clay deposits. The later shell sands at the Bay of Skaill were described as coarse to medium well-sorted aeolian sands, with coarser 'tabular shell fragments'; inclusions of silt and clay-sized particles and lack of stratification in the dunes suggested to de la Vega Leinert *et al.* that there was little winnowing. A coarsening upward trend observed (*ibid.*) was interpreted as resulting from increased energy in the depositional environment over time, with the finer particles indicating reduced aeolian energy, and/or reduced supply of sand and/or freshwater flooding contributions. The impact of soil formation and later land use on this aspect was not discussed by those authors, who were focused primarily on the early phases of machair formation sequences. Presumably some of the fine fraction could also represent later leaching, which was seen in the relatively recent deposits in this study, which date from well within the last two millennia (see below).

Geoarchaeology and soil micromorphology sampling strategy

The geoarchaeological interest was multi-faceted, focusing on soil and sediment assessment at the sites and in the landscape, in a background of local information from geoarchaeological studies of preserved cultural sediments and soils (*e.g.* Card *et al.* 2007; Cluett 2007). Assessment for potential for studies of use-of-space and land use from the historic sites was conducted, and recommendations made based on availability of materials for sampling from the excavations. The sedimentary processes involved in mound development (see *e.g.* Davidson *et al.* 2007) were also preliminarily assessed through excavation and auger survey. In the context of this volume, geoarchaeological observation and sampling aimed to add an extra level of information to excavation-based observations, emphasising the nature and context of sediments exposed by excavation, soil and mound-formation processes, and the relationship of site deposits to the history of the wider landscape. This included inspection of excavation trenches at Snusgar and East Mound, recording and targeted sampling of deposits, small-scale targeted auger survey, and the opening of one small trench for geoarchaeological purposes: Trench 2 on Snusgar.

A series of block samples for soil micromorphology was taken from a variety of deposits and soils (Table 6.1); a set of these was produced and is reported on here, while a further group, considered to be of secondary importance to this stage of reporting, remain to be produced for future research. The thin sections were made by Julie Boreham at Earthslides, following the methodology outlined by Murphy (1986). They were analysed by the author at University College Dublin School of Archaeology using a Nikon Eclipse LV100 POL microscope, following the international guidelines presented by Bullock *et al.* (1985), in plane polarised (PPL), cross polarised (XPL) and oblique incident light (OIL). This chapter presents summary thin section descriptions. All field descriptions and excavation-based interpretations are based on the site context record created by the excavation teams or on the author's field notes, except where explicitly cited. All percentages are visual estimates of area.

Geoarchaeological assessment of the 'Castle of Snusgar' Mound (Trenches 1–4) and its immediate proximity

Excavations on Snusgar produced evidence of midden deposits, agricultural tool marks, and post-medieval kelp burning pits. Soil micromorphology samples were taken from a number of possible buried topsoil horizons exposed in the mound, and from midden and agricultural deposits seen within Trenches 1, 2 and 4 (Table 6.1). Of these, four profiles are discussed in more detail here: sample numbers 2004 14; 2004 18; 2006 contexts 1510-1547; and 2006 45. The first three samples represent typical midden and pit fill deposits seen across the upper mound, while the latter represents a set of tillage marks. Trench 2 was a small trench excavated at the easternmost fringe of the Snusgar mound in 2004, primarily for geoarchaeological purposes.

Trench 1 (incorporating Trench 3)

The earliest dated midden deposits on the sites, found in Trench 1 and associated with the remains of the longhouse, were studied in sample 2004 18 (Contexts 1017-1045-1035), dated to the late 9th-early 11th century AD. Context 1017 was associated with archaeobotanical remains of carbonised cereal grains (oats and barley mainly), small amounts of burnt peat, and rare seeds representing heath/moorland and arable/disturbed ground, as well as burnt seaweed and hammerscale (Chapter 8). Charcoal from this deposit gave a date of cal AD 880–1030 (SUERC-17847). Context 1045 was greyish brown and brown sand, with iron panning noted in the field in the greyish brown zones; this was interpreted as a midden or amended soil deposit (see Fig. 4.12). Charcoal from this deposit produced a date of cal AD 880–1020 (SUERC-17848). Unlike 1017, this deposit had less organic material found through flotation, with rare grains recorded (Chapter 8).

It is very difficult to distinguish between 1017 and 1045 microscopically, but the boundary between them appears to be marked by a linear pore infilling running near horizontally across much of the thin section. This is *c.* 1000 μm thick, and very dark reddish brown (PPL and XPL); in places it appears to be extremely organic and/or iron-stained, and there is a great deal of evidence for iron precipitation. This infilling appears to have accumulated through leaching and translocation.

Context 1017, like many of the midden layers studied (described below), comprises medium to coarse sand with fragments of soil, but it also includes discontinuous banded zones of very fine sand, silt and clay infillings. It is unclear from the thin section if this represents accumulation and depletion zones (a sorted infilling), or a floor type of deposit. There are occasional rounded and subrounded aggregates of yellow clay (PPL and XPL: 10–15%) with

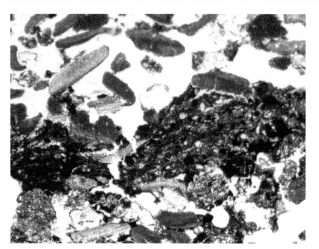 

Fig. 6.1: The boundary between (1045) and (1035) sands, with silty clay pore infilling. PPL (left) and XPL (right). Frame width: 2.5 mm. H. Lewis

densely packed silt grains (80%) and rare very fine sand (5–10%). These relatively well-sorted aggregates appear to be redeposited materials in this profile, with crystallitic fabric and inclusions of micro-organic matter and iron or manganese nodules. This deposit has a greater mixture of mineral components than seen in the other midden materials from the site (described below). There are sandstone fragments with calcareous cement, siltstone fragments, and rare possible chlorite grains. At the base of the layer the sediment becomes matrix-supported, with increased fine fraction, a close porphyric related distribution, and a porosity of 15% (packing pores). There are inclusions of red (PPL) plant remains in a laminar arrangement in pores, which may represent the burnt peat found in the archaeobotanical analysis (Chapter 8), but this is not definite without other diagnostic characteristics.

Context 1045 is similar to the lower part of 1017 being mainly matrix-supported, with mixed single grain and angular blocky structure, the latter being composed of coarse sand grains attached to each other by fine fraction bridges and cappings. The main differences are that overall the fine fraction component is greater, and porosity is both packing pores and interpedal channels (*c.* 100–200 × 1000 μm, straight, with uneven sides) as well as very small possible bone fragments (reddish brown PPL and XPL, <100 μm in size). There are angular and subrounded rock fragments of mixed quartz and calcareous siltstone with occasional very fine sand grains, and frequent iron lenses and nodules. 1045 has rare to occasional organic matter (beyond staining), including occasional charcoal fragments (up to 0.3 cm in size), less frequent than in 1017, as well as very small possible bone fragments (reddish brown PPL and XPL, <100 μm in size). These organic and bone fragments are mainly found mixed into the fine groundmass, but occasionally in pore spaces.

The boundary between 1045 and underlying sand 1035 is slightly undulating but very clear: a near horizontal zone *c.* 0.5 cm thick of medium and coarse sand with soil coatings, cappings, pendants and infillings. These pedofeatures are particularly concentrated in two very fine layers at the top and bottom of this boundary zone, and are organic-stained light to medium brown (PPL), orange to very dark brown (XPL) clay 50%, silt 40% and very fine and fine sand 10%, marking an accumulation zone for fine fraction materials within the overall medium to coarse sand deposit (Fig. 6.1). It is very likely that this represents a zone of structural and/or chemical change in the sandy soil profile. The feature is similar to boundaries seen at the base of Ap (tilled) horizons, at the bases and edges of implement mark cut features, and also at major boundaries of introduced and/or compacted deposits within leaching sands (Lewis 2012; Deak et al. 2017). The idea behind this is that while leaching can be ongoing up to the present day, something in the past created a change at this point in the profile, making this a location for redeposited (leached) material such as clay, silt, organic matter and iron. This often marks a major boundary in the soil, such as a horizon boundary, or a physical/structural boundary such as noted above. However, a change in rock fragment inclusion composition was also noted between 1045 and 1035, and this might have some significance here (see below). The boundary zone has 15% porosity (packing pores), and single grain with intergrain microaggregate structure, but it is matrix-supported.

Context 1035 was described in the field as clean yellow sand. It has single grain with intergrain microaggregate structure, with a porosity of 25–30% (packing pores). The layer comprises calcareous shell sand, including both shell fragments and grains that appear to originate from chalk or chalk-like sources, along with frequent quartz grains, coarse sand-sized rock fragments of quartz sandstones, and occasional quartz-based silt-stones (possibly chert/flint).

In addition there are frequent rounded and subrounded aggregates as described in 1045, of mainly quartz silt (60%) with clay (20%) and very fine quartz sand (20%), with a close porphyric relationship and crystallitic groundmass. In some cases these aggregates appear to be excremental, and probably relate to soil faunal activities. There are occasional <20 μm thick clay coatings, and frequent <10 μm thick calcium carbonate crystal coatings. This appears to be a natural sand layer, mixed with soil material through bioturbation. There are relatively frequent quartz inclusions in the layer, and of source rock fragments for quartz grains, and although most of these deposits were likely transported by wind, there are larger rock fragments (very coarse sand to small pebble sized), which could suggest either much stronger winds, or another means of transport. The meaning of the frequent quartz found here is not clear based on the study conducted to date, but it is a significant variation from the sediments found in the later deposits discussed above, which are mainly shell sand.

Trench 2 (Fig. 6.2)

This small, narrow trench was positioned on the eastern edge of Snusgar, where mound deposits tailed off into the surrounding flat landscape. Trench 2 was not expected to produce structural archaeology, although small features mainly of relatively recent date were encountered, most notably a kelping pit 504.

Late, probable Phase 9, midden deposits examined in thin section from Trench 2 include a sequence of contexts 506-507-508-510-502, sampled in three staggered blocks (samples 14/1-3; Figs 6.3 and 6.4). Context 506 was a pink sand layer underlying a set of spade marks, and overlying (507), the fill of an underlying pit. In thin section, the base of the spade marks comprises almost pure medium to coarse shell sand. There are clay coatings on grain edges, occasional siltstone and quartz sandstone rock fragments, and rare intergrain microaggregates (yellowish-brown (PPL and XPL), <300 μm in size). The porosity of this deposit is 30–45% (packing pores). Other frequently seen features include occasional reddish-brown soil infillings, cappings, coatings and pendants; these are clay (45%), silt (45%), and very fine sand (10%), stipple speckled and organic stained. These types of features represent soil disturbance and leaching and it is likely that they reflect the impact of the digging represented by the spade marks, and/or subsequent disturbance.

Pink sand layer 506 is denser (25% porosity), with frequent infillings and intergrain aggregates of reddish brown clay (PPL and XPL). The main fabric is a loam (medium, fine and very fine sand 50%, silt 20%, clay 30%), and has a granostriated to stipple speckled groundmass. The pink colour of this layer seems solely related to the clay infillings and aggregates; there is no evidence of iron panning or of any combustion features. However, a similar layer below, context 508, was related structurally to burning evidence, and it is possible that 506 also reflects oxidisation of clay-rich soil (*e.g.* burning of clay-rich turf).

Context 507 is greyish brown medium to coarse sand pit fill, overlying 508, and is composed of essentially the same materials as 506, comprising sand with intergrain microaggregates, some found coating grains, but with a porosity of 50%. Other major differences include rare earthworm calcitic granules, attesting to some bioturbation of the deposits. There are rare fragments of brown siltstone with angular coarse silt to very fine sand inclusions, and some particulate organic matter (5%), mainly charcoal fragments (<200 μm, rarely up to 500 μm, in size). These likely originate from a charcoal deposit at the top of layer 508.

At the base of 507 is a sharp, slightly undulating boundary marked macroscopically by colour change and a line of black material. The latter is a zone *c.* 500 μm thick of intermittent charcoal, which appears to be on the surface of 508. Charcoal fragments are frequently found within the upper 0.5 cm of 508, presumably from this deposit. 508 comprises a set of (oxidised) layers of reddened sand. This was interpreted in the field as a possible B horizon underlying a tilled soil, but the microscopic characteristics suggest it is actually a combustion zone, physically overlying 502 (Fig. 6.4). As with 506, the colour of this layer appears to relate mainly to the soil inclusions: the layer becomes less pink (and has fewer soil inclusions) with depth.

Based on the thin section evidence of this sequence, the deposits appear to represent the base of a tilled and otherwise disturbed soil which has seen a great deal of leaching. This soil appears to have grown on top of a pit that may have been related to a combustion event, which is also seen in underlying 510. Black silty sand layer 510, which also overlay 502, comprises frequent micrite and charcoal, the latter mostly very fragmented, but occasionally up to *c.* 1 cm in size, and represents localised burning or hearth rake-out. The finding of micrite in pore spaces was not seen in the other deposits examined, despite the presence of calcareous sands, and in a context with frequent charcoal this could suggest it is related to the other burning indicators seen, particularly to burnt wood. Context 510 also has rare earthworm granules, attesting to some post-depositional bioturbation, and soil fragments and infillings as seen in 507. This layer does not appear to be oxidised (it is not reddened), although it is the most likely of all the deposits described thus far to represent an *in situ* burning episode.

Underlying Context 502 was described in the field as 'clean' yellow sand, but this has frequent soil aggregates within it, mostly crystallitic, and calcareous infillings in pore spaces; the latter further represent disturbance to the overlying profile.

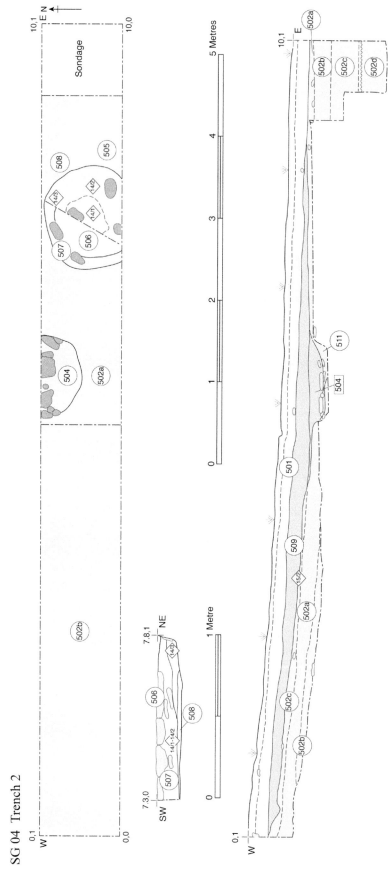

Fig. 6.2: Trench 2, plan and sections: middle section shows location of samples (colour code Fig. 4.43)

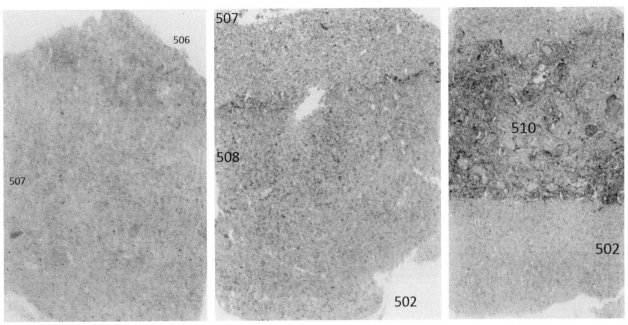

Fig. 6.3: Trench 2, Scanned images of thin sections 14/1 (left), 14/2 (centre), 14/3 (right). Original size: 14/1–2 6 × 10 cm, 14/3 6 × 12 cm. H. Lewis

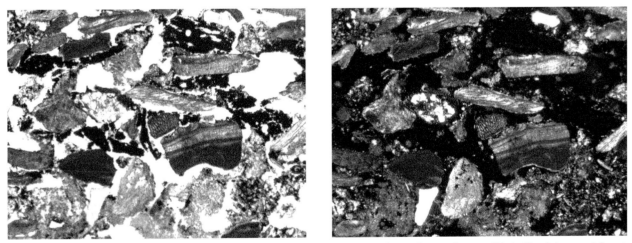

Fig. 6.4: Trench 2, combustion zone features between contexts 507–508, showing charcoal micro-layer visible in Fig. 6.4 centre (above). Reddened microaggregates in 508 can be seen in the lower right corner. Frame width: 2.5 mm; PPL (left) and XPL (right). H. Lewis

Trench 4

The upper part of the Snusgar mound in Trench 4 comprised a series of well-defined midden layers. Context 1508 (ash-rich midden layer) was seen to be overlying a series of implement (possible plough) marks (see below), dating to Phase 3 (10th to mid-11th century). The majority of the aggregates are calcareous (see above regarding calcareous inclusions), but possible peat and/or turf material was seen in thin section. Most of the mineral material in the sample comprises calcareous aggregates and similarly-sized shell sand grains, but unlike underlying layer 1509 (see below), this sand layer has relatively low porosity (30–40%), and occasional dark brown (organic stained) coatings and cappings of grains. Other components include rare micro-fragments of bone, reddened ('rubified') aggregates, rare sand-sized rock fragments of a very strong yellow colour (PPL and XPL) with internal iron nodules, and rare sandstone fragments with iron cement.

Organic components include occasional very fine sand and silt-sized charcoal fragments, and frequent smaller micro-charcoal and 'punctuations', with rare intact plant tissue. At the base of the sample is dark greyish brown (PPL), very dark brown to black (XPL) soil material,

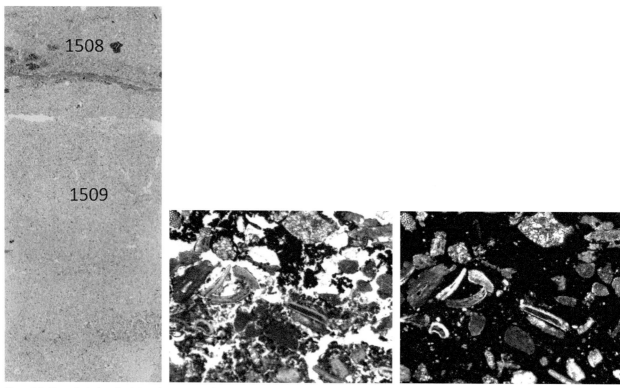

Fig. 6.5: Trench 4, leached fine fraction and iron accumulation zone at the boundary between 1508–1509, and the reddened nature of some of the sediments in the boundary zone. Left: scanned image; original size 6 × 14 cm. Micrograph frame width 2.5 mm, PPL (centre), XPL (right). H. Lewis

with very low birefringence (almost undifferentiated, but stipple speckled, with occasional individual clay zones visible). This material is clay-sized mineral and organic matter (40%), silt (50%) and very fine to fine sand (10%), with occasional possible charcoal fragments. In some places this material is red to reddish brown (PPL & XPL), with very low birefringence, and appears 'rubified' (oxidised, in this case possibly through burning; Fig. 6.5).

Peat was found in the archaeobotanical study (Chapter 8) and much of the black and red material seen in thin section could represent this, but it is not 'ashed' (calcified or silicified), and there is definitely some soil present in the material described above. Burnt peat interpreted as hearth material has been described from a Viking Age building by Dufeu (n.d., 10) as comprising '…rubified fine material (red), …ash, charred…turf and plant residues… (and) small fragments of bones', and at Quoygrew, Simpson *et al.* (2005) found mineral inclusions (in that case of quartz grains) in material interpreted as burnt turf. Turf is likely to have some type of clay fabric, such as that seen at Snusgar, and while the 1508 material appears to be rubified (PPL, OIL) much of it does not appear to be peat. Burnt turf has been distinguished from burnt peat at Belmont through experimental charring (Hamlet and Simpson, n.d.), but no images were presented

in that study for comparison to the Snusgar material. In studies from more recent periods in the region, 'fuel residues' (carbonised organic material with rubified mineral material) and turf (non-carbonised organics) are known to have been built up into middens linked with particular types of arable farming (*e.g.* kailyards), and variations reflecting peaty and more mineral turves are discussed (Adderley *et al.* 2006). Milek (2012) notes pink peat ash at Thvera in an ethnoarchaeological study, which shows clear structural features of peat (unlike the material here), as well as describing very reddened 'turf' soil within the floor sequences studied. Finally, at Gasir microlayers of brown, reddish brown, dark brown, pink and red silty and sandy loams and peat ash, all with inclusions of peat ash, carbonised and decomposing plant remains are interpreted as reflecting hearth rake-out material (Guðmundsdóttir Beck 2011), and proposed to represent Gé *et al.*'s (1993) 'polyphased occupation surfaces'. The peat ash samples in that study have a very organic structure, and reveal organic remains and diatoms, unlike the remains seen here. Given the overall findings from the thin section and the archaeobotany, the 1508 midden material appears to represent a mixed deposit of peat and turf material, or of peaty turves, burned at low temperature. Iron oxides form at *c.* 400°C, while higher temperatures (above 550°C) would lead to loss of organic components (Courty *et al.* 1989; Canti and Linford 2000).

The mixed nature of the Snusgar midden deposits, which was very clear in the field, is also expressed through the variation seen in the thin section samples. Context 1518 is interpreted as a Phase 2 midden deposit, dating to the late 9th–early 11th centuries, with a date on a charred barley grain of cal AD 900–1040 (SUERC-18265). This is a dense soil layer with frequent very fine and very well-preserved, highly-fragmented plant remains and charcoal (10–15% organic components). The soil is clayey silt (35% clay, 50% silt, 15% medium sand), with a medium brown (PPL) and very dark brown to undifferentiated (XPL) groundmass, with clay in a stipple speckled organisation. The material has an angular blocky structure, with 3 cm sized aggregates and 15–20% porosity (channels and packing pores). This type of mixed soil and organic deposit was seen in several places in the mound. Whether or not this is burnt turf or peaty soil is not clear; the very rich dark brown colour of these types of deposits is not typical of a naturally growing *in situ* soil layer, despite its clear soil characteristics, and possibly represents soil material mixed with and influenced by the other types of materials found in the midden.

Context 1547 was interpreted as a Phase 2 midden layer structured by stone. This deposit is very similar to overlying 1518 in structure (angular blocky, 3–7 cm sized aggregates) and texture, but with more frequent organic components (15–20%, up to 40% in some places), including more charcoal and more plant remains, and including modern spores, indicating more recent bioturbation. There are bone inclusions, and zones of soil depleted in both iron and organic matter; these depleted zones appear mainly to be infillings in pore spaces. The fabric is highly organic stained, and there are frequent 'dusty' clay coatings in pores and on grains; this clay is orange (XPL) where not covered with organic staining, with moderate birefringence, and is non-laminated. Depletion, infillings and clay coatings are all representative of leaching and translocation of materials under the impact of rainwater, possibly representing all periods from original deposition of the soil material in that location up to the time of sampling. The fact that these are not seen in the overlying midden layer could reflect some impact of disturbance related to that midden, such as its deposition or later disruption (*e.g.* through tilling), but it could also indicate later processes. 'Dusty' clay suggests relatively strong disturbance of aggregate bonds, and is frequently found on archaeological sites with arable farming, construction, vegetation clearance and other disruptive physical impacts on the soil (*e.g.*Courty *et al.* 1989).

I consider that the variations seen here relate mainly to the materials involved in the midden deposits; *i.e.*

that most or all of these deposits, with the exception of the calcareous aggregates and mineral sands, represent industrial or domestic combustion processes, but of a range of materials – wood, turf (including some clay-rich turf), and probably peat, although no clearly identified peat was discovered in these thin sections. As such, these thin sections confirm the field interpretations, with slight additions to the specifics of the details of each interpreted layer. Due to the small numbers of samples per trench and phase, it is impossible to state whether the variations seen reflect changing activities over time, different depositional processes on different parts of the mound, or simply variations in the natural and preservation environments in different locations.

Agricultural contexts at Snusgar: Trench 4

A set of implement (probably plough) marks was studied in Trench 4 on Snusgar (Fig. 6.6, see also Fig. 4.15). The agricultural sequence investigated in the field comprises contexts 1509, 1554 – the implement marks – and 1581. The thin section study of the base of overlying midden 1508 is discussed above. The plough marks underlay and were partially filled by aeolian sand layer 1509 which was seen in the field to comprise two fine layers: 1) 5–10 cm of white blown sand, and 2) 5–10 cm of grey, slightly organic sand, the latter interpreted as a possible old topsoil horizon in the field.

In thin section, 1509 is a well-sorted deposit of medium to coarse shell sand, and calcareous aggregates of the same size with internal quartz grains. This loose sediment (*c.* 50% packing pores) contains almost no organic matter, with very rare micro-charcoal and rare soil micro-aggregates. The inclusion of quartz in the calcareous aggregates suggests that they originated from somewhere not immediate to this location, and possibly

Fig. 6.6: Trench 4, implement marks (plan, Fig. 4.15) north sign approx. 30 cm

represent a natural deposit (possibly even very calcareous soil material) from elsewhere in the nearby landscape. Similar aggregates were also found in the overlying 1508 deposit interpreted in the field as part of a 'midden with ash', but do not appear to be combustion remains, and are here interpreted as part of the natural landscape. Given their similar size to the shell sand grains in this deposit, it appears that they may also have had an aeolian origin. Archaeobotanical study (see Chapter 8) found no identifiable material.

The implement marks 1554 cut into a <5 cm thick horizon of dark brownish red sand 1581. The marks were clearly seen as greyish-white sand-filled features. Feature 1554 comprised five furrows, labelled A–E. The features tended to have one straight side and one irregular side, and the straight sides alternated (on the right in one mark, on the left in its neighbour etc.), as if the plough were turned around to create the return furrow. The bases of the marks were exposed in plan, and some complete marks were also visible in the western section of the trench. The mark dimensions were 10–15 cm wide at the surviving tops, 10–12 cm deep. No ridges were visible. This phase of ploughing appears to have been short-lived, and no evidence of inter- or cross-cutting marks was seen, but truncation is likely given the absence of ridge remains.

Upon excavation, although the fills were mainly 1509, a few fragments and fine layers of the immediately underlying contexts were seen as inclusions. Clods of 1581 occurred both on top of and under/around marks, suggesting that it was directly associated with the marks as the lower part of a plough zone, and also that mouldboard inversion was seen in a couple of the features, bringing aggregates of this underlying layer into the top of the features. 1581 belongs to Phase 2 (Late 9th–early 11th century AD), and was distinguished by being slightly more organic than 1509.

In thin section, context 1581 is similar to 1509, including the sand and calcareous aggregates, but with soil coatings, including bridges and cappings, on sand grains. Although still of a similar porosity, it has a higher fine fraction proportion, and that fraction is mainly clay and very fine silt, organic stained, with very low birefringence. This layer also contains rare to occasional charcoal fragments. Fine organic coatings are common in well-drained soils seeing strong leaching, with deposition frequently seen at the base of implement marks or tilled soil horizons (Lewis 2012); this translocation of fine materials from above could have happened at any time from the original deposition of the sand layer, including from any topsoil disturbed by the later plough marks. Given the fact that the main constituents of 1581 are the same as those of 1509, it appears that the source of these materials remained the same during these phases – presumably beaches in the vicinity.

The general picture of arable farming and 'farmstead' settlement at Snusgar correlates with discoveries at Birsay (*e.g.* Beachview: Rackham 1996), which also showed collection and burning of seaweed, turf and peat. Plough and ard marks, and possible buried cultivation soils have been found at other sites in the area, dating from at least the Bronze Age (*e.g.* Simpson *et al.* 1998, Rackham and Young 1989) and from other Norse period sites, such as Freswick Links (Morris *et al.* 1995). Regarding the Norse sites, tillage is commonly found very close to farmstead buildings, and ploughing of midden material is often seen.

Buried soil at Snusgar: Trench 4

The Trench 4 extension was excavated in 2005 to expose the edge of the dune mound, and to allow the excavation of a deep sounding through the depths of clean sand found by auger testing in the base of trenches in 2004, underlying the historic cultural deposits on top of the mound. The deep sounding showed that mound topsoil overlay *c.* 1.5 m of alternating medium to coarse yellow and grey sand layers, devoid of obvious cultural remains, which appeared to be windblown and influenced by leaching post-depositionally.

Under the sand towards the mound centre, two organic soil layers were exposed, separated by a thin layer of blown sand, each *c.* 5–8 cm thick. Context 1536a comprised grey sandy silt loam, overlying yellow sand layer 1536b, and appeared to be an old, leached topsoil layer growing on a thin layer of blown sand. A date on a cormorant bone from 1536 was 1710 ± 35 BP (SUERC-17851). Under context 1536b was 1537, a layer of slightly purple greyish-brown silt loam. This also appeared to be an old organic horizon, presumably another thin topsoil layer, which overlay layer 1538, site 'natural'. 1538 gave an OSL date of 2015 ± 210 years BP (SG06-19) (Chapter 5). A Dutch soil auger was put into the excavated base of context 1538, and revealed a further 90 cm depth of yellow and grey 'sterile' sand layers, becoming more grey and wet with depth. The water table was reached at this point (see Fig. 4.3). One soil micromorphology block (sample 2005 11) was taken from this sequence, along with one small bulk sample from each of the buried soil layers for future analysis. The deposits have been phased to pre-Viking Phase 1.

The buried soil layers under Snusgar appeared to have been substantially influenced by the mound, which has undoubtedly compacted them towards the centre, creating the impression that they turn upwards towards the edge of the mound presumably because towards the centre the layers have been pushed downward. The sudden ending of the layers at the mound edge, and the fact that they do not continue down the sides of the mound, suggests that the area adjacent to the later sand mound formation was disturbed or eroded away. It is possible that this erosion relates to ancient and/or modern land use, but no further suggestion of any disturbance, stripping or tilling was seen in profile outside of the mound.

A further auger hole was drilled into the centre of the mound in Trench 4 at its deepest exposed point in 2006 for comparison to the buried soil profile 1536 revealed at the edge of the mound. This revealed 35 cm of yellow sand (under base of mound), over 10 cm of light grey sand on 20 cm of yellow clayey sand (buried soil profile), over 40 cm of grey waterlogged sand with patches of yellow sand and iron stained roots (this equates to *c.* 1.05 m depth from the ground surface). The overall sequence is the same as that seen nearer the edge of the mound and the depths of the buried soil are generally comparable, taking into account the evidence of compaction and tilting of the buried soil layers at the edge of the mound seen in 2005. However, this profile is significantly different due to the presence of a clayey layer in the buried soil. It is difficult to say at present whether the clayey yellow sand layer is part of an initial buried soil profile (*e.g.* a B horizon) which was subsequently lost 'outside' the mound through disturbance and/or increased leaching away of clay due to more exposure to the elements, or whether this clay has translocated under the mound over time through increased clay supply, related to the overlying midden and burning deposits, which, as noted above, include clay-rich soil materials. Unlike the central part of the mound, the slope was primarily sand with stones, and this variation would obviously have had an impact on clay availability for leaching.

A layer of pebbles followed the mound contour and correlated with a stony occupation or construction layer on the mound site, and may represent an early phase in the occupation activity on top of the mound. However, there is some evidence of soil macrofaunal (earthworm) activity in various deposits on Snusgar (see above), and it seems possible that this might in part represent a stone line from faunal sorting.

The general depositional sequence (not matrix) seen at Snusgar through the geoarchaeological assessment is shown in Table 6.2, from the top downwards.

Geoarchaeological assessment of East Mound (Trenches 5 and 7) and its immediate proximity

Trench 5: Buried soils

As in the upper parts of Snusgar Trench 1, relatively organic soil horizons were found high up within and over the cultural deposits in Trench 5. Excavation in this trench revealed that a thick layer of blown sand 2012 within the latest Phase 6 ancillary structure appeared to correlate with a relatively thin layer outside (blown sand 2001); in both cases, these sand layers were immediately under the topsoil profile. The upper sequences in Trench 5 (2005 sections 6–9) revealed modern topsoil (Ah)

Table 6.2: General depositional sequence (not matrix) seen at Snusgar through geoarchaeological assessment, from the top downwards

Description
Modern topsoil
Clean sand (probably windblown)
Thin midden deposits and yellow sand
1509 greyish white buried topsoil
Ploughmarks 1554
1581 midden
Midden layers, stone layers, burnt layers with clay patches at base
Pit 1568 (with burnt 'peat' identified in the field)
Clean sand (probably windblown)
1570
1576
Clean sand (probably windblown) – forming main mound dune
Buried soil profiles 1536/1537
Clean sand (probably windblown)
Sand (waterlogged) with oxidation of roots

overlying a layer of yellow sand 2001, over layers 2002, 2006 and 2028, all dark grey sand with some silt; these buried slightly organic layers appeared to abut the structural remains found in the trench, and probably represent soils growing during phases of stabilisation of the blown sand deposits covering the structures. Overall, the soils evidence suggests that the final 'burial' of some structural areas occurred only relatively recently (the date of the last major sand deposition), and parts of the buildings survived for some time after abandonment as a ruin or earthwork at the surface. Buried soil (*e.g.* contexts 2006, 2024) was seen underneath blown sand on the uphill side of the trench, but not on the downhill side, suggesting some variation in retention of deposits.

Another possible buried soil was also discovered (sample 2007/169, Phase 8, context 2104: Fig. 6.7); this was a 25 cm thick dark greyish brown sand layer underlying the uppermost layer of windblown sand, context 2001, over context 2084. One soil micromorphology sample was taken from the uppermost boundary where 2104 met 2001, which gave OSL dates of 185 ± 130 (SG06-20) and 170 ± 45 years BP (SG06-21) (Chapter 5). Context 2001 is medium to coarse yellow sand, with dark reddish brown 'dirty' clay coatings <5–20 μm thick, laminated where thicker, and includes some calcareous soil fragments as described previously, along with aggregates of underlying context 2104. Context 2104 has the same components,

SG 07 Trench 5
Section 8

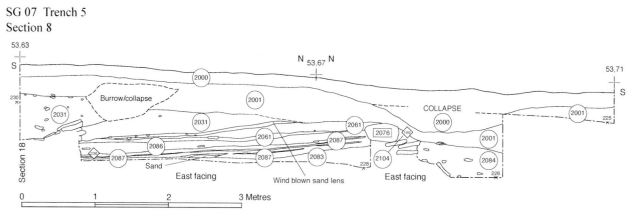

Fig. 6.7: Trench 5, section showing Sample 169 in upper context (2104), under blown sand (2001) and over (2084); sample 236 is shown to the left

but with organic-stained soil coatings and cappings, and frequent small subrounded to rounded aggregates of medium brown soil with silt and very fine sand, as well as calcareous aggregates. This soil profile has 30–35% porosity (increasing with depth to 50%) of packing pores, mixed enaulic and gefuric related distributions, and very rare organic fragments (<100 μm), including some possible charcoal.

Other field observations focused on some agricultural remains, such as the Phase 6 organic layer within the byre end of the main longhouse with hoof marks (apparently of cattle) in its surface (contexts 2239-2164). Beyond its organic nature in the field, this deposit was not seen to be typical of stabling, showing no horizontal lamination, no crusting or panning layers, no trampling indicators, and no obvious dung. It seemed more likely that this was a soil horizon, with an increased organic nature related to temporary animal stalling in a yard; this may have been after abandonment of the longhouse as an intact structure.

Trench 5: Samples from Phase 3–5 floors and surfaces

Several possible floors/surfaces were sampled and these are interpreted in the following sections. Floors 2077-2080 in the earliest ancillary building contexts (Phases 3–4) were investigated with samples 2007 167, 177 and 178; in the metal working yard just to the west with Sample 2008 247, context 2105 (Phase 3); from the later yard in the same area with Sample 2010 A8 (Phase 3); contexts 2119-2202-2203 (Phase 5); and from the yard/area to the north with samples 2007 168 and 2008 236, contexts 2086-2087 (Phase 5).

SAMPLES FROM FLOOR LAYERS IN THE ANCILLARY BUILDING

Soil micromorphology sampling of Phase 3–4 floor layers within the ancillary buildings focused primarily on a series

SG 07 Trench 5
Section 7

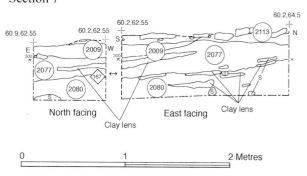

Fig. 6.8: Trench 5, section showing the series of alternating yellow clay and sand layers, interpreted as series of laid floors; Sample 167 position shown (samples 177 and 178 also taken from these layers)

of clay layers, apparently laid floors or structural deposits, associated with early Phase 3 walls 2122-2172 and the Phase 4 remodelling (Table 6.1, samples 2007 167, 177 and 178; Fig. 6.8). Next to and apparently associated with the earliest walls was a series of at least three 2–4 cm thick yellow clay layers separated by sand deposits. Some of these layers were only intermittently seen in plan on excavation, but were extremely clear in profile, where they seemed to be laid floor deposits. In 2008, the areas were re-examined, including a series of apparent clay floors associated with the early building phase. Section profiles appeared to confirm that the clay layers were restricted in horizontal space to an area bounded by and related to the walls of the earliest building phase seen by that date.

Context 2077 was described in the field as a yellow sand layer overlying 2080, which was thought to be disturbed residual material, possibly redeposited. A

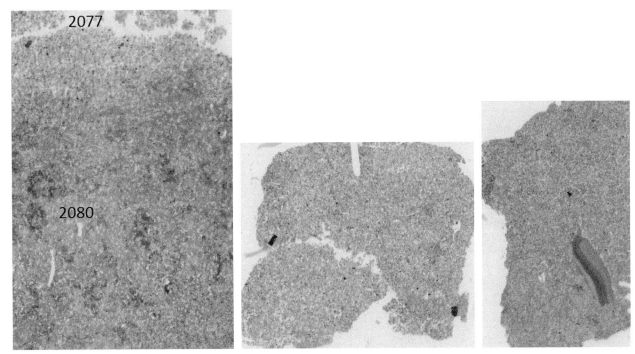

Fig. 6.9: Trench 5, sample 167: sandy 2077 overlying clay-rich 2080. Scales: scanned image (left) original size 6 × 14 cm; Sample 177, context 2080A (centre) scanned image, original size 5 × 8 cm; and sample 178, context 2080B (right), original size 5 × 8 cm. H. Lewis

radiocarbon date on (residual) barley grain from this layer was cal AD 770–980 (SUERC-24701).

Context 2077 was a mixture of sand, calcareous aggregates and soil aggregates, all subrounded, well-sorted, and medium-coarse sand sized, suggesting that perhaps all of the main deposit material was originally deposited through the same process, most likely wind-blown sea sand accumulated as part of dune formation (Fig. 6.9). The soil aggregates are yellow-brown (PPL), light reddish brown (XPL), stipple speckled, with medium and fine sand (15%), silt (60%) and clay (25%), iron-staining and densely packed, with 5% porosity (channels/vughs) internally. Overall the porosity is *c.* 20% (packing pores). Some parts of the deposit have yellow-coloured (PPL) zones related to the frequency of these materials, and showing frequent iron-stained very 'dusty' to 'dirty' clay coatings in all voids, relating to disturbance, leaching and illuviation; in some places there are iron hypocoatings and pendants associated with sand grains. There are also zones with frequent infillings of the calcareous-rich fine sand matrix seen in some of the aggregates noted above, suggesting disaggregation of some of the aggregates and leaching/re-deposition. In the layer as a whole, organic matter is *c.* 2% (extremely small (<1 mm) black fragments, possibly charcoal, with very rare larger charred and iron-replaced fragments (up to *c.* 1.5 mm). Besides the very rare charcoal, there is no cultural material in, or obvious cultural impact upon, this deposit. It is not simply a yellow

sand layer but a deposit of mixed origin, and has been subject to strong impact from overlying disturbed and leaching deposits.

Context 2080 was a clay layer underlying 2077 and overlying a lens of yellow sand. In this discussion, the layer is divided into 2080a-2080b to reflect the microstratigraphy, which shows two clay-rich layers separated by a thin sand layer. 2080 has a date on a barley grain of cal AD 990–1160 (SUERC-24705).

2080A comprised sand with clay-rich soil aggregates. There were also very rare possibly phosphatic deposits, which appear as a kind of cloudy wash of amorphous material. 2080B is a dense clay-rich layer, which is yellowish brown (PPL and XPL), low birefringent stipple-speckled clay (30%) with frequent silt-sized organic and/or iron or manganese 'punctuations' (50%) and silt, very fine, fine and medium sand (20%). Porosity in this layer is <5%, and there are indicators of iron staining and iron-replaced recent root remains. Red (PPL) platy very fine plant fragments are frequently seen. This layer is *c.* 3 cm thick in thin section, and is very different from anything else described thus far; it truly appears to be a clay layer, although it is non-laminated, and might represent a laid clay floor deposit. After this depth, the layer grades into a medium to coarse sand deposit, with frequent clay-rich soil fragments. With depth in the underlying sand layer (no number), the amount of fine matrix decreases, but the clasts are still matrix supported, and porosity is still only about 10–15% (packing pores, possible channels). Charcoal increases with depth, from 5% very fine fragments in the uppermost deposit, to 5–10% (fragments up to *c*. 100 *μ*m), with cellular structure, in the lower part of the thin section.

In this small sequence there appeared to be the history of a clay floor laid on a sandy layer, then probably trampled and exposed, with evidence of some input from phosphatic compounds (possibly leached into the upper layer); this all underlies what appears to be a sedimentary deposit of mixed materials, well sorted and probably deposited together, or at least by the same process creating the sorting, with the only cultural materials being probably redeposited – possibly an abandonment/infill deposit.

SAMPLES FROM THE METALWORKING YARD AND AREA/YARD TO THE NORTH OF THE METALWORKING YARD

1. THE METALWORKING YARD AND LATER YARD IN THE SAME AREA
Immediately on the south side of the yard wall (running west–east to the west of the ancillary building), one sample was taken from Phase 3 context 2105 – Sample 2008 247 (Fig. 6.10). This deposit was a series of 1–2 mm thick layers of spatially discontinuous burnt materials (charcoal, burnt peat, possible burnt clay) with frequent inclusions of metalworking slag, and a willow fragment from this deposit was dated to cal AD 890–1030 (SUERC-24716).

The thin section shows a very dark brown (PPL and XPL) fine matrix with frequent charcoal (up to 1 cm in size), apparently randomly distributed. Although a clay layer was noted by the author within 2105 in the field, no obvious clay layer is seen in the thin section. The sample comprises a number of mixed fabrics, in zones of various sizes. Boundaries between the zones are sharp and often

marked by pore space (packing pores), suggesting these are aggregates mixed together from a variety of origins, including hearth materials, soil or turf materials, and possibly peat. There is a relatively large and somewhat altered bone fragment in one area. The mixed fabrics seen include: 1) wood ash and/or micrite-rich zones with sand, silt and frequent charcoal, with a crystallitic groundmass; 2) light reddish brown (PPL), orange (XPL) clay-supported, iron-influenced soil material (45% clay, 35% silt, 20% very fine, fine and medium sand), with granostriated groundmass and very rare, very fine charcoal; 3) very dark brown to black, stipple-speckled to opaque, organic matter stained and organic-rich loams which are very densely packed, include medium to coarse sand, and with frequent charcoal; 4) the matrix material noted in 3) is also seen as coatings on medium to coarse sand in zones with single grain structure, 40% porosity (packing pores) and frequent charcoal; and 5) depleted fabric zones, light grey (PPL), dark grey to black (XPL) with stipple speckled or undifferentiated groundmass, size sorted with only silt and very fine sand grains, in close to open porphyric related distribution with the fine clay fabric. These zones are often subrounded to subangular, and show calcareous deposits of fabric type 1) in between them, and may be related to faunal activity or redeposited from an area of depleted soil.

Although treated as one context, and clearly very mixed in the thin section, some parts of 2105 may represent a floor layer. In particular, although it was not caught by the thin section sample, an extensive, although discontinuous, deposit of yellow clay (up to 1–1.5 cm thick in places) was noted in the field during sampling, and appeared to be typical of floor deposits located near to a furnace or hearth, with frequent charcoal inclusions often appearing

SG 08 Trench 5
Section 30

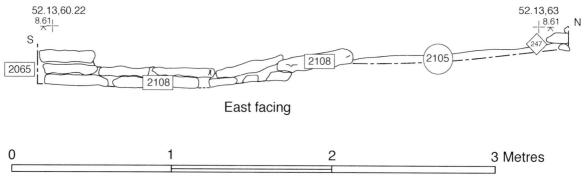

Fig. 6.10: Trench 5, section showing location of Sample 247 just south of wall 2057 on right

Table 6.3: Stratified deposits contained in sample 2010 A8, listed from the top of the sample down, and phased to the 11th–12th century

Context no.	Macroscopic description
2119	3–4 cm thick brown sand layer with frequent charcoal
	Fragments of clay and unidentified red inclusions
217	Yellow sand layer
2202	1 cm thick layer of moist black silt and charcoal, lumps of grey-yellow clay, and fine layers and zones of red sandy clay
	This context was associated with frequent metal slag.
2203	Yellow-brown sand layer

trampled in, deposited as rake-out or possibly as a floor lining proper. The context produced a large assemblage of charcoal; the material suggested both rake-out deposits and wood storage for use (see Chapter 8). Charcoal and ash are well known to have been used in early historic times in northern Europe as floor coverings, apparently for hygiene purposes (against smells, insects).

Immediately adjacent to this series of deposits, and separated by a 'gap' in the wall structures surrounding it, was a profile of thin layers of iron panning and windblown sand, apparently only slightly affected by the depositional processes seen 'inside' and adjacent to the metalworking hearths. Wall 2057 survived as narrow stone foundations and the two sampled areas were apparently not separated by much of a structure. However, some turf was also seen in the wall's upper courses in the field descriptions, suggesting it was originally more substantial, with a turf component.

An additional soil micromorphology sample was taken from later floors within the metalworking area, which post-dated the metalworking activities. Sample 2010 A8 contained the stratified deposits discussed below, listed from the top of the sample down, and phased to the 11th–12th century AD (Table 6.3).

Contexts 2119 and 2202 were found to contain some burnt cereal grains and small amounts of burnt peat, but mainly produced a lot of willow charcoal. The charcoal amount suggested the refuse came from the metalworking that had occurred previously in the same area (Chapter 8). A willow charcoal fragment from the layer was dated to cal AD 970–1150 (SUERC-47149).

Layer 2202 was composed of charcoal fragments and large zones of amorphous organic matter (50%), medium to coarse sand grains (30%) with soil coatings, and aggregates (20%) of various types noted previously: calcareous, red clay-rich, dark brown and medium brown

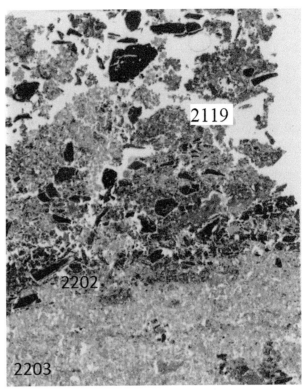

Fig. 6.11: Trench 5, Sample 2010 A8, scanned image (original 4 × 6 cm) H. Lewis

soil aggregates (Fig. 6.11). There are very oxidised iron-rich zones of very strong red (PPL and XPL) stipple speckled clay (60%) with very fine sand and silt (30%), and rare medium to coarse sand (10%), iron impregnation of plant remains, and iron and/or manganese nodule formation in the deposit. These components have been seen in the midden deposits described from Snusgar, and the floor sequences already described, but in this case they are mixed with a great deal of burnt organic material; while there was no structure visible, the amorphous organic matter zones could be interpreted as also representing peat, as noted in the archaeobotany.

The boundary with underlying layer 2203 is clearly marked by a thin layer of charcoal and brown soil, which is contiguous across the thin section. The layering seen in the charcoal suggests this may have been just one fragment of wood. Its position and the nature of the underlying material (see below) suggest perhaps it fell onto this location, as there is no indication of *in situ* firing in this particular place. Rather, this deposit could originally have comprised rake-out deposits from a nearby burning feature, fitting the field description and archaeobotany interpretation.

Context 2203 was described as a later surface after the metalworking area went out of use. It was also very mixed, mainly calcareous sands, calcareous aggregates, zones of the brown soil fabric noted above, and zones of depleted soil. There is occasional charcoal (up to 1.5 mm), and many sand grains have clay or soil coatings. Besides the charcoal and this mixing there is little cultural about it. One small patch in the lower part of the thin section has a lot of charcoal and iron-rich material, perhaps showing mixing in of some 2202.

2. SAMPLES FROM THE AREA/YARD TO THE NORTH OF THE METALWORKING AREA

To the north of the metalworking area, there was an additional area of spatially-delimited possible external surfaces. These covered a depth, as exposed at time of recording, of *c*. 40 cm, and included a sequence of at least ten layers separated by yellow wind-blown sand deposits. Some of the layers appeared similar to layers previously excavated associated with kelp burning (red silt and sand layers), while others comprised compacted grey silt (possibly ash) and grey-brown clay as noted in the metalworking area. There appeared to be some leached layers and iron panning. In this case, however, it was unclear macroscopically if the reddening seen in these layers represented illuviated iron oxide deposits on sand grains, or simply oxidised sand from burning. That issue may be clarified through future thin section study.

Samples 2007/168 and 2008/236, from contexts 2086 and 2087, were taken from the yard area north of the metalworking yard (Fig. 6.12; position at southern limit of Fig. 4.9).

Context 2087 was described in the field as a buried cultural deposit in the field, of grey ashy clay with charcoal, burnt sediment, rich brown clay and windblown sand layers. Only a few cereal and burnt peat remains were noted (see Chapter 8). Context 2086 is part of these layers, being one of the overlying blown sand layers. The contexts are described below as a series of micro-

layers of similar deposits: for example, six layers were seen in sample 236. These deposits occurred in repeated sequences, separated by sand layers, suggesting either repeated storm events, and/or that sand was laid down as part of floor/surface construction sequence. No clear trampling indicators were seen, but the relative density of the soil layers (described as A below), with only *c*. 15% porosity, could perhaps be interpreted as a compaction indicator for the sites studied here, where porosity is generally higher. Sample 236, contexts 2086 and 2087, Fig. 6.13 showed the following layers from top to bottom, in a repeated sequence of soil material on top of a thin layer of organic matter (charcoal and/or burnt peat), over a layer of sand with soil microaggregates:

A) Very dense stipple speckled soil fabric, with zones of yellow clay; texture: clay 30%, silt 40%, very fine sand 5%, fine sand 5%, medium sand 15%, coarse sand 5%. Porosity: 15%, channels (some with iron-replaced root remains inside, 200–500 μm diameter, <500 μm long, accommodated to partially accommodated) and vertical cracks (1000 μm wide × 1.5 cm long, straight); organic matter: 5–10%

SG 07 Trench 5
Section 18

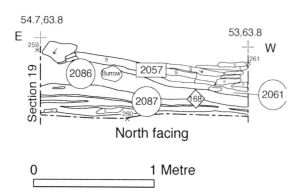

North facing

0   1 Metre

Fig. 6.12: Trench 5, section showing the location of Sample 168

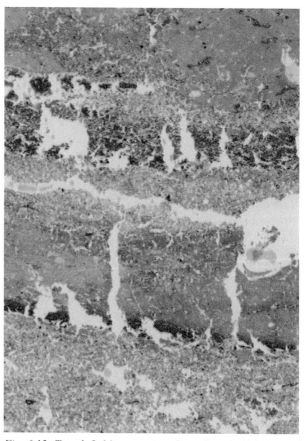

Fig. 6.13: Trench 5, Microstratigraphy in Sample 236. Scan of mammoth thin section; original size (4 × 6 cm). H. Lewis

('punctuations', charcoal, root remains, fungal sclerotia); inclusions of calcareous aggregates as described above.

B) 2–3 mm thick straight layer of dark brown iron-stained organic matter; no charcoal; no soil fabric.

C) 1 cm thick layer of shell sand with intergrain soil microaggregates; these are reddish brown stipple speckled (clay 45%, silt 45%, very fine and find sand 10%); 5% organic matter (mainly charcoal). Porosity 20–30%, packing pores and in places angular blocky zones of soil inclusions (*c.* 1–2 mm in size). All grains have soil coatings up to 200 μm thick in places.

D) Same material as A; organic matter 5–10%.

E) 2 mm thick straight layer of dark brown material; soil similar to A, but extremely organic-coated and with charcoal, charred organics and uncharred tissues in pore spaces (up to 300 μm); the groundmass is mainly undifferentiated; very sharp upper and lower boundaries.

F) Shell sand with intergrain microaggregates, as in C; overall porosity 20% packing pores; occasional charcoal up to 300 μm

Summary

In general, the metalworking area and the central yard both revealed frequent repeated floor layers. The material seen in the metalworking area was extremely mixed: comprising aggregates from many different origins, and no clear floor structuring was seen. Based on the thin sections, it appears that the central yard area saw repeated depositional sequences representing structured activities, while the metalworking area seems to show mixing of many types of deposits with burning materials.

Other samples from East Mound

Trench 7 was an area opened in 2007, and a large, orthostatic wall 4009 was found. There was a possible relationship seen with the uppermost of a series of midden layers, with the wall appearing to be quite late in the overall mound sequence. Mounded midden deposits were cut through by a linear feature, caught both in section and, at least the very base, in plan in the trench. This feature was lined with a 3–4 cm thick deposit of yellow clay. The layers of packing sediment were similar to midden deposits identified elsewhere on this site and on Snusgar (reddish-pink, clay-rich, with charcoal and fine clay fragments). However, in one location, such packing deposits 4012 overlay a <1 cm thick layer of yellow sand, over a greyish-brown soil-rich layer – also apparently a packing layer around the base of the wall footing. This layer, 4012, from Phase 8, was sampled for soil micromorphological study (Sample 2007/416; see Fig. 4.38). When the sample was taken it was possible to see a very thin (<1 cm) layer of yellow clay separating

4012 from underlying sand layer 4013; this is presumably also a structural component of the wall footing, and is included in sample 416. 4012 produced small amounts of cereal grain, which were interpreted as relating to midden deposition (Chapter 8).

Context 4012 was a Phase 8 greyish-brown soil found as wall footing packing, over a thin clay layer (no number given), and under wall 4009. The deposit is rare for this site, as it shows ped formation at a macroscopic level, with angular blocky (1–3 cm) to lenticular/platy (1 × 2–3 cm) aggregates, while microscopically the materials in the deposit were similar to those seen in other parts of the site, with medium and dark brown clayey loam soil microaggregates, calcareous aggregates, and a micro-structure of single grains with bridges and cappings. The macrostructure seen is possibly related to compaction forces, as well as sufficient clay to form these types of aggregates. The internal porosity of the aggregates is 30–35% (packing pores), and there are interpedal cracks (1 mm × 3 cm). Charcoal is rare, and there are very rare clay coatings. In general, this packing material comprises the same clayey soil materials seen as part of midden deposits described above from Snusgar, but without the possible burnt peat and/or turf or other cultural fabrics seen in the middens. Altogether, deliberate choosing of clayey soil material, and avoidance of midden material, is suggested for this wall footing construction.

Deposits between trenches 5 and 7 on East Mound (see Fig. 3.3)

In 2007 a short auger transect was extended from the north-east corner of Trench 5 on the East Mound, out along the 12 m grid line, to just past the north-west corner of Trench 7. This transect represents sediments lying between Trenches 5 and 7. The transect was augered using a Dutch head at *c.* 5 m intervals (except where restricted by spoil heaps), and the most relevant exposed profiles in Trenches 5 and 7 were included as points. Some general sequencing is postulated, but with the known variation in mound archaeological and wind-blown sand deposits, this can only be tentative. The profiles revealed a sequence similar to that seen on the mound through excavation: modern topsoil over windblown sand, overlying a series of midden deposits, and then a sequence of alternating midden and/or soil layers and blown sand layers, as discussed above. The auger profiles were recorded and archived.

Between Snusgar and East Mound (see Fig. 3.3)

An auger transect was carried out between Snusgar and the neighbouring East Mound to assess the immediate surrounds for ancient landscape information, with profiles recorded every 10 m from the lower corner of Snusgar Trench 4 for 64.70 m. No further holes could be recorded after 64.7 m along the line, due to the location of boundary fencing. The transect revealed nothing clearly of archaeological interest, with repeated results of modern topsoil overlying a variety of blown sand layers down to 1.58 m maximum depth. Although the topsoil had a thin stabilised turf horizon, small ridges from modern ploughing were visible from the surface; as such the topsoil is designated an Ap horizon. This was medium brown sandy loam with frequent inclusions of fine to very fine white sand and fine rooting. Near Snusgar mound (0–30 m boreholes) there was some variation in sand deposits underlying the topsoil, possibly related to disturbance and activities on and near the mound, as well as the mound's impact on blown sand deposition. Away from the Snusgar mound, the profile was very simple: Ap over C (yellow sand). Most auger holes were abandoned at less than 1 m depth due to obstructions; the 0 m auger hole was abandoned on reaching the groundwater table, with samples collapsing. It was clear there were no connective archaeological deposits between the mounds; the auger profiles were recorded and archived. At the western extremity of East Mound (the 'Warren Section'), an erosive sand blow-out exacerbated by cattle trampling and rabbit burrows, exposes some of the mound layers. A section was cleaned, drawn and archived, but not sampled. Four separate grey sand layers were recorded: potential buried A horizons or sand layers enhanced with leached amorphous organic matter. These underlay a fine pink layer, with distinctive colouring resembling the oxidised sand in the burning deposits on Snusgar.

Off the mounds

A series of test-pits were machine-excavated during the project in order to expose deposits away from the mounds (Fig. 3.4). Of these, Test Pit 3 (TP3), excavated in an area north of East Mound, revealed a peat layer deeply buried under sand. The stream curves around the East Mound, defining its eastern and southern edges, before running towards the sea. It seems likely that the peat layer found is related to some earlier course of the stream, or to a backwater area of the same. The peat was located under a profile described in Table 6.4.

Full recording of the trench was carried out, along with sampling of the peat to allow for absolute dating and pollen studies. These samples remain in the project archive. Other test-pits merely showed significant depths of sand down to the water table, beneath which it was impractical to continue excavating.

Discussion

The discovery of buried soil horizons 1536 and 1537 (Trench 4) under the thick blown sand of the Snusgar mound was very exciting. The positive results from excavating the deep sounding show how necessary it is to go beyond auger surveying from upper horizons in

Table 6.4: Test Pit 3 (TP3) profile

Depth from ground surface	Description
0–25 cm	A horizon
25–35 cm	Leached sand
305–220 cm	Yellow and grey sand, iron root pseudomorphs in upper metre
220+ cm	Peat (10 cm exposed)

assessing such sites. In trenches 1 and 3 it was simply impossible to get the auger through the various stony horizons associated with the archaeological site on the mound, and blown sand was exposed only down to *c.* 1.5 m depth. Ground-penetrating radar (Fig. 3.7) places Snusgar sediment depth at the mound centre at *c.* 4.5 m above the old ground surface revealed in the extension trench; obviously standard auger assessment will not be appropriate for examining deeply buried layers under these thick sand mounds, and future reconnaissance for buried soils must bear this in mind. Only through targeted and deep excavation would it be possible to reveal that there is a more widespread earlier land surface. The buried soil horizons date into prehistory. It was not possible in the field to determine what type of soil the horizons represented in regard to land use (grassland/forest/cultivated land), besides saying that they are certainly organic enough to represent old A horizons. Future analyses of soil micromorphological and bulk samples taken from these layers may be able to distinguish land use and soil profile histories in these buried horizons.

Dunes begin to form when an obstacle blocks further movement of windblown sand; as they become larger, dunes themselves become obstacles and they continue to grow; they also erode, and are subject to blow-outs. Machair dunes in this part of the world are believed to have formed initially in the mid-Holocene, related to sea level rise, erosion and deposition of calcareous sands (*e.g.* Ritchie 1966; 1979; Provoost *et al.* 2011) in locally-specific developmental sequences (Ritchie and Whittington 1994; Gilbertson *et al.* 1999), although with some broad regional patterns (*e.g.* de la Vega Leinert *et al.* 2000). Past study of dunes at the Bay of Skaill show Neolithic open woodland and grasslands before the first windblown sand depositional episodes (Watt 1820; Spencer 1975; Keatinge and Dickson 1979), with open vegetation related to sand deposition, and possibly to increased storminess and limited prehistoric woodland clearance (de la Vega Leinert *et al.* 2000). Machair environments are believed to have developed over time after about 5000 years ago (*ibid.*). The mounds studied here appear to consist mainly of windblown sand, with possible stand-still events during which topsoil growth could occur. While it was not possible to radiocarbon date any of the buried soils that could indicate standstill horizons on the dunes, we can propose that there are phases of dune formation and dune stability, and if these could be dated and further studied, the area could be compared to other studies, such as that on a phase of soil formation identified to date to the Little Ice Age in the Outer Hebrides (Gilbertson *et al.* 1999). The dune sands are also influenced by post-depositional leaching processes, primarily loss and accumulation of amorphous organic matter and iron, and of clay. Neither of the mounds investigated shows certain construction evidence until historic periods, and it is suggested that they continue to be considered as initially natural dune formations until such time as deeper structural remains are revealed.

The excavated remains on East Mound in particular showed good potential for a study of use-of-space through investigation of soil chemistry (Chapter 7), texture and density, as well as soil micromorphological study. Such studies on other sites (*e.g.* Milek 2001; Milek *et al.* 2014; Simpson *et al.* 2005) have been useful in distinguishing locations of cooking, sleeping and animal penning quarters, as well as discussing how structures such as the longhouse at East Mound were constructed, used and abandoned. Some soil micromorphology samples focused on these aspects at Snusgar and East Mound, and the bulk sampling of a representative proportion of other floor layers was also conducted.

Recent work on plaggen soils and mounds in other parts of Scotland using diatom and soil micromorphological analyses has been able to demonstrate the presence of ashes from turf and organic muds in medieval mound deposits (Stephen Carter 2007 pers. comm.), and it may be possible to further explore both the fuel type used and the processes implied on the mounds here through additional sedimentary analyses of the sampled deposits. These deposits showed burning of several types of fuel, including turf, peat and wood, as part of habitation and industrial activities at these sites. The results support the site interpretations, while adding depth to certain understandings of the deposits. For instance, while archaeobotany has found peat burning evidence, through soil micromorphology it was also possible to see turf or soil burnt as fuel.

Repeated re-laying of floors was noted microscopically, associated with the area outside the metalworking yard on the East Mound, presumably related to repetition of activities over time, and other deposits on both mounds showed industrial activity involving burning. Evidence from the metalworking yard itself suggested a lot of combustion activity in this area. The nature of those deposits and of those 'outside' this area, support the interpretation of intensive industrial activities. Intact *in situ* burning deposits, that appear to represent small one-off combustion features, were also found microscopically at both mounds at varying phases. Repeated phases of 'standstill', with soils growing on dune and midden deposits, were seen and these were also found external to the sites, and could bear future investigation, as could the agricultural history noted on site and further characterised in a few samples in this study.

To broaden the landscape geoarchaeological study, in the future, further sample programmes taken from buried soils at various locations around the Bay of Skaill, Marwick and Birsay Bay could be taken, analysed and interpreted in light of Cluett (2007) and other regional studies, to develop landscape and land use history models and to inform further stages of research. It is already clear that there is a good deal of ancient landscape information available in the area in the form of buried soils from many periods, and the finding of a buried peat deposit demonstrates the potential for borehole, augering and test pit survey, coupled with environmental archaeological study, to reveal landscape and settlement history across the project area.

7

Geochemical intra-site mapping: Inorganic and organic

Roger C. Doonan and Alexandre Lucquin

The deposits, floors and drains of the East Mound longhouse, in Trench 5, were subjected to a regular pattern of soil sampling (see Chapter 4, separate to the soil flotation sampling programme, see Chapters 8–10) with the intention that this material could later be used to further our understanding of the types of activity undertaken within the longhouse and its immediate environs by geochemical analysis and mapping. Only *ex situ* analysis was undertaken, and although the preference in future would be to undertake *in situ* readings, this capability was not available to the site team at the time. All samples came from deposits in phases 3–6. The results presented as spatial plots (Figs 7.1–7.3) provide a broad provisional indication which has some archaeological interest and implications.

Overview
Roger C. Doonan and Alexandre Lucquin

A wide range of human activities have direct influences on the formation and transformation of soils and sediments. Whereas highly invasive activities such as farming, construction and disposal of waste can be widely recognised in the archaeological record, less invasive activities such as food preparation, animal husbandry and crafts may produce highly localised anthropogenic signatures, some of which are only recorded at the elemental and molecular level.

Archaeologists have already had considerable success in deducing activity on a surface from variations in artefact and micro-debris distributions. But a more complete detailed coverage comes from mapping of the chemical composition of the soil. Chemical studies on archaeological soils have focused on bulk variables at first on phosphorus (Arrhenius 1929), completed thereafter by other spot test analyses (Dore and López Varela 2010) and on multi-elemental analyses (Abrahams *et al.* 2010; Wells 2004; Wilson *et al.* 2008) in order to identify areas of activity and their nature.

The processes and mechanisms by which soil is modified by human action are still relatively poorly understood (Wilson *et al.* 2008; Entwistle *et al.* 1998, Middleton and Price 1996) but geochemical patterning has been recognised as providing valuable insights into how past communities have spatially organised a range of activities (Haslam and Tibbett 2004). Interpretive challenges are not restricted to soil ecology but include basic understandings of how specific human practices imprint themselves on open soil contexts. Conventional geochemical analysis operates with restricted sample numbers due to limitations of sampling time and costs of analysis. For these reasons it has rarely been employed to identify spatial patterning at a level of resolution commensurate with human practice, instead being used for broadly descriptive programmes of soil characterisation.

This study reports the analysis (*ex situ*) of soil samples from floor deposits in the Trench 5 longhouse and its ancillary buildings.The samples analysed were retrieved on site by the excavation team in the 2005, 2008 and 2010 seasons. These were taken in a consistent manner from fixed points across the longhouse interior areas, through successive contexts in Phases 3 and 5. Samples were bagged on site taking care to avoid inadvertent admixture or contamination, and kept separate to those taken for archaeobotanical purposes. These were subsequently subdivided, and smaller amounts of each were sent to laboratories at the Department of Archaeology, University of Sheffield (inorganic analysis) and BioArch, University of York (organic analysis). Considerably more samples

Table 7.1: Samples analysed for inorganic residues

Context-sample	P	Location/description	Context-sample	P	Location/description	Context-sample	P	Location/description	Context-sample	P	Location/description
2008-8	6	Midden	2071-16	5	Floor AB	2227-a11	6	Floor LH	2264-a43	3	Floor LH
2009-1	6	Floor AB	2080-a63	5	Floor AB	2227-a15	6	Floor LH	2264-a59	3	Floor LH
2009-2	6	Floor AB	2148-2	3	Fill, drain	2229-a26	6	Surface, Byre	2267-a31	3	Floor Byre
2010-4	6	Floor AB	2156-1	5	Floor, Byre	2232-a19	6	N Sidebench	2267-a40	5	Floor Byre
2010-5	6	Floor AB	2173-1a	5	Floor Byre	2232-a21	5	N Sidebench	2267-a49	5	Floor Byre
2025-1	6	Floor AB	2202-a1	5	Surface MWA	2234-a57	5	Floor MWA	2268-a34	5	Floor Byre
2025-3	6	Floor AB	2202-a2	5	Surface MWA	2240-a46	3	Fill, hearth	2268-a54	5	Floor Byre
2034-2	6	Floor AB	2202-a23	5	Surface MWA	2241-a29	5	Floor LH	2269-a45	3	Fill, hearth
2034-7	6	Floor AB	2203-a22	5	Surface MWA	2241-a33	5	Floor LH	2271-a50	5	Floor, Byre
2034-8	6	Floor AB	2224-a3	5	Floor LH	2245-a24	3	Floor AB	2272-a55	3	Floor, Byre
2034-9	6	Floor AB	2224-a6	5	Floor LH	2255-a32	5	Fill, pit	2273-a42	3	Floor LH
2040-10	5	Floor AB	2224-a7	5	Floor LH	2261-a27	5	Floor LH	2273-a47	3	Floor LH
2040-13	5	Floor AB	2224-a12	5	Floor LH	2261-a41	5	Floor LH	2274-a38	5	Floor Byre
2040-19	5	Floor AB	2224-a13	5	Floor LH	2261-a53	5	Floor LH	2276-a37	5	Floor Byre
2040-4	5	Floor AB	2224-a17	5	Floor LH	2262-a35	3	Floor LH	2277-a36	5	Floor Byre
2053-11	5	Floor AB	2224-a17	5	Floor LH	2262-a44	3	Floor LH	2285-a51	5	Fill, tank
2053-12	5	Floor AB	2224-a20	5	Floor LH	2262-a48	3	Floor LH	2290-a60	5	Cooking pit
2053-15	5	Floor AB	2225-10	6	S Sidebench	2263-a28	5	Floor LH	2294-a56	3	Fill, hearth
2053-23	5	Floor AB	2225-a4	6	S Sidebench	2262-a39	5	Floor LH	2301-a58	5	Fill, hearth
2053-161	5	Floor AB	2226-a5	6	N Sidebench	2263-a52	5	Floor LH	2305-a61	5	Fill, scoop
2071-14	5	Floor AB	2227-a9	6	Floor LH	2264-a30	3	Floor LH	2307-a62	5	Fill, P hole

Detailed results on archive. P = Phase; AB = Ancillary Buildings; MWA = Metalworking Area; LH = Longhouse; P hole = Post-hole

were processed for inorganic chemical analysis (118 in all, including control samples and some taken from Trench 4, the results of which have been archived, but the decision was taken not to proceed with full plotting and reporting due to the relative uncertainty of their spatial placing with regard to structures, in comparison to the excellent resolution of samples from Trench 5). Eighty-four samples from Trench 5 have been plotted (Table 7.1). Fewer samples (21) were processed for organic chemical analysis; this was driven by greater selectivity, focusing on deposits from hearths, floors and drains, coupled with considerations of cost and laboratory capacity.

Inorganic chemical analysis

Roger C. Doonan

Scholars have noted that chemical elements vary in their interpretive value with most agreeing that the elements with the greatest potential to aid archaeological studies include *inter alia* Phosphorous (P), Copper (Cu), Zinc (Zn), and Lead (Pb). Although acknowledging the utility of these elements is an important first step, there remains an interpretive gulf in how their enhancement might relate to practice beyond broad categories of human activity. For instance, the work of Wilson *et al.* (2008) has done much work with ethnohistorical sites to demonstrate the relation between types of practice and soil chemistry, yet in archaeological contexts soil chemistry is most frequently used to highlight increased human activity or simply the presence of 'archaeology'.

A notable exception to such activities is non-ferrous metalworking (Cu) and agricultural/disposal/fire-related processes which have enhanced phosphorus (P). Whereas the wide range of human activities might enhance heavy metal concentrations by small amounts, the practice of copper metallurgy has the potential to enhance soil copper (and other elements) significantly and certainly well beyond crustal or background levels. The characterisation of working areas has been accomplished through systematic soil sampling and laboratory-based analysis (Andrews and Doonan 2003, 42–4; Derhan *et al.* 2013). This is especially powerful when used in combination with geophysical survey (Doonan *et al.* 2003).

Methods and analysis of soil samples

Analysis was undertaken by the author at University of Sheffield using a NITON XLT 3 XRF in laboratory test stand mode. The campaign of analysis was designed to quantify the variability of soil chemistry in the samples taken. In addition to geochemical analysis, magnetic susceptibility was also undertaken. X-Ray fluorescence (XRF) analyses were undertaken on approximately 10 g samples contained within a standard sampling vessel with proline analysis window. Determinations were made using a Niton XLT3 instrument that is equipped with a 50 kV X-ray tube, and an Ag anode with a silicon positive intrinsic negative (Si PiN) detector. The area excited is 8 mm in diameter giving an analytical area of ~50 mm^2. The analytical mode chosen was the standard 'mining' mode using the main, low, high and light filters in conjunction with a helium purge so as to facilitate light element detection (especially P). Analysis time was adjusted to 120 seconds (main 45 s, low 15 s, high 15 s, light 45 s) and determined the following elements: Ba, Nb, Zr, Sr, Rb, Bi, As, Pb, Zn, Cu, Fe, Mn, Cr, V, Ti, Ca, K, Al, P, Si, Cl, Mg, S. (Some of these elements are not regarded as reliably reflective of archaeological activity, so only a selection of the results were plotted, the rest have been archived.)

Magnetic susceptibility was undertaken on the samples subsequent to chemical analysis. Determination was made using a Bartington MS2B benchtop analyser. Samples were weighed to allow a mass-normalised determination. Deviation between LF and HF results was low which meant that all readings were determined at LF.

ANALYTICAL PERFORMANCE

Prior to undertaking field analyses a number of certified reference soils were analysed to determine the accuracy of the instrument under ideal conditions. The performance of hand-held portable XRF (HHpXRF) is now well established for most heavy metals in soils (Kilbride *et al.* 2006).

SAMPLE PREPARATION

Soils from the longhouse floors were sieved to 2 mm and approximately 10 g placed in a standard analytical vessel with a 4 μm proline analysis window. Care was taken to avoid the inclusion of any large pieces of organic material in the sample and to exclude any large (>2 mm) rock fragments. The same samples were also used for magnetic

susceptibility determination. Samples were weighed and MS determined. All results were mass-normalised.

SAMPLES

Table 7.1 shows the list of samples included in the study. Eighty-four samples from Trench 5 (East Mound longhouse and its environs) were analysed and plotted in Figs 7.1 and 7.2. These were taken from floors, hearths and features in the central domestic area and western extensions of the longhouse, in the ancillary buildings to the south, and from surfaces and hearth deposits in the metalworking area at the south-west extent of Trench 5.

Results

Results for soil chemistry are reported in ppm and associated with a spatial coordinate. In producing representations of the distribution of soil chemistry no interpolation was employed, instead point data was plotted as a means to best represent the raw data. The samples were taken systematically based on fixed locations from suitable deposits.

When detected, spatial plots show the variability of selected key elements (P, Cu, Zn, Pb) that are usually associated with anthropogenic activity, together with Magnetic Susceptibility. It is worth noting that these key elements showed marked variability across the site and this certainly holds interpretive potential. The samples were consistently located, driven by the priorities of archaeological excavation. A pure grid strategy might have made it easier to ascertain more detailed 'structure' in some of the data although broad comparative analysis is afforded. As a general guide, a structured anomaly should be considered present when a spatial sequence of chemical data shows a rise and fall across a minimum of 3 data points in close proximity.

MAGNETIC SUSCEPTIBILITY (MS)

The results of MS analysis show striking variation across the East Mound longhouse (Fig. 7.1). Samples ranged from very low (6) to very high (4474). It was clear background MS was very low permitting good anthropogenic visibility across the site. The concentrations cluster around the hearths, there is a general spread in the central hall and ancillary building to the south; an area of raised susceptibility is visible in the western annex of the longhouse around hearth 2290, but by far the highest occurs in the metalworking yard on the south-west periphery of the building complex. Iron (Fe) is included as a comparison, although MS is regarded as a more reliable indicator of past burning processes.

PHOSPHORUS (P)

Variation in Phosphorus was also marked across the sample area (Fig. 7.1) with developed anomalies to the west of the trench. Samples ranged from very low (294 ppm) to very high (10632 ppm). P seemed to indicate marked variation in activities across the site which would benefit from closer contextual scrutiny. There are concentrations in the western annex of the longhouse around hearth (context 2290) and in the ancillary building on the south side of the complex. It would not be unreasonable to infer from this distribution that cooking, eating and intensive animal quartering are represented in the spatial distribution of results.

COPPER (CU)

Copper was rarely detected across the sample area (Fig. 7.1) with the exception of a few samples and one notable high concentration. Results varied from not detected (ND – the norm) to 318 ppm with the majority of measured samples ranging from 30–100 ppm. Such levels are typical of anthropogenic activity but the single high value of 318 ppm (found in the central floor of the longhouse close to the point where the Phase 3 building was extended to that of Phase 5) is a level that may be encountered in metalworking environments (Hanks *et al.* 2015). It is unlikely that this alone can indicate the presence of non-ferrous metalworking in the absence of any other indicators (only ferrous metalworking was identified archaeologically; see Chapter 11).

ZINC (ZN)

Zinc provided a good response across the sample area (Fig. 7.2) with clear structure anomalies visible. Again there was a broad enhancement in the westerly aspect of the structure but a very notable elevation in the southern area associated with the ancillary buildings and the metalworking area. Zn levels ranged from ND (rare) to 360 ppm. The upper ranges are comparable with a number of reports of heavy metal enhancement associated with human activity. It is not possible to tie Zn to any specific activity.

LEAD (PB)

Lead provided an exceptionally clear response across the sample area (Fig. 7.2) with clear structured anomalies visible in the westerly benched area. The result shows a clear differential use of space with distinguishing activities in this area. Pb levels ranged from ND (the norm) to 60 ppm. The upper ranges are comparable with a number of reports of heavy metal enhancement associated with human activity and stand in stark contrast to the values across the site. It should be noted that these values are not high in themselves and most likely do not indicate the practice of lead-working. It is more likely they indicate the use of lead or even the deposition of biological material that has accumulated lead through metabolic processes.

IRON (FE)

The distribution of iron shows a general coverage across the sample area, with the highest concentrations in the metalworking yard and adjacent ancillary structures to the south of the longhouse (Fig. 7.2).

Discussion

The study reported here was based on *ex situ* samples and focuses on a relatively limited sample set. It has produced results which show clear variation and from this perspective the dataset can be considered to have certain interpretive value. Although only *ex situ* analysis was undertaken for this site, utilising soil samples taken up to 2010, the technical feasibility and responsiveness of *in situ* measurement has moved on considerably since then, meaning that future exposures of floors and occupation surfaces in longhouse structures such as this example should now proceed with *in situ* analysis as a preferred approach.

The study has provided information on a number of specific issues. Firstly, it can be established that the variability encountered across the sites is of a magnitude that makes it possible to forecast that intensive *in situ* geochemistry would provide an informative archaeological soil chemistry dataset. It is notable that P, Cu, Zn and Pb perform well in terms of correlating with archaeologically distinct contexts.

MS and Zn appear to show a strong correlation with the metalworking area and the levels of detection would support this proposal. The absence or very low levels of Cu would suggest that the metalworking area was preoccupied with ferrous metallurgy and that copper-alloy working is likely to be absent. Although there are a number of copper-alloy small finds (Chapter 13), there is nothing amongst them to suggest manufacturing or secondary metalworking on site: this therefore bears out the conclusion drawn from the soil chemical analysis alone. The benched area on the western aspect of the longhouse shows the most structured geochemical response with strong anomalies shown for Pb and P. It is difficult to be conclusive about the specific significance of these elemental concentrations but it is clear that the range of activities in this area were very different from the rest of the structure. With this in mind it is possible to suggest that this area of the structure was the focus of routine social activities likely centring on maintaining fire, heating, cooking and eating. It is apparent that these specific activities were relatively contained in this area and were not common elsewhere in the structure.

The key elements assessed are very much standard indicators of human activity (P, Cu Zn and Pb). There seems to be also clear structured patterning in a number of other elements yet at present it is unclear to what extent they assist with the interpretive burden. Correlations with specific small finds or other data (environmental) may

Table 7.2: List of samples analysed for organic residues

Site	Context	Sample	Phase	Localisation	Description	Mass (g)	Concentration (µg g⁻¹)
SG8	2148	2	3		Fill of a drain	2.12	52.7
SG8	2156	1	5	Byre floor	Ash and charcoal	2.02	32.5
SG8	2173	1a	5	Byre floor	Workshop	2.02	39.1
SG10	2240	a46	3	Metal working	Hearth fill	2.21	16.3
SG10	2261	a27	5	Longhouse floor	Near small hearths	2.07	33.5
SG10	2261	a53	5	Longhouse floor	Near small hearths	2.21	40.0
SG10	2262	a35	3	Longhouse floor	Near large hearth	2.04	34.7
SG10	2262	a44	3	Longhouse floor	Near large hearth	2.00	104.7
SG10	2263	a28	5	Longhouse floor	Near cooking pit	2.07	78.1
SG10	2263	a39	5	Longhouse floor	Near cooking pit	2.17	74.7
SG10	2263	a52	5	Longhouse floor	Near cooking pit	2.05	97.5
SG10	2264	a30	3	Longhouse floor	Near large hearth	2.42	79.9
SG10	2264	a43	3	Longhouse floor	Near large hearth	2.06	61.9
SG10	2264	a59	3	Longhouse floor	Near large hearth	2.11	10.8
SG10	2267	a40	5	Byre floor	Animals	2.02	74.6
SG10	2268	a54	5	Byre floor	Workshop	2.15	33.2
SG10	2285	a51	5	Longhouse floor	Fill of storage tank	2.06	153.7
SG10	2290	a5	5	Longhouse annex floor	Fill of cooking pit	2.06	9.9
SG10	2294	a56	3	Metal working	Hearth fill	2.13	49.9
SG10	2301	a58	5	Longhouse floor	Fill of small hearth	2.28	24.0
SG10	2305	a61	5	Longhouse floor	Fill of scoop hearth	2.11	68.2

well serve to enhance the utility of these datasets. In summary, the study has highlighted varying degrees of geochemical variation across the longhouse (Figs 7.1, 7.2). The variability occurs between a number of architectural zones and in some cases correlates (+/−) with geophysical survey (MS).

Organic residue analysis

Alexandre Lucquin

There is much greater variation in the types of organic matter than for the inorganic elements that contribute to a soil as a result of different activity patterns. The potential for using organic biomarkers as signals, first proposed fifty years ago (Den Dooren De Jong, Dauvillier and Roman 1961), has been largely ignored because we tend to believe that post-depositional process lead to their disappearance, even in burial contexts favourable to the conservation of perishable materials. This belief is profoundly wrong, as has been revealed by the systematic recovery of the most perishable of molecules, DNA, at multiple archaeological

and paleontological sites (*e.g.* Hebsgaard *et al.* 2009). By some (as yet unknown) means, organic residues can be recovered in an amorphous form or bound to mineral matrices and can be characterised at the molecular scale. Lipids have been recovered from numerous contexts and can be extracted from ceramic potsherds (Evershed *et al.* 1992). They are relatively stable molecules and can also be recovered from archaeological sediments and floors.

Twenty-one soil samples from 15 contexts of floor deposits from the East Mound longhouse (Trench 5) have been selected and analysed (Table 7.2). Lipids extracted have been characterised at molecular level using gas chromatography mass spectrometry (GC-MS).

Methods and analysis of soil samples

Floor sediment samples were sieved through a mesh of 1 mm and then carefully crushed with a solvent cleaned agate pestle and mortar. The obtained powder was then sieved through a mesh of 200 µm and homogenised. An aliquot of about 2 g was weighed for extraction.

Lipids were extracted using a one-step acid/methanol extraction technique, following previously established extraction protocols (Craig *et al.* 2013; Papakosta *et al.* 2015). Briefly, acid catalysed lipid extraction and methylation with MeOH (70°C, 4 h) was conducted, after which lipids were extracted with *n*-hexane (3 × 2 ml). The samples were dried up under a stream of nitrogen and 10 μg of internal standard of $C_{36:0}$ (*n*-hexatriacontane) was added. Further derivatisation of compounds containing hydroxyl group was realised by silylation with BSTFA at 70°C for 1 h, and then evaporated to dryness under a gentle stream of N2. After resuspension in hexane, the obtained extract was analysed directly with GC-FID and GC-MS.

General screening and quantification of the lipid extract was realised by GC-FID (gas chromatography – flame ionisation detector). Analyses were carried out using an Agilent 7890A gas chromatograph (Agilent Technologies, UK). The injector was splitless and maintained at 300°C and injected 1 μl of sample into the GC. The column used was a 100% Dimethylpolysiloxane DB-1 (15 m × 320 μm × 0.1 μm; J&W Scientific, Folsom, CA, USA). The carrier gas was hydrogen with a constant flow rate of 2 ml min^{-1}. The temperature program was set at 100°C for 2 minutes, rose by 20°C min^{-1} until 325°C. This temperature was maintained for 3 minutes. Total run time was 16.25 minutes. The lower boundaries of interpretable archaeological lipid extract were 5μg g^{-1} of sediment powder corresponding roughly to 10μg of extracted lipids.

GC-MS (gas chromatography-mass spectrometry) analysis was performed with Agilent 7690A Series gas chromatography and Agilent 5975C Inert XL mass-selective detector with a quadrupole mass analyser with Triple-Axis Detector (Agilent Technologies, Cheadle, Cheshire, UK) were used. The splitless injector and interface were maintained at 300°C and 340°C respectively. Helium was the carrier gas at constant inlet pressure. The GC column was inserted directly into the ion source of the mass spectrometer. The ionisation energy was 70 eV and spectra were obtained by scanning between m/z 50 and 800. All samples were analysed using a DB5-ms (5%-phenyl)-methylpolysiloxane column (30 m × 0.32 mm × 0.25 μm; J&W Scientific, Folsom, CA, USA) with the temperature program of 2 min at 50°C, 10°C min^{-1} to 325°C and 15 min at 325°C. The identification of compounds was conducted with the Agilent Chemstation software according to their mass spectrum, their retention time and with the help of NIST 2008 library of mass spectra.

Results

All the samples extracted have yielded an amount of lipids above the minimal boundary accepted (Table 7.2). According to their average concentration, no relation can be clearly established between the phase attributed

to the sample and the concentration (Phase 3, 51.3 ± 31.5 μg g^{-1}; Phase 5, 58.4 ±38.5 μg g^{-1}). The range of concentration is high (between 9.9 and 153.7 μg g^{-1} of sediment) and this is certainly the result of variability of the deposition of organic matter resulting from different human and animal activities. Moreover, the variability within a context can be quite high (*i.e.* in context 2264, the concentration ranges from 10.8 to 79.9 μg g^{-1}). Only the maximum concentration was considered for spatial distribution (Fig. 7.3, plot 1). The highest concentration is found in the fill of the storage tank within the longhouse floor. Concentrations around the cooking hearth (2290) are generally high, as are deposits along the edges of the floors (where corners beside orthostats may have protected the deposits from greater disturbance and degradation). The byre floor (average, 44.8 ±20.1 μg g^{-1}) and the external working area (average, 33.1 ± 23.7 μg g^{-1}) are generally less concentrated than within the longhouse (average, 66.3 ± 38.9 μg g^{-1}). Only the space reserved for animals shows a higher concentration of organic matter.

Molecular characterisation reveals that complex mixtures of organic matter are preserved in the soils. The signatures seem to be the results of both the human activities and environmental deposit. A plant signature is highly predominant and typical of plant epicuticular waxes. It is composed of saturated fatty acid ranging from $C_{12:0}$ up to $C_{34:0}$ with a high proportion of long chain fatty acids (from 30% to 90%), various isomers of unsaturated fatty acids ($C_{16:1}$ and $C_{18:1}$), long chain dicarboxylic acids, and a variety of phytosterols (campesterol, stigmasterol, β-sitosterol) and terpenes. Bacterial and microbial activity is marked with the presence of branched chain fatty acids, 2- and 3- hydroxy fatty acids, but seems to remain limited. Those compounds are certainly related to the organic matter deposited naturally on the site. It has to be noted that the saturated fatty distribution of SG2294-A56, corresponding to the hearth fill in the metal working area is characterised by an unusual amount of $C_{20:0}$. This compound has been found in high concentration in heartwood extract from various wood species (Salem *et al.* 2015) and could be linked to the use of heartwood fuel in this area (see also Chapter 8).

Animal trace is more discreet and mainly related to the presence of cholesterol and its derivative. The spatial distribution of cholesterol is mapped according the concentration of cholesterol normalised to the maximum value (Fig. 7.3, plot 2). A higher concentration of animal organic matter is found in the storage tank in the longhouse floor, the drain and in the animal park area in the byre floor. Consumption or cooking traces in the longhouse and byre floors are also generally high. Areas more dedicated to craft, such as the metal working area, reveal a lower impact of animal traces. These animal traces in the samples from the longhouse floor coming from the hearth

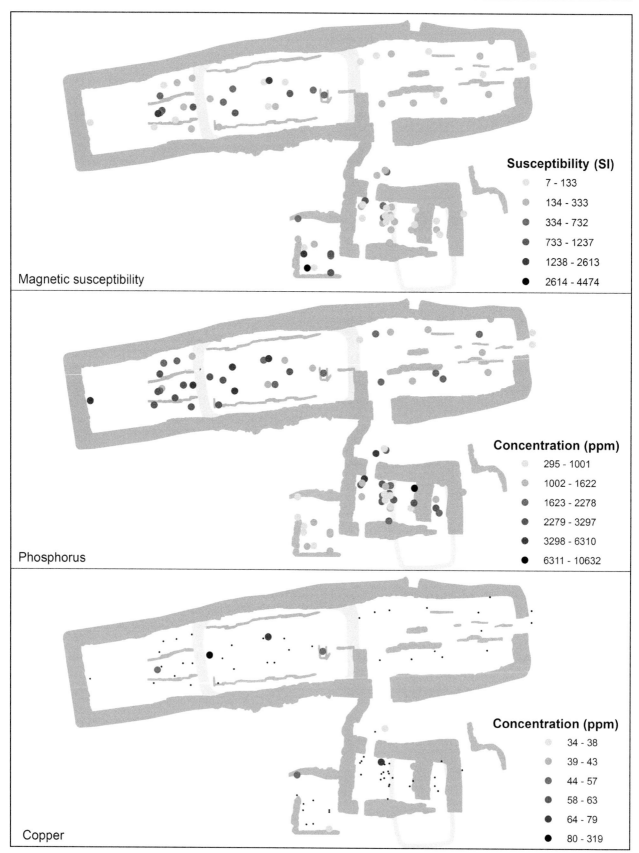

Fig. 7.1: Trench 5, Inorganic soil chemistry distribution plot 1 (black dots = sample with no result or below concentrations presented)

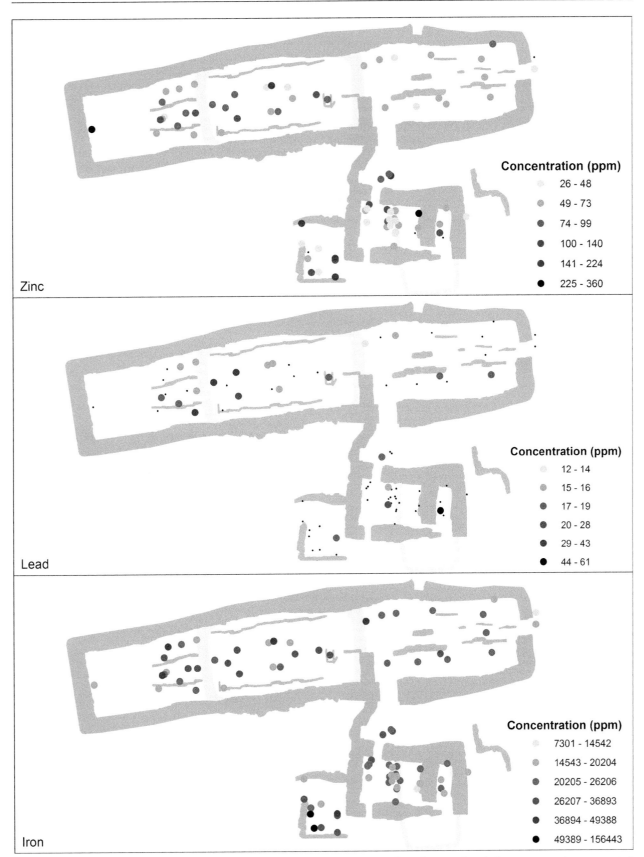

Fig. 7.2: Trench 5, Inorganic soil chemistry distribution plot 2 (black dots = sample with no result or below concentrations presented)

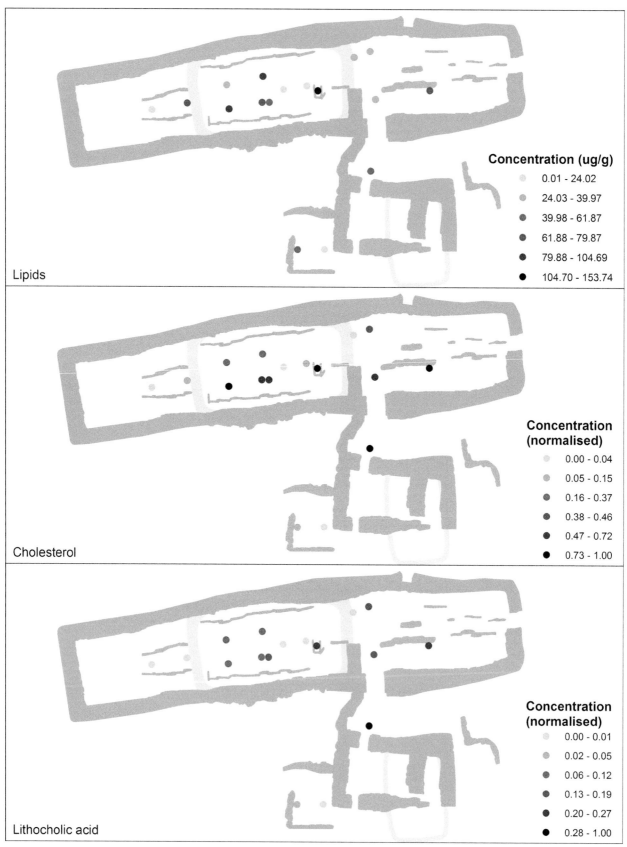

Fig. 7.3: Trench 5, Organic soil chemistry distribution plot

or cooking pits are associated to $C_{18}\omega$-(o-alkylphenyl) alkanoic acids that are only formed by heating C_{18} poly unsaturated fatty acids coming from plants and may be related to cooking residues (Evershed, Copley, Dickson and Hansel 2008). In the animal area of the byre floor, phytanic acids is found at the highest concentration, and despite a possible bacterial origin it has to be noted that it is also abundant in ruminant and aquatic resources (Lucquin *et al.* 2016).

A number of stanol, biomarkers related to faecal deposit, albeit mostly in low amount, can be found on most of the samples (coprostanol, epicoprostanol, cholestenol, 5β stigmastanol, epi 5β-stigmastanol, stigmastanol). The ratios of those biomarkers indicates that herbivorous faeces are predominant in most of the samples. More omnivorous stanol mixtures are limited to the byre floor and drains. Lithocholic acid (bile acid), indicating both herbivorous and omnivorous faeces, is found frequently within the samples, but its spatial distribution (normalised to the maximum concentration) show that it is coming mostly from the drain fill samples (Fig. 7.3, plot 3).

Discussion

Organic residue analysis of floor samples has brought more information on the functionality of the living space of the East Mound longhouse. Despite a large environmental contribution, the communal, central domestic living space of of the longhouse clearly shows the deposit of organic matter related to cooking and food consumption activities. The storage tank within this area may have also contained food residues. The byre area may have been dedicated to more variable activity. Nevertheless, compounds found in the byre area seem to confirm its role as animal housing space, presumably of ruminant species. Finally, the metalworking areas have left few organic residues but their remains suggest the presence of heartwood.

Archaeobotanical evidence: Carbonised plant macrofossils and charcoal

Diane Alldritt

Introduction

A total of 292 bulk environmental samples ('General Bulk Analysis', Dobney *et al.* 1992) taken from seven seasons of archaeological investigation (2004–10) – six seasons at the Bay of Skaill and one season at Marwick in 2009 (Chapter 4) – were fully analysed for carbonised plant macrofossils and charcoal. Of these, only 19 samples were found to be completely sterile of identifiable charred remains, with the remainder producing varied amounts of material ranging from highly abundant remains in some of the hearth fills through to trace evidence in other deposits, largely dependent upon the type of context sampled. Charred material sorted from the sample residues, together with 'spot' finds of burnt material taken during excavation, were incorporated into the results where appropriate. All results have been tabulated but sterile and trace samples have been removed from any further analysis in order to focus on both the most stratigraphically relevant and archaeobotanically significant contexts (see summaries of results given in Tables 8.1 to 8.10). (The full data is in the online archive.)

Throughout the course of the excavations, a systematic and thorough environmental sampling strategy was employed. Samples were examined from Trenches 1–4 from Snusgar, and 5–8 from East Mound. Initial sample assessment undertaken in 2004 indicated a very high potential for further work at the site to produce large amounts of carbonised material, with excellent levels of preservation likely to be encountered as the excavation progressed to deeper sealed deposits. Indeed, this proved to be the case, particularly in Trench 5 on East Mound, with findings of delicate and friable plant parts such as oat chaff and seaweed, together with other rarely found macrofossils such as flax. The sampling strategy aimed to maximise the recovery of carbonised plant remains from across the two mound sites in order to provide potentially significant quantities of data for an economic and environmental interpretation of the local and regional landscapes. Of equal importance was the recovery of suitable material for radiocarbon dating, and the excellent preservation of charcoal and cereal grain enabled nine potential phases of use, occupation and post-occupation/collapse to be proposed (Chapters 4 and 5).

Archaeobotanical studies in the Northern Isles have tended to focus generally on midden remains and their associated settlements, but in recent years there has been a more concerted attempt to integrate various forms of environmental evidence, such as fish bone, charred plant remains and marine shell, with structural evidence and site formation processes, most notably demonstrated through research into farm mounds (*e.g.* Bertelsen and Lamb 1993). The level of interpretation is often constrained by preservation and deposition, with the majority of plant evidence arising from carbonisation.

Previous archaeobotanical work on Viking-Late Norse period sites in the Northern Isles has produced a range of macrofossil finds including charcoal, cereal grain, burnt peat and turf, weed seeds and other remains revealing evidence for the arable economy, woodland resources, use of wild plants and gathered resources, and ultimately trading patterns with the wider world. The often complex pattern of movement of materials around the Norse farmstead, involving midden formation, recycling of materials from different sources, use of plant materials and subsequent reuse of burnt waste, have been well documented by Buckland *et al.* (1993, 513), and in turn these materials have contributed toward the overall formation of some 'farm mound' features visible on the landscape.

Archaeological finds on Orkney of species such as *Salix* (willow), *Betula* (birch) and *Corylus* (hazel) probably represent locally growing scrub vegetation (Dickson 1994), whilst non-native species such as *Picea* (spruce), *Larix* (larch) and *Pinus* (pine) would have been gathered as driftwood from the shore, or perhaps imported for use as building or manufacturing materials (Dickson 1992). Woodland management would have been an important practice in order to provide a continuous and sustainable supply of fuel for metalworking, whilst the exploitation of peat and heath habitats would have provided fuel for cereal drying and domestic hearths, as well as pasture areas for animals (Dickson 1994, Alldritt 2003). Both wood and peat land would also have been used as sources of constructional materials, such as timber supports, roofing and for internal features.

Identification of carbonised grain from archaeological deposits has demonstrated a mixed cereal economy largely reliant upon barley and oats. Indeed the ubiquitous *Hordeum vulgare* var. *vulgare* (six row hulled barley) appears to be the most common multi-period cereal crop recorded from archaeobotanical samples in Scotland (Boyd 1988; Dickson and Dickson 2000, 232). Barley is a hardy crop, well suited to northern climates, and can grow on heavy or light soils. Oat is capable of growing on quite impoverished soils, such as rough wet grassland, and has even been recorded as growing in a completely waterlogged field on Unst, Shetland, accompanied by a drowned sheep (Hinton 1991). In modern cereal agriculture hulled barley has been gradually modified over time to produce a grain more suited to malting to make beer, whilst in the past it is suggested from ethnographic records that it had a multi-purpose use as both food (such as barley bread, bannocks) and to a lesser extent drink (Fenton 1978, 332). It has recently been demonstrated that the 'naked' type of barley (*Hordeum vulgare* var. *nudum*) is actually a more efficient use of the land in terms of human food production, requiring a much lower input of fertiliser than hulled barley or wheat (Steele and Wright 2013). The Norse infield system would have required a large amount of fertiliser to maximise repeated yields of hulled barley. This intensive drain on resources may potentially be one of the reasons why evidence from many sites suggests a move toward increased oat production on rougher areas of land unsuited to barley, into the Late Norse period in order to produce a more sustainable and reliable crop. Oat probably also had an important role as animal fodder in the Late Norse period, as the economy changed more toward pastoral practices reliant upon dairy farming (Barrett *et al.* 2000).

In Orkney, the Viking phases at Pool, Sanday, produced more hulled barley than oats, but during the Late Norse period there was a shift toward increased oat production, and it was suggested that the best arable land was actually reserved not for barley but for flax cultivation (Bond 2007, 205). Whilst in contrast, at Birsay Bay, Donaldson and Nye (1989) mainly found barley, as did Donaldson (1986) at Brough of Birsay, perhaps suggesting consumption of barley as a high status food or drink. Excavations of Norse deposits at Tuquoy, Westray produced six row hulled barley, oats and flax from the Norse house deposits (Owen 1993), but unfortunately no published data is available on the ratios recorded. The analysis of grain and weed seeds from midden and other deposits at Quoygrew, Westray indicated six row hulled barley, oats, flax and traces of wheat, with an increasing use of oats for fodder, and changes in the ratios of barley to oat over time (Adams *et al.* 2012, 166). Flax was a prevalent find from Quoygrew and possibly locally grown using lighter sandy soils, but the wheat grain was probably imported. The Late Norse deposits at Earl's Bu, Orphir produced very large numbers of oat grains, and some hulled barley and flax (Batey and Morris 1992, 38).

On the northern Scottish mainland, midden material from the coastal sites of Geodha Smoo Cave in Sutherland, and from Marymas Green in Caithness produced fairly equal numbers of six row hulled barley and oats from the early Norse deposits, but with a dramatic increase in oat production seen in the Late Norse material from Marymas Green (Alldritt 2003). In Shetland analysis of Pictish and Viking material from Old Scatness produced similar results to Pool, Sanday, with an agricultural regime based around six row hulled barley and oats, with flax introduced as a new crop in the Viking period and an increased emphasis on oats over time (Bond *et al.* 2010, 195). Interestingly, both Pool, Sanday and Old Scatness produced weeds of well manured sandy arable fields, a general reflection of coastal farming perhaps, but at Old Scatness increasing sand blow in the later phases could have triggered the greater emphasis on growing oats as premium farmland was reduced (Bond *et al.* 2010, 195). Further afield findings of hulled barley in Iceland might have been locally cultivated, or could have been imported (Martin 2014, 193), and it is probable that grain was quite widely traded across the Norse sphere of influence (Zori *et al.* 2013, 154).

The Western Isles are not directly comparable to the Northern Isles in terms of soils, environment or building tradition (Bond 2002, 179). However, there are certain archaeological parallels reflecting human response to survival in marginal island environments, and similarities to the constraints placed upon agriculture, which suggest some comparisons can be made (Bond 1998; Bond 2002, 179). Small islands in the Western Isles were able to survive difficult marginal environmental conditions by adaptation and management of local resources combined with external trading (Smith and Mulville 2004). Excavations at Bornais, and at Cille Pheadair on South

Uist produced high densities of six row hulled barley from the Norse phases, alongside an increase in oat and rye (*Secale cereale*), with an expansion in oat cultivation seen in the Norse period (Smith and Mulville 2004; Smith 2005). Rye is a slightly unusual find, but tolerant of poor soils and dry conditions, and could reflect expansion of arable agriculture onto marginal land (Smith 2005, 189). Both Bornais and Cille Pheadair produced flax in large quantities. Spatial analysis of the plant remains from Bornais revealed greater quantities of barley, oat and rye recorded from the kiln/barn structure than from within the Norse house, with chaff remains indicating barley and oat grain were being processed on site in large amounts.

Whilst there are some variations in the ratios of barley to oat found across these previously excavated sites, which might be attributable to consumer/producer differences or status, there does also seem to be a growing body of evidence revealing changes in arable practice occurring over time. There seems to be a general trend toward increased oat production into the Late Norse and medieval periods seen not just in Orkney, but also across Scotland and northern Britain. Part of the problem with trying to compare some of the earlier excavated material is the often lengthy hiatus between excavation and publishing, accompanied by a general lack of solid published radiocarbon dating. Variations in the plant nomenclature used can also cause problems, particularly when reviewing data accumulated many years ago, and it should be beholden upon specialists to attempt to use a standard modern naming system, such as Stace (1997) to prevent confusion.

The environmental samples from Snusgar and East Mound produced highly significant quantities of carbonised plant remains and charcoal, which combined with a thorough radiocarbon dating programme, have enabled a modern, systematic analysis of the economic and environmental processes taking place during the Viking-Late Norse period in Orkney. As such the work has both local and regional significance. Economic data in the form of large quantities of cereal grain, consisting of oats and barley, and other economic plants, such as flax, were recorded, whilst the exploitation of wild resources such as peat, and in later phases seaweed, was also indicated by the range of macrofossils present in some of the deposits. An ecological interpretation of the weed flora has allowed various habitats, both wild and cultivated, to be proposed in the vicinity of the mounds. Some of the weeds were very specific to coastal environments and suggested a mixed habitat of shingle and coastal grassland rich in wild flowers, whilst others indicated highly fertilised sandy arable land such as one would expect in a coastally based infield system. Wood charcoal was found in large amounts in Trench 5, particularly from the metalworking areas in use during Phases 3 and 5, but there was also evidence for the use of birch, alder and Scots pine for fuel and building material during other phases and in different parts of the East Mound longhouse. The reconstruction of everyday life on a Norse farmstead can be proposed, with the main period of occupation on East Mound taking place over about 25–50 years, followed by post-occupation, and the processes of collapse and final abandonment.

Methodology

Bulk environmental samples were processed by project staff and students under supervision using a Siraf style water flotation system (French 1971). Samples were taken from every stratigraphically significant deposit, with standard 10 l sealable sampling tubs utilised to ensure consistency in sample size and eliminate potential sources of contamination. Most samples consisted of a minimum of 10 l per context, with richer deposits yielding up to 120 l. All sample volumes are provided in the summary results tables and online archive spreadsheets for comparative purposes. The resultant light fraction or 'flot' was dried before examination under a low powered binocular microscope typically at x10 to x20 magnifications. The heavier 'residue' portion of each sample was dried and then sorted by eye, with carbonised material subsequently forwarded to the author for identification. All identified plant remains including charcoal were removed and bagged separately by type. Indeterminate grain was counted by the presence of embryo end in order to avoid duplicate counts of multiple fragments.

Wood charcoal was examined using a high-powered Vickers M10 metallurgical microscope at magnifications up to x200. The reference photographs of Schweingruber (1990) were consulted for charcoal identification. Plant nomenclature utilised in the text follows Stace (1997) for all vascular plants apart from cereals, which follow Zohary and Hopf (2000). Ecological groupings are based upon Stace (1997) and Scott and Palmer (1987), the latter being more Northern Isles specific. The term 'seed' is used in the broadest sense to include, achenes, nutlets and so forth.

Results

The environmental samples overall produced large amounts of well-preserved carbonised plant remains. The amounts per sample varied from <2.5 ml up to 40 ml of charred detritus, including cereal grain, charcoal, burnt peat and weed seeds in some of the midden deposits, general hearths, internal layers, floor layers and wall fills, through to some of the extremely abundant metalworking features which produced from 100 ml up to 1660 ml of carbonised material mainly consisting of large fragments of wood charcoal.

Modern roots were recorded throughout the samples in small amounts, along with occasional earthworm egg capsules, suggesting bioturbation of the deposits was minimal, with earthworm eggs situated mostly in the wall fills and later disturbed layers. Internal floor deposits and other layers particularly within Trench 5 were found to be extremely secure. Snail shell was recorded in some of the samples, but mainly related to the later abandonment/ disturbance deposits, and from more recent activity during Phase 9.

The weed seeds were divided into six ecological categories based upon Stace (1997) and Scott and Palmer (1987). These consisted of: 1) Sandy arable land and disturbed ground; 2) Non-sandy arable land and waste places/disturbed ground; 3) Grassland: rough/ grassy arable land, meadows and pasture; 4) Wetland environments: moors, bogs and heath/heathy pasture; 5) Wetland environments: wet grassland, marsh, streamside and ponds; and 6) Shoreline environments: shingle beaches, coastal arable fields. Of course many species can be found to have quite wide ecological preferences and are not strictly specific to any one main habitat, particularly some of the more pernicious disturbed ground and waste-place weeds, which are often prolific colonisers on arable land. The categories are therefore intended as a broad guide to the groups of plant communities that might have existed in the vicinity of the mounds, or arrived from environments that were exploited for resources, and are interpreted as a whole suite of remains in conjunction with the macro-plant evidence for cereal, woodland resources, peat, heather and straw/dung.

Summary results are provided by phase in Tables 8.1 to 8.10. All results are discussed below by phase. For phases see Chapter 4 (Table 4.2).

Phase 2: Late 9th–early 11th centuries AD (Figs 8.1 and 8.2; Table 8.1)

A total of 27 bulk samples were taken from 20 different contexts assigned to Phase 2, covering Trenches 1 and 4 on the Snusgar mound and Trench 5 on the East Mound.

SNUSGAR (TRENCHES 1–4)

Midden deposits from Trench 1 produced large concentrations of carbonised cereal grain, with a combined total of 622 grains from 50 l of sample (12.44 grains per litre of sediment) from contexts 1017 and 1051. The grain consisted mainly of *Avena* sp. (oat) type – which included the cultivated variety *Avena sativa* (common oat) grains preserved within the floret, together with *Hordeum vulgare* sl. (barley) some of which could be identified as *Hordeum vulgare* var. *vulgare* (six row hulled barley). The oat component out-numbered the barley by almost 2:1. Both samples contained a small concentration of burnt peat, accompanied by scarce seeds of *Empetrum nigrum* (crowberry) a heath/moorland plant, and a single specimen of *Stellaria media* (chickweed) a

ubiquitous arable and disturbed ground weed often found on sand dunes, sandy arable fields and shingle beaches in the Northern Isles (Scott and Palmer 1987, 128). Context 1017 was found to be slightly more structured during excavation and also contained burnt seaweed and hammerscale. This suggested deposition of waste from a combination of activities, such as cereal processing/ drying, metalworking and other burning, with this waste perhaps used as stabilising material or representing activities taking place on an outdoor working surface. There was a sharp contrast between the burnt organic content of 1017 with other external deposit 1045 – clearly demonstrated in Table 8.1 – with only trace grain recorded from (1045). The samples produced very similar radiocarbon dates of cal AD 880–1030 (SUERC-17847) for 1017, and cal AD 880–1020 (SUERC-17848) for 1045, although 1045 was stratigraphically earlier. The degraded burnt material from 1045 was possibly trampled into the deposit. Indeed the main carbonised component of 1045 came from a Spot Find sample of charcoal fragments, which included *Salix* (willow) and *Corylus* (hazel), possibly a discrete deposit of fuel waste. The willow charcoal consisted of roundwood fragments of 15 mm diameter with six growth rings, suggesting small branch wood being cut for fuel.

The samples from Trench 4 mostly consisted of midden material producing a smaller concentration of cereal grain than that seen in T1, together with burnt peat, heather stems and rhizome fragments, and a small amount of willow charcoal, seaweed and weeds from arable ground and heathland/boggy places. A total of 250 l of sediment were sampled from the Trench 4 middens from Phase 2 (Table 8.1), resulting in 456 cereal grains (1.82 grains per litre), with 2.18 g of burnt peat, heather stems and rhizomes. The grain suggested a similar range to that seen in Trench 1, with the bulk of material consisting of oat, with fewer barley grains recorded, mixed together with burnt peat fragments and other evidence for the use of peat/heath for fuel. The first midden layers contained grain, peat evidence and a small amount of willow charcoal, mainly focused in shell midden deposit 1561, radiocarbon dated to cal AD 890–1030 (SUERC-17856), but the main concentrations of grain were found in the second extensive series of midden layers 1519, 1529 and 1533 with mostly oat identified. Almost all the complex structured midden layers from Trench 4 produced some evidence for grain and peat, albeit often only in small amounts, and generally in much smaller concentrations than that seen in Trench 1. Some of the general organic layers mixed with sand, such as 1545, 1557, contained only trace degraded material, and are probably not that significant in archaeobotanical terms other than as echoes from nearby activity. Pit fill 1571 was sterile of identifiable material.

EAST MOUND (TRENCHES 5–8)

Three of the Phase 2 samples from Trench 5 produced small quantities of cereal grain and charcoal, and trace evidence for the use of peat (Fig. 8.2). The grain was mainly found to be oat, with traces of barley recorded in midden layer 2152, together with seaweed and charcoal indicating mixed midden material, whilst the longhouse floor 2146 produced occasional barley only. External yard surface 2234 also produced traces of oat and barley along with willow charcoal. No weed seeds were present. Although the evidence was quite scarce from this early phase, it is possible to see some suggestions for divisions in activity, with general agricultural waste in the midden, charcoal from burning in the yard, and barley perhaps waste remains left from cooking on a peat hearth inside the house.

During this phase, the main focus of activity was on the Snusgar mound, with evidence for complex middening practices taking place, involving movement, combination and recycling of burnt waste and other material, such as shell and bone, from a number of sources, and probably as part of an intensive infield agricultural system (Harrison 2013). Some of the burnt waste was probably being used as packing or levelling material to stabilise the mound without the intention of being reused, suggesting plenty of farm yard and other waste available for fertiliser. Evidence from East Mound is slightly more ephemeral during this phase, but hinted at divisions that may be more visible in later phases.

Phase 3: 10th–early/mid-11th centuries AD (Figs 8.3, 8.4, 8.14)

This phase produced 52 samples from 35 different contexts, with only five samples sterile of identifiable remains.

SNUSGAR (TRENCHES 1–4, TABLE 8.2)

Two samples were examined from Trench 1 related to the longhouse building. Context 1019, a layer from within the longhouse, produced a small amount of burnt material, consisting of oat grain, burnt peat and other peat/heath related fuel waste, and a small amount of willow and hazel charcoal. Cereal drying or cooking activity with peat used as fuel on domestic hearths could have been taking place within this structure, with burnt material then trampled or compacted into the floor. External wall fill 1023 contained similar traces of burnt evidence to 1019, but more degraded and probably reflecting material used as packing or swept out of hearths and into crevices in the wall. Seeds of *Plantago lanceolata* (ribwort plantain) in 1023 could have come from turf used in the house construction, or an oat crop grown in grassy fields, whilst the *Chenopodium album* (fat hen) recorded here is a common arable weed, especially on

sandy farmland in the Northern Isles (Scott and Palmer 1987, 118).

In Trench 4 the third series of extensive midden deposition 1508 to 1510 produced small amounts of charred material, with traces of oat and barley in 1508 and 1510, and evidence for *Calluna* (heather) in 1508. A single poorly preserved Poaceae (grass) seed was the only weed recorded from these deposits. Context 1509 was sterile of identifiable material. Degraded indeterminate grain in 1508 and 1510 suggested trampled/re-deposited material, or areas of poor preservation. The plant remains do not form a particularly significant component of this third series, and other activity was probably taking place at this time. Above this the uppermost midden, represented by extensive deposit 1504, radiocarbon dated to cal AD 970–1040 (SUERC-17850), contained slightly more cereal evidence, with oat and barley identified as well as a small amount of burnt peat and some indeterminate degraded grain. Perhaps more significantly 1504 was the first of the midden deposits to produce *Linum usitatissimum* (flax) on the Snusgar mound, albeit a single specimen only, providing tentative evidence for the use of this plant at the site (Fig. 8.3).

Other midden lenses and deposits mixed with wind-blown sand in Trench 4, such as 1507, 1514, 1515, 1516, 1551 and 1552 were either sterile of identifiable material or produced only trace remains and probably represent periods of relative inactivity or changes in focus. In total 155 l of sediment were taken from the Phase 3 Trench 4 middens, but these produced only 82 cereal grains (0.52 grains per litre), with 0.52 g of burnt peat, rhizomes and heather stems, suggesting a general reduction in cereal related burning activity/agricultural midden deposition from that seen in the previous Phase 2. Certainly, less burnt waste was being stored and recycled via midden accumulation, and other types of activity were probably contributing toward the main component of the midden material in Phase 3.

EAST MOUND (TRENCHES 5–8, TABLE 8.3)

Phase 3 on the East Mound was marked by a period of metalworking activity taking place to the west of the north–south ancillary building and activity related to the first hall-building.

INTERNAL AND EXTERNAL DEPOSITS, ANCILLARY BUILDINGS

Samples were taken from a series of floor deposits in the longhouse, western yards and north–south ancillary building, enabling a comparison of deposition of types of burnt remains to be made (Figs 8.4 and 8.5) and potential activity to be proposed. Midden material, and remains from the drain feature were also examined. Midden layers 2254 and 2288 building up to the east and north-east of the ancillary building produced small amounts of cereal grain consisting of six row hulled barley and oats (1.05 grains per litre). Occasional finds of weeds indicating highly fertilised sandy arable land or disturbed ground, probably arrived with the cereal crop. A concentration of burnt peat, rhizomes and heather stems, in total 3.75 g obtained from 20 l of sediment, suggested intensive burning, probably the waste remains from fuel used in cereal drying or internal domestic hearths. Two of the barley grains still had chaff attached and were part-sprouted, suggesting drying of partially processed grain probably after a wet summer. Drying would help prevent further spoilage of a crop in which some of the grain had started to germinate (van der Veen 1989, 303; Fenton 1978, 375). Interestingly *Salix* (willow) charcoal fragments present in these midden deposits, could have derived from metalworking hearth waste combined into the midden. Willow from 2288 dated to cal AD 1010–1160 (SUERC-33721) was found to be roundwood with 12 very tightly packed growth rings, suggesting poor growing seasons, which matched the condition of some of the charcoal found in the metalworking hearths. Traces of burnt seaweed were also recorded and were probably deliberately added to boost the fertilizer content of the midden. Seeds of *Linum usitatissimum* (flax) were found in 2288, probably originating from activity taking place inside the longhouse, which will be discussed further below. Flax appears for the first time at Snusgar and East Mound in Phase 3.

The origins of some of the midden deposits from activities taking place inside the hall-building and the north–south ancillary building can be proposed by the similarities in the material. Hall-building floor deposits produced *Avena sativa* (common oat) preserved in its chaff, as well as *Hordeum vulgare* var. *vulgare* (six row hulled barley) again with some found with chaff attached, with slightly more oat present than barley, producing in total 2.5 grains per litre of sample. Weeds indicating highly fertilised arable land or disturbed ground, mostly *Spergula arvensis* (corn spurrey) and the nitrophilous *Stellaria media* (chickweed) were recorded, and most likely arrived with a cereal crop grown on an infield where manure could be heavily focused to improve sandy coastal soil conditions.

Flax seeds from the floor deposits may have derived from wet plants being hung above a hearth to dry. Interestingly a number of weeds preferring wetland environments were found with the flax, including *Ranunculus repens* (creeping buttercup) and *Ranunculus flammula* (lesser spearwort), suggesting wet grassland, streamside or pond habitats in the vicinity. It is possible these seeds became accidentally incorporated with flax plants retted in nearby ponds or streams, and were brought into the house via that route, or they may have dropped down from turf used as roofing material or fuel. Burnt

peat fragments were found in large amounts, together with occasional finds of heather, rhizomes and seaweed. The peat and other peat related elements totalled 8.28 g achieved from only 52 l of sediment, and indicated that peat was likely being intensively used as fuel for cereal drying activity and general domestic heating. This compacted material probably represents the mixed accumulation of flooring remains with sweepings or scatters of material from day to day processing, cooking, drying and general domestic heating related activity taking place around the hearth places inside the hall (Fig. 8.14). Other evidence for fuel recovered from the floor deposits consisted of *Salix* (willow), *Betula* (birch) and *Pinus sylvestris* (Scots pine), suggesting mixed sources being exploited, although willow dominated.

The floor deposit 2273 from the far west of the hall-building produced a similar broad range of fuel types to the other floors, indicating use of willow, birch and peat, but there was a greater concentration of cereal grain found within this area with 9.5 grains recovered per litre of sediment. The grain consisted of oat and barley, with traces of oat chaff, but no weeds of agriculture were present. The plant evidence largely indicates a clean crop with no weed remains found in this area, concurrent with ready-processed grain being cooked in this area. A single flax seed had also found its way into this context, possibly trampled in. Interestingly a few burnt organic fragments from 2273 may be burnt straw, perhaps flooring material accidentally burnt.

In contrast the floors from the north–south ancillary building were more similar to the main surviving patches of hall-building floor than to floor deposit 2273, producing cereal grain, cereal chaff, sandy arable weeds and evidence for use of peat as fuel, with flax also present. A degree of cereal related activity was probably taking place in the north–south building, with 1.08 grains per litre recovered, but probably only the latter stages such as drying prior to storage, and not in the amounts seen in either the longhouse or annex. Drain fills 2148, 2149 and 2153 produced traces of burnt waste probably trickling down from activity taking place within the structure and not particularly significant.

METALWORKING HEARTHS

The fills of a sequence of four metalworking hearths, 2282, 2281, 2295 and 2293, and also the external metalworking yard floor 2105 were extensively sampled (Table 8.3). These deposits produced large amounts of very well preserved charcoal, with the greatest concentration found compacted into the metalworking yard floor 210, probably including material that had been cleaned out of the nearby hearths as well as remains of stores of charcoal ready for use. This floor material was radiocarbon dated to cal AD 970–1150 (SUERC-24715). Roundwood *Salix* (willow) charcoal was found from the hearth deposits and yard floor, preserved with bark attached, indicating it had not moved far from the original source of charcoaling, with growth rings counted from various pieces indicating wood cut at 7, 9, 11 and 12 years, as well as other fragments of general trunk wood. The bowl hearth rake out 2240 from 2282 dated to cal AD 1010–1160 (SUERC-33700) contained willow with 12 closely packed growth rings, indicating poor or short growing seasons during the trees lifetime. Locally growing small trees and scrub were probably being deliberately managed in order to supply a steady, possibly seasonal, supply of charcoal for the personal metalworking use of the farmstead. A small amount of *Betula* (birch) was also found in 2281 and 2282 suggesting this type was used occasionally but willow was the preferred source. Comparative analysis of the fuel results from these metalworking related features with the longhouse deposits is given in Fig. 8.5. There is a clear distinction between the types of fuel used and the activity taking place in the metalworking area, and agricultural and other domestic-related activities taking place within the living structures. Charcoal fragments were heavily concentrated in the metalworking hearths, whilst peat/turfy peat formed the bulk fuel for day-to-day processes such as cereal drying and domestic heating.

Trace amounts of cereal grain were recorded from the metalworking areas, together with rare fragments of peat, and these were probably trampled in or wind-blown from nearby general activity and not significant or related to the metalworking processes taking place in this area. Grain was present in an extremely low concentration of 0.2 grains per litre, whilst only 0.18 g of peat related items were found from the 135 l of sediment sampled. No agricultural weeds were recovered from these samples. It is possible some of the trampled in cereal grain originated from the subsequent phase, from sealing or material used as levelling deposits.

Phase 4: Transition, mid–end 11th century AD
East Mound only (Trench 5 only) (Table 8.4)
Eight samples from seven contexts broadly dated to Phase 4, produced small trace amounts of carbonised plant material and scarce charcoal. The deposits consisted mainly of wall and building fills that had been disturbed or redeposited. Traces of oat and barley grain, willow charcoal and burnt peat were present but these remains are probably not significant other than as a reflection of activity taking place in the vicinity at various times.

Phase 5: 11th–mid-12th centuries AD (Figs 8.11–8.14, Tables 8.5, 8.6, 8.7)
In total 83 samples were examined from 55 contexts assigned to Phase 5. Two of these samples were found to be sterile of identifiable material, whilst occasional samples contained only small amounts of charred remains, but the majority produced significant quantities of carbonised plant material. Cereal grain was recorded in the largest quantities from Trench 5 in Phase 5, from the west annex cooking area, from the longhouse floors, and from the main hearth 2303 in the longhouse (Fig. 8.14).

Snusgar (Trenches 1–4)
Midden material from Trenches 1, 3 and 4 was examined, producing reasonable concentrations of oat and barley from Trenches 1 and 3 (1.6 grains per litre, and 1.34 grains per litre, respectively), but with far fewer grains or other burnt material recorded from Trench 4 (0.64 grains per litre). Phase 3 had indicated a similar drop-off in numbers, suggesting different constituents in the make-up of the midden deposits. The Trench 1 and 3 middens were quite similar, with *Hordeum vulgare* var. *vulgare* (six row hulled barley), *Avena sativa* (common oat), accompanied by a mixture of weeds originating from arable land, grassland and heath, and fuel remains consisting of mainly burnt peat fragments with some charcoal, indicating waste from cereal drying or cooking with peat used as fuel, so general domestic/farmyard recycled waste. Context 1013 from Trench 1 radiocarbon dated to cal AD 990–1160 (SUERC-17846), produced an interesting peak in flax seeds (Fig. 8.13) suggesting the probable processing/drying of this crop in the longhouse or nearby during Phase 5. The Trench 4 deposits contained only traces of cereal grain, no oat or barley chaff, no weeds of cultivation, no charcoal, and only small amounts of peat, indicating different processes taking place in the formation of this midden.

East Mound
Phase 5 saw the extension of the longhouse with the byre and western ends added: a series of ashy floor layers accumulated in the domestic area, and a sequence of hearths were built. The main hearth 2303 and small metalworking hearth 2301 were in use, whilst in the western annex cooking pits 2291 and 2306 were being used to dry large amounts of cereal grain and flax, and probably also acted as cooking areas. The north–south ancillary building had been re-built as a west–east sub-rectangular building – floors 2053, 2071, 2113 and 2120, and then subsequently reconfigured into a square structure – floor/hearth deposit 2116.

Longhouse internal deposits: Floors in domestic area, western annex, hearths, quenching tank
The longhouse floor deposits 2158, 2224, 2261, 2263, 2265 and 2275 produced equal amounts of oat and barley (Fig. 8.11), with six row hulled barley and cultivated oat both present, along with chaff from both cereals. Grain was present in quite large concentrations of 4.55

grains per litre of sediment. Abundant amounts of sandy arable weeds, grassland and some non-sandy arable/general disturbed ground weeds were found, along with a few heath and wetland types, with particularly large amounts of weeds in 2224, 2261 and 2263. Floor 2224 contained *Ranunculus repens* (creeping buttercup) and *Ranunculus sceleratus* (celery leaved buttercup) which may have arrived accidentally as a by-product of flax retting or dropped from a turf roof. Flax seeds were found carbonised in the floor deposits, perhaps from being dried over nearby hearths, and were particularly notable in 2261. Rare seeds of *Tripleurospermum maritima* (sea mayweed), a plant of shingle beaches in 2224, may have been accidentally gathered with seaweed taken from the shore, as some carbonised seaweed was also found in the floors. Large amounts of burnt peat and peat-related items were found and probably represent general fuel waste trampled into the floors, creating an ashy accumulation. Dry peat may have been laid as flooring, with some dry brown organic fragments, possibly peat/turf found in floor deposit 2263. A few fragments of burnt straw/dung were also compacted into the floor deposits and these may have originated from straw used as flooring or to soak up spillages.

Fill 2304 from hearth 2303 dated to cal AD 1020–1170 (SUERC-33711) contained a high concentration of burnt cereal grain, with 7.47 grains per litre, consisting of slightly more oat than barley, and with chaff from both also present (Fig. 8.12). The main fuel being used in this hearth seems to have been peat, and this was probably an area for cereal drying, and perhaps also cooking. Weeds from the fill indicated a mixture of highly fertilised sandy and non-sandy arable ground being used for agriculture, with crops such as barley or perhaps flax probably grown in the infield, whilst some of the grassland seeds may have arrived with oats grown on rougher marginal land. Wetland and heath plants, in particular sedges and rushes, and grassland plants such as *Bromus* sp. (bromes) in this deposit, may have originated from turf roofing or internal structures, or from peat or turf being used for fuel. In buildings with a turf element to their construction vegetation can become soot blackened by smoke from the hearth, leading to preservation of sedges, docks, grasses, heather and sometimes seaweed (Holden 1998, 29). Flax seeds were also found in this deposit and the hearth was probably being used for suspending retted flax plants to dry, or was near an area where flax plants were processed for fibres.

The contrast between domestic and non-domestic was apparent in the sample from small metalworking hearth fill 2301, which produced no flax and no peat-related items, but did contain charcoal, identified as both *Salix* (willow) and *Pinus sylvestris* (Scots pine) likely being used as fuel. Fill 2301 contained quite a lot of cereal grain, suggesting a

duel use for the hearth, or that burnt waste from the main hearth 2303 was used as a sealing deposit. Quenching tank fill 2285 underlined the link to the metalworking hearth as it produced a good deal of willow charcoal; it also contained burnt peat and a few cereal grains which probably drifted or were swept in from nearby activity.

PIT FILLS

Fills from three pits were examined (2205: external to the ancillary building, 2255: in the western annex and 2296: in the floor of the domestic longhouse area) and revealed different types of burning events taking place and spatial separation in activities. Small pit 2296 contained cereal grain (5.3 grains per litre), flax and a small amount of grassland weeds, this may have been a discrete dump of burnt waste from elsewhere, or a 'scoop hearth' type feature with material burnt *in situ*. The small pit in the western annex 2255 was quite distinctly different, producing trace finds of probably intrusive cereal and charcoal, a small amount of burnt peat and a very large collection of carbonised seaweed fragments. This pit was being used for burning seaweed, with peat used as fuel (Fig. 8.12). The large pit east of the ancillary building 2205 did not leave a particularly strong archaeobotanical signature and it is possible other activities, not producing burnt waste, were taking place here. Only trace amounts of cereal grain (0.8 grain per litre) were found along with a small amount of burnt peat.

WESTERN ANNEX

The western annex produced some very rich samples abundant in cereal grain and other carbonised material. This area was probably used for a number of purposes, including final drying of cereal grain and flax plants, and for extremely large amounts of cooking. Floor deposit 2241 produced a high concentration of cereal grain with a little chaff, and with evidence for both peat and charcoal used as fuel. The charcoal was identified as willow and birch. The grain was found in concentrations of 17.3 grains per litre, indicative of the large amount of processing and cooking activity taking place in this area, with spillages from hearths, sweepings and other general burnt waste compacted into the floor. Scoop 2306 might have been a cooking pit/scoop/hearth-type feature, with the same types of material found here as in the floor 2241, but with more flax, and greater amounts of burnt peat and weeds of cultivation (circular pit 2300 in the main longhouse floor could have been a similar type of feature, although it contained much lower amounts). Circular cooking pit 2291 dated to cal AD 1020–1210 (SUERC-33719) accounted for the largest amount of cereal grain recorded from any deposit on the East Mound, with huge amounts of oat grain (Fig. 8.12) but only traces of barley in fill 2290, producing 20.36 grains per litre, with weeds from arable land and rougher ground. Peat was the sole source of fuel, with no charcoal found. The burning of grain is an accidental occurrence during cereal drying and therefore can be seen as representing only a small proportion of the actual amount processed during an agricultural season. The amounts in 2290 suggested a very large amount of cereal processing was taking place; oat was clearly an extremely important part of the cereal economy during this phase.

BYRE (EASTERN) END OF THE LONGHOUSE

At the byre end of the longhouse different activities were taking place, indeed the samples from this area produced only small concentrations of grain compared to that seen elsewhere, but there was some evidence for peat and charcoal being used for fuel. The byre samples were split into three different types of floor deposit for analysis: work 2173, 2268, 2272 and 2274; animal 2267, 2271 and 2277; and general 2156 and 2276. Floor 2276 produced a date of cal AD 900–1120 (SUERC-47156), whilst 2271 and 2277 produced slightly later dates of cal AD 1010–1160 (SUERC-33712) and cal AD 1020–1170 (SUERC-33716) respectively. The work and animal-related floors both produced large amounts of burnt peat, probably derived from ashy flooring material and general work activity occurring in this structure. Cereal amounts were very low and possibly represent trampled material brought into the area, with weeds of cultivation found in traces only, indicating cereal processing was probably not taking place at the byre end. Interestingly both the work and animal contexts contained straw/dung organic material compacted into the floor deposits, probably representing a straw floor laid down to soak up animal waste or cover damp areas.

EXTERNAL DEPOSITS AND ANCILLARY BUILDINGS

Far fewer carbonised remains were found in the ancillary buildings and external deposits than were recorded from the longhouse (Fig. 8.13). The west–east sub-rectangular building and subsequent square structure produced very little burnt evidence and it is unlikely any cereal processing or cooking activity was occurring here, although the odd trace grain may have been trampled through from the longhouse. These two structures were largely bereft of any burnt remains to indicate what processes may have been taking place, perhaps they were used for storage or different types of activity. The external yard area 2087 and 2089 was similar, with just a few traces of burnt peat and cereals, perhaps this area was regularly swept through, whilst 2109 contained a few fragments of willow charcoal, perhaps remains from general farmyard activity. The other general external layers, 2118, 2119, 2202 etc., contained some burnt cereal grain waste and a little burnt peat, but were more notable for producing a large amount of willow charcoal. The burnt material may have

been dumped out of the longhouse and used as levelling material or accumulated as midden-type storage, whilst the large amount of charcoal suggested re-worked refuse from the metalworking that had occurred in the area in Phase 3.

Phase 6: Later 11th–12th centuries AD (Fig. 8.6, Table 8.8)

Phase 6 produced 53 samples from 31 contexts, with three samples found to be sterile of identifiable material, whilst most were quite low in charred content, although some remains of cereal, peat, charcoal and other macrofossils were recovered.

EAST MOUND (TRENCHES 5–8)

INTERNAL DEPOSITS: WESTERN ANNEX, BYRE FLOOR

Internal deposits and general layers 2009, 2010, 2130, 2141, 2225 and 2226 produced some trace evidence for oat and barley cereals, a little flax, and burnt remains indicating fuel waste and possible structural collapse, such as roofing material and internal wooden supports and fixtures (Fig. 8.6). The grain was only present in amounts of 0.44 grains per litre, so did not form a major constituent of the internal sediments, and may indeed have been churned up from earlier deposits. Burnt straw/dung and seaweed were found mixed in with burnt peat and other peat-related items such as heather stems. Some of this may have been structural, such as flooring or benching material, or collapse from a smoke-blackened turf roof. A range of charcoal was found including *Salix* (willow), *Betula* (birch) and *Pinus sylvestris* (Scots pine), with birch found in the largest amounts. This could have originated from internal wooden supports, roof beams, internal fittings, roof pegs and so forth that have been smoke-blackened over time or accidentally destroyed by fire at some point during abandonment, or perhaps deliberately dismantled and reused for fuel. Interestingly a large amount of grassland and heathland weeds were found in 2225, including *Rumex acetosella* (sheep's sorrel), *Rumex crispus* (curled dock), *Empetrum nigrum* (crowberry) and *Prunella vulgaris* (selfheal), with some of these probably originating from turf walls and roofing material that has subsequently collapsed (Holden 1998, 50) or from turf used as fuel.

The byre floor deposits 2164 and 2169 were cattle-trampled, producing very few remains other than some trace cereal grain, probably churned or trampled through (only 0.65 grains per litre), a tiny fragment of burnt rhizome and two fragments of *Quercus* (oak) charcoal. The oak was unusual and probably came from a structural timber that was burnt.

The western annex floor area 2227 was interesting, with evidence for fuel waste, collapse and burning. There was probably still some, perhaps transient, cereal-related or other domestic activity occurring here during Phase 6, with a cereal concentration of 6.6 grains per litre, including well preserved six row hulled barley and oat. Peat ash remains were found mixed with straw, perhaps flooring material, and this area could have become a scaled back cereal-processing/cooking area, perhaps a temporary living-quarters as the main building was dismantled and took on different uses.

EXTERNAL DEPOSITS AND ANCILLARY BUILDINGS

Midden remains 2008 and 2056 produced scarce traces of charred material, with a few poorly preserved barley and oat grains, and single fragments of burnt peat and *Corylus* (hazel) charcoal. The cereal concentration was very low at only 0.36 grains per litre, indicating agricultural processing waste was not a key component in the make-up of this midden. External surfaces and occupation surfaces possibly trampled by cattle in this phase, for instance 2259, also contained low amounts of grain, with the main constituent being burnt peat mixed with a little charcoal, and occasional finds of straw-like material. The remains in 2259 possibly represent building collapse – turf and trampled waste, or perhaps include mixed organic material used on the floors to soak up cattle waste. External yard surface deposits 2092 and 2093 contained trace, probably wind-blown cereal in a concentration of 0.06 grains per litre, less than recovered from the external yard areas in Phase 5, although it was quite low even then, showing a general reduction in agricultural activity.

The square ancillary building floors roughly spanning Phases 5 to 6, 2040 and 2115, produced small amounts of oat and barley, with some reasonably good preservation of six row hulled barley and cultivated oat, and some sandy arable weeds in 2040 together with burnt peat. The final phase floors 2034 and 2066 contained trace remains only, with grain dropping from a concentration of 0.48 down to 0.08 grains per litre, although this building was probably never really used for cereal-related activity, being more of a storage area.

Phase 7: Immediate post occupation, later 12th–13th centuries AD (Fig. 8.7, Table 8.9)

Phase 7 produced 30 samples from 27 contexts, largely related to disturbance, collapse, later midden material and general post-use. Most samples contained only very small trace amounts of carbonised material.

INTERNAL AND EXTERNAL DEPOSITS: TRENCH 5

This phase produced some evidence for the continuation of cereal agriculture in the immediate post-use of the structures in Trench 5, and around the external surfaces, albeit much scaled-back and possibly with some bioturbation from earlier deposits (Fig. 8.7). Deposits within the remaining longhouse walls 2208 and 2209 produced scarce traces of cereal, all found to be oat, plus

a little burnt peat, possibly residual material mixed from earlier activity. Small concentrations of cereal were found in some of the immediate post-use deposits, mainly 2217 and 2223 consisting of six row hulled barley and oat, but with a high proportion of poorly preserved indeterminate grain, indicating possible mixing and disturbance in the soil. External layer 2035 was similar and also contained quite a few weeds of fertilised sandy arable ground suggesting farming was still taking place in the vicinity. It is possible a small amount of agricultural processing was still taking place here, perhaps using the partially-collapsed structures as a temporary shelter or 'lean-to'. Alternatively, this could be midden-type material dumped into the abandoned building from a nearby settlement (Martin 2014, 202). Byre fill 2238 produced traces of cereal grain, mostly poorly preserved, together with a range of charcoal types, and a few weeds of grassland and heath, possibly from roofing collapse. The charcoal consisted of oak, willow, alder and Scots pine, perhaps from collapse and burning of internal wooden fittings, or opportunistic fuel use from people using the buildings as temporary shelter or farm outbuildings.

MIDDEN MATERIAL: TRENCHES 5, 6, 7 AND 8

The midden remains from all four trenches in this phase did not show agricultural or other burnt waste, such as domestic hearth material, as a major component. Different waste products were going into the middens, with agricultural waste not being stored for reuse on the fields. Midden material mixed with wind-blown sand and stone collapse in Trench 5 produced traces of grain (0.17 grains per litre) with a little willow charcoal, probably not particularly significant. The Trench 6 external midden was sterile of carbonised remains and probably peripheral to any activity. In Trench 7, midden contexts 4016 and 4020 produced some flax and a small amount of cereal, but these were obviously not the main constituent with a grain concentration of only 0.67 per litre. Capping deposit 4015 on top of earlier midden material produced three stray cereal grains and nothing else. Trench 8 consisted of mixed layers, high in seaweed content, indicating disturbance from later kelp-burning activity.

Phase 8: Collapse, robbing 13th–17th centuries AD (Table 8.10)

Phase 8 produced 26 samples from 20 contexts with four sterile samples and the remainder very low in charred content.

INTERNAL AND EXTERNAL LAYERS: TRENCH 5

Mixed and disturbed layers from Trench 5 produced oat and barley cereal grain, possibly bioturbated from earlier deposits, mixed with burnt peat and carbonised seaweed, suggesting kelping activity. Most of the grain came from 2074 and 2131 with the material from 2131 poorly preserved.

MIDDEN AND EXTERNAL DEPOSITS: TRENCH 6 AND 7

Two external layers from Trench 6, 3003 and 3004, were to all intents and purposes sterile, with only a single grain in 3004 mixed with traces of crushed indeterminate charred detritus. This area is not particularly significant with the material probably wind-blown. Trench 7 produced small amounts of cereal grain from midden contexts 4006, 4007 and 4012 possibly indicating some later middening activity.

Phase 9: Modern, 18th century onward, including kelping and cow burial (Table 8.10)

A total of 13 samples from 12 contexts produced two sterile samples, with a number of disturbed and mixed modern contexts containing traces of residual material.

Trench 1 and 4 had been heavily disturbed by modern kelping and cow burials. Kelp pits 1004 and 1540 produced charred seaweed, whilst disturbed layer 1050 contained quite a high concentration of burnt peat, perhaps a single episode dump of fairly recent fuel waste. Trench 5 produced traces of grassland and wetland weeds, possibly bioturbated remains from the structural collapse. Trench 6 was sterile.

Discussion

The agricultural economy

The environmental analysis demonstrated both barley and oats were in use on the Snusgar and East Mounds, with variations in ratio and quantity recovered across the phases (Figs 8.8–8.9). The cereal assemblage consisted of *Hordeum vulgare* sl. (barley), with the better preserved specimens identifiable as *Hordeum vulgare* var. *vulgare* (six row hulled barley), together with *Avena* sp. (oat). The presence of oat chaff indicated the cultivation of *Avena sativa* (common oat), with some whole grains still preserved within the chaff. This range of cereals is similar to other sites of the Viking-Late Norse period and fits the general pattern for Scottish material (Dickson and Dickson 2000). The grain was generally very well preserved, with indeterminate grain more notable in the later phases, suggesting some re-deposition or disturbance was occurring later on. Phases 2, 3 and 5 on both the Snusgar mound and East Mound produced a strong signature for the dominance of oat, with this pattern particularly notable in Phase 5 on the East Mound. In Phases 6 and 7 the ratios between oat and barley evened out slightly with less numerical dominance of one type. During Phase 5 there was marked intensification in oat production – not only did this phase produce, across all deposits, the most oat grains, but also the most oat chaff, and the highest number of weeds of rough grassland, sandy

arable and non-sandy arable land/disturbed ground. This probably reflected an increased need for fodder production to feed cattle (Barrett *et al.* 2000) and also expansion onto land not ideally suited to barley or flax (Bond 1998, Bond *et al.* 2010).

Barley had an important role at both mound sites, and analysis of the weed flora indicated highly fertilised sandy arable land was under cultivation, possibly for the barley crop, but perhaps for flax which prefers a lighter free-draining soil (Bond 2007). Equally, barley could be cultivated on a heavier soil provided sufficient manuring materials were available, and the weeds suggested disturbed ground and non-sandy arable land in the vicinity. Barley cultivation was probably taking place using an infield system, heavily fertilised to improve the yield and prevent soil depletion. Sandy coastal soils such as those in the immediate surroundings of the mounds can be improved by the addition of rotted down animal manure, plus other organic materials such as seaweed, fish bone, ground animal bone and even blood. As an indirect consequence of this manure-rich environment the background arable weed assemblage of *Spergula arvensis* (corn spurrey), *Chenopodium album* (fat hen), *Stellaria media* (chickweed), *Fallopia convolvulus* (black bindweed) and *Euphorbia helioscopia* (sun spurge) would have thrived, and the combined recovery of these types peaked in Phase 5. Scarce seeds of *Tripleurospermum maritimum* (sea mayweed) as well as more frequent finds of *Galium aparine* (cleavers) may have arrived on the farm with seaweed harvested for fertiliser from shingle beaches, or could suggest sandy arable fields extending directly down to the shore (Scott and Palmer 1987, 282).

The 'plaggen' or 'proto-plaggen' system utilising organic manures, such as animal dung mixed with hay from byre floors, combined with domestic waste and compacted floor material has been demonstrated as taking place in the Northern Isles (Fenton 1978, 274; Guttmann *et al.* 2003). Stalling of animals indoors has been attributed as the cause of the build-up of compacted organic floor material accumulated at sites such as Scalloway in Shetland (Sharples 1998) and at Howe, Orkney (Dickson 1994), which in turn would then enable a feedback of useful organic material into a plaggen-type system. It is however important to remember that the material analysed from midden remains is the material that has not been put on the fields, but this in turn can reflect changes in economic focus, for instance from agriculture to fishing.

Both settlements were involved in the creation of agricultural produce to feed people and animals. Barley and oats could have been used for both food and drink. Probably the simplest way to produce food was by mixing barley and oat grain together, drying until parched, grinding and then eating with milk, like a cold porridge, but barley could also be boiled into a broth or soup, or made into bannocks (Fenton 1978, 395). Hulled barley could also have been brewed into beer during the Norse period, but perhaps only reserved for special social occasions such as feasting (Zori *et al.* 2013). The presence of sprouted barley grains may provide some indication as to whether brewing was taking place, but caution is advised. In modern brewery samples every single grain in a given assemblage will usually be found to have sprouted (author's own observation). Small quantities of sprouted grains were found on the East Mound, with single grains in Phase 3 midden contexts 2254 and 2288, whilst two grains were present in the western annex floor deposit 2227 in Phase 6. The bulk of sprouted barley was found in Phase 5, although this amounted to only 18 grains out of more than 550 identified. Most of the sprouted grains came from scoop hearth 2305 in the western annex and from main domestic hearth 2304 in the longhouse. There was possibly some intermittent small-scale household or seasonal festive brewing occurring on East Mound, but equally, wet weather could have caused some of the grains to begin sprouting. At Quoygrew, Westray the scarce presence of sprouted grains is explained as poor storage conditions or the grain not being dried properly (Adams *et al.* 2012, 165). In the Northern Isles the practice of drying whole ears of barley or fully processed grain after a wet summer, in order to prevent further spoilage of a crop in which some of the grain had started to germinate is well documented (van der Veen 1989, 303, Fenton 1978, 375), and that is most likely what is being seen in the bulk of the material here.

On the Snusgar mound during Phase 2 the Trench 1 midden deposits produced abundant cereal grain, with a large concentration of oat outnumbering barley by almost 2:1. The Trench 4 midden samples also contained oat and barley, in lower quantities, but with oat dominating by over 3:1. During Phase 3, the amount of carbonised material in general was greatly reduced with small amounts of oat recorded in the longhouse 1019 in Trench 1, whilst the Trench 4 midden produced traces of oat and barley. Charred material was not a major component of the Trench 4 midden in Phase 3, indicating a slight shift in activity focus, with this accumulation mainly found to be shell midden. In Phase 5 there was a slight increase in carbonised deposition in the Trench 1, Trench 3 and Trench 4 middens, but not on the scale seen earlier in Phase 2. These later middens contained a greater peat/heath component than seen earlier, perhaps the fuel waste from domestic hearths, byre and floor waste, with Trench 3 also containing seaweed.

On East Mound during Phase 2 small traces of oat and barley were found in the hall-building and midden deposits. By Phase 3 there was a marked increase in cereal presence, particularly notable in the hall-building

floors 2262 and 2264, and some of the north-east ancillary building floors, with some spatial difference in activity. Early in the next phase the western annex floor 2273 produced a good concentration of cooking waste, mainly clean grain with only traces of oat chaff and no weeds suggesting primarily a consumption area, whilst the longhouse floors produced oat and barley grain and chaff plus agricultural weeds, suggesting mixed processing/cereal drying and cooking waste in the main building. The north–south ancillary floor deposits were more closely matched to the hall-building and probably represent areas of processing. There is a possibility some clean grain might have come from the Snusgar settlement for cooking at the East Mound hall-building during Phase 3.

In the main Phase 5, cereal production greatly increased: by this time the agricultural focus had probably largely moved away from Snusgar over to East Mound, with abundant oat grain, oat chaff and barley grain recovered. There was marked intensification in oat production during Phase 5, with rougher more marginal areas of land under cultivation, probably to meet the demands for animal fodder, but perhaps also to increase overall grain production by bringing other areas of land unsuited to barley into agricultural use (Bond *et al.* 2010, 193). Very intensive cooking activity was taking place in the western annex, but this area also took on a multi-purpose role with evidence for processing and final drying of grain in 2305 and 2290. In the central area of the longhouse, the main focus of cereal drying and cooking was hearth 2304, with extensive processing taking place. Very little cereal evidence was recorded from the byre end suggesting other working practices taking place here.

By Phase 6 the western annex was still being used for some cereal processing, and might have been a scaled back living area or temporary shelter as the building ran into decay, or acting as an outbuilding for a nearby farm. Maybe the younger men moved away to more lucrative fishing work, whilst others stayed to tend the cattle and agriculture took on a lesser role in the economy. The spatial differentiation between the longhouse and the byre seen in Phase 5 was largely lost in Phase 6 when the deposits became amorphous and churned together by cattle. A slight resurgence in cereal agriculture was visible in Phase 7, mainly from the post use and external deposits, maybe indicating some temporary or short-lived attempts at resettlement, or reuse of the structures as midden retainers.

Other economic plants: Flax

The plant evidence indicated that flax production played an important role in the local economy, particularly on the East Mound, and flax seeds were first seen in both the Snusgar and East Mounds during Phase 3. At Snusgar this was as a single find in a Trench 4 midden, whilst on the East Mound small concentrations were found in both midden 2288 and longhouse floors, with single stray finds in the north–south ancillary building and metalworking hearth 2294. Flax recovery increased in Phase 5 with a good concentration found in the Trench 1 midden layers at Snusgar, whilst larger amounts were found on the East Mound. These were mainly focused in the longhouse floor deposits, particularly 2261, in the western annex scoop 2305 and in the main domestic hearth 2304 (Figs 8.11 and 8.12). A few seeds were found in the byre end: these were generally less well preserved suggesting they had been trampled or scattered through from the longhouse. Traces were found in Phase 6 but mostly in the cattle trampled floor deposits suggesting possible bioturbation from earlier activity. Phase 5 therefore saw the main peak in flax production with activity focused primarily around the hearth places in the longhouse and western annex.

Bond (1994) suggested the intensive farming of flax in Orkney during the Viking period, and certainly Orkney had a very successful 18th-century flax linen industry (Fenton 1978, 491). Flax production was potentially a very important part of the Norse farming economy, with a growing body of data for its presence in Orkney and further afield (Dickson and Dickson 2000; Smith 2005; Bond 2007; Bond *et al.* 2010; Adams *et al.* 2012). Indeed, the introduction of flax has been seen as a distinctive marker of Viking settlement in the Northern Isles (Bond 2007), with significant repercussions to the local farming economy, as its growing requirements would place it in direct competition with barley for the best land (Bond *et al.* 2010, 195). In the complexity of the interaction between barley, oats and flax crops, combined with factors such as dairying and environmental change, the influence of flax growing on increased oat production has perhaps been overlooked (Bond *et al.* 2010, 193).

Flax could be grown for linen and for linseed oil production, and there are a number of possible pathways that could result in flax seeds being recorded in the deposits. The flax plant is harvested by pulling up the whole plant and then retting in order to separate the fibres, with bundles placed into pools, specially prepared pits or flowing streams (Gale and Cutler 2000, 153). The harvested plant, with roots and seeds intact could then either be dried outside, weather permitting, or taken indoors for drying over hearths. Retting in fresh water supplies could result in pollution of streams and Hall (pers. comm. in Gale and Cutler 2000, 153) reports that retting in Viking York was only allowed in certain areas due to risk of water contamination. A number of seeds belonging to marsh, streamside or pond plants, were found in the same deposits as the flax in Phase 5, and these may well have arrived accidentally with flax that had been soaked in the nearby burn or a tributary.

The location of the burnt flax seeds indicated retted plant material was probably hung from the roof over the hearth areas resulting in some seed drop (Dickson and Dickson 2000, 254). Certainly, a number of the flax seeds recovered from 2261, 2296 and 2304 appeared deflated and soggy, as if they had been waterlogged prior to carbonisation. The process of 'rippling', where the top ends of dry flax bundles are pulled through a nail board or comb, effectively deseeds the flax and could result in a scattering of material into the hearths or onto the longhouse floor. Breaking, beating and finally hackling with a fine comb polishes the plant fibres ready for weaving into linen, resulting in further addition of organic material to the floor deposits if this process is carried out indoors.

Flax seeds collected from the rippling process could be turned into oil. In modern practice this involves warming the seed, gently squashing it, slowly heating again through a series of controlled levels so as not to burn the seed, before putting through a press to extract the oil (Newkirk 2015, 5). During the Viking period this was probably a much rougher hit and miss affair, the dry seed could have been put straight to a press, but more oil could be extracted by pre-warming and crushing the seeds in pots over the hearth, and this may have resulted in some falling into the fire. The majority of flax seeds from the East Mound were found in very good condition, suggesting they were not pressing waste, but had more likely come from the drying and processing stages of linen manufacture.

Fuel and building resources

WOODLAND

Charcoal identification demonstrated the use of woodland resources for fuel and building materials on Snusgar and East Mound. Small amounts of charcoal were recorded from the Trench 1 and Trench 4 midden deposits at Snusgar during Phases 2 and 3, consisting of willow and hazel types. These probably originated from hearth waste from within the Snusgar settlement. The East Mound revealed a number of woodland types in use, which expanded in range as time progressed. This began with trace hints for willow being used as fuel in Phase 2, through to the intensive exploitation of willow charcoal for use on the metalworking hearths in Phase 3. During Phase 5 there was a broadening out in the range of types used, to include birch and Scots pine, although willow still held a dominant presence. By Phase 6 willow decreased with a more opportunistic use of the local landscape, using scrub hazel, birch and collecting more Scots pine driftwood from the shore. Some of the charcoal in Phase 6 is probably related to building collapse, such as birch and pine used for roofing and other structural materials. Oak was recorded from the byre floor in Phase 6 and may have been from a collapsed roof beam or support.

In Phase 7 the byre produced oak, willow, alder, Scots pine and other conifer, again probably related to collapse of the structures and opportunistic fuel use.

Overall the internal longhouse, byre and annex floors and ancillary building floors on both mounds did not produce particularly large amounts of charcoal, with fragments recovered from the longhouse floors in Phases 3 and 5, and from the north–south ancillary building in Phase 3 (Figs 8.8 and 8.9). Discrete larger concentrations of willow charcoal were recorded from internal metalworking hearth (2301) and quenching tank 2285 in Phase 5, indicating some industrial activity taking place here. The general low recovery of charcoal in the internal deposits is most likely because peat was being used as the main source of domestic hearth fuel, with charcoal reserved for metalworking (Fig. 8.10). The metalworking yard 2105 and Phase 3 metalworking hearths, particularly 2294 and 2240 on the East Mound, produced the main peak in charcoal use seen across the settlements, and this consisted almost entirely of willow charcoal, with lesser amounts of birch. In Phase 5 willow continued to be recorded in quite high amounts from the external work areas and general layers suggesting general farmyard type repairs, smithing and so forth were occurring using charcoal as fuel.

Charcoal clearly held a special role in the East Mound settlement, its use was largely reserved for metalworking, there was probably less natural woodland available in the immediate location than peat, and it is highly likely that during Phase 3 willow stands were being specifically locally grown and managed for use in metalworking. The presence of native woodland on Orkney has been clearly established from previous research, notably Dickson and Dickson (2000, 64) who identified 14 different types of native wood from Skara Brae, including alder, willow, hazel, birch, rowan and various cherry types. In addition they recorded four types of North American coniferous driftwood mainly spruce. In modern day Orkney this list is considerably reduced to six indigenous woody plants that can reach the stature of trees (or small shrubs), consisting of aspen, downy birch, hazel, juniper, rowan and willow, largely restricted to sheltered areas and gullies such as Berriedale on the Isle of Hoy (Dickson and Dickson 2000, 65). The Late Iron Age deposits from Howe broch indicated alder, birch, hazel and rowan being used for fuel and constructional materials, but perhaps most notably in comparison to the East Mound metalworking area, were the extremely large concentrations of willow charcoal found in the hearth places and furnace (Dickson 1994). By the Late Iron Age and Viking Age, with woodland much reduced, effective management of fast growing tree and shrub/bush types such as willow would have enabled local supplies of charcoal to be maintained for metalworking, albeit on a seasonal or intermittent basis. Interestingly

at Old Scatness, Shetland, Francis *et al.* (2010, 197) identified native alder, willow and hazel, indicating local fuel sources were being exploited alongside peat, as well as coniferous types which probably arrived as driftwood. As with the later phases of the East Mound, some of the charcoal at Old Scatness may have come from old recycled wood from collapsed or disused structures or from artefacts.

In the East Mound metalworking area, hearth rake-out 2240, floor 2105 and hearth fills 2269 and 2294 produced small branch willow roundwood with growth rings indicating a 7–12 year growing period, with tightly packed growth rings indicative of inclement weather and short growing seasons. The majority of charcoal identified from the external metalworking area was in good condition and not heavily heat damaged indicating firing temperatures above 300°C, but below 800°C when significant structural damage would start to occur (Gale and Cutler 2000, 12). Above 800°C charcoal takes on a glassy vitrified appearance as the cell structure begins to fuse, and at very high temperatures is often not identifiable. Glassy fragments were found in the longhouse floors 2264, 2261 and 2224 and in longhouse hearth 2301, suggesting some processes involving higher temperatures could have been occurring in that internal hearth feature.

PEAT AND TURF

Peat and peaty turf/turf had an everyday role as domestic fuel and in the construction of buildings. The weed flora indicated there was a plentiful supply of peat, heathland and other wetland resources in the vicinity, whilst the grassland weeds provided strong evidence for the use of turf. Exploitation of peat areas may have been tightly controlled with each family group owning cutting rights over the turves (Fenton 1978, 210). Peat or heathy turves were the primary source of fuel for domestic heating and cereal drying at both sites (Fig. 8.10). Large amounts of burnt peat were found in association with cereal grain in East Mound Phase 5 in the main domestic hearth 2304, western annex cooking pits 2305 and 2290, and forming the ashy floor build-ups in the longhouse, annex and byre. Whilst some of the more grassy turves may have been used to keep the fire in at night or as an occasional fuel supplement, it is unlikely that turf was used as the main source of domestic fuel on the East Mound, as it is difficult to dry and contains a high inorganic component consisting of several centimetres of soil (Dickson and Dickson 2000, 53). In areas of Orkney with few peat resources, such as the island of Sanday, the inhabitants imported peat from nearby Eday during the 19th century, exchanging grain for peat, but were known to stretch out meagre supplies by using cow and horse dung for fuel (Fenton 1978, 213). The prevalence of burnt peat fragments in the archaeological deposits suggested the occupants of East

Mound had access to good quality peat and heath land for fuel – whether by trading resources or direct ownership of the land – but if necessary could also have diversified to use other sources, such as turfy peat, dung and seaweed (see Chapter 6) – more turfy material 'peaty turves' was being burnt in Trench 4; also in the Phase 5 Trench 5 yard there was evidence for peaty turf burning.

Peat and heathy turves were probably also being used to make internal fittings and laid on the floor as litter, and used as bedding or padding on internal stone benches, and this is particularly notable in Phases 5 and 6 on the East Mound. Icelandic and ethnographic parallels show peat often supplemented hay on the floors in both human and animal habitation, making interpretation slightly difficult, as peat is not just used as fuel (Buckland *et al.* 1993, 518). In Phase 5 longhouse floor deposit 2263 produced 'dry' brown peat, a straw/dung organic burnt mixture and carbonised seaweed, indicating possible mixed flooring material combined with ashy build-up from hearth sweepings. Organic material consisting of straw/dung together with peat was found in the Phase 6 floors, 2227, 2225 and 2259, during the period when cattle were trampling about, probably a mixture of material put on the floors to soak up the mess, and churned up floor deposits, indeed ashy organic floor 2224 from Phase 5 was very similar to 2259.

Roofing materials may have consisted of turf tied together with heather and secured with wooden support pegs. Plant macrofossil finds such as seeds of grasses, sedges, docks, and larger carbonised elements such as heather may reflect various structural elements originating from smoke-blackened turf roofing (Holden 1998, 29). During the lifetime of an organic roof, regular patching would be required to prevent it falling into disrepair, particularly during bad weather. Originally writing in 1920, Firth (1974, 13) described the conditions inside a typical Orkney farmstead as having an all pervading smoke, whilst during wet weather the soot would literally run in slow streams like tar down the walls. Some of the grassland and wetland seeds recorded from the Phase 5 longhouse floors and internal hearth places may reflect smoke blackened turf material that has fallen from the roof during occupation.

Following collapse, up to 1 m of organic roofing deposit may accumulate (Holden 1998, 17). The full deterioration and collapse of the East Mound roof probably started in Phase 6, before final abandonment in Phase 7. The turf layer noted during excavation was probably the roof, with collapse and cattle trample noted in 2259, 2164 and 2169. In particular 2259 contained lots of peat and grassland weeds, indicative of heathy or grassy turves. Birch and conifer wood in Phase 6 probably came from collapsed roof beams and internal fittings – the closest comparisons to this are Icelandic structures which have

turf laid over stone slabs supported by driftwood timbers and birch branches. The supporting walls are made of interlocking turves placed upon stone foundations, and only if sufficient resources allow do they cap the whole roof with a waterproof layer of thatch (Buckland *et al.* 1993, 511). The East Mound roof may have been bare turf tied down with other organic material, such as heather and wood, possibly with the turf laid grassy side up so the structure formed a grassy living mound (Fig. 25.1).

An abandoned structure may subsequently become a dumping ground for external material, with midden waste from nearby settlement deposited in the ruined buildings (Martin 2014, 202). This may explain some of the 'post-use' cereal grain and other agricultural waste deposition occurring in Phase 7, effectively beginning the formation of a post-abandonment midden.

Summary

The environmental samples contained well preserved and often abundant quantities of carbonised plant remains including wood charcoal, cereal grain, weed seeds, burnt peat and other material. Evidence from the Snusgar mound came mostly from midden material and revealed an agricultural system involved in relatively large-scale production of oat and barley during Phase 2. Changes in economic practice were suggested as the emphasis changed from agriculturally-influenced deposition, to middens largely dominated by shell and fish remains during Phases 3 and 5. This change may also reflect a shift in settlement or importance as the influence of East Mound became more prominent on the landscape.

Archaeological evidence from East Mound was more extensive allowing a fuller reconstruction of the settlement and its place within the environment. The agricultural remains indicated a mixed cereal economy involved in the cultivation of barley and oats during Phases 3 and 5, probably locally-grown using an infield/outfield system, and with the final stages of processing/drying and cooking taking place within the longhouse. The western annex was used primarily for cooking, and during Phase 5 this expanded to include some processing activity too. Oat grain dominated the assemblage and probably reflected the need to create enough surplus fodder for the over-wintering of animals as well as increasing the grain yield for human consumption. High-quality barley grain was being consumed primarily as food, with the possibility of some seasonal brewing also occurring but evidence for this was scarce with very few sprouted grains recorded. Spatial separation can be demonstrated within the Phase 5 longhouse, with the living quarters and hearth end mostly involved in domestic activity, whilst the byre end was largely free of agricultural waste. The internal hearth at the eastern end of the domestic area was an exception, and may have seen processes requiring high heat. Small amounts of charcoal indicated a degree of work activity taking place in the byre end. Flax production was occurring locally with drying and processing activity taking place in the domestic area of the house.

The peak in metalworking activity during Phase 3 involved the intensive use of willow charcoal on the external hearths, probably grown locally and charcoaled at source, requiring a degree of woodland management to sustain seasonal activity. The internal metalworking taking place around the small longhouse hearth mentioned above during Phase 5 also used willow.

The environmental analysis has enabled a reconstruction of the East Mound longhouse as a living organic structure within the landscape, utilising local materials such as turf and peat in its construction. The building probably had a

turf roof supported by wooden beams, possibly made from locally growing birch supplemented with pine driftwood. Peat or straw laid on the floor and combined with ashy deposits from the hearths would have soaked up waste from messy processing activity, animals and wet plant material such as flax hung from the roof. By the very Late Norse period there was a general decline in activity as the use of the longhouse changed from a farmstead into a cattle shelter, and the structure fell into disrepair. Some transient agricultural processing was probably still taking place in the western annex and this may have been a temporary shelter as the surrounding buildings collapsed. A brief post-use resurgence in activity was seen in Phase 7, perhaps involving use for storage, or dumping rubbish, before the structures were finally abandoned.

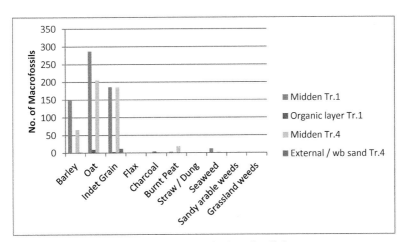

Fig. 8.1: Snusgar Mound, Phase 2: all deposits

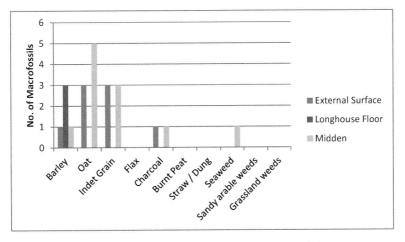

Fig. 8.2: East Mound, Phase 2: internal and external deposits

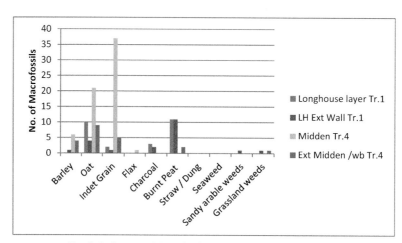

Fig. 8.3: Snusgar Mound, Phase 3: internal and external deposits

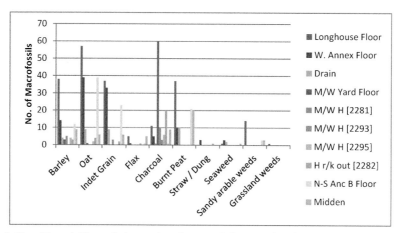

Fig. 8.4: East Mound, Phase 3: internal and external deposits, longhouse and ancillary building

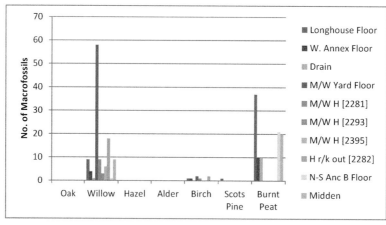

Fig. 8.5: East Mound, Phase 3: comparison of fuel types

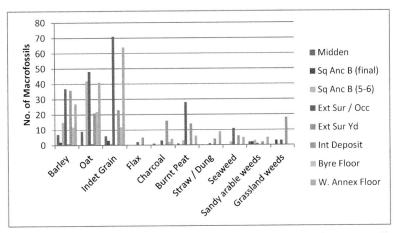

Fig. 8.6: East Mound Phase 6: internal and external deposits, longhouse and square ancillary building

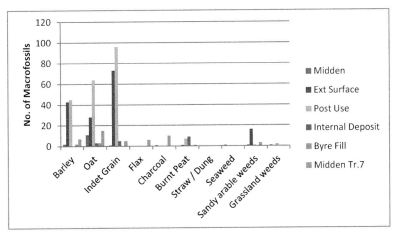

Fig. 8.7: East Mound, longhouse, Phase 7: internal and external deposits

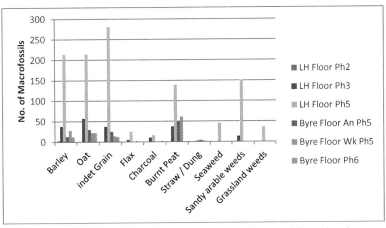

Fig. 8.8: East Mound, longhouse: comparison of internal floors by phase

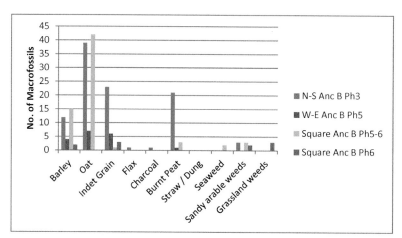

Fig. 8.9: East Mound, ancillary buildings: comparison of Phases 3, 5 and 6

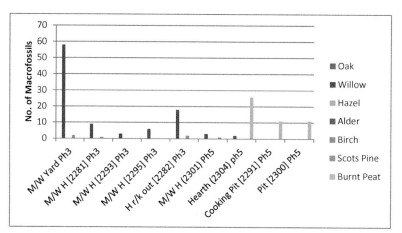

Fig. 8.10: East Mound longhouse: comparison of fuel types used in metalworking yard and domestic hearths and cooking pits

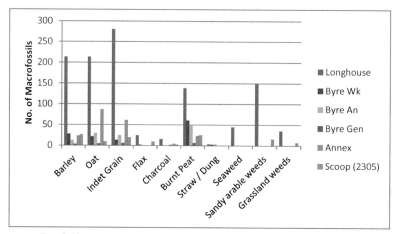

Fig. 8.11: East Mound longhouse, Phase 5: internal deposits (floors)

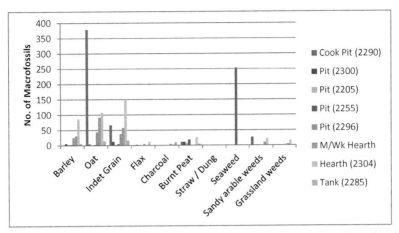

Fig. 8.12: East Mound longhouse, Phase 5: internal deposits (pits, hearths and tank)

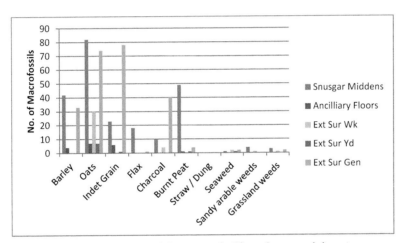

Fig. 8.13: Snusgar and East mounds, Phase 5: external deposits

Fig. 8.14: Trench 5, Grains per litre distribution plot

Table 8.1: East Mound and Snusgar. Carbonised plant macrofossils and charcoal. Summary phased table: Phase 2

	Midden	Organic layer	Midden	Ext layer/wb sand	External surface	Longhouse	Midden
Trench	Tr.1	Tr.1	Tr.4	Tr.4	Tr.5	Floor Tr.5	Tr.5
Contexts	1017, 1051	1045	1517, 1518, 1519, 1529, 1533, 1547, 1556, 1558, 1560, 1561	1545, 1557, 1559	2234	2146	2152
Total sample volume (litres)	50	10	250	45	15	20	30
Cultivated plants: cereal grain							
Barley: hulled	22	0	19	2	0	1	0
Barley: indet	127	0	47	0	1	2	1
Barley: chaff	0	0	0	0	0	0	0
Total barley grain	149	0	66	2	1	3	1
Oat: cultivated	8	0	2	0	0	0	0
Oat: indet	279	9	203	1	3	0	5
Oat: chaff	8	0	2	0	0	0	0
Total oat grain	287	9	205	1	3	0	5
Other indet. grain	186	3	185	12	3	0	3
Total grain	622	12	456	15	7	3	9
No.grains per litre sediment	12.44	1.2	1.82	0.33	0.46	0.15	0.3
Charcoal							
Willow	0	3 (3.67 g)	2 (0.11 g)	0	1 (0.02 g)	0	1 (0.04 g)
Hazel	0	1 (0.11 g)	0	0	0	0	0
Wild plant resources							
Burnt peat	3 (3.46 g)	0	18 (0.98 g)	1 (0.30 g)	0	0	0
Heather stems	0	0	2 (0.03 g)	0	0	0	2 (<0.01 g)
Rhizomes	0	0	17 (0.73 g)	2 (0.13 g)	0	0	0
Seaweed	12 (0.11 g)	0	2 (0.01 g)	0	0	0	1 (<0.01 g)
Weed ecology							
Sandy arable land	1 (1sp)	0	2 (2sp)	0	0	0	0
Grassland	1 (1sp)	0	0	0	0	0	0

Table 8.2: Castle of Snusgar: mound internal and external deposits. Carbonised plant macrofossils and charcoal. Summary phased table: Phase 3

	Longhouse layer	LH Ext Wall	Midden	Ext midden/wb sand
Trench	*Tr.1*	*Tr.1*	*Tr.4*	*Tr.4*
Contexts	*1019*	*1023*	*1504, 1508, 1510*	*1507, 1509. 1514, 1515, 1516, 1551, 1552*
Total sample volume (litres)	*20*	*10*	*60*	*95*
Cultivated plants: cereal grain				
Barley: hulled	0	1	1	4
Barley: indet	0	0	5	0
Total barley grain	0	1	6	4
Oat: indet	10	4	21	9
Oat: chaff	0	0	0	0
Total oat grain	10	4	21	9
Other indet. grain	2	1	37	5
Total grain	12	6	64	18
No. grains per litre sediment	0.6	0.6	1.06	0.18
Cultivated plants: non-cereal				
Flax	0	0	1	0
Charcoal				
Willow	2 (0.54 g)	2 (0.19 g)	0	0
Hazel	1 (0.07 g)	0	0	0
Wild plant resources				
Burnt peat	11 (9.93 g)	11 (0.69 g)	0	2 (0.06 g)
Straw/dung	0	0	0	0
Heather stems	3 (0.06 g)	0	1 (0.03g)	3 (0.07 g)
Rhizomes	4 (0.34 g)	0	6 (0.36g)	2 (<0.01 g)
Weed ecology				
Sandy arable land	0	1 (1sp)	0	0
Grassland	0	1 (1sp)	0	1 (1sp)

Table 8.3: East Mound longhouse: internal, external deposits and ancillary buildings. Carbonised plant macrofossils and charcoal. Summary phased table: Phase 3

Contexts	Longhouse floor 2262, 2264	W. Annex floor 2273	Drain 2148, 2149, 2153	Ext surface M/W yard floor 2105	Ext M/W hearth[2281] 2269	Ext M/W hearth[2293] 2292	Ext M/W hearth[2295] 2294	Hearth bowl rk/out[2282] 2240	N–S Ancilliary B Floor 2080, 2155, 2160, 2162, 2231, 2245	Midden 2254, 2288
Total sample volume (litres)	52l	9	148l	56	28	1.0	15	35	68	20
Cultivated plants: cereal grain										
Barley: hulled	12	7	0	1	2	0	0	3	5	3
Barley: indet	26	7	4	2	3	0	4	0	7	6
Barley: chaff	4	0	0	0	0	0	0	0	0	0
Total barley grain	38	14	4	3	5	0	4	3	12	9
Oat: cultivated	7	2	0	0	0	0	0	0	2	0
Oat: indet	50	37	9	1	0	0	2	4	37	6
Oat: chaff	11	2	0	0	0	0	0	0	3	0
Total oat grain	57	39	9	1	0	0	2	4	39	6
Other indet. grain	37	33	9	0	3	0	0	2	23	6
Total grain	132	86	22	4	8	0	6	9	74	21
No. grains per litre sediment	2.5	9.5	0.14	0.07	0.28	0	0.4	0.25	1.08	1.05
Cultivated plants: non-cereal										
Flax	5	1	0	0	0	0	1	0	1	5
Charcoal										
Willow	9 (0.72 g)	4 (0.93 g)	1 (0.02 g)	58 (43.0 g)	9 (3.89 g)	3 (1.02 g)	6 (8.51 g)	18 (12.33 g)	1 (0.02 g)	9 (4.86 g)
Birch	1 (0.05 g)	1 (0.20 g)	0	2 (0.59 g)	1 (2.41 g)	0	0	2 (4.81 g)	0	0
Scots pine	1 (0.03 g)	0	0	0	0	0	0	0	0	0
Wild plant resources										
Burnt peat	37 (8.20 g)	10 (1.70 g)	10 (0.18 g)	0	0	0	0	0	21 (1.88 g)	20 (3.71 g)
Straw/dung	0	3 (0.05 g)	0	0	0	0	0	1 (0.15 g)	0	0
Heather stems	11 (0.06 g)	1 (<0.01 g)	0	0	0	0	0	0	6 (0.09 g)	7 (0.04 g)
Rhizomes	1 (0.02 g)	0	2 (0.02 g)	1 (0.03 g)	0	0	0	0	0	0
Seaweed	1 (0.02 g)	3 (0.02 g)	2 (<0.01 g)	0	0	0	0	0	0	1 (<0.01 g)
Weed ecology										
Sandy arable land	14 (2sp)	0	0	0	0	0	0	0	3 (2sp)	3 (1sp)
Grassland	1 (1sp)	0	0	0	0	0	0	0	0	0

Table 8.4: East Mound longhouse: Walls fills, layers and middens. Carbonised plant macrofossils and charcoal. Summary phased table: Phase 4

Contexts	Wall fill 2011	Wall fill 2018	Wall fill 2054	Internal layer 2077	Wall fill 2084	Midden 2170
Total sample volume	*10*	*20*	*20*	*40*	*20*	*10*
Cultivated plants: cereal grain						
Barley: indet	0	0	1	7	1	1
Oat: chaff	0	0	0	0	1	0
Other indet. Grain	0	0	0	5	0	0
Total grain	0	0	2	12	3	2
No. grains per litre sediment	0	0	0.1	0.3	0.15	0.2
Charcoal						
Willow	3 (0.73 g)	0	0	0	0	0
Indet	0	0	0	0	1 (0.02 g)	0
Wild plant resources						
Burnt peat	0	0	0	0	2 (0.04 g)	1 (0.03 g)
Seaweed	0	0	0	1 (0.02 g)	0	0
Weed ecology						
Docks	0	0	1	0	0	0

Table 8.5: East Mound: longhouse and byre, internal deposits. Carbonised plant macrofossils and charcoal. Summary phased table: Phase 5

Contexts	Longhouse floor 2158, 2224, 2261, 2263, 2265, 2275	Byre floor: work 2173, 2268, 2272, 2274	Byre floor: animal 2267, 2271, 2277	Byre floor: general 2156, 2276	Annex floor 2241	Scoop in W. annex floor 2305
Total sample volume (litres)	155.5	68	40	50	10	10
Cultivated plants: cereal grain						
Barley: hulled	124	4	2	0	8	16
Barley: indet.	90	14	11	4	16	11
Barley: chaff	1	0	0	0	0	0
Total barley grain	214	28	13	4	24	27
Oat: cultivated	2	0	1	0	1	1
Oat: indet.	212	22	29	5	86	9
Oat: chaff	3	0	1	0	2	2
Total oat grain	214	22	30	5	87	10
Other indet. grain	281	14	25	6	62	20
Total grain	709	64	68	21	173	57
No. grains per litre sediment	4.55	0.94	1.7	0.42	17.3	5.7
Cultivated plants: non-cereal						
Flax	25	2	0	1	1	10
Charcoal						
Willow	14 (1.49 g)	1 (0.26 g)	0	2 (0.02 g)	3 (0.28 g)	0
Birch	2 (0.12 g)	0	0	0	2 (0.23 g)	2 (0.21 g)
Scots pine	0	0	0	0	0	1 (1.12 g)
Wild plant resources						
Burnt peat	139 (16.45 g)	61 (5.57 g)	50 (11.82 g)	7 (0.80 g)	24 (5.89 g)	26 (9.20 g)
Straw/dung	4 (0.40 g)	3 (1.15 g)	4 (0.08 g)	0	0	0
Heather stems	11 (0.07 g)	9 (0.13 g)	0	0	0	0
Rhizomes	0	0	0	0	3 (0.06 g)	0
Seaweed	45 (0.19 g)	0	0	0	1 (<0.01 g)	1 (0.02 g)
Weed ecology						
Sandy arable land	151 (3sp)	1 (1sp)	0	0	0	16 (16 (3sp)
Grassland	36 (4sp)	0	1 (1sp)	0	0	8 (1sp)

Table 8.6: Snusgar and East Mound: external deposits and ancillary buildings. Carbonised plant macrofossils and charcoal. Summary phased table, Phase 5

	Midden	Midden	Midden	W–E Subrect Anc B	Ext Surface	Ext Surface	Ext Layer
Trench	Tr.1	Tr.3	Tr.4	Floors	Work	Yard	General
Contexts	1013, 1037	1039, 1049, 1056	1502, 1503, 1513	2053, 2116, 2071, 2120, 2113	2109	2087, 2089	2118, 2119, 2125, 2161, 2178, 2180, 2202, 2218, 2233
Total sample volume (litres)	30	50	50	135	30	70	156.5
Cultivated plants: cereal grain							
Barley: hulled	8	4	0	1	0	0	7
Barley: indet.	8	20	2	3	0	0	24
Total barley grain	16	24	2	4	0	0	33
Oat: cultivated	4	4	0	0	5	0	4
Oat: indet.	20	37	17	7	25	7	74
Oat: chaff	4	4	0	0	5	0	4
Total oat grain	24	41	17	7	30	7	74
Other indet. Grain	8	2	13	6	0	1	78
Total grain	48	67	32	17	55	8	185
No. grains per litre sediment	1.6	1.34	0.64	0.12	1.83	0.11	1.18
Cultivated plants: non-cereal							
Flax	18	0	0	0	0	0	1
Charcoal							
Willow	2 (0.07 g)	0	0	0	4 (0.26 g)	0	40 (26.76 g)
Hazel	1 (0.01 g)	1 (0.12 g)	0	0	0	0	0
Scots pine	0	6 (1.18 g)	0	0	0	0	0
Wild plant resources							
Burnt peat	0	14 (4.02 g)	35 (1.40 g)	1 (0.03 g)	0	1 (0.02 g)	4 (0.03 g)
Heather stems	41 (0.40 g)	17 (0.17 g)	0	0	1 (<0.01 g)	0	0
Rhizomes	1 (0.05 g)	4 (0.16 g)	17 (0.67 g)	3 (0.03 g)	0	0	1 (<0.01 g)
Seaweed	0	1 (0.01 g)	0	0	2 (<0.01 g)	1 (<0.01 g)	2 (<0.01 g)
Weed ecology							
Sandy arable land	2 (1sp)	2 (1sp)	0	0	1 (1sp)	0	0
Grassland	1 (1sp)	2 (2sp)	0	0	1 (1sp)	0	2 (2sp)

Table 8.7: East Mound longhouse: internal deposits, pits, hearths and stone tank. Carbonised plant macrofossils and charcoal. Summary phased table, Phase 5

	Cooking pit (circular)	Circular pit	Large pit	Small pit	M/Wk hearth	Main hearth remains	Stone tank
Contexts	2290	2300	2205	2296	2301	2304	2285
Total sample volume (litres)	22	26	10	20	11	40	18
Cultivated plants: cereal grain							
Barley: hulled	0	1	1	14	13	40	6
Barley: indet.	2	5	2	11	18	47	0
Barley: chaff	0	0	0	0	0	1	0
Total barley grain	2	6	3	25	31	87	6
Oat: cultivated	8	0	0	0	4	15	0
Oat: indet.	371	4	0	44	88	102	14
Oat: chaff	13	0	0	0	6	15	0
Total oat grain	379	4	0	44	92	107	14
Other indet. Grain	67	13	2	37	58	150	16
Total grain	448	23	8	106	181	299	36
No. grains per litre sediment	20.36	0.88	0.8	5.3	16.45	7.47	2
Cultivated plants: non-cereal							
Flax	0	2	0	5	0	12	0
Charcoal							
Willow	0	0	0	0	3 (0.35 g)	2 (0.26 g)	9 (1.15 g)
Scots pine	0	0	0	0	1 (0.15 g)	0	1 (0.02 g)
Wild plant resources							
Burnt peat	11 (0.96 g)	11 (1.86 g)	8 (0.71 g)	0	0	26 (11.83 g)	5 (1.86 g)
Straw/dung	0	0	0	0	0	0	1 (0.10 g)
Heather stems	0	0	3 (<0.01 g)	0	0	5 (0.11 g)	1 (<0.01 g)
Weed ecology							
Sandy arable land	27 (2sp)	0	0	0	10 (2sp)	22 (2sp)	0
Grassland	0	0	0	2 (1sp)	4 (2sp)	16 (3sp)	1 (1sp)

Table 8.8: East Mound longhouse: internal, external deposits and ancillary buildings. Carbonised plant macrofossils and charcoal. Summary phased table: Phase 6

	Midden	Square Anc B floor (final phase)	Square Anc B floor (phase 5–6)	External surface/ occupation surface	External surface: yard	Internal deposit/ layer	Byre floor	W. Annex floor
Contexts	2008, 2056	2034, 2066	2040, 2115	2003, 2013, 2051, 2060, 2061, 2062, 2197, 2229, 2259	2092, 2093	2009, 2010, 2130, 2141, 2225, 2226	2164, 2179	2227
Total sample volume (litres)	60	60	120	190	30	180	70	20
Cultivated plants: cereal grain								
Barley: hulled	1	0	10	15	0	10	0	7
Barley: indet	6	2	5	22	1	26	12	20
Barley: chaff	0	0	0	0	0	0	0	5
Total barley grain	7	2	15	37	1	36	12	27
Oat: cultivated	0	0	2	0	0	0	0	0
Oat: indet	9	0	40	48	1	21	22	41
Oat: chaff	0	0	2	0	0	0	0	0
Total oat grain	9	0	42	48	1	21	22	41
Other indet. Grain	6	3	1	71	0	23	12	64
Total grain	22	5	58	156	2	80	46	132
No. grains per litre sediment	0.36	0.08	0.48	0.82	0.06	0.44	0.65	6.6
Cultivated plants: non-cereal								
Flax	0	0	0	2	0	5	0	0
Charcoal								
Oak	0	0	0	0	0	0	2 (0.09 g)	0
Willow	0	0	0	1 (0.04 g)	0	4 (0.86 g)	0	4 (0.21 g)
Hazel	1 (0.03 g)	0	0	0	0	0	0	0
Birch	0	0	0	2 (0.06 g)	0	6 (2.41 g)	0	0
Scots pine	0	0	0	0	0	6 (1.66 g)	0	0
Wild plant resources								
Burnt peat	1 (0.06 g)	0	3 (0.19 g)	28 (11.92 g)	0	14 (29.66 g)	0	6 (0.58 g)
Straw/dung	0	0	0	1 (<0.01 g)	0	4 (0.03 g)	0	9 (0.21 g)
Heather stems	0	0	0	0	0	8 (0.10 g)	0	1 (<0.01 g)
Rhizomes	0	1 (0.03 g)	4 (0.04 g)	1 (<0.01 g)	0	4 (0.19 g)	1 (<0.01 g)	0
Seaweed	0	0	2 (0.01 g)	11 (0.02 g)	0	6 (0.02 g)	0	5 (<0.01 g)
Weed ecology								
Sandy arable land	2 (1sp)	2 (2sp)	3 (2sp)	1 (1sp)	0	2 (1sp)	0	5 (2sp)
Grassland	0	3 (1sp)	0	3 (3sp)	0	18 (2sp)	0	0

Table 8.9: East Mound: internal and external deposits. Carbonised plant macrofossils and charcoal. Summary phased table: phase 7

	Midden/wb sand	External layer/ surface	Post-use	Internal deposits	Byre fill	Midden/ capping
Trench	Tr.5	Tr.5	Tr.5	Tr.5	Tr.5	Tr.7
Contexts	2007, 2015, 2029, 2043	2035, 2044, 2171	2127, 2139, 2217, 2223	2208, 2209	2238	4015, 4016, 4020
Total sample volume	80	50	40	30	10	40
Cultivated plants: cereal grain						
Barley: hulled	2	17	26	0	2	2
Barley: indet	0	26	19	0	0	5
Total barley grain	2	43	45	0	2	7
Oat: cultivated	0	2	1	0	1	0
Oat: indet	11	26	63	3	2	15
Oat: chaff	0	5	2	0	1	0
Total oat grain	11	28	64	3	3	15
Other indet. grain	1	73	96	5	0	5
Total grain	14	144	205	8	5	27
No. grains per litre sediment	0.17	2.88	5.12	0.26	0.5	0.67
Cultivated plants: non-cereal						
Flax	0	0	0	0	0	6
Charcoal						
Oak	0	0	0	0	1 (0.48 g)	0
Willow	1 (0.47 g)	0	0	0	2 (0.62 g)	0
Alder	0	0	0	0	3 (1.19 g)	0
Scots pine	0	0	0	0	4 (1.72 g)	0
Wild plant resources						
Burnt peat	0	1 (3.36 g)	7 (0.43 g)	9 (0.58 g)	0	1 (0.03 g)
Heather stems	1 (<0.01 g)	0	3 (<0.01 g)	1 (<0.01 g)	0	1 (<0.01 g)
Rhizomes	0	0	0	1 (<0.01 g)	0	0
Seaweed	1 (0.01 g)	0	0	0	0	0
Weed ecology						
Sandy arable land	0	16 (3sp)	1 (1sp)	0	3 (3sp)	0
Grassland	1 (1sp)	0	2 (1sp)	0		0

Table 8.10: East Mound: post-use. Carbonised plant macrofossils and charcoal. Summary phased table: phases 8 and 9

	Phase 8	Phase 8	Phase 8	Phase 9	Phase 9	Phase 9
Trench	*Tr.5*	*Tr.6*	*Tr.7*	*Tr.5*	*Tr.6*	*Tr.7*
Feature type	*Ext+int/dist*	*Ext layer*	*Midden/ext*	*Burrow*	*Midden*	*Midden*
Total sample volume (litres)	*175*	*40*	*160*	*20*	*20*	*40*
Total carbonised volume (ml)	*20*	*<2.5*	*10*	*2.5*	*0*	*5*
Cultivated plants: cereal grain						
Barley: hulled	16	0	9	0	0	0
Barley: indet.	23	0	15	0	0	4
Total barley grain	39	0	24	0	0	4
Oat: cultivated	1	0	0	0	0	0
Oat: indet.	69	1	57	0	0	21
Oat: chaff	1	0	0	0	0	0
Total oat grain	70	1	57	0	0	21
Other indet. Grain	42	0	36	0	0	32
Total grain	151	1	117	0	0	57
No. grains per litre sediment	7.55	0.02	11.7	0	0	11.4
Charcoal						
Willow	1 (0.04 g)	0	0	0	0	0
Hazel	1 (0.04 g)	0	0	0	0	0
Wild plant resources						
Burnt peat	3 (0.09 g)	0	0	0	0	0
Rhizomes	3 (0.04 g)	0	0	0	0	0
Seaweed	3 (<0.01 g)	0	0	0	0	0
Weeds of cultivation						
Sandy arable types	0	0	1 (1sp)	0	0	0
Non-sandy arable types	1 (1sp)	0	1 (1sp)	0	0	0

9

Archaeozoological evidence:
The faunal assemblages

Ingrid Mainland, Vicki Ewens and Cecily Webster

Introduction

A sizeable faunal assemblage was recovered during the 2004–2010 excavations. This report focuses on the hand-recovered mammalian, avian and marine molluscan evidence; the fish-bone assemblage is reported elsewhere (Chapter 10, below). The chapter aims to provide an overview of the assemblage as a whole, focusing in particular on the spatial distribution of faunal material across the excavated areas, the species representation therein and the identification of any general taphonomic biases, which may have affected the quality of the data set. A more detailed analysis of the assemblage was undertaken on selected midden and floor deposits securely dated to the Viking-Late Norse periods (Phases 2–6). Here the aim is to assess evidence for any variation in midden derived faunal assemblages between Snusgar and East Mound, diachronic trends in species representation, and for East Mound (Trench 5), evidence for variation between Viking-Late Norse middens and floor deposits associated with the longhouse. Mammal bone was also recovered from the heavy residues of flotation soil samples processed for carbonised plant remains. Analysis of this fraction focused only on specific contexts associated with the longhouse floor and is reported upon below. The full data is in the online archive (Archive spreadsheets 9.1–9.7).

Methodology
Identification and recording system

All mammal and bird fragments were weighed and whenever possible were identified to species, anatomical element and body side. Where this was not possible fragments were assigned to one of the following size classes: L.ung (large ungulate – *e.g.* cattle/horse/red deer); S.ung (small ungulate – *e.g.* sheep/goat/pig); S.mam (small mammal sized – *e.g.* dog/cat); Mam (indeterminate land mammal) and I.sea (indeterminate sea mammal); L.avian (large avian, *e.g.* cormorant-sized and above); S.avian (small avian, *e.g.* ducks, guillemots, puffin-sized); S.passerine (small song bird – sparrow, etc.). Vertebrae and ribs were not identified to species (or side for rib) but were grouped into one of the size classes above. The presence of particular diagnostic zones on elements were also recorded and specifically whether 50% or greater of the zone was present. This system allows for quantification and a study of fragmentation within the assemblage. Epiphyseal fusion was also recorded for all bones identified to species, any bone completely fused and not displaying signs of erosion was measured using criteria set out in von den Driesch (1976). Finally, all fragments were examined for signs of pathology, butchery, recent breaks, erosion or weathering, burning and canid gnawing. For the purpose of this report, species relative frequency has been assessed using the total number of identifiable fragments (NISP).

Mammalian and avian species identification was achieved using the modern reference collection in the Division of Archaeological, Geographical and Environmental Sciences at the University of Bradford, the UHI Archaeology Institute, University of the Highlands and Islands, Orkney College, and with reference to identification manuals such as Schmidt (1972), Cohen and Serjeantson (1986), Boessneck (1969), Halstead *et al.* (2002) and Halstead and Collins (n.d.).

Marine molluscs were identified using Oliver (2004) and Gibbons (1991). Univalue species (such as periwinkle) were recorded only if the apical end and columella were almost complete, while bivalve species (like the queen scallop and limpet) were recorded if the umbo or apex, respectively, was present (Claassen 1998).

Quantification of species and skeletal elements

Relative frequencies of species and body part were estimated using the total number of identifiable fragments (NISP).

Ageing

Age-at-death (mortality profile) was assessed using tooth eruption and wear following Payne (1973; 1987), Mainland and Halstead (2005) and Jones (2006) for ovicaprid, Halstead (1985) for cattle, and Grant (1982) for pig.

Sexing

Diagnostic features were studied to determine sex in the domestic animals present in the assemblage. To do this morphological differences of the pelvis in ovicaprids (Boessneck 1969) and cattle (Grigson 1982) and the presence or absence of an open root canine in pigs were noted (Schmidt 1972).

Sheep/goat identification

Sheep and goat bones were distinguished using Boessneck (1969) for cranial and postcranial remains and Halstead *et al.* (2002) for mandibles and teeth.

Metrical Data

Metrical information was taken on any completely fused bones not displaying signs of damage or erosion following criteria set out in von den Driesch (1976).

Butchery

Evidence of butchery was recorded by producing a sketch of the element, illustrating the position and type of mark. Marks were classified as either cut (produced by a knife) or chop (using heavier action like that of a cleaver).

Pathology

The assemblage was analysed for signs of trauma (such as fractures), degenerative changes (arthropathies etc.), congenital and dental diseases. Each case was described and, if possible, an aetiology presented.

Results

Distribution of mammal, bird and mollusca

A total of 15,628 fragments of mammal and 832 of avian bone were recovered from phased contexts (Table 9.1), of which 6838 were identified to species. The one fragment of human bone (metacarpal), from context 2123, is not included in these figures. 2932.85 g of marine molluscs were recovered, representing a minimum of 23,012 individual shells and/or valves (Tables 9.1 and 9.2). Just

Table 9.1: Mammal, avian and marine mollusca, hand-collected bone only

Trench	Mammal		Avian		Shell	
	n	%	n	%	n	%
1	3061	19.59	68	8.17	1437	6.24
2	26	0.17	0	0.00	12	0.05
3	374	2.39	0	0.00		
4	3273	20.94	292	35.10	5935	25.79
5	8728	55.85	464	55.77	15,274	66.37
6	93	0.60	4	0.48	117	0.51
7	24	0.15	4	0.48	237	1.03
8	49	0.31	0	0.00		0.00
Total	15,628		832		23,012	

For mammal and avian, total bone counts are given; for marine molluscs only designated zones were recorded: see methodology for further details

Table 9.2: Relative frequency of marine mollusca and marine invertebrates in Viking–Late Norse deposits (hand collected shell only)

Species	n	%
Blunt tellin	2	0.01
Common cockle	2	0.01
Cockle	10	0.05
Common mussel	6	0.03
Mussel	34	0.17
Common oyster	1	0.005
Dog whelk	67	0.33
Flat periwinkle	67	0.33
Edible periwinkle	5200	25.81
Great scallop	2	0.01
Variegated scallop	1	0.00
Queen scallop	3	0.01
Tiger scallop	1	0.005
Scallop	9	0.04
Heart cockle	1	0.005
Limpet	14,719	73.05
White tortieshell limpet	3	0.01
Oyster	4	0.02
Thick trough shell	1	0.005
Painted topshell	12	0.06
Topshell	3	0.01
Total	20,148	
Crustacean	26	0.09
Sea urchin	1	0.01

over half of the faunal remains came from Trench 5 (East Mound) with a further *c.* 40% being derived from Trenches 1 and 4 on the Snusgar mound (Table 9.1). Smaller amounts of bone and shell were found in the remaining trenches. A small assemblage (n=143) of microfauna (rodents, voles, etc.) was recovered from wet-sieved samples.

Across the site 204 contexts securely relate to the Viking-Late Norse periods (Phases 2–7). These contained 13,337 (85%) of the 15,628 mammal fragments recovered from the site. The remaining 51 contexts cover a broad chronological span from the 13th to the 17th centuries AD (Phase 8, 23%) and into the post-medieval to modern (Phase 9; 18th century onwards, 6%). Average fragment frequency per context is reasonably low (59), and in only seven were there more than 300 fragments of bone (1012, 1017, 1019, 1504, 1511, 1533, 2008) most of which were described as midden spread or layers. The largest bone deposit (n=649) was derived from context 1504, a Phase 3 shell-rich, structured midden including a working surface in Trench 4 (Snusgar mound).

Of the 127 phased contexts containing avian remains, 103 could be attributed to the Viking-Late Norse period representing 89% (n=740) of the avian assemblage. Most contexts contained between 1 and 10 fragments of bird bone (mean number of fragments per context = 20). Context 1504 again provided the largest assemblage and at 180 fragments represents *c.* 1/5 of the total avian bone recovered. This context is atypical in its emphasis on one species, the gannet (n=111). Bird bone was also found in 18 contexts dating to the early post-Norse period to 17th centuries (Phase 8, 9%) and 6 contexts relating to 18th century to modern kelp pit/rabbit activity (Phase 9, 2%). A single cormorant coracoid was recovered from an Iron Age, pre-Viking buried soil (context 1536) (Phase 1), which was radiocarbon dated to cal AD 240–410 (SUERC-17851).

Shell occurred in 188 Viking/Norse contexts with on average 107 shell/valves per context. There were seven contexts with fragment numbers in excess of 300: 2204, 2008, 2053, 1012, 2254, 1502 and 1504. Like the mammalian and avian assemblages, context 1504 was once again the largest deposit excavated with nearly 4000 shells/valves represented, mainly of limpet (n=3311) and periwinkle (n=576).

Taphonomy

To explore the general taphonomic processes affecting the assemblage analysis considered evidence of mammalian bone modification (recent breaks, erosion, burning, butchery, weathering and carnivore gnawing) (Table 9.3). General preservation was also assessed by the proportions of loose teeth (this indicates the fragmentation of a robust element, the mandible).

The taphonomic indicators analysed suggest broadly similar processes operating on the bone deposited in the three main Trenches, 1, 4 and 5 (including 8). Generally low numbers of weathered and eroded bones in these areas of the site (<3%) and of loose teeth (<6%) demonstrate that bone was not unduly affected by soil pH, nor was it exposed long to the environment before burial. The low numbers of bones which bore evidence of having been modified by dogs in Trenches 1 and 4 (1.6%, 0.89%, respectively) further supports this interpretation. In Trench 5, however, a greater frequency of damage through carnivore activity was observed (10.25%) and this likely reflects the fact that the assemblage was collected from internal floors and middens close to domestic structures on the East Mound. Gnawed bone is more prevalent in the bone recovered from floor surfaces (n=222, 15.35%) in Trench 5 although at not greatly different frequencies from those found in the middens and other deposits in this area of the site (midden: n=126, 10%; other deposits:

Table 9.3: Taphonomic indicators

Trench	Phase total	RB		GN		ER		FR		WE		BUT		BRT		LT	
		n	%	*n*	%	*n*	%	*n*	%	*n*	%	*n*	%	*n*	%	*n*	%
1	3061	315	10.29	49	1.60	47	1.54	2	0.07	11	0.36	144	4.70	86	2.80	173	5.65
2	26	3	11.54	0	0	2	7.69	0	0	3	11.54	1	7.69	0	0	8	30.77
3	374	3	0.80	2	0.53	0	0	0	0	0	0	31	8.29	20	5.34	19	5.08
4	3273	570	17.41	29	0.89	53	1.62	47	1.44	39	1.19	117	3.57	319	9.75	191	5.84
5	8728	1510	17.30	895	10.25	240	2.75	71	0.81	89	1.02	367	4.20	162	1.86	548	6.28
6	93	16	17.20	1	1.06	1	1.06	5	5.37	3	3.23	2	2.15	5	5.37	9	9.68
7	24	1	4.17	1	4.17	0	0	0	0	2	8.33	0	0	3	12.5	2	8.33
8	49	20	40.82	8	16.32	0	0	0	0	0	0	5	10.20	0	0	2	4.08

Lists for each trench, the total number and % of fragment (n) which are recently broken (RB), show evidence for modification by dogs (GN), of bone surface weathering (WE), erosion (ER), butchery (BUT) or burning (BRT). The final column indicates the numbers of loose teeth (LT) per trench. Mammal bone from phased contexts only (hand collected bone only) n=547, 9.08%). This indicates perhaps that the original source of the bone found within the middens was waste from butchery and food preparation activities from the house floors and other domestic working areas to which dogs had access.

The Trench 4 mammal bone deposits exhibited a greater frequency of burning (9.75%) than elsewhere. This was associated in particular with four large midden contexts, 1502, 1533, 1547 and 1559 all of which had numbers of burnt bone in excess of 20% of the total bone per context. 667 fragments displayed evidence of butchery and there was no particular variability in relative frequency for this observed between the Snusgar and East Mounds. Butchered bone was evident in all mammal species represented in the assemblage, with an emphasis on cattle and sheep/goat: cat = 1, cow = 201, dog = 2, horse = 4, pig = 48, red deer = 3, rabbit = 1, sheep/goat = 79, whale = 2, L.ungulate = 167, S.mammal = 4, S.ungulate = 155, unidentified = 5. All appear to have been caused by metal tools (knives and cleavers), due to the long straight nature of the cuts and the spalling or delamination of the bone surface (Binford 1981).

Species representation

OVERVIEW

The following mammal species were represented: cattle (_Bos taurus_), sheep/goat (_Ovis aries/Capra hircus_), pig (_Sus scofra_), horse (_Equus caballus_), red deer (_Cervus elaphus_), dog (_Canis familiaris_), cat (_Felis catus_), rabbit (_Oryctolagus cuniculus_), whale (_Cetacaea sp._), seal (cf. _Phoca/Halichoerus sp._), Orkney vole (_Microtus arvalis_), house mouse (_Mus musculus sp._) and rat (_Rattus sp._). Where species distinction was possible for ovicaprid remains, sheep were identified with only three exceptions: goat astragalus context 2193 (Phase 7, longhouse/annex spread), goat metacarpal context 2198 (Phase 6 external surface, south of longhouse) and goat skull and horn core, context 2206 (Phase 3 external surface, east of ancillary building). Twenty avian species were recorded, mostly non-domesticates, including seabirds such as guillemot (_Uria aalge_), gannet (_Sula bassana_) and cormorant (_Phalacrocorax carbo_); water fowl – ducks, swan, goose; birds of moorland and mire – grouse and snipe. Nineteen species of marine mollusc were recovered from Phase 2–7 deposits, with the most frequently found being the common limpet (_Patella vulgata_) (n=14719, 73%) and the edible periwinkle (_Littorina littorea_) (n=5200, 26%) (Table 9.2).

The vertebrate assemblage is dominated by the domestic species cattle (n=2808), sheep/goat (n=2310) and pig (n=816) which make up 38% of the total phased assemblage while horse (n=96), dog (n=46), cat (n=110) and domestic fowl (n=23) only represent a small proportion (1.75%). Wild species were also rare: only

1.5% were from non-domesticated mammals: red deer (n=55), rabbit (n=175), whale (n=3) and seal (n=5). Rabbit is likely to be intrusive, as this species was not present in Scotland before the mid-13th century (Yalden 1999, 160) and is concentrated in specific areas of the site within deposits disturbed by burrows. The presence of butchery on one fragment of rabbit, a pelvis recovered from context 2193, Phase 7 (12th–13th century AD) a disturbed organic spread in the uppermost layers of the long house/ byre floors does suggest that at least some of the rabbit present in the later phases could have an anthropogenic origin. As the introduction of this species to Orkney is generally assumed to have been significantly later than on the Scottish Mainland, during the 16th–17th centuries AD (Harland 2012), the presence of a butchered fragment in Phase 7 contexts is nevertheless anomalous and likely indicates some bioturbation where modern rabbit activity prevails. Birds are predominately of wild species, from diverse habitats but with an emphasis on marine. Few species are represented by more than ten fragments, with two notable exceptions, gannet (n=258) and guillemot (n=91). Domestic fowl (_Gallus gallus_), with 23 fragments, is the third most common species though clearly the emphasis is on wildfowl. 188 fragments of eggshell were retrieved: these were roughly evenly divided between chicken and domestic goose (pers. comm. John R. M. Stewart, Bioarch, University of York). Ten fragments of goose were recovered from Snusgar, all of which derived from a large species, likely _Anser sp._ which would not be inconsistent with domestic geese (Gotfredson 2014; Best and Mulville 2014).

The majority of molluscan remains are from marine species: edible periwinkle (_Littorina littorea)_, common limpet (_Patella vulgata)_, flat periwinkle (_Littorina littoralis_), dogwhelk (_Nucella lapillus_), common cockle (Cerastoderma edule), common oyster (Ostrea edulis), queen scallop (_Chlamys opercularis_) (Table 9.2). Fragments of the species' thick trough shell (_Spisula solida_), painted topshell (_Calliostoma zizyphinum_) and blunt tellin (_Arcogapia crassa_) were also noted.

All the molluscs identified can be found in the North Atlantic so it is likely that they were collected locally. The most numerous shells found on site are the common limpet and edible periwinkle. Both are found on rocky shores, the limpet living from the upper shore downwards, while the periwinkle is most commonly found clinging to rock and grasses in the middle tidal level. Likewise, the dogwhelk occurs in middle to lower zones of rocky coasts, usually in large numbers. The middle zone of the shore is uncovered at every low tide making these species of molluscs easily accessible. Thick trough shells are found buried in sand anywhere from the upper shore (always accessible) down to the lower shore, which is only accessible during spring tide lows. Blunt tellin also live in muddy sand and gravel. Oysters are found in dense beds in muddy or stony locations where they can be harvested, while queen scallops swim in large shoals over the sea floor, but are attached to rocks when young and frequently wash up on beaches. It is possible that the flat periwinkles in the assemblage may have been accidentally introduced to site as they are found mostly on the surface of brown seaweed (wracks) on which they feed and are too small to be edible (Gibbons 1991).

SPATIAL AND TEMPORAL VARIATION IN THE VIKING AND LATE NORSE DEPOSITS

The assemblage comprises faunal material excavated into different areas of two mounds, Snusgar and East Mound. As these could potentially reflect distinctive areas of settlement, an intra-site analysis was undertaken to explore whether there was any evidence of spatial and temporal variation in the faunas deposited across the excavated areas. The larger of the excavation Trenches, 1 and 4 from Snusgar and Trench 5 (including 8) from East Mound produced virtually all of the faunal assemblage, and therefore the more peripheral trenches 2, 6 and 7 were excluded. Analysis focused on species representation for mammals and birds (Tables 9.4–9.7) and skeletal element representation for the main domesticates: cattle, sheep/goat and pig (Figs 9.1–9.3). Although all phases are reported in Tables 9.4–9.6, analysis concentrated on those dating to the Viking-Late Norse period (*i.e.* Phases 2–7) (Table 9.6; Figs 9.1–9.3). To enable adequate sample sizes for certain analyses, these phases were grouped into Viking (*i.e.* Phases 2–3) and Late Norse (*i.e.* Phases 4–7). Context of deposition was also considered to assess the nature of faunal remains deposited in areas with potentially different functions within East Mound. Here analysis focused on floor layers associated with the Trench 5 ancillary buildings, Trench 5 longhouse byre floors, Trench 5 longhouse domestic floors and the middens. To enable sufficient sample size, analysis of context-related variation was focused on the Viking-Late Norse period as a whole (*i.e.* Phases 2–7 inclusive) (Table 9.8).

Variability in faunal deposition is evident across the two mounds. Whilst in each trench, the overall emphasis is on domesticates – cattle, sheep/goat and pig in that order – differences are found in the relative proportions with which these occur. Overall, sheep/goat tends to be more common in the Snusgar mound Trench 4 deposits and cattle in the Trench 1 area (Table 9.7). Pig bones are relatively more frequent in East Mound Trench 5 deposits, *i.e.* the deposits associated with the longhouse, particularly in the Viking Age (Phases 2–3; Table 9.7). In this area of the site, a decline in pig is evident through time while sheep/goat becomes relatively more common by the Late Norse period (Phases 4–7; Tables 9.4–9.7). Trench 4 at Snusgar has comparatively more sheep/goat in both the

Viking and Late Norse periods, an association which increases through time. Cattle tend to be more common in the Trench 1 area of the site, a focus that becomes more pronounced in the Late Norse period (Phases 4–7). This is the only area of the settlement showing an increase in cattle in the Late Norse period.

Figures 9.1–9.3 illustrate skeletal anatomical representation for the Norse period as a whole (Phases 2–7) for each of the main excavation Trenches. These present the ratio of upper limb bones to lower limbs, feet and mandibles to explore any variability in depositional practice, and hence differential utilisation of animal carcasses across the two mounds. To minimise the impact of differential fragmentation due to skeletal elements of differing bone density and size, only bone ends (proximal, distal) are included for the long bones and the skull elements are represented by mandibles with at least one tooth *in situ*. For cattle and pig the overall the pattern of representation is similar to what is expected should entire carcasses have been deposited, suggesting that there was little movement of animal body parts into or out of the different areas of the site for these species. For pig, the variability evident in Trench 4 likely reflects the biasing effects of smaller sample size (n=15) rather than actual depositional practice. Sheep/goat element representation shows a greater degree of deviation from the expected with Trench 1 in particular showing a higher than expected frequency of upper limbs and correspondingly fewer elements of the foot. This may reflect an importation of meatier joints of sheep into this area of the site.

The East Mound longhouse and its associated deposits are also distinctive in their relatively lower frequency of wild mammalian fauna (red deer, whale, seal) with the only exception being rabbit, which is likely to be intrusive (ratio of wild to domestic mammal fauna: Trench 1 = 11: 1153 [1%]; Trench 4 = 19: 1015 [2%]; Trench 5 = 1: 2475 [0.04%]). In contrast, the minor domestic species (horse, dog and cat) were more commonly found in Trench 5 on East Mound. Horse relative frequency, for example, was greatest in Trench 5 (n=60), and derives mostly from Late Norse deposits (Phases 4–7) (n=58). These latter consist of skull and mandible fragments and loose teeth deposited in context 2008, a Phase 6 midden (NISP=35; MNI=2). There are too few fragments of horse bone to conclusively identify trends in skeletal element representation though elements of the foot and (metapodials, phalanges, n=20) and skull (mandibles, maxilla, skulls, loose teeth, n=41)) are more frequent than limb fragments (n=8). An articulated hoof and lower leg (metacarpal, phalanges 1–3, LHS) was recovered from context 2087, a Phase 5 working surface within the yard area north of the western yard of the ancillary square building. Two fragments of butchered horse bone were recovered from within the Phase 5 longhouse (context

Table 9.4: Trench 1. Mammal and avian species representation by phase

	Species	2	3	Ph2–3 combined		4	7	Ph4–7 combined		9
		n	*n*	*n*	*%*	*n*	*n*	*n*	*%*	*n*
Domestic mammals	Cow	121	167	*288*	*20.65*	196	47	*243*	*25.23*	162
	Sheep/Goat	77	118	*295*	*13.98*	122	26	*148*	*15.37*	80
	Pig	30	57	*87*	*6.24*	35	9	*44*	*4.57*	26
	Horse	2	2	*4*	*0.29*	3		*3*	*0.31*	14
	Cat	1	6	*7*	*0.50*	5		*5*	*0.52*	1
	Dog		2	*2*	*0.14*	18		*18*	*1.87*	1
Wild mammals	Red Deer	3	6	*9*	*0.65*	2		*2*	*0.21*	6
	Rabbit				*0.00*				*0.00*	10
	Seal				*0.00*				*0.00*	
	Whale				*0.00*				*0.00*	
Other	Large ungulate	122	351	*473*	*33.91*	217	66	*283*	*29.39*	133
	Small ungulate	117	192	*309*	*22.15*	160	27	*187*	*19.42*	62
	Small mammal		1	*1*	*0.07*	4		*4*	*0.42*	
Bird	Cormorant		1	*1*	*0.07*				*0.00*	2
	Domestic Fowl		3	*3*	*0.22*	3	1	*4*	*0.42*	3
	Gannet	2	5	*7*	*0.50*	9		*9*	*0.93*	3
	Guillemot	1	7	*8*	*0.57*	11	1	*12*	*1.25*	7
	Pigeon	1		*1*	*0.07*	1		*1*	*0.10*	
	Duck				*0.00*				*0.00*	
	Goose				*0.00*				*0.00*	
	B. Guillemot				*0.00*				*0.00*	
	Manx Shearwater				*0.00*				*0.00*	
	Shag				*0.00*				*0.00*	
	Grouse				*0.00*				*0.00*	
	H. Gull				*0.00*				*0.00*	
	Razorbill				*0.00*				*0.00*	
	Curlew				*0.00*				*0.00*	
	Puffin				*0.00*				*0.00*	
	Snipe				*0.00*				*0.00*	
	Starling				*0.00*				*0.00*	
	Swan				*0.00*				*0.00*	
	Raven				*0.00*				*0.00*	
Unidentified	Mammal	16	25	*41*		11	1	*12*		32
	Avian	1	2	*3*		4		*4*		
Total id.		477	918	*1395*		786	177	*963*		510
Total unid.		17	27	*44*		15	1	*16*		32
Total (TNB)		494	945	*1439*		801	178	*979*		542

Table lists the number (n) of fragments identified to species (NISP) for each phase group in Trench 1 at Snusgar (hand collected bone only)

2141, distal metatarsal, RHS; context 2261, ulna, LHS) and one fragment was found deposited in a Phase 6 external surface layer (context 2003, distal metacarpal). A butchered horse ulna (LHS) was recovered from the Phase 5 longhouse floor (context 2261). Only nine fragments of horse bone were recovered from the Snusgar mound (Trench 1, n= 7; Trench 4, n=2) from within the Phase 2 middens (contexts 1017, 1511) and internal contexts

Table 9.5: Trench 4. Mammal and avian species representation by phase

	Species	2	3	Ph2–3 combined		5	Ph 4–7 combined		8	9
		n	*n*	*n*	*%*	*n*	*n*	*%*	*n*	*n*
Domestic mammals	Cow	264	182	*448*	*17.97*	46	*46*	*14.98*	23	21
	Sheep/goat	163	206	*369*	*14.80*	46	*46*	*14.98*	28	41
	Pig	68	26	*94*	*3.77*	6	*6*	*1.95*	6	6
	Horse	2		*2*	*0.08*			*0.00*	1	
	Cat	1	1	*2*	*0.08*			*0.00*		
	Dog	2		*2*	*0.08*			*0.00*		
Wild mammals	Red Deer	3	14	*17*	*0.68*			*0.00*		
	Rabbit		1	*1*	*0.04*	1	*1*	*0.33*	4	1
	Seal			*1*	*0.04*	1	*1*	*0.33*		
	Whale				*0.00*		*0*	*0.00*		
Other	Large ungulate	384	204	*588*	*23.59*	84	*84*	*27.36*	47	6
	Small ungulate	443	358	*801*	*32.13*	97	*97*	*31.60*	88	81
	Small mammal		2	*2*	*0.08*	3	*3*	*0.98*		
Bird	Cormorant				*0.00*			*0.00*		
	Domestic fowl		3	*3*	*0.12*	3	*3*	*0.98*		
	Gannet	20	120	*140*	*5.62*	19	*19*	*6.19*	5	1
	Guillemot	2	17	*19*	*0.76*	1	*1*	*0.33*		
	Pigeon				*0.00*			*0.00*	1	
	Duck	1		*1*	*0.04*			*0.00*		
	Goose		3	*3*	*0.12*			*0.00*		
	B. Guillemot				*0.00*			*0.00*		
	Manx Shearwater				*0.00*			*0.00*		
	Shag				*0.00*			*0.00*		
	Grouse				*0.00*			*0.00*		
	H. Gull				*0.00*			*0.00*		
	Razorbill				*0.00*			*0.00*		
	Curlew				*0.00*			*0.00*		
	Puffin				*0.00*			*0.00*		
	Snipe				*0.00*			*0.00*		
	Starling				*0.00*			*0.00*		
	Swan				*0.00*			*0.00*		
	Raven				*0.00*			*0.00*		
Unidentified	Mammal	180	91	*271*		14	*14*		16	4
	Avian	25	51	*76*		19	*19*			
Total id.		1353	1137	*2493*		307	*307*		203	157
Total unid.		205	142	*347*		33	*33*		16	4
Total (TNB)		1558	1279	*2840*		340	*340*		219	161

Table lists the number (n) and relative frequency (%) of fragments identified to species (NISP) for each phase group in Trench 4 at Snusgar (hand collected bone only)

associated with the longhouses in Phase 3 (contexts 1019, 1021) and Phase 5 (context 1012). Butchered horse bones were also found in Trench 1, within the Phase 2 longhouse (context 1011, metatarsal [RHS]).

Dog and cat shows a similar spatial distribution to horse with most fragments of these species associated with the Late Norse deposits in Trench 5 (Tables 9.4–9.6), reflecting deposition in diverse context types, both

Table 9.6: Trench 5 Mammal and avian species representation by phase

	Species	2 n	3 n	Ph2–3 combined n	%	4 n	5 n	6 n	7 n	Ph 4–7 combined n	%	8 n	9 n
Domestic mammals	Cow	46	96	142	17.64	93	267	346	299	1005	18.65	193	9
	Sheep/Goat	51	67	118	14.66	83	305	269	269	926	17.19	146	5
	Pig	24	47	71	8.82	41	120	105	105	371	6.89	54	8
	Horse	1	1	2	0.25	1	12	43	2	58	1.08	9	
	Cat	2	3	5	0.62	3	56	16	11	86	1.60	2	
	Dog	10		10	1.24	4	13	5	7	29	0.54	2	
Wild mammals	Red Deer				0.00						0.00	1	
	Rabbit				0.00	1	3	34	34	72	1.34	67	11
	Seal				0.00						0.00	1	
	Whale				0.00			1		1	0.02		
Other	Large ungulate	56	115	171	21.24	110	246	590	289	1235	22.92	186	11
	Small ungulate	88	172	260	32.30	134	397	422	422	1375	25.52	189	11
	Small mammal	4	6	10	1.24	7	35	28	28	98	1.82	31	1

Table 9.6: (Continued)

Species	2 n	3 n	Ph2–3 combined n	Ph2–3 combined %	4 n	5 n	6 n	7 n	Ph 4–7 combined n	Ph 4–7 combined %	8 n	9 n
Bird												
Cormorant	2	1	3	0.37	1	1	1		3	0.06	2	
Domestic fowl			0	0.00	1	2	1	2	6	0.11		
Gannet	3	3	6	0.75	1	8	24	19	52	0.97	15	
Guillemot	3	2	5	0.62	6	8	9	10	33	0.61	5	
Pigeon		1	1	0.12	1	1	1	1	4	0.07		
Duck				0.00				1	1	0.02		
Goose				0.00		3	1	2	6	0.11		
B. Guillemot		1	1	0.12		2	1	1	4	0.07		
Manx shearwater				0.00		1			1	0.02		
Shag				0.00						0.00		
Grouse				0.00	1	1	1	1	4	0.07		
H. Gull				0.00		3	1	2	6	0.11		
Razorbill				0.00		2			2	0.04		
Curlew				0.00			1		1	0.02		
Puffin				0.00			1		1	0.02		
Snipe				0.00				1	1	0.02		
Starling				0.00			2		2	0.04		
Swan				0.00		1			1	0.02		
Raven				0.00		3	1		4	0.07		
Unidentified												
Mammal	76	183	259		172	268	195	372	1007		21	13
Avian	32	7	39			57	72	64	193		40	
Total id.	290	515	805		488	1490	1904	1508	5390		903	45
Total unid.	108	190	298		172	325	267	436	1200		61	13
Total (TNB)	398	705	1103		660	1815	2171	1944	6590		964	58

Table lists the number (n) and relative frequency (%) of fragments identified to species (NISP) for each phase group in Trench 5/8 at East Mound (hand collected bone only)

Table 9.7: Relative representation of cow, sheep/goat and pig by phase and trench

Trench	Phase grouping	NISP	Cow (%)	Sheep/goat (%)	Pig (%)
All	Phases 2–3	1811	48.43	37.66	13.91
All	Phases 4–7	3165	45.24	40.51	14.25
Snusgar T1	Phases 2–3	570	50.53	34.21	15.26
Snusgar T4	Phases 2–3	911	49.18	40.50	10.32
East Mound T5	Phases 2–3	331	42.90	35.65	21.45
Snusgar T1	Phases 4–7	435	55.86	34.02	10.11
Snusgar T4	Phases 4–7	98	46.94	46.94	6.120
East Mound T5	Phases 4–7	2302	43.66	40.23	16.12

NISP = combined total for cow, sheep/goat and pig (hand collected bone only)

Table 9.8: Species representation by context type and trench (T) for selected features

	Species	T1 middens		T4 middens		T5 middens		T5 ancillary floors		T5 long house floor		T5 byre floor	
		n	%	n	%	n	%	n	%	n	%	n	%
Domestic mammals	Cow	165	51.56	404	38.11	81	25.71	56	37.84	78	36.28	86	27.04
	Sheep/goat	87	27.19	370	34.91	129	40.95	48	32.43	81	37.67	135	42.45
	Pig	45	14.06	90	8.49	69	21.90	16	10.81	44	20.47	42	13.21
	Horse	2	0.63		0.00	1	0.32		0.00	2	0.93		0.00
	Cat	1	0.31	2	0.19	5	1.59	5	3.38		0.00	47	14.78
	Dog		0.00		0.00	15	4.76	13	8.78		0.00		0.00
Wild mammals	Red deer	5	1.56	10	0.94		0.00		0.00		0.00		0.00
	Rabbit		0.00	2	0.19		0.00		0.00		0.00		0.00
	Seal		0.00	1	0.09		0.00		0.00		0.00		0.00
	Whale		0.00		0.00		0.00		0.00		0.00		0.00
Avian	Domestic fowl	2	0.63	6	0.57	1	0.32	0	0.00	0	0.00	2	0.63
	Wild avian: land	2	0.63	3	0.28	1	0.32	1	0.68	3	1.40	2	0.63
	Wild avian: sea	11	3.44	172	16.23	13	4.13	9	6.08	7	3.26	4	1.26
Total		320	100	1060	100	315	100	148	100	215	100	318	100

Table lists the number (n) and relative frequency (%) of fragments identified to species (NISP) for each context type with data from phases 2–7 combined (hand collected bone only)

within and outside the house structures (Table 9.9). One articulated bone group of dog was recovered, a partial lower spine along with ribs likely to be from the same individual beneath a paving flag in a Phase 5 floor layer within the ancillary building (context 2115). Two fragments of dog bone bore evidence of butchery, a paired left and right femur from context 2171, a Phase 7 external surface adjacent to the ancillary building. Fragment counts for cat are elevated by the presence of a pair of partial cat skeletons in Phase 5 context 2268, recovered from beside an orthostat close to the threshold between the Trench 5 byre and the passageway to the

domestic longhouse. For the remaining cat assemblage, no specific selectivity in deposition can be identified, with both axial and appendicular elements well represented. A butchered lumbar vertebra, likely of cat, is derived from context 2056, a midden adjacent to the square ancillary building in Phase 6.

Non-domesticated avians are found in each of the Trenches but with a relatively higher frequency in Trench 4 (Viking, Phases 2–3, 6.54%; Late Norse, Phases 4–7, 6.51%) than in the other areas of the site (Trench 1, Phases 2–3 1.1%, Phases 4–7 2.28%; Trench 5, Phases 2–3 1.99%, Phases 4–7 2.45%). This Trench

Table 9.9: Species representation within the main deposit types in Trench 5 (%)

	Middens	Ancillary floors	Long house floor	Byre floor
Cow	25.71	37.84	36.28	27.04
Sheep/goat	40.95	32.43	37.67	42.45
Pig	21.90	10.81	20.47	13.21
Horse	0.32	0.00	0.93	0.00
Cat	1.59	3.38	0.00	14.78
Dog	4.76	8.78	0.00	0.00
Red deer	0.00	0.00	0.00	0.00
Rabbit	0.00	0.00	0.00	0.00
Seal	0.00	0.00	0.00	0.00
Whale	0.00	0.00	0.00	0.00
Domestic fowl	0.32	0.00	0.00	0.63
Wild avian: land	0.32	0.68	1.40	0.63
Wild avian: sea	4.13	6.08	3.26	1.26
Total NISP (n)	315.00	148.00	215.00	318.00

Table lists the relative frequency (%) of fragments identified to species and the total NISP for each context type; data from phases 2–7 combined (hand collected bone only)

Table 9.10: Animal bone species representation in the Trench 5 floor samples

	Total frequency (n)	Frequency of burnt	Total weight (g)
Cow	15	7	99.94
Pig	7	1	6.45
Sheep/goat	17	2	26.83
Cat	1	0	0.08
Vole	1	0	0.12
Large ungulate	22	5	42.29
Small mammal	1		0.14
Small ungulate	80	15	78.33
Microfauna	5	1	0.08
Unidentified mammal	621	313	93.94
Unidentified avian	6	0	1.52
	761	337	249.78

Wet-sieve residues: >4mm fraction

4 emphasis can be attributed to one species, gannet, and is associated in particular with context 1504 a Phase 3 midden layer used as a working area, which is responsible for 70% of the gannet bone in this area of the site. Gannet humerii in this and other deposits across the site exhibit a systematic butchery pattern in which the bone has been broken across the mid-shaft region of the bone reflecting removal of the wing, as process documented in the recent past by bird fowlers in the Western Isles (Beatty 1992).

Looking more specifically at species variation across deposit types within East Mound broadly confirms the trends identified above (Table 9.9, Fig. 9.4). An association is apparent between cat and the byre floor deposits, and between dog and the floor layers of the ancillary building. Cattle bones are also more common in the floor layers of the ancillary building, as are bones derived from marine birds. Pig and horse are more frequently deposited within the longhouse floors. Cattle are less well-represented in the midden deposits than any other of the main domesticates. This and the correspondence between relative frequencies of sheep/goat and pig in both midden and longhouse floors deposits may suggest that the middens derive predominately from cleaning and removal of detritus from the longhouse floors, and thus reflect waste from meat on the bone consumed within the hall. Cattle meat

will have been eaten (by humans) inside the longhouse and, on overall relative frequency of older calves and adult individuals (*i.e.* wear stages C+, Tables 12 and 13) and absolute body size, will have made a major contribution to the diet even with the relatively high numbers of individuals culled at or around birth (*e.g.*, Minimum Number of Individuals for sheep/goat at wear stages C+ = 20, for cattle = 13; average live weight of small modern 'primitive' cattle breed *c.* 400–500 kg (McCormick 2002); average live weight of hill-reared Shetland sheep = 20–30 kg (Shetland Sheep Society 2018). The spatial distribution of cattle bone, however, indicates that primary butchery and secondary processing of the carcasses prior to consumption may have occurred elsewhere on site, perhaps in and around the area of the ancillary building. Sample sizes are too small to explore this further by addressing spatial variation in anatomical representation as was undertaken above for each species at the level of context type. However, using the same anatomical categories as in Figs 9.1 to 9.3, but including shaft fragments as well as bone ends, a relatively higher frequency of cattle meat-bearing bones (*i.e.* upper and lower limbs) is apparent in the middens (69%) and the longhouse house-floor layers (70%) and of feet and mandibles (*i.e.* waste/primary butchery) in the ancillary building floor (44%), providing some support for this interpretation. The prevalence of dog and horse in the middens and the longhouse floors is interesting, and together with evidence of butchery may suggest some consumption of these species within the longhouse.

Table 9.11: Molluscan species representation in the Trench 5 floor samples

	Total frequency (n)	Frequency of burnt	Total weight (g)
Blue rayed limpet	2		0.021
Cockle	1		0.61
Common top shell	2		0.7
Edible periwinkle	112		111.8
Flat periwinkle	14	1	4.23
Limpet	1367	161	629.89
Mussel	43		3.242
Oyster	1		0.25
Razor shell	1		0.17
Rough periwinkle	1		0.07
Eea urchin	2		0.26
Shell unidentified	64	3	10.89
Crustacean claw	11	6	1.81
Total	1621	171	763.943

wet-sieve residues: >4mm fraction

Table 9.12: Animal bone representation in the Trench 5 floor samples

	Total frequency (n)	Frequency of burnt	Total weight (g)
Cat	1		0.12
Mus musculus	2	1	0.04
Microtus arvalis	3		0.016
Microfauna	17	3	0.156
Unidentified mammal	374	200	10.695
Amphibian	12		0.16
Bird	2		0.04
Total	411	204	11.227

wet-sieve residues: 2–4mm fraction

Table 9.13: Molluscan species representation in the Trench 5 floor samples

	Total frequency (n)	Frequency of burnt	Total weight (g)
Crustacean claw	9	2	0.36
Shell unidentified	780	5	27.53
Total	789	7	27.89

wet-sieve residues: 2–4mm fraction

TRENCH 5 FLOOR SAMPLES

A spatial analysis of the distribution of faunal remains and marine molluscs within the floor layers of the longhouse and associated buildings was undertaken as part of a wider analysis of use of these structures. To enable comparison with other ecofactual evidence, this focused on the assemblages recovered from the wet-sieve residues (for full methodologies, see Chapter 8). This data is presented in Tables 9.10–9.13 and Fig. 9.13.

Just over 500 fragments of animal bone were recovered from the wet-sieve residues of Trench 5 floor samples (Table 9.10 and 9.12). The vast majority of this bone was unidentifiable to species. For the identified wet-sieve residue fractions, the emphasis was on the domesticates, in particular the smaller species sheep/goat and pig which, as outlined above, also tend to be more frequent in the hand collected material from the longhouse floors (Figs 9.12–9.13). Evident also were bones of mice and voles, identified from the dentition as *Mus musculus*, the house mouse, and the Orkney vole, *Microtus arvalis*. Unburnt mammal bone was relatively poorly represented in the byre floors. Larger amounts were evident in the longhouse, longhouse annex and ancillary building (see also Chapters 7 and 25). The highest concentration of animal bone was evident in the north-west corner of the ancillary building, the south-east corner of the longhouse and in the floors of the annex (Fig. 9.13). This distribution suggests detritus from food consumption, preparation and other uses of bone being overlooked in the corners of rooms for the two former structures. For the annex, the more dispersed distribution of bone may indicate a working surface. Burnt mammal bone shows three particular concentrations, in the opening between the longhouse and byre; the upper north-west corner of the longhouse and the southern side wall of the ancillary building. This latter distribution mirrors that of unburnt bone, and may again indicate general refuse being moved to the edges of the floors during cleaning activities.

2410 fragments of shell (marine molluscs) and crustacean were recovered from the floor layers in Trench 5 (Tables 9.11 and 9.13). These were more readily identified to species with a wide range of species represented. As with the hand collected material, limpets and edible periwinkle were the most abundant species. The presence of tiny shells of mussels, flat periwinkles and edible periwinkles, too small to be used for food or bait, on all floor types suggest that at least some of this material must have been brought into the buildings attached to seaweed, for bedding or fodder, or along with shell sand, used for example for covering/cleaning floor surfaces.

Unburnt marine molluscs were found throughout the floor layers in Trench 5, with no specific clustering apparent. Relatively higher concentrations were recovered from the ancillary building floors but this partially reflects a greater density of sampling in this area of the site. Limpets and edible periwinkle were particularly associated with the floor layers of the longhouse (40% and 19% of each species in the >4 mm fraction, respectively) suggesting consumption of both and not a use of limpets primarily for bait, as has been argued for this species elsewhere in Norse Orkney (*e.g.* Rackham 1989). Fragments of sea urchin and burnt crustacean claw were recovered from the ancillary building and byre floors but not from the longhouse floors.

681 fragments of mammal bone were recovered by hand from the floors of the longhouse and the ancillary buildings, with the greatest concentrations being found in the byre (47%) and longhouse (31%) and a lesser quantity in the ancillary building (22%) (Table 9.9). Figure 9.12 shows the spatial distribution of bone density for the hand-collected sample (for a discussion of species representation see above). These fragments, being hand-collected, will tend to reflect larger pieces of bone than recovered from the wet-sieve samples discussed above. The relatively higher representation of this fraction in the byre may indicate that floors in this area of the settlement were not kept as clean and free of larger bone fragments than the hall and ancillary building, reflecting perhaps the use of these structures as living/working areas.

Ageing

Thirty-five cattle mandibles were assigned to one of the age stages described by Halstead (1985) (Tables 9.14 and 9.15; Figs 9.5 and 9.6). Mortality profiles calculated using this method indicate high numbers of neonatal deaths, together with a secondary emphasis on individuals which had reached maturity and were likely quite old before being culled, particularly in the later phases of occupation at the site (Table 9.15). This profile is commonly found within Norse sites in the North Atlantic islands and is considered indicative of a dairying economy in which milk and other milk products, cheese, butter, yoghurts, were being emphasised. Changes in culling pattern are apparent through time, with a greater frequency of cattle culled between *c.* 1–3 years, *i.e.* at prime meat-bearing age in Phases 2–3 (36%) than in Phases 4–7 (22%). This may be interpreted as a shift away from the combined use of cattle for milk and meat towards a greater specialisation in milk products, an economic change also evident at other sites of this date in the Northern Isles (Harland 2012).

The sheep/goat profile, based on 40 mandibles, suggests a herding strategy focused on meat with a reasonably steady culling from one month onwards and a peak age-at-death falling between six months to three to four years, when individuals would have been at their prime (Tables 9.16 and 9.17; Figs 9.7 and 9.8). Although there were no mandibles from neonatal lambs, other skeletal elements from foetal/neonatal individuals were recovered and it is thus likely that sheep were being reared in the vicinity. As with the cattle, there is an increased emphasis on secondary products, in this case wool, in the

Late Norse period, represented by a higher frequency of animals culled as mature and old adults (age category G–I) (Table 9.17; Fig. 9.8) The few pig mandibles indicate a culling strategy focused entirely on juveniles, and is consistent with use of this species for meat (Table 9.18; Fig. 9.9).

Table 9.14: Cattle mortality profiles: phases 2–3

Age stage	n	%	Survivorship (%)
A: 0–1 month	3.3	25.38	74.62
B: 1–8 months	0	0.00	74.62
C: 8–18 months	2.7	20.77	53.85
D: 18–30 months	0	0.00	53.85
E: 30–36 months	2	15.38	38.46
F: young adult	0	0.00	38.46
G: Adult	2	15.38	23.08
H: old adult	1	7.69	15.38
I: Senile	2	15.38	0.00
Total	13		

Table 9.15: Cattle mortality profiles: phases 4–7

Age stage	n	%	Survivorship (%)
A: 0–1 month	3	13.63	86.36
B: 1–8 months	8	36.36	50.00
C: 8–18 months	2	9.09	40.91
D: 18–30 months	2	9.09	31.82
E: 30–36 months	1	4.55	27.27
F: young adult	1	4.55	22.73
G: Adult	0	0.00	22.73
H: old adult	2.3	10.45	12.27
I: Senile	2.7	12.27	0.00
Total	22		

Table 9.16: Sheep/goat mortality profiles: phases 2–3

Age stage	n	%	Survivorship (%)
A: 0–1 months	0	0	100.00
B: 1–4 months	2.4	15.00	85.00
C: 4–13 months	1.9	11.88	73.13
D: 1–2 years	4.1	25.63	47.50
E: 2–3 years	3.6	22.50	25.00
F: Young adult	3	18.75	6.25
G: Mature adult	0	0.00	6.25
H: Mature adult	1	6.25	0.00
I: Old adult	0	0.00	0.00
Total	16	0	

Table 9.17: Sheep/goat mortality profiles: phases 4–7

Age stage	n	%	Survivorship (%)
A: 0–1 months	0	0	100.00
B: 1–4 months	3.8	15.83	84.17
C: 4–13 months	2.6	10.83	73.33
D: 1–2 years	2.85	11.88	61.46
E: 2–3 years	7.75	32.29	29.17
F: Young adult	2.3	9.58	19.58
G: Mature adult	1.2	5.00	14.58
H: Mature adult	1.2	5.00	9.58
I: Old adult	2.3	9.58	0.00
Total	24	0	

Table 9.18: Dental eruption/wear stage data for pig: phases 2–7 combined (after Grant 1982)

Stage	Age	Frequency	%	% age survival
A	Birth	1.5	12	88
B	8 months	1.5	12	77
C	13 months	3	23	54
D	16–20 months	6	46	8
E	young adult	1	8	0
F	adult	0	0	0

Biometry

Metrical data for this assemblage is presented in Archive spreadsheet 9.5. Withers height in cattle was calculated for whole metapodials (Table 9.19) using Fock's equations (presented in von den Driesch and Boessneck, 1974) and the greatest length measurements. This produced withers heights of between 1.00 m and 1.13 m for the animals in this assemblage, which is a relatively small stature equivalent to the modern Dexter breed (Alderson 1984). Withers height was established in the ovicaprids using calcaneum, femur, metacarpal and metatarsal greatest length measurements with Teichert's formula (in von den Driesch and Boessneck 1973) (Table 9.20). This produced a withers height of between 0.50 m and 0.60 m, which approximates the height of Soay sheep (Wilson 1978). Small ponies, the size of modern Shetlands, are indicated from withers heights calculated using greatest length measurements from a horse metacarpal and metatarsal (1.17 m and 1.24 m, respectively, *c.* 11–12 hands).

Pathology

109 pathological specimens occurred in the assemblages, of which 100 derived from securely dated Norse

Table 9.19: Cattle withers heights

Element	Context	GL (mm)	Withers height (m)
Metacarpal	1021	164	1.00
Metacarpal	1515	166.5	1.02
Metacarpal	2193	176.2	1.07
Metacarpal	1533	184.5	1.13
Metacarpal	1019	185	1.13
Metacarpal	1013	183	1.12
Metacarpal	1012	172	1.05
Metatarsal	1012	193	1.05

GL = greatest length calculated using Fock's (von den Driech and Boessneck 1974) formula for metacarpals (GL × 6.1); metatarsals (GL × 5.45)

Table 9.20: Sheep/goat withers heights

Element	Context	GL (mm)	Withers height (m)
Calcaneus	1017	53.99	0.58
Calcaneus	2216	52.25	0.56
Calcaneus	2193	45.97	0.50
Femur	1012	152.38	0.54
Metacarpal	2198	109.3	0.53
Metacarpal	2193	114.2	0.56
Metacarpal	2216	119.9	0.59
Metacarpal	1012	110.31	0.54
Metatarsal	1013	124.66	0.57
Metatarsal	1041	131.1	0.60
Metatarsal	2227	132.1	0.60
Radius	2262	142.6	

GL = greatest length, mm = millimetres, m = metres; Calculated using Teichert's (von den Driech and Boessneck 1974) formula for calcaneus (GL × 10.78); femurs (GL × 3.53); metacarpals (GL × 4.89); metatarsals (GL × 4.54)

contexts (*i.e.* Phases 2–7). Pathologies were categorised according to lesion type and then aetiology (where possible). A full description is provided in Archive spreadsheet 9.6. Here, only broad trends are considered, with a focus on specimens for which aetiology was discernible.

Arthropathy

Abnormalities of the joint (arthopathies) were the most common lesion identified (n=73), being found mainly in cattle (n=44) but also in sheep/goat (n=22), pig (5), small ungulate (1) and in one unidentifiable fragment. In cattle these are predominately sub-chrondrial cystic lesions, or depressions, of the joint surfaces (n=38) with most examples deriving from the bones of the foot (n=35). A similar pattern is observed for sheep/goat (foot joints = 14 out of 20 sub-chondrial lesions) and pig (foot joints = 4 out of 5 sub-chondrial lesions). Baker and Brothwell (1980) recognised three forms (types 1–3) in the phalanges, a classification subsequently added to by Telldahl (2012) who identified a further two types (4–5). All five were identified in these assemblages in a wide range of elements. The aetiology of sub-chondrial cystic lesions is likely complex and is currently poorly understood. Thomas and Johanssen (2011) have suggested osteochrondrosis for type 1, 3 and 4 facets (accounting for 52% (n=32) of these cases), attributing formation to a combination of hereditary factors and environment, which may include rapid growth, diet and lack of exercise. This condition would have caused a degree of lameness in the affected animals. Type 2 facets (n=7, 11%), however, are thought to reflect a 'benign developmental condition' with little impact on individuals concerned (Thomas and Johanssen 2011, 53).

Telldahl (2012) has argued that type 5 lesions have a different aetiology and suggests that these pronounced groove-like depressions are associated with degenerative non-infected arthritis indicative of the onset of spavin. In this assemblage type 5 lesions were found in three cattle metapodials (context 2150–metacarpal, context 2170 – metatarsal, context 2129 – metatarsal) a cattle navicular-cuboid (context 2016) and a sheep/goat metacarpal (context 2224). In addition, a cattle navicular-cuboid (context 2251) displayed fusion with adjacent tarsals bones, a more advanced form of this arthropathy. Spavin is an inflammation of the 'hock' joint resulting in fusion of the bones of the ankle, likely reflecting deformation through prolonged use and excessive loading. It is prevalent in animals used for traction, but not exclusively so, also being found in other livestock species as well as in non-domesticates, including red deer (Bartosiewicz and Gal 2013).

Six cattle first phalanges (contexts 1013, 1557, 1559 and 2031) display bone thickening (exostosis) on palmar surfaces and eburnation consistent with osteoarthritis (Baker and Brothwell 1980, 115). Eburnation was also recorded in a further five elements (calcaneum – context 2176, pelvis – context 2139, three metacarpals – contexts 2150, 2170, 2129) while lipping (hypertrophy) of articulatory surfaces was evident in four first phalanges (contexts 2033, 2127, 4077, 2156), a second phalange (context 2077) and a metatarsal (context 2156). Eburnation and exostosis were also found in two sheep/goat phalangeal joints (contexts 2267, 2227 both second phalange) and in a sheep proximal humerus (context 2077). The absence of other pathological indicators (such as trauma-related deformity) in all these fragments again points to

osteoarthritis. Like spavin, osteoarthritis is associated with joint strain and degeneration, often manifesting in traction animals (Telldahl 2012; de Cupere *et al.* 2000) but equally may be a symptom of age-related joint wear in older individuals (Bartosiewicz and Gal 2013).

INFECTION

Seventeen lesions identified as potentially indicating infection were either associated with non-specific bone loss (lysis), non-specific bone formation (proliferation) or a combination of the two (cattle n=5, dog n=2, large ungulate n=8, small ungulate n=1, sheep/goat n=1). A cattle navicular-cuboid (context 2206) exhibited strongly exaggerated fossa on the lateral side of proximal articulation with linear lesion/deformity extending onto the articular surface and with the entirety of the distal lateral articulation deformed into a lesioned and porous surface. Similar lesions were attributed by Baker and Brothwell (1980, 124–5) to infection of the foot, often associated with damp conditions. The massively lesioned (lytic) and porous superior articular surface of large ungulate cervical vertebrae (likely cattle on size) from context 1533 may reflect a blood-borne or soft tissue infection of the back (Baker and Brothwell 1980, 124–5).

Two articulating large ungulate (likely cattle on size) lumbar vertebrae from context 2201 exhibit enlarged/deformed foramina on the left ventral surface and a further lumbar vertebra, again large ungulate, from context 2224 displays a unilateral depression/cavity on left of caudal edge of vertical process. Enlarged foramina are widely reported (*e.g.* Wooding 2010; Baker and Brothwell 1980, 35) but their aetiology remains uncertain. Wooding (2010, 342) has argued that extreme examples, as here, may reflect disease and inflammation of the spinal cord or blood vessels.

A minor periostal infection, perhaps following trauma or knocking of the limb is indicated by a small area of hypertrophic and lytic bone, characterised by circular pits, in the distal shaft (medial) of a cattle humerus from context 2180. More significant bone infection, consistent with osteomyelitis or osteoperiostitis (*e.g.* Baker and Brothwell 1980, 69) is found in two bones of dog: a fourth metacarpal from context 2057 exhibits thickening and bone proliferation across the proximal shaft and throughout the thickness of the bone and, a heavily remodelled (hypertrophic) and deformed distal humerus shaft (context 2193).

TRAUMA

Four cases of trauma were recorded: a large ungulate (likely cattle, context 1504) and small mammal (likely dog, context 2115) rib exhibited hypertrophic calluses consistent with healed fractures. Mid-shaft calluses and deformity consistent with healed greenstick fracture were evident in a pig second metatarsal (context 2009) and a cow tibia (context 2206).

DENTAL PATHOLOGY

An ovicaprid third molar from Phase 3 context 1504 showed signs of linear enamel hypoplasia, resulting from early environmental and/or nutritional stress (Ewens 2010; Suckling 1980). Further occurrences of enamel hypoplasia occur in contexts 2002 and Phase 7 context 2127, an ovicaprid and pig, respectively. The maxilla of a pig skull from Phase 3 context 2204 showed deformity of the molar row typical of osteomyelitis contracted from infected local soft tissue, such as that pierced by coarse fodder or forage (Baker and Brothwell 1980, 71, 150–1).

DISCUSSION

Pathological specimens were identified in low numbers across all phases at Snusgar (Viking n=22 (0.4%); Late Norse n=78 (0.9%)). Of the domesticated livestock species, cattle exhibited the highest frequency, both in absolute and relative terms (cattle n=51 (2% of cattle assemblage), sheep/goat n=25 (1% of sheep/goat assemblage), pig n=8 (1% of pig assemblage)). Dog was the only other species to display pathologies with three of the 45 fragments identified (*i.e.* 6%) showing signs of disease, all of which came from different phases and are thus unlikely to represent the same individual.

The range and generally low frequency of pathologies present appears to reflect a generally healthy population, with osteoarthritis indicating some individuals living to a considerable age and/or the use of some cattle for traction. This corresponds well with the pathological profile at Quoygrew (Harland 2012, 152), which also shows an occasional trend of infected joints with a few aged animals and healed injuries. The occasional traumatic injuries, and what may be damp-related infections of the limbs, suggest the use of rough pasture at some times of the year. Sub-chondrial lesions, if reflecting osteochrondrosis, may indicate periods of rapid weight and/or fattening of stock and will have been associated with lameness. However, the presence of early neonatal animals in the assemblage and of hypoplasia, demonstrating an episode of environmental stress or nutritional deficiency, suggests some animals were kept in a byre/infield context during winter/early spring, where fodder was insufficient. The pathological profile is in contrast to that at the later (Viking era) stages at Pool (Bond 2007), where most pathology related to traction and stress changes in the hindlimbs of cattle and horses, and dental disease among sheep was more common.

Palaeodiet

The faunal assemblages from Trenches 1–5 were included in an ongoing research project into the dynamics and resilience of pastoral herding economics in Viking and Late Norse Orkney (Mainland *et al.* 2015; 2016). This has involved a synthesis of zooarchaeological data (species representation, mortality profiles, palaeopathological and metrical data) from 16 sites spanning the Late Iron Age to Late Norse period in Orkney and Shetland together with palaeodietary analysis via stable isotopes and dental microwear. Bone stable isotope analysis (carbon, δ13C, and nitrogen, δ15N) sampled collagen from sheep/goat (n=62), cattle (n=59) and pig (n=41) mandibles from six sites: Earl's Bu, Swandro, the Cairns, Beachview, Brough Road and this assemblage using standard analytical approaches (Ascough *et al.* 2012). This included 21 sheep/goat, 24 cattle and 10 pig mandibles from Snusgar. Analysis is ongoing and will be published in full elsewhere (Mainland and Batey 2019). Preliminary results, however, suggest that cattle and sheep/goat mostly grazed on terrestrial grazing. Sheep/goat may indicate a slight enhancement of carbon, δ13C, and nitrogen, δ15N through time, perhaps indicating an expansion of herds via grazing of coastal pastures and heathlands and a greater interest in secondary products from this species in the Late Norse period, *i.e.* wool, as has been argued for Quoygrew on similar evidence by Barrett (2012). Stable isotopes in Late Iron Age to Late Norse pigs in Orkney indicate a more variable diet than the other species with some evidence of foddering on marine products as indicated by enhanced δ15N values. Individuals from Snusgar, however, seem more likely to have fed in the terrestrial biosphere than at other sites.

Discussion

Like most assemblages of this date in the Northern and Western Isles, and indeed across the North Atlantic, the Viking-Late Norse deposits at the Bay of Skaill are dominated by domesticated species, with an emphasis on cattle, sheep/goat and pig (Mainland and Halstead 2005; Mainland *et al.* 2016; McGovern *et al.* 2010; Bond 2007). The cattle were short in stature, similar in size to modern Dexters, and raised primarily for milk and dairy products. Evidence for intensive dairying, indicated, as in this assemblage, by a slaughter profile in which high numbers of calves are culled within the first month of life is found extensively in Norse North Atlantic settlements from Viking period onwards, as well as in the preceding Iron Age in the Western and Northern Isles (Mainland *et al.* 2016; Mulville *et al.* 2005). Here, mortality profiles indicate a shift in the utilisation of dairy products through time, with greater specialisation evident in the Late Norse period. Culling patterns indicative of intensification in milk production in the Late Norse period are found at several other sites in Orkney and Shetland, such as Quoygrew in Westray and Sandwick in Shetland (Harland 2012; Bigelow

1992). Arguably an adaptation to constraints of arable production in this region (Halstead 1998; Mainland and Halstead 2005), dairy products played an increasingly important role in the Northern Isles for payment of taxes and tithes from the 11th centuries onwards (Bigelow 1992; Harland 2012).

The sheep were slender but relatively long-limbed, comparable with Soays or North Ronaldsays, the extant primitive breed of sheep from Orkney. Slaughter profiles indicate that ovicaprine husbandry was focused on prime meat production in the earlier phases of occupation, shifting towards a greater use of wool in the Late Norse period, and especially from Phases 5 to 7, mirroring the increasing emphasis on secondary products of cattle in this period. A slight rise in the relative frequency of sheep is also evident in Phases 4–7, and also may point to a greater interest in the use of sheep and of wool during this period. An intensive exploitation of this resource as a product for trade, as is, for example, evident in many of the Icelandic Viking-Late Norse assemblages (*e.g.* McGovern *et al.* 2010) is not, however, apparent.

Cattle are numerically more frequent than sheep/goat and, by virtue of their larger size, will have made a greater contribution to diet even with the relatively high culling rates of neonates and calves. In its greater overall emphasis on cattle, this assemblage differs from some other of the 9th to 11th century settlement sites in Orkney, such as Pool, Buckquoy and the early Norse phases at Quoygrew, where sheep/goat predominate. Cattle denoted elevated socio-economic status across the Norse North Atlantic and an association between a herding economy focused on cattle and the higher status settlements, as indicated by hall size and pastoral capacity, is evident within faunal assemblages of this date from Greenland and Iceland (Zori *et al.* 2013; McGovern *et al.* 2010). In Orkney, however, it is the greater relative frequency of pig remains which characterises the faunal assemblages from two of the historically attested highest status Viking Norse sites in Orkney, the Earl's Bu and the Brough of Birsay, residences and estate farms of the Earls of Orkney (Mainland *et al.* 2015; 2016; Harland 2012) (Fig. 9.10). In the Northern Isles, intra-site variability in cattle representation is evident, but an association between status and a high frequency of cattle is less clear (Fig. 9.11). This is particularly so for the Late Norse period where cattle representation at likely lower status sites such as Quoygrew in Westray is similar to that evident at the Earl's Bu (Fig. 9.11). The bone assemblage for Trench 5, *i.e.* the area associated with the longhouse, exhibit the highest frequency of pig remains across the excavated areas and at *c.* 21% in the earlier phases of occupation (Phases 2–3) is not dissimilar to the Earl's Bu in the same period (phase M, 'Viking' – 24%). By

Phases 4–7, pig has decreased in importance. If it were accepted that pig is equated with higher-status households in Norse Orkney, this would suggest that the East Mound longhouse was a relatively high status household in the earlier period (Phases 2–3) but that this importance had subsequently changed or even declined. This change in status may also be reflected in the changing economic orientation of cattle and sheep/goat husbandry in which meat production, and by extension consumption, is replaced by increasing specialisation in secondary products, *i.e.* milk and wool. In this respect, the difference in species representation between the settlement areas of Snusgar and East Mound with cattle and sheep/goat more abundant in the former, especially in Phases 4–7 period may hint to a spatial differentiation in socio-economic status. However, this intra-site variability could equally reflect zoning of activities across the wider landscape (see below).

Variability in the faunal assemblages from different excavation areas (Table 9.21) indicate the likelihood of some spatial organisation in and/or restriction of activities undertaken around the settlement. Of particular note, is the focus on non-domesticated species (red deer, whale, seal) in the Snusgar mound and the prevalence of burnt bone in specific midden locations in this area. Several of the Trench 4 midden layers were also used as working areas and it may be that these served as processing areas for animal carcasses. The absence of minor domesticates, cat, dog and horse in this area might then be consistent with a largely non-food usage of these species. Nevertheless, all of the latter species do exhibit butchery marks, albeit in low frequencies. Butchery in cat and horse is not uncommon in Viking/Norse contexts and is often interpreted as opportunistic use of species for food, as well as for skins and furs (Harland 2012), although the early church in Scandinavia appears to have placed prohibitions on the consumption of horse flesh (Jennbert 2011, 148–9). Each of these species also has significant symbolic connotations for the Pagan Norse, and the possibility that both consumption and deposition reflects ritual or sacrificial acts must be borne in mind (Jennbert 2011). The spatial distribution of cat, for example, indicates a particular association with the longhouse structure, with a potential cat burial foundation deposit at the juxtaposition of the domestic dwelling and the byre, and a further emphasis on this species evident in the latter structure. A similar 'paired' cat burial is also found at Pool (Bond 2007, 214). Dog is also represented by at least one partial burial (Phase 7 middens), while articulated forelimbs of horse are found in the middens associated with the long house. The presence of butchery marks on dog is notable, this being only very rarely found within a Norse context, suggesting a taboo on the regular consumption of this species. There is some indication, however, that

Table 9.21: Characteristics of faunal remains compared across trenches and between phases

| | Faunal remains | | | | | |
| | Snusgar T1 | | Snusgar T4 | | East Mound T5+T8 | |
	Phases 2–3	Phases 4–7	Phases 2–3	Phases 4–7	Phases 2–3	Phases 4–7
General	Low numbers of weathered and eroded bones					
	Inc. in diary specialisation over time: not intensification					
	Very little carnivore (dog) gnawing				More carnivore gnawing	
			More burnt bone			
					W/s: little, unburnt mammal bone in byre: more, burnt in longhouse/ anc. building	
Cattle	Dominate all areas and phases					
	Whole carcasses represented					
	Rel. more cattle: inc. assoc. over time					
					H/c: anc. building floors: rel. more frequent	
Sheep/goat			Rel. more s/g: inc. assoc. over time			
	Import of meatier joints				W/s: longhouse floors: rel. more frequent	
Pig	Whole carcasses represented					
					H/c: rel. more pig: dec. assoc. over time	
					W/s and h/c: longhouse floors: rel. more frequent	
Wild mammals	Relatively more (but small amounts)				Less wild fauna	
Wild avian			Most: gannets		H/c: anc. building floors: rel. more frequent	
Horse, cat and dog						H/c: rel. more
					H/c: longhouse floors: horse rel. more frequent	

dog, along with horse and other non-food animals such as bear were sacrificed and perhaps even consumed during ritualised feasting events (the *blót*) (Magnell and Iregen 2010). In the Trelleborg well deposits, for example, Gotfredsen *et al.* (2014) identify butchery marks are evident on dog skeletons consistent with meat removal associated with food refuse assumed to derive from *blót* feasting events. Fine knife marks are evident on the proximal shaft of a pair of dog femurs from a Phase 7 (*i.e.* 12th–13th century AD) external surface adjacent to the Trench 5 ancillary building. This date is rather late for Pagan activity and an alternative explanation may be disarticulation and de-fleshing of a carcass for skinning/ furs, though consumption arising from dietary stress, as has been argued for dog butchery in Norse Greenland (Buckland *et al.* 1983), cannot be ruled out. The ancillary building with its emphasis on cattle, and in particular feet

and heads, marine molluscs and wild avian fauna may also have functioned as an initial processing area for cattle carcasses and seabirds as well as shellfish.

Within the microfauna, of interest is the mouse in Trench 5, in Phase 7 context 2044, which is described as a possible later trample/occupation layer within the angle of a wall and context 2294. In each case, the skulls have been identified as those of house mouse (*Mus musculus domesticus*). The find in Phase 3 context 2294 has been radiocarbon dated to a late 10th century date range (SUERC-47148). Genetic studies of the European house mouse have shown that while this species was likely introduced into Britain from continental Europe during the Iron Age, its spread in the North Atlantic islands and in Scandinavia can be attributed to the Vikings (Searle *et al.* 2009; Jones *et al.* 2012). Moreover, it has been argued that the direction of movement was from the British Isles to

Norway rather than vice versa (Searle *et al.* 2009). House mouse remains were identified in Iron Age deposits from Shetland at the site of Old Scatness, though these have not been dated (Nicholson *et al.* 2005). Well-stratified examples are currently lacking in Iron Age contexts in Orkney, but this species is found in 11th–12th century middens from Quoygrew and Earl's Bu. The house mouse is currently the earliest, well stratified and radiocarbon dated remains of this species to have been found in Orkney.

The greater exploitation of wild sea birds evident here, in particular in comparison to domestic birds, is a common pattern noted on Viking-Late Norse sites in Orkney and an emphasis on sea birds is evident at Norse period sites such as Buckquoy (53%) (Serjeantson 1988), Beachview, Birsay (60%) (Allison and Rackham 1996), Pool (Serjeantson 2007) and Quoyrew (Harland *et al.* 2012). On these sites gannet, guillemot and shag/cormorant are found in the greatest numbers (Serjeantson 1988). This pattern partly reflects the abundance of sea birds in the Northern Isles, but also their breeding habits. Gannet and guillemot in particular come together in large colonies to breed which provides a rich seasonal resource. At all these sites, as at Snusgar, domestic fowl are present but in significantly lower numbers than wild sea birds. Relative frequencies of domestic fowl and larger geese (Anser sp.) assumed to be domestic are comparable with those evident at other Norse sites in Orkney, including Quoygrew and Pool (*c.* 2–3%). Domestic fowl are rare in Scotland before the Norse period (Best and Mulville 2014), but it is not necessary to rear domestic birds to supply eggs, feathers and meat if there is a large wild source (Serjeantson 1988). The practice of exploiting sea birds for food and trade was common in Orkney up to the present day, but it was not without danger. Historical evidence of methods include the use of nooses (*grins*) slipped over sleeping birds' heads, nets spread across the cliff into which startled birds flew, and men descending cliffs and stacks on ropes to collect eggs and birds (Fenton 1978). Fowlers used ropes of straw when swine hair was not available and, although sticks were used to avoid friction and wooden stakes as support, many men slipped to their deaths on the rock or drowned (Fenton 1978). While guillemots and cormorants could have been caught locally in these ways, the capture of gannets from offshore islands or stacks required seaworthy boats and a large number of men (Serjeantson 1988; 2001). Despite this, many Norse sites in the North Atlantic exploited gannet such as Pool, Buckquoy, Quoyrew and the Udal (Serjeantson 2001).

Fracture patterns for the large gannet bone deposit in Phase 3 context 1504 (Trench 4) and elsewhere across the sites indicate a very consistent butchery process; most of the humeri present have been broken across the mid-shaft region in almost the same position. These fracture/butchery patterns are comparable with

ethnographic accounts of wing removal during the capture and processing, on a semi-industrialised scale, of gannet in post-medieval periods (Beatty 1992). The nearest breeding colony for gannet today is the Sule Stack, 50 km to the west of Orkney. Historically, exploitation of gannets on Sule Stack was in the control of the Earl of Orkney (Serjeantson 2007), though it is not known how far back in time this right extends.

The molluscan assemblage is dominated by two species, periwinkle and limpet. The periwinkle has long been considered a food source and has been eaten in Orkney even until relatively modern times, usually by the poor in times of scarcity (Fenton 1978). While limpet can and has been used for food, it is also essential bait for craig fishing. In Orkney and the Northern Isles craig fishing, fishing from the rocks on the shore with a rod and line, has been practised since at least the Norse period. The limpets were prised from the rocks, parboiled and then either attached to the hook or mashed and put in the water as a lure (Fenton 1978). It is possible that the other species, which are present mainly in small numbers, were gathered accidentally either with other species and seaweed, or represent opportunistic finds on the shore.

Conclusions

The faunal assemblages indicate a settlement cluster focused primarily on domestic animals and in particular cattle and sheep/goat. For the assemblage as a whole, cattle were the preferred species and would have provided the bulk of the meat consumed as well as supplying dairy products such as milk, cheese, butter and yoghurt. A potential association is indicated between pig consumption in the East Mound longhouse and socio-economic status, and there is some suggestion that this area of the site at least may have seen a decline in importance through time. A shift in the economic focus of animal husbandry from the Viking (Phases 2–3) to Late Norse (Phases 4–7) occupation has been identified: from meat to specialisation in secondary products. An emphasis on secondary products is evident elsewhere in Orkney at this period, and has been equated with increasing levels of taxation by the Orkney earls to finance their aspirations within the Scandinavian and Scottish courts (Barrett 2012; Crawford 2013). The faunal evidence here thus suggests changes in social standing, with the occupants of the longhouse less interested in providing high status foods for consumption in the hall than goods such as milk and wool, which could be used for exchange and/or taxation. Sea fowling was a smaller, but likely significant, part of the economy and again there is a suggestion in the systematic exploitation of gannet that something more than subsistence production is being indicated for the settlement(s) at the Bay of Skaill during the Viking-Late Norse periods.

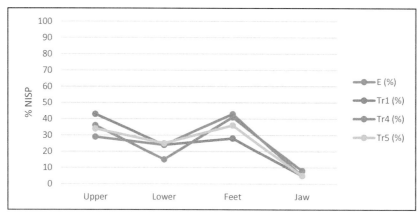

Fig. 9.1: Sheep anatomical representation (Phases 2–7): lists for the primary excavation Trenches (T1, T4, T5) the ratio (expressed as a %) of upper limbs (scapula, pelvis, humerus, femur), lower limbs (radius, ulna, tibia), feet (metacarpal, metatarsal, phalanges 1–3) and head (mandible). For comparison the expected ratio in which these elements occur within an entire carcass is also given (E)

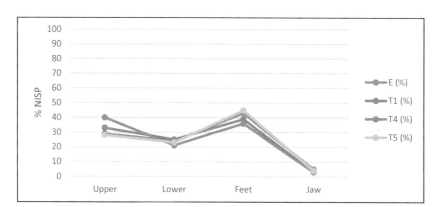

Fig. 9.2: Cattle anatomical representation (Phases 2–7): lists for the primary excavation Trenches (T1, T4, T5) the ratio (expressed as a %) of upper limbs (scapula, pelvis, humerus, femur), lower limbs (radius, ulna, tibia), feet (metacarpal, metatarsal, phalanges 1–3) and head (mandible). For comparison the expected ratio in which these elements occur within an entire carcass is also given (E)

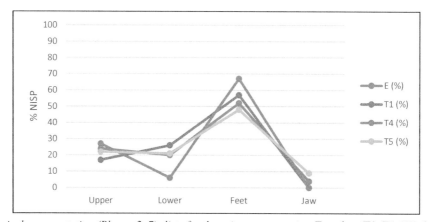

Fig. 9.3: Pig anatomical representation (Phases 2–7): lists for the primary excavation Trenches (T1, T4, T5) the ratio (expressed as a %) of upper limbs (scapula, pelvis, humerus, femur), lower limbs (radius, ulna, tibia), feet (metacarpal, metatarsal, phalanges 1–3) and head (mandible). For comparison the expected ratio in which these elements occur within an entire carcass is also given (E)

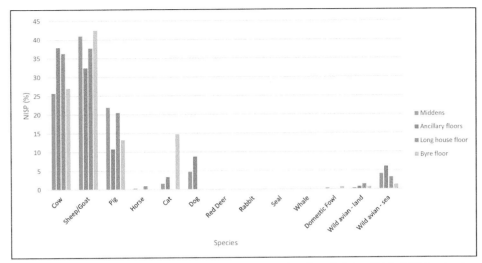

Fig. 9.4: Spatial variation in species representation within Trench 5 (see Table 9.21 for data)

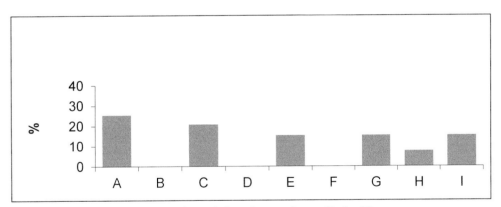

Fig. 9.5: Phases 2–3 cattle mortality profile (n=13)

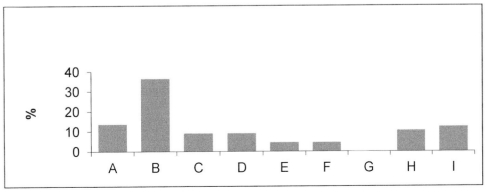

Fig. 9.6: Phases 4–7 cattle mortality profile (n=22)

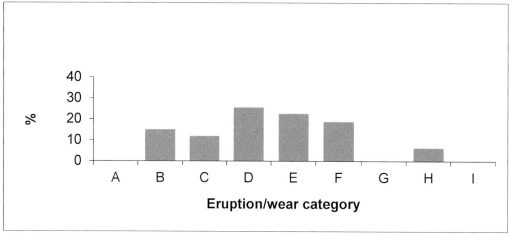

Fig. 9.7: Phases 2–3 sheep/goat mortality profile (n=16)

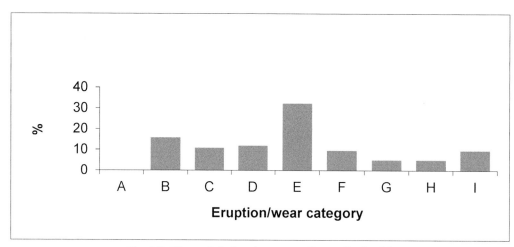

Fig. 9.8: Phases 4–7 sheep/goat mortality profile (n=24)

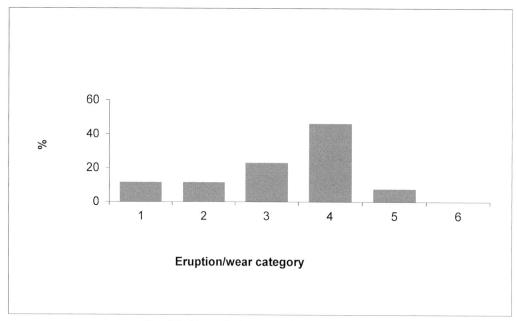

Fig. 9.9: Phases 2–7 pig mortality profile (n=13)

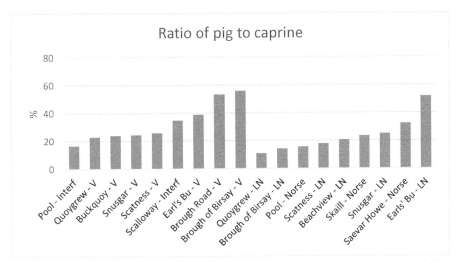

Fig. 9.10: Pig: caprine (sheep/goat) ratio for Viking (V) and Late Norse (LN) sites in Orkney and Shetland (Snusgar = all trenches 1–8; Skaill = Skaill Deerness)

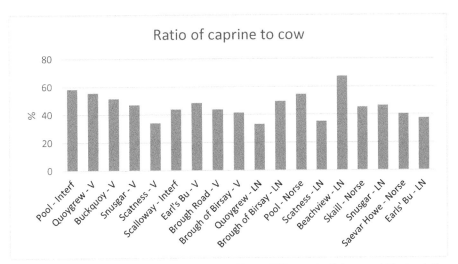

Fig. 9.11: Cow: caprine (sheep/goat) ratio for Viking (V) and Late Norse (LN) sites in Orkney and Shetland (Snusgar = all trenches 1–8; Skaill = Skaill Deerness)

Fig. 9.12: Trench 5 Hand-collected bone count by phase

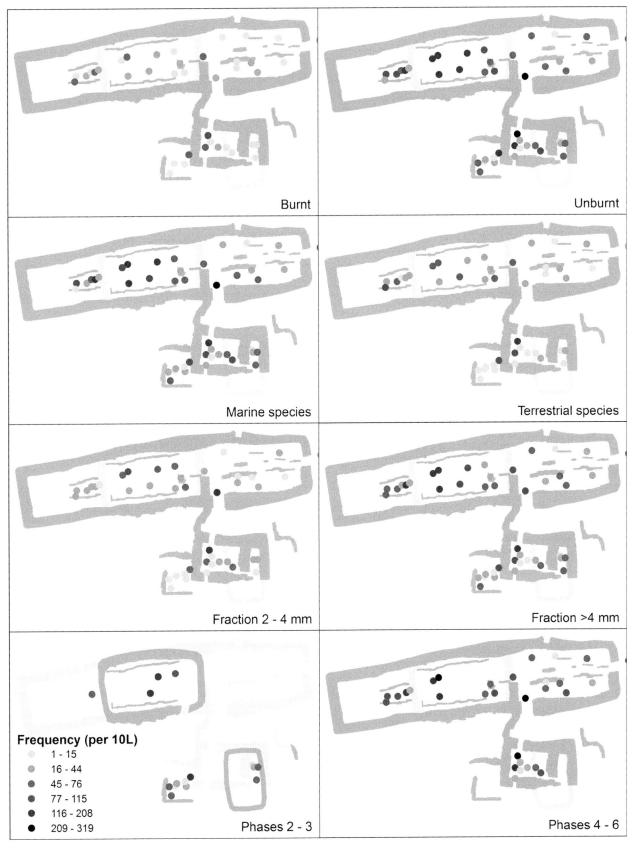

Fig. 9.13: Trench 5 Wet-sieve residues, bone and shell

10

Fish remains

Rebecca A. Nicholson

Introduction

The excavations at the Bay of Skaill resulted in the recovery of several thousand fish bones. These were collected from a wide range of deposits, including occupation/trample horizons, wind-blown sand layers, middens and the fills of walls and other features dating from the earliest to latest phases. However, the majority of securely-phased bones came from stratified Viking-Late Norse midden spreads from Trenches 1 and 4 (Snusgar) and, in greatest numbers, from floor surfaces and soil layers from the longhouse, ancillary buildings and associated middens discovered in Trench 5 (East Mound). Most of the occupation deposits which produced fish remains date to Phases 3–6 (10th to 12th centuries)

Around 83% of the identified fish bones were recovered by hand during the excavations, with approximately 18% extracted from the residues of the 292 10-litre bulk soil samples, which were each sieved and sorted to 2 mm. Almost all of the sieved bone came from samples taken from the structures and middens in Trench 5, with a very much smaller assemblage deriving from Trench 4. The analysis was conducted primarily to compare the assemblages from Snusgar and East Mound in terms of species representation, fish size/age and element representation in order to investigate whether fishing and fish consumption changed between the Viking and Late Norse periods (Phases 3–6) and, specifically, whether there was any evidence for the large-scale production of dried fish for export or, conversely, of the importation of these stored fish. Additionally, for East Mound, to explore whether there is any evidence for differential refuse disposal between the middens and the floor deposits associated with the longhouse. Very much smaller amounts of fish remains from Trenches 6 and 7 were

recorded. The full data is in the online archive (Archive spreadsheet 10.1).

Identification and recording

The majority of recovered fish remains were identified to species, or other taxonomic level where appropriate, using the author's comparative collection. Bones not generally considered identifiable to family or species level include bones such as those of the branchial arch and fins, which are difficult to speciate apart from in a few specific cases such as the diagnostic spines of gurnards (Triglidae) and flatfish anal pterigiophores. Where present, most or all were consistent with large cod family fish (Gadidae) and while these bones are not included in the fragment counts their presence has been noted. Scales were likewise recorded as present but counts have not been tabulated. The anatomical side (left or right) has been recorded for key cranial elements but no attempt was made to pair bones because the generally fragmented nature of the remains, and the asymmetrical nature of some paired bones in the comparative collection, made this unwise.

Where possible, measurements were taken using vernier callipers to 0.1 mm on the dentary, premaxilla and otolith, following Wheeler and Jones (1976) and Jones (1991). Other measurements were taken occasionally following Morales and Rosenlund (1979). Biometrical analysis of fish bones has certain limitations, however, not least because the bones are relatively small and measurement error consequently likely, especially for the smallest fishes. Where measurements were not taken, approximate fish size has been reconstructed by comparison with reference specimens of known length, although in the largest size categories (>1 m fish) size estimation was limited by the lack of comparative material. Where sizes are indicated for gadid fish (fish of the cod family, Gadidae) the following sizes apply: tiny (under 0.15 m length); small (0.15–0.30 m); medium (0.30–0.7 m); large (0.7–1 m); extra-large (over 1 m) and extra, extra large (over 1.5 m). To reconstruct fish lengths more accurately, the regression formulae of Barrett (1995) were used for the dentary and premaxilla of cod, saithe and ling (see Archive Spreadsheet 10.1); where two measurements were taken on the dentary (D1 and D2), size reconstructions using D2 has been found to be more accurate (Barrett 1995, 231), but this measuring point may be more likely to be eroded (Jones 1991, 331). Some ling premaxilla measurements may exaggerate the size of the fish because it can be difficult to insert the callipers fully into the notch at the base of the condyle (as discussed by Jones 1991, 331).

All bones were scanned for butchery marks and other pre-depositional modifications such as burning and gnawing. Any observed pathologies or abnormalities were also noted. Where present these traits were noted in the record and the butchery marks described. Barrett (1995; 1997, Fig. 7) has classified butchery marks on gadid fish into six inferred butchery categories: consistent with tongue or cheek removal (category 1), gut, tongue or cheek removal (category 2), decapitation (category 3), gutting (category 4), axial splitting (category 5) and severing the vertebral column (category 6). These categories are particularly useful in interpreting the cut and chop marks found on gadid skeletal elements, and where appropriate have been added to the butchery descriptions in this report.

Crab claw and carapace fragments consistent with the edible crab *Cancer pagrus* were present in a few contexts and have been recorded and tabulated, even though these are, of course, crustaceans rather than fish.

Preservation

Bone condition was recorded on a subjective five point scale – as 'very good', 'good', 'fair', 'poor' or 'very poor' with 'very good' bone appearing fresh and with no evidence of erosion, 'good' preservation equating to bone with intact surfaces and very minimal flaking and 'poor' bone exhibiting significant fragmentation and erosion of diagnostic features. Bone in 'very poor' condition was frequently too eroded and fragmented to be identifiable and consequently was rarely recorded. Occasionally groups of bones (particularly vertebrae) were recorded together, and in this case, condition was scored as variable, if appropriate.

Generally, the fish bones from all phases of excavation were in good or fair condition; a few contexts contained bone in a poor, eroded, state but equally some contained bone that appeared almost fresh. A few deposits contained bones in a range of preservation states, but in most cases, bone condition was consistent within contexts, suggesting

a single depositional event rather than redeposition and mixing. Burned bones and gnawed bones were extremely rare, and the presence of several sets of probably articulating vertebra indicates that most waste was buried fairly rapidly.

Quantification and location of the data

The representation of taxa is here presented mainly as fragment counts. All identifiable fragments were used rather than just anatomically discrete areas, because in practice very few fresh breaks were evident and few fragments seemed to have originated from the same bone as another; to use only discrete portions of the bones would have ignored many bones not represented by any other fragments. The minimum number of individuals (MNI) is not a very useful statistic in fish bone studies, as fish bones are generally subject to extensive post-depositional decay rendering the figure almost meaningless (Wheeler and Jones 1989, 151–2). No attempt was made to estimate original population sizes, a comprehensive critique of which has been given by Leach (1986). Full records will be available as spreadsheets in the archive (Archive spreadsheets 0.1, 10.2).

The assemblage

The total assemblage of identified fish remains comprised 5437 hand collected fish bones as well as 1270 fish bones extracted from the sieved residues, only 87 of which came from Snusgar mound. In addition, several thousand fragments including large quantities of gadid rays, ribs, branchial bones and skull fragments were recovered but not specifically recorded. The bone was distributed fairly evenly between contexts; there were few large dumps of fish.

Unsurprisingly, the hand retrieved assemblage was largely composed of bones from large and very large fish, almost entirely gadid (Tables 10.1–10.7); the majority were from large (0.7–1 m) cod, *Gadus morhua* L. (Table 10.1). Other related taxa represented in a number of contexts included: saithe (coalfish), *Pollachius virens* (L.); pollack, *Pollachius pollachius* (L.); ling, *Molva* cf *molva* (L.); torsk (cusk), *Brosme brosme* (Ascanius); haddock, *Melanogrammus aeglefinus* (L.) and hake, *Merluccius merluccius* (L.). There were also rare finds of three-bearded rockling, *Gaidropsaurus vulgaris* (Cloquet), as well as flatfish – both left eyed (Bothidae) and right-eyed (Pleuronectidae), wrasse (Triglidae), small salmon or trout (Salmonidae), rays (Rajidae), spurdog, *Squalus acanthias* (L.) and dogfish (Scyliorhinidae).

The sieved assemblage was slightly more diverse but again gadid bones were numerically dominant, comprising over 95% of the assemblage (Table 10.7). In contrast to the hand retrieved bone, small fish (<0.35 m) were at least as common as large (>0.7 m) specimens in the sieved

Table 10.1: Number of hand collected fish and crustacean remains, by phase

Phase	2	2 or 3	3	4	5	3–5	6	7	8	9	Unphased	Total
Elasmobranch	1		8		1							10
Shark					1							1
Spurdog			3									3
Dogfish	3											3
Ray			1									1
Salmonid								1				1
3-bearded rockling									2			2
Gadid	49		118	43	284	3	197	96	67	2	8	867
Cod	149	1	320	176	1127	13	655	614	210	11	7	3283
Saithe	7		45	4	57	1	12	10	6			142
Pollack	2		12	1	3		11	4	2			35
Saithe/pollack	3		23	4	24	1	9	7	4		1	76
Cod/saithe/pollack	34		184	34	265	2	54	92	36		4	687
Haddock	6		1	1								8
Hake			4	1	9		6	1	1			22
Ling	17		9	8	73		36	34	20		2	199
Torsk	2		4	2	10		5	6	3			32
cf. Torsk					1		1					2
Ling/torsk	4		2	6	11		12	5				40
Wrasse					4							4
Ballan wrasse							2	1				3
Mackerel			1									1
Left eyed flatfish					1							1
Right-eyed flatfish	1		2	1	1			2				7
Unidentified fish									4	3		7
Crab			1		5		7	2	4			19
Total	278	1	738	281	1860	20	1008	880	355	13	22	5456

assemblage, a reflection of the important role of inshore fishing. Apart from large and small cod, saithe, pollack and ling, several contexts included bones from tiny eel, *Anguilla anguilla* (L.); herring, *Clupea harengus* L.; small dogfish or ray (Elasmobranchii); three-bearded rockling; 4-bearded rockling, *Rhinonemus cimbrius* (L.); 5-bearded rockling, *Ciliata mustela* (L.); butterfish, *Pholis gunnellus* (L.); eelpout, *Zoarces viviparus* (L.); ballan wrasse, *Labrus bergylta* (Ascanius); cottid(s) (Cottidae); garfish, *Belone belone* (L.); halibut, *Hippoglossus hippoglossus* (L.); right eyed flatfish; small salmonid, probably trout, *Salmo trutta* L.; sandeel (Ammodytidae); as well as possibly snake blenny, *Lumpenus lampretaeformis* (Walbaum) and tadpole fish, *Raniceps raninus* (L.).

Fish as export commodities

Most of the occupation deposits which produced fish remains date to Phases 3–6 (10th to 12th centuries), a period of economic change across much of the North Atlantic region, with the development of commercial fishing and trade alongside traditional mixed farming and subsistence fishing. Any discussion of fish remains from Viking and Late Norse sites in the Northern Isles of Scotland inevitably centres on the topic of dried fish as an exported commodity. The dominance of mature gadids, particularly cod but also saithe and ling is typical of Norse assemblages in Orkney, as elsewhere in the North Atlantic at this time and has been termed the 'fish event' by Barrett *et al.* (1999; 2000; 2004). Fishing activity appears to have been almost entirely devoted to the capture of these large fish, which could be dried for export and/or to provide a stored food for use in winter and spring. The commercialisation of fishing in the North Atlantic went hand in hand with a change from the use of fish as a subsistence food and as a commodity for local exchange and demonstration of chiefly prestige to the large scale production of dried cod family fish – stockfish – as a cash crop, with international value (Perdikaris 1996; 1998, 130–139; 1999). The development of the trade in preserved fish is thought to have begun around the end of the first millennium AD (Barrett *et al.* 2004).

Detecting the production or consumption of cured fish, and if present the scale, is therefore one way in which the nature and status of a household in this region can be determined. In order to establish involvement in commercial production or consumption a number of parameters can be examined. Firstly, the sizes of fish provide an indication of the type of fishing practised: from the shore, from small boats fishing inshore or from more seaworthy vessels fishing in deep water. Secondly, the relative numbers of bones from suitably large-sized fish can provide a good indication of the importance of fishing to a settlement. Commercial fishing and fish preparation generates huge quantities of fish bones at producer sites. Thirdly, the distribution of skeletal elements can provide a strong indication of stockfish production or consumption: head bones are discarded at the processing location while cleithra and some vertebrae – particularly posterior caudal vertebrae – are left in the prepared fish to provide structure. Cutmarks may also provide some indication of the methods used for fish preparation, although butchery marks on fish bones tend to be scarce due in part to bone erosion. Finally, the preparation of fish for commercial export would take place close to the shore, rather than within a domestic dwelling.

Large fish middens dating to the Late Norse/Medieval periods have been discovered at several sites in Northern Scotland and the Northern Isles including Robert's Haven and Freswick Links (Caithness), Quoygrew (Westray) and at Sandwick (Shetland), where the remains may be interpreted as evidence for the production of stockfish, possibly for export (Colley 1983, Bigelow 1984; Jones 1995; Barrett 1997). There is some circumstantial historical evidence to suggest that the Earldom of Orkney was participating in the fish trade in the 12th century (Pálsson and Edwards 1978), and fish midden at St Boniface, Orkney may include the remains of fish prepared for export dating from the 11th century (Lowe 1998). Determining the origin of stockfish production in the Northern Isles is of significant interest, but it is likely that it grew out of local, small-scale trade and consequently may be difficult to establish.

Diachronic and spatial distribution of fish remains

The assemblage is considered by excavation area and phase in the following discussions, with the midden-derived fish remains from Snusgar and East Mound, and the floor and midden-derived bones from deposits associated with the East Mound longhouse and ancillary buildings, examined for any diachronic and spatial variation. Both hand collected and bones from sieved soil samples are considered from Phases 2–7. No fish remains were identified from Phase 1 deposits, and those that were found from Phases 8 and 9 are from insecure deposits and/or very broadly phased deposits, and consequently are of little significance.

Trenches 1 and 3: Midden spreads and fills associated with the Snusgar longhouse (Tables 10.2 and 10.3)

ALL PHASES (SEE CHAPTER 4, TABLE 4.2)

Deposits excavated in Trenches 1 and 3 (Tables 10.2, 10.3) included sequential midden spreads to the north and south of the longhouse, as well as later 18th- and 19th-century layers and kelp pits. The fish remains considered here are from Viking-Late Norse middens and fills associated with the longhouse: 1012, 1013, 1017, 1019, 1020, 1021, 1022, 1038, 1039, 1041, 1045, 1046 and 1056.

None of these middens contained especially large collections of fish bones, and some contexts contained only one or two fragments. The only midden layer with more than a couple of fish bones in Trench 1 was 1017, to the north of the longhouse and dated to Phase 2. Most of the bones came from the heads and anterior part of the spine (precaudal vertebrae) of large cod, with a few bones from saithe and pollack of similar size. One cod maxilla had cuts around the articulation, suggesting dismemberment of the head, possibly to remove the tongue.

Table 10.2: Number of hand-collected bones, Trench 1

Phase	2	3	5	Total
Elasmobranch		3	1	4
Gadid	2	11	3	16
Cod	13	31	15	59
Saithe	3	17	2	22
Pollack		2	1	3
Cod/saithe		1		1
Saithe/pollack	2	7	1	10
Cod/saithe/pollack	2	14		16
Total	22	86	23	131

Table 10.3: Number of hand-collected bones, Trench 3 midden

Phase	3	7	8	Total
Gadid		6	2	8
Cod	1	14	1	16
Ling		4	1	5
Total	1	24	4	29

Internal layers from within the longhouse, Trench 1, dating to Phase 3 and Phase 5 contained similar suites of bones from the heads and anterior spines of large and very large cod and saithe, with a few medium-sized individuals also present, including pollack. Several posterior (caudal) vertebrae also came from large and medium-sized fish, and a small elasmobranch vertebra, probably from dogfish, has been chopped through, probably when cutting the body of the fish into portions (steaks). A vertebra from a small-medium sized shark, probably tope, *Galeorhinus galeus* (L.) from a Phase 5 layer within the longhouse 1012, is evidence that these fish were occasionally caught and eaten.

The Trench 3 middens, from south of the Snusgar longhouse comprised mainly bones from the heads and anterior spine of large and very large cod and saithe, with saithe perhaps proportionately more important than cod in this midden, although with only 58 identified bones this is not conclusive. A medium-sized elasmobranch vertebra, again probably from tope, was also recovered. A single sample (sample 23 from 1056) included only a few bones from the head and anterior spine of large and very large cod and possibly saithe.

These middens and internal layers provide some slight evidence for the production of dried fish, in that those bones which would be discarded from a dried product are represented while those which would be retained within the product are missing or under-represented. However, these bones were almost all hand collected, and caudal vertebrae – particularly those towards the tail of the fish – are smaller and so less easily seen. Cleithra, also left in the dried product, are easily fragmented and this could explain their under-representation (Jones 1991, 334; Nicholson 1992).

Trenches 4–8

PHASE 2

TRENCH 4: SNUSGAR (TABLE 10.4)

Many of the 86 identified hand collected bones from the Phase 2 middens in Trench 4 came from large and very large cod and ling, some well in excess of 1.2 m. A ling dentary from midden context 1533 came from an enormous fish of well over 2 m long. While cod was the most frequently identified fish, with both cranial bones and vertebrae from all parts of the spine present, ling, saithe and haddock were also identified, together with occasional vertebrae from a small shark or ray and right eyed flatfish (plaice, flounder or dab). Butchery marks were confined to a single large ling post-temporal, where cuts to the dorsal surface probably indicate beheading of the fish. Large and medium-sized cod dominate the small sieved assemblage, with occasional bones from small saithe or pollack and a single rare find of herring, which could have come from the gut of a larger carnivorous fish.

Table 10.4: Number of hand-collected bones, Trench 4

Phase	2	3	5	9	2–3	Unphased	Total
Elasmobranch	1	5					6
Spurdog		3					3
Gadid	23	16	12			1	52
Cod	41	19	12	1	1		74
Saithe	2	10	10				22
Pollack		4					4
Saithe/pollack		4	10				14
Cod/saithe/pollack		5	1				6
Haddock	5	1					6
Ling	13	1					14
Wrasse			4				4
Right-eyed flatfish	1	1					2
Total	86	68	50	1	1	1	207

TRENCHES 5 AND 8: EAST MOUND (TABLE 10.5)

A fairly small group of fish bones, 170 identified fragments, was hand retrieved: some from the earliest hall-building floor 2146 and, particularly, the midden to the east of the ancillary building 2152. Both contexts produced bones from the heads and spines of large and very large gadids, including cod, saithe, pollack, ling, torsk and haddock, many from fish of over a metre long, with few bones from fish under 0.6 m. Measurements taken on the premaxilla indicated cod of between 1 and 1.2 m. Cut marks on one very large cod cleithrum were probably inflicted as the fish was being filleted. Several smaller elasmobranch vertebrae were probably from dogfish. Soil samples taken from the same two contexts produced only 31 fish bones, mostly from small gadids, particularly saithe. The similarity of fish remains from the internal floor and the external midden is perhaps surprising and is explored further below. It would seem inherently unlikely that large fish heads and spines were left to rot on the floor of an inhabited building, although those bones discovered on the floor were predominantly from material trapped under the cross-wall during the re-configuration of the hall-building into the longhouse.

PHASE 3

TRENCH 4: SNUSGAR

The small hand collected assemblage comprised only 68 bones, including three spurdog dorsal spines, all from midden deposits (mainly 1504). In addition to medium and large-sized cod saithe, pollack and haddock, several small elasmobranch vertebrae were identified, probably from

Table 10.5: Number of hand-collected bones, Trench 5 (incorporating Trench 8)

Phase	2	3	4	5	6	7	8	9	3–5	Unphased	Total
Dogfish	3										3
Ray		1									1
Salmonid						1					1
3-bearded rockling							2				2
Gadid	24	91	43	265	197	89	65	1	3	7	785
Cod	95	269	176	1081	655	599	209	9	13	7	3113
Saithe	2	18	4	25	12	10	6		1		78
Pollack	2	6	1	1	11	4	2				27
Saithe/pollack	1	12	4	8	9	6	4		1	1	46
Cod/saithe/pollack	32	164	34	238	54	92	36			4	656
Haddock	1		1								2
Hake		4	1	9	6	1	1				22
Ling	4	9	8	72	36	30	19			2	180
Torsk	2	4	2	10	5	6	3				32
cf. Torsk				1	1						2
Ling/cf. Torsk	4	2	6	11	12	5					40
Ballan wrasse					2	1					3
Mackerel		1									1
Left eyed flatfish					1						1
Right-eyed flatfish		1	1	1		2					5
Unidentified fish					1	1	4				6
Crab		1		5	7	2	4				19
Total	170	583	281	1729	1008	852	351	10	20	21	5025

dogfish as well as a single partial anal pterygiophore from a right eyed flatfish (plaice, flounder or dab). Fifty-three identified remains from six sieved samples included six otoliths from large and small gadids as well as vertebrae from gadids of various sizes and small elasmobranchs. The preservation of otoliths, which are distinctive structures composed of calcium carbonate found in the inner ear, is a consequence of the calcareous nature of the sandy soils.

Trench 5: East Mound

A large range of contexts contained a few fish bones, and these were generally from deposits within the hall-building and ancillary building. The hand collected material comprised 583 identified bones, recovered from 21 contexts which included a disturbed floor in the ancillary building 2080, metalworking yard floor 2105, drain fill 2148, ancillary building floor 2160 and middens east of the ancillary building 2204, 2254 and 2236 with working surface 2206. Again, deposits both within and outside the ancillary and yard structures contained bones from large and very large fish, mainly cod heads and vertebrae from fish of 0.7–1 m long, with a few larger and smaller fish and also occasional saithe, pollack, ling, torsk and hake. There were rare finds of mackerel from floor 2155 in the north–south ancillary building and right eyed flatfish (plaice, flounder or dab) from midden 2254, a midden deposit to the south-east of Trench 5. Both head bones and vertebrae were present in the assemblage of around 300 hand collected bones from 2254, from a minimum of five cod, two saithe, two pollack, one ling, one torsk and one hake. While cleithra appeared to be slightly under-represented, posterior caudal vertebrae were common and since these bones would be expected to be retained within a dried fish it seems likely that in general whole fish frames were dumped in the midden. Cleithra fragment fairly easily and consequently may be rendered undiagnostic more frequently than other more robust skeletal elements. One large cod precaudal vertebra had been chopped through transversely, probably while splitting the body of the fish (butchery category 6 in Barrett 1995, 239). A small cut to the dorsal aspect of a large cod post-temporal and to a large gadid supracleithrum (Barrett's category 3, *ibid.*)

may have occurred during beheading, as may several cuts to large gadid branchiostegal rays.

The 240 sieved bones came from internal and external contexts as well as from drain fill 2148. Many of the internal deposits, including hall-building ashy floor surfaces 2262 and 2264 and floors in the ancillary building including 2245, contained the remains of small, medium and large gadids, mainly cod and saithe, probably indicating that ash midden was used in the build-up of these surfaces. Some bones may also have derived from fish prepared in the longhouse, or possibly from fish hung up to dry and smoke, although there is no indication from the skeletal element distributions for beheaded or split fish. Rare elements from herring and butterfish demonstrate the advantageous conditions for bone preservation within the ashy layers. While midden deposit 2254 mainly included bones from young saithe, the peat ash midden 2288, to the east of the ancillary building and dated to cal AD 1010–1160 (SUERC-33721), was evidently used for the disposal of larger waste since most of the fish remains were of large cod, with both heads and major parts of the spine present. Flax seeds were also found in 2288 which is interpreted as possible evidence for the drying of flax above the domestic hearth, so evidently this midden included waste from a range of activities taking place in and around the longhouse and ancillary building. Drain fills 2148, 2149 and 2153 included 42 bones from young saithe and larger gadids, with cuts to a large gadid branchiostegal ray indicating the butchery of this fish.

PHASE 4: TRANSITION

The assemblage from Phase 4 came entirely from East Mound, Trench 5. Samples producing fish remains came from wall fill 2084 and sandy midden 2170 east of the ancillary building, as well as construction cut fills 2054 and 2077. With only 39 identified bones, no sample was particularly rich; most bones were from large cod and medium-sized saithe and pollack with a few bones from juvenile saithe and indeterminate small gadid. Rather more (281 identified fragments) were hand collected, again from middens but also from poorly stratified deposits including wall fills, windblown sand layers and disturbed fills. Midden 2170, to the east of the ancillary building, contained an assemblage of bones from a minimum of four large cod, saithe, ling and flatfish – probably halibut. A large cod dentary and a premaxilla, as well as a large saithe premaxilla, had been chopped through the symphysis, possibly in an attempt to open the mouth and remove a hook (category 1, Barrett 1995). Other cuts (n=3) were to cod supracleithra and a cleithrum, consistent with beheading (category 3, *ibid.*). Most of the cod were around 0.9–1.2 m long, although a few smaller fish (0.5–0.7 m) were also present.

PHASE 5

EAST MOUND

The largest quantity of hand recovered fish remains came from middens and floors dated to the 11th–mid-12th century. Over 1700 bones were hand recovered, almost all of which came from Trench 5 (Table 10.1 and 10.5). Bones extracted from the sieved residues from 74 samples included very small numbers of eel and dogfish bones in addition to the ubiquitous large, medium and small gadids. Most of the bones, which were of variable condition, came from longhouse floor deposits 2158, 2224, 2261, 2263, 2265 and 2275 and from within the ancillary building, and many were very from large fish. Based on measurements on the dentary and premaxilla, ling from ashy longhouse floor 2224 and ancillary building floor 2113 and 2016 were in excess of 1.5 m long. Hand collected material from a late floor within the western annex 2241 included cranial and post-cranial elements from one or more large cod and other large gadid(s), probably from fresh fish prepared here.

Carbonised seeds, including flax, from floors within the longhouse seem likely to relate to activities taking place around the hearth, such as flax drying, and possibly also accidentally imported in peat for the fire and turves used for roofing. It is difficult to view the fish remains in this light, since entire, large, fish seem to have been present; the presence of fish heads indicates that these fish were not dried and stored. A very similar suite of skeletal elements, from similarly large fish, is present in the byre and external middens. While the evidence from carbonised plant remains indicates that different activities were taking place at the byre end of the longhouse, this cannot be deduced from the fish remains, which show a consistent pattern of midden-type material scattered fairly uniformly through all parts of the longhouse and outbuildings.

Floor deposits from the byre end of the longhouse 2267, 2271, 2277, dated to cal AD 1010–1160 (SUERC-33712) and 2276, dated to cal AD 900–1120 (SUERC-47156) also included significant quantities of bones from large and very large fish, including ling of over 1.5 m. Several sets of vertebrae were articulated, indicating the deposition of whole or partial fish or fish frames. It is possible that fish waste may have been used for animal feed, although no evidence for distorted, chewed or digested fish remains was recovered.

The fill of large pit 2205 in the south-eastern midden area produced 122 identified fish bones by hand collection, mainly large and very large cod but also including a maxilla and caudal vertebrae from ling, two vertebrae from medium-sized flatfish (0.35–0.5 m fish) and a precaudal vertebra from a large hake. This pit also contained cattle bones and the articulated remains of a dog. Both the hand collected fish assemblage and that from the one sieved sample (sample 8) were unexceptional; bones from small saithe, medium-sized and large cod as well as a single vertebra probably from a tadpole fish are likely to be from general domestic rubbish. One of the few gnawed bones came from this pit: a cod supracleithrum from a large fish.

Butchery evidence in the form of chops and cut marks was observed on 20 bones, mainly from large and very large cod, but also on a large ling dentary and post-temporal and a torsk articular. Cuts to the jaw elements are likely to result from attempts to remove a deeply seated hook or to access the tongue, although removal of the tongue can also be effected through the gills. These cuts have been classified by Barrett (1995) as Type 1. Five cod jaw elements also exhibited Type 1 butchery. The most frequent butchery (n=8) was to the supracleithrum and post-temporals, either chopped through or cut from the dorsal or ventral side. This butchery is consistent with decapitation, and is Barrett's Type 4 (*ibid.*), as are cut marks on a cod basioccipital. Small cuts to the dorsal aspect of a cod ceratohyal probably derive from removal of the fish tongue (Barrett's Category 2, *ibid.*). Cuts around the edge of the anterior facet of two cod precaudal vertebrae may have been inflicted when separating the musculature from the vertebrae (Barrett's Category 5, *ibid.*). One large cod parasphenoid had been chopped through in the saggital plane, possibly to remove the brain, while a chopped symplectic is harder to explain, but may have been damaged when the meaty 'cheeks' were removed.

SNUSGAR

Fifty hand collected bones were identified from middens 1502 and 1503. The remains were a typical mix of bones from the heads and spines of very large, large, medium-sized and small cod, saithe and ling, as well as four vertebra from small wrasse. Cod of 1.04 m and saithe of 0.88 m, 0.54 m and around 0.30 m were indicated by measurements on the dentary and premaxilla.

PHASE 6

All fish remains from Phase 6 came from East Mound Trench 5, from external surfaces and middens and deposits relating to the end of use of the longhouse and its byre and the square ancillary building. Virtually all of the 1008 identified hand collected specimens were from large and very large gadids, mainly cod but also saithe, pollack, ling and torsk, with abundant cranial and post-cranial elements present. The only exceptions were two ballan wrasse precaudal vertebrae from disturbed occupation deposit 2031 in the longhouse, and a small number of large hake jaw elements and a single vertebra from several midden and disturbed occupation deposits from within the longhouse and ancillary building. Based on calculations from the dentary and premaxilla

measurements, the majority of cod were 0.8–1.2 m in length (Archive spreadsheet 10.2). Butchery evidence was limited to cuts at the distal part of cod dentaries: in one instance across the tooth row behind the symphysis, all probably inflicted when removing a hook or the tongue (Category 1 cut marks, Barrett 1995, 239). Fine cuts to branchiostegal rays, a quadrate and an articular may have occurred when removing the tongue through the gill slits, although the former may also result from gutting. Cuts to cod post-temporals (Barrett's Category 3, *ibid.*) are consistent with beheading, as are cuts to several cleithra. A single precaudal vertebra had been cut on the ventral surface, lateral aspect (Barrett's category 4). Pathological changes were noted on a large cod post-cleithrum (excess bone growth), a large saithe dentary (slightly displaced symphysis) and a torsk premaxilla, which exhibited a slight lump mid-way along the tooth row, all of unknown aetiology.

The sieved samples reveal a different picture: as in earlier phases, these produced some bones from very much smaller fish, albeit mainly gadids, with small salmonid (probably trout) in disturbed longhouse occupation deposit 2031, herring from longhouse layer 2226, eel from midden 2008 and sandeel from external surface 2003, although at least the last two bones may well be accidental inclusions, from the guts of larger fish or from a seabird catch, for example. A large halibut caudal vertebra came from working surface 2060.

After the longhouse was abandoned, midden deposits including 2225 accumulated in the western annex. Fish remains from 2225 include heads from at least 4 large and very large cod, as well as a precaudal vertebra from a ling of more than 1.2 m, a cleithrum fragment from a ling or torsk of similar size and a torsk precaudal vertebra from a fish of 0.6–0.7 m.

PHASE 7

Over 850 identified bones were recovered from Phase 7 middens, collapsed wall fills and general layers from Trenches 5, 6 and 7. Although the number of bones deriving from middens was small (151 identified hand collected bones) there was some evidence of spatial variation, those from midden 2043, west of the ancillary building, and midden 2015 south of the ancillary buildings mainly comprised post cranial and a few cranial bones from large cod, while the assemblages from midden 4020 in the south-west corner of the site was mainly composed of cranial bones, from the heads of medium and large sized cod and ling. Butchery marks were seen on seven bones, one very large cod atlas vertebra and two large cod posterior precaudal vertebrae had small cuts to the dorsal surface, one large cod precaudal vertebra had been chopped through transversely, one large cod supracleithrum had a cut to the dorsal surface, a large cod quadrate had a fine cut to the lateral aspect and the articulation and a large gadid (probably cod) cleithrum had cuts to the anterior margin. Taken together, these cuts and chops evidence decapitation in front of the cleithrum, division of the fish mid-way along the body, and separation of the vertebrae from the musculature (as Barrett 1995, category 3, 5 and 6), and possible removal of the meaty 'cheeks'.

Two pairs (precaudal and caudal) and one set of three (precaudal) cod vertebrae were fused together, a pathology previously seen on both modern and archaeological specimens by the author; the set of three precaudal vertebrae were also significantly compressed, which would have given the fish a 'humpback' appearance.

Sieved samples included the remains of entire small gadids, mainly saithe, as well as larger gadids and rare other taxa including ballan wrasse. A sample from midden 4020 included occasional burnt fish bone, probably raked out from a domestic hearth.

PHASE 8

The hand collected and sieved bones from the Phase 8 windblown sands, disturbed soil layers and wall fills number almost 400 items. Overall, the remains are very similar to those recovered from earlier phases and it is very likely that the bones have been reworked from the Viking-Late Norse middens, although bone condition was generally good. A few bones had cut marks consistent with gutting and hook removal. Three gadid caudal vertebrae were compressed and fused together, as described above.

Discussion

Fish, fishing and the distribution of fish remains

Notwithstanding the likely effects of centuries of midden accretion and degradation, it is clear that the fish represented in the Viking and Late Norse assemblages from the excavations are the product of a selective fishing strategy, specifically targeting mature gadids, especially cod, saithe and ling. The hand-collected assemblage almost exclusively comprises the remains of these large and very large gadids, especially cod, but even in the sieved material, apart from small gadids, the absence of inshore dwelling fish, which could have been caught locally, is striking and again indicates careful resource selection. Absent, or largely so, are flatfish, gurnards, cottids, butterfish and so on which would have been present in and around the Bay of Skaill. As a comparison, cod and related gadids also dominated the smaller fish assemblage from Norse middens excavated at Skaill, Deerness, but there, bones from a wide range of other taxa were also present in what was a fairly small assemblage, despite the absence of sieving at the site (Nicholson 1997). These included grey gurnard, *Eutrigla gurnardus* (L.), conger eel, *Conger conger*

(L.), Ballan and cuckoo wrasse, *Labrus mixtus* (L), sea scorpion, *Taurulus bubalis* (Euphrasen), thick lipped grey mullet, *Crenimugil labrosus* (Risso) and mackerel, as well as several species of flatfish, dogfish, tope shark, *Galeorhinus galeus* (L.) and possibly bass, *Dicentrarchus labrax* (L.). The more restricted range of taxa particularly evident in Phases 5 and 6 at East Mound, is likely to reflect a deliberate strategy related to the aspirations of, and resources available to, the occupants of the site, perhaps the 'chiefly provisioning' identified by Perdikaris (1999). Eel and trout, abundant in the Neolithic middens at Skara Brae (Jones, n.d.), were also almost entirely absent at Snusgar and East Mound despite the proximity of the Burn of Snusgar, next to the sites, and the nearby freshwater Loch of Skaill.

An offshore fishing strategy based around the capture of large gadids using many hooked lines is typical of most Viking and Late Norse sites in Northern Isles and nearby Caithness, but is in contrast to the much more local, inshore and shore-based fishing which seems to have been consistently practised in the Iron Age (*e.g.* Nicholson 2004). Supplementing this catch at the Bay of Skaill, as elsewhere in the region, was a significant quantity of much smaller gadids, largely saithe, the remains of which are generally only found when soil samples are sieved (Tables 10.6 and 10.7 and Figs 10.4 and 10.5).

Prior to the introduction of long-line fishing in the 16th century, the islanders would have fished for cod, saithe and ling up to ten miles from the shore, using small boats, probably similar to the small clinker-built Ness yoles and fouraenings (4-oared boats) of Scandinavian origin which are still used in the Northern Isles today (Irvine 1987, 96; Goodlad 1971, 76; Fenton 1997, 552). Attention should here be drawn to the antler fairlead (SF 257), from the byre end of the East Mound Trench 5 longhouse (Chapter 15), which demonstrates the presence of fishing technology among the material culture of the Bay of Skaill settlements.

Small fish, particularly first and second year saithe or coalfish (sillocks and piltocks) would have been abundant and probably available close to the shore for much of the year. Fenton (1997, 530) records that sillocks were numerous around the shores of Birsay and were best in June, July and August, although fishing in Hamnavoe (Stromness Harbour) traditionally took place from September to March. Around the Orkney coast, ideally around sunken rocks and tangled beds, fishing for sillocks and piltocks is likely to have been by simple handline made of horse-hair with an iron or bone hook, from small boats close to the shore; this kind of fishing was known as 'eela' fishing, based on the Old Norse 'ili' or 'ile', a stone used as an anchor (Fenton 1997, 528). Traditionally, chewed limpets were used as bait to attract

Table 10.6: Number of fish and crustacean remains from bulk samples, by phase

Phase	2	3	4	5	6	5 or 6	7	8	9	Unphased	Total
Shark/ray		2		1							3
Dogfish			1	2							3
Eel		1		3	2		1				7
Salmonid					1						1
Herring	1	1			1						3
Gadid nfi	41	97	12	244	101	1	74	22		15	607
Cod	10	78	5	72	61		18	5	1	11	261
Saithe	5	42	7	29	31		10	5			129
Pollack			2	4			2				8
Saithe/pollack	5	31	11	25	23		17	4			116
Cod/saithe/pollack		10		12	7		1				30
Haddock							1				1
Saithe/pollack/haddock				2			1				3
Ling			1	13	2		2				18
Torsk					2						2
Ling/torsk				1	1						2
Hake					1		1				2
5-bearded rockling	1			1							2
cf. Tadpole fish				1							1
Butterfish		1									1
cf. Snake blenny					1						1
Sandeel					1						1
Garfish				1							1
Cottid				2							2
Ballan wrasse				1			1				2
Flatfish nfi		3		1			1				5
Right eyed flatfishes				1							1
Halibut					1						1
Unidentified fish	2	10		19	16		7	1		1	56
Crab				3	1						4
Total	65	276	39	438	253	1	137	37	1	27	1274

nfi = not further identified

shoals of fish which could then be caught easily (*ibid.*, 527–9). These smaller fish are likely to have been a fairly regular source of food and were an economic necessity during times of agricultural failure in the eighteenth and nineteenth centuries. They could be eaten fresh or split and dried, or smoked. Soured fish may also have been eaten, and the livers may have been boiled to extract oil, as in later centuries (*ibid.*, 529).

LARGER GADIDS

It is tempting to interpret the abundance of large gadid remains as indicative of stockfish – in other words to view the assemblage in terms of Barrett's producer or consumer sites (Barrett 1997). A wealthy landowner might well have been involved in the fish trade, which was an important part of the Norse economy and that of the earldoms of Orkney and Shetland, from at least the 11th century (*ibid.*). While dried fish were exported to Norway, partly as Crown Rents from at least the 12th century, the trade in fish from Orkney and Shetland expanded in the later medieval centuries, with exports largely controlled by Hanseatic merchants from around the early 14th century until about 1500 (*ibid.*; Smith 1984, 7). However, from the excavated evidence at Snusgar and East Mound, direct involvement in this trade as a producer site seems unlikely. While it is possible that the abundance of head bones in some contexts may represent

Rebecca A. Nicholson

Table 10.7: Distribution/estimated size of gadid skeletal elements

	No in 1 fish	Large/ extra large	Medium	Small
Vomer	1			1
Frontal	1	1		
Otolith	2	8	1	8
Parasphenoid	1	1		1
Basioccipital	1			3
Dentary	2	2	2	3
Maxilla	2	3	1	5
Premaxilla	2	1	1	1
Articular	2			2
Quadrate	2	5		
Palatine	2	1		1
Ectopterygoid	2	1		3
Ceratohyal	2	1	1	3
Epihyal	2	1		
Hyomandibular	2	2		1
Symplectic	2	2		
Opercular	2			1
Preopercular	2	1		1
Interopercular	2	1		1
Subopercular	2	1		
Cleithrum	2	1		
Post cleithrum	2		1	
Post temporal	2	1		
Supracleithrum	2	2		3
Coracoid	2	2		
Abdominal vertebra (PC1)	4	3		10
Middle precaudal vertebra (PC2)	5 (4–6)	2	4	4
Posterior precaudal vertebra (PC3)	8 (7–8)	14	9	33
Precaudal vertebra nfi				10
Anterior caudal vertebra (CV4)	14 (13–16)	4	3	10
Posterior caudal vertebra (CV5)	17 (15–19)	37	13	4
Caudal vertebra nfi		2	5	33
Vertebra nfi		6	2	91
Total result		106	43	149

nfi = not further identified

the bones discarded during the preparation of fish for drying as 'stockfish', the over-representation of posterior caudal vertebrae in other contexts suggests that some previously

dried fish were eaten at the site (cleithra and vertebrae from the tail area of the fish were typically left in the dried fish). If stockfish were prepared as a commodity for export, then it could be expected that those bones not included in the final product would have been discarded close to the processing station, or at least in midden deposits rather than within a domestic dwelling or communal hall.

To explore the issue further, the bones recovered from soil samples have been used to investigate the proposition that occupation and floor deposits from inside structures would include bones from smaller fish than those found in middens and other external soil deposits. This would seem to be a reasonable hypothesis given that smaller bones could be expected to survive better in an internal, protected environment. Also, it could be anticipated that more obvious and malodorous waste would be disposed of outside, in the midden, while smaller 'kitchen waste' may have collected in crevices and around the hearth. However, when the fish remains recovered by sieving were grouped into large/extra-large gadid, medium gadid, small gadid and other taxa, and the sampled deposits into internal (floor/occupation deposits or ashy deposits overlying floors), midden, wall fill and external (the last including a variety of deposit types including dumps, wall collapse, windblown sand etc.), no clear patterning was found (Fig. 10.4). The same was true when only Phase 5 contexts were considered and deposits grouped by structure (Fig. 10.5). Wherever the fish were prepared for drying or for immediate consumption, it would seem that their bones, having presumably been discarded on a midden, were then redistributed with other midden material within as well as without the dwellings, deliberately used for wall packing and floor levelling, as discussed in detail by Harrison (2013). The consequent redistribution and mixing of material is likely to have distorted any patterning relating to activities and activity areas, since it is likely that specific kinds of midden material were valued for particular kinds of construction (*ibid.*), and so the 'right' kind of midden could have been brought in from an outlying area for a specific task. This is particularly likely to have been the case for wall fill and levelling deposits, but these may, of course, have been mixed in with floor surfaces after the abandonment and collapse of the structures. Consequently, the lack of patterning within and between the various kinds of deposits is perhaps to be expected.

There was also no clear evidence from the relative frequency of skeletal elements within the East Mound longhouse, outbuildings or middens to indicate any specialised kind of fish processing, but again the general mixing of midden material may have obscured any spatial trends. The distribution of skeletal elements within Phase 5 deposits at East Mound (Trench 5) shows a bias in favour of posterior caudal vertebrae in larger gadids

(Table 10.7), although elements from the head and other parts of the spine were also present and cleithra – which would be retained in a dried fish – were not over-represented. An under-representation of cleithra may be explained by preferential fragmentation of this bone (Jones 1991, 331), but the smaller posterior vertebrae are usually more prone to disintegration and decay than larger elements of the spine (Nicholson 1991; 1992), so an under-representation of these bones could be indicative of stockfish. Consequently, it is likely that in all periods the majority of bones are from the remains of whole fresh fish prepared for consumption, with some fish probably dried at or close to the site for storage. It is possible that some fish may well have been traded locally or further afield, but the evidence is far from conclusive.

While the fish remains seem to be distributed across all areas of the site, the recovery of several spurdog spines from midden 1504 on Snusgar mound may be significant, as these were not found elsewhere. There appears to have been a greater proportion of bones from non-domesticated species (including red deer, whale and seal) in the Snusgar mound, and, taken in conjunction with the faunal evidence (see Chapter 9), suggests that Trench 4 may have served as a processing area for carcasses.

Conclusions

In general terms, this assemblage appears similar to that recovered from other roughly contemporary sites such as Sandwick South, Unst (Shetland) (Bigelow 1984), Freswick (Caithness) (Jones 1991; 1995) and Pool (Sanday, Orkney) (Nicholson 2007), where the fish remains indicate a significant offshore fishery in the Viking-Late Norse centuries, but not at a level which would demonstrate the systematic production of stockfish for export. All these sites have produced fish assemblages which seem to represent both the consumption of whole, fresh, fish and

probably some limited stockfish production, which may have been simply to preserve the fish for later consumption by the local inhabitants. Overall, it would seem that here, as at most Viking and Late Norse sites in the Northern Isles, and elsewhere in the North Atlantic region, fishing was one part of a broad subsistence base, together with arable agriculture and pastoralism, with some fowling, hunting and collecting also practised. The dominance of bones from large fish which would have been caught some way offshore does, however, indicate a reasonable level of wealth, since even part-ownership of a boat would have required significant investment and would consequently have conferred some control over resource distribution. This indication of elevated socio-economic status is consistent with the greater proportion of cattle remains in the faunal assemblage, and with the size of the longhouse. The very large size of some of the fish is also consistent with elevated status, since considerable resources would have been used in their capture. Whether some of these foods were eaten in feasts is open to conjecture. Also worthy of consideration is the possibility that fish caught for export were processed closer to the shore, and their remains dumped in middens which have eroded away, been completely reworked or are yet to be discovered.

Although some floor deposits may contain refuse from meal preparation, or the preservation of fish by drying, the homogeneous nature of the fish remains in many deposits from within the domestic area of the East Mound longhouse, especially within the byre and outside the structure, suggests that much originated in reworked midden material. The presence of fairly complete and large fish bones in later surfaces (Phase 7) implies that those bones were incorporated into the deposit after the main period of use, while other more complete examples in earlier phases survived on the edges of floors and yards, against walls and stones.

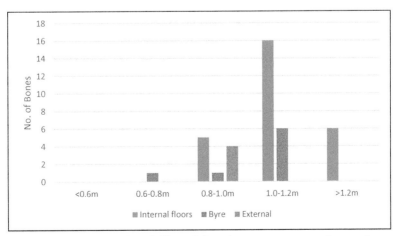

Fig. 10.1: Predicted lengths of gadid fish from East Mound, Phase 5, based on measurements taken on the premaxilla (after Jones 1991 and the regression formulae of Barrett 1995)

Rebecca A. Nicholson

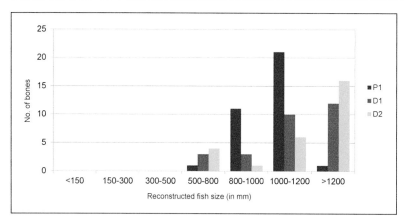

Fig. 10.2: Reconstructed fish size, based on cod premaxilla and dentary measurements (after Jones 1991 and Barrett 1995), East Mound, Phase 5

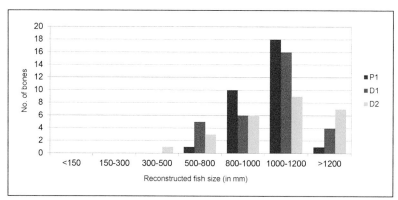

Fig. 10.3: Reconstructed fish size, based on cod premaxilla and dentary measurements (after Jones 1991 and Barrett 1995), East Mound, Phase 6

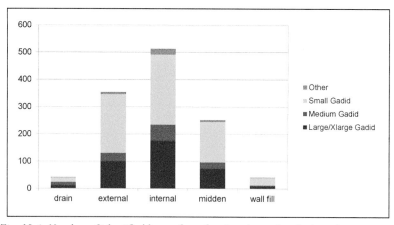

Fig. 10.4: Number of identified bones from the sieved samples, by broad context type

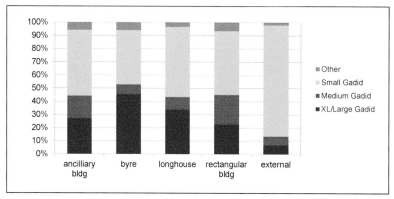

Fig. 10.5: Proportion of identified fish remains from the Phase 5 sieved material by broad context grouping

11

Ferrous metalworking: Vitrified material

Dawn McLaren

Overview

A substantial assemblage of vitrified material and associated debris (23.57 kg) was recovered from the 2004–11 excavations at the Bay of Skaill. The assemblages can be divided into three broad categories: vitrified debris indicative of ferrous metalworking, non-diagnostic vitrified material such as fuel ash slags and other low-density slags that could have resulted from a range of high-temperature pyrotechnic processes and are not necessarily the result of metalworking, and finally, non-vitrified material including iron pan, fired clay and burnt sand. Despite the presence of large amounts of material which is not readily associated with metalworking, over 12.6 kg of waste derives from ferrous metalworking. Where it is possible to determine the stage of the ironworking process being undertaken, bloom or blacksmithing debris is dominant. No waste suggestive of iron smelting or non-ferrous metalworking was identified amongst the debris from any of the excavated areas.

Two distinctive assemblages of vitrified material were recovered from the two mounds. That from Snusgar (Trenches 1–4) is predominantly undiagnostic sintered material not indicative of metalworking activities accompanied by a very limited residual scatter of ferrous metalworking waste which suggests that ironworking was taking place in the vicinity of the site. The ferrous metalworking debris from Snusgar is not morphologically characteristic of a particular stage in the ironworking process and could not be related to a specific structure or area of the excavated building. In contrast, the assemblage from Trenches 5–8 at East Mound are predominantly debris produced or related to iron smithing; a craft which appears to have taken place particularly during Phase 3 in a specialised metalworking area or yard, with further limited metalworking activity taking place within the main longhouse structure itself in Phase 5.

Methodology

The vitrified material was visually examined allowing it to be broadly categorised on the criteria of morphology, density, colour, vesicularity and magnetic level (Bachmann 1982; McDonnell 1986). During iron production a range of slag types are produced but few, such as tapped slag and hammerscale, are considered truly diagnostic of a particular stage in the ironworking process (McDonnell 1994; Starley 2000; McLaren and Heald 2006). Where discernible they appear to fall into two types: a wide range of debris indicative of ironworking, specifically bloom or blacksmithing, and those created as a result of a range of pyrotechnic processes, not necessarily associated with ironworking. A full catalogue of the material is presented in the archive.

The following report will outline the broad categories of vitrified material, burnt material and other deposits recovered during the excavations. As there is a significant overlap in terms of the categories of material found at both East Mound and Snusgar the material categories will be discussed in detail with specific reference to the residues from the East Mound excavation. These descriptions will be referred to in the discussion which considers the Snusgar evidence (Trenches 1–4), to avoid repetition.

Snusgar (Trenches 1–4)

Over 5.9 kg of vitrified material, associated heat-affected materials and other fragments were recovered from excavations at Castle of Snusgar mound (see Table 11.1). The excavations at Snusgar were more limited than those at East Mound and this is reflected in the more

Table 11.1: Summary of vitrified material etc. recovered from trenches 1–4 (Snusgar Mound)

Type	Mass (g)
Vitrified material (ironworking)	
Bloom (B)	0
Hammerscale and magnetic residue (HS)	0
Plano-convex slag cake fragments (PCSC)	101.4
Slag amalgam (SA)	0
Smithing pan (SP)	0
Unclassified iron slag (UIS)	33.9
Non-diagnostic vitrified material	
Magnetic vitrified residues (MVR)	55.2
Non-magnetic vitrified residue (NMVR)	0
Fuel ash slag (FAS)	1.9
Low-density slag (LDS)	4518.8
Vitrified ceramic (VC)	0
Other (heat-affected material)	
Fired clay	6.5
Heat affected sand/earth/turves	239.1
Fuel residues (charcoal/cinder/peat/amorphous burnt plant material)	420.8
Vitrified stone	28.0
Other (unmodifed)	
Bog ore	0
Iron pan	388.5
Iron spalls	14.3
Raw clay	34.0
Natural stone, bone, shell etc	74.7
Total	5917.1

and small to allow confident identification of the stage in the ironworking process that it relates to but on the basis of its thickness, magnetic quality and morphology it is likely to be the product of bloom or blacksmithing. It was recovered from a Phase 5 midden layer south of the longhouse 1038.

In addition to the ferrous metalworking waste already discussed, small quantities of magnetic residues (55.2 g) came from midden deposits of Phase 2 to Phase 5 date (1039, 1048, 1510, 1513, 1514, 1517, 1519, 1551, 1558, 1578). None of this material includes recognisable diagnostic micro-debris of ferrous metalworking activities (*e.g.* hammerscale flakes or spheres from smithing) making a connection to metalworking difficult to argue for with certainty.

The majority of the vitrified material from this excavated area (4.5 kg; 76% of the assemblage) comprises low density, silicate-rich, sintered material and fuel ash slags. The problems with identifying the process that led to the creation of this low-density sintered material have already been outlined and the material is not well understood. The majority of this waste (3.2 kg) came from a late, Phase 8, disturbed layer relating to kelping and rabbit activity 1006 associated with an 18th/19th century kelp burning pit (feature 1003). It is possible that this heat-affected material relates to a preceding phase of kelp burning or could be heat-affected fuel residues resulting from a domestic hearth which was kept burning for long periods of time. More restricted quantities of similar waste came from various midden-rich layers and dumps associated with the longhouse, layers outwith the structure, and disturbed or residual contexts.

Small quantities of other heat-affected but not vitrified materials are also present, none of which can be directly related to metalworking activities. These comprise 58.2 g of cinder, burnt shale and charcoal fragments and 362.6 g of amorphous pieces of burnt plant material which are likely to represent waste from domestic fuel. With the exception of 13.5 g of cinder from a possible working surface 1504 the rest of the material within this category came from incidental or late deposits. Similarly, small fragments of amorphous burnt plant material was scattered across 21 Phase 2 to 5 contexts and is particularly well represented in ash-rich midden layers, strengthening the interpretation made here that this material represents domestic fuel waste. A fragment of heat-affected clay (6.5 g) came from a Phase 2 midden layer 1017 and various amorphous pieces of heat-affected earth, sand and turves (236.2 g) were recovered from contexts relating to Phase 2 to 9 activity.

The other materials amongst the assemblage from Snusgar are unmodified and unrelated to ironworking. These include small pieces of iron pan, raw clay, natural stone, shell and bone.

restricted range and quantity of waste recovered. Very little of this waste has been identified as slags relating to metalworking but where present, the processes represented are limited to bloom or blacksmithing activities.

Only 135.3 g of vitrified material diagnostic of ironworking were recovered from Snusgar in the form of a plano-convex slag cake fragment (101.4 g) and small fractured pieces of unclassified iron slags (33.9 g). Although this type of vitrified material is indicative of ironworking, it cannot be related to a specific stage in the ironworking process and could be rake-out material from a smelting furnace or smithing hearth. The unclassified iron slags came from a Phase 2 midden layer (5.5 g, 1533), a Phase 3 working surface (6 g, 1504), deposits within the longhouse interior (5.4 g, 1012; Phase 3) and late disturbed material (17 g; context 1501). The plano-convex slag cake fragment (101.4 g) is too fragmentary

Discussion

The quantity and range of vitrified material recovered from the excavations at Snusgar suggest that ferrous metalworking was taking place in the vicinity of the longhouse structure contemporary with its main period of occupation. This is indicated by the recovery of a fragment of possible smithing hearth bottom from a midden layer external to the longhouse (1038; Phase 5) and from scatters of unclassified ironworking slag amongst midden layers and redeposited midden-rich sands. The secondary or residual context of much of this material makes it impossible to identify closely both where and when this metalworking activity was taking place with any confidence. Yet the presence of unclassified slag from deposits relating to Phase 2 through to Phase 8 activity implies that ferrous metalworking was in progress during or before the late 9th century AD. In the absence of any metalworking structures associated with the Snusgar longhouse (*e.g.* smelting furnaces or smithing hearths) it is unclear where the focus of this activity was but, like the evidence uncovered at East Mound, it is likely that ferrous metalworking was taking place somewhere within the unexcavated complex of ancillary structures associated with the main longhouse building.

Despite the small quantity of waste recovered, the more diagnostic of pieces are indicative of bloom or blacksmithing activities; no waste suggestive of iron smelting or non-ferrous metalworking are present amongst the assemblage from Snusgar. The level of metalworking activity here is difficult to assess based on the 135 g of ironworking waste recovered but low-level bloom or blacksmithing is suggested. No debris suggestive of the smelting of iron ore or non-ferrous metalworking activities was present.

As demonstrated by Table 11.1, the vitrified material assemblage from the Snusgar mound is dominated by low-density sintered slags. The interpretation of this heterogenous heat-affected material is not certain but aspects of its morphology indicate that it was debris produced during an extended, low-temperature pyrotechnic process probably related to the processing or burning of organic materials such as turves, seaweed or dung. The proximity of the greatest concentration of this material at Snusgar to a possible kelping pit suggests that, in this instance, the majority of the low-density debris may be a by-product of post-medieval kelp burning.

East Mound (Trenches 5–8)

A large and comprehensive assemblage (21.2 kg) of ironworking debris and a range of associated vitrified and burnt materials were recovered from the longhouse building and ancillary structures at East Mound. Vitrified material was found throughout the excavated area, deriving from over 150 contexts across the site. The

majority of this waste was concentrated outwith the longhouse structure, focusing on a discrete area to the south of this building and to the west of the north–south aligned ancillary structure. The metalworking activities that this waste represents appears to have been unenclosed or only partially enclosed at the time of metalworking activity but was later built over by a series of ancillary structures. The ironworking debris from this area derives from a series of small bowl-shaped hearths set into the ground surface that were the focus of iron smithing and appears to represent a smithy in use during Phase 3. Further evidence of iron smithing comes from a hearth and associated features within the longhouse itself but the scale of the debris in this instance is much more restrictive and may represent smaller scale activity taking place during Phase 5. Debris from metalworking and a range of other pyrotechnic processes has resulted in the spread of large quantities of vitrified material both in the interior and exterior of the excavated structures. In most instances, this spread of residual waste appears to be incidental. Significant quantities of ironworking waste and other burnt materials were found spread across the floor of the byre (Phase 5). This burnt waste may have been gathered up alongside charcoal-rich fuel debris and cinders and deliberately spread across byre to create an absorbent floor level.

Due to the incidental incorporation of ironworking waste within many midden layers and levelling layers used throughout the structures, it is unclear whether the two distinct foci of metalworking activity were contemporary.

Introduction

A wide range of vitrified material is represented amongst the East Mound assemblage, dominated by waste indicative of ferrous metalworking activities. The assemblage comprises a number of small, compact plano-convex slag cakes, unclassified iron slag, vitrified ceramics and large quantities of low-density non-magnetic vitrified material including fuel ash slag (Table 11.2). No residues diagnostic of iron smelting or non-ferrous metalworking were identified amongst the assemblage.

The assemblage from East Mound can be classified under four broad categories: vitrified material diagnostic of or indicative of ironworking, non-diagnostic vitrified material which has been formed under a high-temperature pyrotechnic process but is not necessarily associated with metalworking, heat-affected material and, finally, unmodified material.

Vitrified material (ironworking)

12.7 kg of ironworking debris recovered at East Mound consists of fragments of plano-convex slag cakes, slag amalgams, unclassified iron slags, possible bloom

Table 11.2: Summary of the East Mound vitrified material assemblage by type

Type	Mass (g)
Vitrified material (ironworking)	
Bloom (B)	323.6
Micro-debris (Hammerscale flakes and spheres) (HS/SS)	2925.3
Plano-convex slag cake fragments (PCSC)	3300.5
Slag amalgam (SA)	116.0
Smithing pan (SP)	468.7
Unclassified iron slag (UIS)	5235.7
Part-forged objects	325.5
Non-diagnostic vitrified material	
Magnetic vitrified residues (MVR)	946.2
Non-magnetic vitrified residue (NMVR)	29.9
Fuel ash slag (FAS)	54.0
Low-density slag (LDS)	3868.1
Vitrified ceramic (VC)	2224.5
Other (heat-affected material)	
Fired clay	51.2
Heat affected sand/earth/turves	25.6
Fuel residues (charcoal/cinder/peat/amorphous burnt plant material)	686.8
Vitrified stone	0
Other (unmodified)	
Bog ore	31.0
Iron pan	2.5
Iron spalls	33.2
Iron nodules	1.5
Raw clay	540.8
Natural stone, bone, shell etc	92.6
Total	21,283.2

fragments, micro-debris (hammerscale flakes and spheres), smithing pan and possible part-forged objects. Diagnostic pieces, such as the plano-convex slag cakes and micro-debris indicate that the waste derives from iron smithing, the manufacturing of artefacts from the iron bloom, bar or scrap (McDonnell 1994, 229).

POSSIBLE BLOOM FRAGMENTS

A limited quantity of possible iron bloom or very iron-rich slag (323.6 g) was recognised amongst the assemblage. During the later prehistoric and early medieval periods, the bloom produced by smelting tended to be fairly heterogeneous in composition, containing quantities of trapped slag and fuel residues (Bayley *et al.* 2001, 13). These blooms would require refining to produce metal

of sufficient quality to forge into objects. There is no evidence amongst the slags from East Mound to suggest that iron smelting was undertaken at the site meaning that raw iron, either in the form of refined blooms, billets or scrap iron would have been brought to site for working. This material is similar in external appearance to amorphous unclassified iron slags but are denser and intensely magnetic. Without chemical analysis it is not possible to classify these pieces with confidence but based on the suite of associated smithing debris, the presence of fragments of possible unworked bloom is not out of place.

PLANO-CONVEX SLAG CAKES

Plano-convex slag cakes, also known as plano-convex cakes or smithing hearth bottoms, are circular or sub-circular plano-convex accumulations of slag, silica and often fuel, which form at the base of a pit, hearth or furnace during ferrous metalworking activities. These dense slag cakes can form during smelting or smithing but the size and composition differs significantly between the two processes, with those produced during smelting being larger in size, heavier and typically having large charcoal inclusions trapped within the slag matrix (McDonnell 1994, 230; 2000, 219). In contrast, smithing hearth bottoms are recognisable by the characteristic plano-convex form, typically having a rough convex base and a vitrified upper surface which is flat or even slightly hollowed and smoothed as a result of the downward pressure of the air from the bellows and are typically magnetic. It is not always possible to differentiate the debris produced as the result of the two ironworking processes on visual examination alone, but in general, cakes resulting from smithing tend to be smaller in diameter and more compact. A useful caveat to this is where several phases of smithing waste have been allowed to build up within a hearth, producing a much larger accumulation of slag. In such an instance, the identification may only be resolved by a series of chemical analysis (Heald *et al.* 2011, 20–1).

A total of 25 fragments of plano-convex slag cakes were recognised amongst the assemblage from East Mound representing a minimum of 19 individual cakes which weigh over 3.3 kg in total (Table 11.3). These cakes were recovered from 12 contexts across the site, concentrating in the metalworking area (8 in total) defined by walls 2068 and 2108, located to the west of the north–south aligned ancillary building. The recovery of a further five examples from Area 1 implies that the construction of structure 1 disturbed and incorporated material from the earlier metalworking area. A further example came from hearth 2301 located immediately to the west of the central partition within the longhouse and suggests that this feature saw use on at least one episode as a metalworking hearth rather than a domestic fire.

Table 11.3: Summary of form and size of surviving plano-convex slag cakes

Context	Context description	Phase	% of cake present	Shape	Super-imposed	Diameter (mm)	Thickness (mm)	Weight (g)
2015	Midden layer	7	100	sub-circular	n	93	41	165
2105	Area of dismantled hearth	3	100	oval	n	98.5	50	188
2148	Drain fill	3	100	sub-circular	n	97	23 to 37	259.5
2178	Dump relating to metalworking	5	100	sub-circular	n	103	50.5	349
2016	Disturbed floor layers	5	90	oval	n	76	34	175.1
2202	Dismantling of metalworking area	5	90	sub-circular	n	98	34	268
2204	Midden	3	90	sub-circular	n	96	42	259
2202	Dismantling of metalworking area	5	*c.*80; edges missing	sub-circular	n	70	31	160
2202	Dismantling of metalworking area	5	*c.*80; edges missing	sub-square	n	77	23	127
2301	Hearth	5	*c.*80; edges missing	sub-oval	n	88	17.5	153
2063	Midden mix sand	6	70	sub-circular or sub-oval	n	90	40.5	297
2202	Dismantling of metalworking area	5	65–75	sub-oval	n	75	31	212.5
2015	Midden layer	7	small frag. proportion unknown	?	n	42	19	29.5
2016	Disturbed floor layers	5	small frag.; proportion unknown	?	n	?	28	116
2152	Midden layer	2	small frag.; proportion unknown	?	n	36.5	20	20.5
2178	Dump relating to metalworking	5	small frag.; proportion unknown	sub-circular	y	65	45	162.5
2180	External: floor covering over flags	5	damaged edge frag.; proportion unknown	?	y	72	33	133.9
2202	Dismantling of metalworking area	5	small frag.; proportion unknown	?	n	65	19	62.5
2239	Disturbed: later use in byre	6	small frag; proportion unknown	?	y	64.5	42.5	162.5

Twelve cakes are substantially complete (*e.g.* more than 65% surviving), with a further seven incomplete examples. Detailed examination of the more intact examples reveals that the slag cakes from East Mound are generally sub-circular or sub-oval in plan, presumably reflecting the original shape of the smithing hearth itself. One more unusual sub-square cake is also present, deriving from 2202. The plano-convex slag cakes amongst the assemblage range in diameter from 70–103 mm with an average diameter of 91 mm and average thickness of 31 mm, consistent with the dimensions anticipated for cakes resulting from smithing activities (McDonnell 1994, 230). Many of the cakes, both complete and fragmentary, have distinct convex upper surfaces created by the downward pressure of the air from the bellows and most have small charcoal inclusions and impressions, particularly on the rounded basal surfaces and curving edges. Two substantially complete cakes from 2002 preserve small hammerscale flakes on the upper surfaces, confirming their origin as the debris resulting from bloom or blacksmithing.

Three of the heavily fragmentary plano-convex cakes from contexts 2178, 2180 and 2239, appear to be accumulations of waste from more than one phase of bloom or blacksmithing activity. One piece from 2178 survives as a thick, wedge-shaped fragment from a red-brown, vesicular, sub-circular plano-convex slag cake. In section, two clear and distinct layers are visible which are likely to represent two superimposed thin cakes, each around 16 mm in thickness. The rounded base is coated in a sand-rich fused material, possibly surviving residues from the hearth lining. Similarly, a robust wedge-shaped fragment of a dense grey plano-convex slag cake from 2239 can be seen in section to be two slightly misaligned, angled, cakes. The uppermost cake is approximately 15.5 mm in thickness; the lower is 20 mm in thickness. In this instance, the two layers are separated at the external curving edge by a vesicular, bubbly mass of low-density grey slag (probably fuel ash slag) but towards the projected centre of the cake, the layers fuse together into one dense layer. The implication of these superimposed cakes is that the smith allowed the slag that had accumulated at the base of the hearth to cool before beginning further episodes of metalworking activity. The accumulations of slag were only removed when they became too large and interfered with the efficiency of the hearth (Heald *et al.* 2011, 20).

HAMMERSCALE AND SMITHING PAN

Hammerscale consists of fine micro-debris produced during the hot working (forging and welding) of iron and generally comprises two main types: hammerscale flakes and spheres (McDonnell 1986; 1994, 230; Dungworth and Wilkes 2009; Young 2011, 26). Hammerscale flakes are small plates or scales that fall from the iron during forging whilst spheroidal hammerscale has recently been demonstrated as being produced during forge welding (Dungworth and Wilkes 2009). Both forms of micro-debris tend to be found in the immediate vicinity of the smithing hearth and anvil and when found in sufficiently large quantities can be helpful in identifying possible areas were smithing took place (Heald 2002, 70–1). 2.9 kg of hammerscale was recovered from East Mound with concentrations in contexts 2105, 2202, 2269, 2285 and 2294. In some exceptional circumstances these residues

are trampled into the floor and can become cemented together by iron corrosion to form a compact but brittle amalgam referred to as smithing pan (Bayley *et al.* 2001, 14, Fig. 20). 468.7 g of smithing pan, consisting of fused lumps of hammerscale flakes representing trampled pieces of floor surface from around the smithing hearth or anvil were identified amongst the assemblage.

UNCLASSIFIED IRON SLAG

As is typical for any slag assemblage, there is a significant amount of material (4.9 kg), much of it small and fragmentary, which cannot be assigned to a specific process (Crew and Rehren 2002, 84). These comprise amorphous, fractured lumps of red-brown or dark grey vitrified material displaying a range of textures, colours, densities and both magnetic and non-magnetic fragments are present. Many of the pieces have charcoal inclusions or impressions representing trapped fuel residues. This type of slag is almost certainly rake-out material resulting from iron smelting or smithing but it is not possible to differentiate between the debris from these two processes on macroscopic examination alone. The association of the majority of this material at East Mound with diagnostic residues from smithing (*e.g.* hearth bottoms and hammerscale) suggests that this material is smithing waste, raked-out from the smith's hearth whilst forging iron objects.

An associated material are slag amalgams, which at East Mound comprises fragments of unclassified iron slag fused to pieces of vitrified ceramic. A total of four fragments weighing 116 g were recovered from 2269.

PART-FORGED OBJECTS

Sixteen possible unfinished or off-cut pieces of iron are present amongst the assemblage. Many of these had been included within the overall iron assemblage but were recognised during analysis (Chapter 12) as being potentially incomplete or unfinished. None of the items come from recognisable objects and consist principally of bar and sheet fragments. The torn and distorted edges and ends of some items, such as SF 246 and SF 274, suggest that they may have been detached from larger bars and could represent discarded off-cuts whilst sheet fragments SF 417 and SF 371 are poorly defined and may have been in the process of hammering out to shape.

Non-diagnostic vitrified material

MAGNETIC AND NON-MAGNETIC VITRIFIED RESIDUES

Not all magnetic material is indicative of ironworking and there is a small quantity of magnetic residues (946.2 g) from East Mound that lack association with diagnostic micro-debris such as hammerscale flakes or spheres. This can include small fragments of slag blisters which can appear superficially similar to hammerscale flakes but are actually just angular fractured pieces of larger, undiagnostic pieces of vitrified material (Young 2011, 28). Amongst the magnetic residues are also broken up surface spalls from iron objects and heavily heat-affected material. A range of non-magnetic residues are also present (29.9 g). These are vitrified and fused in appearance but not magnetic, and lack distinctive characteristics to allow it to be more clearly classified.

FUEL ASH SLAG

Fuel ash slag is a type of slag that derives from a high temperature reaction in a hearth between the ash of the fuel and siliceous material such as clay and sand (McDonnell 1994, 230). When found amongst archaeological assemblages it is typically in the form of amorphous, low-density, porous and sometimes glassy nodules displaying a range of colours from white, green through to dark brown. This type of slag can form during a range of pyrotechnological processes, including domestic hearths, and is not diagnostic of metalworking processes (*ibid.*, 230). A total of 54 g of this material was recovered amongst the assemblage.

VITRIFIED CERAMIC

Over 150 fragments, totalling 2.2 kg, of vitrified ceramic were recovered. The vitrified faces of these fragments of burnt clay indicate that they had been used as hearth lining. While this material cannot be related specifically to ironworking, the contextual associations and often slag-attacked faces of the fragments suggest that at least some of this material derives from the hearths related to ironworking.

LOW-DENSITY VITRIFIED MATERIAL

Over 3.8 kg of low-density, sintered and partially vitrified material is present amongst the assemblage. This material ranges in colour from a buff brown, pale grey to pale red-brown and is heterogeneous in composition with frequent multi-directional cracks and voids. Some areas of the slags are heat-affected, brittle and fused with a granular texture and pockets or inclusions of a light-grey/green, vesicular, glassy vitrified material. These glassy inclusions and patches are similar in appearance and texture to fuel ash slag or clinker (also known as cramp; Spearman 1997, 165; Photos-Jones *et al.* 2007) suggesting a high silicaceous and organic content but lacks the porous structure of the former and the high-organic content of the latter. Scientific analysis of clinker or 'cramp' from prehistoric burial sites in Orkney suggest that this material is a fusion of sand and seaweed (Photos-Jones *et al.* 2007) and similarly, that from the Neolithic settlement at Barnhouse, Orkney, was determined to be a combination of naturally-occurring sandy-silt earth with marine plant ash and possibly animal bone (Stapleton and Bowman 2005).

A scatter of this sintered low-density material was found across the excavated area at East Mound but the largest concentration (3.4 kg) came from pit 2205. Although this feature was interpreted in the field as a metalworking hearth due to the presence of large quantities of vitrified material, this sintered and partially vitrified waste has no characteristics present to suggest that it is associated with metalworking. The process in which it has formed is not well understood but similar materials are known from other contemporary and later sites and may at least provide useful information on the technology of the formation of this material.

Small quantities of non-magnetic sintered slags were recovered from the Norse farmstead excavated within Mound 3 at Bornais, South Uist. These were dominated by pale grey to creamy yellow pieces of sintered sand and glassy slag (Young 2005, 174). Analysis of these slags, which appear to have been dispersed from a grain drying kiln and domestic hearth were considered to have a non-metallurgical origin (*ibid.*, 176). At Mound 1, none of the slags recovered appeared to derive from metallurgical processes but instead are thought to be a product of reactions between iron-bearing peat ash, the calcareous sands of the machair and, in some instances, fragments of rock, within hearths and ovens (Young 2012, 289). This material comprised friable, sintered waste, but also included pockets of denser material which was more heavily fused and vitrified, like the material from East Mound. Young's analysis of this material suggests that they were produced as the result of high temperatures within a hearth, which was maintained for an extended period of time, allowing slags to be generated through sintering of sand into which the hearths were cut as well as through reactions with peat fuel (*ibid.*, 289). The peat ash from the fuel would have provided a source of silicates, and the peat ash would have contributed a fluxing effect leading to the partial vitrification of some of the sintered material (*ibid.*, 294).

Small quantities of similar sintered sand and clay are also known from 14th century contexts at Edinburgh Castle where it was suggested to have had a similar origin to clinker. At Edinburgh Castle, this material was interpreted as the result of a lower fire temperature and/or lower organic content in the original mixture (Spearman 1997, 165).

Although the process by which this material has been produced is unclear, the similarity of this low-density sintered material to that at Bornais Mounds 1 and 3 suggests that the material at East Mound represents debris resulting from an external hearth which was maintained over an extended period of time allowing elements of sand the hearth was dug into, ash from the turf or peat fuel and possible other organics such as kelp to compress and fuse together.

NON-VITRIFIED, HEAT-AFFECTED MATERIAL

In addition to the categories just described, small quantities of heat-affected but non-vitrified material were also recovered. These comprise 51.2 g of fired clay, a mixture of heat-affected sand/earth and turves (25.6 g), various fuel residues including amorphous burnt plant material (686.8 g).

Other

Further unmodified materials are also present. These include very small quantities of possible bog ore (31 g), naturally occurring iron pan (2.5 g), iron spalls from unidentified iron objects (33.2 g), iron nodules (1.5 g), raw clay (540.8 g) and other natural materials (92.6 g).

Distribution

Vitrified material including large quantities of ferrous metalworking waste were recovered from 153 contexts within and around the longhouse and ancillary structures uncovered in Trenches 5, 6 and 7. The range and mass of material by context is detailed in spreadsheet for in the online archive and summarised in Table 11.4.

No significant metalworking evidence is present in association with the earliest phase of construction and use of the Phase 3 longhouse and the earliest ancillary building. Exceptions to this are restricted to a small quantity of residual ferrous metalworking waste incorporated within a Phase 2 midden 2152 within the area of a curvilinear wall 2289/2373. This suggests early metalworking activity at East Mound, perhaps contemporary with the initial construction of the buildings. A further ephemeral quantity of waste, consisting of a fragment of bloom and a possible partly forged object (SF 246) came from 2146 alongside very limited quantities of amorphous burnt plant material. It is unclear where the focus of metalworking was during this period as the level of re-building and modification to structures within the excavated area is such that any early

metalworking features are likely to have been obliterated by later phases of activity.

As the west–east hall-building or first longhouse and north–south ancillary structure begin to be modified during Phase 3 to allow changes in entrance orientation and access routes, it is possible to recognise further scatters of residual metalworking waste becoming incorporated within midden levels 2204 and the fill of a re-configured drain 2191.

During this period of occupation in the 10th to early 11th centuries (Phase 3) ferrous metalworking evidence becomes more significant in scale and also in visibility. Significant concentrations of ferrous metalworking waste (11.2 kg) were found to the west of the north–south ancillary building in association with a series of floor level, bowl-shaped hearths 2282, 2281, 2295 and 2293 which imply that this discrete area was used as a smithy or forge, albeit episodically or intermittently. Initially, this focus of metalworking activity appears to have been conducted in the open, sheltered by an existing wall to the south but lacking any formal enclosure. This phase of metalworking activity is broadly contemporary with the first detectable alterations to the hall-building.

After the start of ironworking within the smithy, the longhouse was extended with the addition of a byre to the east of the main domestic building. A series of fine ashy floor layers built up within the western, domestic, end of the longhouse relating to the day-to-day activities and occupation of the structure. Residual quantities of ferrous waste and other vitrified materials of possible domestic origin were found within many of these layers. The inclusion of this debris within floor layers and midden material appears to be the result of incidental human action, trampling and, in the byre, the purposeful spreading of ash-rich deposits as flooring material. Cut into these floor layers within the longhouse, immediately west of the partition between the byre and the domestic half of the structure, was a small bowl-shaped hearth 2301 that contained small quantities of ferrous metalworking waste suggestive of smithing; this feature has been dated to 1010–1160 cal AD (Phase 5). Closely situated to this hearth was a stone-lined tank or box 2285 which contained small amounts of ferrous micro-debris in the form of hammerscale and smithing pan. It is possible that this feature was used as a quenching tank in association with the metalworking hearth but this may not have been its primary or subsequent function. The smithy, which appears to have seen episodic use throughout the early 11th century, appears to have gone out of use by this point, indicating a change both in focus of metalworking activities to within the main longhouse structure itself and potentially a decrease in the scale of ironworking.

It is during this period (Phase 5), that the ancillary buildings to the south of the longhouse were substantially

Table 11.4: Summary of distribution of vitrified material across the excavated areas

Area/feature	Quantity (g)
Smithy or workshop: includes dismantled hearths, rake-out spreads, dumps of metalworking waste and metalworking debris incorporated within floor deposits	11,215.2
Longhouse: stone-built tank (2285). Metalworking?	82.7
Longhouse: hearth (2301):metalworking?	736.3
Pit/hearth fill (2204): not metalworking	3552.9
Residual spreads of metalworking debris	4933.9
Residual spreads of undiagnostic vitrified material	761.7

reconfigured; the smithy area to the west of the north–south ancillary structure was built over and a large pit 2222 was dug into midden deposits to the east in the south-east midden area. It contained over 3.5 kg of vitrified material (Context 2205). This feature was interpreted in the field as a possible metalworking hearth but no metalworking related material was associated. Rather, the waste it contained was dominated by sintered low-density slags that appear to be the result of a low-temperature but long burning bonfire or hearth (Young 2012, 289).

THE METALWORKING YARD OR SMITHY: SOUTH-WEST CORNER OF TRENCH 5

A small square ancillary building located to the south-west of the main longhouse structure in the south-west corner of the excavated area was the focus for ironworking activities at East Mound with over 11.2 kg of ferrous metalworking waste and associated vitrified materials being recovered from this area alone. Excavation revealed a series of at least four small bowl-shaped hearths associated with a range of diagnostic and non-diagnostic vitrified materials which demonstrate that iron smithing was undertaken within this building. No evidence for iron smelting was identified amongst the excavated material. The sequence of hearths revealed during excavation demonstrates that these hearths represent successive phases of ironworking rather than all four being in use contemporaneously.

Amongst the latest phases of activity relating to this structure was a clay levelling layer 2118 and a construction layer 2119 that were cut by a later wall 2042 which was constructed to define a small enclosed square yard. The construction layer 2119 contained very little in the way of vitrified material. Only 8.5 g of undiagnostic magnetic vitrified residues and 0.8 g of amorphous burnt plant residues were recovered. Context 2118 encompassed over half a kilogram of vitrified material, including 412 g of unclassified iron slag and 147.5 g of vitrified ceramic. Also recovered from this layer was a partly forged iron bar, broken at both ends (SF 152). This later clay layer 2118 overlay deposit 2105, which contained abundant evidence for ferrous metalworking waste (3.9 kg). This layer has been characterised as a demolition and levelling episode. The presence of large quantities of micro-debris in the form of hammerscale flakes (619.1 g) and smithing pan (316.4 g) as well as a fragmentary plano-convex hearth bottom (188 g) demonstrates that this deposit consists of debris removed from the interior of smithing hearth and floor areas around an anvil. In addition to the residues already noted, over 1.2 kg of unclassified iron slag, almost certainly hearth rake-out material, small quantities of fuel ash slag (24 g) and magnetic vitrified residues (200.2 g) were also recovered. 787.5 g of vitrified ceramic probably derives from the lining of the dismantled metalworking hearths.

The lower spits of 2105 comprised contexts 2202, 2203, 2218. Context 2202 is similarly rich in metalworking debris to that of 2105 and appears to represent a mixed layer created by partial dismantling of the hearths and the spreading out of debris across the floor to create a level surface. A total of 4 kg of diagnostic and non-diagnostic vitrified material was recovered from this deposit and includes plano-convex slag cake fragments (830 g), large quantities of hammerscale (1.4 kg) as well as significant quantities of unclassified iron slag (1.1 kg) which indicate that iron smithing activities took place within this structure. Also associated were 53 g of magnetic vitrified residues and 430 g of vitrified ceramic which are likely to be fragments of hearth lining. In contrast to 2202, context 2203 was void of any vitrified materials and 2218 revealed only residual quantities of vitrified material (106.2 g), including small pieces of unclassified iron slag and vitrified ceramic. Below these deposits were the truncated and dismantled remains of four hearths, all of which contained small quantities of ironworking waste indicative of smithing activities and sealed by an ash-rich clay layer which made up the surface of the yard 2234. Only small, residual pieces of slag were present (68.5 g) including 44.5 g of unclassified iron slag. It is likely that this material had been incorporated within the clay surface due to disturbance of underlying deposits during construction.

The earliest and best preserved hearth 2282 was found in the south-east area of the structure. The surviving sub-oval bowl of the hearth was 0.5 m in diameter and only 0.4 m deep and its fill 2240 contained a very small quantity of micro-debris in the form of hammerscale flakes (181 g), indicative of iron smithing.

The second hearth 2281 survived half a metre to the west of 2282. Like this earlier hearth, 2281 survived as a sub-oval bowl-shaped pit which had been truncated by later hearth 2295. It was 0.46 m wide and nearly a metre long, orientated west to east. The sides of the cut were near vertical. The fill 2269 contained 952 g of vitrified material including 369 g of hammerscale flakes and spheres, 125 g of smithing pan, a fragment of slag amalgam (116 g) and a small quantity of unclassified iron slag (254 g). Also present was a small amount of possible hearth lining in the form of small pieces of vitrified ceramic (88 g).

The northernmost hearth within the structure was 2295. It was similar in dimensions to 2282 but slightly different in plan, oriented north-east to south-west with evidence of rake-out material to the south-west. This hearth truncates hearth 2281 and is therefore stratigraphically later. Only small quantities of vitrified material came from this hearth feature 2294 but includes 222 g of hammerscale and 15.5 g of smithing pan suggesting that this feature saw use as a smithing hearth. Small quantities of vitrified ceramic (31 g) were also present, probably deriving from the lining of the hearth.

The fourth and final hearth 2293 was cut through the upper layers of 2234 which sealed all the other hearths. It had been heavily truncated by later activity and only a restricted amount of rake-out 2292 from this feature survived, which contained 16 g of hammerscale from iron smithing.

Linked to deposit 2105 was a dump of metalworking waste on the yard surface 2178 which contained over 1 kg of vitrified material dominated by smithing residues including fragments of bloom, hammerscale and smithing pan.

Ironworking features within the longhouse

Small, residual quantities of vitrified material, including a fragment of possible bloom were recovered from an early floor layer within the longhouse (2146, Phase 2). As discussed previously, it is unclear where the focus of metalworking activities was during this early phase at East Mound but the context of discovery implies that it was residual debris, possibly introduced to the structure amongst midden-contaminated soils used as flooring.

A small bowl-shaped hearth 2301 was located immediately to the west of the partition that divides the longhouse into an eastern byre and a western domestic building. It was partially stone-lined as suggested by the presence of two burnt stones in the north-east side. It is possible that this hearth functioned as a smithing hearth, indicated by the presence of a plano-convex hearth bottom fragment (153 g), a possible bloom fragment (7.8 g) and small quantities of unclassified iron slag (22.5 g). Also present were fragments of vitrified ceramic (110 g) and magnetic vitrified residues (443 g). The fact that there are no diagnostic micro-debris associated with this feature leaves the interpretation as a metalworking related hearth uncertain but the suggestion is bolstered by the presence of significant quantities of hammerscale (71 g) and smithing pan (3.3 g) being recovered from the adjacent stone-lined tank or box 2285 alongside an incomplete or possibly unfinished forged iron object. The object is a flat, short, sub-rectangular strip, lentoid in section and broken at one end (SF 452); its corroded condition precludes precise identification but it may be a broken fitting or scrap intended for recycling or a partly forged item. It is likely that this stone-lined feature may have seen use as a quenching trough although this may not have been its function during later periods of use of the longhouse. The general paucity of spreads of hammerscale in association with this hearth is of interest; concentrations would be expected had the hearth and tank been used for an extended period of time. This implies that it was perhaps only used on an expedient and/or singular basis or that the floor layers surrounding the hearth were regularly cleared out.

Dump of non-metalwork-related vitrified material [2222]

At a later date, contemporary with the reconfiguration of the buildings to the south of the longhouse, a pit 2222 was dug into the south-east midden. The fill of this pit 2205 contained one of the largest concentrations of vitrified material on site comprising over 3.5 kg of vitrified and heat-affected debris in association with shell and fish bones. The vitrified material recovered lead to this feature being interpreted in the field as a metalworking hearth. No diagnostic ironworking debris or material indicative of metalwork was recovered from this feature to suggest that metalworking activities had taken place here. But large quantities of low-density, silicate rich vitrified material was present (3.4 kg) as well as small amounts of magnetic vitrified residue, fuel residues and raw clay. The purpose of this hearth or dump is not clear but by similarities to slags from Bornais, South Uist, it is likely that the waste is the result of an external hearth being maintained over an extended period of time (Young 2012).

Residual material (including metalworking waste)

Limited background quantities of waste material, including micro-slags and small fractured pieces of bulk slags, were found as low-density scatters within 56 contexts across the excavated area of East Mound, including trampled floor layers and surfaces. This material probably derives from nearby *in situ* metalworking features within the longhouse itself, and from the smithy or metalworking yard to the south of the longhouse. Layers of ash and burnt material, particularly within the byre end of the longhouse, demonstrate that hearth waste from domestic fires and possibly also from the metalworking hearths was deliberately spread in this area with the dual purpose of creating a floor surface but also the ash acting as an antiseptic and odour absorbent. It is likely that the majority of the vitrified material and metalworking debris found within these floor surfaces had been incidentally introduced into the longhouse by this action. The remaining 761 g of material comprises a spread of waste considered to be undiagnostic of metalwork activities and are likely to represent vitrified or burnt mineral components of fuel residues (such as fuel ash slag and low-density slags) and heavily burnt fragments of ceramic from the lining of domestic hearths.

Discussion

Iron objects are ubiquitous finds on Viking and Late Norse-period settlement sites in Scotland. And yet very little is known of their production or point of origin. The ferrous metalworking debris from East Mound represents a rare and significant example of well-dated, securely stratified evidence of blacksmithing activity associated with the Longhouse and the surrounding activity zones.

Two distinct foci for metalworking activity have been identified: the first, and earliest, dates to Phase 3 in the form of a small metalworking yard, probably a smithy or forge, and took place to the west of the north–south aligned ancillary structure, to the south of the Phase 3 longhouse; the second, potentially slightly later activity, dating to Phase 5, focuses on a hearth within the domestic area of the expanded longhouse (Phase 5). Ephemeral traces of a possible earlier phase of metalworking evidence is suggested by a small quantity of ferrous metalworking debris within Phase 2 midden material but no surviving evidence remains of where the focus for this activity took place due to the extent of modification and rebuilding across the excavated area.

The metalworking yard or smithy was found to consist of five sequential bowl-shaped hearths set into the ground. Each appears to have been lined with clay and were filled by, and surrounded by, re-deposited waste indicative of blacksmithing. Although no above ground features in this area survived, it is entirely possible that further hearths elevated from the ground surface were originally present. Similarly, no trace survived of the original setting of the anvil but the quantities of micro-debris in the form of hammerscale found in this area, as well as the traces of smithing pan representing a trampled floor surface leave little doubt that such a tool would originally have been present. The smithy itself appears to have only been partially enclosed at the time of use by a wall to the south and west but it remains unclear whether this ephemeral structure was ever roofed. The reconfiguring of this and the adjacent ancillary structures in Phase 4 effectively dismantled the metalworking features and there may have been a short hiatus of metalworking activities at East Mound prior to small scale smithing resuming within the Longhouse itself during Phase 5.

The configuration of the smithy at East Mound appears to be somewhat less substantial than that at some other broadly contemporary sites such as the smithy at Freswick Links (Building III), Caithness (Curle 1939, 81, pl. xxxix) with a series of massive central hearths, or that from Brough of Birsay, Structure 6 (Hunter 1986). Dedicated structures for metalworking activities have also been recognised at Jarlshof, Shetland; Udal, North Uist; Pool, Skaill, Deerness and Tuquoy, Orkney (Hunter 1986; Ballin Smith forthcoming; Hunter *et al.* 2007; Buteux 1997; Owen 1995). At Pool, a suite of Viking and Late Norse period structures and deposits were encountered consisting of a range of domestic and potentially non-domestic buildings. To the south of building 25, an earlier cellular structure had been converted into a smithy with a central elevated hearth associated with quantities of metalworking waste (Hunter *et al.* 1995, 277; Hunter 2007). Although the site remains largely unpublished, traces of metalworking activities at the Udal, North

Uist, are known to have come from deposits of 10th to 11th century date and in association with a possible non-domestic structure (Ballin Smith, forthcoming). An ancillary structure to the main domestic building at Tuquoy, dating to the Late Norse period, has been interpreted as a smithy on the basis of ferrous waste and floor-set, stone-built boxes which are plausible quenching troughs like that in the Phase 5 Longhouse at East Mound (Owen 1995). A possible Norse-period smithy was also noted at Whithorn, Galloway (Graham-Campbell and Batey 1998, 203–4; Hill 1997, 229–32). Unlike at East Mound, the workshop identified at the Brough of Birsay and metalworking waste at St Boniface and Lavacroon, Orphir, Orkney (Hunter 1986; McDonnell 1998, 143; Batey with Freeman 1986) revealed evidence for both copper-alloy and ironworking.

Fieldwalking around a mound at Lavacroon, Orphir, recovered a range of artefacts and industrial debris including possible Norse-period stone moulds and crucibles associated with copper alloy casting and approximately 17 kg of vitrified material representing ironworking waste (Batey with Freeman 1986). Two pieces of the collected iron slag were analysed and have been interpreted as the products of either blacksmithing or bloom reduction (*ibid.*, 296) and fragments of slag-attacked hearth lining were found suggesting the presence of disturbed metalworking furnaces or hearths. The date of this activity is unknown but it suggests the potential of the presence a workshop for ferrous and non-ferrous metalworking, roughly contemporary with that at East Mound. Small quantities of smithing slag were associated with Norse-period structures at Bostadh, Lewis, but the focus for this craft activity was not identified within the excavated area (McLaren and Heald, in Neighbour *et al.* forthcoming). Similarly, at Beachview, Birsay, Orkney, small quantities of smithing slag were found amongst deliberately dumped waste from a nearby structure and yet no metalworking residues were recovered in direct association with the building itself leaving a question over where the focus for metalworking was at this site (McDonnell 1996). In contrast to comprehensive metalworking evidence from East Mound, metalworking residues and structures at the Norse Farmsteads excavated at Mound 3 at Bornais, South Uist, and Buckquoy, Orkney were conspicuously absent (Sharples 2005, 194; Ritchie 1977).

The scale of metalworking at East Mound is hard to judge due to the level of truncation caused by later modification to the buildings. This process of re-building and reconfiguration of structures has resulted in metalworking waste from the smithy being dispersed across the site, becoming incorporated into midden layers, deposits and spreads. The use of midden-rich material as levelling deposits and floor materials has caused further mixing of material meaning that ironworking waste is found across the excavated area, throughout the phases of activity, despite only two main foci and periods of activity being identified. Despite this, the quantity of waste in relation to the number of potential metalworking hearths identified on site is relatively small and suggests that ironworking at East Mound was modest in scale and perhaps episodic, rather than continuous. This considers the evidence that the hearths focused in the smithy area to the south of the longhouse were built consecutively rather than being in contemporary use and the number of hearth bottoms identified amongst the assemblage represent an estimated minimum of 23 episodes of smithing activity in total. This implies that small-scale manufacture and maintenance of iron objects was undertaken at East Mound, probably for the use of the household rather than a larger scale of production intended to service the wider community. A similar picture was suggested from the recovered residues at Freswick Links, Caithness, where the waste was interpreted as debris from small-scale industry (Morris *et al.* 1995, 260). This concurs with an earlier suggestion that on-site smithies of Viking and Late Norse periods in Scotland were principally domestic in scale of production (Graham-Campbell and Batey 1998, 221).

All of the diagnostic ironworking slags from East Mound are indicative of blacksmithing activities. No smelting slags were recognised amongst the assemblage to suggest that the processing of ore into useable blooms or billets was undertaken on site. This opens up the question over what the smith was using as a raw material with which to forge new products or to conduct repairs to existing items. Analysis of the iron objects from the site (Chapter 12) and the small clench bolts in particular, suggest that timber from clinker-built boats was being reused within the structure. Based on this principle of reuse and modification of existing resources, it is possible that any broken or redundant iron implements or fixtures could also have been appropriated for re-working but the use of scrap metal for recycling may have been an erratic and unreliable resource. The evidence of both part-forged or scrap iron objects as well as reused iron fittings found during excavation imply that iron objects were recycled and reforged, as well being made from

raw iron on site, as indicated by the presence of bloom and bar fragments.

Although slag suggestive of ironworking activities have been found on many Viking and Late Norse period sites in Scotland, the majority of this waste appears to be debris from iron smithing rather than smelting. Despite Graham-Campbell and Batey's (1998, 221) suggestion that local sources of bog ore must have been exploited during the Viking and Late Norse periods, evidence for this in the form of debris from primary iron production (*e.g.* smelting) has rarely been recognised amongst slag assemblages of this period in Orkney. The assemblage of vitrified material recovered from the late Iron Age and Norse structures at Bostadh, Lewis, was dominated by smithing slags (McLaren and Heald forthcoming). Small quantities of diagnostic smithing debris in the form of slag spheres were recovered from the Norse period structure and middens but no foci for metalworking activity were recognised on site and no debris from smelting was identified. At Freswick Links, Caithness, the industrial residues were dominated by iron smithing debris; enough material was present to suggest that a smithy was located nearby, outside the excavated area (Spearman 1995, 132–3). Similarly at Birsay Bay, hammerscale, fuel ash slag and fired clay was recovered from Area 1 suggesting small scale industrial activity (Morris 1989, 109–27, 300). At the Biggings, Papa Stour, Shetland, iron and slag were present in small quantities in all but the first structural phase of activity (Crawford and Ballin Smith 1999). It was noted that although it was possible that some iron was smelted on the island there was no evidence for this from the recovered debris from the site (*ibid.*, 126). In contrast, all stages of the iron production/working process were present at Dornoch, Sutherland (Photos-Jones 2008, 15). Analysis of the residues suggested that low-intensity metalworking took place in a distinct area of the settlement over a prolonged period of time, broadly spanning the 9th to 11th centuries.

This hint at an imbalance between surviving evidence for primary and secondary ironworking evidence during the Viking and Late Norse periods in Scotland is intriguing and potentially significant but not well understood. A similar picture has been noted on later prehistoric sites in the Hebrides (McLaren, forthcoming).

12

Iron and lead finds

Colleen E. Batey

Iron

Due to the largely sandy preservation conditions, the overall condition of the ironwork from the Bay of Skaill is highly variable and in a number of cases, without the aid of the X-rays, it would have been impossible to discern the artefact type. Numerically dominant within the overall assemblage however are the nails (71 finds) and the clench bolts/roves (35 clench bolts or part thereof and 23 roves, including two multiple rove plates). In the case of both these larger elements in the assemblage, Phase 5 dominates numerically. Smaller groups of other artefact types include buckles and parts of buckles (four finds from as many phases in Trench 5), mounts (three finds from two phases in Trench 5), several knife blades (eight, of which one is from Trench 4 and the remaining from Trench 5, and spread across several phases) and a small group of miscellaneous tools (seven of which all are from Trench 5 and several phases). In addition, there are nine finds of metal plate, some of which may have been part of nails or clench bolts but now indeterminate – again Trench 5 and several phases are represented.

Buckles (Table 12.1)

There is one example of a complete simple oval-framed buckle lacking its pin (SF 205) (Fig. 12.1). The type is ubiquitous and considered most likely to be a personal belt item. This is solely based on size, following Patrick Ottaway's distinction at Meols, where horse buckles were distinguished as being larger than 50 mm (Ottaway 2007, 203). This example is from Trench 5, Phase 2, but the type is long-lived. The second buckle frame section (SF 239) is from Phase 6, and is of squared form, likely to be similar to an example from London – although that had a tin coating (Egan 2002, 68–69, SF 267, illus. 41)

and was dated by Geoff Egan to the 15th century. This indicates that a simple form continues unchanged for a substantial period. Egan suggested the London example was a personal buckle.

Three finds are suggested here as buckle tongues, SF 346 of Phase 5, SF 321 of Phase 7 and SF 62 of Phase 8. These are not chronologically very sensitive items; the bulky nature of SF 321 could indicate an association with horse-gear.

Mounts (Table 12.2)

Three finds are assigned to the category of mounts, SF 215 from Phase 2 (Fig. 12.4), and SFs 418 (Fig. 12.4) and 436 from Phase 5. The earliest piece here (SF 215) (Fig. 12.2) has a plate and a probable securing nail at one end. The most likely suggestion is that this piece is a fitting to be applied to a box or similar. Several items of this type are noted from Anglo-Scandinavian contexts at 16–22 Coppergate, York (Ottaway 1992, 640–643). The form is barely sufficiently clear to further identify even on X-ray.

SF 436 (Fig. 12.2) is a stapled hasp. It is elegantly worked with a spatulate end and a securing rivet at its mid-point with remains of a curving terminal at the opposite end. Such finds have been noted in earlier contexts at Coppergate (Ottaway 1992, 645), although the delicate form of this working suggests it originally may have been a box fitting rather than something more structural. SF 418 (Fig. 12.4) is potentially the most significant of this small group. The piece itself is incomplete and both long edges are damaged, but X-ray indicates nine matching pairs of bright points on the larger fragment and a further four on the smaller fragment which may be conjoining. The bright points are likely to be applied decoration in another metal, but metallurgical investigation would be needed to confirm this.

Table 12.1: Iron buckles

SF no.	Context no.	Object type	Description	Dimensions (mm)	Phase	Trench
205	2146	Buckle	Flattened oval, undecorated	L 38 × W 23 × T 5	2	5
346	2224	Buckle tongue?	X-ray indicates a loop at one end and a curve at opposite	L 26 × W 5 × T 4	5	5
239	2169	Buckle	Section of rounded buckle frame with squared interior	L 28 × W 13 × T 4	6	5
62	2045	Buckle tongue?	Corroded length with curved loop end. Shank broken but squared in section	L 32 × W 10 × T 7	8	5
321	2209	Buckle tongue?	Badly corroded loop, indeterminate	L 38 × W 20 × T 10	7	5

Table 12.2: Iron mounts

SF no.	Context no.	Object type	Description	Dimensions (mm)	Phase	Trench
215	2146	Mount?	Indeterminate, highly corroded and misshapen. Possible signs of a perforation or rivet?	L 53 × W 20 max × T 5	2	5
436	2268	Stapled hasp?	Elegantly shaped piece with one end spatulate and the other curved. Substantial rivet or loop at midpoint?	L 62 × max W 17	5	5
418	2265	Decorated plate?	2 conjoining fragments of plate which have approx. 11 pairs of small bright spots on x-ray. Possibly applications or decoration. Function unclear, but probably decorative	Overall L 60 × W 15 × T 3	5	5

L = length, W = width, T = thickness

Table 12.3: Iron knife blades

SF no.	Context no.	Object type	Description	Dimensions (mm)	Phase	Trench
15	1519	Knife blade	Small intact blade with tapering tang. Triangular section with flat back, slightly offset. Slightly curved blade. Whittle Tang Type C? (Goodall 2011, 106). Possible organic remains in corrosion	Overall L 84; blade L 44 × D max 8 × T 5	2	4
355	2146	Knife blade?	Possible large bladed knife tip, damaged edge and slightly bent	Overall 40 × D 15 × T 6	2	5
384	2224	Knife blade	Central part of blade with offset tang. Clear shoulder and choil. Triangular section blade. Whittle Tang Type D (Goodall 2011, 106–7)	Tang L 38; blade L 44 × D max 18 × T 10–5	5	5
412	2268	Knife blade	Most of blade, triangular section and part of tang. Whittle Tang Type F (Goodall 2011, 106–7). Back curving towards broken tip	Blade L 55 × D 10 × T 4 max; Tang L 16	5	5
363	2225	Knife blade	Segment of blade and offset tang. Triangular sectioned blade and traces of possible organics in corrosion at junction of blade and tang. Whittle Tang with blade heavilyoffset to tang.	Overall L 56; blade L 18 × D 10 × T max 5	6	5
365	2225	Knife blade	Tip of knife blade, pronounced triangular section, possibly part of 384 but slightly damaged at break so conjoin not exact	L23 × Dmax 8 × T 7	6	5
136	2127	Knife blade	Tip of triangular sectioned plate. Possibly in manufacture as narrower edge is blunt. Straight back, but could be end of a stepped back form Whittle Tang H (Goodall 2011, 106–7)	L 40 × D 100 × T max 4	7	5
25	2012	Knife blade?	Indet plate, slightly triangular in section	L 32 × D 12 × T 4	8	5

L = length, D = depth, T = thickness

Fig. 12.1: Buckle SF 205

Fig. 12.2: Stapled hasp SF 436

Fig. 12.3: Knife SF 15

Knife blades (Table 12.3)

There are eight finds from this category, representing a maximum of six or seven different knives, as SFs 384 from Phase 5 and 365 from Phase 6 are likely to be from the same knife blade, broken in antiquity. In addition, two blade fragments, SF 355 of Phase 2 and SF 25 from Phase 8 are uncertain identifications in this category. The remaining pieces are clearly whittle tang knife blades: SF 15 (Phase 2), SF 384 (Fig. 12.3), SF 384 (Phase 5), SF 412 (Phase 5), SF 363 (Phase 6) (Fig. 12.4) and SF 136 (Phase 7), *i.e.* six knives in total. The various types of whittle tang knives have been studied by Goodall (2011), and his type letters are applied here. The simple knife

form uses a tang inserted into the handle, and differs from the scale tang knives which have riveted handles, both types are known in the early medieval period. It is rare for handles to survive in the medieval period, but wood was the most common material. The assemblage of iron knives from Quoygrew, Westray, numbering 23 in total, includes two wooden handles, one in oak and the other a hard wood which might be a local product (Rogers *et al.* 2012, 249).

SF 15 (Fig. 12.3) is a small intact blade of triangular section with a flat curved back which is slightly offset. It is of the type Goodall Type C (Goodall 2011, 106) and has possible remains of organic (wood) preserved in the corrosion products at the blade/handle junction. SF 384 (Fig. 12.4) is the central part of a blade with offset tang and a clear shoulder (Type D, Goodall 2011, 106–7). SF 412 comprises most of the blade and part of the tang, with the back curved towards the broken tip (Type F, Goodall 2011, 106–7). SF 136 is a tip only of a straight-backed knife, possibly in the process of being manufactured and tentatively identified as part of a stepped back knife (Type H, Goodall 2011, 106–7). SF 363 does not easily fit into Goodall's categories and is a blade and tang segment where the blade is markedly offset to the tang.

Ottaway made an extensive study of the knives from Coppergate and sub-divided them by the form of the back. In his categories, SF 363 (Fig. 12.2) with its very distinct angle at the tang/blade junction can be paralleled in 2871 and 2954 (Ottaway 1992, 567, 573, Figs 231 and 235) from 10th century levels. The small and scattered nature of this part of the assemblage suggests only that the knives were used for a common range of activities, much as today. Broken blades would have been discarded and blunt ones would have been repeatedly sharpened by hones (Chapter 18).

Tools (Table 12.4)

There are a variety of object types within this overall category, ranging from two awls (SFs 168, Phase 2 (Fig. 12.2) and SF 357, Phase 7) and a possible punch (SF 85, Phase 6), to a possible key (SF 55, Phase 7), a hook (SF 335, Phase 7) to a candlestick (SF 109, Phase 5), and a ploughshare (SF 329, Phase 7, Fig. 12.4).

The two awls are of very different lengths (SF 168, Fig. 12.4). The earlier of the two is 75 mm long, the other 104 mm, and may have been utilised in leather preparation. Examples of this type are recorded from Winchester (Goodall 2011, Fig. 6.3 *e.g.* E55) as well as Coppergate (Ottaway 1992, Fig. 222). The tang-less punch (SF 85) is more robust and suggests some working of stone (*e.g.* Goodall 2011, Fig. 4.3). The tool would have been held in the hand and whilst some are suggested as being for iron working, this is not an obvious use of a metal tool that is used in the working of hot metal.

SF 55 is tentatively identified as a key. One end is spatulate and presumed to be the handle end, the other broken, but the whole is bent in an S-shape and may

have worked with a rather large padlock. A hook, SF 335, is a ubiquitous find, in this case highly corroded and indeterminate in detail.

The candlestick from Trench 5, Phase 5 (SF 109, Fig. 12.4) is very similar in form to two examples from Coppergate, from a 10th century context (Ottaway 1992, 680, 3674 and 3675), although one of those was angled. Goodall illustrates many of the type, several dating into the 14th–15th centuries with stems bent at right angles to the ferrule (Goodall 2011, 317, Fig. 11.8). However, there are also examples that have straight stems (*ibid.*, 315, Fig. 11.7) and a date range beginning in the 12th century. This object, in two conjoining pieces is a simple upright socketed holder which would have been stuck directly into a horizontal surface – perhaps a table or a beam. The point is intact and the 'ferrule' of approximately 15 mm in diameter would have held a flammable source, conceivably a beeswax candle (which would have to have been imported) or simple rushes. This is an unusual find for the Northern Isles.

SF 329 (Fig. 12.4) is suggested to be a ploughshare or perhaps a shoe for a hoe. The metal plate is curved as if to embrace a wooden tip of a share beam and the blade end is irregular as if damaged by wear. Similar finds have been noted in medieval contexts, such as at St Neots, Cambridgeshire (Addyman 1973, 94, Fig. 19.30) and the type is discussed and illustrated by Goodall (2011, 77 and 85, Fig. 7.2 F5).

Nails (Table 12.5)

In common with many similar sites, the iron assemblage is dominated numerically by the nails (69 finds). For

Table 12.4: Iron tools

SF no.	Context no.	Object type	Description	Dimensions (mm)	Phase	Trench
168	2146	Awl	Slightly narrowed at slimmer end. Broader in middle with squared section and slightly damaged ends. Possibly for leather working? cf.Goodall 2011, fig. 6.3, E50/E51.	L 75 × max Diam. 5	2	5
109	2115	Candlestick?	Two conjoining pieces of square sectioned and tapering point with hollow expanded socket.	L 120 × Diam. 15	5	5
85	2062	Punch?	Slightly curved at tip, flat rectangular section along length of possible tool.	L 90 × max W 14	6	5
329	2208	Ploughshare?	Blade squared and possibly distorted through wear. Hafted by incurved metal anchors around a rectangular flat shaft.	L 122 × W 91 × T 4	7	5
335	2209	Hook	Tapering to the point and highly corroded at broader end, possibly concealing plate.	Overall 38 × 15 × T 17	7	5
357	2228	Awl?	Square sectioned long piece of iron with both ends complete but blunt, slightly bent.	L 104 × max Diam. 7	7	5
55	2007	Key?	2 fragments, conjoined. Sinuous, one end flattened, other missing. Square sectioned.	Overall 160 × T 6	7	5

L = length, W = width, T = thickness, Diam. = diameter

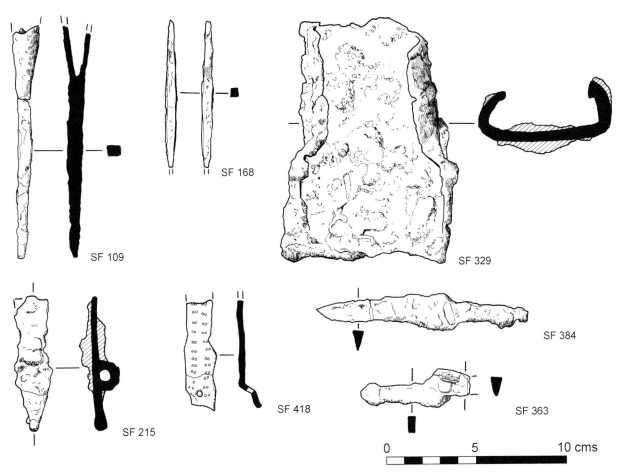

SF 168

SF 109

SF 329

SF 384

SF 215

SF 418

SF 363

0   5   10 cms

Fig. 12.4: Iron finds: tools, household and dress accessories

example at Quoygrew on Westray, recent excavation yielded over 157 nails but only 8 clench bolts (Rogers *et al.* 2012, 249). The different types of nails distinguished here follow the nomenclature of Goodall (2011, 163–164, Fig. 9.1). In his 2011 study, Goodall combined data from several different medieval sites in England, but the comment that nails are ubiquitous and to be measured in their thousands in purchase terms (*ibid.* 163), is as relevant in Orkney as elsewhere. Within the assemblage here, the nails that can be assigned to a specific type are predominantly Goodall's Type 1 ('Flat head of square, rectangular or rounded shape', *ibid.* 164; see also Ottaway 1992, 608, Fig. 253). The type is simple, functional and clearly conservative in its form. This makes it difficult to make a specific comment about dating, as the type is inevitably long-lived. It does indicate however that wooden elements were likely to be present on site, and in a treeless landscape such as Orkney, this observation is more important than it might otherwise indicate. The limited number of complete examples could indicate careful recycling, or on-site production as indicated in the roves. Nails are easier to remove intact from

wood which is to be reused than the clench bolts discussed below, although they may be survivals of wooden elements which have now disappeared. Type 1 is represented by 37 examples (or 38 depending on the form of one piece from Phase 8), which is just over 53% of the group. On site these are predominantly to be found in Phase 5 of Trench 5 (18 examples). Amongst this group, ten survive as complete examples with both head and tip intact. The next largest concentration of the Type 1 can be found in the succeeding Phase, 6 (with seven examples including two complete). Other phases outside 3–5 have low figures for this type, but two are from the earliest phase represented (Phase 2) and three from Phase 8.

Goodall's Type 2 is a type with 'raised head of circular or rounded rectangular shape' and identified specifically in only three cases across all the assemblage. Type 3 has a 'flat head of narrow, rectangular shape' and is limited to Phase 8 where there are two examples and dated there to the last stages of the site's use. It is easy to confuse this head form with that of Type 1, however, if the head has been broken. Type 6 has a 'flat rectangular head

Table 12.5: Iron nails

SF no.	Context no.	Object type	Description	Dimensions (mm)	Phase	Trench
3	1504	Nail	Large headed, slightly domical. Shank short and incomplete. Type 2?	L 18 × Head Diam. max 20	3	
24	1504	Nail	Shank of oval section.	L 23	3	
38	1547	Nail	Flat-headed nail with most of shank remaining. Type 1.	L 34 × Head Diam. max 18	2	4
275	2152	Nail	Possible squared nail? Shank. Indeterminate type.	L 24	2	5
251	2146	Nail	Flat headed nail, square section, indeterminate on x-ray. Type 1?	L 30 × Head Diam. max 17	2	5
4	1507	Nail	Flat-headed nail with shank slightly bent at tip. Type 1.	L 19 × Head Diam. max 13	3	1
45	1551	Nail	Shank only, indeterminate section.	L 35	3	4
391	2236	Nail	Headless nail, shank complete. Type 8.	L 50	3	5
404	2264	Nail	Indeterminate head and small part of shank. Type 1.	L Shank 7 × Head Diam. max 17	3	5
320	2219	Nail	Heavily corroded, section indeterminate, possibly complete head and shank. Type 1.	L 25	3	5
4020	1019	Nail	Wedge shaped shank. Head undifferentiated. Goodall 2011, 164, Type 6.	L 34	3	1
	2204	Nails	Shank fragments and indeterminate.	Largest 31	3	5
405	2264	Nail	Bent shank with curved flat head. Type 1.	Head 15 × 10; shank L 17	3	5
160	2084	Nail?	Shank with flattened spatulate end, tip slightly bent. Type 8.	L 32	4	5
4027	1038	Nail	Flattened head with tapering shank, bent at tip. Type 1.	L 20 × Head Diam. max 10	5	3
100	2087	Nail	2 conjoining pieces of nail shank, head small and end of nail beaten. Possibly Type 1?	L 30	5	5
101	2087	Nail	Broken head and shank with beaten end. Type 1?	L 30	5	5
118	2040	Nail	Segment of shank only, possibly squared in section.	L 34	5	5
195	2087	Nail	Slightly bent shank and flattened head. Type 1.	L 25 × Head Diam. max 13	5	5
196	2087	Nail	Slightly domical nail head and shank of slightly squared section, tip missing. Type 2.	L 20 × Head Diam. max 11	5	5
197	2087	Nail	Angled flat head and shank section. Type 1.	L 20 × Head Diam. max 12	5	5
203	2087	Nail	Flat headed nail, lacking tip. Head at angle to shank. Large head Type 1.	L 30 × Head Diam. max 14	5	5
209	2087	Nail	Shank with expanded head mass, head possibly flat. Type 1.	L 34 × Head Diam. *c.* 15	5	5
228	2087	Nail	Part of shank and flattened head. Type 1.	L 20 × Head Diam. max 16	5	5
334	2202	Nail	Multiple fragments of long nail shank, square sectioned.	Largest L 21	5	5
360	2163	Nail	Round, flat-headed nail with offset bent shank, complete. Type 1.	L 18 × Head Diam. max 15	5	5
386	2224	Nail	Long nail with small flat head. Type 1.	L 50	5	5

SF no.	Context no.	Object type	Description	Dimensions (mm)	Phase	Trench
390	2173	Nail	Flat headed nail with short shank. Type 1.	L 22 × Head Diam. max 20	5	5
398	2265	Nail	Indistinct of x-ray. Could be bent shank.	L 30	5	5
409	2265	Nail/Stud	Domical? Head and short length of shank. Type 12?	Shank 10 × Head max Diam. 26	5	5
410	2261	Nail	Flat headed nail with shank bent. Type 1?	L 30 × Head Diam. *c.* 10	5	5
413	2265	Nail	Shank only.	L 28	5	5
414	2265	Nail	Small nail, head and bent over shank, tip complete. Type 1.	L max 21	5	5
427	2265	Nail	Short shank remaining, large flat head. Type 1.	L 28 × Head Diam. max 18	5	5
434	2277	Nail	Slightly expanding nail shank. Totally disintegrated and indeterminate.	Largest L 22	5	5
466	2263	Nail	Flat headed nail and incomplete long shank. Type 1.	L 32	5	5
452	2285	Nail	Sample 66, 2 indeterminate, 1 nail shank and flat top. Type 1?	L 20; Head Diam. max 18	5	5
221	2087	Nail	Expanded at both ends, possible flat head. Type 1?	L 34	5	5
28	1038	Nail	Hollow long shank, damaged head. Type 1.	L 43	5	3
225	2087	Nail	Shank fragment.	L 20	5	5
400	2265	Nail?	Curved fragment possibly shank.	L 24	5	5
221a	2087	Nails	Multiple fragments, including nail shank pieces. Indeterminate type.	Largest 14 × 8	5	5
393	2224	Nails	2 fragments, one possibly a shank and the other indicates squared section at point and indeterminate other end. Types unidentified.	Largest L 35	5	5
43	2031	Nail	Flat headed with short shank remaining, angled. Type 1.	L 15 × Head Diam. max 11	6	5
51	2031	Nail	Flat head and tapering squared shank, tip missing. Type 1.	L 35	6	5
60	2031	Nail	Shank only.	L 37	6	5
67	2046	Nail	Slightly domical headed nail with broken shank. Type 2?	L 10 × Head Diam. max 123	6	5
86	2062	Nail	Flat head and tapering shank. Type 1.	L 33 × Head max D 10	6	5
116	2031	Nail	Flat headed and long broken shank. Large Type 1.	L 28 × Head Diam. 20	6	5
128	2034	Nail	Flat headed, tip missing. Type 1?	L 25	6	5
141	2130	Nail	Small headed nail and shank? Indeterminate.	L 6 × Head Diam. max 20	6	5
183	2063	Nail	Shank fragment.	L 25	6	5
235	2164	Nail	Flat headed nail with round-sectioned shank, complete. Type 1.	L shank 23 × Head Diam. max 14	6	5
88	2056	Nail	Bent shank and possible head. Indeterminate form.	Overall 22 × 15	6	5
68	2062	Nail	Long narrow shank, incomplete and substantial flat head. Type 1.	L 55 × Head Diam. max 20	6	5

Table 12.5: Iron nails (Continued)

SF no.	Context no.	Object type	Description	Dimensions (mm)	Phase	Trench
134	2107	Nail	Complete with incomplete round flattened head, bent shank of squared section and tip remaining. Large Type 1.	L 65 × Head Diam. max 19	7	5
146	2139	Nail	Slightly bent shank and flattened head. Type 1.	L 20 × Head Diam. max 12	7	5
169	2139	Nail	Short angled shank and flat round head.	Head 17 × 14; shank 15	7	5
307	2209	Nail	Shank only.	L 35	7	5
57	2028	Nail	Small tack-like nail, broken shank. Type 1/3?	L 13 × Head max Diam. 11	8	5
59	2036	Nail	Flat-headed nail with bent shank, complete. Type 1.	L 34 × Head Diam. max 10	8	5
75	4004	Nail	Complete thin nail. Type 3.	L 38 × Head Diam. 10	8	7
77	4004	Nail	Small headed nail, flattened and shank bent at right angles. Type 1.	Length *c.* 38	8	7
93	2045	Nail	Indeterminate head, fully corroded and stump of shank. Type 1?	Overall 15 × 13	8	5
73	2001	Nail	Length of slightly flattened shank. Indeterminate type.	L 42	8	5
481	2304	Nail?	From residues, sample 76. Corroded and no x-ray, possible nail shank with head of indeterminate form.	L 13 × Diam. 11	8?	6
389	2248	Nail	Length of thin shank. Indeterminate.	L 28	9	8
370b	2146	Nails	Two nail shank fragments, one with indeterminate head.	24 × 20 × 20; 35 × 8	2	5
170	Unstrat	Nail	Broken shank, with possible simple head. Type 1?	L 16 × Head Diam. max 8	Unstrat	

L = length, Diam. = diameter

formed by flaring, wedge shaped shank'. There is one from Phase 3, and this has remained complete particularly due to its form (SF 4020). Type 8 is a 'headless nail' and represented by two examples only, one from Phase 3 and one from Phase 4, both surviving complete. A single nail of Type 12, 'stud with circular head', survives incomplete in Phase 5. All remaining nail finds are indeterminate types (a total of 24 in total across most phases), due to being damaged and incomplete, and surviving only as shanks. The lack of heads (and indeed bent shanks), however, could be indicative of the attempt to remove nails from wood to be recycled (as also noted by Ottaway at York, 1992, 614), and see below where it is suggested that some of the plate pieces could be heads now divorced from the nail.

Across the assemblage there is a variety of shank sections, ranging from oval (*e.g.* SF 24 from Phase 3) to square (*e.g.* SF 251, Phase 2), but this information is limited to a number of examples where conservation has been undertaken or the shank is otherwise visible other than on X-ray which does not allow for this detail to be clarified. Most examples have broken shanks, lacking the more vulnerable tips, and in a few cases the shank itself is bent (*e.g.* SF 4 and SF 405 from Phase 3; SF 360 from Phase 5). Commonly the shank is seated roughly centrally on the head, although there are examples where this is not the case, a good example of this is SF 360 from Phase 5.

In terms of functions indicated here, use in structural timber is likely, particularly given a concentration in Phase 5. Where it is possible to gauge the full length of the nail, a length in the region of between *c.* 19 and 50 mm is represented (SF 4 and SF 391 from Phase 3), and up to 65 mm in SF 134 of the later Phase 7. There is a small number across the phases that have the heads angled to the shanks (*e.g.* SF 203 from Phase 5). This could be post depositional damage or damage during removal from a timber, or it could even indicate the specific angle of the nail as originally placed at a junction.

In terms of additional functions indicated by these nails, some of the smaller ones are likely to have been associated with house fittings or in the case of the shortest complete shanks, even part of chests or furniture as indicated at Coppergate (Ottaway 1992, 613). This variety of use is perhaps clearer however in the clench bolts discussed below, where it is possible to see in some cases the full original thickness of the wood.

Clench bolts/roves (Table 12.6)

The clench bolts are here defined by the presence of part of a shank with a rove, and a complete example includes both head and rove and thus indicating the full thickness of the original timber it embraced. There are 35 clench bolts that have been identified in this assemblage, of which only nine (just over 26%) remain complete and allow for the timber thickness to be assessed. They are predominantly recovered from Phase 5, with 19 examples of which five are complete. There are a further two from Phase 2, one from Phase 3, two from Phase 4, five (one complete) from Phase 6, three from Phase 7 (one complete and one repaired) and one from Phase 8 (one complete).

The roves (also known as clench plates) are distinguished here as only the perforated plate remaining and no shank traces at all. Twenty-one roves have been identified and again the predominance is in Phase 5, where 13 roves including seven squared, three large squares, one rectangular and two indeterminate original form were identified. This has the added significance of two rove strips being discovered there and indicating production or repair (SFs 186 and 194) (Fig. 12.5). Phase 2 has three roves, of which two are square (both large and small) and indeterminate; Phase 3, two squared roves; Phase 7, one squared and one rectangular; and Phase 8, one indeterminate original form.

The roves, numbering 21 finds, are most commonly of square form, varying in size from approximately 20 mm square to larger ones of approximately 30 mm (*e.g.* SFs 397 and 421 from Phase 5). A clear diamond form is noted on the clench bolt (SF 229) of Phase 5 (Fig. 12.5) and a more rectangular shape is represented in SF 330 of Phase 7 and clench bolt (SF 97) of Phase 5. The actual size is related to the fastening required, so a larger piece of timber needs more securing, but whether the difference in actual shape is significant is difficult to ascertain. Notably the two perforated strips from which roves could be offcut, SFs 186 and 194 with three and two perforations respectively, would have produced complete roves of approximately only 14–17 mm across, and these are clearly at the smaller end of the square range. The two general shapes are also matched in the larger assemblages from Coppergate, York, where Ottaway discusses the rectangular/square form as well as the diamond shape examples (Ottaway 1992, 615).

There are only a few examples of complete clench bolts, with head, shank and rove remaining and which therefore enable an assessment of the thickness of wood secured. In these cases, the wood is of variable thickness and the lack of straightness of the shanks in some cases must indicate that they were removed from the wood forcibly, presumably with a claw hammer. From Phase 5, there are five complete examples, with wood indicated as being variable between as little as 7 mm (SF 229), 10 mm (SF 230) (Fig. 12.5) or up to 19 mm in the case of SF 208 (Fig. 12.5). Two examples which may indicate repair of roves/clench bolts are SF 72 from Phase 5 as well as SF 165 from Phase 7. In these cases there are two perforations in very close proximity on the roves, and these are likely to be too close to indicate use at the same time.

The use of clench bolts is most commonly associated with ship-building technology, where clinker-built vessels required a double thickness of wood to be joined. However, in items such as doors where there is a similar need to secure double pieces of wood together this would require similar technology, and indeed it is not unknown for ships' timbers to be recycled in domestic structures. In a recent study by Bill in relation to clench bolt finds from Woodstown, Ireland, he notes that in seagoing Viking ships the normal plank would be in the region of 20–25 mm at its edge for securing, so to fasten two pieces together would require a bolt of 40–50 mm. At Woodstown, this size of clench bolt is rare, and more commonly timbers of 10–15 mm needed to be spanned, resulting in functioning clench bolts of 20–30 mm (Bill 2014, 151). However, in the case of SF 230 (Fig. 12.5) or SF 229 from Phase 5, where the clench bolt is angled, this could have accommodated a fine scarf joint, effectively only representing the thickness of a single timber (as illustrated by Ottaway 1992, 617, Fig. 257).

To gain a fuller idea of the actual size of the clench bolts however, where it is also likely that some of the longer nails broke or were extracted and broken in the course of that activity, the width of the nail shank itself may be more helpful. This information is not easily available on many examples that are identified through corrosion products seen on X-ray, but an average of between 5 and 8 mm would seem to be common, which interestingly is the same as Bill notes for the boat rivets from a Viking grave at Kiloran Bay, Colonsay (Bill 2014, 152). The size of most of the roves would seem to corroborate this size comparability. In the case of Woodstown, Bill interprets this as indicating small vessels of varying sizes being represented (*ibid.* 152) in the assemblage. It is possible that small vessel timbers were in use at Skaill also, probably in the form of reused timbers. The size range though may also be consistent with door furniture, window covering or even cart fittings (c.f. Fyrkat, Denmark; Roesdahl 1977, 84–90, Figs 109 a–d, 110), or in some of

Table 12.6: Iron clench bolts/roves

SF no.	Context no.	Object type	Description	Dimensions (mm)	Phase	Trench
2	1504	Clench bolt	Long bent shank with flat head and rove displaced to part way up shank, possible shadow of second rove?	Overall 48 × 35 × 24	3	
371b	2146	Clench bolt	Length of shank and plate which could be a rove.	Shank L 30; Plate 17 × 15	2	5
366	2146	Clench bolt	Shank and rove/head.	Rove/head 20 × 10 × 5. Shank L 15	2	5
263	2146	Rove	Probable segment of plate, clearly perforated.	26 × 20 × 8	2	5
367	2146	Rove	Large square rove, off centre perforation.	25 × 20 × 8	2	5
370a	2146	Rove	Small square rove.	Rove 20 × 16 × 6	2	5
258	2105	Rove	Squared plate, rove?	25 × 25 × 8	3	5
435	2262	Rove	Complete, square with central perforation.	23 × 22 × 7	3	5
271	2170	Clench bolt	2 fragments, nail head, shank and perforated square rove.	Rove 26 × 26 × 4	4	5
74	2056	Clench bolt	Rove and shank, head is quadrant shaped. Shank is short and broken.	L 18 × Head Diam. 28	4	5
194	2118	Rove strip?	Strip of flat metal with two perforations. Slightly bent.	L 40 × W 17 × T 4	5	5
71	2053	Clench bolt	Multiple fragments, formerly small rivet with rove and shank.	Shank L (wood T) 8	5	5
72	2040	Clench bolt	Possible repair evidence. Rove with perforation and adjacent shank which looks as if it is secondary (intercutting perforation).	Rove 15 × 20; Shank L 14	5	5
97	2087	Clench bolt	Rectangular rove with virtually headless nail.	Rove 23 × 10 × 4; Shank L 18	5	5
184	2156	Clench bolt	Small stub of shank and indet plate? Rove.	Overall 24 × 15 × 12	5	5
222	2087	Clench bolt	Flat headed nail with shank and angled rove and tail of nail tip.	Head *c.* 10 × 10; Rove *c.* 15 × 15; wood T 14	5	5
227	2087	Clench bolt	Flat headed nail and most of rove. Thickness of wood.	Head D 15; Rove 23 × 17; wood T 11	5	5
229	2087	Clench bolt	Small nail, flat head and diamond rove, angled.	Head 17 × 12; Shank (wood T *c.* 7); Rove 20 × 21	5	5
230	2087	Clench bolt	Flat headed nail with off centre shank, rove of narrow rectangular form. Thickness of wood.	Head D 15; Shank/wood T *c.* 10; Rove 9 × 12	5	5
150	2125	Clench bolt	Complete flat headed nail, shank slightly bent and squared in section, diamond rove.	Head D 14; Rove 18 × 26; wood T approx. 15	5	5
208	2087	Clench bolt	Complete, full width of wood indicated. Flat head, damaged. Plus small rove mostly complete, narrow rectangular form. Shank bent.	Head 14 × 16; Shank L 19; Rove 18 × 12	5	5
352	2163	Clench bolt	Nail and rove visible on x-ray only.	Rove 30 × 20 × 5; Shank L 15	5	5
226	2087	Clench bolt	Broken shank and squared rove.	Shank L 8; Rove 20 × 20	5	5
318	2218	Clench bolt	Small and square, traces of shank.	20 × 17 × 15	5	5

Table 12.6: (Continued)

SF no.	Context no.	Object type	Description	Dimensions (mm)	Phase	Trench
358	2224	Clench bolt	Small square perforated rove with stump of shank.	Rove 18 × 15 × 5	5	5
361	2163	Clench bolt	Small part of rove remaining with end of shank.	25 × 15 × 8	5	5
138	2119	Clench bolt	Fully concealed in corrosion, small stump of shank with rove/head.	Max 22 × 20 × 15	5	5
351	2163	Clench bolt	2 fragments, one possible square rove.	Rove 16 × 15	5	5
475	2224	Rove	Indeterminate plate fragment, possibly with perforation?	16 × 15 × 3	5	5
347	2163	Rove	Small square perforated plate.	14 × 14 × 5	5	5
179	2156	Rove	Squared with off centre perforation.	20 × 22 × 5	5	5
198	2163	Rove	Large square plate with central perforation.	22 × 25 × 5	5	5
202	2163	Rove	Square, off centre perforation.	25 × 20 × 6	5	5
223	2087	Rove	Rectangular, incomplete, badly corroded. Perforated.	18 × 12 × 3	5	5
280	2173	Rove	Complete, square with central perforation. Large.	25 × 25 × 4	5	5
397	2263	Rove	Large and complete, square with signs of perforation on x-ray only.	30 × 28 × 7	5	5
421	2265	Rove	Large and complete squared, twisted and with central perforation.	31 × 25 × 10	5	5
448	2158	Rove	Small square perforated.	15 × 15 × 3	5	5
402	2261	Rove	Complete square.	24 × 26 × 5	5	5
201	2087	Rove	Squared and with trace of perforation, slightly bent.	21 × 15 × 4	5	5
456	2265	Rove	Amorphous, slight indication on x-ray of central perforation	Overall 20 × 18	5	5
186	2087	Rove strip	Length of plate with three perforations, strip of uncut roves. cf. Goodall 2011, 189, Fig. 9.11, H252.	L 46 × W 14 × T 4	5	5
224	2087	Clench bolt	Flat headed nail/rove and shank. Shank bent.	Shank L 32 × Rove/Head Diam. 22	5	5
277	2087	Clench bolt	Broken shank with hammered end and angled plate/rove (?)	Shank L 8 × Head max 17; wood T max. 8	5	5
387	2224	Clench bolt?	Very amorphous, solid possible clench bolt fragment?	Overall Diam. 22 × 23	5	5
47	2031	Clench bolt	Complete short nail with traces of small square rove and head. Full timber thickness and traces of wood in corrosion products.	Rove: 15 × 15; Head Diam. 15; wood T c. 10	6	5
76	2061	Clench bolt	Small nail with rove, slightly diamond shaped.	Rove 20 × 18	6	5
296	2197	Clench bolt	Section of shank and part of rove.	Rove 20 × 22 × 7. Shank L 14	6	5
102	2092	Clench bolt	Rove and shank, very distorted and indeterminate on x-ray.	Rove 20 x 15. Shank L c. 8	6	5
105	2092	Clench bolt?	Very amorphous, detail obscured by corrosion even on x-ray.	Overall 34 × 20	6	5
130a	2044	Clench bolt	Hollow tapering nail shank and plate fragment.	Overall L 21	7	5

Table 12.6: (Continued)

SF no.	Context no.	Object type	Description	Dimensions (mm)	Phase	Trench
313	2209	Clench bolt	Complete, full width of wood indicated. Flat headed.	Head Diam. 15; Shank/wood T *c.* 10.	7	5
165	2139	Clench bolt	Rove with large and misshapen perforation and shank. Possible repair?	Rove 35 × 22 × 4; Shank L 10	7	5
312	2209	Rove	Complete squared rove with perforation.	24 × 20 × 7	7	3
330	2209	Rove	Rectangular, off centre perforation.	30 × 25 × 5	7	5
87	2045 = 2032	Clench bolt	Diamond rove, flat headed nail and short shank.	Rove 30 × 20 × 2; Head Diam. 20; wood T *c.* 11	8	5
140	2131	Rove	Heavily corroded, x-ray indicates perforation.	17 × 20 × 5	8	5
480	2240	Clench bolt	From residues, sample 63. Bent shank and squared rove.	Rove 20 × 20 × 5; Shank L 22		

L = length, T = thickness, Diam. = diameter

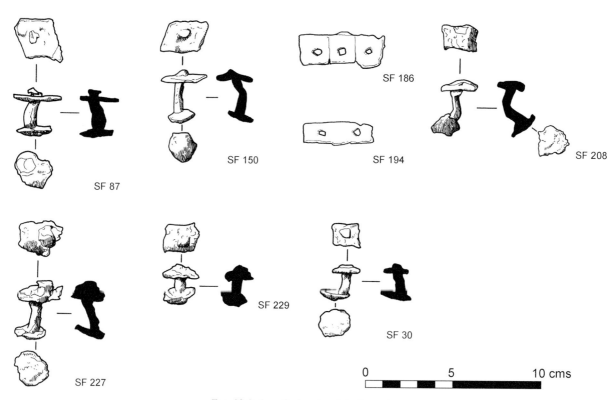

Fig. 12.5: Iron finds: clench bolts and roves

the smaller cases, such as SF 227 (Phase 5) (Fig. 12.5) it may have been part of a chest. The numbers of clench bolts represented here is too small to indicate large scale production, although repair and expedient production can be suggested, especially in Phase 5.

Plate (Table 12.7)

The nine finds of metal plate span from Phases 2 to 7. In all cases they cannot be further distinguished to specific artefact types, and as noted in relation to the clench bolts and nails, it is possible that amongst this small group are pieces that were formally parts of nail heads.

Miscellaneous (Table 12.8)

There are two finds that come into this category, one of which, SF 316 from Phase 5 is indeterminate. SF 166, Phase 7, is a damaged length with a slight curve at one end, more of a hook-form.

Discussion

The ferrous metalwork assemblage is numerically dominated by the large number of nails and clench bolts/roves, which make up 44.10% and 34.20% respectively. The quantity of nails alone is not necessarily indicative of either production or indeed large-scale recycling of wooden timbers. The number of clench bolts/roves is more diagnostic, with 58 identified, spanning all phases but with a marked concentration in Phase 5 (32 out of the 58), and including the two rove strips (SF 194 and 186) (Fig. 12.5) being recovered from two different contexts in that phase. The possible repair of roves is also notable here (SF 72 from Phase 5). This could be interpreted as evidence of production and re-utilisation of timber resources in this phase, although perhaps not numerically large enough to suggest the dismantling or construction of a timber phase.

Amongst the rest of the assemblage, both tools and knives suggest activities within the buildings and in adjacent areas, with the quantity of broken knives of particular note here, presumably discarded rather than repaired. There is strong structural and depositional evidence of smithing at East Mound in Phases 3–5 (Chapter 11, above), and the relatively plentiful use of iron at the settlement for domestic and agricultural tools, domestic building and possible boat-building, was evidently based on a mix of imported, manufactured and recycled objects.

Lead

A single piece of worked lead was recovered from Phase 6 (SF 63). It is an offcut of a lead bar of indeterminate function, but which has been cut at one edge obliquely and broken off at the other. Lead is commonly underrepresented on sites in the Northern Isles, and even where relatively extensive metalwork assemblages are recovered, for example at Quoygrew, Westray, which had 530 iron finds, 33 copper alloy and only two lead pieces, including a simple rolled piece which is suggested as part of a line weight (Rogers *et al.* 2012, 245 and 252). Likewise at the Biggings on Papa Stour, Shetland, just two items were noted, including a whorl and a line weight fragment (Ballin Smith 1999, 171).

Table 12.7: Iron plate

SF no.	Context no.	Object type	Description	Dimensions (mm)	Phase	Trench
176	2146	Plate	Flat and indeterminate	21 × 12 × 4	2	5
287	2105	Plate	Small segment of?plate. Indeterminate	20 × 10 × 3	3	5
399	2263	Plate	5 flat fragments, possibly conjoining	Largest 28 × 10 × 12	5	5
482	2305	Plate	From residues, sample 79. Double thickness plate	20 × 15 × 4	5	5
459	2277	Plate	Heavily corroded, square piece of metal, possible plate?	34 × 31 × 10	5	5
187	2016	Plate	Flat and indeterminate	15 × 12 × 3	5	5
380	2227	Plate	2 fragments. Flat conjoining segments. Indeterminate	Overall 20 × 29	6	5
175	2139	Plate	Length of indeterminate plate of even thickness	35 × 10 × 4	7	5
241	2171	Plate	Flat fragment slightly distorted at one edge, possible perforation visible on x-ray	40 × 38 × 3	7	5

Table 12.8: Miscellaneous iron

SF no.	Context no.	Object type	Description	Dimensions (mm)	Phase	Trench
316	2202	Indeterminate	Dense square-sectioned section.	41 × 15 × 20	5	5
166	2139	Loop	Now broken loop head and adjoining shank possibly squared in section. Long and fragile shank, slightly bent at broader end	L 45 × 4	7	5

L = length, W = width, T = thickness

13

Copper-alloy finds

David Griffiths

Introduction

There are eleven copper-alloy objects from the excavations at Snusgar and East Mound, nine of which are from deposits within or closely related to the longhouse uncovered in Trench 5 (Table 13.1). This total is comparable to that from similar Viking-Late Norse settlement phases of sites in Orkney, especially once the extent and duration of excavations is taken into account. Published catalogues give comparable totals as follows: Pool, Sanday, Phases 7 and 8 (17); Skaill, Deerness, all phases, non-differentiated (23); Beachview, Birsay, Studio Site (10); Quoygrew, Westray, Phases 1 to 2–3 (8), all amounting to around 3% or less of total finds. The Brough of Birsay has produced a higher number (Curle 1982 lists 53 items of 'Bronze' from the 1930s excavations alone, all phases), but this is a specialised site group with an acknowledged pre-Viking tradition of non-ferrous metalworking; it is a distinctive archaeological complex which has undergone significantly more extensive excavation over many decades, so may not be directly comparable to the individual site excavations noted above. These very modest totals indicate that copper-alloy was not a material in large-scale or frequent use in Viking Age and Late Norse Orkney, although it was represented in all of the major and medium-ranking settlements. It tended to be reserved for personal dress ornaments, such as studs, pins, brooches and rings. Some later comb types have copper-alloy rivets (Ashby 2014, 120), but all of the combs with rivets remaining from Snusgar and East Mound use iron, which is more common in the earlier types of Viking comb.

The relative scarcity of copper-alloy may also partly be explained by the fact that as a material it is relatively easy to recycle, although evidence for non-ferrous metalworking is also relatively rare, especially in the Viking/Norse periods. The use of copper-alloy is almost exclusively seen in objects of relatively small physical size, weight and thickness. Within the Snusgar/East Mound assemblage, copper-alloy objects seem to have survived in the ground very well, with items such as the ringed pin (SF 39) bearing little or no trace of corrosion. Other copper-alloy objects are in a more fragmentary state, but this is more likely to be indicative of wear and breakage before they were deposited, rather than of *in situ* corrosion afterwards.

Table 13.1: Copper-alloy finds by trench and phase

SF no.	Context no.	Trench	Phase	Description
01	1506	4	3	Finger ring
375	2224	5	5	Backplate of a disc brooch
446	2263	5	5	Decorated quatrefoil stud
396	2263	5	5	Small strip
451	2285	5	5	Small strip
39	2031	5	6	Ringed pin
256	2164	5	6	Clasp
416	2227	5	6	Curved mount or strip with rivet
218	2164	5	6	Small fragment(s)
349	2228	5	7	V-shaped mount fragment
4002	1002	1	9	Strip with tapered end

Personal/dress items

SF 39, Trench 5, 2031 external surface (Phase 6) (Fig. 13.1)

Ringed pin, intact, with ring still mobile. The head is decorated on both sides with a single incised and tooled rectangular border and a central vertical dividing line producing a simple pattern of two parallel horizontal rectilinear panels. The ring is simple and undecorated, and the shank is also plain; it is bent at a single oblique angle, an apparently deliberate feature, probably done at the manufacturing stage and intended to improve its holding power upon garments. L 114 mm, W (head) 8 mm, T (shank) 3 mm max.

SF 39 conforms to the crutch-headed, stirrup-ringed class identified by Fanning (1994, 41–6) amongst the large number of ringed pins from Dublin. Their distinctive T-shaped head (also seen on many closely-related non-ringed examples) allows a slim semi-circular ring to be attached on tiny pointed tenons at either side, rather than using a heavier, cast circular ring which passes through the head, as in other, generally earlier, sub-groups of the ringed pin type. This example is slightly plainer than most of the examples illustrated by Fanning, and its panel-type head decoration is unusual, with the heads and rings of many Dublin examples being decorated with lines and groups of ring-and-dot motifs. The crutch-headed, stirrup-ringed type was seen by Fanning as a relatively late variant within the Dublin corpus, as none of this group was found in levels that were coin-dated to earlier than the 11th century. Hence this class of ringed pin is normally seen as an 11th to 12th-century variant. A similar pin of this type, with a single panel decorating its head, was found at Pool, Sanday (PL 4483), from Phase 8.2.3, the latest Norse phase on the site (Smith 2007, 437). Other examples of the crutch-headed stirrup-ringed class, together with a similar stick pin (both with ring-and-dot rather than panelled head decoration), have been found at Jarlshof, Shetland (Hamilton 1956, 127), and two examples respectively from Cnip, Uig, Lewis (Close-Brooks 1995, 271–2, Illus. 10, 15 (plain) and 16 (ring-and-dot), both lacking their rings), and from Whithorn (Hill 1997, 369), one of which (7) has a similar incised rectangular decorative panel on the head but inside which is diagonal incised decoration.

The ringed pin, with its long (often, as in this case, characteristically bent) shank and small head and ring, with all its variation is a highly distinctive object, with the

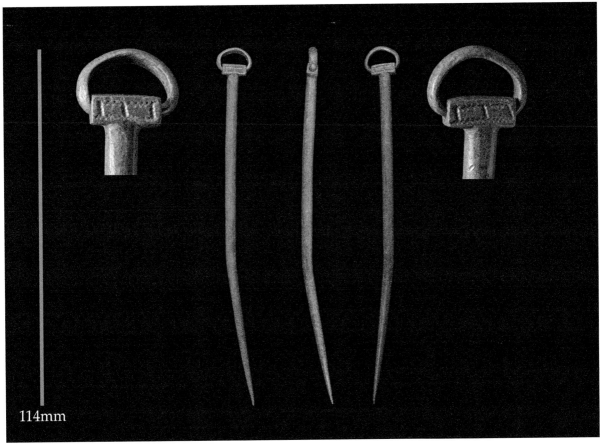

114mm

Fig. 13.1: Ringed pin SF 39

preponderance of find locations principally associated with Ireland, the Irish Sea region and Northumbria. The largest individual concentration of examples, and so far the only indubitable evidence for manufacture, occur in Dublin (263 examples found in excavations between 1962 and 1981), and Thomas Fanning's 1994 Dublin monograph remains the key published source on them. Single examples occur from Scandinavia, across the North Atlantic settlements, to L'Anse aux Meadows in Newfoundland, Canada. In Britain, larger groups occur at towns and trading sites such as York, and Meols (Mainman and Rogers 2000; Griffiths *et al.* 2007), and individual examples are well-represented amongst finds from furnished graves in Orkney, elsewhere in Atlantic Scotland, and in northern England, such as the fine example of the polyhedral-headed type from a furnished grave excavated in 1970–71 at Buckquoy, Birsay (Ritchie 1977, 200). A silver polyhedral-headed ringed pin was amongst the objects in the 1858 Skaill Hoard. Its shank is bent into a fish-hook shape (Graham-Campbell 1995, 117).

SF 375, Trench 5, 2224 longhouse floor (Phase 5) (Fig. 13.2)

Sub-circular backplate of a disc brooch, with a corroded hinge and catchplate for the pin, which is no longer attached, and a worn trace of the support for a pin-lug. The object is worn and was evidently incomplete when deposited. D 30 mm, T 0.5 mm, H (of catchplate) 2 mm.

Viking-Age brooches commonly had a composite form, with an (often openwork) decorative front plate attached to a plain, solid back plate. Circular brooches are normally identified and dated on art-historical grounds based on the decoration on the front, which is missing in this case. Kershaw (2013, 161–2) describes the various ways in which pins were fitted and fastened to clothing, identifying a Scandinavian preference for pin-lug on the right and catchplate on the left. Unfortunately, whilst this piece may conform to this convention, the lack of decorative scheme on the front makes it impossible to be certain which way up the brooch would have been worn.

SF 1, Trench 4, 1506 windblown sand lens within midden (Phase 3) (Fig. 13.2)

Finger ring, complete, with a fine, circular hoop of sub-square cross-section and simple, flat lentoid bezel. The ring is worn and showing evidence for surface corrosion. The hoop has faint ribbing on its outer circumference. D 22 mm, H (bezel) 3 mm, T (hoop) 1 mm.

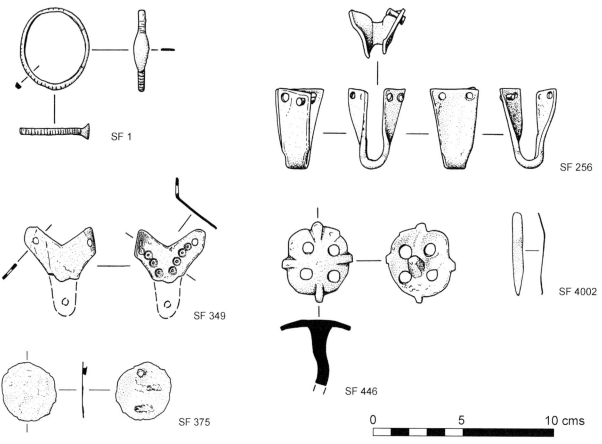

SF 1

SF 256

SF 349

SF 4002

SF 446

SF 375

0   5   10 cms

Fig. 13.2: Copper-alloy finds

The most convincing parallels for such simple ring forms are Roman or mid/late Anglo-Saxon, with the emphasis of probability falling towards the Anglo-Saxon examples. Possible parallels consistent with a Roman date are ribbed finger-rings from Baldock, Hertfordshire (Stead and Rigby 1986, 129, Fig. 54). Anglo-Saxon parallels include a copper-alloy ring dated as 10th–11th century from Thetford, Norfolk (Goodall 1984, Fig. 110, nos 12 and 13), and similar examples reported to the Portable Antiquities Scheme from Buttercrambe-with-Bossall, near York (LVPL-B45BB6), and 'near Stamford Bridge' (YORYM-0248F2). The form, if not the metal, is paralleled by silver Anglo-Saxon rings with bezels bearing Trewhiddle-style motifs, such as those from Flixborough, Lincolnshire (Evans and Loveluck 2009, 27, Fig. 1.11, no. 203) and from Ropley, Hampshire, reported to the Portable Antiquities Scheme (HAMP-C25EF3). It bears little similarity to simple rings of the high medieval period from London (Egan and Pritchard 1991, 331–3) or from Meols (Griffiths *et al.* 2007, 162–3).

Attachments, mounts and compound items

SF 446, Trench 5, 2263 longhouse floor (Phase 5) (Fig. 13.2)

Decorated stud in quatrefoil form. 20 × 19 mm, T (plate) 2 mm, L (rod) 13 mm, T (rod) 3 mm max.

The plate (the part of the object which was intended to be seen) has four symmetrical lobes with drilled round openings (slightly asymmetrically situated), and there are raised barbs mid-way along each of the four outside edges, forming a trilobate appearance on each axis. Traces of gilding suggest the object was once more impressive and perhaps more complex in appearance. The quatrefoil, lobed decorative scheme, although simple, could possibly bear a slight affinity with aspects of the Ringerike Style of the early 11th century, for example as seen on a decorated slab from the City of London (Fuglesang 1980, pl. 54). The plate caps centrally a plain cylindrical rod which forms its attachment, presumably to a leather, metal, or wooden object such as a bridle or scabbard. An object of somewhat similar type was found in a Late Norse longhouse at Sandwick, Unst, Shetland (G. Bigelow, pers. comm.). The Portable Antiquities Scheme in England has recorded several comparable pieces, mostly loosely described as post-medieval, although all are unstratified and found by metal-detectorists. Of these, the closest in appearance, if not quite identical, is HAMP-9005E2, a quatrefoil stud or mount from Soberton, Hampshire.

SF 349, Trench 5, 2228 post-abandonment layer (Phase 7) (Fig. 13.2)

V-shaped fragment of a mount (originally trefoil in shape) decorated with an inconsistent line of eight ring-and-dot motifs, with two attachment holes. W 19 mm, T 0.3 mm. The back is plain. Very thin and with one end folded.

SF 256, Trench 5, 2164 byre floor (Phase 6) (Fig. 13.2)

Clasp formed of a slightly asymmetric bi-concave strip with terminals bent into a U-shape and twisted; each has two attachment holes (one copper-alloy rivet remains). Plain apart from a thin decorative line along the outside edge of the slightly larger of the two heads. W (head 1) 12 mm, W (head 2) 11 mm, H 41 mm, L (rivet) 6 mm, T (rivet) 0.8 mm.

SF 416, Trench 5, 2227 layer of rough flagging in longhouse annex (Phase 6)

Thin, curved bar-shaped mount or strip, with one rivet protruding from its back. Plain. L 20 mm, W 6 mm, T 1 mm.

Simple strips and fragments

SF 4002, Trench 1, 1002 layer beneath topsoil, disturbed (Phase 9) (Fig. 13.2)

Elongated strip with tapered end. L 48 mm, W 4 mm, T 0.4 mm. It may be a strap or lace terminal but if so, is unfinished.

SF 396, Trench 5, 2263 longhouse floor (Phase 5)

Small strip with apparent cut mark on one end. L 18 mm, W 5 mm, T 1 mm.

SF 451, Trench 5, 2285 fill of stone slab storage tank set in longhouse floor (Phase 5).

Strip with hole or notch mid-way. One end is rectangular, the other offcut at an angle. L 21 mm, W 7 mm, T 0.6 mm.

SF 218, Trench 5, 2164 byre floor (Phase 6)

Small fragments of copper-alloy, probably all or part of a small object which has disintegrated in the soil. L (max) 4 mm.

Discussion

The copper-alloy finds include only two complete objects; one well-preserved ringed pin of a fine standard (SF 39), and a finger ring (SF 01). Most of the others are parts of larger objects, or fragmentary. The strips, and broken objects (*e.g.* SF 375) may plausibly indicate that some items were intended for recycling, which may suggest that some non-ferrous metalworking (probably re-working rather than primary smelting) was taking place somewhere in the vicinity (although no metallurgical or structural evidence for this was found in the excavations). SF 4002 and SF 349 are obviously residual by a considerable length of time, and are probably redeposited within the site. SFs 39, 256, 416 and 218 come from contexts within the relatively late occupation Phase 6, so may also be residual or might have been in circulation for a relatively long time, but the rest are plausibly within their original contexts of deposition, or very closely related ones in time. SF01 (the finger ring) comes from Viking-Age Phase 3. The copper-alloy assemblage, with the exception of SF 39, reveals little about the wealth or external contacts of the settlements at Snusgar and East Mound. In all probability, any better-quality non-ferrous items were removed between the end of Phase 6, when the longhouse was turned over to animal use, and its subsequent abandonment in Phase 7.

14

Combs

Steven P. Ashby

Introduction

The combs from the excavations at the Bay of Skaill are an important resource for the writing of narratives for rural and maritime societies in early medieval northern Europe. Furthermore, in the particular context of recent excavations in Viking-Late Norse Orkney and Shetland, the collection is numerically significant, and closely comparable to collections from the sites of Pool, Sanday (Smith 2007b) and Quoygrew, Westray (Ashby and Batey 2012) (Table 14.1). The collection comprises 21 fragments, probably equating to 19–20 combs, though few fragments are large enough to allow cross-matching to be investigated (Table 14.2). All combs and comb fragments are of the single-sided composite type (see Galloway 1976); there are also elements of comb cases, no doubt relating to combs of the same type. Traditionally all the combs and cases would be identified as 'Viking' on morphological grounds; herein they are categorised according to Ashby's (2011) typology. Most are of antler rather than postcranial bone, and there is no clear evidence for the use of non-local species. In the form of two fragments of probable working waste, Trench 1 has revealed some of the first evidence for Viking-Age comb-making in northern Scotland although the rest of the material suggests that the people living at the Bay of Skaill were mainly provisioned with combs from outside their own area. It seems, however, that the source of these was not Norway, but either southern Scandinavia or (more likely) somewhere else in Ireland or the British Isles: the Irish Sea region being their most probable origin.

Below, each of the comb fragments is catalogued, the collection is characterised according to its chronology, and its significance considered in local and regional perspective. The combs are discussed using the terminology of Galloway (1976) and MacGregor (MacGregor 1985; MacGregor *et al.* 1999). Most early-medieval combs were of composite construction, consisting of at least two 'connecting plates' that ran along the length of the comb, and a variable number of 'toothplates' and 'endplates', each of which was riveted in place between the connecting plates. Recent work by the author and others has shown raw materials, comb form, ornament, and the materials and placement of rivets to be regionally and chronologically variable (*e.g.* MacGregor 1985; Riddler 1990; Smirnova 2005; Ashby 2011, 2013a). Where discernible, these phenomena are recorded in the catalogue below. Raw materials are classified as 'bone' or 'antler', and, where possible, to species level, using proteomic techniques (Buckley *et al.* 2009; Van Doorn *et al.* 2011; von Holstein

Table 14.1: Total numbers of comb fragments from selected Viking Age/Late Norse sites in Orkney

Site	Date of excavation (publication)	No. frags/combs
Snusgar/East Mound	2004–10 (this volume)	21/19–20
Brough of Birsay	1934–74 (Curle 1982)	38/ (primarily pre-Norse)
Pool, Sanday	1983–88 (Smith 2007)	/24 (inc. antiquarian finds)
Quoygrew, Westray	1999–2006 (Ashby and Batey 2013)	34/26

Table 14.2: Bone comb material by trench and phase

SF no.	Context no.	Trench	Phase	Description
4004	1017	1	2	Comb endplate
4003	1012	1	5	Piece of worked antler debitage
4006	1012	1	5	Piece of worked antler debitage
4013	1016	1	8	Comb endplate
17	1504	4	3	Comb toothplate
18	1504	4	3	Comb connecting-plate frag.
19	1504	4	3	Comb connecting-plate fragment
20	1504	4	3	Comb toothplate
21	1504	4	3	Comb toothplate
22	1504	4	3	Comb connecting-plate frag.
139	1504	4	3	Comb toothplate and frag. connecting plate
265	2152	5	2	Long plate from comb case
310	2204	5	3	Frag. comb connecting plate
40	2013	5	6	Comb connecting plate frag.
61	2008	5	6	Comb toothplate
64	2008	5	6	Rectilinear piece of bone with remains of 4 iron rivets
83	2061	5	6	Long plate from a comb case
108	2115	5	6	Almost entirely complete single-sided composite comb
182	2063	5	6	Comb frag. connecting plate
364	2225	5	6	Comb toothplate
479	2209	5	7	Frag. comb connecting plate

et al. 2014; see also Ashby 2009; Ashby *et al.* 2015). Where proteomic identification is to 'red deer (*Cervus elaphus*)/roe deer (*Capreolus capreolus*)/fallow deer (*Dama dama*)', roe deer can usually be ruled out on morphological criteria, and it is appropriate to exclude

fallow deer on biogeographic grounds. Thus, red deer is the probable raw material in these cases. Similarly, where proteomic spectra leave 'bovid' as a possible identification, this can be ruled out if the fragment is demonstrably antler on macroscopic grounds.

Catalogue

In the following, measurements are given in millimetres. Raw materials are identified on macroscopic grounds (after techniques described in Ashby 2013b; first trialled in Ashby 2009) and using proteomic protocols (outlined in Buckley *et al.* 2009; Van Doorn *et al.* 2011), successfully trialled on comb material (von Holstein *et al.* 2014; see also Ashby *et al.* 2015). Macroscopic identifications may be: bone/antler/indeterminate, and may be qualified with 'probably' (after O'Connor 1987). Proteomic analyses are listed as: species or groups of species; indeterminate (*i.e.* spectrum cannot be precisely matched with current data) or no spectra (sample produced, no useable data). Tooth gauge, where present, is recorded as n per 1 cm.

SF 4003, Trench 1, 1012 layer internal to longhouse (Phase 5) (Fig. 14.1)

A piece of worked antler debitage, possibly from comb production. The piece is rectangular in profile and section, and appears to have been roughly broken at one end. Proteomic identification: bovid/cervid (*C. elaphus. C. capreolus, or D. dama*). Max W 18 mm, Max H 9 mm Max T 3 mm.

SF 4006, Trench 1, 1012 layer internal to longhouse (Phase 5) (Fig. 14.2)

A piece of worked antler debitage, possibly from comb production. The piece is rectangular in profile with a slightly tapering section (reminiscent of a combtooth

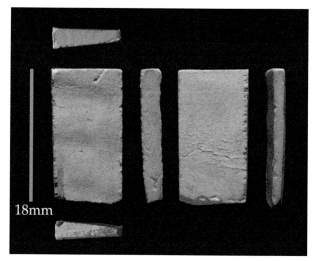

Fig. 14.1: Antler comb-making waste SF 4003

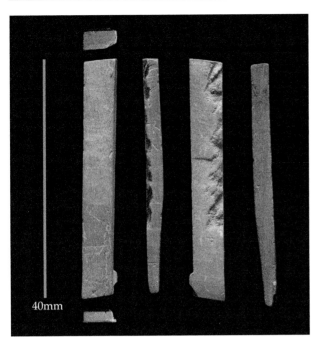

Fig. 14.2: Antler comb-making waste SF 4006

profile), with damage to one face. Proteomic identification: bovid/cervid (*C.elaphus. C.capreolus, or D. dama*). Max W 40 mm, Max H 5 mm, Max T 3 mm.

SF 4013, Trench 1,1016 disturbed layer (Phase 8)

Endplate from a single-sided composite comb. Straight terminals and flat top, graduated teeth. Teeth unbeaded; no obvious striations, square section. Tooth gauge *c.* 5 per cm. Single perforation in upper, outer corner, surrounded by corrosion from iron rivet (now lost). Probably Type 5 or 6. Antler. Macroscopic identification: antler; proteomic identification: no spectra. Max W 17 mm, Max H 31 mm, Max Th 3 mm.

SF 4004, Trench 1, 1017 midden (Phase 2)

Endplate from a single-sided composite comb. Straight terminals and concave top edge, indicating profiled comb back. Graduated teeth. Teeth beaded; no obvious striations, square section. Tooth gauge *c.* 5 per cm. Large perforation in upper, inner corner, with extensive corrosion from iron rivet (now lost). Additional perforation in lower, outer corner, intended for suspension or (more likely) attachment of a case. Probably Type 6. Macroscopic identification: antler; proteomic identification: no spectra. Max W 16 mm, Max H 23 mm, Max T 3 mm.

SF 17, Trench 4, 1504 midden (Phase 3)

Toothplate from a single-sided composite comb. Type unknown. Slightly profiled upper edge, corrosion staining on broken upper edge suggests use of iron rivets on at least one toothplate edge. Teeth are cut obliquely, so that

they run slightly short of vertical. No evidence of beading. Tooth gauge *c.* 4 per cm. Macroscopic identification: antler; proteomic identification: no spectra. Max W 19 mm, Max H 23 mm, Max T 2 mm.

SF 18, Trench 4, 1504 midden (Phase 3) (Fig. 14.3)

Connecting-plate fragment from a single-sided composite comb. Section is subtriangular, reconstructed profile would be plano-convex. Some evidence of toothcuts along lower edge. Evidence of corrosion staining; likely iron rivets. Type 8a, decorated with incised line ornament (paired marginal lines, and grouped vertical lines). Macroscopic identification: antler; proteomic identification: red deer/ roe deer/fallow deer. Max W 22 mm, Max H 10 mm, Max T 2 mm.

SF 19, Trench 4, 1504 midden (Phase 3)

Connecting-plate fragment from a single-sided composite comb. Type 8a, decorated with paired central longitudinal lines, dividing the area into two fields, each of which is filled with ring-and-dot motifs. The ornament is redolent of designs common in the Irish Sea region (see Dunlevy 1988). Macroscopic identification: antler; proteomic identification: indeterminate. Max W 39 mm, Max H 13 mm, Max T 3 mm.

SF 20, Trench 4, 1504 midden (Phase 3)

Toothplate from a single-sided composite comb. Rivet perforation through one edge. Type unknown. Macroscopic identification: antler; proteomic identification: no spectra. Max W 16 mm, Max H 26 mm, Max T 2 mm.

SF 21, Trench 4, 1504 midden (Phase 3)

Toothplate from a single-sided composite comb. Very large perforation through centre of plate, and no evidence of iron-staining. Second perforation through one edge. Tooth gauge *c.* 5 per cm. Teeth striated, but not beaded. Type unknown. Macroscopic identification: antler; proteomic identification: red deer/roe deer/fallow deer. Max W 12 mm, Max H 28 mm, Max T 2 mm.

SF 22, Trench 4, 1504 midden (Phase 3) (Fig. 14.3)

Connecting-plate fragment from a single-sided composite comb. Sub-triangular section, probably plano-convex reconstructed profile. Type 8a, decorated with paired central longitudinal lines, dividing the area into two fields, each of which is filled with ring-and-dot motifs. Traces of iron rivets at either end of fragment, and an additional perforation (diameter 3 mm) crudely placed through middle of decorated area, perhaps suggesting reuse as a mount or similar. Toothcuts decoratively added on lower edge. Macroscopic identification: antler; proteomic identification: indeterminate. Max W 39 mm, Max H 12 mm, Max T 3 mm.

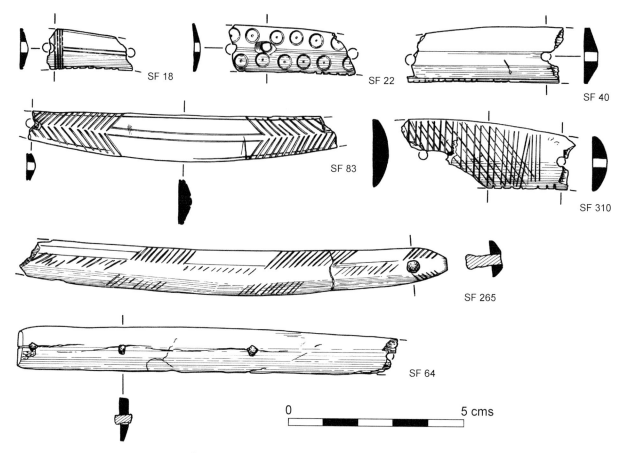

Fig. 14.3: Comb, comb case plates and possible handle

SF 40, Trench 5, 2013 occupation layer external to longhouse (Phase 6) (Fig. 14.3)

Connecting-plate fragment from a single-sided composite comb. Deep plano-convex section, unclear profile. Undecorated. Given the small size of the preserved fragment, its type is unclear, though it is clearly of a relatively gracile, single-sided composite form, and possibilities include Types 8c and 9. There is no evidence of corrosion, so the use of either iron or copper-alloy rivets or bone pegs is possible. Macroscopic identification: antler; proteomic identification: red deer/roe deer/fallow deer. Max L 47 mm, Max W 14 mm, Max T 4 mm.

SF 61, Trench 5, 2008 midden (Phase 6)

Toothplate from a single-sided composite comb. Flat upper and side edges, with rivet perforation through one edge (no evidence of corrosion or staining). Type unknown. Tooth gauge *c.* 5 per cm. Toothbases are heavily beaded and striated, and all teeth are now lost: heavily worn. Macroscopic identification: antler; proteomic identification: no spectra. Max W 25 mm, Max H 14 mm, Max T 3 mm.

SF 64, Trench 5, 2008 midden (Phase 6)

Rectilinear piece of bone, preserving the remains of four iron rivets (three intact) placed along its length. No evidence of toothcut marks. Potentially a plate from a Type 4 riveted mount, though this form is unknown in the Northern Isles, and the use of four rivets on a *c.* 100 mm plate would be unusual. An identification as a plate from a knife or implement handle is perhaps more likely. Macroscopic identification: Postcranial bone, probably a rib from a medium-sized mammal. Proteomic identification: Indeterminate. Max L 108 mm, Max W 12 mm, Max T 2 mm.

SF 83, 2061, Trench 5, external surface (Phase 6) (Fig. 14.3)

Long plate from the case for a single-sided composite comb. Profile is concavo-convex, and cross-section is triangular, mimicking the Type 8a comb form; Decorated accordingly, with paired central longitudinal lines, and grouped opposing obliques (chevrons) close to terminals. Likely for a comb of Type 6. Traces of two iron rivets at either end. Well polished. Macroscopic identification: antler; proteomic identification: red deer/roe deer/fallow deer. Max L 90 mm, Max W 13 mm.

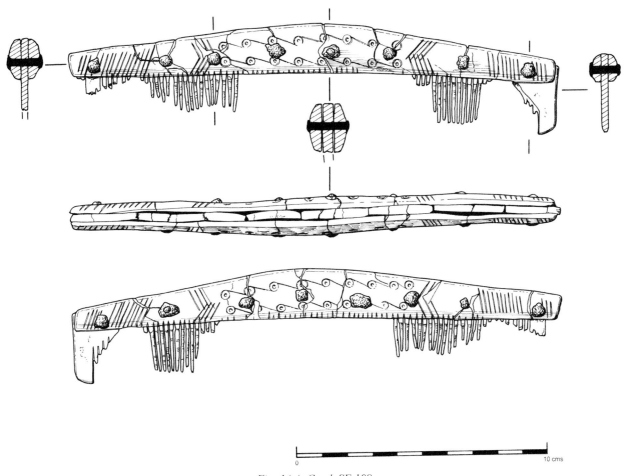

Fig. 14.4: Comb SF 108

SF 108, Trench 5, 2115 floor deposit in ancillary building (Phase 6) (Figs 14.4, 14.5)

Almost entirely complete single-sided composite comb. Type 8a, decorated with scrolling ring-and-dot motifs, incised line, and chevron motifs. The two connecting plates are decorated in identical fashion. Two lines of interconnected ring-and-dots form a sort of primitive guilloche that runs across the central portion of the plate, bounded at each end by a group of 3–4 opposing knife-cut obliques. The terminals are decorated with a wide group of knife-cut incisions, some of which are oblique, others approaching the vertical. There are eight iron rivets, apparently arranged ornamentally. The teeth are very worn, with significant beading, breakage, and loss, and there are irregular toothcut marks along the underside of both connecting plates. Macroscopic identification: antler; proteomic identification: red deer/ fallow deer. One may exclude fallow deer on grounds of historical biogeography. Max L 192 mm, Max W 36 mm, Max T 13 mm.

The general impression is of a professionally produced but rather roughly decorated comb. The nicely arranged

Fig. 14.5: Comb SF 108 in situ *as found*

ring-and-dot motifs appear somewhat at odds with the rough knife-cut incisions. The comb is clearly an ornate variant of the Type 8a form common in 10th-century Ireland (Dunlevy 1988), England (MacGregor 1985, 90; Ashby 2011) and, to some extent, the southern Baltic (*e.g.* Cnotliwy 1973; 2013). The ornamental use of iron rivets might suggest its production by a craftworker familiar with Scandinavian Type 9 combs, and their decorative employment of copper alloy rivets. Strings of ring-and-dot motifs connected by tangential obliques do seem to be more common on combs of Types 8a and 8b than on other Viking-Age forms, and examples are known from York (MacGregor *et al.* 1999), though there are none there that precisely match the arrangement seen on SF 108. Neither is the design well-represented in Pictish art (c.f. Curle 1982; Porter 1997). In Ireland, the design has its origin in pre-Norse material culture, and persists into the Viking Age, where it is a recognisable feature of Type 8a and 8b combs (Dunlevy 1988, *passim*). In terms of ornament, there are some close parallels from Atlantic Scotland: two Type 9 combs from Sandwick Unst (ARC 654.94) and Phase V at Jarlshof (1958.1096) feature very similar rudimentary strings of ring-and-dot motifs, as does a fragment of a (probable) Type 8 comb from North Uist (NMS GT 1037). The comb then, is something of an enigma: it clearly dates to the 10th or 11th centuries, but its geography is unclear. It displays form and technology consistent with a comb produced in Britain, Ireland, or the southern Baltic, while simultaneously echoing the aesthetics of northern and western Scandinavian combs. Anecdotally then, the comb supports an idea first suggested by the author (Ashby 2006, 234–6; see also Ashby 2015): that Type 8 combs may be a southern and western response to the popularity of the Scandinavian Type 9 comb.

The comb was discovered in a context sealed from above by a flagstone, carefully laid flat on compacted ashy floor, in conjunction with an iron candlestick (SF 109), three glazed whiteware pottery sherds (SFs 107, 110, 111) and part of a whetstone (SF 113). Given the apparent late date of the whiteware pottery (Chapter 20), it is possible that this interesting group was a 'closing deposit' (the comb by then being an heirloom of perhaps a century or more in age), possibly marking the point when human occupation of the building complex ceased (see Chapter 25).

SF 139, Trench 4, 1504 midden (Phase 3)

Toothplate and fragment of connecting plate from a single-sided composite comb. Rivet perforation through one edge. Decorated with groups of incised vertical lines. Teeth appear tapered; light beading. Comb type unknown. Macroscopic identification: antler; proteomic identification: no spectra. Max W 9 mm, Max H 23 mm, Max T 8 mm.

SF 182, Trench 5, 2063 external surface (Phase 6)

Fragment of connecting plate from a single-sided composite comb of unknown type. It features a line of three small, unconnected ring-and-dot motifs. No evidence of riveting. Type unknown. Macroscopic identification: antler; proteomic identification: no spectra. Max W 9 mm, Max H 13 mm, Max T 2 mm.

SF 265, Trench 5, 2152 midden (Phase 2) (Fig. 14.3)

Comb case: a long plate (largely complete) from the case for a single-sided composite comb. Profile is concavo-convex, and cross-section is trapezoidal, mimicking the Type 8b comb form. Decorated accordingly, with chequerboard pattern made up of fields of oblique lines within longitudinal guidelines. Probably for a comb of Type 6. Traces of an iron rivet at one end, and staining at the other. Macroscopic identification: antler; proteomic identification: red deer/roe deer/fallow deer. Max L 125 mm, Max W 13 mm, Max T 3 mm.

SF 310, Trench 5, 22\04 midden (Phase 3) (Fig. 14.3)

Fragment of connecting plate from a single-sided composite comb. The fragment is of plano-convex section, and features a field of incised cross-hatch, bordered by grouped vertical lines. The object is unusual within this collection; the only example from Skaill of this form and ornament. Probably Type 7. Some evidence of iron staining at one end. Very abraded surface. Macroscopic identification: antler; proteomic identification: red deer/ roe deer/fallow deer. Max L 52 mm, Max W 17 mm, Max T 4 mm.

SF 479, Trench 5, 2209 disturbed layer of wall fill (Phase 7)

Fragment of connecting plate from a single-sided composite comb. The fragment is of slightly faceted subtriangular section, and features a central longitudinal line, flanked on either side by lines of ring-and-dot motifs. Probably Type 8a. Some evidence of iron staining at one end. Macroscopic identification: antler; proteomic identification: indeterminate. Max L 18 mm, Max W 7 mm, Max T 2 mm.

SF 364, Trench 5, 2225 deposit internal to longhouse (Phase 6)

Toothplate from a single-sided composite comb. Iron rivet with corrosion halo at one edge. Highly polished. Type unknown. All teeth complete and intact, but highly beaded; very worn. Macroscopic identification: probably bone; proteomic identification: indeterminate. Max W 17 mm, Max H 31 mm, Max T 3 mm.

Discussion

As a whole, the Bay of Skaill assemblage makes an important addition to the corpus of combs from Atlantic Scotland, and provides a useful 'fingerprint' for a mid-/ high-status Viking-Age settlement in the region. The

Table 14.3: Combs and comb fragments from Bay of Skaill excavations by type (Ashby 2011)

Type	5	6	7	8 (8a)	9	11	12	13	14	Case	Unknown	Other	Total
N (frags)	1	2	1	3	0	0	0	0	0	1	13	1 (non-comb)	21

combs are generally of middling quality of workmanship, and on typological grounds date primarily to the 10th and 11th centuries AD. Interestingly, few examples are well paralleled in western or northern Scandinavia, and the closest analogies come from England, Ireland, southern Scandinavia and the south coast of the Baltic, though most of the combs are too fragmentary to precisely characterise or parallel.

Table 14.3 lays out the site's type profile, using Ashby's (2011) classification, which grew out of multivariate analysis of hundreds of combs from northern England, Scotland, and Scandinavia (see, for example, Ashby 2009). The most common comb form at Skaill is probably Type 8, though there are also probable examples of Type 7, and while a number cannot be closely typed, many of these were identified as most likely Type 8a. The presence of comb cases, frequently associated with comb Type 6, and not common in Orkney (though see Batey and Morris 1992), may also be significant. In this regard it is also noteworthy that the furnished grave found to the west of Skara Brae in 1888 also contained a Type 6 comb with a case: an unusual set of equipment for a Viking burial in Orkney (Chapter 22). It is interesting to note the apparent absence of the pre-Viking Types 11, 12, and 1c; the early Viking (9th–early 10th century) Type 5 (just one possible example), and the Late Norse (latest 10th–12th century) Type 9. Neither are later medieval types (13, 14b) represented. The finds are thus consistent with the site being occupied in the 10th and 11th centuries, and the patterning of finds across phases offers some support to the overall site chronology.

Table 14.4 summarises the stratigraphic distribution of the combs. Most were recovered from Phases 3 (10th to early/mid-11th century) and 5 (11th to mid-12th century), with residual material in later phases. It should also be noted that most of the material comes from Trenches 1, 4 and 5, the only concentration is from midden layer 1504 in Trench 4. Few of the combs are complete, and most are heavily fragmented, having been recovered predominantly from middens, floors and disturbed contexts. The single find from a protected, sealed context (SF 108) is substantially complete.

A brief aside on SF 108 is justified. This comb is most closely paralleled by examples from elsewhere in Atlantic Scotland, which might suggest an insular point of manufacture and ornament. Certainly, neither the form of the comb nor the crude knife-cut ornament is typically Norwegian, though the scrolling ring-and-dot motifs are

Table 14.4: Distribution of comb types by phase at the Bay of Skaill (number of fragments)

Type (Ashby 2011) Phase	5	6	7	8a	Cases	Unknown
1 (pre-Viking)	0	0	0	0	0	0
2 (late 9th–early 11th century)	0	1	0	0	1	0
3 (10th–early/mid 11th century)	0	0	1	3	0	4
4 (mid–end 11th century)	0	0	0	0	0	0
5 (11th–mid-12th century)	0	0	1	0	0	0
6 (late 11th–12th century)	0	0	0	0	1	5
7 (mid 12th–13th century)	0	0	0	1	0	1

consistent with work seen in western Scandinavia. The comb's ornament is not well paralleled in the southern Baltic (see Cnotliwy 1973; 2013; Tempel 1970; 1979), and an origin somewhere in Britain and Ireland, perhaps on the coasts of the Irish Sea, does seem most likely.

The combs from the excavations feature iron rather than copper-alloy rivets, but fragmentation meant that detailed study of rivet placement was rarely feasible. Nonetheless, one may observe that three of the four loose toothplates feature rivet perforations and/or staining on only one edge, which at least suggests that the 'alternating edge' model frequently encountered in Viking-Age Britain, Ireland (Ashby 2005) is represented here (the other plate is centrally riveted). The absence of copper-alloy rivets is striking, given that the site's life extends through the 11th century, a time at which copper-alloy riveted combs become popular across the majority of Scandinavian settlements in the North Atlantic.

The combs are, as a whole, manufactured with proficiency, though few ornate examples are present. The level of fragmentation also precludes any detailed study of patterning in tooth beading and use wear, but it suffices to say that where evidence is present, it is consistent with regular use.

Comb-making debris, blanks, or semi-manufactures are largely unknown from Viking Age and medieval sites in the Northern Isles (c.f. Ashby and Batey 2012), suggesting that the majority of the combs used were brought in from beyond Orkney, either as carried possessions or as imports (von Holstein *et al.* 2014). In this context, finds SFs 4003 and 4006 are of note, as they constitute such meagre evidence of manufacture as we have from Orkney. In such small quantities the evidence is equivocal, but nonetheless tantalising. Were manufacture/repair activities taking place at Snusgar? If so, this is significant, as direct evidence for comb manufacture in early medieval Scotland is extremely rare. The best known example comes from Mound 2A at Bornais, South Uist, but this is a relatively small deposit, interpreted by the excavator as residue of the activities of an itinerant artisan. Moreover, close dating of adjacent stratigraphic levels demonstrate that the deposit was quickly built up in the later phases of activity on the site: sometime in the 14th century (Smith 2004; Sharples pers. comm.). There is also evidence at the pre-Viking site of Traigh Bostadh, Lewis (Neighbour and Burgess 1996), for which we await full publication.

Table 14.5: Results of ZooMS raw material analysis

SF no.	Type	Species
4003	–	Bovid/cervid (red/roe/fallow)
4006	–	Bovid/cervid (red/roe/fallow)
18	8a	Cervid (red/roe/fallow)
19	8a	Indeterminate
21	Unknown	Cervid (red/roe/fallow)
22	8a	Indeterminate
40	Unknown	Cervid (red/roe/fallow)
83	Case	Cervid (red/roe/fallow)
108	8a	Indeterminate
115	Unknown	Bos
265	Case	Cervid (red/roe/fallow)
310	7	Cervid (red/roe/fallow)
364	Unknown	Indeterminate
479	?8a	Indeterminate

Thus, while the quantity of evidence from Skaill is small, its presence is potentially significant. Found in Trench 1 midden layers associated with the longhouse on Snusgar, these two fragments of probable red deer antler – one a surface offcut, the other a waste section produced when working a toothplate billet – may point to either a more substantial deposit outside the limits of the excavation, or alternatively the actions of a small-scale (possibly travelling?) artisan.

The observation that manufacture was rare in Atlantic Scotland is supported by patterning in raw material analysis; the majority of the combs are of antler, a material thought to be in poor supply in mid-Viking Age Orkney (Mulville 2015; Table 14.5).

While the fragments were not identifiable to species on macroscopic grounds, ZooMS analysis and interpretation allowed us to ascertain that most – including comb SF 108, the complete example – were made of red deer antler. The absence of reindeer antler here, so common on other sites in the region (see von Holstein *et al.* 2014) suggests that wherever these combs were made, it was not in western Scandinavia. Given the lack of evidence for manufacture in Orkney, one might suppose an origin somewhere in the southern Baltic or, more likely in the British Isles: a good candidate might again be the Irish Sea region. Whether these combs reached the Bay of Skaill as imports or in the hands of settlers, we are seeing a society that did not look solely east to Norway, but also maintained contacts to the south and west.

Together then, raw material, form, and manufacturing technique seem to speak of connections with parties other than those in western Scandinavia, where copper-alloy riveted Type 9 combs were the norm (see Wiberg 1987; Flodin 1989; Hansen 2005). Such a connection is interesting, as it sets the site rather apart from other broadly contemporary sites in the region (*e.g.* Quoygrew, Westray; Pool, Sanday; the Brough of Birsay; and Skaill, Deerness) (Ashby and Batey 2012; Smith 2007b; Curle 1982; Porter 1997; see Table 14.6).

Was this a distinctive population, tied into a different social and economic network? Or might it simply reflect the absence of later and post-Viking Age phases of activity?

Table 14.6: Comparative numbers of 'Viking-Age' and 'medieval' combs by type (including small fragments) from sites in Orkney

	Type 5	Type 6	Type 7	Type 8a	Type 8b	Type 8c	Type 9	Type 13	Type 14b	Total
Snusgar/E Mound	1	1+1 (2)	1	3	0	0	0	0	0	12
Brough of Birsay	2	0	0	0	1	0	1	0	0	4
Pool	7	0	0	0	2	0	2	3	1	15
Quoygrew	0	2	0	2	0	4	7	1	1	17

Data collated from Ashby (2006: drawing on Curle 1982; Smith 2007b, and updated using Ashby and Batey 2012)

Perhaps what we are picking up here is chronological variability that relates to wider social dynamics in the Northern Isles; perhaps the material culture of the early part of the Orcadian Viking Age was less dominantly 'Norse' than has been argued in previous work, with the distinctive Scandinavian signature only really becoming clear from the later 10th or 11th centuries (Chapter 1, above). It is difficult to be sure, as so many of Orkney's early excavations suffered from serious stratigraphic confounds, while there are similarities between the 10th-century combs (*e.g.* Type 8) of England, Ireland, northern continental Europe, and southern Scandinavia. Nonetheless, the absence of forms common in later 10th and 11th-century western Scandinavia is genuine and significant, and it would be interesting to assess whether the pattern is replicated in other forms of material culture at Skaill, and at other recently excavated Viking-Age sites, such as Pool, Sanday.

Summary

The majority of the combs catalogued here fall into Types 8a and 8b; making a marked contrast with the situation seen at a generally later date at Quoygrew, Westray, where the comb collection appears to suggest a mixed, but dominantly Scandinavian-facing society (Ashby and Batey 2012). Type 8 is entirely represented by Type 8a, pointing to a date in the 10th and 11th centuries, rather than the 11th and 12th. Moreover, the presence of Type 8 combs, together with possible examples of Types 6 and 7 and associated cases, is likely indicative of contact with Ireland, the Irish Sea or the Western Isles at this time.

The absence of pre-Viking Age and early Viking Age Types 1c, 5, 11 and 12 is clearly consistent with the site's mid-Viking Age to medieval date on other

criteria, while the absence of Type 9 is unusual for a 10th/11th-century site in the North Atlantic region. The lack of evidence among the combs for direct contact with western Scandinavia, and the absence of Types 9 and 13 is striking, particularly given the fact that other sites in northern Scotland (*e.g.* Freswick Links, see Batey 1987; the Brough of Birsay, Curle 1982; Pool, Sanday, Smith 2007b; Skaill, Deerness, Porter 1997; Jarlshof, Hamilton 1956; Quoygrew, Ashby and Batey 2012) have yielded significant numbers of Type 9 combs. To provide an example, at Quoygrew, the presence of Type 9 combs – manufactured in Oslo, Trondheim, or, more probably, Bergen – was interpreted as evidence of long-distance trade with western Scandinavia; the inhabitants of the farm were exporting bulk goods such as butter, grain, and stockfish in exchange for the trappings of an elite (or sub-elite) Scandinavian lifestyle – Eidsborg hones, steatite bakestones, and antler combs. In contrast, the Snusgar/ East Mound assemblage appears to be looking westward, and was perhaps trading its collected resources for combs manufactured in an Irish milieu. It is even possible that combs were being made – or at least repaired – close to the site. This tells us much; it suggests that both the economic and social context of life at the site had an important Irish Sea component.

Of course, it would be simplistic to attempt to use the comb remains in isolation to understand long range trade and contact. Rather, the distributions of this particular form of artefact arise from particular contexts of contact and interaction, and must be interpreted alongside other forms of material and environmental evidence. Nonetheless, the findings are evocative, and when studied in this fashion, may allow the reconstruction of local, regional and long-range networks of communication and trade.

15

Worked bone

Colleen E. Batey

The preservation conditions at the Bay of Skaill excavations are such that bone work has survived in excellent condition, and as indicated below there is a wide range of artefact types to be discussed. The sandy matrix, mixed in many cases with rich midden debris, elicits close comparison with other northern Scottish coastal sites, most particularly Pool on Sanday, Orkney, and Freswick Links in Caithness. In due course, when the full published records are released, the excavations undertaken in North and South Uist (Western Isles) at The Udal, Bornais, and Cille Pheadair will be available to be fully integrated into these discussions. Combs are covered in Chapter 14.

Bone toggles (Table 15.1) (Fig. 15.1)
Three of the five perforated pig metapodial bones are from Phase 7, a disturbed horizon in and around the longhouse/byre in Trench 5 (SFs 133, 300, 304), another is unstratified (SF 294) and the final example, SF 36, is from midden deposit 1504 (Phase 3). This is a common artefact, usually termed a 'toggle' which could imply a button-like function, but a viable alternative identification is as a child's toy, a 'buzz-bone'. The additional trimming, as on SF 300 or the off-centre perforation as in SF 36, may have been in turn aesthetic modification or functional improvement, and do not assist with an identification of the function of these complete finds. Examples from Scandinavia have been discussed in relation to material from Århus in Denmark (e.g. Andersen et al. 1971, 196–7) and from Northern Scotland from Jarlshof, Shetland (Hamilton 1956, 146, nos 61–3) and Freswick Links, Caithness (Batey 1987, 229), from contexts spanning the 10th to the 12th centuries.

Table 15.1: Bone toggles

SF no.	Context no.	Description	Dimensions (mm)	Phase	Trench
133	2127	Complete metapodial bone with mid point circular perforation through full thickness	L 60 × W 15 max; perf. Diam. 4	7	5
294	Unstrat	Complete metapodial bone with mid point circular perforation through full thickness. Weathered surface	L 54 × W 14 max; perf. Diam. 5	US	5
300	2208	Complete metapodial bone with mid point circular perforation through full thickness. One end cut flat and length has light paring	L 49 × W 13 max; perf. Diam. 5 (oval)	7	5
304	2209	Complete metapodial bone with mid point circular perforation through full thickness. Slight chip at one end	L 60 × W 14 max; perf. Diam. 5	7	5
36	1504	Complete metapodial bone with slightly off-centre medial circular perforation	L 48 × W 15 max; perf. Diam. 9	3	4

L = length, W = width, perf. = perforation, Diam. = diameter

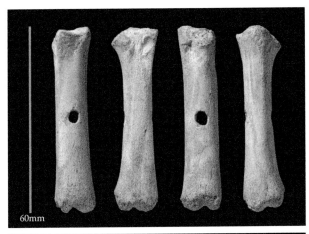

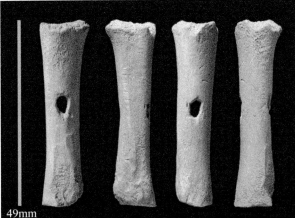

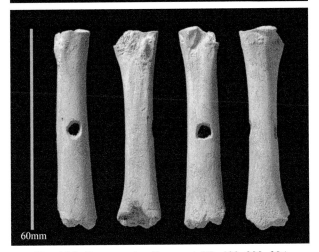

Fig. 15.1: Bone toggles (from top) SFs 133, 300, 304

Femur-head whorls (Table 15.2) (Fig. 15.2)

There are two finds of femur head whorls in this assemblage, one (SF 295) from Phase 7 (dated to the 12th–13th century) and the other (SF 4031) probably from an original context within the longhouse from Phase 3 dated to the 10th–11th centuries. Both are cut from cattle femur heads, with SF 295 being from a partially fused bone, the illustrations show clearly that the drilled perforation in each case is not of the characteristic hourglass form, but simply drilled from one side only. Walton Rogers notes in relation to the finds from 16–22 Coppergate, York (where 56 such whorls were identified) that the average diameter is between 35–48 mm and only a little larger than the Anglo-Scandinavian stone whorls from the site (Walton Rogers 1999, 1964–1965). Predominantly dating from the 10th–11th centuries, there are later examples recovered in more disturbed contexts at that site, a situation apparently mirrored here. These are indicative of domestic textile manufacture on site. This is a commonly identified find type, and for example at Freswick Links, Caithness, 37 examples were discussed (Batey 1987, 224–5, pl. 32 C) and a wide date range is recognised, from the Iron Age to the 13th century.

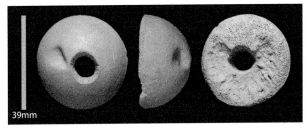

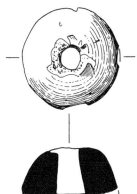

Fig. 15.2: Bone femur-head whorls SFs 295, 4031

Table 15.2: Bone femur-head whorls

SF no.	Context no.	Description	Dimensions	Phase	Trench
295	2193	Complete, slightly eccentric roundperforation and partially trimmed based, rest is unfused. Slight natural depression adjacent to perforation	Diam. 39; H 19 max; perf. D 12	7	5
4031	1023	Complete with slight chipping on lower edge and damage around central perforation	Diam. 40; H 17; perf. D 8	3	1

Diam. = diameter, H = height, perf = perforation, D = depth

Table 15.3: Bone needlecase

SF no.	Context no.	Description	Dimensions (mm)	Phase	Trench
4024	1021	Complete length of bird bone, with cut ends and 2 medial perforations	L 76 × Diam. 8; perfs 4 × 4 and 4 × 3	3	1

L = length, Diam. = diameter, perf. = perforation

Table 15.4: Bone panel/mount

SF no.	Context no.	Description	Dimensions (mm)	Phase	Trench
115	2004	Rectangular section of cortical bone with three perforations roughly along midline, two at opposing ends and oneoff-centre. All marked by iron staining reflecting rivet positions. One narrow end is damaged at perforation. Undecorated mount applied with iron rivets	L 69 × W 21× T 1	7	5

L = length, W = width, T = thickness

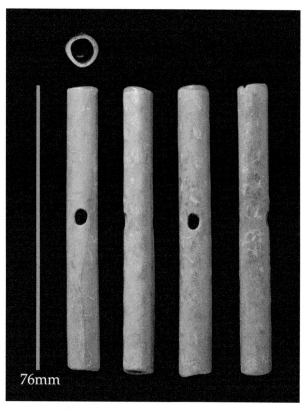

76mm

Fig. 15.3: Bone needle case SF 4024

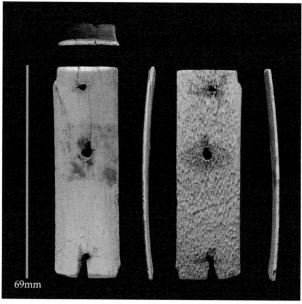

69mm

Fig. 15.4: Bone mount SF 115

Needlecase (Table 15.3) (Fig. 15.3)

The section of trimmed bird wing ulna (possibly goose), SF 4024 was recovered from Phase 3 in Trench 1, in an internal longhouse deposit dated to the 10th–11th centuries. Designed to enable needles to be rolled in fabric and then secured via the opposing perforations within the bone case, these items are most commonly found in grave contexts. Examples are noted from Cnip, Lewis (Welander

et al. 1987, 157), Càrn a' Bharraich, Oronsay (illustrated in Graham-Campbell and Batey 1998, 7.2, 117) and Pool (Smith 2007b, 502, illus 8.8.21).

Mount (Table 15.4) (Fig. 15.4)

with Steven P. Ashby

SF 115 was found in Trench 5, Phase 6. It is a piece of worked cortical bone, cut from the split rib of a medium/large mammal, with bevelled terminal edges (suggesting that the piece is complete), and three perforations along its centre line. There is evidence of iron corrosion around these perforations, suggesting that they are rivet holes, and a 15 mm wide rectangular zone of corrosion lies around the central perforation, perhaps suggesting that there was originally a larger metal component (a plate of some kind?) present. The piece has a flattened section, and appears to have been used as some form of mount or fitting. Proteomic identification: cattle.

Although hard to date specifically on the basis of the simple form, a number of comparable riveted mounts have been noted from Coppergate, York (MacGregor *et al.* 1999, Fig. 912, 1953) where they are concentrated in contexts of the mid 10th–mid 11th century. The specific function is unclear, although there is potential for this to have an industrial or craft function. An earlier close parallel, but using bone pegs rather than iron, is from Iron Age deposits at the Broch of Burrian, Orkney (MacGregor 1975, 78, find 131).

Pins and needles (Fig. 15.5)

This section has been sub-divided into two in the attached catalogue. Pins are defined as either being perforated at the head or unperforated, and of a form which would not be usable as a needle due to the marked expansion of the head in relation to the shank. Here, needles are distinguished by having a perforation but crucially a head which is streamlined to the shank. These categories form numerically the largest part of the worked bone assemblage here considered.

Pins without perforations (Table 15.5)

There are fifteen individual pins which fall clearly into this category. Of these, seven were recovered from phases dated to the 9th–10th centuries, one unfinished example from the 10th–11th centuries, six from the period 11th–12th centuries and one from disturbed Phase 7. Of the two examples which are in the process of manufacture (SF 4025 from Phase 3 and SF 177 from Phase 4) it is assumed that these are local productions, made of readily available bone fragments. Two others have indeterminate head forms (SF 4022, Phase 2; SF 359, Phase 5) and further comment cannot be made. A further six pin/needle tips are also classed as indeterminate, adding simply to the overall numbers within the two combined categories here discussed. Despite the variety of head forms, the overall lengths of virtually all the pins mark them out as Viking Age rather than pre-Viking, and this is confirmed by the lack of hipped modification of the shafts.

There is a single find of crutch-headed form, SF 4029 from Phase 2, which it is currently not possible to match to other published assemblages. However, the flat-headed type, sometimes called nail-headed, is more commonly found, and there are four in this group. Assemblages from Pool on Sanday (Smith 2007b, illus 8.8.9 *e.g.* PL 0006, 478–9) and from Quoygrew, Westray (Ashby and Batey 2012, Fig. 13.5, 241) have provided close parallels here from Norse contexts.

The ball-headed (or spherical-headed) pin, SF 106 from Phase 6, is of a type which has particularly good longevity. With similar examples spanning all periods from the Roman period into beyond the 10th century, but this example is similar to one from York, Coppergate find number 6824, which is described as 'unusually substantial' (MacGregor *et al.* 1999, Fig. 907, finds 1948–9).

The spatulate form of pinhead, marked by a splaying of the head, is a distinctive form. There are five examples in this group, spanning Phases 2 to 7. In the case of SF 4026 from Phase 2, dated to the 9th–10th centuries it also has some simple dot decoration on one flat face which was designed to be visible during use. The further elaboration of the splayed head has been noted at a number of other sites, including Quoygrew (Ashby and Batey 2012, Fig. 13.5, Test Pit Find 1983) and this has strong Scandinavian parallels. SF 344 is likely to be made of walrus ivory and has incised lines beneath the splayed head. A shorter ivory pin with simpler head has been recorded from an early context at the Earl's Bu, Orphir, Orkney (Small find 2487, Phase K), and is indicative of the introduction of walrus ivory into the region.

Perforated pinheads (Table 15.6)

The spatulate type of pinhead is similar to those which are perforated and a combination of punched decoration, as in SF 4035 from Phase 3 or for SF 301 from Phase 7 which seems likely to have had a double perforation at its head, although there is extensive damage at that area, seem to be cognate items. Smith discusses this pin form in relation to Pool, and there is a double-perforated pin illustrated (Smith 2007b, 480–1, illus 8.8.10, PL 0035), although unfortunately it is an unstratified find.

Needles (Table 15.6)

There are five pieces that have been identified as needles, with one from a disturbed context in Phase 7, the date range on site is essentially from the 10th to the 12th century. These examples have perforated heads which are streamlined to the shaft, commonly for more open-weave fabrics, although SF 114 is very finely made and of narrow gauge, seemingly broken at the perforation. SF 161 is a small pin with a round head dominated by a large perforation, and classed here as a needle. However, it is worth noting that the same form was distinguished by Smith at Pool as a ring-head pin, although actually longer than the SF 161 example, it also shows very slight hipping and suggests a Pictish date (Smith 2007b, 482–3, illus. 8.8.11, PL 2388). The presence of needles does however unite this part of the assemblage with the femur head whorls and the needle case discussed above and demonstrates domestic textile making activities

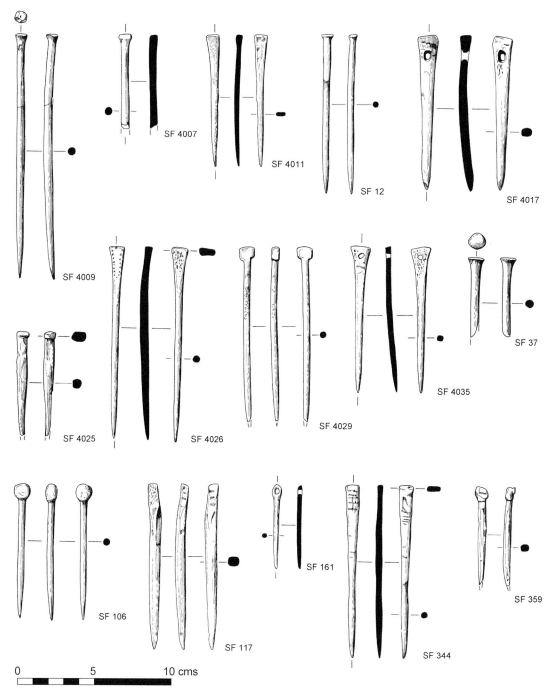

SF 4007

SF 4011

SF 12

SF 4017

SF 4009

SF 4025

SF 4026

SF 4029

SF 4035

SF 37

SF 106

SF 117

SF 161

SF 344

SF 359

0   5   10 cms

Fig. 15.5: Bone and ivory pins

Miscellaneous worked bone (Table 15.7)
(Fig. 15.6)

Within this category of seven finds, one (SF 4001) is considered to be relatively modern and identified as a bone/worn ivory cutlery handle, from the latest phase. Fragments of longbone with cut marks, such as SF 4005 or SF 188 may have served as simple chopping surfaces, although SF 188 was originally perforated and SF 156

is flat and tapering and of uncertain function. SF 478 is a worked bone point, of ubiquitous form and function, although having been found on the byre floor in Trench 5, may have acted in this capacity. It is clearly homemade. SF 94 is a multi-perforated sheep scapula from Phase 6. The perforations are sub-square in form and form a loose row of three down the centre, with other smaller random holes. It shows apparent signs of gnawing at the proximal

Table 15.5: Bone pins

SF no.	Context no.	Type	Description	Dimensions (mm)	Phase	Trench
4007	1017	Flat headed	Upper section of approximately half of long pin with polished surface. Head is irregular and follows form of knuckle, otherwise is trimmed and flat	L 57 × Head Diam. max 12	2	1
4011	1012	Spatulate head	Complete small fibula (?) shank, tip intact and splayed head trimmed on upper edge.	L 81 × Head W max 7 × T 2	5	1
344	2225	Spatulate head	Complete long pin with spatulate trimmed head. Polished light-coloured bone. Very slight expansion/hipping towards tip. Incised lines beneath expanded head	L 106 × Head W max 8 × T 3	6	5
37	1545	Flat headed	Upper part of flat headed pin, weathered and signs of ossicles beneath head which is complete except for slight chip on one edge	L 48 × Head Diam. max 10	2	4
106	2004	Ball headed	Complete mid-sized ball headed pin. Polished surface and traces of ossicles on head surface	L 82 × Head Diam. max 10 × 7	6	5
4026	1017	Spatulate head	Complete long pin with dot design (17 dots) profiling the spatulate head on one face. Polished along length	L 119 × Head W max 10 × T 3	2	1
359	2232	Indeterminate head	Complete short pin with incompletely worked head, crudely worked. Pared shank	L 59 × Head W max 11 × 10	5	5
12	1519	Flat headed	Complete long pin with flat, nail-from head, of slightly irregular form. Polished along full length	L 95 × Head W max 10	4	4
4029	1045	Crutch headed	Complete long pin with slight chipping at tip. Flat crutch-form head	L 108 × Head W max 10 × T 9	2	1
4025	1023	Unfinished	Crudely worked flat-headed pin with broken tip. Damaged cortical area towards head end	L 64 × Head W max 8	3	1
322	2208	Spatulate head	Expanded head is broken, full length and tip complete. Very fine bone, slightly curved	L 83 × Head W 9	7	5
266	2152	Spatulate head	Expanded head is broken, full length and tip complete, crudely made, squared section	L 82 × Head Diam. Max 9	2	5
4022	1017	Indetermin-ate head	Complete tip and shank, damaged and indeterminate head area, crudely worked with porous bone exposed at slightly spatulate head	L 108 × Head W max 8 × T 4	2	1
42	1533	Pin/needle tip	Lower part of shank only, sharp intact point. Slightly flattened shaft	L 41 × W 9	2	4
8	1504	Pin/needle tip	Length of long shaft, tip intact. Polished along length	L 89 × W 10	3	4 e × t
9	1504	Pin/needle tip	Complete tip and short length of shaft, slightly flattened shaft	L 30 × W 4	3	4
376	2229	Pin/needle tip	Lower length of polished shank, flattened in section, tip intact	L 65 × W 10	6	5

Table 15.5: (Continued)

SF no.	Context no.	Type	Description	Dimensions (mm)	Phase	Trench
299	2193	Pin/needle tip	Lower length of polished shank, flattened in section, tip slightly chipped.	L 71 × W 4	7	5
4021	1019	Pin/needle tip	Lower length of polished shank, rounded in section, tip intact	L 61 × W 9	3	1
4009	1012	Pin	Complete polished bone pin with flat nail-form head. Modern break near head, slightly curved towards tip	L 151 × D 5 × Head Diam. 6	5	1
177	2072	Preform pin	Full length of worked bone pin with head end squared and unfinished. Tip complete	L 100 × W 12	4	5

L = length, W = width, Diam. = diameter, T = thickness, D = depth

Table 15.6: Bone needles/perforated pins

SF no.	Context no.	Object type	Description	Dimensions (mm)	Phase	Trench
4017	1013	Perforated fibula	Complete, broad shank, expanded head with perforation at mid point. Polished shank, paring at tip and head cut flat along top edge	L 95 × Head W max 12 × T 5, perf. Diam. 5	5	1
161	2086	Perforated round head	Complete short highly pared shank with flattened rounded head with central perforation	L 50 × Head Diam. 5, perf. Diam. 3	6	5
114	2103	Needle	Long narrow shank with broken head across perforation. Trimmed shank and area around head	L 80 × W max 3 (below perf.)	7	5
4034	1038	Perforated pin	Complete bone pin with perforated head, crudely trimmed and incomplete thickness of bone visible at head end. Slightly irregular towards point	L 105 × W 10 × T 4 max	5	3
4035	1019	Perforated	Complete (in 2 conjoining sections) with flat spatulate head, cleanly cut by a knife; head has possible random dots accentuating the ossicles. Polished and slightly flattened shank	L 90 × Head W max 11 × T 3	3	1
4023	1019	Needle head	Fragment of head with eye	L 55 × W 7	3	1
13	1504	Needle head	Head and shank of perforated needle. Polished along length and misshapen hole is large for the size of the bone width. Flattened section	L 56 × W 7	3	4
4016	1013	Needle head	Burnt upper segment of a worked fibula needle head. Perforated at expanded part, broken across large round perforation. Knife pared	L 43 × W 10 max × T 5	5	1
301	2209	Needle head	Well-made pin/needle head, 1 complete perforation and possible traces of 2nd one immediately above at break. ?repair or functional. Circular cross-section, tapering thickness at head	L 42 × W 13 × T 5	7	5

L = length, W = width, Diam. = diameter, T = thickness

Table 15.7: Miscellaneous worked bone

SF no.	Context no.	Object type	Description	Dimensions (mm)	Phase	Trench
94	2092	Perforated scapula	Left sheep scapula, broken at narrow end and possibly trimmed at broader edge. Line of 3 perforations from upper part of blade, and 2 with a 3rd at blade edge from under part of the bone. Function unknown	Overall: max L 112 × max W 68; perf. Diam. Av. 9	6	5 ext
4005	1012	Worked	Longbone fragment with cut marks on one face. Indeterminate	L 43 × W 6 × T 10	5	1
306	2208	Worked	Sliver of longbone, weathered and slightly tapering. Indeterminate	L 50 × W 10 × T 3	7	5
188	2156	Worked	Length of bone with cutting at narrow end and incomplete perforation at broad end. Indeterminate	L 41 × W 18× T max 13	5	5
4001	1002	Handle	Highly worked, round ended cutlery handle, socketed to take tang	L 44 × W 14 × T 8	9	1
478	2268	Point	Highly worked bone point with incomplete/crude broader end. Tip in tact and polished	L 72 × W 9 × T 7	5	5
156	2127	Worked	Flat length of bone, trimmed on both narrow edges and slightly burnt at one broken end. Wear at opposite end could be deliberate tapering. Indeterminate	L 72 × W 12 × T 3	7	5

L = length, W = width, Diam. = diameter, T = thickness

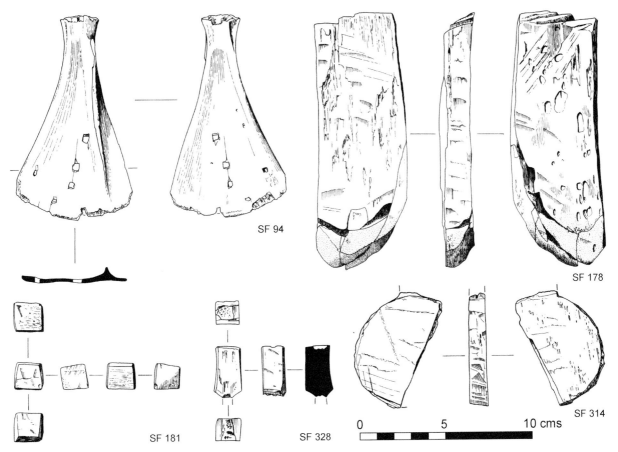

Fig. 15.6: Worked bone and whalebone objects

end and around the edges and the spina scapula has been partially removed. It may be a crude strainer, perhaps used in dairy activity, which was gnawed by a dog after discard. A similar perforated scapula has been recorded from 16–22 Coppergate, York (MacGregor *et al.* 1999, Fig. 929, find 7065, 1973), however the perforations that would have allowed drainage when the scoop was in use, are more regularly positioned. It is dated to the 12th–13th centuries in York, but this find is potentially somewhat earlier.

Whalebone (Table 15.8) (Fig. 15.6)

Two finds in this category may be related to pastimes: SF 181 from Phase 5, byre floor, is an incomplete dice and SF 314 is half of a disc which resembles an incomplete gaming piece, from Phase 6 within the wall of the ancillary building in Trench 5. The use of whalebone for dice is uncommon, and suggests expedient use of a locally available resource and it is not possible to comment on the potential numbering or symbol system to be employed on the completed object (see discussion in relation to finds from York in MacGregor *et al.* 1999, 1982–1985). The half

disc is reminiscent of the complete decorated example, from Childe's excavations at Freswick Links (Batey 1987, 8.13.2, Fig. 42D, 228–9) which has a Norwegian parallel dated to the 12th–13th centuries.

SF 328 from Phase 7, in a disturbed layer, and SF 178 from a primary deposit Phase 2, longhouse floor, are both heavily trimmed whalebone pieces, both of indeterminate function. SF 328 appears to have been possibly socketed, although incomplete and the five conjoining fragments of SF 178, form a flat section of even thickness and burning traces at one end.

Antler boat fitting (fairlead) (Table 15.9) (Fig. 15.7)

SF 247 from Phase 5, the byre floor, is a significant piece. It is complete, and forms a fitting for a boat, as a fairlead for use with a fishing line, and would have been affixed by the two perforations to the upper strake of the vessel. A similar piece was identified from Grave 11, a boat grave at Westness, Rousay, Orkney (Kaland 1980; (Kaland 1980; https://canmore.org.uk/site/2204/rousay-westness). This is probably indicative of some boat repair activity, as this

Table 15.8: Whalebone

SF no.	Context no.	Object type	Description	Dimensions (mm)	Phase	Trench
328	2209	Trimmed	Roughly rectangular offcut. 4 flat sides, one cut end (narrower) with indications of incomplete working to form a square socket? Other end has 2 parts of cutting towards a central broken section.	L 22 × W 14 × T 12	7	5
178	2146	Trimmed	5 conjoining fragments of flat trimmed whalebone of roughly even thickness. One flat end has chopping grooves and opposite end, trimmed to a rounded form with slight traces of burning which has resulted in modern fracturing	Overall L *c.* 132 × W 51 × T 15	2	5
181	2156	Dice?	Small cube of whalebone, incomplete and irregular dice?	L 15 x W 13 x T 13	5	5
314	2209	Gaming piece	Roughly half of a worked whalebone disc, possibly preform for gaming piece	D 64 × T 10	6	5

L = length, W = width, T = thickness, D = depth

Table 15.9: Antler boat fitting/fairlead

SF no.	Context no.	Description	Dimensions (mm)	Phase	Trench
247	2173	Complete highly worked antler section. Trimmed brow tine and beam with extensive wear along beam which is smoothed and has two grooves from rope friction in the angle of the two tines. Rear face is trimmed to allow fitting adjacent and over an upper boat strake and two perforations enabled attachment. Upper part seems water worn	Overall L 170 × max H 75, T 5–20	5	5

L = length, H = height, T = thickness

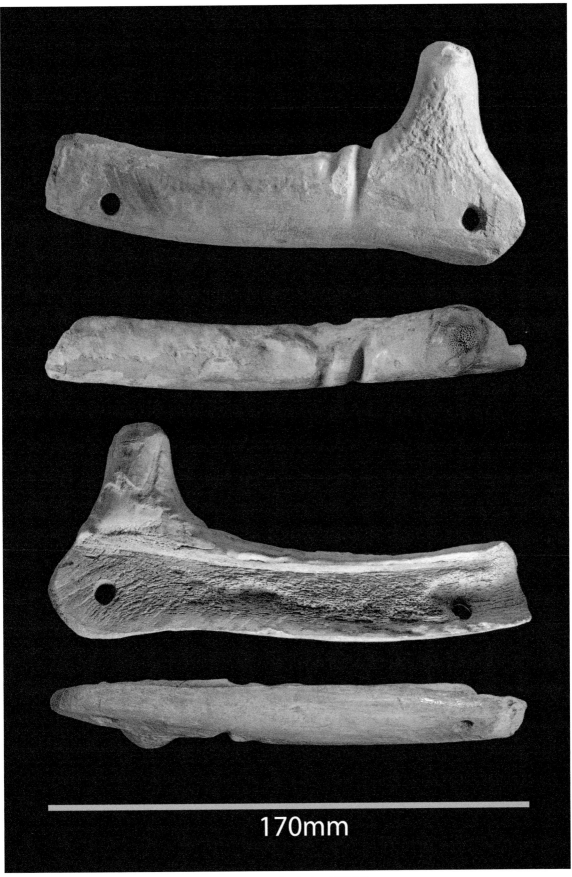

Fig. 15.7: Antler fairlead SF 247

example is clearly well used and has clear signs of rope friction at the junction with the tine.

James Graham-Campbell comments: The Westness parallel for this antler fairlead (cited above) is extremely close, having likewise the appearance of a rowlock, although on the small size for such a purpose and lacking the essential grommet hole or loose thole pin. The Westness boat (in Grave 11) also has a second antler fairlead which differs from this example in having a pair of projecting tines. According to Arne Emil Christensen (pers. comm.), such two-pronged fairleads (or vabein) are typical in Norway, where they change little from the late Neolithic in Finnmark to medieval layers at Bryggen (Bergen). This example, and its parallel from Westness, are thus atypical, with further examples of the standard two-pronged type being known from both the Broch of Burgar, Orkney (Allen 1996, 12, pl. 5), and Jarlshof, Shetland (Hamilton 1956, 124 and Fig. 57, 1–2).

16

Glass and amber beads

Birgitta Hoffman and Colleen E. Batey

There are three beads from the Bay of Skaill excavations, all recovered from Trench 5 in Phases 4, 5 and 6 (Table 16.1). They are of different types and colours, two are complete and one is very fragmentary. It is clear that at least in the case of polychrome bead SF 249 from Phase 5, and amber bead SF 142 from Phase 4, where the surface condition is worn or weathered, they have long biographies and variable origins.

SF 249 (Fig. 16.1) is made of white opaque glass decorated with royal blue double swags; it has a drum-form and weathered surface. The irregularity of the perforation indicates use-wear. Beads of similar form and decorative scheme are found in Scandinavian contexts, although the colour combination in SF 249 is not recorded (Callmer 1977, types B0160 and B0180). The most recent detailed consideration of beads by Margaret Guido (Guido 1999, 32–3, 197–200) does however supply information of this and related types,

as Group 3iiia. These beads are most common in the Rhineland, Netherlands/Belgium and Northern France region, defined as Koch 34 (Koch 1977), with forms ranging from annular to globular. Brugmann has studied the English distribution of this type and combines Guido and Koch classifications (Koch 34 blue). The continental and English examples of Koch 34 date mostly from the period 580–650 AD, and the variety of shapes suggest at least one workshop. This bead type spread from the Low Countries into southern Germany and Anglo-Saxon England south of the River Trent. More than half of the type in England are known from Kent and East Anglia (Brugmann 2004, 81, Fig. 61; Guido 1999, 32–3). Almost identical beads have been noted for example from the Hadleigh Road cemetery, Ipswich (Layard 1907, pl. VII). In a Viking context these are most likely to have been dispersed via contacts with the Lower Rhine/Pas de Calais area. A long circulation period for beads is not unexpected, they were a highly portable and durable

Table 16.1: Glass and amber beads

F no.	Context no.	Description	Phase	Trench
142	2084	Frag. flat annular amber bead Diam. 26 mm, Int Diam. 3.3 mm, H 9 mm	4	5
249	2173	Polychrome bead. White opaque glass decorated with royal blue double swags Diam. 13.6 mm, Int Diam. 4.5 mm, H 13 mm	5	5
44	2031	Dark blue biconical bead Diam. 11 mm, Int Diam. 5.8 mm, H 9 mm	6	5

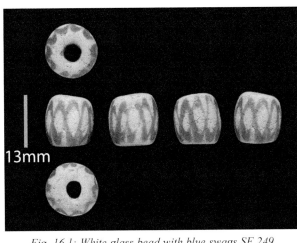

Fig. 16.1: White glass bead with blue swags SF 249

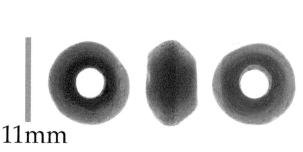

11mm

Fig. 16.2: Blue glass biconical bead SF 44

17mm

Fig. 16.3: Amber bead SF 142

status symbol, of intrinsic value for their beauty and distant origins, and may have become heirlooms.

Earlier Continental and Anglo-Saxon beads are not uncommon in Viking contexts (Havernick 1968) and indeed within Orkney, at Lavacroon, Orphir, fieldwalking activities near the Norse Earl's Bu produced a distinctive drum-shaped polychrome bead of red and yellow colours (RF 18). Clearly of a Saxon origin, the type is identified at Schretzheim where it is dated to the period 545–600 AD (Batey with Freeman 1986, 298 and illus. 9). Also from Lavacroon, a second bead is tentatively identified as being of similar date range (*ibid.*, SF 12 and illus. 9). Contacts between Anglo-Saxon England and Orkney are commonly identified with finds including Anglo-Saxon coins (*e.g.* those summarised by Stevenson 1986, 339–41). Notably however, these are somewhat later than the bead discussed here, and earlier contacts implying direct trading connections with England and the Continent are much harder to demonstrate.

SF 44 (Fig. 16.2), is a dark blue biconical bead which has similarities with Anglo Saxon forms (Guido 1999, 52 and 264–5), although it is best compared to Callmer's type A176, which comes from Scandinavian contexts dating to 790–860 AD, with a few later examples. Beads of similar form have been illustrated from the extensive Viking era cemetery at Birka, Sweden (Arbman 1940, Taf 121, 8b and Taf 122 12 h) and in Scotland, examples have been found in variably dated contexts (Gregory 2001, 199, illus. 19), there is no reason to assume that SF 44 is earlier than the Viking era, and is probably to some extent residual in Phase 6.

SF 142 (Fig. 16.3) is a fragment of a flat annular amber bead which has seen much wear and was recovered from a floor layer. Amber beads have a long and widespread currency; there are numerous amber deposits around the globe that can be differentiated by scientific analysis. The closest and largest deposits to Scotland are in the Baltic Sea region (succinite) and large quantities continue to be swept onto the southern shores of the Baltic and eastern Scandinavia. There are also very occasional quantities in East Anglia (Kosmanowska-Ceranowicz 1999). Amber was a particularly popular exchange commodity in the Viking period and fragments have been recovered from several sites, both worked and unworked. SF 142 has a cracked and worn surface caused by dehydration, and extensive bruising along the broken edges indicates that it was broken in antiquity. It is a discarded fragment, about 20–25% of the full bead. Flat annular amber beads occur during the Viking period and in the continental Iron Age. Those from the Iron Age are often grooved, but this example lacks that feature. In the Viking period amber workshops, often associated with glass bead working, appear to have been common in the larger urban centres. 9th and 10th-century workshops have been noted at Staraja Ladoga (Kirpichnikov 2004), Hedeby (Graham-Campbell 1980, 461) and Dublin (Panter 2000, 2517). At York, several sites have produced evidence for amber working (Clifford Street, Coppergate and Piccadilly; Panter 2000). Indeed the flat annular beads were one of the products of the Coppergate workshop (Panter 2000, Fig. 1219, 2505); York may therefore have been the origin of this bead, although the traded nature of the raw material means that this cannot be confirmed by material analysis.

17

Glass linen smoother

Colleen E. Batey, with a contribution from Justine Bayley

SF 425, Context 2241, Trench 5, Phase 5. Approximately 80% of a glass linen smoother which has been broken on one side. Standard pontil mark on under side and slight secondary scarring on working face. Diam. 74 mm × H approx 32 mm.

A circular object of dark glass (black or dark green), with convex upper surface and lower concave face depressed with central pontil scar. In terms of function such objects are identified as linen smoothers, used for pressing pleats in linen garments, for which there are a number of modern analogies both in Scandinavia and Scotland (Anderson 1880, 63–4).

The context for this find, in the western annex to the East Mound longhouse in a floor layer dated to Phase 5, would be within the known date range for the object type. It is however impossible to know how long it was in use prior to discard, indeed it may still have been usable after it was damaged, and the break does not appear to be raw. Hence its arrival at the site could have been somewhat earlier, possibly in Phase 3.

The type is of a standardised form, with diameters being typically between 70 and 90 mm and 25–40 mm high (Bayley 2009, 257). They have been categorised by both Rygh (Type 446, 1885, 24) and Petersen (Type 178, 1951, 328–9), and Petersen cites 28 Norwegian examples 'probably from early medieval graves' (Petersen 1951, 328–9). Elsewhere several others are from grave contexts *e.g.* Kilmainham, Ireland (Harrison and Ó Floinn 2014, 170), Ballinaby, Islay (Grieg 1940, 38, Fig. 20), as well as Birka in Sweden (*e.g.* Graves 963 and 973 Arbman 1940, taf. 153; 1943, 388 and 398). Although relatively rarely found together, they are functionally paired with whalebone plaques (c.f. Scar, Sanday; Owen and Dalland

80mm

Fig. 17.1: Glass linen smoother SF 425

1999, Fig. 97, 141) with a rare potential archaeological association noted at Kilmainham-Islandbridge (Harrison and Ó Floinn 2014, 170). There are also several of these smoothers that have also been recovered from settlement contexts, including from recent excavations on the Brough of Deerness, Orkney (J. Barrett, pers. comm.), from Coppergate, York and many from France (see below). The scientific search for the source of production has been recently presented in detail. The glass of SF 425 has not corroded and its highly polished black appearance, together with its density, suggests the glass is probably lead-rich. Examination of 41 examples from the excavations at Coppergate in York, by C. Mortimer, from contexts that date from the 10th to 12th/13th centuries, identified five made of lead-rich glass, which were suggested as being local products (Mortimer 1995). However, more recent analyses have shown that the composition of this type of lead-rich glass (Bayley 2009, 258, Table 3) does not match that of the glassworking evidence cited by Mortimer, and it is not used to make any other objects. Gratuze *et al.* (2003) analysed 79 French linen smoothers and found 13 of them had the same lead-rich composition, which also matched that of the lead-smelting slag from Melle (near Poitiers, the source of much of the silver used for the Carolingian coinage); they suggested the slag had been recycled into linen smoothers. Their further work, including lead isotope measurements, reinforced this suggestion; 48 lead-rich linen smoothers are known from all over France (19% of those analysed, with higher proportions in the areas around Melle) and at least 17 others from Dublin, York, Hedeby, Ribe, Kaupang, and Novgorod (Gratuze *et al.* 2014).

18

Worked stone (non-steatite)

Dawn McLaren, with geological identifications by Fiona McGibbon

Snusgar (Trenches 1–4)

Introduction

Two items of worked stone were recovered during excavations at the Castle of Snusgar Mound, comprising a small finely produced perforated stone pendant or touchstone (SF 4030) and a siltstone whetstone (SF 123) (see Table 18.1). The unusual lithology of the perforated stone suggests that it was an import. In contrast, the siltstone cobble used as a whetstone was probably sourced from the local beach. Both objects are consistent with a Viking-Late Norse date.

Touchstone or pendant SF 4030 (Fig. 18.1)

The small bar-shaped pendant or touchstone is a notable find both for its careful manufacture and its striking lithology. It derives from 1012, an internal layer of peat-ash rich material in Trench 1 (Phase 5). In form it resembles a perforated bar-shaped whetstone, yet this item is distinctive because of its small size, lack of any obvious evidence of wear through sharpening metal blades and the aesthetic quality of the rock type used. The stone, a laminated hornfelsed turbiditic mudstone or argillite, was undoubtedly selected due to its striking, distinctive,

banded appearance which highlights contrasting natural foliated layers of dark brown and pale sage green stone. The extent of modification to the surfaces of the stone as the result of shaping and finishing means that it is impossible to determine whether this object was produced from an erratic pebble or an outcrop source.

Being only 43.9 mm in length, its restrictive size would make effective use as a whetstone doubtful but not

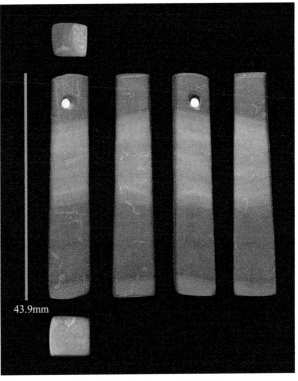

Fig. 18.1: Touchstone SF 4030

Table 18.1: Worked stone finds from Snusgar Mound

SF no.	Context no.	Description	Phase	Trench
4030	1012	Touchstone or pendant	5	1
123	1561	Square-sectioned siltstone whetstone bar with one blunt rounded end surviving	2	4

impossible. Had it been used regularly to sharpen metal blades it would be anticipated that evidence of such wear would be present on the surfaces of the stone including scratches from abrasion or dished ground facets such as those observed on many of the whetstones from East Mound. Instead, all four extensive faces of the bar-shaped stone have a light sheen suggestive of contact with a soft material, perhaps the result of rubbing against an item of clothing made from textile or hide, and light linear scratchmarks. Under high magnification of the surfaces, ephemeral bands of possible metalliferous deposits were observed on the long edges of the stone which was subject to non-destructive surface tests. A series of analyses using ED-XRF was undertaken at various points on the object's surfaces by Gemma Cruickshanks (Scottish History and Archaeology Department, National Museums Scotland, Edinburgh), but no surviving metallic residues were detectable.

Polishing around the circumference of the perforation from wear confirms that the item was suspended, perhaps on a string or thong around the neck or from a belt. Small perforated pendants of similar form are known from elsewhere, such as that found with an amber bead around the neck of a crouched child inhumation within a Viking-Age cemetery at Cnip, Lewis (Cowie 1995, 726, illus. 5:2), from Birka, Sweden (Arbman 1940, 103, no. 3) and an example from York which was found with a copper-alloy ring *in situ* within the perforation (Mainman and Rogers 2000, 2497–8).

Although interpretation as a decorative pendant is entirely possible, as illustrated by the comparable examples cited, the lithology and colour of this stone may be significant in determining an alternative function. It is also possible that this object was used as a touchstone, a tool used for scratch-testing the quality of metal (Kars 1983; Ježek 2013). Hard, dark coloured stones were favoured for touchstones; soft precious metals, such as gold, would leave a trace on the stone when scored against its surface, whereas minerals that simply looked like precious metal, such as pyrites, would not. This would provide a simple but effective way of testing the quality of gold, or other precious metals, by the comparison of its streak on the touchstones surface (Anon 1892, 50). Unfortunately, the analysis undertaken failed to detect any metal residues on the surfaces of the object to add weight to this interpretation. No items of precious metal were noted amongst the Castle of Snusgar assemblage, nor does the assemblage of vitrified material from the site include fragments indicative of non-ferrous metalworking.

Possible examples of touchstones from another Viking-Age site in Britain are known from 16–22 Coppergate, York (Mainman and Rogers 2000). At York, three possible touchstones were recognised simply on the basis of their

unusual lithology which stood out from the large and fairly homogenous assemblage of sandstone, schist and pylite hones/whetstones (Gaunt in Mainman and Rogers 2000, 2491, 2497, Fig. 1210: no. 9606–8). These possible touchstones are all small, unperforated, bar-shaped stones and other than their distinctive lithology they are not markedly different in form, shape or size to the rest of the whetstone assemblage. A possible fourth example, perforated with a copper-alloy ring *in situ*, was originally published as a perforated whetstone (Roesdahl *et al.* 1981, YTC18, 127) but re-appraisal suggests it could be a touchstone or pendant (Mainman and Rogers 2000, 2498). A slender hone or touchstone also came from a late 10th to 12th century context at Fishergate, York (Rogers 1993, 1313, Fig. 635, no. 4446).

Scandinavian examples are more frequently recognised and are known from Kaupang (Resi 2008; 2011, 391), Dorestad (Kars 1983, 25–6) and Hedeby (Resi 1990, 39–40). Four of five examples discovered at Kaupang are small perforated plates or bars of black calcitic mudstone or greenschist (Resi 2011, 392; Fig. 14.18.1 and 2) of similar size to the stone discussed here. Although many come from coastal settlements and trade centres around north-western, central and eastern Europe they are also known from funerary contexts. Touchstones can also be found in association with balance scales and weights within early medieval graves, items typically associated with prosperous merchants. Such items in a funerary context can be interpreted as a sign of the deceased individual's access to resources of precious metals (Ježek 2013, 715).

The bold, banded colouration of SF 30 and its fine craftsmanship certainly suggest that the object's inherent aesthetic qualities were valued and displayed. Two very similar complete grey-green banded pendant whetstones or touchstones come from a chieftain's farm at Borg in Northern Norway (Johansen *et al.* 2003, 152–3, Fig. 9B.14) and colourful banded touchstones, both with traces of an iron ring fitting surviving within the perforations, come from at Valsgärde, Uppland, Sweden (Ježek 2013, 717, Fig. 4, no. 12 and 15).

Whetstone SF 123

In contrast to the finely crafted touchstone or pendant already discussed, the whetstone SF 123 from Snusgar (Trench 4) utilises a naturally water-rounded siltstone pebble which saw little modification to its form prior to use for sharpening metal blades. The stone itself was probably collected from the local beach. Such tools were easily procured and often readily discarded. The recovery of the whetstone from 1561, a shell-rich midden layer (Phase 2), implies that the whetstone was deliberately discarded after breakage. Similar makeshift whetstones come from the Beachview 'Studio Site' at Birsay, and from Saevar Howe (Batey and Lambden 1996, 89; Batey and Morris 1983, 99, 36–8).

East Mound (Trenches 5–8)

Introduction

A small but comprehensive assemblage comprising 17 worked stone objects were recovered from the longhouse and ancillary structures excavated at East Mound (see Table 18.2). Most numerous amongst the assemblage are whetstones (five in total), which include several examples produced from imported pale grey schist likely to derive from southern Norway, as well as those that have been made from locally-available rock types. Also present are

Table 18.2: Worked stone finds from East Mound

SF no.	Context no.	Description	Phase	Trench
78	2032	Thick, bar-shaped whetstone fragment	8	5
113	2115	Abraded tip from a tapering square-sectioned whetstone		5
153	2118	Whetstone with ancient stepped break at one end		5
260	2170	Whetstone		5
333	2196	Whetstone		5
236	2156	Short rectangular quartzite burnisher		5
264	2146	Short, rectangular, square-sectioned burnisher	8	5
49	2031	Flattened globular spindle whorl	6	5
90	2063	Pounder (light-use)		5
213	2164	Possible heat-affected rubbing stone		5
285	2158	Possible smoother		5
455	2273	Possible strike-a-light	3	5
200	2146	Approximately 25% of a decorated upper disc quern		5
95	2063	Pot lid or palette		5
231	2164	Flaked stone, possible tether stone		5
474	2307	Notched stone fragment		5
278	2176	Flint core	8	5

a small group of cobble tools used for a range of domestic activities, two possible burnishers, some flaked stone items including a possible pot lid or palette, a struck flint, a spindle whorl and a fragment of an unusual decorated rotary quernstone.

In addition to the worked stone objects discussed and catalogued here, a dressed block of stone built into one of the main walls of the longhouse (SF 98) and a series of socketed stones incorporated into paving in the byre passageway were recorded in the field but have been left *in situ* within the structure.

Looking at the assemblage as a whole, the worked stone is dominated by simple tools reflecting a variety of commonplace domestic tasks and household craft activities such as the day-to-day maintenance of sharp bladed metal tools, fire-lighting, small-scale textile production as well as hints of hide processing. In terms of date, very few of the objects are chronologically sensitive but their contexts of recovery indicate that most of the worked stone comes from Phases 5 and 6. Possible residual prehistoric material is suggested by the presence of a single struck flint from Phase 8, and a possible Iron Age-early historic rotary quern fragment which was re-used as a sharpening stone.

Whetstones

Whetstones are typical finds on Viking-Age and early medieval settlement sites and are considered to be essential equipment for everyday maintenance of sharp-edged iron or steel tools (Resi 2011, 374) such as the knives discussed in Chapter 12. A total of five whetstones were found in association with the structures at East Mound, accounting for over 29% of the worked stone assemblage. Three distinct forms of whetstones are represented in this small group mirroring the composition of the Viking-Late Norse 'hone' group from Jarlshof, Shetland (Hamilton 1956, 119). These three types consist of small pale grey schist bars made on non-local stone, a perforated bar-shaped example, also not local stone, and a robust blocky tool made from locally procured sandstone.

The group of whetstones (three in total) is dominated by pale grey psammitic schist bars, each of which is heavily worked resulting in flattened and concave abrasion of the surfaces. It is common on these types of whetstones for wear to be found on all four faces of the stone. This results in distinct concave abrasion facets developing on each worked face, causing the stone to taper at the waist or towards one end. This form of wear gives the tools their distinctive 'haunched' appearance and are often referred to in earlier excavation reports as 'haunched hones' (Hamilton 1956, 114, Fig. 54:15). Their worn tapered form would have made them vulnerable to breakage during use, as two examples from East Mound demonstrate (Allen 1999, 181). This soft grey schist is not local to

Orkney and has almost certainly been brought to the site either from Shetland or from Scandinavia, probably from southern Norway (McGibbon, *infra*; Moore 1978; Resi 2011, 373). At the Biggings, Papa Stour, a large quantity of tapering schist whetstones are thought to derive from schist outcrops on Shetland rather than a Norwegian source (Allen 1999, 180–2).

Elongated bar-shaped whetstones of grey schist are typical finds on settlement sites of Viking to early medieval date across Britain and Ireland. This includes Viking-Late Norse assemblages associated with a smithy at Freswick, Caithness (Curle 1939, 106) and Pool, Sanday, Orkney (Clarke 2007, 377). The preference for using imported Norwegian grey schist as whetstones continued into the medieval period (Ellis and Moore 1990; Allen 1999, 181) so although useful in confirming the broad date span of occupation of the longhouse at East Mound, this small group of implements cannot of themselves provide much chronological resolution beyond suggesting an early 9th century or later date.

In addition to the common bar-shaped schist whetstones, there is also a carefully shaped, perforated whetstone of phyllite which, like the pelitic schist stones just described, is not local to Orkney. The perforation at one end for suspension suggests that this was a personal item, worn on the person, perhaps suspended from a belt. This stone has seen extensive wear and re-working: a corner has broken off over the perforation but the fractured surface has been smoothed down and re-fashioned to enable it to continue to be suspended and fine scores have been made across all four faces in a narrow band towards the unperforated end. It seems as though this item, which was probably brought to the site from Scandinavia, was a treasured item either because of its provenance or perhaps because a replacement from the same source would have been difficult to obtain. Small pendant whetstones are frequently recovered both from settlement contexts, such as Jarlshof, the Biggings, Papa Stour, Shetland and

Brough of Birsay, Orkney (Hamilton 1956, 114, Fig. 54, 17; Allen 1999, 181–2, illus. 99; Curle 1982) as well as graves of Norse to early medieval date. Those associated with graves in Scotland have been usefully summarised by Grieg (1940) to which more recent finds, such as that from Cnip, Lewis (Welander *et al.* 1987), Cruach Mhor, Islay (Gordon 1990, 155) and a 10th century grave at Buckquoy, Orkney (Ritchie 1977, 190–1), *inter alia*, can be added.

With the exception of one item, SF 78, the whetstones are all small, portable objects of a size and form entirely consistent with personal tools used for day-to-day maintenance of small knife blades and other sharp-edged tools. SF 78 is a little larger and may have been used in conjunction with larger blades. The difference in the form of this item is reflected in its potentially later date, deriving from 2032 relating to Phase 8 activity, although it may of course be residual having originated in an earlier phase.

Despite the strong representation of whetstones amongst the East Mound assemblage, their number is not particularly large considering the abundance of evidence relating to ironworking. In contrast to the large number of whetstones associated with a structure used as a smithy at Freswick, Caithness (Curle 1939, 106), only one whetstone, SF 113 (Fig. 18.2) came from the floor of the metalworking area at East Mound.

Burnishers

Two short, fine, bar-shaped stones (SF 236, Fig. 18.3 and SF 264, Fig. 18.4) were originally identified in the field as whetstones but closer examination suggests that these

Fig. 18.2: Whetstone SF 113

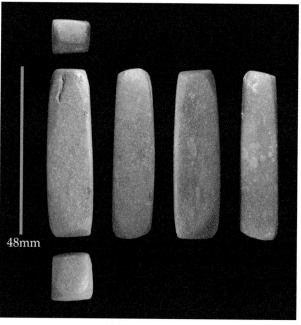

Fig. 18.3: Burnisher SF 236

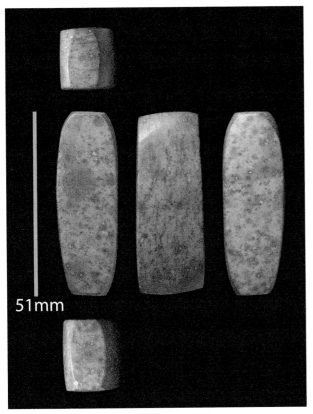

Fig. 18.4: Burnisher SF 264

Fig. 18.5: Spindle whorl SF 49

are best described as burnishers as their morphology and wear implies a distinct function from the whetstones just described. These tools stand out amongst the worked stone due to the fineness of their craftsmanship and the aesthetic qualities of the stones used. They have been produced on hard, coarse grained quartzite in hues of orange, red and green and are likely to have derived from a source on the Scottish mainland or Scandinavia. As the schist whetstones may come from a southern Norwegian source, it is possible that the burnishers derive from a similar area.

In contrast to the whetstones that are bar-shaped with parallel faces, the surfaces of the burnishers are convex with vertical edges which taper gently towards squared ends. The form of the wear on these items is also distinct from the whetstones as the rounded faces are smoothed and polished with no evidence of whetting present; bevelled abrasion is restricted to the squared ends and rounded corners of both stones only.

The care of manufacture and particular selection of the stones suggests that they were tools intended for a specific purpose; the facetted and bevelled abrasion on the ends and corners of the tool suggest fairly intricate use to grind, smooth or polish but for what purpose is not entirely clear. It is possible that like the whetstones already described, they had a metal- or metalworking-related function but use

in conjunction with finishing items of stone, wood, bone or leather should also be considered. The term 'slickstone' or polisher has also been used to describe similar quartzite tools known from mainland Scotland (Anon 1892, 50; *e.g.* NMS: x.AL 5, x.AL 6 from Bankhead Moss, Ayrshire and Knockneen, Galloway).

Items of similar shape and size but made from locally-sourced stone are known from Freswick Links and Crosskirk Broch, Caithness and from Scalloway, Shetland but have been interpreted whetstones or hones (Batey and Healy 1995, 129, Fig. 94C; Fairhurst 1984, 125; Clark 1998, 147, no. 4483). Fairhurst (1984) noted a distinction between these more finely made, convex faced 'hones' to the more expedient whetstones from Crosskirk Broch, Caithness, but did not make comment on differences in function.

Textile production

A single spindle whorl (SF 49, Fig. 18.5) produced from locally available stone came from 2031, a layer of sandy occupation material to the exterior of the longhouse (Phase 6). Although only one stone spindle whorl was recognised amongst the assemblage, further examples in steatite are present (see Chapter 19).

Cobble tools

Four cobble tools, produced from locally sourced water-rounded beach cobbles are present. In each case, the wear displayed is ephemeral, suggesting only light use prior to discard. Cobble tools are often seen as general purpose tools or hand-held tools linked to food processing tasks but even where function is not readily apparent, detailed examination of the wear resulting in use can help to distinguish between groups of tools used for distinct tasks, particularly in larger assemblages such as that from The Howe, Orkney (Ballin Smith 1994) and Burland, Shetland (McLaren and Hunter 2014).

A single lightly-used strike-a-light, used for fire-lighting, came from 2273, a charcoal and ash rich deposit deriving from the hearth area within the East Mound longhouse (Phase 3). Wear is indicated by distinctive rust-coloured strike-marks across one or both faces of the stone, and in some extensively used examples, the naturally smooth surfaces of the stone can be completely obscured with strike-marks. The example from East Mound, in contrast, appears only lightly used with a few distinct linear scores towards the edge of one face. Large quantities of strike-a-lights were found in association with a metalworking structure at Berst Ness, Knowe of Skea, Westray where many saw extensive use (Moore and Wilson forthcoming).

Other craft activities represented amongst the cobble tools appear more prosaic and domestic in character. The rubbed and stained surfaces of smoothers from Dunadd, Argyll, have been interpreted as wear and residues remaining from use as hide smoothers in leather production (Lane and Campbell 2000, 178, 179, 185). Only one example of a possible smoother (SF 285) was noted amongst the finds from East Mound but it suggests that small-scale hide preparation may have taken place within the longhouse. A lightly used pounder (SF 90) and fragment of heat affected rubbing stone (SF 213) are entirely consistent with the domestic setting of their recovery; the latter clearly has seen reuse and fragmentation prior to discard.

Rotary quern fragment SF 200 (Fig. 18.6)

One of the most intriguing items amongst the worked stone assemblage from the longhouse on East Mound is a fragment of a substantial disc-shaped upper rotary quernstone. Although quern fragments are not uncommon on Viking and Late Norse settlement sites, this item is notable for several reasons: the atypical handling system, the decoration present on the upper surface and the reuse of the stone after breakage.

When complete, this would have been used alongside a lower rotary stone to grind grain into flour. However, the fragmentary condition of the piece from East Mound casts an element of doubt over whether it ever saw such use on site contemporary with the occupation of the longhouse. The quern fragment that survives represents only about 25% of the upper stone of a thick disc-shaped quern made from fine grey sandstone. The stone has split adjacent to a horizontal U-shaped handle slot which has been sunk into the upper surface of the stone at one edge. The grinding surface has certainly seen use, as indicated by the concentric abrasion that has resulted from the upper and lower stones rotating against one another, but the surface has become so smooth through wear that it may not have been particularly efficient at grinding grain at the time of breakage. Traces of reuse of this smoothed, abraded face are present in the form of a cluster of sharpening grooves that could be the result of sharpening the edge of blades or from finishing points/ pins of various materials. Secondary wear such as this is not uncommon on quernstones and similar examples are known from Iron Age assemblages such as that from Broxmouth (McLaren 2013, 314). The position of the sharpening grooves on the East Mound stone suggest it was already broken when reuse took place.

Rotary quernstones with U-shaped horizontal handle slots are not commonplace but are increasingly recognised within later prehistoric contexts in Scotland, particularly in Orkney and Shetland (McLaren and Hunter 2008). Horizontal handle slots sunk into the surface of the quern's upper surface, perpendicular to the feeder pipe, are not the typical handling system for disc querns but they are

230mm

Fig. 18.6: Rotary quern fragment SF 200

widely distributed in Scotland (*ibid.* 2008; 2013, 289). A review of querns with this form of handling system suggests a floruit of use in the Roman Iron Age (McLaren and Hunter 2008, 112–4) but they often see reuse in later contexts such as those from Burland, Shetland (McLaren and Hunter 2014).

The deeply incised radial decoration flanking the handle slot is not readily paralleled and appears to be unique. It is assumed that the radial decoration extending away from the U-shaped handle slot was symmetrical and a similar series of short pecked U-shaped slots would have originally flanked the handle slot on the lost portion of the quern. Despite the unusual form of this decoration, it is broadly consistent with the limited suite of decorative schemes noted on rotary quernstones from Scotland (McLaren and Hunter 2008, 114–7, table 3). A similar, but more extensive radial motif is recognised on an upper quern from Nybster Broch, Caithness (Anderson 1901, 141, Fig. 21).

On current evidence, both the handling system and radial decorative motif displayed on the quern's upper surface suggests that this quern may be Iron Age-early historic in date and its use as a quern may pre-date the East Mound longhouse by several centuries.

Flaked stones

A small, flat, ovoid disc of siltstone (SF 95) came from amongst deposits to the west of the ancillary buildings. It has been crudely bifacially flaked to shape and may have functioned as a pot lid, similar to those known from the Jarlshof, Clickhimin, and Kebister, all Shetland (Hamilton 1956, 53, 62, 69; Hamilton 1968, 82–3; Clarke 1999, 157). Faint, ephemeral scratches on the surface of the disc could suggest limited, perhaps expedient, use as a palette. An asymmetric flaked slab (SF 231) which was found amongst deposits on the byre floor may have originally been set within the wall of the structure for use as a tether stone.

The notched stone (SF 474) consists of a squared corner fragment of a larger plate, broken across a crescentic notch or circular perforation. This item is coated on one face with heat-affected clay. The interpretation offered here is that this stone acted as a support for a clay tuyère which would have protected the organic nozzle of a set of bellows used to stoke the fire in a hearth, possibly related to metalworking or other high-temperature pyrotechnic process. It was recovered from 2307, the recut fill of a posthole within the main longhouse building.

Flint

One small fragment of worked flint (SF 278) from 2178 (Phase 8) is likely to be early prehistoric in date, and represents a residual piece from earlier activity on site. Small quantities of struck lithics have been found

in association with Viking-early medieval settlement contexts in Orkney and elsewhere such as at the Brough of Birsay (Hunter 1986, 192–6), Pool, Sanday (Finlayson 2007), Freswick Links, Caithness (Batey and Healy 1995, 125, pl. 49). As Batey and Healy discuss in reference to the flints from Freswick, the use of flint tools contemporary with the use of the structures should not be ruled out but in this instance the find was clearly residual.

Distribution and contextual analysis

No concentrations or clusters of worked stone were found at East Mound; the stone tools were recovered throughout the excavated area including occupation deposits within the longhouse, ash-rich layers within the byre, from deposits associated with the ancillary structures and from external deposits of occupation material and midden.

Worked stone was absent from Phases 1 and 7. The majority of items were associated with Phases 5 and 6 dating to the later stages of occupation of the longhouse and ancillary structures. The earliest finds come from Phase 2 and consist of a rotary quern fragment (SF 200) and burnisher (SF 264) from context 2146. The rotary quern may well be an earlier artefact that pre-dates the excavated structural evidence which was appropriated and re-used as a sharpening stone. The burnisher has been identified as a possible import from Scandianvia and may have been an early loss within the early longhouse floor deposits. From Phase 3 deposits, the earlier period of occupation, is a strike-a-light (SF 455) which was found amongst ash-rich floor deposits within the longhouse. Four out of five of the whetstones from East Mound came from Phases 4 and 5. The perforated whetstone (SF 260, Fig. 18.8) was the earliest of these to be deposited but the evidence of re-working and extended use suggest that this item may have been curated or retained in use for some time. Artefacts from Phase 5 are dominated by schist whetstones. The most significant item, in terms of the context of recovery, is a whetstone (SF 333, Fig. 18.7) which was found jammed in between the stones of the double-faced west–east aligned wall 2196 of the longhouse. This placement is unlikely to be incidental.

In contrast to the restricted range of items present in Phase 5, no whetstones were associated with Phase 6, and the range of tools present are wide ranging consisting of a pounder (SF 90), pot lid (SF 95), spindle whorl (SF 49), heat affected rubbing stone fragment (SF 213) and a possible tether stone (SF 231). These tools derived mainly from external deposits, including external working areas and possible re-deposited occupation material.

Geographical setting and access to resources
by Fiona McGibbon

The locality of the excavations at the Bay of Skaill is in an area of outcrop of part of the Middle Old Red Sandstone

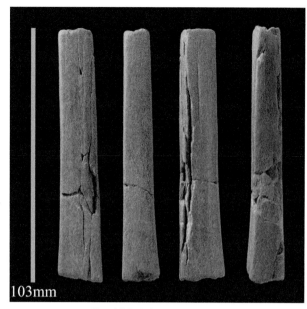

Fig. 18.7: Whetstone SF 333

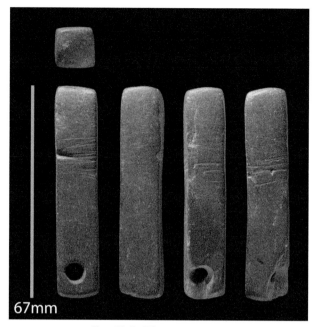

Fig. 18.8: Whetstone SF 260

succession, of Devonian age. The typical lithologies are siltstone and fine sandstone of the Caithness Flagstone Group. The most common rock type in this group is finely laminated lacustrine mudstones but fluctuations in relative sea level lead to some deltaic and even marine deposition. There were also periods of subaerial exposure leading to desiccation. Glaciation has left many examples of scratched (striated) outcrops as well as an array of exotic lithologies which are noticeable against the limited *in situ* range. Glacially transported pebbles of granite, gabbro, gneiss and Norwegian rhomb porphyry are noted in the boulder clay on other islands such as Westray. Nodular flint is also found, as are chalk pebbles – both are derived from submarine exposures in the North Sea and Moray Firth.

Most of the objects examined were of siltstone or fine sandstone considered to be of local provenance. One flint object could be sourced from local drift deposits. Several objects stood out due to both their lithologies and their fine crafted shape. Whetstones SF 113, SF 153 and SF 333 are of identical lithology of a very fine grained pelitic schist. The metamorphic rock type is not unusual and is common in outcropping rocks in the Highlands, but not on Orkney. These outcrops are part of the Caledonides, a mountain belt that is part of a larger orogenic belt that also occurs in western Scandinavia.

Three other objects that are highly shaped and also crafted from metamorphic lithologies are a whetstone (SF 260, Fig. 18.8) and two burnishers (SF 236 and SF 234). The burnishers are of quartzite which is also common to the Caledonides and could come from the same source as the pelitic schist of SF 113, SF 153 and SF 333. Quartzite could also be locally available as glacially transported

material as it is noted for its hardness and long life in the erosive environment.

Conclusions

The assemblage of worked stone from Snusgar and East Mound is dominated with tools reflecting a range of domestic tasks and household craft activities. Most of the artefact types represented, such as the schist whetstones and spindle whorl, are typical of other Viking-Age and early medieval sites excavated in the Northern Isles, and in Atlantic Scotland more generally. The assemblage is not extensive enough to provide the basis for meaningful comparative analysis but is consistent in terms of date and function with a domestic assemblage broadly of 9th to 13th century date.

Despite the periods of occupation demonstrated by the well-dated sequence of deposits within the longhouse and the ancillary structures, the worked stone assemblage is surprisingly small. Many of the items recovered from within midden deposits are broken or in a damaged condition, implying the deliberate disposal of non-functioning tools, whilst others, such as the re-worked perforated whetstone may well have been curated for some time. The possibility that this item was brought to the site by the occupants when the longhouse was first constructed suggests that the whetstone may have been kept in use over a long period of time as it was no longer possible to easily procure a replacement of the same stone or quality, or that it was a favoured tool. The combination of tools from both local sources and those that appear to have been imported, either from the

Scottish mainland or from Norway, is a recurrent feature of the assemblage.

Catalogue

Abbreviations: L, length; W, width; T, thickness; Diam., diameter; D, depth.

Touchstone or pendant
SF 4030 (FIG. 18.1)

Very fine bar-shaped perforated stone, produced from an attractive banded fine-grained rock with natural contrasting bands of dark brown and pale green stone. In form it is a short, square-sectioned bar, perforated towards the narrowest end with a small, slightly off-set bipartite bored hole (Diam. 3 mm), the stone expanding gently in width and thickness towards the flat squared end. The edges of the perforation are lightly polished as the result of rubbing during suspension and a light sheen from rubbing is present on all four flat faces. L 43.9 mm W 7.5–8.5 mm T 7–8.5 mm. Trench 1, Context 1012, layer of loose mid-brown silty/sandy loam within structure (SG04).

Whetstones and whetstone fragments
SF 123

Square-sectioned siltstone bar with one blunt rounded end surviving; opposite end lost and original length unknown. Two opposing surfaces are smoothed and gently dished through abrasion with a corresponding light sheen across the worn surfaces. A linear band of iron-pan staining overlies one worked surface and fractured end. Remaining L 68 mm W 23 mm T 24.5 mm. Trench 4, Context 1561, ashy, organic shell dump (SG 06).

SF 78

Thick, bar-shaped fragment of a larger slab or block of fine sandstone, broken at both ends and across one face; only one flat face and two steep-sided, near vertical weathered edges survive. The original surfaces are heavily weathered suggesting this stone was exposed on the surface for an extended period of time. One flat face is smoothed towards one broken end, possibly the result of use as a whetstone but this is unclear due to the extent of weathering. L 100.5 mm W 60.5 mm T 47.5 mm. Trench 5, Context 2032.

SF 113 (FIG. 18.2)

Abraded tip from a tapering square-sectioned whetstone produced from imported pale grey schist. The stone has broken at the widest point and the stone has split longitudinally towards the flat squared tip. The stone has been heavily worked on all four faces resulting in significant dishing through abrasion on all surfaces, particularly on two opposing faces. Irregular red-brown staining is also present from use. Remaining L 50 mm W 9–14.5 mm T 4.5–11 mm. Trench 5, Context 2115.

SF 153

Irregular thin rectangular peltic schist bar with ancient stepped break at one end which has resulted in loss of corner and much of one end of the stone leaving a narrow blunt projection with recent damage at tip. Stone tapers asymmetrically along length creating distinctive 'haunched' profile towards fish-tail shaped wide end. Both edges and one face are smoothed with dished abrasion from use. Opposing face is lightly abraded indicating limited wear. The lithology of the stone is not local; a typical Caledonite metaphorphic rock that could be sourced in Highland Scotland or Scandinavia. Remaining L 117 mm W 27–32.5 mm T 6–9 mm. Trench 5, Context 2118.

SF 260 (FIG. 18.8)

Short, rectangular, square-sectioned, non-local, phyllite (fine peltic schist) bar, squared by facetted abrasion at both ends and each of the four faces ground to shape. A biconical perforation (Diam. 6–6.5 mm) has been sunk 5 mm from one end to allow suspension. The conical hollows bored from opposing faces are misaligned but adjustment of the position of the hollow on one face has successfully perforated the stone. The perforation is damaged towards one edge of one face resulting in the loss of the corner of the stone. It is unclear if this occurred during manufacture or later use but the corner has been reworked after breakage to extend the use of the perforation. The fractured surfaces have been abraded to smooth and a vertical angular notch has been created from the squared end to edge of perforation with distinct tool marks remaining in the interior of the notch. Wear from use as a whetstone is evident on all four faces: each surface has gentle dished abrasion towards unperforated squared end. At the narrowest point on all four faces are a series of parallel and cross cutting horizontal sharpening grooves; two faces display more extensive use. The rock type used is a typical Caledonide metamorphic rock that could be sourced in Highland Scotland or Scandinavia. L 67.5 mm W 12.5–13.5 mm T 13.5–14 mm. Trench 5, Context 2170.

SF 333 (FIG. 18.7)

Conserved haunched tapering bar of non-local grey pelitic schist. Angular squared breaks at both ends with no attempt to smooth or finish. Each of the four flat faces is smoothed with dished abrasion through use towards one end creating tapering shape. Abrasion through use is associated with bands of dark brown staining on each face. One surface has short, shallow, sharpening groove along long axis towards narrow squared end. The rock type used is a typical Caledonide metamorphic rock that could have been sourced in Highland Scotland or Scandinavia. L 104 mm W 14.5–18.5 mm T 11–15.5 mm. Trench 5, Context 2196.

Burnishers

SF 236 (Fig. 18.3)

Short rectangular bar of non-local quartzite which ranges in colour from salmon pink to buff to a blue-grey-green suggesting the pebble was selected not just for its fine-grained texture but also its striking colouring. All surfaces have been carefully ground to shape, the stone gently tapering towards one squared end. Both ends have bevelled abrasion facets and two corners of both ends have been rounded by abrasion from use. All four faces are gently rounded, smoothed and highly polished. Although produced from a ubiquitous rock type, the shaping suggests a provenance from the same source as SF 264 and could have been sourced in Highland Scotland, Scandinavia or could have been fashioned from a glacially transported local material. L 48 mm W 11–13.5 mm T 10–11.5 mm. Trench 5, Context 2156.

SF 264 (Fig. 18.4)

Short, rectangular, square-sectioned bar of a non-local feldspathic quartzite with a dappled appearance, ranging in colour from a greeny-buff to brown matrix with blooms of red-brown iron-rich staining. The shape of the stone is slightly trapezoidal due to asymmetric abrasion at both squared ends. All surfaces have been ground to shape, creating gently convex smooth faces. Two faces are rounded and smoothed, one with facetted bevelled abrasion towards both squared ends. The adjacent sides are flattened by abrasion with a high degree of polish and light longitudinal and transverse striations from use. The rock used is a typical Caledonide metamorphic rock that could have been sourced in Highland Scotland, Scandinavia or fashioned from glacially transported local material. L 51 mm W 18.5–20 mm T 8.5–17.5 mm. Trench 5, Context 2146.

Decorated rotary quern fragment

SF 200 (Fig. 18.6)

Approximately 25% of a decorated upper disc quern produced from a large coarse-grained sandstone slab, broken across central circular biconical feeder pipe (Diam. 58–65 mm), parallel to a horizontal U-shaped handle slot. The quern has a naturally flat upper surface and rounded edges which have been pecked to shape with clear peck marks remaining from manufacture. The edge immediately adjacent to the handle slot is straight but it is unclear if this is by design or simply reflects the original shape of the slab. The handle slot is U-shaped: 36.5 mm wide at edge, tapers to a rounded tip (W 20 mm) and is 37 mm deep. The slot is slightly undercut at the opening of the slot but this does not

continue along the full length and peck marks remain from manufacture in the interior of the slot. Flanking the handle slot on the surviving face are three deep, short, equidistant, horizontal radial slots which graduate in length, becoming shorter further away from the handle slot (L 84.5 mm W 17–27.5 mm Dth 17 mm; L 66 mm W 10–19 mm D 12 mm; L 54.5 mm W 8.5–12 mm D 8 mm). It is likely that this decoration was symmetrical and an identical series of slots would originally have been present on the other side of the handle slot. In profile the stone slopes and tapers in thickness towards the feeder pipe. The grinding face is smoothed with patches of concentric striations and pitting through use. Secondary expedient use of the grinding face is indicated by a band of parallel shallow sharpening grooves which extend from one fractured edge towards the rounded edge of the stone but it is unclear whether this wear pre-dates the breakage of the stone. The stone used is typical of deltaic sands known to form discrete layers within the Caithness flagstone group and is likely to have been procured locally. Approximate original Diam. 440–460 mm; T 73–81 mm. Trench 5, Context 2146.

Spindle whorl

SF 49 (Fig. 18.5)

Flattened globular whorl produced from light brown mudstone. The edges are D-shaped, smoothed and rounded with a slightly off-centre bored perforation Central drilled perforation (Diam. 8.5–9 mm). D 28 mm T 15.5 mm. Mass 12.1 g. Trench 5, Context 2031.

Cobble tools

SF 90

Pounder (light-use). Flattened ovoid water-rounded fine sandstone cobble. Two small pecked facets (11 × 14.5 mm; 11.5 × 14.5 mm) are present off-centre at the rounded tip at the narrowest end of the stone. L 116.5 mm W 92.5 mm T 61 mm. Trench 5, Context 2063.

SF 213

Possible heat-affected rubbing stone. Rounded tip of a plano-convex ovoid muscovite-flecked sandstone cobble. Only one original rounded end and small area of flattened face survive; rest of cobble lost, possibly due to heat damage. Surviving face is convex on longitudinal axis with light abrasion through use although the 'grain' of the stone is still clear implying limited wear. Patches of dark brown staining on abraded face. Dark patch of black sooting present on curving edge and tip of abraded face is pitted from heat damage. Remaining L 80 mm Remaining W 144 mm T 75 mm. Trench 5, Context 2164.

SF 285

Possible smoother. Large ovoid water worn local sandstone or quartzite cobble. One rounded face has light abrasion and a slight sheen towards the centre and dark staining across surface. L 141.5 mm W 86 mm T 71 mm. Trench 5, Context 2158.

SF 455

Possible strike-a-light. Small smooth ovoid water worn pebble of local fine-grained sandstone/siltstone with small oval patch (10 × 33 mm) of dark brown staining on one rounded edge of flat face. Although obscured by the darkened stain, an overlapping configuration of fine, ill-defined V-shaped striations or strike-marks are visible suggesting limited use as a strike-a-light. L 54.5 mm W 40 mm T 26.5 mm. Trench 5, Context 2273.

Flaked stone

SF 95

Pot lid or palette. Flat oval fine sandstone disc, with rounded edges around *c.* 80% of the circumference, two opposing edges of the remaining straight portion of the edge are damaged. Both faces display attempts to thin and flatten. The surfaces of the stone are weathered. Very faint ephemeral series of fine scratch marks are present towards the centre of one face and may indicate expedient use as a palette or working surface. L 102 mm W 83.5 mm T 3.5–4 mm. Trench 5, Context 2063.

SF 231

Flaked stone, possible tether stone. Substantial flat sub-square siltstone cobble. One straight edge has natural, stepped notch which creates the appearance of the shoulder of a bladed instrument. From this notch extends a short, rectangular projection (L 72 mm W 69.5 mm), bifacially fractured at tip. The opposing edge is curved with patches of unifacial flaking probably from use rather than an attempt to shape. One further rounded corner is flattened by unifacial fracture damage. L 265 mm W 170–200 mm T 31 mm. Trench 5, Context 2164.

SF 474

Notched stone fragment. Right-angled corner fragment from a flat sub-square local siltstone plate broken across sub-circular notch or perforation. Only one original edge survives; the other edges are angular and chipped. Both flat faces are heat affected; one with an adhering patch of fired-clay. The adhering clay and heat-damage could suggest this was a component of, or support to, a ceramic tuyere. Remaining L 61 mm Remaining W 50 mm T 7.5–11 mm. Trench 5, Context 2307.

Other

SF 278

Flint core. Large angular fragment of a water worn nodular flint pebble, the unmodified cortex surface survives on one face. One end and much of opposing face is fractured with facetted percussion marks indicating expedient removal of flakes. Likely to have been procured locally from drift deposits. L 53.5 mm W 45.5 mm T 26 mm. Trench 5, Context 2176.

19

Steatite

Amanda K. Forster, with a contribution from Richard Jones

Steatite (soapstone) was used for cooking vessels and other purposes. The assemblage of steatite artefacts from Snusgar and East Mound consists of 85 small find records, comprising 118 individual fragments and amounting to 22.6 kg of material (Table 19.1). Of the total assemblage, 62 finds represented steatite vessels, including a total of 89 fragments. Together, the vessel fragments account for 92% of the total mass of steatite artefacts recovered. Other artefact types include whorls (four examples) and bakestones (two possible examples), with the remainder (17) classified as miscellaneous fragments which are too small and/or degraded to ascribe to a particular type of object.

The high percentage of vessel fragments and low variation in steatite artefact types is typical of an Orcadian Norse assemblage. These characteristics suggest that those living at the settlement had a reasonably consistent access to worked steatite vessels, that they repaired and re-worked broken fragments but did have access to (or perhaps the desire to) import raw material itself. The character of the assemblage contrasts markedly with contemporary groups from Shetland, where access to quarries is evident by the diversity of artefact categories and often the presence of offcuts and small fragments of raw material (for example, see Forster 2010). In addition, Orcadian assemblages also differ from those recovered from further reaches of Norse influence such as the Western Isles, Iceland and the Faroe Islands, where access to any steatite objects is limited and unpredictable. Here, fragments tend to be limited either in number (such as in the Western Isles and Faroe) or from considerable reuse (evident in Iceland). For a discussion on the use of steatite in Orkney, see Forster (2005).

Whorls and worked discs

SF 65, 2008, Phase 6, Trench 5, Whorl (Fig. 19.1)
SF 281, 2158, Phase 5, Trench 5, Drill whorl (Fig. 19.2)
SF 302, 2209, Phase 7, Trench 5, Whorl (Fig. 19.3)
SF 465, 2263, Phase 5, Trench 5, Whorl blank
Only four objects described as whorls or worked discs were recovered at Bay of Skaill, with one definite example of a spindle whorl, one probable, a blank and a drill whorl. One other spindle whorl was recognised within the finds assemblage – a light mudstone example of local provenance (SF 49, Chapter 18). The group is not substantial enough to discuss implications for textile production at these sites.

Table 19.1: Assemblage summary

Artefact type	No (SF Units)	Frags	% frags	Weight (kg)	% weight	Av. weight per frag. (g)
Vessels	62	89	75	20.7	92	232
Bakestone	2	2	2	1	4	500
Whorl	4	4	3	0.3	1	75
Misc	17	23	19	0.6	3	26
Total	85	118		22.6		191

Fig. 19.1: Whorls and worked discs, SF 65

Fig. 19.2: Whorls and worked discs, SF 281

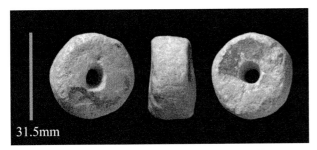

Fig. 19.3: Whorls and worked discs, SF 302

All of the artefacts in this group appear to have been reworked from vessel fragments. Only one can be confidently categorised as a spindle whorl (SF 302), recovered from a deposit 2209 from within the longhouse associated with the north side bench. A second find, SF 465, appears to be a blank for a spindle whorl, and is almost identical in size to SF 302, but lacks the central perforation. SF 65 was also recovered from within the longhouse, from floor deposit 2263. Both finds are around 30 mm in diameter (SF 465 35 mm; SF 302 31 mm) and 19 mm thick. SF 302 weighs 31.5 g, and has been fully perforated, with a biconical hole 8.2 mm in diameter drilled through the centre. One other find which may have been used as a spindle whorl is SF 65, recovered from a midden deposit 2008 from the east of the ancillary building. This worked disc is less well made, with the perforation off centre and a more wedge-like profile.

The diameter is larger, *c.* 38 mm and it weighs 47 g. There are examples of asymmetrical whorls from other sites, suggesting they were usable as spindle whorls (see PL2296, Pool, Smith and Forster 2007, 429).

The rectangular profile of SFs 302 and 465 would be identified as a 'B' profile using the classification developed by Walton Rogers, based on finds from 16–22 Coppergate, York (1997, 1736). These B type examples have flat faces of equal diameter, essentially being rectangular in profile; other examples from the York series (such as whorls with oval, domed or conical profiles) are not present in this assemblage, but are not uncommon throughout the Northern Isles (*e.g.* Pool, Smith and Forster 2006, 428, and Old Scatness, Forster 2010, 290). The propensity for B type whorls in assemblages across the Northern Isles and further afield may relate to the reuse of vessel fragments; although such whorls can be shaped more finely, often only minimal effort is applied and no attempt made to further shape the profile and overall appearance.

It is also common to find roughs, blanks and unfinished whorls which have broken during manufacture. At Borg, a Viking-Age chieftain's farm in Lofoten, Northern Norway, the process of manufacture from vessel sherd to finished article was illustrated using examples from each stage recovered from the site (Johansen *et al.* 2003, Fig. 9B.4, 145). The blank (SF 465) is a very nearly complete whorl, lacking only the perforation. Examples from Quoygrew also included partially manufactured whorls (Batey *et al.* 2012, Fig. 12.8, 217).

This group of finds are a good example of the common practise or reusing broken vessel sherds to make usable objects. The presence of sooting on all the whorls indicates that these examples are all recycled and objects of secondary manufacture. This contrasts with evidence from Pool, where a larger collection of steatite whorls is linked to an earlier phase of that settlement. The majority of the whorls at Pool were recovered from Viking-Age contexts and include examples which appear to have been purpose-made and not reworked from broken vessels (Smith and Forster 2007, 428). Presumably the earliest Viking settlements included an imported toolkit, which the Late Norse period was replaced with locally available materials. At the Bay of Skaill, the small number of steatite whorls of steatite and other finds types is interesting. Whorls were used to spin wool into a yarn after being combed or carded, the whorl providing a weight on a spindle, allowing the yarn to spin faster and produce a tighter yarn (see Scott and Jolie 2008 for an interesting discussion of yarn production in Norse Greenland). Although not the most common artefact type within an assemblage, whorls are almost always recovered from Norse settlement sites. In one Icelandic site, Sveigakot, the steatite whorls were more numerous than the poorly preserved collection of vessel fragments (Gísladóttir and Forster 2014).

Finally, the most distinctive object within this group is a drill whorl, SF 281 (Fig. 19.2). This drill whorl was also recovered from deposits making up the longhouse floor. This find is much larger in diameter and weight (at 92 mm and 215 g) and has been decorated with radial lines emanating out from the perforation. The perforation itself is 13 mm in diameter and polished from use. The whorl is 22 mm thick and clearly a reworked vessel fragment, both in its profile and the remnants of sooting on what would have been the external face. Similar sized whorls were recorded at Kebister (1809 and 2057, Sharman 1999, 177) and at Jarlshof, Shetland (Hamilton 1956, 185, classified as loomweights), recognised by Simon Buttler as drill whorls by comparison with similar examples in use up to the end of the 19th century in Iceland, Faroe and Norway (Buttler 1984, 34). Four examples recovered from Borg, Lofoten, weigh between 106 and 318 g (Johansen *et al.* 2003, 145 and Fig. 9B.5, 145).

Bakestones

SF 35, 2016, Phase 5, Trench 5
SF 315, 2204, Phase 3, Trench 5 (Fig. 19.6)
Only two finds have been classified as bakestones, both very different in their morphology and possible origin. SF 35 has a very laminar appearance and could be a very burnt and badly preserved example of a Norwegian schist bake stone. However, the fragment lacks the typical deep scoring that is usually present on both faces of the stone. Although not common, the Hardanger type bakestone has been recorded across the Northern Isles, most significantly The Biggings where 87 fragments were recorded (Smith with Buttler and Weber 1999, 134 f). Fewer numbers of the same type have been noted at Kebister (Sharman 1999, 173), Sandwick South (Bigelow forthcoming) and Quoygrew (Batey *et al.* 2012, 219). This example was recovered from disturbed floor layers (2016) dating to the 11th–early 12th century.

The second example, SF 315, is more typical of a Shetland bakestone. These are worked in a similar manner to the Norwegian type with clear scoring on both surfaces. They tend to be thicker (this example is 19 mm thick) and would have been large rectangular slabs. It is impossible to gauge from this example how big it may have been as it is very worn and degraded. The earliest identification of the Shetland stones is in Orkney, at Pool, where examples seem to have been imported to the site from the second half of the 10th century (Phase 8.1, Smith and Forster 2007, 432). This fragment was recovered from midden 2204 to the east of the ancillary buildings.

The vessels

Research into the morphology of steatite vessels across the North Atlantic region developed a basic and broadly defined typology of vessels. Despite the apparent variability of vessels, there are only seven broad types which feature regularly within North Atlantic assemblages (see Forster and Jones 2017, for discussion). The following discussion references the vessel type series developed by the author. The series is particularly relevant to the steatite vessels recovered across the medieval North Atlantic region and aims to provide a consistent method of recording morphological types. As part of a wider project utilising science-based provenance studies to help shed light on the development of Norse settler societies in the North Atlantic region, a number of vessel fragments from the assemblage have been analysed with an aim to determining provenance (see Forster and Jones 2017). A summary of this work can also be found below.

Individual vessels can be inconsistent in wall thickness, form, treatment or use-wear, and the nature of the burial environment can also influence preservation and appearance of fragments. This can make the confident identification of individual vessels challenging unless conjoining fragments can be located. As a result, the following discussion focuses on vessel groups which comprise fragments associated by form, preservation and surface treatment (*e.g.* from working and/or use-wear). As well as providing a useful mode of describing the nature of the assemblage, vessel groups provide a basic estimate of how many individual artefacts may be represented. The Snusgar/East Mound steatite assemblage includes approximately 15 individual vessels, with groups described below. In addition to the fragments included in groups, there are a number of individual finds (n=20) recovered which are too small, burnt or worn to allow a reasonably full description of the morphology – these have been denoted at Group 0 in the catalogue. In addition, six of the finds are vessel base fragments and cannot be associated with any particular vessel group due to being poorly preserved (SF16, SF149, SF272, SF383, SF392 and SF457). Finally, three finds have been reworked substantially (SF281, SF388 and SF470) and the primary vessel morphology is difficult to determine.

Vessel typology

Four vessel types are recorded in the assemblage (see Fig. 19.4). Type 1 (hemispherical circular vessel) is the most common type within Scandinavia and provides a standard morphology to which a number of attributes can be added. Within the North Atlantic region, Type 1 vessels have been recorded at sites in every area (for examples see Old Scatness, Shetland, Forster 2010, 258; Pool, Orkney, Smith and Forster 2007, 412). The common factor of Type 1 vessels is quality; a consistent wall thickness, reasonably symmetric shape and curved profile. Type 2 is a less accomplished curved vessel, with thicker walls, a

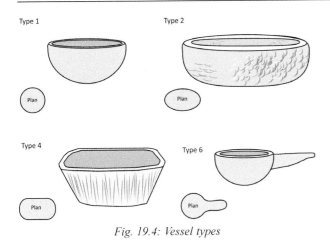

Type 1   Type 2

Type 4   Type 6

Fig. 19.4: Vessel types

Fig. 19.5: Vessel SF 305

flatter base and rougher finish. This vessel is not strongly recognisable as either Norwegian or Shetland in origin. Type 4 is a very typical Shetland type vessel; it is sub-rectangular and flared from the base with rounded corners. Both square and sub-rectangular vessels had developed by the second half of the 10th century, appearing in Orkney at this time at the multi-period settlement of Pool, Sanday (Smith and Forster 2007, 432). Type 6, a handled scoop or ladle, has a wide distribution across areas of Scandinavian influence but generally recovered in small numbers, with one or two finds recorded at most Viking and Norse period sites.

Group 11 Type 1 hemispherical and circular vessel, wall thickness 11–14 mm

SF 305, 2209, Phase 7, Trench 5 (Fig. 19.5)

This is a well-manufactured vessel, probably with a large diameter and a consistent wall thickness. The fragment was recovered from a 12th–13th century deposit associated with the disturbed layers of the north bench within the longhouse (2209). This type of vessel is the most representative of the Norwegian soapstone bowl and could be considered the basic model for medieval soapstone vessels. This form would have been imported with Norwegian pioneers and then settlers both as the physical artefacts and part of a cultural idea and blueprint (see Forster 2005 for discussion). Although this particular vessel could have been manufactured in either Norway or Shetland, the form is very much linked to the homeland. Comparable examples are numerous within the Northern Isles and span the Viking and Norse periods. From early Viking contexts at Norwick in Shetland examples ranged from 160 mm in diameter to 480 mm (Forster 2006), and an example of 500 mm recorded at the Brough of Birsay dating from the mid-9th to early-11th century (SF 5414, Hunter 1986, 189 f). Later examples can be found, but in fewer numbers, and it is not inconceivable to think that some of the earlier imports may have been curated for a

couple of generations within the settlement. A possible late example was also recovered from Quoygrew dating to the 13th century (Sf 62160, Batey *et al.* 2012, 214).

SF 305 appears well-used with scouring on the internal walls and blackened residue on the external faces. As a wall fragment, the specific morphology of rim type and base cannot be discussed, although the overall vessel is likely to have been plain, consistent in appearance and bowl shaped in profile. The diameter cannot be estimated accurately, but is likely to have been between 380 and 480 mm.

Group 2 Type 1 hemispherical and circular vessel, wall thickness 8–17 mm and 140 mm diameter

SF 54, 2041, Phase 7, Trench 5, Vessel rim and wall, illustrated (Fig. 19.6)

This Type 1 vessel is relatively small compared to Group 11 and is reminiscent of the plain hemispherical vessels common in Norway. It is only 8 mm thick at the rim, and slightly thicker at the wall (17 mm) and would have been about 140 mm in diameter. The form is unlikely to have been manufactured in Shetland and is therefore a likely import from Norway. This particular example is relatively deep compared to its diameter, with an upright and slightly curved profile. Both surfaces have been smoothed and the vessel looks well used and the fractures are very worn. Sooting is visible on both external and internal surfaces.

In the Northern Isles, high numbers of Type 1 vessels tend to be indicative of earlier Viking phases (such as Pool in Orkney and Old Scatness in Shetland, see Forster 2005 for discussion). This example was recovered from later

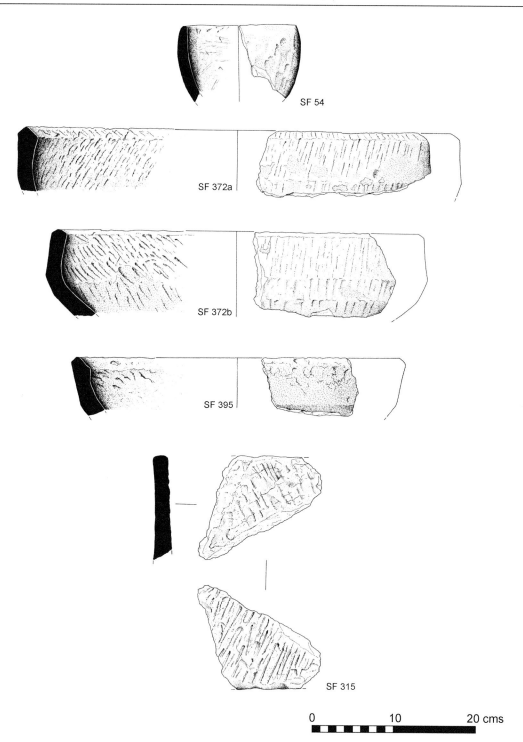

0   10   20 cms

Fig. 19.6: Steatite finds, Groups 1–5 and bakestones

deposits – a 12th–13th century fill from a collapsed wall, although likely to be a residual 11th century find. During the Viking settlement period, Norwegian settlers would have brought vessels into the region as goods associated with setting up a new home (rather than reflecting trade). A very similar sized vessel is recorded at Pool from Viking period contexts (SF 5230, Phase 7.2, Smith and Forster 2007, 415) and another, similarly dated, from Toftanes, Faroe (Stummann Hansen 2013, 68). A slightly larger example from Orkney, also from Pool, is dated to the later 11th–mid-12th centuries (SF 340, Smith and Forster 2007, 420).

GROUP 1 TYPE 2 CARINATED OVAL VESSEL, WALL THICKNESS BETWEEN 19 AND 24 MM, APPROXIMATELY 500 MM LENGTH AND 130 MM DEEP

SF 372 (a and b), 2224, Phase 5, Trench 5, Two rim sherds, both illustrated (Fig. 19.6)

SF 395, 2263, Phase 5, Trench 5, One rim sherd, illustrated (Fig. 19.6)

These three rim fragments were all recovered from two contexts relating to the East Mound longhouse floor. Although there may be two or even three separate vessels (owing to the differing profiles of the rim sherds), they share similar characteristics and could feasibly be from the same vessel. All have carefully bevelled rim profiles emphasised by shaping on the external and internal surfaces. The vessels have a carinated profile, with a slightly inturned profile and the carination sitting about 50 mm below the rim. Although the basic morphology of this vessel is quite typical, the decorative treatment of the working and careful shaping of the rim and carination would indicate an important vessel which is likely to be of Norwegian origin. A very similar example with a finely worked rim and carination was recovered from Quoygrew dating to 11th–12th century deposits (Sf 61990, Batey *et al.* 2012, 215).

The vessel type is large and curved in plan, probably oval rather than circular and at least 500 mm in length. Although it is difficult to estimate a depth, the vessel type is likely to have been quite wide and shallow; open in profile rather than tall and closed. Below the carination, the wall curves towards the base which would have been hemispherical, though flattened through wear, and without a defined wall to base angle. There is no vessel base fragment which can be linked to these particular examples; base fragments are often badly burnt and worn, often the first point on the vessel to fracture and break.

The careful nature of the working visible on these fragments would suggest a Norwegian origin, however from a purely morphological perspective the vessels could have been manufactured in Shetland or Norway.

GROUP 13 TYPE 2

SF 473, 2268, Phase 5, Trench 5

This vessel, recovered from deposits in the byre floor and workshop area, is a large plain thick-walled vessel which would have been circular in plan with a curved profile. The vessel wall is 22 mm thick with plainly worked surfaces and sooting evident on both wall faces. The external surface is heat damaged and may be from the lower part of the vessel wall. The fragments are all badly worn and burnt. The vessel is perhaps more similar to examples from Shetland than Norway, with comparable examples from Old Scatness, Norwick and Jarlshof (personal observation). However, this form of

vessel is not regionally sensitive to the same degree as Types 1, 3 and 4.

GROUPS 6 TO 10, AND 12 TYPE 4, FLARED SUB-RECTANGULAR VESSEL WITH FLAT BASE

GROUP 6 (ALL TRENCH 5)
SF 103, 2095, Phase 7
SF 120, 2043, Phase 7
SF 323, 2219, Phase 3 (Fig. 19.7)
SF 378, 2227, Phase 6
SF 429, 2248, Phase 9
SF 377, 2251, Phase 7 (Fig. 19.7)
SF 445, 2251, Phase 7 (Fig. 19.7)
SF 423, 2273, Phase 3

GROUP 7
SF 143, 2084, Phase 4 (Fig. 19.7)
SF 432, 2275, Phase 5

GROUP 8 (ALL TRENCH 5)
SF 10, 2008, Phase 6
SF 238, 2076, Phase 2 (Fig. 19.7)

GROUP 12 (ALL TRENCH 5)
SF 33, 2007, Phase 7
SF 185, 2087, Phase 5
SF 217, 2152, Phase 2

GROUP 9 (ALL TRENCH 5)
SF 32, 2007, Phase 7
SF 48, 2009, Phase 6
SF 46, 2018, Phase 4
SF 50, 2034, Phase 6
SF 219, 2132, Phase 5
SF 298, 2193, Phase 7
SF 401, 2241, Phase 5 (Fig. 19.6)
SF 407, 2241, Phase 5
SF 424, 2273, Phase 3

GROUP 10 VESSEL BASE (ALL TRENCH 5)
SF 324, 2219, Phase 3
SF 326, 2219, Phase 3
SF 327, 2219, Phase 3
SF 356, 2227, Phase 6
SF 369, 2232, Phase 5

By far the most common type of vessel in the assemblage, Groups 6 to 10, and Group 12 are all part of the Type 4 family of sub-rectangular vessel. This form represents a typical Shetland vessel morphology strongly linked to the development of square and rectangular vessels manufactured within the archipelago. Type 4 vessels are large, sub-rectangular and flat-based. They can be up to 600 mm in length and are rectangular in plan, with sub-rounded corners. Some examples are close to being

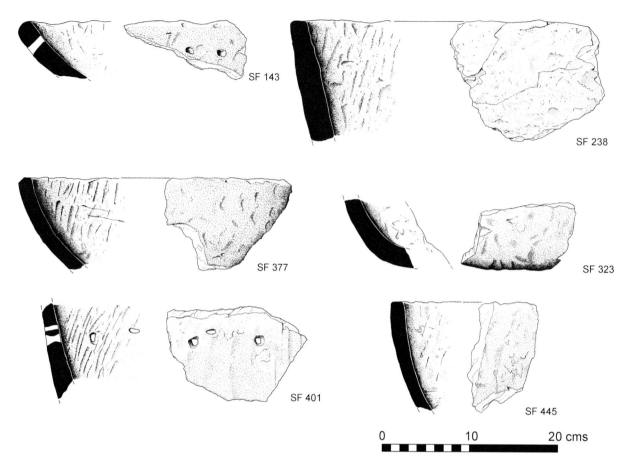

Fig. 19.7: Steatite finds, Groups 6–12

oval but the Type 4 vessel is always definable by having discernible corners. The form was developed in Shetland soon after the establishment of Viking settlements in the islands (as seen at Norwick and Old Scatness) and grew to become the predominant vessel type of the following period. The appearance of Type 4 vessels in Orkney is recorded at Pool, Sanday, from possibly as early as the mid-9th century. This is an important moment, indicating that Type 4 was well on its way to becoming a common Shetland export to Orkney and beyond (as discussed in Forster 2005; Smith and Forster 2007, 432).

The latest dated examples from Quoygrew, Orkney, where fragments were recovered from a 15th century deposit (Batey *et al.* 2012, 216). There is the suggestion that the latter example was possibly residual and the authors' note that the active use of steatite at Quoygrew was from Phases 1 to 3 (10th–14th century; *ibid.*). In Shetland, the site of The Biggings, Papa Stour, provides evidence that some steatite vessels were in use in later phases, with fragments associated from floor deposits in a dwelling house dating from the 15th to early 17th century (Smith *et al.* 1999, 143).

The six groups in this Type 4 category represent at least five vessels and includes one group comprising fragments

from a vessel base (Group 10). Although all these vessels all sit within the Type 4 classification, they do demonstrate the wide variation found between individual examples. From the straight-sided and sharp-angled (Group 8) through to examples with curving profiles and rounded corners (Group 6), Type 4 is a versatile staple of the medieval domestic assemblage in Orkney.

Group 6 is a well-manufactured example with a rim thickness of 11 mm and wall thickness of between 22 and 25 mm. The distinctive tooling is present on both internal and external surfaces, and the vessel has been well worn through cleaning and use. The external surface is sooted and residue is present. Whilst it is very difficult to reconstruct the dimensions of a vessel from a few sherds which may or may not have been from the same artefact, this is a large and thinner walled example. Complete it would have been up to 50 cm in length, with a depth of at least 20 cm. The walls flare from the base at an angle of between 60 and 70 degrees, which would result in a large and stable vessel with a high capacity in terms of volume.

Although the finds are from different contexts, there does appear to be a reasonable spatial grouping within the longhouse, with the majority from deposits dating to Phase

3 and 6. Later finds are associated with a disturbed surface (2095) and an area of wall collapse (2251), Phase 7, and one fragment was recovered from a much later kelping pit.

Group 8 (SF 10, SF 238) is a classic Type 4 vessel being recognisably sub-rectangular with a straighter profile than Group 6, though still flared from the base. This straighter profile tends to be consistent with a more angular plan, essentially worked to have clear corners between the four wall faces and the base. This vessel could be as substantial as Group 6, though the size cannot be ascertained from the extant sherds. The rim here is thicker and has a squarer profile (thickness is 17 mm at rim, 25 mm at wall).

Both finds are associated with the ancillary building; 2008 midden layer to the east of the ancillary building and 2076 is from wall core material.

Group 9 (SF 32, SF 48, SF 46, SF 50, SF 219, SF 298, SF 401, SF 407, SF 424) is a large group representing at least one vessel which has similar characteristics with regards to size and appearance to Group 6. This was a substantial vessel type with a thickness of 18 mm at the rim and up to 25 mm at the wall. A few of the fragments in this group have signs of conservation in the form of perforations and iron staining from rivets (SF 32, SF 298, SF 401, SF 407, SF 424). One sherd, SF 32, has the remnants of a rivet in place.

Group 7 (SF 143, SF 432) (Fig. 19.7) are very flared examples of rim sherds, which also include evidence for repair. The walls are reasonably thick, from 11 to 14 mm at the rim and up to 20 mm at the wall. It is very difficult to assign particular sizes for this vessel as the surviving sherds are small. The presence of repair perforations is an important indication that vessels when broken could be repaired and conserved relatively easily.

Group 12 (SF 33, SF 185, SF 217) represents a probable single vessel of a slightly odd morphology. Though sub-rectangular in plan, this vessel appears to have been very shallow compared to others in this Type 4 category. It may be an example of a vessel which has been reworked due to a fractured rim, resulting in a shallower than normal vessel. The vessel was well-used, with degradation visible on the external surface of SF 33, and thick sooting on SF 185 and SF 217.

GROUP 4 TYPE 6 LONG-HANDLED VESSEL/LADLE

SF 31, 2007, Phase 7, Trench 5, Handle from long-handled vessel/ladle (Fig. 19.8)

Type 6 vessels are not numerous but have often been recovered as single examples from Viking and Norse sites in the Northern Isles. This type is also known in Norway, where Skjølsvold considered them strongly associated with the Viking period in Norway (1961, 15). There has not yet been a systematic study of all examples (including other materials, such as wood) which may narrow down the dating of these long-handled vessels. It is possible that

Fig. 19.8: Long handled vessel fragment SF 31

the chronological trends associated with them across the North Atlantic region will differ markedly from the Viking period association suggested by Skjølsvold for Norway.

This find is from Phase 7, and specifically to a midden layer dating to the 12th to 13th centuries, to the south of the abandoned ancillary buildings. As with the Type 1 vessel, the dating for these finds is traditionally earlier. Examples from Shetland tend also to be associated with the Viking Age, such as at Jarlshof where examples were recovered from Phases 1–3, AD 800–1000, and Old Scatness, where a complete example is contemporary with the Viking-age remodelling of an Iron Age wheelhouse (SF 14950, Forster 2010, 266). A similar find from Norwick, Shetland is also dated to earlier Norse phases, although the dating here is not as complete (Forster 2006). Later examples of ladle vessels do exist, but are relatively unique in design and should perhaps be seen as one-off examples. These include finely worked examples in Shetland from Sandwick South (Bigelow, forthcoming) and another from Kebister (Sharman 1999, 174–5), both suggesting a small and more refined vessel type.

SF 31 comprises the handle, which has detached from the bowl along with a small part of the vessel wall and is broken at the tip. The handle is 105 mm long and between 50 and 60 mm in circumference. Working is visible on both the handle and the internal face of the bowl. There is burning on the bottom of the handle but no sooting or residue is visible internally or on the fracture. The find is worn and was clearly well used prior to breakage.

Residue analysis

Many of the steatite artefacts are sooted and some show possible signs of encrustation with food residues. Scientific study of these may yet yield useful information on foodstuffs, diet and agriculture. The material is available in archive for future enquiry.

The provenance of the steatite vessels: preliminary findings

Richard Jones and Amanda Forster

The above catalogue of the vessels from the site suggests, in some cases, a broad provenance of some of the vessel groups to either Norway or Shetland. This idea of provenance is based on the morphological features of the vessels, comparing examples from sites across the North Atlantic region and considering the most likely source. Typological work is based on the extensive survey of hundreds of artefacts from across the region, including finds from the major source areas of Norway, Shetland and Greenland (Forster 2004). However, without the input of science-based analysis, these characterisations can only ever be hypothetical. An ongoing project led by the authors of this summary report (named *Homeland to home*) and part-funded by the US National Science Foundation (as part of the *Comparative Island Ecodynamics in the North Atlantic Project*), is gathering morphological and science-based data in order to more fully examine the question of provenance of steatite artefacts in the North Atlantic region (Forster and Jones 2017).

The material from The Bay of Skaill has provided 14 additional samples from this well stratified and dated site (Table 19.2), with the range of evidence and identifiable steatite vessel fragments suiting the needs of the study. This data is unable to be fully interpreted with regards to precise source at the time of writing. However, analysis does provide some intriguing insights into the range of potential sources and the comparison of the finds both within the site and with finds from other Orcadian Viking/Late Norse settlement sites such as Pool and Quoygrew. For example, despite the similar typological nature of vessel groups present in Bay of Skaill and Quoygrew, none of the potentially Norwegian examples at Bay of Skaill seem to relate to the Quoygrew 'outliers' which have been taken to be Norwegian (see Batey *et al.* 2012, 207f). In addition, vessel sherds which are suggested to be Norwegian and Shetland vessel groups based on typological attributes have broadly similar rare earth element (REE) compositions and moreover several of them compare well with analysis of samples from the large quarry site of Catpund, Shetland. This should suggest that *either* one or more Norwegian

Table 19.2: Vessel fragments from Bay of Skaill excavations with samples taken for science-based provenance analysis

SF no.	ICP-MS	XRF	Vessel group	Likely source suggested by morphology
31	✓	✓	Group 4	Shetland
50	✓		Group 9	Shetland
54	✓	✓	Group 2	Norway
143	✓	✓	Group 7	Shetland
219	✓	✓	Group 9	Shetland
238	✓	✓	Group 8	Shetland
272	✓	✓	Base fragment	Shetland?
298	✓		Group 9	Shetland
305	✓	✓	Group 11	Norway
372a	✓	✓	Group 1	Norway?
372b	✓	✓	Group 1	Norway?
378	✓		Group 6	Shetland
395	✓	✓	Group 1	Norway
445		✓	Group 6	Shetland

sources have compositions very similar to those recorded at Catpund in Shetland, *or* the morphological indicators are unreliable in the North Atlantic context. For the moment it is likely that these various scenarios all hold elements of truth, but until a fuller composition database for the many Norwegian quarry sites becomes available, the first scenario cannot be reliably tested.

Discussion

Amanda Forster

The evidence from the Bay of Skaill would suggest that steatite was a material familiar to the inhabitants at the site, and one which was almost exclusively associated with imported vessels. In terms of chronology, the site spans the period around which steatite would have been commonly used across the Northern Isles and the assemblage reflects those recovered from settlements of a similar date in Orkney and Shetland. There are no examples of raw material recovered and very few examples of the small miscellaneous flakes which might be indicative of on-site manufacture or modification. The vessels would certainly have been imported as complete and finished artefacts, mostly of the sub-rectangular type strongly associated with Shetland. Typologically, there are very few changes or developments in the use of steatite vessels from the mid-10th century through to their falling out of favour around the end of the 13th century. However, this group is a typical Viking-Late Norse assemblage.

The vessels recorded at the site are generally large (in both size and volume), which is not unusual for Norse period steatite vessels. Flat-based sub-rectangular vessels would have provided both large capacity and stability, presumably sitting on or near to the hearth as an almost permanent fixture (they would have been very heavy). The distribution of the fragments seems to bear this out; many of the larger fragments were recovered from around the hearth area in the longhouse, perhaps not falling too far from where the vessel may have broken. Once the material had been transported as far as the midden, fragments tended to be smaller in size and in weight.

The finds at Bay of Skaill are well used, with evidence of scouring (from cleaning, *e.g.* SF 388) and sooting visible on most vessel fragments. The vessels would seem to have been used in the domestic context and associated primarily with the longhouse, disposed of when broken and occasionally reworked. The smaller portable objects recorded at the site (*e.g.* the spindle whorls and drill whorl) were reworked from broken vessel sherds. It is possible that some of the larger steatite vessel sherds were retained within the longhouse as a useful material for recycling into other objects.

Provenance and form

The greatest number of vessels from the site were imported from Shetland, with just a small number of well-made examples originating in Norway. This identification is based on typological characteristics. Science-based provenance provides some interesting comparisons with other Orcadian Norse sites, and suggests tantalising differences between the assemblage recovered from Quoygrew, to those from Bay of Skaill and perhaps Pool. The scientific data is not yet conclusive, but these

apparent groupings are promising. There seems to be a strong case that the majority of material could be linked positively to the Catpund quarry – the largest quarry in the southern Mainland of Shetland and one which would be a logical source. The potential for some vessels to be from Norwegian quarries cannot be ruled out at this stage, and the typological evidence attests to either a direct source, or a knowledge and replication of Norwegian vessel forms.

The emphasis on sub-rectangular vessels is consistent with the dating of the site, and only the Type 1 and Type 6 examples would look at home in an earlier assemblage. In such small numbers these few vessels are not out of place in later contexts, but would have been different to the rest and perhaps provided something special and more exotic. The carinated examples (Group 1) may only represent a single vessel, but it would have been very different in appearance to the chunky sub-rectangular vessels imported from Shetland. How it came to be at the site could provide an interesting story and one which reflects the status of the settlement and its links to more exotic goods – would such a vessel be a result of travel, or a gift from a higher status individual or visitor to the site.

Spatial distribution

Despite the fact that structures, middens and many other artefacts of comparable date were retrieved from Snusgar, only two steatite fragments (SF 5 and SF 119) were recovered from Trench 4, with the vast majority coming from East Mound (Trench 5; n=111 fragments; weight = 22 kg). Three fragments were recovered from Trench 8 (SFs 377, 445 and 429), with one residual piece from later deposits in Trench 6 (SF 126).

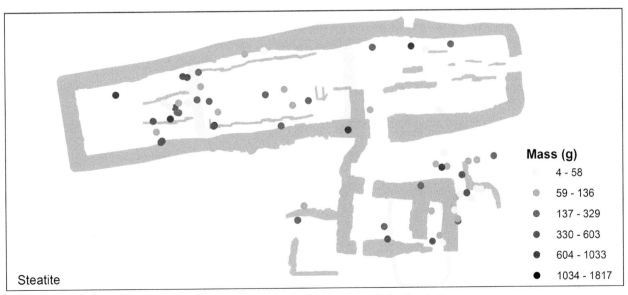

Fig. 19.9: Distribution plot of steatite finds, Trench 5

This distribution would suggest that the use of steatite artefacts is very much associated with the occupation of the longhouse at East Mound (Fig. 19.9), with a strong representation of finds associated with the longhouse floor and annex (c. 29 finds), the byre/workshop (6), the ancillary building (c. 9), and its adjoining external midden (c. 14). A few finds made their way into wall cores – perhaps providing a useful levelling stone or included in the midden brought in as wall core material.

Conservation and curation

As is common with many assemblages, there are examples of vessels which have been repaired (*e.g.* SF 143, SF 401) and smaller portable objects carved from broken sherds (*e.g.* the whorls). These few examples of re-working and conservation suggest that steatite vessels could be reasonably easily replaced when broken, but were worth recycling if possible. The overall preservation of the assemblage is good in terms of fragmentation, with an average vessel fragment weight of 232 g. For comparison, the large assemblage recovered from Norwick, Shetland, has a vessel fragment average weight of 285 g, and at Old Scatness the same figure is 148 g for Viking and Norse period vessels (personal observation). In Iceland, where steatite finds are few in number and were presumably very difficult to replace, the average can be as low as 35 g, such as at Hriesheimar (Forster 2014).

There is some suggestion that examples of the Norwegian imported vessels reminiscent of Viking-type bowls may have been curated. These vessels would have been harder to replace and perhaps held greater significance than the Shetland type vessels. Unfortunately, as we are unable to date the manufacture of these objects, and they were known to have been common in Norway throughout the medieval period, we cannot rule out their introduction to the site at a later date.

Range of artefacts

The range of artefact types in use at the site is limited mainly to vessels, with a small number of whorls and two probable bakestone fragments. The lack of raw material should not be a huge factor in determining the variety of artefact types present in the assemblage; many of the regulars within Norse assemblages, such as weights and whorls, are manufactured from re-worked vessels fragments. Instead, it seems more likely that specialist activities took place in other areas of the settlement and although this is difficult to establish from the finds alone, it is this lack of certain finds within the assemblage which could be one of the most interesting aspects of it.

The very low numbers of spindle whorls from the whole assemblage (including other materials) and the apparent lack of loomweights or fishing weights is unusual for longhouse sites in the Northern Isles. The animal bones recovered at the site do indicate wool was a likely product of the sheep reared by the site's occupants, and the fish recorded suggests off-shore fishing, which would have required line sinkers and weights (Chapter 10).

Producing and processing wool would have been a staple activity within the settlement and the recovery of only two whorls seems striking. The presence of numerous vessel fragments within the longhouse attest to deposition of objects within the occupation surfaces of the structure (*e.g.* they were not simply all cleaned out). In fact, the contexts that include the largest numbers of steatite finds are found in longhouse floor deposits 2219, 12 fragments weighing 2.2 kg, and 2224, 11 fragments weighing 2.7 kg. The average weight of the finds in both these contexts indicates they were not simply the small fragments which had fallen between the cracks and crannies of the floor surface.

At Quoygrew, the partial Phase 2 deposits of House 5 included only steatite vessels (see Barrett 2012, 278), however, the later Phase 3 House 1, which was more complete, did include a wider variety of artefact types, with vessels, spindle whorls and loom weights present within the structure (*ibid.,* 284). At Old Scatness, a cache of large broken steatite vessels fragments, alongside cobbles and finished loom weights numbering 60 in total, was recovered from an occupation surface in Structure 34 (Forster 2010, 283). At Jarlshof, a cache of 52 weights was recovered from House 7, dating to the 11th century (Hamilton 1956, 183). One site which does have a similarly low number of steatite fishing and loom weights within the settlement complex is Pool, Sanday. Here, vessels and bakestones were the most prevalent finds, although 23 spindle whorls were also recovered (Smith and Forster 2007, 433). One fishing weight was recovered and no steatite loomweights, however, a number of sandstone weights were attributed to the Viking and Late Norse phases (n=9) (see Clarke 2007, 381). Larger caches of weights at some sites seem to suggest that areas of specialist activity were present within settlement complexes, whereas others illustrate how smaller numbers of objects can often find their way into occupation areas. At the Bay of Skaill, the faunal evidence (Chapter 9) is perhaps the best indicator that these activities would have been part of the day-to-day economy of the site, but that the objects and tools associated were not kept or used within the longhouse or adjacent buildings excavated.

20

Ceramics

Derek Hall and Michael J. Hughes

These excavations produced 52 sherds of pottery and one spherical clay object (see Table 20.1). Thirteen of the pottery sherds are a distinctively decorated glazed pottery and 39 are sherds of an unglazed greyware fabric. The standard deviation errors in the elemental signatures for those sherds in these fabrics that were scientifically analysed suggest that they may be from only two vessels.

The glazed whitewares

The whiteware sherds (Fig. 20.1) are glazed amber brown and four of them have applied decorative clay pads glazed brown (SF 107, SF 339, SF 408, SF 112). Three sherds, a rim (SF 262), a body sherd with a pronounced cordon (SF 110) and a baluster basal angle (SF 430) provide some evidence for original vessel form. All of these

Table 20.1: Ceramics by phase

Phase	Context	SF no	Description	Context description
3	2219	SF 331	13 sherds of Coarseware including joining basal angle and bodysherds	Longhouse floor
3	2273	SF 419	1 sherd of Coarseware	Annex floor
3	2275	SF 443	1 sherd of glazed French pottery	Longhouse floor (possibly intrusive)
5	163/2146	SF 430	1 bodysherd from glazed French pottery	Longhouse floor/deposit internal
5	2115	SF 111	3 sherds of glazed French pottery	Ancillary building floor
5	2146	SF 248, SF 262	2 sherds of glazed French pottery (one is a rimsherd SF262)	Longhouse floor
5	2163/2146	SF 430	1 basesherd from glazed French pottery	Longhouse floor/deposit internal
5	2241	SF 403	5 sherds of Coarseware (base and sidewall)	Annex floor
5	2241	SF 411	2 bodysherds of Coarseware	Annex floor
5	2261	SF 408	1 sherd of Coarseware	Longhouse floor
6	2197	SF 135	1 sherd of glazed French pottery	External surface
6	2226	SF 339	1 sherd of glazed French pottery	Deposit internal
6	2227	SF 345	8 bodysherds of Coarseware (1 with drilled hole)	Annex floor
6	2227	SF 353	1 sherd of glazed French pottery, 8 sherds of coarseware (rim and seven bodysherds)	Annex floor
8	2044	SF 84	1 bodysherd Coarseware	External
8	2200	SF 297	1 sherd of glazed French pottery	Disturbed

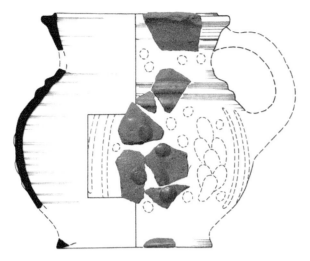

Fig. 20.1: Glazed whitewares, vessel reconstruction

Fig. 20.2: Coarsewares

sherds appear to come from a single glazed jug with a rim diameter of 80 mm and pronounced cordons around its neck that is decorated with applied clay pads glazed brown, it also had a baluster base (Fig. 20.1). It does not match the established parameters of any pottery currently known from the Scottish mainland, and is an unusual continental import (see below, Discussion and conclusions).

The coarse greywares (Figs 20.2 and 20.3)

The greyware sherds are unglazed and come from a vessel with a flat-topped rim (SF 348), a rim diameter of 165 mm and a flat base (SF 403 and SF 331). A rim sherd (SF 345) has a 5 mm diameter hole drilled through it 35 mm from the top of the rim. This was presumably used for either suspending the vessel or to hold in place a cover. Some of the sherds show traces of smoke blackening suggesting that this vessel was used for cooking. These greyware fabrics are also difficult to provenance and date, imported greywares are known on the Scottish mainland from the Low Countries, Denmark and East Anglia dating to the 12th/13th centuries (Hall and Chenery 2005) but these sherds share none of the characteristics of these fabrics. There are no known parallels for such fabrics in the Craggan Type Ware tradition of the Scottish west coast and Islands and again these sherds would appear to be from an imported vessel (Cheape 1993).

Site locations, contexts and phasing

All of the ceramic finds come from Trench 5, and are associated with the East Mound longhouse and its environs. The sherds from the single decorated glazed vessel come from 2163/2146 (SF 430) 2275 (SF 443), internal longhouse floors (Phase 5); 2115 (SF 111) ancillary building floor (Phase 5); 2197 (SF 135) external surface (Phase 6); 2226 (SF 339) deposit internal (Phase 6); 2227 (SF 353) annex

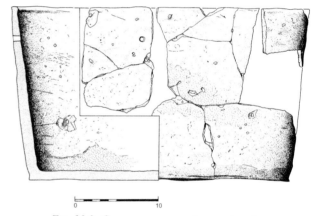

Fig. 20.3: Coarsewares, vessel reconstruction

floor (Phase 6); 2200 (SF 297) disturbed (Phase 8) and seem to have been widely distributed across the trench.

The sherds from the single coarseware cooking vessel (Fig. 20.3) come from 2219 (SF 331) longhouse floor (very disturbed) (Phase 3), 2273 (S F419) annex floor (Phase 5), 2241 (SF 403, SF 411) annex floor (Phase 5), 2261 (SF 408) longhouse floor (Phase 5), 2227 (SF 345, SF 353) annex floor (Phase 6) and 2044 (SF 84) external (Phase 8) and would seem to represent a cooking vessel that is in use in an annex to the longhouse.

Scientific analysis

In 2007 a sherd of glazed whiteware (SF 135, from 2197) and a sherd of coarse greyware (SF 84, from 2044) were thin sectioned and chemically sourced by the late Alan Vince. In his report Dr Vince stated that, 'The glazed ware is consistent with a Tertiary French source but to be honest contains rocks and inclusions which have a wide outcrop.' The handmade thick-walled unglazed cooking pot was seen to be packed with rounded fragments of volcanic rocks, which seemed to Dr Vince to be (a) not Orcadian and (b) quite fresh, *i.e.* probably tertiary and therefore not mainland Scottish either. He felt that Ulster was a strong possibility as a source for this fabric.

In 2013 further chemical analysis using Inductively-coupled plasma spectrometry (ICPS) was carried out on nine sherds in both fabrics by Dr Michael Hughes (five glazed wares and four coarsewares). The two previous analyses of sherds by Alan Vince (V5018 and 5019) from the site were available and were compared against the new set of analyses, as were relevant databases of analyses of pottery.

The samples were numbered 1–9 and their full site numbers and ICPS are available in the online archive, and summarised as follows: visual examination of the data showed that the sherds fell into two very distinctive chemical patterns: sherds 1–5 (and V5018) were of a high alumina clay, low in iron, magnesium, calcium and sodium and unusually low in potassium – a whiteware clay; the other four sherds 6–9 (and V5019) had a very unusual chemical analysis, with extremely high transition metal trace elements chromium, nickel and vanadium – this chromium level in pottery is higher than virtually anything previously seen by the author. The two distinct chemical patterns suggest the sherds were from two very different clay sources. Close inspection of the full range of element analyses shows extremely similar analyses for the sherds of each pattern, such that they very probably represent just two pots. The relative standard deviations for sherds 1–5 were 2–5% for the major elements and 4–5% for many trace elements; these are comparable to the percentage error associated with the analytical process coupled with the small variations expected within a single clay pot. Sherds 6–9 have only slightly higher figures than these but are also consistent with fragments of a single pot. It is less likely, though possible, that the sherds include more than one pot made in identical clay.

Sherds 1–5

Sherds 1–5 have a chemical pattern consistent with production in the Parisian area. When compared to the average analyses by X-ray fluorescence (XRF) of northern French highly decorated whitewares from a number of sites (Boivin *et al.* 1996), their Rouen group b in beige sandy fabric and Poissy fabric a (Boivin *et al.* 1996, 76, table 4) had slightly higher aluminium than sherds 1–5 but all other elements are comparable. In particular sherds 1–5 share the distinctively higher iron content of highly decorated wares made in the northern Ile de France, which included these sherds found at Rouen and Poissy (Boivin *et al.* 1996, 78). In contrast, highly decorated wares produced in the area of Rouen have a lower iron content (average 1.57%) than the finds at Poissy (average of 3.09%; A. Bouquet-Lienard, pers. comm.); sherds 1–5 contain the higher iron level of the latter. Of XRF analyses

of sherds from other French sites, those from the Villadin workshop also had higher aluminium but lower iron than sherds 1–5 (*op cit.*, table 6), but those from St Omer and Metz had quite different chemical profiles (Boivin *et al.* 1996).

The difference in iron content appears to be a key defining feature, allowing sherds 1–5 to be associated with production in the north of Ile de France rather than Rouen. Vince (2011) carried out a number of ICPS studies on northern French whitewares (analyses available at Vince 2010), comparing them to earlier X-ray fluorescence analyses of whiteware sherds found at Bergen (Deroeux *et al.* 1994), and found a distinctive chemical pattern for the whitewares produced in the region of Rouen. He earlier used the statistical technique of factor analysis to compare the ICPS analyses of the products of the Carolingian period kiln at La Londe; northern French whitewares found at Southampton (Hughes 2002–3); 10th–11th century glazed wares from various sites in Rouen; and late 12th and 13th century Rouen-type glazed wares from various sites in Europe (Vince 2005; 2011, 200). This showed a common chemical cluster which included the La Londe wasters, the Rouen early glazed wares, the later Rouen glazed wares, and the Southampton whitewares. However, although sherds 1–5 have similar analyses to the La Londe sherds they show minor differences – lime, sodium and the rare earths were slightly higher in 1–5, and titanium, chromium and yttrium were higher in La Londe. Examination of the original ICPS datasets of Alan Vince shows slightly different chemical profiles among northern French whitewares, for example of the eleven La Londe sherds analysed, two had significantly higher rare earth element concentrations, similar to sherds 1–5, while the remainder had levels about half these. The same bimodal pattern of rare earth elements was found among the Southampton whitewares (Hughes 2002–3), but not the two from Wood Quay, Dublin (Vince 2006: CMC10 and 15) which had lower rare earth elements but were otherwise like sherds 1–5. Four examples of Normandy Gritty wares had relatively high rare earths and similar chemical features to other Rouen wares (Hughes 2002–3). The bimodal pattern of rare earth elements merits further investigation, while the multiple but related chemical profiles suggests multiple workshops using different sources and clay preparation techniques. Dufournier (1981) analysed the major chemical elements in numerous clay samples collected in northern France and showed an area of clay straddling the Seine which had an average analysis very similar to that of sherds 1–5.

The XRF analyses which provided confirmation that the excavated sherds originated in the north of the Ile de France were for major elements only, so it is not clear whether trace elements also distinguish highly decorated wares from the Parisian area from Rouen wares. However, there are indications of differences in other elements such as the rare earth elements, but further analyses are needed to investigate this possibility.

Sherds 6–9

Sherds 6–9 have a very unusual analysis: very high iron (it is very rare for iron oxide in pottery to exceed 8%); extremely high chromium; and high vanadium (very rare to contain over 150 ppm) and nickel (again, rare to exceed 100 ppm). The magnesium is also significantly high for a pottery clay (2–3% is more common). Thorium and uranium are by contrast distinctly lower than usual, but the rare earths are a typical level for pottery. Ulster has been suggested as the origin of this handmade pottery, and the Antrim basalts – rich in iron and magnesium – contain just such a combination of elements as found in the Snusgar handmade sherds. The Antrim basalts (Antrim Lava Group) cover a large area whose southern boundary is from Lough Neagh to Belfast, extending east to the coast and north to Ballycastle (Simms 2000, 331: Fig. 8). The British Geological Survey of Northern Ireland geochemical map for nickel shows high levels coincident with the occurrence of the basalt. Red palaeosols derived from the basalt occur at its junction with the underlying Ulster White Limestone, and major weathered horizons occur on the Causeway Coast of north Antrim, while grey clays derived from the weathering of rhyolitic ash are found west of Lough Neagh (Simms 2000, 328). For example, a basalt from Co. Antrim (Simms 2000, 329, table 2) contains high levels of iron (14.1%), magnesium (15.4%), titanium (1.5%) and sodium (1.41%), with low potassium (0.31%) and high nickel (497 ppm) and vanadium (245 ppm) – chromium was not analysed. The basalt and a grey clay from Coagh (a few miles W of Lough Neagh) share similar analysis features to the handmade sherds. Without further analyses of clays from this area, it is not possible geochemically to suggest a specific origin within the province, but it is clear that clays matching the unusual chemical pattern of the sherds of the handmade pot exist in Ulster and are consistent with an origin there. The British Tertiary Volcanic Province, of which the Antrim basalts are a part, extends across western Scotland, including Skye, Ardnamurchan and Mull (Emeleus and Gyopari 1992). Analyses of sherds from Baliscate, Mull included ten examples of Craggan-type (Hall *et al.* 2017), but none showed the very distinctive combination of chemical features of these handmade sherds. However, two of the Craggan sherds contained 10% iron (the rest

7–8%), *c.* 200 ppm chromium (others 74–140 ppm) and *c.* 250 ppm vanadium (others 92–300 ppm), though with 'normal' levels of magnesium and potassium, indicating derivation from basaltic material.

Comparanda

This pottery assemblage is very different from those larger groups of ceramic examined by the author at Quoygrew (Orkney) and Robert's Haven (Caithness) where any pottery present is either of local manufacture (Organic tempered Craggan type wares) or imported from the Scottish mainland and occasionally continental Europe (Scottish Redwares and Scottish White Gritty wares; Rhenish Stonewares) (Hall *et al.* 2012; Hall forthcoming). This author has, so far, not seen the pottery fabrics present here from anywhere else in Scotland.

Discussion and conclusions

Scientific analysis shows that these sherds fall into two distinct chemical patterns: the first is consistent with the analyses of highly decorated wares from the north of Ile de France. The second is of a clay chemical profile not previously recognised among archaeological pottery, but consistent with an Ulster origin, specifically Antrim, associated with clays derived from the local basalt and rhyolite.

Discussions with ceramic colleagues from France indicate that the very distinctively decorated glazed pottery sherds from these excavations originate from Northern France (probably Poissy to the west of Paris). Although the precise/earliest date of its manufacture is not known, on currently published and anecdotal evidence such vessels are not normally dated any earlier than the later 12th century (Fabienne Ravoire, pers. comm.), which falls within the 95.4% probability range of AD 990–1250 given by a radiocarbon date from context (2115) (SUERC 59189). In fact, in France comparable vessels become more frequent in the 13th century (Ravoire 2014 a and b, 58, 60, 119, Fig. 51, no. 11; 120, Fig. 52, no. 1–5; 125, no. 2, 10).

Chemical analysis suggests that the coarse greywares are from Ulster, specifically Antrim. It has not been possible to confirm this postulated identification by comparison with samples from Ulster as no chemical sourcing has yet been carried out on these fabrics in Northern Ireland (C. McSparron pers. comm.). It has also not yet been possible to find an exact parallel for this particular fabric in the published literature.

The 1858 Skaill Viking-Age silver hoard

James Graham-Campbell

The 10th-century silver hoard discovered in 1858 at the Bay of Skaill, Sandwick, Orkney (a selection of objects from which is shown in Fig. 21.1), is amongst the largest and most important find of Viking treasure known from

Fig. 21.1: Brooches and rings from the Skaill hoard, found in 1858, now in National Museums of Scotland © NMS

Scotland. It consists of over 8 kg of silver, with the next largest Orkney hoard, that from Burray (found in 1889), having an estimated weight of *c.* 2 kg (Graham-Campbell 1995, 127, 141). Detailed descriptions and full discussion of the non-numismatic contents of the Skaill hoard, numbering 115(+) pieces, are available in the present author's catalogue of *The Viking-Age Gold and Silver of Scotland* (Graham-Campbell 1995, no. 24). The 21 surviving coins, which include Islamic dirhams, have been published by Robert Stevenson (1966, nos 69, 177 and 715–33). Michael Dolley's proposed deposition date for the hoard of *c.* 950 (Dolley 1966, 50, no. 84) has since been revised to *c.* 960–80 (see below). The following account summarises this earlier work on the Skaill hoard, but provides greater detail concerning the locality of its discovery in March 1858, in the light of the researches presented in this volume, which were summarised provisionally in Griffiths (2013).

Discovery and recovery

The primary source for the discovery and subsequent recovery of the Skaill (1858) hoard is the well-known Orkney antiquary, George Petrie (1818–75),[1] who visited Sandwick only a couple of days after its discovery to interview the finders and to obtain the silver in their possession, as Treasure Trove, on behalf of the then Sheriff-substitute. The relevant Petrie papers form two groups of Society of Antiquaries of Scotland manuscripts (in NMS):

(i) SAS 487: 'Correspondence etc of George Petrie re the recovery of relics in the silver hoard at Skaill'; and

(ii) SAS 378 (stored with SAS 487): a draft and fair copy of his 'Notice of a large collection of Fibulae, Torcs and other silver ornaments and Coins discovered in the Parish of Sandwick in Orkney', together with two drafts and a fair copy of his 'Inventory of ancient Silver ornaments &c ...'.

The Petrie papers (SAS 378) include a first draft (no. 221),[2] a revised draft dated 5 April 1858 (no. 221d)[3] and the final manuscript of his 'Inventory' (no. 221e),[4] as eventually published in *Proceedings of the Society of Antiquaries of Scotland* 3 (1857–60), 247–9, headed:

> Inventory of Ancient Silver Ornaments, &c., found buried between the Parish Church and the Burn of 'Rin,' and a short distance from the shore of the Bay of Skaill, in the Parish of Sandwick, Mainland of Orkney. The greater portion of the articles were discovered on 11th March 1858 by some country people – the hook and a few fragments having been picked up by a boy the previous week at the mouth of a rabbit-hole.

This will have accompanied the hoard from Kirkwall to Edinburgh, where it was exhibited to the Society of Antiquaries of Scotland on 12 April by Professor Aytoun, Sheriff of Orkney (*ibid.*, 107). The following year it was donated by the Exchequer to the Museum, on 14 June 1859 (*ibid.*, 245).

Petrie's draft manuscript (no. 221b) 'Notice of a large collection ...' is dated 1 November 1858 and was thus completed by him over six months after the hoard's discovery (in March).[5] The content of this 'Notice', replete with crossing-outs and re-writes in Petrie's own hand, was that from which Graham-Campbell quoted *in extenso* in 1995 (p. 124). However, since then, Petrie's fair copy of his (12-page) final version, with the same date, has been located among his papers (SAS 378,2), presumably in the form in which it would have been submitted to the Society of Antiquaries in Edinburgh, although nothing is seemingly known as to why it was never published. The following passage therefore provides his own definitive account of 'the discovery of the Treasure as communicated to me by the finders':

> In the beginning of last March (1858) a lad sauntering near the Parish Church of Sandwick not far from the Shore on the north side of the Bay of Skaill observed something of a bright metallic appearance lying in the Sand. A closer examination led to the discovery of several articles scattered about apparently cast up by rabbits burrowing there. They consisted of a hook with ring attached (No. of the Inventory accompanying this)[6] and a penannular ring with several fragments of other ornaments. It was only some days afterwards that the lad found out that they were silver. On this becoming known to the neighbours they resolved

> to examine the place in the hope of finding some more Silver Relics and on the morning of Thursday 11th March some of them being at the Bay of Skaill collecting Sea Weed, and waiting for the landing of a quantity which was drifting about in the surf and not likely to be cast ashore for some time, one of them proposed that they should in the meantime go and examine the Spot where the Silver had been found. This being readily agreed to, they accordingly proceeded thither, and one of them thrust his 'ware pick' into a rabbit-hole and on attempting to withdraw it found that it had hooked on to something in the hole. On pulling it out a glance was sufficient to satisfy the searchers that the ring-like objects in the groups of the 'pick' were somewhat more valuable than 'tangles' or sea-weed which it was at first thought the pick or fork had hooked and an eager scramble commenced, each trying to secure as much as possible of the treasure. On the whole they seem to have divided it pretty equally among them. Subsequently the sand all around the spot was thoroughly sifted, and examined, and a number of fragments were discovered. It was two days afterwards that I heard of the discovery and obtained possession of the articles as already described.

It is perhaps worth adding Petrie's slightly more extended version of the penultimate sentence from his draft (Graham-Campbell 1995, 124):

> Subsequently a number of boys and others visited the place and have carefully sifted the sand thereabouts and discovered a number of fragments of Ring Brooches, and Torcs, and coins &c. the most of which it is believed has been given up.

The first printed account of the hoard's discovery appeared in the local newspaper, *The Orcadian*, on Monday 29 March 1858. A further report was published the following month in the *John O'Groat Journal* (24 April 1858), quoted in the *Gentleman's Magazine* (1858), 542.

Location

As documented above, the Skaill hoard was found in 1858 on the north side of the Bay of Skaill, on the property of Edward Irvine of Quoyloo, the extent of which is marked on the (1834) 'Plan of the Township of Scarwell' (Fig. 2.6) as consisting of the large field (now subdivided) containing part of the 'Castle of Snusgar', bounded then, as now, by a track along its eastern side. Irvine's property did not extend as far south as the Burn of Rin/Snusgar; it is evident therefore that the find-place cannot have been as far south as indicated on Graham-Campbell's location map (1995, fig. 49), where it is located on the wrong side of this dyke, but rather to the east side of the mound, towards 'a small spring head which runs seasonally and feeds the Burn of Rin/Snusgar' (Griffiths 2013, 506).[7]

The RCAMS *Inventory of Orkney* (1946) contains no further information, noting only that this 'very remarkable hoard' had been 'found between the parish church and the Burn of Snusgar, near the Bay of Skaill' (*Orkney & Shetland*, vol. II, 270, no. 734).

In 1980, while researching the find-places of the Viking hoards from Orkney and Shetland, Olwyn Owen collected information from descendants of those involved in the discovery of the Skaill hoard, notably James, grandchild of William Brass, and his wife Edna. Owen's observation (pers. comm.) was that 'local people were very clear in their accounts of their grandparents' discovery of the hoard and its exact findplace', with the result that she was 'fairly happy that the Skaill hoard came from the east side of the mound known as the Castle of Snusgar'.

This combined documentary and local evidence for the find-place of the Skaill hoard, on the east side of the mound known as the Castle of Snusgar, meets all the criteria that can be established from Petrie's own accounts: it being located between Skaill Church and the Burn of Rin/Snusgar, not far from the shore, and in a sandy area with rabbit activity. This location also accords with the understanding of J. Storer Clouston, the Orcadian author and historian (1870–1944), that 'the find had been made about 800 m north of the mansion-house of the estate' (as reported in Grieg 1940, 133), which description places it in the vicinity of the burn (as opposed to the church). Clouston was one of the gentlemen who 'most courteously assisted' Sigurd Grieg during his 1925 visit to Kirkwall (1940, 10).[8]

There was, however, one somewhat divergent voice which caused Grieg to comment that 'about the locality itself the information varies somewhat' (1940, 133). In his 'Introduction' to 'Viking antiquities of Scotland', Grieg records that 'I am also indebted, for a great deal of important information, to Mr. *J. W. Cursiter*, who happened to be staying at Kirkwall in the summer of 1925' (*ibid.*, 10), and what Cursiter told him was that 'the Skaill hoard was brought to light "on the north side of the bay, very near the Church on the west side of the road"' (*ibid.*, 133). It is important to note that Cursiter was only a small boy in 1858 when the hoard was discovered (too young to have had any personal recollection of the event) and was in his mid-seventies when he communicated his version of its find-place to Grieg.[9] There is no obvious explanation for this contrary account other than mistaken memory, given that Cursiter's version of the location varies quite significantly from the eye-witness accounts collected by Petrie at the time, in placing it to the north-west, rather than on the east side, of the Castle of Snusgar. Petrie believed that he had 'obtained a tolerably correct account of the discovery', as given by him in his draft 'Notice'. Graham-Campbell's previously published transcription of this draft has been mentioned above (1995, 124), but to

this should be added the first sentence of its subsequent paragraph:

> There are traces of ruins of a Building a short distance from the spot where the Relics were found and I was informed that Stones were discovered set on edge in the form of a Cist into which it is believed the Silver articles had been deposited.

In Petrie's 'fair copy', the equivalent passage states:

> At a short distance from the place where the Relics were discovered there are traces of the ruins of a large building, but there is nothing to connect the treasure with the building.

Whatever the nature and date of this ruined building (see above, Chapter 2), the excavations reported here have amply demonstrated occupation in both the Castle of Snusgar mound and the adjacent 'East Mound' around the time of the hoard's deposition in the second half of the 10th century (*c.* 960–80), within the area of settlement activity, if Cursiter's otherwise unattested whereabouts for its deposition is rejected in favour of that documented here.

On balance, therefore, it seems that the location of the hoard was most probably more or less correctly plotted on the (1902) OS map (Fig. 2.7), not having been shown on the first (1882) edition.

Contents

Petrie's final 'Inventory' of the contents of the Skaill hoard, including the coins, as submitted by him on 5 April 1858, contains 120 entries; however, there are now 115(+) items of silver bullion on record (as listed below, nos 1–6), with the addition of 21 coins (NMS: X.IL 103–13):

1. The 'Treasure Trove' (NMS: X.IL 1–102)
2. Cursiter: 2 ring fragments (Hunterian Museum: B.1914.696 and 699)
3. Storer Clouston: 1 'ball-type' penannular brooch (NMS: X.IL 742)
4. Collins/Milsom: 3 rings (NMS: X.IL 385–7)
5. Grant: 4 pieces, including a pin (NMS: X.IL 514–17)
6. Robertson: 2 pieces, including a brooch pin (NMS: X.IL 840–1)

No unofficial 'escapes' seem to have come to Petrie's attention between the completion of his official 'Inventory' and the writing of his 'Report', over six months later, which would have provided him with a good opportunity to put any further material on record. The fact remains, however, that there are twelve pieces of silver now known from the Skaill hoard (some substantial; nos 2–6, listed above) that were not included in his 'Inventory', thus accounting for the increase in the weight of the hoard from 'sixteen pounds avoirdupois' (7.26 kg), when officially weighed on 15 April 1858 (*Proceedings of the Society of Antiquaries of Scotland* 3 (1857–60), 249) to the current 8.11 kg, as calculated by Graham-Campbell (1995, 127). It is noteworthy in this connection that the last two pieces to come to light (no. 6: a large 'ball-type' brooch pin and a separate pin-head) were purchased by NMS (in 1981) from a direct descendant of the James Robertson who was the Sheriff-substitute of Orkney when the hoard was discovered (Graham-Campbell 1984; 1995, 127).

There seems to have been no great dishonesty on the part of the original finders in handing over their shares of the hoard, despite some initial suspicion to the contrary (see Graham-Campbell 1984, 294; 1995, 126). However, one of them (David Smith) admitted to Petrie that, not knowing the value of his finds, he had at first 'left them within reach of his children, and of parties who came to see them & he thought some of the things had gone missing', but later (on 18 March) he wrote to Petrie concerning the articles 'lost in consequence of my little boy getting at them and scattering them about our Garden', for he was 'happy to report that all of them or nearly so have been found', with the result that 'six armlets' were subsequently delivered up to Petrie in Kirkwall, on 20 March, but there was 'a pin which is still yet lost' (Graham-Campbell 1995, 126).

There exists therefore the possibility that a few pieces of the Skaill hoard may yet be missing, although some (such as Smith's pin) might be accounted for amongst those listed above as having come to light during the 20th century, but there is nothing to demonstrate that anything much else has definitely been lost. Finally, it should be noted that, although Olwyn Owen was told in 1980 that 'some metal detecting activity has been taking place around the Castle of Snusgar' (pers. comm.), no finds of Viking silver have been reported from anywhere in the Bay of Skaill since 1858. In consequence, it seems reasonable to conclude that the original contents of the Skaill hoard are now most probably known almost in their entirety.

Dating

The coins from the Skaill hoard have conveniently been summarised by Michael Metcalf (1995, 20):

> With the artefacts there were only twenty-one coins, of which nineteen were dirhams, mostly battered fragments. The latest legible pieces were dated AH 330 and 334 (AD 941/2 and 945/6). There was one coin of Athelstan and one swordless St Peter of York. The date of concealment may have been significantly later than that of the latest coin. The coins are all illustrated in the Edinburgh sylloge (Stevenson 1966).

On this basis, Metcalf (1995, 20) felt it desirable to revise Dolley's (1966, 50, no. 84) oft-quoted deposition date of

c. 950, as adopted by Blackburn and Pagan (1986, 296, no. 129), to a bracket of c. 950–70. This was in fact in line with Stevenson's own suggestion (1966, xiv) that 'from the style of the brooches a deposition well into the second half of the century would be acceptable', regarding '950' as an 'approximate *terminus post quem*' (*ibid.*, vi). However, in a letter to Ingmar Jansson (pers. comm.), dated 19 April 1971, in response to his paper on 'Wikingerschmuck und Münzdatierung' (Jansson 1970), Stevenson wrote that:

> As can be seen from the accounts of the other coin hoards in Scotland, the occurrence at Skaill of one very early 10th century Anglo-Saxon coin and one pre 940 but none of the very common Edred 946 onward makes Skaill correspond much more closely to the large Skye hoard of the second quarter of the century than to the numerous hoards of 970–90 period in which just a few earlier coins survive. This confirms the oriental coins significance. Even if all the Skaill coins were not recovered, as Anderson implies, the probability that they were buried much after 950 is slight.

On the other hand, Gareth Williams has recently suggested that Metcalf's dating should be advanced by a decade, to c. 960–80, 'so as to allow for a slightly longer period for the circulation of the nineteen dirhams' (Graham-Campbell 2011a, 18, note 12).[10]

This later deposition bracket brings Skaill more into line with the dating of the two 'Irish Sea' hoards with which its contents have most often be compared: Chester (Castle Esplanade), deposited c. 965, and Ballaquayle, Isle of Man, deposited c. 970 (see below). In addition, it removes the art-historical problem relating to the dating of the Mammen style of Viking art which is used to decorate some of the brooch terminals (Fuglesang 1991, 94, 103), in the manner of the ornament on the Mammen axe itself which has a *terminus ante quem* of 970/71 for its manufacture, from the dendrochronological date for the construction of the chamber-grave in which it was deposited (see Graham-Campbell 1995, 46, with refs).

Discussion

Context

In his recent review of 'The Context of the 1858 Skaill Hoard', Griffiths (2013, 522) suggested that its find-spot might have been 'next to the spring', mentioned above as the small spring-head, located 'some 15 m beyond the eastern flank of the mound … which runs seasonally and feeds the Burn of Rin/Snusgar' (*ibid.*, 504 and 506). Such would allow for the possibility that it had been irretrievably deposited in a wet place for 'sacred' reasons (cf. Graham-Campbell and Sheehan 2009), as 'an act of "votive" deposition in the last years of pagan practice', rather than 'within or very close to a substantial building complex', with a view to its subsequent recovery (Griffiths 2013, 522). However, as Griffiths goes on to observe, 'the record of the silver being found in rabbit burrows points to the [latter], these being less evident on the boggier ground around the spring, than on the mound'. Even if 'the "sacred" alternative cannot be dismissed' – and, indeed, various possible reasons can be advanced for the ritual deposition of Viking silver hoards (cf. Graham-Campbell 2011b, 106–11; Arrhenius 2013) – a further fact needing to be taken into account in this case is that the silver is said to have been protected by some stones 'set on edge in the form of a Cist', suggesting that it had been concealed with sufficient care to ensure that it could be recovered in its entirety when required – or at least safe to do so.

It appears therefore that the Skaill hoard was most probably buried deliberately, for reasons of security, in the east-facing slope of the mound known as the Castle of Snusgar, close to a Norse settlement-site now known to have been established at the time of its deposition in the period between about 960 and 980.

Contents

The Skaill hoard contains a mixture of silver penannular brooches (some with Mammen-style decoration), neck- and arm-rings (including a quantity of 'ring-money'), ringed pins, ingots and hammered bars, together with some miscellaneous fragments, to a total of 115(+) pieces, and the relatively small number of 21 coins, to a total weight of 8.11 kg (Graham-Campbell 1995 and Stevenson 1966, as above). The following observations are edited excerpts from the author's earlier discussion of 'The nature of the hoard', where greater detail and full references are to be found (Graham-Campbell 1995, 34–48 at 47–8):

> A low number of coins is a notable feature of late tenth- to eleventh-century mixed hoards from Scotland containing 'ring-money'. The most obvious comparisons for the Skaill hoard are to be made with those from Tarbat, Ross-shire, Quendale, Shetland, and Burray, Orkney. The latter is of particular relevance in this context; weighing about two kilograms, it contained only something over a dozen coins in relation to its 140 items of bullion.
>
> On the basis of their wear, the 'ball-type' brooches with Mammen-style decoration had certainly not been newly commissioned, but it is difficult to conceive that they had already come to be regarded as so-old fashioned that their presence in the hoard was simply to provide a source of raw material for a silversmith (although one does consist only of a detached terminal). There is, indeed, a small number of fresh pieces, including some of the neck-rings and the magnificent animal-headed arm-ring, but much of the rest, including the 'ring-money', is in good ordinary condition; this material is not in evident

need of recycling, although there are a few repaired or modified twisted-rod rings. In addition, there are only two or three part-manufactured items and a couple of rod fragments that might be considered as silversmith's waste. On balance, the Skaill hoard has the appearance of a normal mixed hoard for tenth-century Scotland, even it is the largest known, equivalent in size to the largest Viking-age silver hoards found in mainland Scandinavia (Graham-Campbell 1993, 180).

There is a more-or-less constant low level of nicking throughout the Skaill ornaments and hack-silver, with an average of four nicks, slices or pecks per object, whilst most of the coins have been tested by bending. Only some fifteen pieces of the bullion are without any nicks, including two of the 'ball-type' brooches with Mammen-style ornament, whereas there are fourteen that have over ten, with a maximum of thirty-four (on an ingot terminal).

In conclusion, the Skaill hoard combines a mixture of prestige ornaments in usable condition and more mundane pieces, in the form of 'ring-money', although this includes a number of ornate examples, together with a small stock of hack-silver, amongst which the few coins should be included. This substantial treasure was clearly 'active' on more than one socio-economic level and so is not to be categorized simply as a merchant's hoard. On balance, therefore, it would seem most reasonable to interpret the Skaill hoard as the accumulated capital of a Norse chieftain or other leader, or of the most prominent family within the local community, given that the Bay of Skaill represents one of Orkney's prime settlement locations.

The contemporary Viking silver hoard from Britain and Ireland most similar to Skaill is that from Ballaquayle (Douglas), Isle of Man, where it was found by workmen – and partially dispersed – in 1894 (Graham-Campbell 2011a, 157–8, 250–3, no. 13, pls 72–6). The Ballaquayle hoard, which was deposited *c.* 970 (Blackburn and Pagan 1986, no. 165) is, however, considerably smaller than Skaill, with an estimated weight of *c.* 2 kg, although it included many more coins (with an estimated total of between 500 and 1000). According to Kristin Bornholdt Collins (2003, vol. 2, Appendix viii, 44), the Ballaquayle coins were

> …drawn from the active currency pool circulating in and around Man in the 970s, probably on a single occasion or at least over a relatively short period, rather than being added to sporadically over time like a savings account.

The Ballaquayle hoard is distinctive in containing a gold arm-ring, but its 'ball-type' brooch fragments, neck-ring terminal and 'ring-money' arm-rings belong in common with the contents of Skaill. Another shared feature is the comparatively small number of ingots in both hoards, given that there is only one in Ballaquayle.

David Wilson (1974, 40) has commented that

> ... it is possible that the Douglas [Ballaquayle] hoard is the treasure of a single family who were one of the richest in the community living on what was later one of the rich medieval farms of the island.

This interpretation has since been endorsed by both Graham-Campbell (1983, 69; 2011a, 157) and Bornholdt Collins, who has calculated that the complete contents of the hoard 'could have bought a flock of at least 330 sheep, and probably closer to 450–500 sheep' (2003, vol. 2, Appendix viii, 43).

It has been suggested that the large mixed hoard from Chester (Castle Esplanade) found in 1950 (Webster 1953), which is similar in size (by weight) and has some clear similarities to the Ballaquayle hoard, might have been the property of a merchant from Ireland or the Isle of Man (Graham-Campbell 2011a, 13). The hack-silver cut from ornaments in this Chester hoard, deposited *c.* 965 (Blackburn and Pagan 1986, no. 144), relates closely to that in Ballaquayle, but the greater part of its non-numismatic silver was in the form of (at least) 98 ingots, 23 of which are complete. On the other hand, there are also some other major differences between these two near-contemporary hoards, and Bornholdt Collins has demonstrated (2003, 294–5, tables 5.10 and 6.5) that the mint structure of the numismatic element in the Chester (1950) hoard is unique and not drawn directly from the contemporary Manx, Irish or Scottish currency pools, or even from a well-circulated general 'Irish Sea' stock. Instead, it appears to be a composite, gradual accumulation of a Chester-based merchant who traded both locally and in and around the Irish Sea over an extended period (elements within the hoard are therefore likely to have been acquired in Man, but the hoard itself was not assembled there).

Unlike any of these Irish Sea hoards, the Skaill hoard is distinctive in containing Islamic dirhams, but from elsewhere in Scotland there is a mixed hoard from Machrie, Islay (1850), which is known to have included a dirham fragment amongst its 120(+) Anglo-Saxon coins, with one Anglo-Viking and one Continental also on record (Blackburn and Pagan 1986, no. 168, dep. *c.* 970; Metcalf 1995, 20–1, dep. *c.* 970–80). This too has an extended age-structure, which Metcalf (*ibid.*) compares to that of a coin hoard from Derrykeighan, Co. Antrim (Blackburn and Pagan 1986, no. 164, dep. *c.* 970); however, Machrie's (lost) bullion element was slight and poorly recorded (Graham-Campbell 1995, 104, no. 18).

A closer parallel for Skaill is therefore provided by another mixed hoard recently discovered (in 2011) at Furness, in south-western Cumbria (Ager *et al.* 2012, 27, 29–30), if also much smaller in size, although once again containing considerably more coins. This consists of 27 fragments of arm-rings and ingots together with 79 coins, most of which are Anglo-Saxon, but with some Anglo-Viking and two dirhams (*ibid.*, 30), deposited 'anywhere within the period 955–*c.*965' (*ibid.*, 31).

Overall, in line with the interpretation of the Ballaquayle hoard proposed above, and in light of the survey and excavation results reported here, it would still seem 'most reasonable' (as previously quoted from Graham-Campbell 1995, 48)

> ... to interpret the Skaill hoard as the accumulated capital of a Norse chieftain or other leader, or the most prominent family within the local community, given that the Bay of Skaill represents one of Orkney's prime settlement locations.

However, the manner of its accumulation remains perforce a matter for speculation – as to whether (or in what combination) its contents constitute 'the profits from peaceful trading contacts ... the loot from piratical raiding or the proceeds of tribute collecting'. In conclusion, the Skaill hoard can indeed be said to represent 'a pragmatic concealment of a huge asset of worldly wealth, within a dynamic phase of the establishment of mature Scandinavian authority over Orkney' (Griffiths 2013, 522).

Notes

1 George Petrie was then Clerk to the Commissioners of Supply, becoming Sheriff Clerk of Orkney in 1868; for an outline of his life and work, see 'Notes on George Petrie, 1818–1875, Antiquary and Sheriff Clerk', compiled by Margaret Watters, Stenness, and Bill and Sheila Cormack, Lockerbie (privately published, 1995).

2 This consists only of nos 1–54.

3 This includes nos 1–118.

4 This has the addition of nos 119 and 120, acquired from J. Linklater on 5 April 1858, the date on which it was completed.

5 I was thus mistaken in supposing that Petrie had drafted his 'Notice' in order for it 'to accompany his official inventory, dated 5 April 1858' (Graham-Campbell 1995, 124).

6 No. 49 in Petrie's 'Inventory' (Graham-Campbell 1995, no. 24, 51: a silver ringed pin).

7 This suggestion for the location of the find-place of the Skaill hoard, on the southern perimeter of the Castle of Snusgar, was made without knowledge of the 1834 'Plan of Township of Scarwell' and 1849 'Map of Crown Lands' (with their detailed information as to the ownership of the relevant fields), which I am grateful to David Griffiths for having brought to my attention.

8 In 1931, Clouston acquired a penannular brooch which had been 'in private possession' since the discovery of the

hoard (Corrie 1932; see also Grieg 1940, fig. 61; Graham-Campbell 1995, 122–3, 126, no. 24, 111, pl. 20).

9 At some stage, Cursiter acquired two pieces of hack-silver from the hoard, from an unknown source, together with some replica pieces (of unknown origin), which formed

part of his collection given to the Hunterian Museum in about 1920 (C. 74–5: Grieg 1940, 132; Graham-Campbell 1995, 126, no. 24, 114–5, pls 36 and 49).

10 In an unpublished paper delivered at the 17th Viking Congress, Lerwick, 2013.

The 1888 Skaill Viking grave

James Graham-Campbell

In April 1888, W. G. T. Watt of Skaill House 'was informed that a human jaw-bone had been picked up among loose stones in a sandy brae on the south side of the bay, close to the boat-house' (Watt 1888, 283). On learning of this discovery, Watt stated that he 'immediately visited the place, and on removing a little sand satisfied myself that there was an interment in a stone cist, and had it opened up'.

The Skaill boat-slip (HY 2297 1874) is located to the west of Skara Brae with adjacent to it a 'a prominent mound now exposed in the sand-cliffs' (The 'Boat House mound', see Chapter 2) (Morris 1985, 82). This was surveyed by Morris and colleagues in 1978 and 1982, when it was established that 'there can be little doubt that [it contained] at least two, if not three, major structural phases ... separated by large deposits of windblown sand' (*ibid.*, 88). This eroding settlement-mound corresponds so exactly to Watt's description of 'a sandy brae on the south side of the bay, close to the boat-house' that it is almost certainly where the grave was discovered in 1888 (*ibid.*, 89), given also that there is some evidence to suggest that it had indeed been dug into midden deposits (see below).[1]

The construction and layout of the grave will be described later, following a review of its contents,[2] commencing with Watt's own description in his 'Notice' of the discovery which he communicated shortly afterwards to the Society of Antiquaries of Scotland, at its meeting on 23 April 1888, as subsequently published in the *Proceedings*:

> The bones were much scattered and damaged by the falling in of the cover stones. The skull lay in the west corner. Close to the head stone lay the head of a spear of iron (Fig. 3), measuring 15½ inches in length. The socket was under the head. About a foot from where

the skull lay, and lying parallel to the south-west side of the cist, an ornamented bone comb came in sight, along with several pieces of carved bone, which have since been put together by Dr Anderson, and turn out to be the case (Fig. 1)[3] ... A little farther along, among the bones of the hand, was an iron weapon 6 inches long, probably a knife, with some remains of the handle attached to the tang. Alongside of this a large iron rivet, and another iron weapon of small size, which from appearance may be an arrow-head; also a small whetstone (Fig. 2), about 2½ inches long, with a hole bored through the top end. At the foot of the grave was a rough stone disc, and near it a large bone, thought to be one of the leg bones of a horse. At the head of the grave on the north-west side there were some bones of small birds; and a bit of the jaw, with teeth, of the frog-fish. There was also a small knuckle-bone of some animal. (Watt 1888, 283–4)

After Watt's 'Notice' had been read, 'the Secretary announced the gratifying fact that ... Mr Watt ... has generously presented the whole of the objects above described to the National Museum' (*ibid.*, 285).

The contents (Figs 22.1 and 22.2)

The objects were registered by the National Museum as IL 230–5, 'from grave in Links of Skaill, Orkney – W. G. T. Watt, 1888', and listed in *NMAS Catalogue* (1892), 279, as:

IL 230 and 231: 'Dressing Comb of Bone and Bone Case for the Comb', illustrated with the Figure from Watt's 'Notice' (1888, Fig. 1);

IL 232: 'small whetstone of sandstone, 2 7/16 × 5/16 in., with perforation at one end';

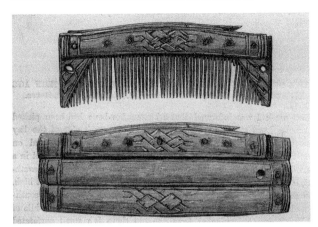

Fig. 22.1: Skaill grave: the comb and comb-case (after Watt 1888, fig. 1)

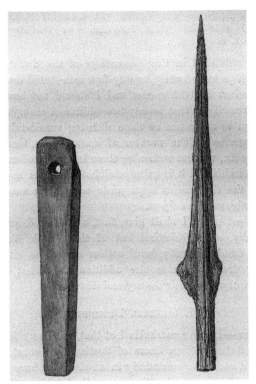

Fig. 22.2: Skaill grave: the whetstone and spear-head (after Watt 1888, figs 2–3)

IL 233: 'iron spear-head, 15½ in. long';

IL 234: 'blade of iron knife, with portion of wooden sheath attached to blade';

IL 235: 'and fragments of bones and iron.'

The iron 'fragments' include Watt's 'large iron rivet' (see below), but there is no mention of his additional 'iron weapon of small size, which from appearance may be an arrow-head'. But then there appears to have been nothing meeting this description available for Sigurd Grieg to

catalogue during his study-visit to Edinburgh in 1925, even though he was aware of Watt's account of 'another small weapon' having been found 'alongside' the knife, supposing himself that this might 'possibly' have been 'a spear-head' (Grieg 1940, 84). On the other hand, Anton Brøgger followed Watt more closely in listing 'an iron arrow-head' among the Skaill grave-goods, in *Ancient Emigrants* (1929, 122), his general survey 'of the Norse settlements of Scotland', but none such was included in his more detailed account of the burial in his subsequent monograph (1930, 182–4). It seems most probable that Watt's original identification was mistaken and that the poorly-preserved piece of iron in question had originally formed part of the knife (having likewise been found 'among the bones of the hand'). However, Brøgger's one reference to this – seemingly non-existent – 'arrow-head' has inevitably lead to it making the occasional appearance in subsequent publications,

Grieg's listing of the contents of the Skaill grave is as follows (1940, 81–4, figs 45–6):

(a) and (b) 'Bone-comb' and damaged 'Bone case';
(c) 'Small needle-whetstone, of black slate, perforated at the upper end';
(d) 'Iron knife';
(e) 'Iron spear-head';
(f) 'Iron rod';
(g) 'Three small indeterminable iron fragments, perhaps originally belonging to f';
(h) 'Small iron nail with big head'; and
(i) 'Some very small animal bones'.

Grieg noted that the knife (d) had 'the remains of the handle attached to the tang' (*ibid.*, 84). His miscellaneous iron pieces (f) and (g) are most readily accounted for as being derived from the knife and the spear-head; in the case of the latter (e), it is important to note that, although originally recorded as being 15½ ins long (*c.* 39 cm), it was by then (1925) reduced to its 'present length [of] about 22 cm', with the 'point as well as the socket broken off, only fragments of the latter being preserved'.

In addition, Grieg mentions only that 'some human remains' were recovered, including the above-mentioned skull (1940, 83) and 'the bones of the hand' (*ibid.*, 84), but then there is no evidence for them having accompanied Watt's donation of 'the whole of the objects' to the Museum. Indeed, they may well have been re-interred, as was the case (initially at least) with the remains of two individuals recovered from 'Skerrabrae' (Skara Brae), likewise in the late 19th century (Garson 1884) (see above, Chapter 2).

Both the spear-head and the comb belong to recognisable Scandinavian types and will be discussed further below during consideration of their dating. Small pendant whetstones (cf. SF 4030, Chapter 18) are also well-known objects from Viking-Age settlements and graves both in Scandinavia, as at Kaupang (Resi 2011, 389) and Birka (Arbman 1940, pl. 186), and elsewhere in the Viking world, including Jarlshof (Hamilton 1956, 114, figs 54, no. 17, and 65, nos 17–18). and the much worn example in the male grave from Buckquoy (see below). The example found in 1888, which is of imported black slate, has been classified as a 'needle-whetstone', although it seems unlikely to have been intended for such use, unlike that of fine-grained quartzite found alongside a needle-case in the well-equipped female grave at Cnip, Lewis ('Burial A' in Dunwell *et al.* 1995, 720; see Welander *et al.* 1987, 157, 170, illus. 8, nos 6–7). On the other hand, although the Skaill example does display some slight wear, it is hardly well suited for general knife-sharpening purposes. It is therefore most probably to be counted among the pendant 'whetstones' identified by Martin Ježek as touchstones (Ježek 2013; 2014; see also Chapter 18).

The single iron rivet from the Skaill 1888 grave is not immediately explicable, although another solitary example was found in the Cnip female grave (Burial A) where its presence was likewise considered 'somewhat perplexing', although with the suggestion that it might represent an unidentified wooden item (Welander *et al.* 1987, 159, 170, illus. 8, no. 11). However, the Skaill rivet could well have been residual, derived from the settlement mound into which the grave was dug. Indeed, it seems most unlikely, on comparative grounds, that the remaining contents of the burial, as recorded by Watt – an unidentified 'rough stone disc' and a small miscellany of dispersed animal/bird/fish bones – had been deliberately placed in the grave, rather than being redeposited midden material.

Grave construction and layout

The grave was aligned north-west to south-east and measured 5 ft 11 ins long (1.8 m) by 2 ft 2 ins wide (66 cm); it was 2 ft deep (60 cm). There was a lining of stone slabs, with that 'forming the southwestern side being the full length of the grave', and it was 'roughly paved with flat shore stones'.

It would appear that the spear was first laid diagonally across the paving and then the body placed on top, given that the spear-head socket was found under the skull 'in the west corner'. The comb (in its case) appears to have been deliberately placed alongside the upper right arm, being 'about a foot from where the skull lay, and lying parallel to the south-west side of the cist'. It is uncertain, however, whether the knife and pendant whetstone were suspended from a belt (on the right side of the body) – or whether one or other (or both) had been placed in the hand of the deceased, among the bones of which they were found.

Finally, the grave was closed with 'several large flat stones above which there seems to have been placed a heap of smaller sea-worn boulders'. It appears therefore that a cairn was deliberately constructed over the long-cist burial, thus adding to the prominence of its bay-side location on top of the extant settlement-mound.

Dating

In Brøgger's opinion, the Skaill spear-head belonged to 'a form which in Norway goes back to the 7th and 8th centuries' (1929, 122), being itself 'certainly from the 8th century' (*ibid.*, 131; cf. 1930, 182–3). He concluded therefore that the Skaill grave contained '*en norsk innvandrer til Orknøyene alt for 800*, antagelig engang i siste halvdel av 8, årh.' (1930, 183). However, Brøgger's assertion that 'it cannot be denied that this find is an argument for Norse settlement in the Orkneys in the 8th century' (1929, 122) was later disputed by Shetelig (1945, 45–6, note 59), as described below, but this was not until after Grieg's publication of the Skaill grave in which he stated that 'the form of this object recalls Norwegian spear-heads from the 6th and 7th centuries' (1940, 82).

F. T. Wainwright, writing in the late 1950s, drew attention to the fact that there existed 'a divergence of opinion' about the dating of the Skaill spear-head, in that Brøgger had 'attributed it firmly, perhaps too firmly, to the 8th century' (1962, 132–3), whereas 'Shetelig, rejecting this attribution, saw no reason why any of the Scandinavian graves in the Northern Isles need be earlier than 800' (*ibid.*, 133 citing Shetelig 1954, 101–2). Wainwright's own comment was simply that the 'stone-lined grave at Skaill' contained 'the comparatively early burial of a man' (1962, 148, pl. xvi, reproducing the same illustrations used by both Brøgger and Grieg). The rather general nature of this conclusion no doubt influenced Morris (*et al.*) who simply observed that the burial 'can be placed in the Viking period, probably the 9th century or later' (Morris (ed.) 1985, 82).

It is essential therefore to consider Shetelig's divergent opinion more closely (as first published by him in 1945):

> The find from the Links of Skaill, the Mainland of the Orkneys, suggests a question of central importance, as Professor Brøgger, has assigned it to about 800 A. D. or perhaps to a somewhat earlier period. His conclusion is based on the type of spear-head whose form is similar to certain spear-heads used in Norway during the 7th and 8th centuries. To judge from the photograph the argument is not absolutely convincing. The specimen from Skaill certainly presents an outline recalling the said Norse spears of the Merovingian period, but the original line is to some extent obscured by rusty deformation, and the general shape of the blade is markedly different. We dare not accept this early dating as a contribution to the history of Viking settlements in Orkney. (Shetelig 1954, 101–2)

Shetelig further observed, in a footnote (*ibid.*, 110–11, note 63), that:

> the chief characteristic of the Merovingian type quoted by Brøgger and Grieg is a flat blade with the central rib slightly raised from the level surface, while the Skaill-spear is thicker with a central ridge, which is not set off in relief. More probably this spear should be determined as the slender Viking type, Jan Petersen type K, Fig. 21.

Petersen's K-type spears (1919, 31–3, Figs 21–2) are one of the later Viking-Age types and Solberg (1985, 86–7, 96) has dated the main variant, with 66 Norwegian examples, to the period *c.* 900–50, with some later examples (Subtype VII.2B). It is 'the predominant form' at Kaupang, in Norway, where a dating 'to the first half of the 10th century ... would seem to be correct for most of our specimens' (Blindheim and Heyerdahl-Larsen 1999, 96, 182). In Ireland, it should be noted that only two of the 59 spear-heads known from Viking graves have been classified as probably of this type, both of which are from Kilmainham-Islandbridge, Dublin, and are considered to 'display potential local influences, perhaps suggesting local manufacture' (Harrison and Ó Floinn 2014, 99–100, illus. 48).

Brøgger supported his 8th-century dating of the Skaill grave, on the basis of the spear-head, by reference to the comb, the decoration of which he likened to that on one of those from the Oseberg ship-burial, although considering the form of the Skaill example to be typologically earlier (1930, 183). On the other hand, Shetelig concluded his footnote on the Skaill spear-head by withdrawing his own early dating of the comb (1954, 111, note 93):

> The bone comb found in association with the spear from Skaill does not admit of a very precise dating. In a preliminary account of the British Viking graves, delivered in 1933, I dated the comb to about 800 A.D. (*Vikingeminner i Vesteuropa*, Oslo 1933, p. 83). But this opinion is hardly maintainable. Cf. the comb from Vendel, grave IX, dating from the middle of 10th century, Hj. Stolpe and T. J. Arne, *Graffältet vid Vendel*, Stockholm 1912, pl. xxvi (cf. Stolpe and Arne 1927, 37, pl. xxvi, with comb-case).

Vendel grave IX is a lavishly equipped male boat-burial which included half a Samanid dirham, of Nasr ben Ahmed (914–43), amongst its numerous grave-goods (Stolpe and Arne 1927, 36). It is not surprising therefore that Steven Ashby, following his recent detailed study of Viking-Age combs (2009, with refs), has concluded that the early dates suggested for the Skaill grave are 'unsupportable' because the comb belongs to his (2007) Type 6 (= Ambrosiani class B):

> This form is relatively rare in both Norway and northern Scotland but emerges in southern and eastern

Scandinavia no earlier than the start of the 10th century. Allowing time for the comb to reach Orkney, [the Skaill grave] must date to the first half of the 10th century, and is thus probably among the later pagan burials in Scotland (Ashby 2014, 131).

Over the last 85 years, the dating of the Skaill grave has therefore been adjusted by some 150 years – from the speculative 'second half of the 8th century' to the 'first half of the 10th'.

Conclusions

Ashby's observation (2014, 131) that the Skaill comb and case are 'suggestive of contacts with Denmark or the Low Countries – links not frequently stressed in Viking Scotland' means that they contribute to our wider picture of the overseas contacts of this 10th-century Norse inhabitant of Skaill Bay, when taken together with the Scandinavian K-type spear-head and imported slate 'whetstone'. However, in this case, the links need not have been direct, given that Type 6 combs are found in England and Ireland, even if rarely in Scotland (Ashby 2009, 8).

If the pendant 'whetstone' is more correctly to be considered a touchstone, as suggested above, then this imported artefact signifies the socio-economic standing of the deceased more clearly than his weaponry, consisting of only a single spear, although such does in fact accord with the general reduction in weapon-kit evident from other such 10th-century burials in Scandinavian Scotland.

Finally, this careful burial, in a stone cist covered by a cairn, prominently sited on the top of a settlement-mound overlooking the Bay, brings to mind that at Buckquoy, beside Birsay Bay (Ritchie 1977, 190–1) (Chapter 2, above). This is a male burial dating from no earlier than the mid-10th century, given the inclusion of a silver coin in the form of a cut halfpenny of the Anglo-Saxon king Edmund (939–46). His weapon was also just a spear, and he was likewise buried with his knife and a pendant whetstone (in this case much worn), but with the addition of an Hiberno-Scandinavian ringed pin.

A further Viking grave from Sandwick, possibly from the Bay of Skaill?

John Fraser overlooked the (1888) Viking burial from Skaill in his paper on the 'Antiquities of Sandwick parish' (delivered to the Orkney Antiquarian Society on 13 December 1923) and, indeed, his brief summary of the 'Ancient graves and burial mounds' (Fraser 1923, 28) contains no mention of any possible Viking graves, although there exist 19th-century references to two further relevant finds from the parish.

Daniel Wilson (1851, 551) records the discovery of 'a bronze pin ... found in a tumulus at Sandwick, in Orkney', accompanied by an illustration of a plain-ringed, polyhedral-headed pin (cf. Fanning 1994, 25–36). This is the commonest type of Viking-Age ringed pin from Scotland (Fanning 1983, 327, although the Sandwick example is omitted from his catalogue), with an exceptional silver example being known from the Skaill hoard (*ibid.*, 336, no. 18; Graham-Campbell 1995, 117, no. 24, 51, pl. 46, a–b). Wilson's woodcut of the Sandwick pin allows it to be identified with that (now lost) known to have been in the possession of Captain (then Lieutenant) F. W. L. Thomas, RN, who was surveying in Orkney in the winter of 1849 (Thomas 1852).

Given the archaeological evidence for settlement reported upon here, including the 1888 grave, it is not unreasonable to suggest that this mid-19th century find was made at the Bay of Skaill. On the other hand, tumuli were being excavated elsewhere in the parish of Sandwick during the 19th century, including one containing a Viking cremation grave at Lyking, some time before 1870 (*NMAS Catalogue* 1892, 276; Grieg 1940, 80; *Orkney & Shetland* 1946, vol. II, 272, no. 758; Graham-Campbell and Batey 1998, 59, Fig. 4.3).[4]

Notes

1 *Orkney & Shetland* 1946, vol. II, 273, no. 767: 'Viking Burial, Bay of Skaill'. There can be no doubt that the next entry in the RCAMS *Inventory* (*ibid.*), transcribed independently from the OS map, refers to the same find (from the same year): '768. Cist, Bay of Skaill. At the S. end of the Bay of Skaill, the O.S. map records: "Stone Cist and Spear-head found A.D. 1888."'

2 A more detailed description of the contents of the Skaill grave will be included in Graham-Campbell and Paterson, forthcoming.

3 It should be noted that the comb-case as currently reconstructed is no longer quite 'as put together by Dr Anderson', on the basis of his representation of it (reproduced here) which was in any case somewhat idealised (see Graham-Campbell and Paterson, forthcoming).

4 According to Canmore (ID 1615), citing the Orkney SMR (n.d.): 'There is some confusion over this site and whether the finds-spot refers to the Lyking in Sandwick or the Lyking of Holm', although no such doubts have yet been expressed in print (cf. *Orkney & Shetland* 1946, vol. II, 272, no. 758).

23

A Viking-Age bone strap-end from near St Peter's Kirk

Caroline Paterson

Orkney Museum: no. 543, Donated Nov. 1931 by Mr Ritch. Found 'in a ditch on the west side of Sandwick Parish Kirk' (Anne Brundle, Orkney Museum, 1989, pers. comm.). L: 64.3 mm, W 15.3 mm, T 4.5 mm.

This bone object almost certainly functioned as a strap-end on account of its form, with terminal at one end, and a trace of an original split end at the other, which is now largely broken away. Much of the original surface of the tag has laminated away. A small section of incised vertebral ring-chain survives close to the tip on one face (Fig. 23.1). This comprises two truncated triangular midrib sections with attendant side loops truncated by a horizontal bar towards the tip, below which is a small sunken triangle which reduces the otherwise rather abrupt termination of the midrib. The ornament surviving on the other face (Fig. 23.2) comprises a more lightly incised, centrally aligned, simple herringbone motif.

Viking-Age bone strap-ends are relatively rare survivals in the Northern Isles, though there are slightly later forms with more rounded tongues, from both York and Dublin. A close parallel to this example was found in 1993 during landscaping of the churchyard at Mail, Cunningsburgh, Shetland (*Discovery and Excavation* 1993, 106, ARC 1993.353). It is likewise decorated on both sides; one face with paired rows of double ring-and-dot, and the other with a slender hatched mid-rib which splays at both ends to accommodate further double ring-and-dot motifs. Unfortunately the ground works involved the importation of soil from neighbouring Dunrossness, so there can be no certainty that the find originally came from Mail, though the recovery of Pictish and Norse finds from the modern

Fig. 23.1: Bone strap-end from St Peter's Kirk, Bay of Skaill: upper side © Orkney Museum

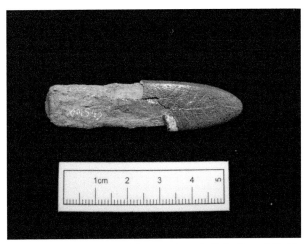

Fig. 23.2: Bone strap-end from St Peter's Kirk, Bay of Skaill: lower side © Orkney Museum

graveyard suggests it overlies later settlement associated with the nearby broch.

Examples of vertebral ring-chain executed in bone include two motif or trial pieces from High Street and Christchurch Place, Dublin, which are clearly important in indicating that local craftsmen were *trying out* the motif in 10th-century Dublin (Graham-Campbell 1980, 290, no. 477). Vertebral ring-chain was particularly prevalent in the Irish Sea region during the later 9th and 10th centuries, and is a signature motif of the sculptor Gautr on several of the Manx cross slabs. One of its earliest appearances is on an originally silver-plated cast iron sword hilt from the cremation burial at Hesket, Cumbria (Cowen 1934, Fig. 2). As a portable artefact this may have come from elsewhere, but the vertebral ring-chain motif seems to have taken hold in Cumbria, with three panels adorning the upper faces of the Gosforth Cross (Bailey and Cramp 1988, illus. 297 and 301), together with several other local sculptural renditions (Richardson 1993, 92–7), including a recently excavated fragment from St Michael's, Workington, and a copper-alloy strap-end decorated in a 'stopped plait' version of the motif from the same site (Paterson forthcoming).

Traditionally ring-chain motifs have been ascribed to the Scandinavian Borre style (Wilson and Klindt-Jensen 1966, 88). However, 'vertebral' depictions like this example with its mid-rib of truncated triangles seem to be an Insular variation (*ibid.,* 108), which appealed to Hiberno-Scandinavian tastes. There are few instances of this particular interlace construction within Scandinavia during this period, and it is possible that the classic example illustrated from Sundvor, Rogaland, Norway

(*ibid.,* Fig. 49) could even have originated in Ireland or Britain. In addition to the copper-alloy strap-ends decorated with vertebral ring-chain from Fishamble Street, Dublin (Lang 1988, Fig. 122) and Blo Norton, Norfolk (Margeson 1997, Fig. 24) there are now approximately ten such finds recorded by the Portable Antiquities Scheme and coming largely from East Anglia.

Given numerous occurrences of the vertebral ring-chain motif in the Irish Sea region it is likely that this find may have originated there or been influenced by the dominant Hiberno-Scandinavian culture from that area during the 10th century. The simple herringbone motif on its other side is less diagnostically helpful, as there are Irish and Pictish parallels alike, though it is handled with a similarly light touch on an altered penannular brooch from Aberdeenshire, which may be of Irish manufacture (Wilson, in Small *et al.* 1973 vols 1–2, 85, Pl.XLIVc).

The Mr Ritch who donated it was probably the same Mr Ritch who reported to RCAHMS the discovery of four skeletons in the mound south of the church during road improvements a few years later ('Mound A', see Chapter 2). Although there are no details of the immediate context of the find (other than a ditch, in the 1930s), its location on the west side of St Peter's Kirk is relevant, for the church site may well have early medieval origins. It is therefore possible that this artefact may originally have accompanied a Viking-Age burial. This need not have been a pagan burial, but perhaps rather one of a transitional nature, such as those from Carlisle Cathedral, where burials in consecrated ground included dress accessories (Paterson 2017, 155).

24

The 'Fin King' folktale

Tom Muir

The Orkney folklorist George Marwick (1836–1912) collected and told a traditional story: The Death of the Fin King: which refers to the Bay of Skaill, in particular its north side, mentioning St Peter's Kirk and the mound known as the Castle of Snusgar (known as Castle o' Snoosgarth in the tale). The story makes incidental reference to severe weather events and to sand-blow covering up dwellings around the bay. There are similarities in the details of the story to folklore from northern Norway, suggesting a common origin. The Death of the Fin King forms part of the collection published as 'The Mermaid Bride' (Muir 1998); and is also referred to in 'George Marwick, Yesnaby's Master Storyteller' (Muir and Irvine 2014).

The Fin Folk were believed to be creatures that live under the sea in a fine city called Finfolkaheem, or during the summer on beautiful floating islands that could sometimes be seen shimmering on the surface of the sea. The fishermen who sailed from Skaill Bay had offended the king of the Fin Folk by trespassing on his fishing grounds and he had used his magic powers to put a spell on all the fish so that none of them would take a hook. They swam around them, looked at the bait, then went away uninterested. This caused great hardship among the local families who relied on fish as an important food source. A spae-wife (witch) was consulted and she taught them the counter-charm that they needed to break the Fin King's spell. A six-oared boat was needed, with a volunteer crew of seven unmarried men – six rowing and one steering. They had to have four strongly made small barrels and a baited hand-line with a sinker stone attached to it. A boat called the *Ram* was borrowed from Thomas Marwick of South Unigar and the crew set off on their perilous journey. On reaching the disputed fishing grounds a charm was said over the sinker stone and the hand-line was cast into the sea, where they immediately caught a cod. They turned the boat and rowed back to shore as fast as they could, heading towards the church, but the Fin King, who was as big as a peat stack, rose up from the deep, roaring with rage. As he neared the boat the steersman threw the first barrel to him, which he stopped to attack, tearing it into splinters. Once he had finished, he set off after them again, but a second barrel was thrown to him, which he stopped to tear to pieces. Unfortunately, when the third barrel was thrown to him, he didn't stop swimming, but tore it apart while he swam towards the boat. With jaws open wide, he raised his huge webbed hand to grab the boat, but the young man on the stroke oar, Johnny Brass, grabbed the last barrel and threw it with as much force as he could, right at the Fin King's head, breaking his skull and causing his death. With that, the boat grounded on the shore and many willing hands pulled it to safety up the beach.

The men were given a hero's return, especially Johnny Brass. This young man had been courting Jeannie Irvine of Newgarth, but her mother was not so keen on him. After his heroic action she embraced him and said that she was proud of him and that there was no question about him marrying her daughter. The dying Fin King was pulled away from the sea and a funeral pyre was built to burn his body. The burn, called 'Rin', was renamed the Burn o' Snoosgarth to commemorate the Fin King's dying sounds, which was said to be a snoozing noise. The body was burnt and the reddened stones of the pyre were called the Castle o' Snoosgarth. Johnny Brass and Jeannie Irvine were married the following year, during a westerly gale. As they walked back from the church they met a fiddler from Harray who had come to play at the wedding. He struck up a tune on top of Sandfiold Hill and the wedding company danced so furiously that, together with the gale of wind, it was said that all the sand blew off the top of the hill and completely buried a house in the valley called the 'Fan'. Wind-blown sand in this area was obviously recognised as a major problem, even in stories, to the extent of houses being completely buried in single, catastrophic weather events.

The tale mentions a number of people who are known to have lived in the area in the early 19th century (Muir and Irvine 2014), but this probably reflects a reworking for the benefit of folk who were alive around that time, and its origins are likely to be much earlier.

What intrigued me about this tale was how different it was from other stories. Throwing the kegs to the monster to attack was new to me in all my years of folk tale research. Had Marwick made it up himself? Then I was asked by my friend, Ole J. Forset, to help with the translation of the works of the 19th century Norwegian folklorist, Olaus Nicolaissen. Ole is the director of the Sør-Troms Museum at Trondenes, Harstad, and wanted to make available Nicolaissen's work, which was originally published in the 1870s. Nicolaissen was a museum conservator and teacher and he collected tales from the Arctic region of northern Norway, mostly around the Lofoten and Vesterålen Islands. The stories that he collected differ greatly from those collected further south by Asbjørnsen and Moe, which are more akin to the northern European types as collected by the Brothers Grimm.

Nicolaissen's stories are about the sea and have more akin with the Orkney tales. In his story *Jenegga,* which is the name of a fishing ground about seven miles north-west of Vesterålen, a fisherman dream of how to find this great fishing ground and that he would need seven oak barrels fastened with iron bands. He sailed to this fishing ground, following the landmarks (meads) given to him in the dream, until he found the richest fishing ground he had ever seen. Once the boat was full of fish the fisherman and his sons turned the boat around and sailed back to the islands. Suddenly, a furious sea troll gave chase, and the father threw a barrel to it, which it stopped to attack. They had got a mile away by the time the sea troll set off after them again and another barrel was thrown. By the time that they were still a mile off shore there were no more barrels left and the monster opened its jaws wide to attack the boat. The father threw his iron bladed knife into the monster's open mouth and the troll turned to stone. There it remains as a skerry known to fishermen as the 'Black Ox'.

The term 'Fin Folk' has always interested me. The 19th century collector, Walter Traill Dennison (1825–1894), stated that they were called that because they were covered all over with fins, like a fish, but they were powerful sorcerers and could use their magic to make the fins look like clothing, fooling the unsuspecting humans who came into contact with them. He also stressed that their name had nothing to do with the Finns of Finland or Finnmark, who we know today as the Sámi. In the sagas and in Nicolaissen's collections, the Sámi are called Finns and are credited with magical powers. In Shetland the Finns are Sámi – humans with magical powers, not supernatural creatures. I believe that the Fin Folk in Orkney form a much older tradition and that the Vikings gave them the name because this was how they understood them. Their powers were like those of the Finns of northern Norway and so we get stories migrating from the far north of Norway to Orkney, or vice-versa, which culturally links these two North Atlantic communities.

25

Synthesis and discussion

David Griffiths

Marwick, the Bay of Skaill and Birsay Bay – the origins of Viking settlement

The landscape fieldwork reported upon in Chapter 3 and the excavations in Chapters 4–20 has revealed a range of new information about the archaeology of the three bays and their hinterlands especially during the Viking and Late Norse periods, but has also posed new challenges and questions. As discussed in the introduction, sites of existing archaeological importance based on previous excavation have been usefully re-contextualised in their landscape. Geophysical and topographical survey has added to evidence derived mainly from coastal erosion. A clearly-demonstrated example of such an outcome is the small complex of two scheduled sites at Marwick, which were subjected to survey and partial excavation. The chapel site (SM 2934) has been re-established in its landscape context, and the extent of the neighbouring settlement mound (SM 2884) mapped. Limited excavation of the latter in 2009 produced two near-identical radiocarbon dates form carbonised grain, the combined range of which covers cal AD 770–980 (SUERC 33697 and 33698), hinting at the Pictish-Viking transition. This raises the potential for Marwick's importance in the wider debate about the date and nature of the early Viking presence. The proximity of mound and chapel is unambiguous, but their chronological relationship could only be further explored through excavation of the chapel.

At the Bay of Skaill, the two excavated mounds and settlement sites at Snusgar and East Mound were evidently not located upon or formed around sites of recognisable pre-Viking settlement significance (see below). However, they were not imposed in a barren, empty landscape. The prehistoric tumuli excavated by Low and Banks in 1772 remain visible features in the centre of the bay, and must

have been more prominent a millennium ago. The broch now known as Knowe of Verron would have been a conspicuous feature overlooking the northern edge of the Bay of Skaill. Like other Iron Age brochs in the Northern Isles such as at Gurness, Orkney, and Old Scatness, Shetland (Dockrill *et al.* 2010), it may have attracted a transitory phase of early Viking occupation, perhaps as a prelude to more substantial settlement elsewhere around the bay. The geophysical programme undertaken on the northern half of the bay hinterland, and its counterpart on the south surrounding the World Heritage Area (Fig. 3.1), indicate extensive potential for further in-depth understanding of the Prehistoric and pre-Viking landscape.

At Birsay, on the Brough, the Buckquoy peninsula, Birsay Links and in the area of the Palace Village, it has been demonstrated by excavations over the years that Viking occupation did take place upon or in very close proximity to areas already settled in the pre-Viking period. In no single case, however, is direct continuity of domestic occupation demonstrated. There is considerable evidence for Pictish activity on the Brough of Birsay and at Buckquoy. On the Brough, spreads of metalworking evidence and artefacts discovered by Richardson and Curle in the 1930s imply the presence of an influential, specialised pre-Viking site, with possible ecclesiastical connections suggested by the symbol stone (Curle 1982). However, accompanying structural evidence for this is surprisingly difficult to identify. No unambiguously pre-Viking building remains have been identified on the Brough, despite strenuous efforts by successive generations of excavators. The belief, favoured by Radford and Cruden in the 1960s, that the Norse church is located within a pre-Viking *vallum* or enclosure has been discredited (Hunter 1986, 28), and an eight-sided stone-lined well once considered to be Pictish cannot securely be associated with a pre-Viking phase so has been left 'floating' (Morris 1996, 230). Conversely, Morris's excavation of a figure-of-eight-shaped Pictish structure at Red Craig on the Brough Road, Buckquoy (Morris 1989), lacks a clear stratigraphic relationship with Viking-period deposits. Fieldwork undertaken for this project in 2003 did however show that the Buckquoy Peninsula was probably divided from the mainland by a boundary feature (the date of which is as yet unknown), which connects to the southern shore in the close vicinity of Red Craig, and that a possible longhouse style settlement may exist near a gap part-way along it. Farrer's excavations at Saevar Howe in the 1862 and 1867 would appear to give us a demonstrable case where a clear pre-Viking and a Norse phase occurred in the same mound. However, Hedges's excavation in 1977, whilst confirming a Norse presence, was unable to identify any trace of Farrer's alleged cist-cemetery, and the stratigraphic connection between that and the Norse buildings remains speculative.

Anna Ritchie's excavations at Buckquoy provide the most convincing example of a multi-phase mound with both Pictish and Viking evidence co-located, and as such (perhaps above all because of its rarity as such) has become seen as a classic type-site for this cultural and chronological transition. The buildings as described by Ritchie span the Pictish-Viking transition. The artefacts from the domestic deposits, even from the Viking phases, are largely insular or locally-made types of object, largely in bone and stone, which are consistent with Pictish occupation. The combs are largely Pictish in style. The site lacks the types of evidence such as steatite and larger amounts of discarded iron which betray Viking occupation. As with the more recently excavated material from Old Scatness, Shetland (Dockrill *et al.* 2010), Buckquoy may well give us a glimpse of a fleeting 'intermediate' phase of early Viking involvement in a still-largely Pictish dominated society, without as yet dominantly Scandinavian cultural forms coming into play. The strongest Scandinavian artefactual signatures at Buckquoy come in fact not from the 'Norse' buildings, but from the furnished Viking grave. Considering this, along with the Viking grave found in 1888 near Skara Brae (Chapter 22), it seems more likely that Pagan Viking settlers, in this area at least, used existing settlement mounds for funerary practices, as opposed to establishing their own domestic settlement upon them.

Bay of Skaill: The Snusgar and East Mound excavations

The development of the settlements

The two main excavation areas at the Bay of Skaill produced a remarkably consistent and contained

archaeological picture, with little of consequence pre-dating or post-dating Viking-Late Norse Phases 2–7. There is next to nothing in the results of these excavations and surveys to indicate that there was a significant presence of earlier structures or activities at or under either of the two mounds, and nothing which appears to differ culturally from the Viking-Age to Late Norse character of the principal deposits uncovered. Deep inside the Snusgar mound, at a level similar to the current ground surface, Trench 4 context 1536, a thin buried soil, produced a cormorant bone which gave (after calibration to include the marine reservoir effect) a radiocarbon date of 489–774 cal AD at 95.4% probability (SUERC-17851), indicating that the entire superstructure of the mound above this point post-dates the late Iron Age. This is, however, not entirely to discount the possibility that some part of the extensive spread of the mound may conceal earlier archaeology; we may continue to hypothesise that a smaller mound or tumulus, perhaps similar to those excavated by Banks and Low in 1772 (Chapter 2) may have acted as a wind-break and point of accumulation of windblown sand, creating a mound which then attracted later settlement. However, despite some very tenuous echoes on the radargrams (Chapter 3; Fig. 3.7) there is no coherent signal visible buried structures. Moreover, very few identifiably pre-Viking objects were retrieved from any of the trenches, and none of the artefacts or ecofacts excavated at either Snusgar or East Mound is unequivocally likely to have been redeposited after disturbance *in situ* from a layer pre-dating Phase 2 at the earliest. We must therefore conclude, on the basis of the available excavated evidence (which is of course based on a modest area percentage and subject to further investigation) that Snusgar, and very probably East Mound as well, are wholly or predominantly accumulations of the Viking Age onwards, and which show strong evidence of relatively rapid formation.

At Snusgar, the presence of the deeply buried soil horizon (1536) does not in itself indicate the beginning of sustained settlement activity on this site, although it may reflect influences from nearby (Chapter 6). It is separated from later layers by an overburden of clean sand. The first sustained traces of settlement activity occur with a series of stone and organic layers with pits, imposed over a layer of windblown sand. These occurred in Phase 2 and were clearly intended to stabilise the site, but their presence implies a more sustained episode of mound-building associated with the construction of a substantial longhouse. At this time that the northern and western flanks of Snusgar probably took on a shaped or graded character, which is still detectible today. The 'Castle of Snusgar' which was first recorded in the *Old Statistical Account* (Chapter 2) may well have been something of a misappropriated description resulting from the observation, or even partial exposure, of the stone masonry of this Viking-Age building on the western flanks of the mound. As implied by Walden's Plan (Figs 2.2, 2.5) parts of the longhouse may have been partially preserved above ground and still visible into the 18th century, giving the impression of a substantial if ruined building, prior to their disappearance due to land improvement and stone robbing. (It is likely that any above-ground traces of the building had disappeared by 1858, as it is not mentioned in any of the accounts of the discovery of the Skaill Hoard.) Geophysical results (Figs 3.5, 4.10) strongly suggest that the Snusgar longhouse is centred on the north-west sector of the mound, although the fragmented remains of its walls, floors and associated middens were perceptible in the excavation of Trench 1 in the north-eastern sector. The northern (east–west) long wall of this building observed in Trench 1 had an impressive stone foundation, apparently supporting a substantial but now-vanished stone and turf superstructure. Later centuries of disturbance and stone robbing have taken their toll,

and its southern and eastern walls especially were largely damaged to the point of disaggregation and disappearance. We are not precisely sure of the exact position of the eastern end of the longhouse or of its dimensions. It is difficult, from the partial extent of excavation, coupled with the limited survival of the structure and its internal deposits, to be sure whether the building's internal layout echoed that of other comparable and roughly contemporary structures with byre areas, domestic floors, internal sub-divisions and opposed entrances. External deposits were better preserved in Trenches 1, 3 and 4, and it is from these that what remains of the story of the Snusgar settlement can best be pieced together.

Life in longhouses

ARCHITECTURE, SPACE AND GENERATIONAL CHANGE

The Snusgar longhouse (Fig. 4.10), which arose in Phase 2, was probably the earliest building in the Viking-Late

Table 25.1: Architecture, space, and generational change

Phase	Events in phase (Snusgar) (Trenches 1–4)	Events in phase (East Mound) (Trenches 5–8)	Events elsewhere in survey area/more widely in Northern Isles
1	Land surface, followed by influx of wind-blown sand.	No evidence of settlement activity; windblown sand	Occupation at Marwick spans Pictish/ Viking-Age chronology? Hints of early Viking activity at Buckquoy, Pool, and Scatness
2	Longhouse construction, roughly date of deposition of Skaill Hoard.	Beginnings of smaller 'ancillary' buildings to south of subsequent longhouse construction	Buckquoy settlement closed with grave. Grave at Skaill (found in 1888) inserted into top of Prehistoric settlement mound
3	Longhouse occupied, middens deposited, surfaces stabilised with stone and midden, seabird harvesting.	Completion of Phase 3 hall-house, ferrous metalworking yard established, consumption of younger animals hints at emerging central place role	Early longhouses at Brough of Birsay, Jarlshof, Pool, Skaill Deerness. Conversion to Christianity, possible adoption of earlier (pre-Viking) church sites
4	Not recorded at Snusgar.	Reconfiguring of ancillary buildings, metalworking yard built over	Transition from Viking to Late Norse periods. Christianity now dominant
5	Longhouse goes out of use.	Full extent of longhouse, byre and western annex added, consumption of older animals; shift towards farming production. Some metalworking at hearth inside longhouse hall	Developed Norse economy starts to take shape across Orkney. Increase in fishing and stockfish trade Established landholdings take shape. Longhouses more common, often near churches
6	Little demonstrable activity.	Longhouse goes out of use and becomes roofless animal enclosure, ancillary building(s) reconfigured to smaller square plan	Late Norse settlements, emergent parishes and townships castles on Wyre, Rousay and at Cairston near Stromness, development of larger churches and cathedrals
7	Site abandoned, structures robbed of stone.	Evidence of farming in vicinity, building of field walls on mound	Later period of Norse Earldom of Orkney
8	Plough damage, influx of wind-blown sand.	Influx of deep wind-blown sand, site largely disappears from view	Scottish rule, rentals of 1492, 1502–3
9	Kelp burning, disturbance, animal burial and stone robbing.	Rough grazing, small shelter occupies last visible trace of walls above the ground	Improvement overwrites earlier landscape layout, new agricultural methods, new roads, harbours and housing constructed

Norse phases on either of the two excavated mounds, although on East Mound the earliest (north–south aligned) building of the series of small ancillary buildings and yard at the southern extent of the excavated area also dates to the same period. It is likely that such Phase 2 activity was broadly coincident with the deposition in the later 10th century of the Skaill hoard (Chapter 21), implying that the silver objects were deposited around the time that the Snusgar settlement was becoming established. East Mound was probably also experiencing some construction at this time, although apparently as yet of relatively small and utilitarian buildings. The Snusgar longhouse continued, from Phase 2 into Phase 3, to form the focus for occupation and the creation of surrounding midden deposits, which form a large part of the structure of the mound as it exists today. Layers were laid down over bands of windblown sand which had accumulated over Phase 2 middens interleaved with windblown sand. On the basis of present (limited) evidence, the development of the Snusgar settlement appears to have lost impetus in Phase 3, and ceased altogether by the end of Phase 5. Few of the primary contexts in Trenches 1–4 post-date Phase 3, and these appear to relate to wall collapses and small reconfigurations rather than to major innovation or extension. Midden deposition continued in Phase 5, but some of this may have involved the redistribution of older deposits from within the longhouse. Thereafter, the archaeology of Trench 1 in particular jumps to Phases 8 and 9, telling a story of widespread disturbance from kelping pits and dumping, coupled with the removal of building stone from the longhouse complex, in some part very probably to construct the 18th and 19th century field dykes seen across the site today.

East Mound, however, saw major reconfigurations and new building in Phase 3. The small north–south aligned building to the south of the complex was established with curving side-walls and a surrounding sunken drain. Immediately to its west, a ferrous metalworking area was constructed, surrounded by small walls probably acting as wind-breaks and/or a light roofed shelter. North of these, dug into the sand and slightly down-slope in elevation, an east–west aligned, bow-sided longhouse or 'hall-building' was established. The main internal space or 'hall' had narrow side-benches, and the roof was evidently supported towards either end by wooden posts. It did not have a formal or kerbed central hearth, but a series of informal smaller hearths were created, used and re-positioned in the central floor area. It had a door in its south wall near to the metalworking area which was later blocked up (in Phase 5) but remained a visible feature in the masonry. The western end of the Phase 3 longhouse lay slightly to the west of the point where the side-walls of the western annex were later joined on to the side-walls of the Phase 3 longhouse. Some of the Phase 3

floor layers continue into this liminal area, and two of the Phase 3 western wall's foundation stones remain at floor level. The position of its eastern end is more problematic to identify, although it seems unlikely there was any enclosed byre area towards its eastern end in Phase 3. These elements were comprehensively overwritten by the construction of the Phase 5 entrances, internally-dividing stub wall, and larger and more elaborate byre area to the east. We are also unsure from the current extent of excavation as to whether there were further (as yet unidentified) attendant buildings during Phase 3. Due to the depth of sand overburden, the geophysical and GPR surveys of East Mound (Chapter 3) were inconclusive on this point. Hints of an opposed-facing element in the masonry of the outer edge of the north wall of the East Mound longhouse could mean that the interior of another substantial structure lies parallel to its north, utilising the same side-wall, however it is not clear which phase this may relate to.

By the early 11th century, a distinctive and important cluster of stone and turf buildings had emerged upon East Mound, representing a powerful household which was centred upon a substantial stone-walled, turf-clad longhouse, equipped with outbuildings and a small but productive metalworking yard. At this time the neighbouring longhouse on Snusgar was evidently still occupied, but was apparently ceding its primacy of place towards the newer complex on East Mound. The East Mound longhouse also left its mark on the surrounding exterior surfaces in the form of middens (mainly deposited to its south and east, down-wind on the prevailing westerlies), and cast-out spreads from the four metalworking hearths which were particularly concentrated, as might be expected, around the periphery of the hearth enclosure wall.

The Phase 3 buildings evidently did not remain in stasis for very long, however, possibly for only one generation, or two to three decades at most. The complex was reconfigured extensively, starting with the beginnings of a repositioning of southern ancillary outbuildings in (intermediate) Phase 4, and culminating in a substantial enlargement of the main longhouse structure in Phase 5. The formerly north–south aligned southern outbuilding was superseded in Phase 4 with a strengthening, filling and repositioning of some of the existing walls as foundations. These became, as fully developed in Phase 5, a rectangular building orientated on an east–west alignment, the western wall of which encroached upon the metalworking yard, covering up part of one of the Phase 3 bowl hearths. The metalworking activity in this part of the site swiftly declined; the former door in the south wall of the Phase 3 longhouse was blocked up and the intermediate space filled with windblown detritus and sand. The access and egress point from the ancillary rectangular building was

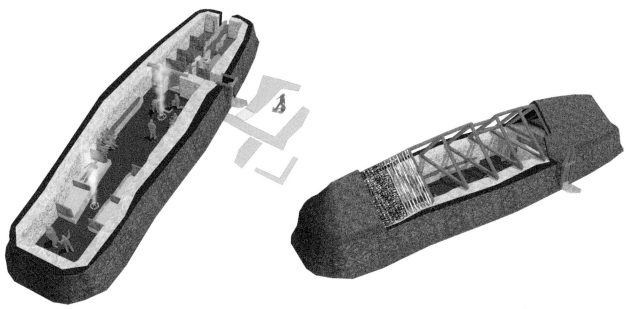

Fig. 25.1: East Mound longhouse, Phase 5, digital reconstructions with conjectured roof

reordered to near its north-western corner and a flight of six stone steps constructed, leading down to a newly-defined and flagged central yard, which was constructed over a network of stone-lined drains. The western end of this yard was blocked from the prevailing weather by a wall, and the consequent right-turn formed the threshold for a new, substantially constructed flagstone entrance into the extended longhouse (Fig. 25.1). An impressive portal 1.2 m wide, it is strikingly similar to the flagged entrance into the building known as 'Room VII' in the Lower Norse Horizon on the Brough of Birsay (Morris 1996, 235). This new main entrance into the East Mound longhouse was constructed just east of what became the central division of space within the longhouse, marked by a new dividing wall abutting, but not meshing with, the existing stonework of the Phase 3 southern wall. Upon entering the main longhouse building, a flagged and kerbed stone passageway formed a T-junction. Turning west, past the end of the new stub wall and through an intermediate space (possibly with a pantry or cupboard against the north wall), a door (the jamb pinion stone of which survived *in situ*) marked the entrance into the hall and domestic chambers. Turning east, the stone passageway continued through the centre of a roofed byre area, connecting to a door in the centre of its eastern wall, evidently intended for human and animal use, and then fanning out as a kerbed walkway onto the eastern exterior.

The domestic space of the extended East Mound longhouse in Phase 5 centred upon a reuse of the Phase 3 hall, but with a further substantial annex to its west. The hall remained a relatively open space, much as it had during Phase 3; although its ends were altered and access

Fig. 25.2: Excavation team in 2010 sitting on side benches in East Mound longhouse central hall, from E

points changed, the side walls and side benches remained much the same. As demonstrated by the excavation team in 2010, it could seat comfortably up to 20 people on its narrow side-benches, facing each other across the central space (Fig. 25.2). A small central hearth was used for cooking, heating and some ferrous metalworking, with a sunken stone-lined quenching box placed alongside. We may infer that the hall was used as a social or meeting space at times, but at other times functioned as a sleeping or cooking area. The metalworking activity may have been a restricted episode, as its noxious presence would have made domestic life in the hall very unpleasant. These functions possibly diversified from Phases 3 to 5.

West of the hall, the former end-wall of the Phase 3 longhouse was removed above its foundations and a new annex constructed with much wider side benches than the hall, and consequently a narrow and more confined central floor, in the middle of which a cooking hearth was created (Fig. 4.32), the heavy and prolonged use of which has left vivid red organic stains on and around it, and is marked by a strong concentration of steatite and carbonised grain deposition. This hearth was not bounded by a rigid rectilinear stone surround, as witnessed in many other Viking-Age longhouses, but like the metalworking hearths of Phase 3, it was dug as a circular bowl into the underlying sand. The side-benches were probably used for sitting, sleeping and storage. On the walls behind the side benches in both the hall and western annex, at the correct height to have been carved by a child whilst standing or an adult whilst seated, are a series of faint inscribed lines denoting 'tally marks' and other, less clear palimpsests of scratches (Fig. 4.44). In its roofed state, the longhouse interior would have been dark, hot and smoky, but an iron candle holder amongst the Phase 5 finds (SF 109; Fig. 12.4) denotes that wall-mounted interior lighting was used. We may infer that some wooden surfacing of walls and benches, with the use of textiles, rugs, animal skins and hay, probably made the domestic environment relatively well-insulated and comfortable. At some point, flax was dried above the hearth, leaving its traces in the floor layers.

East of the main entrance of the East Mound longhouse, the byre area was more utilitarian in its lay-out. The central passage has flat, cornered cut slots carved into some of its kerbstones, supporting a series of modest wooden uprights forming roof supports either side of a corridor. To the south of the central passageway were small stalls with beaten earth floors in which (apparently relatively modest-sized) farm animals were kept. To the north of the passage is a less clearly-organised area, the finds from which (including a number of iron tools) suggest a workshop area, possibly with a workbench.

The internal floors of the East Mound longhouse were, apart from the flagstones around the entrance door and the stone-lined passage in the byre, made up of successive fine spreads of peat ash, organic materials and sand. These may have been covered with matting but we do not have clear surviving evidence of this. The floor layers were relatively soft and their build-up preserves the chemical signatures of occupation, with iron concentrations around the hearths reflecting the influence of metalworking, phosphorus denoting human and animal excrement, and food consumption (Chapter 7). Magnetic susceptibility shows the limited but apparently deliberate extent to which burnt material was spread from its sources in the hearths. Organic chemical traces show a broad spread of indicators in the floors, mainly in the central hall area (confirming

this was the likely location of food consumption), with food waste, excrement and bilary acids marked by lipids, cholesterol and lithocholic acids concentrating in the lowest depositional features, notably in under-floor drainage system near the main entrance and the byre and the sunken stone box feature (the 'quenching tank') in the main domestic hall.

By the mid to late 11th century, therefore, as the Snusgar longhouse apparently waned somewhat in importance, the East Mound settlement had evolved into a significant farmstead with an internal byre, which compares well with comparable buildings from prominent Viking and Late Norse sites in the Northern Isles and elsewhere in the North Atlantic (Fig. 25.3). With an overall length of 26.3 m, it is exceeded in size only by House 1 at Jarlshof. Its method of construction – double-skinned walls of about 1–1.5 m width faced internally with flat vertical masonry and filled with stone and midden, is characteristic of other contemporary sites in Orkney and Shetland, notably Jarlshof and the Brough of Birsay. Likewise, the floors were not flagged throughout, but were a mixture of flagging and soft deposits (indeed the central yard is the most complete area of flagging seen on the site). The Phase 3 'bow-sided' hall was retained, but was rebuilt and extended at both ends.

ARTEFACT AND ECONOMY

A rotary quern fragment (SF 200; Fig. 18.6) found in an early floor longhouse floor layer in Trench 5 may be a rare case of a pre-Viking object reused in the Phase 2/3 settlement. Most of the other Phase 2 finds are broadly similar in style and material to those of later periods, suggesting a characteristically Viking-style material culture was emerging in tandem with occupation at this time, which became established across the excavated sites, and which owed little to any previous period or occupation. A handful of steatite sherds, iron objects and worked bone imply a modest level of economic activity across the excavated sites in Phase 2, with the numerical emphasis upon Trenches 1–4 (Snusgar). Relatively few finds are demonstrably associated with Phase 2, although some of those from later phases may be to some extent residual. A small number of steatite sherds from middens and wall core material indicate contacts with Shetland, whereas (discounting those of unknown provenance) the sherds identifiable as Norwegian imports are all from Phase 5 or later. A significant measure of residuality between phases is implied by two of the beads (SF 249 and 44; Figs 16.1, 16.2), which are dated respectively to between AD 580–650 and AD 790–860, but were deposited in Phases 5 and 6. A worked flint fragment (SF 278) is from the prehistoric period but was found in the comparatively modern Phase 8.

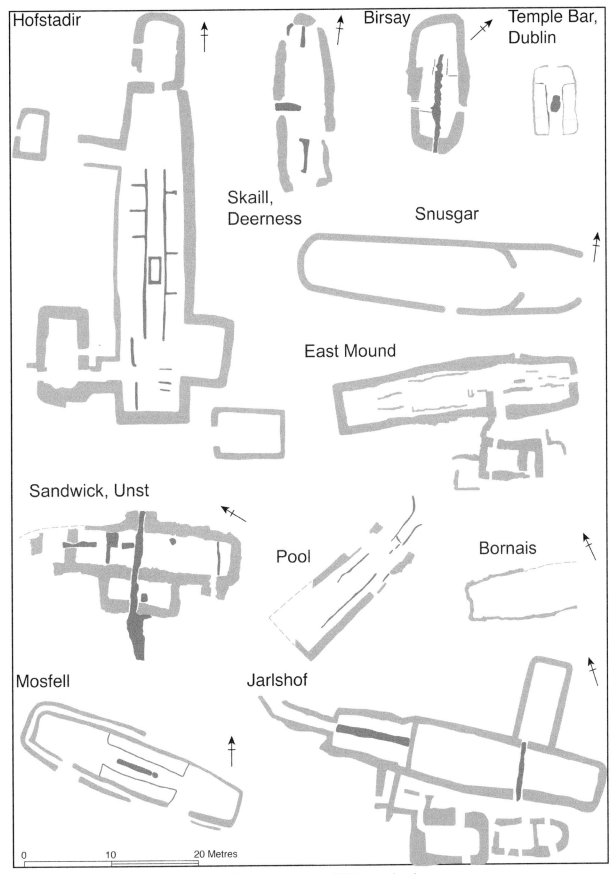

Fig. 25.3: Comparative plans of Viking-Age longhouses

The artefacts from the clusters of structures exposed here are broadly comparable in scale and type to assemblages from other well-known Norse-period settlements in Atlantic Scotland, such as the Brough of Birsay (Curle 1982), Skaill, Deerness (Buteux 1997), Pool, Sanday (Hunter 2007), Jarlshof, Shetland (Hamilton 1956), and the South Uist machair sites of Bornais (Sharples 2005) and Cille Pheadair (Parker Pearson *et al.* 2004a). The majority of objects found are of relatively mundane raw materials which for the most part were probably sourced by local trade within the area of the Norse earldom of Orkney (including Shetland and Caithness), such as bone, antler and steatite, although many of the bone and antler objects are well-made and decorated with simple but recognisable motifs such as symmetrical cross-hatching and herringbone patterns, and linked ring-and-dots. Small bone pins and needles, and decorated antler-comb fragments, fall into type groups of the 10th to 12th centuries associated with Viking-Late Norse sites elsewhere in Orkney and the western Viking world. The combs are exclusively of iron-riveted rather than copper-riveted types, strengthening their date attribution to the earlier phase of the Viking comb tradition. Metal finds have predominantly been small iron objects such as ties and nails, many of which probably formed part of the wooden superstructure (Fig. 25.4). Small quantities of pottery and larger quantities of steatite offer insights into food storage, cooking and eating. Gaming pieces, beads and objects such as the glass linen smoother SF 425 (Fig. 17.1) illustrate the indoor domestic crafts and occupations of the inhabitants, whereas iron tools, whetstones, and objects such as the antler fairlead (SF 247) (Fig. 15.7), speak more of the exterior world of building, farming, and fishing.

The building forms are similar to those observed elsewhere in the northern world, but the material culture of the settlements is far from defined exclusively by Scandinavian traits. Objects such as the amber bead, the Norwegian steatite sherds, and the green/brown banded whetstone (SF 4030, Fig. 18.1) carry Scandinavian cultural associations, yet in this respect seem to be in something of a numerical minority. Perhaps most striking is a group of objects which point towards the Irish Sea region as a source of cultural reference. The attribution of the crutch-headed ringed pin to a Dublin provenance is a near-certain one, as the city accounts for by far the predominant number of ringed pins found, coupled with the only archaeologically demonstrable evidence for their manufacture. There is a strong Irish and correspondingly weak Scandinavian flavour to the comb assemblage (Chapter 14). Some of the coarse greyware sherds (Chapter 20) also have a possible Irish Sea provenance in Ulster. More spectacular as a signifier of Irish Sea, and more particularly Manx, links are some

of the more elaborate silver ornaments within the Skaill Hoard (Chapter 21). Outside local intra-earldom trading dependencies, contacts with the southern North Sea, and with Dublin and the Irish Sea, are perhaps the most surprising yet persistently visible amongst the finds. The activities in Ireland of the 11th-century Orkney earls are well-known, including most famously Sigurd the Stout (father of Thorfinn) who died carrying the Raven banner at the Battle of Clontarf in 1014. Hiberno-Norse influences may have acted in Orkney itself to distance the ethnic self-perception of the settled population from the traditional Viking homeland in Norway in the 11th and 12th centuries, and in so doing perhaps helped to establish a genuinely distinctive Orcadian identity for the first time.

Archaeobotanical evidence from the sites (Chapter 8) points towards the dominance of oat and barley cultivation. Dryland weeds such as corn spurrey and chickweed suggested that the surrounding sandy land was in use for infield cultivation. The barley, but perhaps more so the oats, may have been intended both for human consumption and for animal fodder. Burnt grain found in domestic hearth contexts suggests not only cooking but drying of corn after a wet harvest, although we did not find evidence for a separate corn-drier, which is a common feature of later Norse and Medieval longhouses, such as at Beachview, Birsay (Morris 1996), and was often located at the corner of the building. Flax was also dried over the longhouse hearths. Textile working is implied by finds of spindle whorls and bone needles. The beginnings of flax production appear in Phase 3 at both Snusgar and East Mound, albeit on a smaller scale than in the later Phase 5. This implies that the natural dune slacks within the Links of Skaill were subject to exploitation for flax retting (which must be done in non-brackish water) and their naturally soft, unstable sides were probably strengthened with stone and wooden planks for ease of access to the water. Arrangements would have had to be made to obtain drinking water from the nearby burn for people and animals from upstream of any noxious and polluting flax-retting area. The close link between the settlements and the freshwater dune slacks and lochs around the Bay is suggested by the discovery amongst the archaeobotanical material of wetland weed flora such as sedge, club-rushes and crowberry.

Archaeobotanical evidence also points towards the various fuels used. Willow, birch and scots pine were found in the metalworking areas in Trench 5, within the complex sequence of floors re-laid with the inclusion of much metalworking waste. These wood species were needed to produce the intense heat required for smithing, and would not have been easy or inexpensive to obtain. Some may have come from driftwood, but this would have been an unreliable source. By contrast, locally-available peat and probably general refuse was burnt to generate the

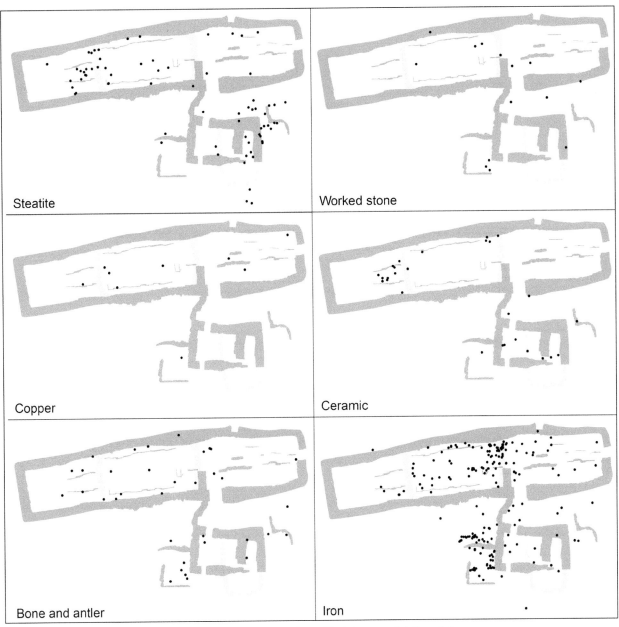

Fig. 25.4: Distribution plots of finds by material, Trench 5

more modest temperatures required in domestic hearths for heat and cooking.

As might be expected from such a coastal location, the marine and shoreline environments were exploited throughout the life of the settlements, although the emphasis and diversity of such exploitation varies from one phase to another. Context 1504, a Phase 3 midden in the upper part of the Trench 4 sequence on Snusgar, contained a large number of fractured gannet humeri which have led to Ingrid Mainland's suggestion that particular seabird species were being exploited in a systematic manner (Chapter 9). Fish remains occur in most midden

and occupation deposits, but are not disproportionately abundant (Chapter 10). They are dominated by gadids (particularly cod, with the larger size dominant but smaller sizes also represented; and saithe, Pollack, ling, hake and torsk) together with smaller amounts of herring, garfish, halibut, mackerel, eel, dogfish, snake blenny, ray or shark and salmon or trout. Layers dated earlier in the excavated sequence, particularly Phase 2 and 3 middens from Snusgar, are less dominated by gadids than those of later phases in the early to mid-11th century and later. This picture is consonant with studies on comparable data from elsewhere (*e.g.* Barrett 2005; 2012) which chart the rise of cod fishing as a North Atlantic commodity in the 11th century. It is unlikely that significant levels of fish-processing activity for export occurred here, unlike at more specialised sites such as Quoygrew and St Boniface (Orkney), and Freswick and Robert's Haven (Caithness), although Nicholson notes that cod head bones are common in the assemblage, suggesting the possible preparation of a storable product such as stockfish, albeit on a less ambitious scale than these other sites and probably for domestic consumption.

The archaeozoological material favours cattle, sheep/ goat and pig (with many instances of butchery) together with lower incidences of red deer, cat, dog, horse and seal. There are hints in the archaeozoological material of a change in some of the functions of the East Mound longhouse. In Phase 3, the majority of animals slaughtered were young, implying a pattern of meat consumption, which may echo the 'feasting' deposits seen elsewhere. This was coupled with the high-point of on-site smithing in the metalworking area. In Phase 5, we can detect a swing towards older animals (both cattle and sheep), suggesting that milk and wool were more important, and a decline in metalworking. It would be easy to over-state the implications of this, and the pattern may well reflect broader changes in the settlement and economy of Orkney, but they appear to point towards an increasingly powerful household in Phase 3 which required a large meeting space, and which consumed resources from a wide agricultural and natural capture in a relatively profligate manner, but which by Phase 5 had evolved into a prosperous farmstead more dependent on its own animal husbandry and cultivated infields, demonstrated by ploughing and soil formation (Chapter 6). Hence in determining the high-point of the social and political status of the settlement, referencing merely the gross size of the longhouse itself may not be a very accurate guide. The smaller version seen in Phase 3 may actually have had more local political impetus as a focus for consumption, whereas by Phase 5 we see a change towards an established farmstead for an extended family (by this stage, the locus of local political power may have shifted yet again), and operating on a more locally productive agricultural model.

Later phases, abandonment and disappearance

As inhabitants of settlements built upon sand, facing the full wrath of the Atlantic Ocean, with the ever-present problem of maintaining a stable ground-surface and viable agricultural activity around them, the people who constructed and dwelt in the Snusgar and East Mound longhouses did not allow their homesteads to stay the same for very long. The fairly short chronology between phases observed in the radiocarbon data in particular (Chapter 5) suggests that deterioration of

soft and vulnerable construction materials was an ever-present challenge, and major changes were wrought to the building complexes at about the interval of one or two generations upon each other. The ever-present need to maintain and refresh occupation surfaces with new material is evident in the soil micromorphological data (Chapter 6). Architectural traits of Viking derivation, such as the basic longhouse form itself and its bow-sided morphological elements, which are visible in the geophysical traces of the Snusgar building and in the Phase 3 hall on East Mound, did not stand in the way of pragmatic change and re-ordering on a frequent basis. Longhouses (and their attendant buildings) were a form of dwelling open to endless reconfiguration, as their inhabitants' needs changed. Drystone walls, soft floors, essentially portable internal elements such as flagstones and orthostatic uprights, and components of their timber and turf superstructures, functioned like a large jigsaw puzzle, elements of which could be pulled apart, moved, opened up, filled in, and reused as desired or required. Buildings, in effect, became their own construction quarries as ongoing change occurred, although new constructional materials were certainly made and brought in from elsewhere. This has created an exceptionally complex three-dimensional archaeological picture across the excavated areas, where earlier deposits were frequently reused as parts of later ones, such as former floor or hearth materials subsequently becoming wall-fill.

The Phase 5 longhouse on East Mound did not have a particularly long life as a fully inhabited space. Like many examples from more recent times in Orkney, what had been the dwelling-house was demoted to being a byre or steading, and people moved on elsewhere, perhaps nearby at this initial point or perhaps somewhat further away. The large turf-covered roof, which was heavy and difficult to maintain, may possibly have suffered irreparable damage in a winter gale, and this possibility, perhaps coupled with death or an outbreak of disease amongst the occupants, may have led to a downgrading of the settlement during Phase 6 in the later 11th and into the 12th century, from a dwelling to a mainly animal-utilised complex. Animals began to occupy what had been formerly the domestic spaces, trampling, disturbing and adding to the floors which now included turf material from the roof, and their hoofprints (see Fig. 4.33) remained fixed in the latest layers, preserved by the windblown sand which filled the interior after it was abandoned. Parts of the eastern end of the longhouse were demolished to make animal entry easier, and possibly some of the stone was robbed for other purposes. A small V-shaped entrance of a type often seen in later cattle fields was created in the north-east wall, which itself became part of a roughly-built probably square stock enclosure extending northwards by 13 m to Trench 7, where its northern extent was demonstrated.

The rectilinear 'ancillary' building to the south of the longhouse was shortened to a square shape, re-floored and flagged, and provided with orthostats dividing its interior space. A wall aperture like a small, low entrance capped with a lintel was created in its southern wall opposite its main entrance in its north-west corner, evidently as a run for small animals or poultry. Under the new flagging and near a corner hearth, a series of artefacts was discovered, including an impressive comb (SF 108; Fig. 14.4), and pieces of glazed whiteware pottery from a table jar probably made in France, which may be amongst the latest imported material to arrive at the site (Chapter 20). These may possibly have represented a special deposit, perhaps a statement 'closing' the site as a dwelling-house and signifying its new and more humble role as a steading or hut. The reconfiguration of the southern ancillary building into its squarer Phase 6 form, was itself evidence that people were still investing in the site, albeit now for mainly agricultural purposes. Soil chemistry, notably phosphorus (Figs 7.1, 7.2) implies a continued presence of animals, and the surrounding later fish middens imply some fish processing and midden dumping continued into Phase 7.

It is hard to say when the East Mound settlement disappeared entirely. Parts of its western end remained above the turf long enough to become part of a very roughly-constructed sheep fold in Phase 9, but it is quite likely by this stage that the significance of these stones, as parts of a much larger buried building, had long become lost and forgotten. An OSL date taken from the middle sand overburden in the centre of the longhouse gave a date of 620 ± 125 BP, indicating that significant amounts of windblown sand had begun to fill the abandoned longhouse by the 14th century, blanketing but also preserving the remains. Thereafter, the East Mound settlement was entirely lost to posterity until it was rediscovered in 2005. The Snusgar settlement did not vanish quite so completely, but as apparently with its neighbour, its former status became lost to recorded history. We do not know if the 1795 observation of the 'Castle' and its tiny (if apparently somewhat fancifully-complete) depiction in Walden's 1772 plan owe anything to a genuine surviving perception locally of its historical status, or just represent educated guesswork of the later 18th century. Either way, neither observation was enough to prevent it subsequently being robbed and part-destroyed by 19th-century dyke-builders and disturbed by kelping activity, sundry agricultural dumping, and random animal burials through to the mid-20th century.

The name Snusgar (rendered as 'Snoosgarth') also features in the folk-tale *The Death of the Fin King* (Chapter 24). The precise antiquity of such tales is of course virtually impossible to establish, as they result from an oral tradition. However, the pedigree of this one

is good, as it forms a part of the collections of George Marwick. Whatever its origins, there is undoubtedly some more recent and probably anachronistic gloss on detail within the tale. Nevertheless, one or two details stand out in archaeological terms. The sea monster (the 'Fin King') which had been terrorising the community around the Bay of Skaill, was killed, and its carcass burnt upon a pyre of stones called the 'Castle of Snoosgarth', and it adds 'You can still see the stones that were burnt on the fire' (Muir 1998, 88). The Burn o' Rin, where the people drank whilst cremating the monster, was renamed the Burn o' Snoosgarth. The hero of the tale married his sweetheart in the Kirk at Skaill, and after the wedding (which took place in a gale), the wedding party danced so hard to the music of a fiddle that they disturbed the sand, which blew and completely buried a house called 'The Fan'.

The historic landscape of the Bay of Skaill

As seen at Snusgar and East Mound, the principal Viking-period settlement loci did not necessarily retain their dominance for very long. It is possible that the landholding, manor or estate mattered more than the individual domestic buildings, and that new structures could arise across the landscape in each generation. The Snusgar and East Mound settlements are so close together in space and time that it is difficult to see them as representing separate or rival landholdings. They were probably households belonging to successive generations of the same, evidently important, extended family. It is as yet unconfirmed as to whether the two mounds nearer the shore, Mounds A and B, conceal contemporary settlement deposits, which could substantially add to this picture.

These mounds present a dominant phalanx of past occupation traces on the northern side of the Bay of Skaill. Rather more extensive than the smaller mound cluster on the south side of the bay within which Skara Brae was discovered, they nevertheless share with these a position part-sheltered from the open sea by the presence of higher ground to the rear, and stand in immediate proximity to a supply of fresh water. The poorer land in the middle seems to have divided the bay landscape into separate north and south foci. Iron Age brochs dominate the northern and southern extents of the Bay, at Verron (Fig. 2.8) and in the south overlooking the Loch of Skaill at HY 238 183 (Fig. 3.1). A hint of early historic importance on the northern side of the Bay is the Parish Kirk of St Peter, which is located 300 m north-west of Snusgar. The present building dates from 1836, and its predecessor was built in 1670, but evidently on a much older site. The bone strap-end reported upon in Chapter 23 implies burial at the kirk in the Viking Age. Opinion is divided as to whether the Petrine dedication may possibly imply a pre-Viking origin. The argument of Raymond Lamb (Lamb 1993, 262) that the Peterkirks represent perhaps the earliest

(Pictish) churches in Orkney remains controversial. In the Viking Age, it is clear that churches were situated elsewhere in Orkney in close proximity to powerful farms, many of which bear the Norse place-name Skaill (ON *Skáli*), a name which may have either aristocratic or humble associations elsewhere, but in Orkney is accepted as denoting the presence of a significant farmstead or 'drinking hall'. Thomson stated: 'These … occupy high-status coastal sites in arable districts. … these features are consistent with a special type of high-status hall appearing on already-settled prime sites. 'Skaills' (see also Lamb 1997) are often found in close association with a church of a district chapel, suggesting that they flourished at a time when church organisation was being consolidated, perhaps in the eleventh or twelfth centuries' (1995a, 55–7). The prominence of the settlement mounds on the north side of the Bay of Skaill, and their proximity to St Peter's Kirk, arguably endows them with the status that elsewhere may have attracted the description of a (now deserted) rural manor.

As mentioned above, the 'Castle of Snusgar' is a name of uncertain antiquity demonstrable only from 1795. The truncated stony mound at Linnahowe (Fig. 2.9) has an even more tenuous status as a 'Castle'. In neither case can a true castle be proven. Norse Castles are a well-known phenomenon in Orkney. Three are mentioned as *kastali* in *Orkneyinga Saga* (Cubbie Roo's Castle, Wyre; Damsay, on the Bay of Firth; and *Kjarrekstaðir*, probably Cairston near Stromness). These were studied, and in the case of Cairston excavated, by J. Storer Clouston (Clouston 1929; 1931). Other significant and probably semi-fortified Late Norse aristocratic residences include the Earl's Bu, Orphir; Tuquoy, Westray; and 'The Wirk' at Westness on Rousay. All have significant proximate relationships with churches, and are located on sites of significance earlier in the Viking period. 'Snusgar' has no saga reference. But could it be a late introduction as a replacement for a *Skáli*? The likelihood of an association of the [Bay of] *Skáli* name with the settlement remains exposed on Snusgar or East Mound is not entirely unproblematic, however. The principal objection to this is the presence, on the south side of the bay, of an apparently undeniable claim on the *Skáli* name in the form of Skaill House, although even if accepted as of medieval antiquity, this in itself does not reduce the claim of Snusgar or its neighbours, as there may have been more than one such centre around the bay.

Further evidence suggesting the northern side of the Bay of Skaill was once at least as important as the southern side are to be found in the history of township development and medieval tax ('skat') rentals. The earliest rentals to survive intact are the Sinclair assessments of 1492 and 1500, compiled just after the transfer of Orkney and Shetland from Denmark–Norway to the Scottish Crown in 1468 (Peterkin 1820). Pennylands, which approximated

to one farm, formed the basic unit of land assessment, 18 of which counted as an ounceland ('Urisland'). Townships were sub-parish units, fundamental to the distribution of agricultural land types between households, which occurred with varying multiples of pennyland values. It is, however, less clear how far back these land apportionments may be taken chronologically, and the view popular amongst an earlier generation of historians, that as a whole they represent an unchanged inheritance from the Viking period has been refuted in more recent years. Thomson's most recent account prefers the 12th century as the period when this system crystallised across Orkney (Thomson 2001, 218). Their documented form is clearly later medieval in character, but there are hints in the values of different townships of older land divisions being maintained within this system. These concern those townships which reproduce within their values clear whole or half multiples of the 18-pennyland ounceland (Clouston 1923; Marwick 1952).

Most Orkney townships are far too small even to include one whole ounceland. The Bay of Skaill, however, is characterised by larger values. Snusgar lies within the township of Scarwell, which was rated in the 1492 and 1500 rentals as 45 pennylands or 2.5 ouncelands. The neighbouring township to the north-west, Northdyke, is also a 45 pennyland/2.5 ounceland township. These may in fact represent equal divisions of an original 5 ounceland township, which would certainly have been the dominant land unit bordering the bay. Southerquoy, however, which includes Skaill House, rated 24 pennylands, a less obvious multiple of the basic unit of 18. To equate multiple values of 18 with relict Norse estates is to invite scepticism from some quarters, however it does appear that not only were Scarwell and Northdyke together equal in value to five ouncelands, but if combined in area extent, both St Peter's Kirk and the Snusgar mound complex stand at their geographic centre. The relatively high value of Scarwell in particular seems curious today, as unlike Northdyke, a large part of the south of the township bordering the bay is now very poor-quality agricultural land with only a thin veneer of grassed topsoil above deep deposits of wind-blown sand, which only provides rough grazing. Much of this sand inundation is, however, most likely to be later medieval in date. A climatic downturn and trend towards oceanic cooling, coupled with an increase in cyclonic storminess, began to assert itself in the 13th century and intensified in the 15th and 16th centuries (Lamb 1982, 171ff; Dawson *et al.* 2011; Griffiths 2015). The skat value of Scarwell township may therefore suggest that a richer and more productive landscape around the Bay of Skaill, which had been agriculturally viable prior to the 13th century, was being covered up and lost to wind-blown sand at this time. An OSL date taken from the fill overlying the buildings in East Mound was determined at

620 ± 125 BP (SG06-22), confirming that the sand covered the by-then abandoned settlement remains in the 13th to 14th centuries AD. The 1492 rentals show that North and South Sandwick, and to a slightly lesser extent Marwick, were amongst the Orkney districts with the largest rent reductions due to unproductive or untenanted land. North Sandwick returned only 18.2% of its old (meaning pre-impignoration) or 'full' value (Thomson 2008, 109), indicating not only a widespread diminution in productive capacity but also a useful standard within living memory by which this diminution could be measured. The loss of productive land to windblown sand may well be a reason for the decline, particularly in coastal areas, although other factors may also have been present.

The abandonment of the buildings on Snusgar and East Mound may have happened for very localised, personal or idiosyncratic reasons and we cannot be sure from the excavated data exactly when people stopped living in them. Use of the mound sites at Saevar Howe and Buckquoy beside Birsay Bay similarly did not outlive the Viking Age. The settlement mound on the foreshore at Marwick (SM 2884) was also abandoned, possibly in favour of a *skáli* further inland, which was apparently divided somewhat later into the farms of Langskaill and Netherskaill.

However, the movement of settlement areas away from the bay frontages towards higher ground to the east, which is visible at Birsay, Marwick and Skaill, points towards a more general process of settlement shift in the middle ages. In all three bay hinterlands, the principal farmsteads of the medieval and post-medieval periods are located away from the shore frontage, and are associated with localised spreads of 'plaggen' soils. The Birsay Be-south quoylands, lining the higher ground on the hillside to the south-east of the bay (Thomson 1995b), are paralleled above the Bay of Skaill by Quoyloo, containing the important farm of Stove (its satellites Midstove and Netherstove overlook the links from the edge of the arable land to the north). These, arguably, are the successor settlements to Snusgar and its neighbour on East Mound. Aristocratic settlement seems also to have developed inland in the north-west Mainland, with the important farm of Housebay by Sabiston Loch (Crawford 2006) perhaps taking on enhanced significance as the focus of dues and obligations. Unlike in comparable situations elsewhere, such as Skaill, Deerness, on the East Mainland, the medieval successor settlements did not occur in close proximity to the Viking/Norse focus at the Bay of Skaill. This may be due to the particularly energetic and intractable nature of the wind-blown sand regime on the West Mainland, facing the full force of the North Atlantic. It is apparently this reason why the historic importance of the coastal zone was lost to later generations, with only the seemingly-isolated parish kirk and the cluster of grassy mounds concealing deeply-buried abandoned settlements left to denote its former significance. In this respect it has parallels elsewhere in Atlantic Scotland, notably in the shift away from the machair on to the Blacklands in the Uists (Parker Pearson *et al.* 2004b, 161–8).

26

Conclusion

David Griffiths and Jane Harrison

As described in the foregoing chapters, an investigation encompassing extensive geophysical survey, topographic analysis of mounds and earthworks, and a targeted but detailed series of excavations, has probed further than hitherto into the human occupation and landscape of these parts of Orkney's West Mainland. The fieldwork and other research reported on in this monograph have contributed a stock of new archaeological information on the areas covered, which has been synthesised as far as possible with the pre-existing picture of evidence discussed in Chapter 2. The landscape surveys reported upon in Chapter 3 revealed a wide range of possibilities for further investigation, for which time and funding only permitted a modest sample to be realised. Excavations, the results of which occupy the majority of the volume from Chapter 4 onwards, were intended partly to test, confirm or eliminate the geophysical and other survey results. They were however also undertaken in a concentrated and substantial enough manner so that a coherent picture could emerge of past occupation, economy, environment and chronology in the deposits and structures selected for exposure, something which a series of test-pits and auger-samples alone could never adequately provide. The excavations have provided a rich haul of site data, which is comparable in many ways to that from other Viking-Age settlement excavations in Orkney and elsewhere.

A conclusion is a good place to return to the opening reasons for spending a good deal of time, money and energy on pursuing a long-running research project – in this case over a 15-year period. It was intended that this project, in its origins and subsequent evolution, would provide a new insight into the history of the coastal landscape of Orkney's West Mainland. The planned work was aimed at establishing how far extensive geophysical survey was a useful way forward as a means of investigation, and at building a new basis upon which coastal management could proceed, in the greater knowledge of what lies behind and away from the eroding edge of the land, facing the ever-hungry sea. It sought to go further, with selective excavation, in order to explore initial survey results. Techniques of excavating in and around windblown sand were a particular point of interest and challenge. Above all, the project has helped to build a new narrative for this landscape, by bringing together old and new evidence, making greater sense of a series of unanswered questions and wonderings about the lives of people here in the past.

In 2003, the utility of archaeological geophysics on sandy coastal landscapes was seen as less than proven, and as yet little practiced in Orkney. In retrospect, from the vantage of 2018, its role seems unsurprising, even predictable; it is now beyond doubt seen as a valid and worthwhile approach, one which is now a mainstream aspect of field research. However, this project has elucidated some essential interpretative pitfalls and caveats, which we should consider. Initially, it was all-too easy to over-interpret what the eye was seeing in the plots of data, against the expectations conditioned by knowledge of the existing archaeology of the locality. In fact, the gestation of our final interpretations was long, reflective and challenging. It was only when the combinations of geophysical techniques' results were evaluated together, and the area of the investigations was dramatically increased over the initial coverage, that site-specific surveys began to make greater sense at a landscape scale. Wind-blown sand, affecting the majority (but not all) of the areas examined, is now better-understood as an aspect of preservation and destruction, blanketing archaeological deposits from sight but also inviting the attentions of quarrymen, rabbits and other agents of disturbance. In excavating, it took experience and care to learn how best to disentangle deposits, how to gauge past disturbance, and understand the way in which stone masonry and other deposits had been assembled, altered, reassembled, moved, repurposed or dismantled.

It is perhaps surprising that such a dominant, near-exclusive proportion of the excavated evidence presented here is restricted to the Viking Age and subsequent Late Norse period between the 10th to 13th centuries AD. This was, to these authors in particular, a welcome focus, if not one which was necessarily expected. The Viking Age is doubtlessly an extremely significant juncture in Orkney's history, but of course by no means the only one. The later, post-medieval landscape of the bay hinterlands is documented here, but is mainly a story of decline, abandonment, wasteland, and emptiness; evidence was found of the foul and poverty-driven occupation of kelping, which was followed eventually by improvement and modernity. Prior to the Viking Age, the picture is yet more hesitant and diffuse, with nothing pre-dating the later Iron Age having been demonstrated in any of our investigations in the mounds of Skaill and Marwick. The close proximity of internationally-important Neolithic sites, most notably at Skara Brae, but also at Brodgar and Stenness, and the nearby megalith quarry on Vestra Fiold, perhaps makes this perplexing. The excavations could of course have gone further, deeper and more destructively, exposing the hearts of our mounds. Ground-penetrating radar was used to try to illuminate any such potential, but whilst it did contribute important information on the structure of the mounds, it did not point the way to any underlying archaeology such as a lost Neolithic settlement beneath. Such may yet be found to exist by future investigations, but we consciously stopped short of doing what may have been necessary to answer that question conclusively. We were satisfied that what we had found gave a coherent picture of one major era, at the dawn of the historical age, and we were unwilling to destroy or dismantle the beauty and completeness of the structures we had discovered (now carefully protected and backfilled intact), in an uncertain quest for something yet older beneath.

The preceding chapters detail a series of glimpses of a landscape and society dominated by access to the sea, perhaps rather more so than in more recent times. For several centuries during the Norse period, people worked this landscape and seascape as a productive whole, supplementing their cultivated barley, flax and oats, and the meat and milk of domesticated cattle and sheep, by gathering the bounty of the cliffs and ocean. The inhabitants of Snusgar and East Mound were evidently relatively prosperous and well-connected people by the standards of their time. Their possessions included imported glass, amber, ceramics and steatite, and they maintained their hair with delicate antler combs. They were skilled farmers, fishers, wildfowlers, builders and metalworkers, having a small but productive smithy on their premises. The central hall in the East Mound longhouse (Fig. 26.1) remains an impressive space, roofless now of course, but still enclosed and upstanding to chest-height in places, with its side-benches, central hearth and well-made stone walls, in some places lightly scratched with tally-marks. Important gatherings took place here a thousand years ago, and for a time it was probably the hall of the district's head household. This was not a palace or grand fortress, such as an earl may have inhabited, but it fits well the upper-middle ranked notion of a *skáli*. The nearby longhouse on Snusgar was probably similar, perhaps pre-dating it by a generation, but has not survived as a structure or deposits nearly so well. Change was evidently fast and far-reaching, and the longhouses on both mounds were relatively short-lived as dwelling spaces. On East Mound, the more complete of the two complexes, the central dwelling passed from hall-house to extended farmstead, to outbuildings, to a roofless animal enclosure, within three or four generations. It disappeared largely from view under deep sand, with one corner serving as a low rubble wall, until it was rediscovered and re-exposed in 2005. The closely-dated sequence of deposits reported upon here suggest that short occupation phases, changes of use, and frequent structural modification were characteristic of Norse building cultures, perhaps more so than has hitherto been perceived.

This research has succeeded in illustrating some details of the broader history of the area, but inevitably, the imprint of these excavations is tiny compared to the scale of the landscape. How typical or atypical were these settlements? Hints of comparable structures in the project area have been found in the geophysical surveys, but these are yet to be explored further. At the Bay of Skaill, Marwick and Birsay, a fresh perspective has been cast on the movement of people away from the oceanic margin to colonise and fertilise the higher ground further inland. The reasons for this transition are complex, and any specific case-study of settlement will be to some extent atypical in its process, reasons or date of abandonment. However, the move away from the sea is a more general phenomenon, evident not just in Orkney but in Shetland, the Hebrides, and beyond. Climate change towards cooler, stormier weather in the medieval period may underlie this movement, with effects such as increased sand-blows, but there remains no predictable basis on which to account for individual human perceptions and decisions.

As we present our results in this publication, it is the authors' hope that we have made a significant

Fig. 26.1: East Mound longhouse from E, Trench 5 excavation and site tour in progress, 2010

contribution to the archaeology of Orkney, and to the wider understanding of landscape, history and archaeology in the North Atlantic and the Northern World. The radiocarbon and OSL chronology, structural and environmental data presented here can now be compared to those from other Viking-Age sites. We took great inspiration from other comparable projects, especially in their application of different research methods, yet none were adopted without adaptation to the needs and nuances of the particular deposits and structures we were working with. Some of the analyses presented here are provisional, and indeed there have been numerous technical advances in site and data science even since 2010. Lidar (only now in mid-2018 becoming available in extensive and detailed resolution for Orkney) and drone photography, allowing rapid and detailed recording, will inevitably improve the possibilities for visualising landscape and structural detail. More extensive and effective modelling of radar and other geophysical techniques will take us nearer to a long-sought-after ability to image sub-surface archaeology in three dimensions. Microscopy will continue to enhance soil, mineral and environmental science. Isotopes from organic materials are already adding huge potential to our understanding of diet, agriculture, social and economic change. We have tested some different approaches, and

the opportunity exists to carry forward the research in future using the materials in the project archive. We have made our decisions and expended our resources: here are the results as we see them. We hope, with the finds and samples and data deposited, and this monograph as a guide, that future researchers will use, reuse, and reinterpret them, perhaps in ways going well beyond our present perceptions and capabilities.

Fig. 26.2: Endpiece, tea-break for the excavation team at the Bay of Skaill

Bibliography

Abrahams, P. W., Entwistle, J. A. and Dodgshon, R. A. (2010) The Ben Lawers Historic Landscape Project: Simultaneous Multi-element Analysis of Former Settlement and Arable Soils by X-ray Fluorescence Spectrometry. *Journal of Archaeological Method and Theory*, *17*(3), 231–48.

Adamiec, G. and Aitken, M. J. (1998) Dose-rate conversion factors: new data. *Ancient TL* 16, 37–50.

Adams, C. T., Poaps, S. L. and Huntley, J. P. (2012) Arable Agriculture and Gathering, the Botanical Evidence. In J. H. Barrett (ed.), 161–98.

Adderley, W. P., Simpson, I. A., Lockheart, M. J., Evershed, R. P. and Davidson, D. A. (2000) Modelling traditional manuring practices. Soil sustainability of an early Shetland community? *Human Ecology* 28, 415–31.

Adderley, W. P., Simpson, I. A. and Davidson, D. A. (2006) Historic landscape management, a validation of quantitative soil thin-section analyses. *Journal of Archaeological Science* 33, 320–34.

Addyman, P. V. (1973) Late Saxon settlements in the St Neots area, the village or township at St Neots. *Proceedings of the Cambridge Antiquarian Society* 64, 45–99.

Ager, B., Boughton, D. and Williams, G. (2012) Viking hoards: buried wealth of the Norse North West. *Current Archaeology* 264 (March 2012), 26–31.

Aitken, M. J. (1985) *Thermoluminescence Dating*. London, Academic Press.

Aitken, M. J. (1998) *An Introduction to Optical Dating*. Oxford, Oxford University Press.

Alderson, L. (1984) *Rare breeds*. Aylesbury, Shire Album 118, Shire Publications.

Alldritt, D. M. (2003) Economy and Environment in the First Millennium AD in Northern Scotland and the Northern Isles. Unpublished PhD Thesis, University of Glasgow.

Allen, A. (1996) *Orkney's Maritime Heritage*, London, National Maritime Museum.

Allen, J. W. (1999) Whetstones. In B. E. Crawford and B. Ballin Smith, 180–2.

Allison, E. and Rackham, J. D. (1996) The bird bones. In C. D. Morris, 171–3.

Andersen, H. H., Crabb, P. J. and Madsen, H. J. (1971) Århus Sondervold, en byarkaeologisk undersøgelse. Copenhagen, Jysk Arkaeologisk Selskabs Skrifter, Bind IX.

Anderson, J. (1880) Notes on the contents of two Viking graves in Islay, discovered by William Campbell, Esq. of Ballinaby; with notices of the burial customs of the Norse sea-kings, as recorded in the sagas and illustrated by their grave-mounds in Norway and in Scotland. *Proceedings of the Society of Antiquaries of Scotland* XIV, 51–89.

Anderson, J. (1901) Notices of nine brochs along the Caithness coast from Keiss Bay to Skirza Head, excavated by Sir Francis Tress Barry, Bart, M.P. of Keiss Castle, Caithness. *Proceedings of the Society of Antiquaries of Scotland* 35, 112–48.

Andrews, K. and Doonan, R. (2003) *Test Tubes & Trowels, Using Science in Archaeology*, Stroud, Tempus.

Anon. (1892) *Catalogue of the National Museum of Antiquaries of Scotland*. Edinburgh, Society of Antiquaries of Scotland.

Arbman, H. (1940) *Birka I. Die Gräber. Vol. 1*. Stockholm, Kungliga Vittenhets Historie och Antikvitets Akademien.

Arbman, H. (1943) *Birka I. Die Gräber. Vol. 2*. Stockholm, Kungliga Vitterhets Historie och Antikvitets Akademien.

Arneborg, J., Heinemeier, J., Lynnerup, N., Nielsen, H. L., Rud, N. and Sveinbjornsdottir, A. E. (1999) Change of diet of the Greenland Vikings determined from stable carbon isotope analysis and ^{14}C dating of their bones. *Radiocarbon* 41, 157–68.

Arrhenius, B. (2013) Finds of treasure and their interpretation with special reference to some hoards found in Birka and on Björkö. In A. Reynolds and L. Webster (eds), *Early Medieval Art and Archaeology in the Northern World: Studies in Honour of James Graham-Campbell*. Leiden/Boston, Brill, 843–58.

Arrhenius, O. (1929) Die Phosphatfrage. *Zeitschrift Für Pflanzenernährung, Düngung, Bodenkunde*, *14*(3), 185–194.

Ascough, P. L., Church, M. J., Cook, G. T., Dunbar, E., Gestsdottir, H., McGovern, T. H., Dugmore, A. J., Friðriksson, A. and Edwards, K. J. (2012) Radiocarbon reservoir effects in human bone collagen from Northern Iceland. *Journal of Archaeological. Science* 39(7), 2261–2271.

Ashby, S. P. (2005) Zooarchaeology, Artefacts, Trade and Identity, The Analysis of Bone Combs from Early Medieval England and Scotland. In A. Pluskowski (ed.), *Just Skin and Bones? New Perspectives on Human-Animal Relations in the Historical Past*, December 2003, 41–3. Oxford, British Archaeological Reports, International Series 1410, Archaeopress.

Ashby, S. P. (2006) Time Trade and Identity: Bone and Antler Combs in Northern Britain c AD 700–1400. Unpublished PhD thesis, University of York.

Ashby, S. P. (2007) *Bone and Antler Combs*. Finds Research Group AD700–1700, Datasheet 40.

Ashby, S. P. (2009) Combs, Contact and Chronology, Reconsidering Hair Combs in Early-Historic and Viking Age Atlantic Scotland. *Medieval Archaeology* 53, 1–33.

Ashby, S. P. (2011) An atlas of medieval combs from northern Europe. *Internet Archaeology* 30. Available online at http://intarch.ac.uk/journal/issue30/ashby_index.html. (accessed 1/2/17).

Ashby, S. P. (2013a) Making a Good Comb, Mercantile Identity in 9th to 11th-century England. In L. Ten-Harkel and D. M. Hadley (eds), *Everyday Life in Viking Towns, Social Approaches to Towns in England and Ireland c. 800–1100*. Oxford, Oxbow Books, 193–208.

Ashby, S. P. (2013b) Some Comments on the Identification of Cervid Species in Worked Antler. In S. O'Connor and A. M. Choyke (eds), *From These Bare Bones, Raw materials and the study of worked osseous materials*. Oxford, Oxbow Books, 208–22.

Ashby, S. P. (2014) *A Viking Way of Life, Combs and Communities in Early Medieval Britain*. Stroud, Amberley Publishing.

Ashby, S. P. (2015) Disentangling trade, combs in the North and Irish Seas in the Long Viking Age. In J. H. Barrett and S.-J. Gibbon (eds) *Maritime Societies of the Viking and Medieval World*. Leeds, Maney and the Society for Medieval Archaeology, 198–218.

Ashby, S. P. and Batey, C. E. (2012) Evidence of exchange networks, the combs and other worked skeletal material. In J. H. Barrett (ed.) *Being an Islander. Production and identity at Quoygrew, Orkney, AD 900-1600*. Cambridge, McDonald Institute Monographs, 229–43.

Ashby, S. P., Coutu, A. N. and Sindbæk, S. M. (2015) Urban Networks and Arctic Outlands, Craft Specialists and Reindeer Antler in Viking Towns. *European Journal of Archaeology* 18, 679–704.

Ashmore, P. (1999) Radiocarbon dating: avoiding errors by avoiding mixed samples. *Antiquity* 73, 124–30.

Bachmann, H. G. (1982) *The identification of slags from archaeological sites*. London, Institute of Archaeology Occasional Paper 6.

Bailey, R. N. and Cramp, R. J. (1988) *British Academy Corpus of Anglo-Saxon Stone Sculpture Volume 2, Cumberland, Westmorland and Lancashire North-of-the-Sands*. Oxford, Oxford University Press.

Baker, J. and Brothwell, D. R. (1980) *Animal Diseases in Archaeology*. London, Academic Press.

Ballin Smith, B. (1994) *The Howe, Four millennia of Orkney Prehistory*. Edinburgh, Society of Antiquaries of Scotland Monograph Series 9.

Ballin Smith, B. (1999) 4.3 Metal. In B. E. Crawford and B. Ballin Smith, 170–2.

Ballin Smith, B. (forthcoming) Excavations of the multi-period site at The Udal. Edinburgh.

Banerjee, D., Murray, A. S., Bøtter-Jensen, L. and Lang, A. (2001) Equivalent dose estimation using a single aliquot of polymineral fine grains. *Radiation Measurements* 33, 73–94.

Barber, J. (1996) Excavations at St Magnus Kirk, Birsay. In C. D. Morris, 11–31.

Barber, J. (2011) Characterising Archaeology in Machair. In D. Griffiths and P. Ashmore (eds), *Aeolian Archaeology, The Archaeology of Sand Landscapes in Scotland*. Edinburgh, Scottish Archaeological Internet Report 48, Society of Antiquaries of Scotland, 37–54.

Barber, J., Crone, A. and Toolis, R. (2003) *Bronze Age farms and Iron Age farm mounds of the Outer Hebrides*. Edinburgh, Scottish Archaeology Internet Reports 3, Society of Antiquaries of Scotland.

Barnes, M. P. (1994) *The Runic Inscriptions of Maes Howe, Orkney*. Uppsala, Runrön 8.

Barnes, M. P. and Page, R. I. (2006) *The Scandinavian Runic Inscriptions of Britain*. Uppsala, Runrön 19.

Barrett, J. H. (1995) 'Few Know an Earl in Fishing-clothes' Fish middens and the Economy of the Viking Age and Late Norse Earldoms of Orkney and Caithness, Northern Scotland. Unpublished PhD thesis, University of Glasgow.

Barrett, J. H. (1997) Fish trade in Orkney and Caithness, a zooarchaeological approach. *Antiquity* 71, 616–38.

Barrett, J. H. (2005) Economic intensification in Viking Age and medieval Orkney, Scotland, excavations at Quoygrew. In A. Mortensen and S. V. Arge (eds), *Viking and Norse in the North Atlantic, Select Papers from the Proceedings of the Fourteenth Viking Congress, Tórshavn, 19–30 July 2001*. Tórshavn, Annales Societatis Scientarum Færoensis Supplementum 44, 264–83.

Barrett J. H. (ed.) (2012) *Being an Islander. Production and identity at Quoygrew, Orkney, AD 900–1600*. Cambridge, McDonald Institute Monographs.

Barrett, J. H., Beukens, R. and Nicholson, R. A. (2001) Diet and ethnicity during the Viking colonization of Northern Scotland, evidence from fish bones and stable carbon isotopes. *Antiquity* 75, 145–54.

Barrett, J. H., Beukens, R., Simpson, I., Ashmore, P., Poaps, S. and Huntley, J. (2000) What was the Viking Age and when did it happen? A view from Orkney. *Norwegian Archaeological Review* 33(1), 1–39.

Barrett, J. H. and Gibbon, S.-J. (eds) (2015) *Maritime Societies of the Viking and Medieval World*. Leeds, Maney and the Society for Medieval Archaeology.

Barrett, J. H., Locker, A. M. and Roberts C. (2004) The origins of intensive marine fishing in medieval Europe, the English evidence. *Proceedings of the Royal Society of London B.* 271, 2417–21.

Barrett, J. H., Nicholson, R. A. and Cerón-Carrasco, R. (1999) Archaeo-icthyological evidence for long-term socio-economic trends in Northern Scotland, 3500 BC to AD 1500. *Journal of Archaeological Science* 26, 353–88.

Barry, G. (1808) *History of the Orkney Islands*, second edition with corrections and additions by J. Headrick. London, Longman.

Bartosiewicz, L. and Gal, E. (2013). *Shuffling Nags, Lame Ducks: The Archaeology of Animal Disease*. Oxford, Oxbow Books.

Batey, C. E. (1987) *Freswick Links, Caithness. A re-appraisal of the Late Norse site in its context.* Oxford, British Archaeological Reports, British Series 179.

Batey, C. E. and Freeman, C. (1986) Lavacroon, Orphir, Orkney. *Proceedings of the Society of Antiquaries of Scotland* 116, 285–300.

Batey, C. E. and Healy, E. (1995) The Stone. In C. D. Morris, C. E. Batey and D. J. Rackham, 125–9.

Batey, C. E. and Lambden, G. (1996) The artefactual assemblage. In C. D. Morris, 89–96.

Batey, C. E. and Morris, C. D. (1983) Part II, The finds. In J. W. Hedges, Trial excavations on Pictish and Viking settlements at Saevar Howe, Birsay, Orkney. *Glasgow Archaeological Journal* 10, 85–105 (73–124).

Batey, C. E. and Morris, C. D. (1992) Earl's Bu, Orphir, Orkney, Excavation of a Norse Horizontal Mill. In C. D. Morris and D. J. Rackham (eds), 33–41.

Batey, C. E., Jesch, J. and Morris, C. D. (eds) (1993) *The Viking Age in Caithness, Orkney and the North Atlantic, Select Papers from the Proceedings of the Eleventh Viking Congress, Thurso and Kirkwall.* Edinburgh, Edinburgh University Press.

Batey, C. E., Forster, A., Jones, R., Gaunt, G., Breckenridge, F., Bunbury, J. and Barrett, J. (2012) Local Availability and Long-range Trade, the Worked Stone Assemblage. In J. H. Barrett (ed.), 207–27.

Bayley, J. (2009) Early medieval lead-rich glass in the British Isles – a survey of the evidence. In K. Janssens, P. Degryse, P. Cosyns, J. Caen and L. Van't dack (eds), *Annales du 17e Congrès de l'Association Internationale pour l'Histoire du Verre,* 255–60. Brussels, University Press, Antwerp.

Bayley, J., Dungworth, D. and Paynter, S. (2001) *Archaeometallurgy.* London, English Heritage.

Beatty, J. (1992) *Sula, the Seabird Hunters of Lewis.* London, Michael Joseph.

Bertelsen, R. and Lamb, R. G. (1993) Settlement mounds in the North Atlantic. In C. E. Batey, J. Jesch and C. D. Morris (eds), 544–54.

Best, J. and Mulville, J. (2014) A Bird in the Hand: Data Collation and Novel Analysis of Avian Remains from South Uist, Outer Hebrides. *International Journal of Osteoarchaeology* 24, 384–96.

Bigelow, G. F. (1984) Subsistence in Late Norse Shetland. An Investigation into a Northern Island Economy. Unpublished PhD Thesis, University of Cambridge.

Bigelow, G. (1992) Issues and Prospects in Shetland Norse archaeology. In C. D. Morris and J. Rackham (eds), 9–32.

Bigelow, G. (forthcoming) *Excavations of the Sandwick South Site, Unst, Shetland, a case study in maritime settlement archaeology.* Lerwick, Shetland Heritage Publications.

Bill, J. (2014) 7.2 Nails. In I. Russell and M. Hurley (eds) *Woodstown, a Viking Age Settlement in County Waterford,* 141–55. Dublin, Four Courts Press.

Binford, L. R. (1981) *Bones, ancient men and modern myths.* New York, Academic Press.

Blackburn, M. and Pagan, H. (1986) A revised check-list of coin hoards from the British Isles, c.500–1100. In M. A. S. Blackburn (ed.), *Anglo-Saxon Monetary History: Essays in Memory of Michael Dolley.* Leicester, Leicester University Press, 291–313.

Blindheim, C. and Heyerdahl-Larsen, B. (1999) *Kaupang-Funnene, Bind II. Gravplassene i Bikjholbergene/Lamøya Undersøkelsene 1950–1957. Del B. Oldsaksformer, Kulturhistorisk tilbakeblikk.* Oslo Norske, Oldfunn 19.

Boessneck, J. (1969) Osteological differences between sheep (*Ovis aries linné*) and goat (*Capra hircus linné*). In D. Brothwell and E. Higgs (eds), *Science and Archaeology,* 351–8. London, Thames and Hudson.

Boivin, A., DuFournier, D. and LeCler, E. (1996) Nouvelles données sur la céramique très décorée présumée rouennaise. In D. Piton (ed.), *La céramique très décorée dans l'Europe du Nord-Ouest (Xe-XVe siècle),* Actes du colloque de Douai (7–8 avril 1995), 61–84. Berk-sur-Mer, Numéro spécial de Nord-Ouest Archéologie, Musée de Berck.

Bond, J. M. (1994) Change and Continuity in an Island System, the Palaeoeconomy of Sanday, Orkney. Unpublished PhD Thesis, University of Bradford.

Bond, J. M. (1998) Beyond the Fringe? Recognising Change and Adaptation in Pictish and Norse Orkney. In C. M. Mills and G. Coles (eds) *Life on the Edge. Human Settlement and Marginality, Symposia for the Association of Environmental Archaeology No. 13.* Oxford, Oxbow Monograph 100, 81–90.

Bond, J. M. (2002) Pictish Pigs and Celtic Cowboys, food and farming in the Atlantic Iron Age. In B. Ballin Smith and I. Banks (eds) *In the Shadow of the Brochs, the Iron Age in Scotland,* 177–84. Stroud, Tempus.

Bond, J. M. (2007) The Bioarchaeological Evidence. In J. Hunter *et al.* (eds), 169–286.

Bond, J. M., Summers, J. R. and Cussans, J. E. (2010) Macrobotanical Remains. In S. J. Dockrill *et al.*, 178–95.

Bornholdt Collins, K. (2003) Viking-age coin finds from the Isle of Man: a study of coin circulation, production and concepts of wealth during the Viking Age. Unpublished PhD thesis, University of Cambridge.

Bornholdt Collins, K., Fox, A. and Graham-Campbell, J. (2014) The 2003 Glenfaba hoard (*c.*1030), Isle of Man. In R. Naismith, M. Allen and E. Screen (eds), *Early Medieval Monetary History: Studies in Memory of Mark Blackburn.* Farnham, Ashgate, 471–514.

Boyd, W. E. (1988) Cereals in Scottish Antiquity. *Circeaea* 5, 101–10.

Brend, A., Card, N., Downes, J. and Edmonds, M. (eds) (in prep) *Landscapes Revealed: Remote sensing around the Heart of Neolithic Orkney World Heritage Site.*

Bronk Ramsey, C. (1995) Radiocarbon calibration and analysis of stratigraphy, The OxCal program. *Radiocarbon* 37, 425–30.

Bronk Ramsey, C. (1998) Probability and Dating. *Radiocarbon* 40, 461–74.

Bronk Ramsey, C. (2001) Development of the radiocarbon calibration program. *Radiocarbon* 43, 355–63.

Bronk Ramsey, C. (2009) Bayesian analysis of radiocarbon dates. *Radiocarbon* 51, 337–60.

Brugmann, B. (2004) *Glass Beads from Early Anglo-Saxon Graves, A study of the Provenance and chronology of glass beads from Early Anglo-Saxon Graves, Based on Visual examination*. Oxford, Oxbow Books.

Brundle, A. (2005) The unimportance of early Birsay. In O. Owen (ed.), *The World of Orkneyinga Saga*. Kirkwall, Orkney Museums and Heritage, 75–88.

Brundle, A., Lorimer, D. and Ritchie, A. (2003) Buckquoy Revisited. In J. Downes and A. Ritchie (eds), 95–116.

Brøgger, A. W. (1929) *Ancient Emigrants, A History of the Norse Settlements of Scotland*. Oxford, Clarendon Press.

Brøgger, A. W. (1930) *Den Norske Bosetningen på Shetland-Orknøyene, Studier og Resultater*, Skrifter av Det Norske Videnskaps-Akademi i Oslo II, Hist.-Filos. Klasse 3, Oslo.

Buck, C. E., Cavanagh, W. G. and Litton, C. D. (1996) *Bayesian approach to interpreting archaeological data*. Chichester, John Wiley and Sons, Ltd.

Buckland, P. C., Sveinbjarnardottir, G., Savory, D., McGovern, T. H., Skidmore, P., and Andreasen, C. (1983) Norsemen at *Nipaitsoq*, Greenland: A paleoecological investigation. *Norwegian Archaeological Review* 16, 86–98.

Buckland, P. C., Sadler, J. P. and Smith, D. N. (1993) An Insect's Eye-View of the Norse Farm. In Batey, C. E. *et al.* (eds), 506–27.

Buckley, M., Collins, M., Thomas-Oates, J. and Wilson, J. C. (2009) Species identification by analysis of bone collagen using matrix-assisted laser desorption/ionisation time-of-flight mass spectrometry. *Rapid communications in mass spectrometry* 23, 3843–54.

Bullock, P., Fedoroff, N., Jongerius, A., Stoops, G. and Tursina, T. (1985) *Handbook for Soil Thin Section Description*. Wolverhampton, Waine Research Publications.

Buteux, S. (ed.) (1997) *Settlements at Skaill, Deerness, Orkney, Excavations by Peter Gelling of the Prehistoric, Pictish, Viking and Later Periods 1963–81*. Oxford, British Archaeological Reports, British Series 260, Archaeopress.

Buttler, S. J. (1984) The Steatite Industry in Norse Shetland. Unpublished PhD thesis, University of Liverpool.

Bøtter-Jensen, L. (1988) The automated Riso TL dating reader system. *Nuclear Tracks and Radiation Measurements* 14, 177–80.

Bøtter-Jensen, L. (1997) Luminescence techniques: instrumentation and methods. *Radiation Measurements* 27, 749–68.

Bøtter-Jensen, L., Bulur, E., Duller, G. A. T. and Murray, A. S. (2000) Advances in luminescence instrument systems. *Radiation Measurements* 32, 523–8.

Callmer, J. (1977) *Trade beads and bead trade in Scandinavia ca. 800–1000 AD*. Lund Acta Archaeologica Lundensia.

Canti, M. G. and Linford, N. T. (2000) The effects of fire on archaeological soils and sediments, temperature and colour relationships. *Proceedings of the Prehistoric Society* 66, 385–95.

Card, N., Cluett, J., Downes, J., Gater, J. and Ovenden, S., (2007) Heart of Neolithic Orkney World Heritage Site, building a landscape. In M. Larsson and M. Parker Pearson (eds), *From Stonehenge to the Baltic, Living with Cultural Diversity in the Third Millennium BC*. Oxford, British Archaeological Reports International Series 1692, 221–31.

Childe, V. G. (1931) *Skara Brae, A Pictish Village in Orkney*, London, Kegan Paul.

Cheape, H. (1993) Crogans and Barvas Wares, Handmade pottery in the Hebrides. *Scottish Studies* 31, 109–27.

Claassen, C. (1998) *Shells*. Cambridge, Cambridge University Press.

Clarke, A. (1998) Miscellaneous stone tools. In N. Sharples, 144–9.

Clarke, A. (1999) The coarse stone tools. In O. Owen, and C. Lowe (eds), 151–64.

Clarke, A. (2007) The Coarse Stone. In J. Hunter (ed.), 353–88.

Clarke, D. V. (1976) *The Neolithic Village of Skara Brae, 1972–3 excavations, an interim report*. Edinburgh, HMSO.

Clarke, D. V. (ed.) (forthcoming) *Skara Brae Excavations 1972–73*. Edinburgh, National Museum of Scotland.

Close-Brooks, J. (1995) Excavation of a Cairn at Cnip, Uig, Isle of Lewis. *Proceedings of the Society of Antiquaries of Scotland* 125, 253–77.

Clouston, J. S. (1918) The Old Chapels of Orkney, 1. *Scottish Historical Review* 15(58), 89–105.

Clouston, J. S. (1923) The Orkney Pennylands. *Scottish Historical Review* 20, 19–27.

Clouston, J. S. (1929) Three Norse strongholds in Orkney. *Proceedings of the Orkney Antiquarian Society* 7, 57–74.

Clouston, J. S. (1931) *Early Norse Castles*. Kirkwall, The Orcadian.

Cluett, J. P. (2007) Soil and sediment-based cultural records and The Heart of Neolithic Orkney World Heritage Site buffer zones. Unpublished PhD thesis, University of Stirling.

Cnotliwy, E. (1973) *Rzemiosło Rogownicze na Pomorzu Sczesnośredniowiecznym (= Antler Handicraft in Early Medieval Pomerania)*. Wroclaw, Polska Akademia Nauk Instytut Historii Kultury Materialnej.

Cnotliwy, E. (2013) *Przedmioty z poroża i kości z Janowa Pomorskiego (=Antler and Bone objects from Janów Pomorski), Truso Studies II*. Elblag, Museum of Archaeology and History, Polish Academy of Sciences.

Colley, S. (1983) The role of fish bone studies in economic archaeology, with special reference to the Orkney Isles. Unpublished PhD Thesis, University of Southampton.

Cohen, A. and Serjeantson, D. (1986) *A Manual for the Identification of Bird Bones from Archaeological Sites*, London, Alan Cohen.

Corrie, J. M. (1932) A Viking brooch of silver from Skaill Bay, Orkney. *Proceedings of the Society of Antiquaries of Scotland* 66 (1931–32), 84–5.

Courty, M. A., Goldberg, P. and Macphail, R. (1989) *Soils and Micromorphology in Archaeology*. Cambridge, Cambridge University Press.

Cowen, J. D. (1934) A catalogue of objects of the Viking period in the Tullie House Museum, Carlisle. *Transactions of the Cumberland and Westmorland Antiquarian and Archaeological Society* 34, 166–87.

Cowie, T. (1995) Excavation of a child burial, 1991 (Burial B). In A. Dunwell, *et al.*, 719–52.

Craig, O. E., Saul, H., Lucquin, A., Nishida, Y, Taché, K. and Jordan, P. (2013) Earliest evidence for the use of pottery, *Nature* 496 (7445, 351–4).

Crawford, B. E. (ed.) (1987) *Scandinavian Scotland*. Leicester, Leicester University Press.

Crawford, B. E. (2006) Kongemakt og jarlemakt, stedsnavn som bevis? Betydningen av Housebay, Harray og staðir navn på Orkenøyenes West Mainland (Royal power and Earldom power, the meaning of place-names? The meaning of Housebay, Harray and staðir names on Orkney's West Mainland). *Viking* 69, 195–214.

Crawford, B. E. (2013) *The Northern Earldoms, Orkney and Caithness from AD 870 to 1470*. Edinburgh, John Donald.

Crawford, B. E. and Ballin Smith, B. (1999) *The Biggings Papa Stour, Shetland. The history and archaeology of a royal Norwegian farm*. Edinburgh, Society of Antiquaries of Scotland Monograph Series 15.

Cressey, M. and Anderson, S. (2011) A Later prehistoric settlement and metalworking site at Seafield West, near Inverness, Highland. *Scottish Archaeological Internet Reports* 47. Available online at: http://archaeologydataservice.ac.uk/archives/view/sair/contents.cfm?vol=47 (accessed 7/1/18).

Crew, P. and Rehren, T. (2002) High temperature workshop residues from Tara, iron, bronze and glass. In H. Roche (ed.), Excavations at Ráith na Ríg, Tara, Co. Meath, 1997, *Discovery Programme Reports 6*. Dublin, Royal Irish Academy, 83–102.

Cuenca-Garcia, C. (2012) The Interface of Geophysical and Geochemical Survey at Scottish Archaeological Sites, Exploring the Potential of an Integrated Approach for Archaeological Prospection. Unpublished PhD Thesis, University of Glasgow.

Curle, A. O. (1939) A Viking settlement at Freswick, Caithness. Report on excavations carried out in 1937 and 1938. *Proceedings of the Society of Antiquaries of Scotland* 73, 71–110.

Curle, C. L. (1982) *Pictish and Norse Finds from the Brough of Birsay 1934–1974*. Edinburgh, Society of Antiquaries of Scotland, Monograph Series 1.

Cuthbert, O. D. (ed.) (2001) (George Low, 1773) *A History of the Orkneys, Introduced by a Description of the Islands and their Inhabitants*. Kirkwall, Orkney Heritage Society.

Dalland, M. (1999) Sand Fiold, the excavation of an exceptional cist in Orkney. *Proceedings of the Prehistoric Society* 65, 373–413.

Davidson, D. A., Harkness, D. D. and Simpson, I. A. (2007) The formation of farm mounds on the island of Sanday, Orkney. *Geoarchaeology 1*(1), 45–59.

Dawson, A., Dawson, S. and Jordan, J. (2011) North Atlantic climate change and Late Holocene windstorm activity in the Outer Hebrides, UK. In D. Griffiths and P. Ashmore (eds), 25–36.

Deak, J., Gebhardt, A., Lewis, H., Usai, M.-R. and Lee, H. 2017. Soils disturbed by vegetation clearance and tillage. In Nicosia, C. & Stoops, G. (eds) *Archaeological Soil and Sediment Micromorphology*, 233–264. Chichester: John Wiley & Sons.

De Cupere, B, Lentacker A, Van Neer W, Waelkens M and Verslype L (2000) Osteological evidence for the draught exploitation of cattle: first applications of a new methodology. *International Journal of Osteoarchaeology* 10, 254–67.

De la Vega Leinert, A. C., Keen, D. H., Jones, R. L., Wells, J. M. and Smith, D. E. (2000) Mid-Holocene environmental changes in the Bay of Skaill, Mainland Orkney, Scotland, an integrated geomorphological, sedimentological and stratigraphical study. *Journal of Quaternary Science 15*(5), 509–28.

Den Dooren De Jong, I. E., Dauvillier, M. M. S. and Roman, W. B. (1961) On the formation of adipocere from fats. *Antonie van Leeuwenhoek, 27*(1), 337–61.

Derham, B., Doonan, R., Lolos, Y., Sarris, A. and Jones, R. E. (2013) Integrating geochemical survey, ethnography and organic residue analysis to identify and understand areas of foodstuff processing. In Voutsaki, S. and Valamoti, S. (eds), *Diet, Economy and Society in the Ancient Greek World, Proceedings of the International Conference Held at the Netherlands Institute at Athens on 22–24 March 2010*, 47–54. Pharos Supplement (1), Peeters, Leuven.

Deroeux, D., Dufournier, D. and Herteig, A. (1994) French medieval ceramics from the Bryggen excavations in Bergen. In A. Herteig (ed.), *The Bryggen Papers*, 161–208. University of Bergen, Supplementary series 5.

Dickson, C. (1994) Plant Remains. In B. Ballin Smith (ed.), 125–39.

Dickson, C. and Dickson, J. H. (2000) *Plants and People in Ancient Scotland*. Stroud, Tempus.

Dickson, J. H. (1992) North American Driftwood, especially *Picea* (Spruce), from archaeological sites in the Hebrides and Northern Isles of Scotland. *Revue of Palaeobotany and Palynology* 73, 14, 49–56.

Dobney, K., Hall, A. R., Kenward, H. K. and Milles, A. (1992) A Working Classification of Samples Types for Environmental Archaeology. *Circeaea*, 24–26.

Dockrill, S., Bond, J. M., Nicholson, R. and Smith, A. (2007) *Tofts Ness, An Island Landscape through 3000 year of Prehistory*, Investigations in Sanday, Orkney 2. Kirkwall, The Orcadian, in association with Historic Scotland.

Dockrill, S., Bond, M., Turner, V., Brown, L. D., Bashford, D. J., Cussans, J. E. and Nicholson, R. A. (2010) *Excavations at Old Scatness, Shetland, Volume 1, The Pictish and Viking Settlement*. Lerwick, Shetland Heritage Publications.

Dolley, M. (1969) New light on the 1894 Douglas hoard. *Journal of the Manx Museum* 7:85, 121–4.

Dolley, R. H. M. (1966) *Sylloge of the Coins of the British Isles: the Hiberno-Norse Coins in the British Museum*. London, British Museum.

Donaldson, A. M. (1986) Carbonised Seeds and Grains. In J. R. Hunter (ed.), 216–9.

Donaldson, A. M. and Nye, S. (1989) The Botanical Remains. In C. D. Morris, 62–267, and Fiche.

Doonan, R. C. (2003) Specialisation and Spatialisation, the use of soil studies in defining the spatial articulation of Iron Age metallurgy. In G. Fuleky (ed.), *Soils and Archaeology, Proceedings of the 1st International Conference on Soils and Archaeology, Százhalombatta, Hungary, 30 May-3 June 2001*. Oxford, Archaeopress, 61–6.

Dore, C. D. and López Varela, S. L. (2010) Kaleidoscopes, Palimpsests, and Clay: Realities and Complexities in Human Activities and Soil Chemical/Residue Analysis. *Journal of Archaeological Method and Theory, 17*(3), 279–302.

Downes, J. and Ritchie, A. (eds) (2003) *Sea Change, Orkney and Northern Europe in the later Iron Age, AD 300–800*. Balgavies, Orkney Heritage Society/Pinkfoot Press.

Dufeau, V. (no date) Micromorphological investigations of two profiles from a Viking Age building. Við Kirkjugarð in Sandur, Sandoy. Unpublished manuscript held at University of Stirling Division of Biological and Environmental Sciences.

Dufournier, D. (1981) L'analyse des materieres premieres argileuses dans la recherche de l'origine de fabrication des ceramiques. *Revue d'Archeometrie, supplement III*, 83–93.

Dunbar, E., Cook, G. T., Naysmith, P., Tripney, B. G. and Xu, S. (2016) AMS ^{14}C dating at the Scottish Universities Environmental Research Centre (SUERC) Radiocarbon Dating Laboratory. *Radiocarbon* 58, 9–23.

Dungworth, D. and Wilkes, R. (2009) Understanding hammerscale, the use of high-speed film and electron microscopy. *Historical Metallurgy* 43, 33–46.

Dunlevy M. M. (1988) A classification of early Irish combs. *Proceedings of the Royal Irish Academy* 88, 341–422.

Dunwell, A. J., Cowie T. G., Bruce, M. F., Neighbour, T. and Rees, A. R. (1995) A Viking Age cemetery at Cnip, Uig, Isle of Lewis. *Proceedings of the Society of Antiquaries of Scotland* 125, 719–52.

Egan, G. and Pritchard, F. (1991) *Dress Accessories 1150–1450*. Medieval Finds from Excavations in London, 3, London, Museum of London, HMSO.

Ellis, S. E. and Moore, D. T. (1990) The hones. In M. Biddle (ed.), *Object and Economy in Medieval Winchester*, Winchester Studies 7, 2, 868–91. Oxford, Clarendon Press.

Emeleus, C. H. and Gyopari, M. C. (1992) *British Tertiary Volcanic Province*. Geological Conservation Review, Joint Nature Conservation Committee. London, Chapman and Hall.

Entwistle, J. A., Abrahams, P. W. and Dodgshon, R. A. (1998) Multi-element analysis of soils from Scottish historical sites, interpreting land-use history from the physical and geochemical analysis of soil. *Journal of Archaeological Science* 25, 53–68.

Evans, D. H. and Loveluck, C. P. (2009) *Life and Economy at Early Medieval Flixborough c AD 600–1000*, Excavations at Flixborough Volume 2. Oxford, Oxbow Books.

Evershed, R. P. (2008) Organic residue Analysis in Archaeology: the Archaeological Biomarker Revolution. *Archaeometry*, 50(6), 895–924.

Evershed, R. P., Copley, M. S., Dickson, L. and Hansel, F. A. (2008) Experimental Evidence for the processing of Marine Animal Products and other commodities containing polyunsaturated fatty acids in Pottery Vessels. *Archaeometry*, 50(1), 101–13.

Evershed, R. P., Heron, C., Charters, S. and Goad, L. J. (1992) Chemical analysis of organic residues in ancient pottery: methodological guidelines and applications. In *Organic residues in archaeology: their identification and analysis*. UKIC Archaeology Section, 11–25.

Ewens, V. (2010) An odontological study of ovicaprine breeding strategies in the North Atlantic Islands. Unpublished PhD Thesis, University of Bradford.

Fairhurst, H. (1984) *Excavations at Crosskirk Broch, Caithness*. Edinburgh, Society of Antiquaries of Scotland Monograph 3.

Fanning, T. (1983) Some aspects of the bronze ringed pin in Scotland. In A. O'Connor, A. D. V. Clarke (eds), *From the*

Stone Age to the 'Forty-Five, Studies presented to R. B. K. Stevenson. Edinburgh, John Donald, 324–42.

Fanning, T. (1994) *Viking Age Ringed Pins from Dublin*, Medieval Dublin Series B, Vol. 4. Dublin, Royal Irish Academy.

Farrer, J. (1862) The Knowe of Saverough. *The Gentleman's Magazine* 213, July–Dec 1862, 601–4.

Farrer, J. (1863) Account of the Discoveries at the Knowe of Saverough. *Proceedings of the Society of Antiquaries of Scotland* 5, 10–12.

Farrer, J. (1868) Note respecting various articles in bronze and stone; found in Orkney and now presented to the museum. *Proceedings of the Society of Antiquaries of Scotland* 7, 103–5.

Fenton, A. (1978) *The Northern Isles, Orkney and Shetland*. Edinburgh, John Donald.

Finlayson, B. (2007) The Flint. In Hunter, J. R. *et al.* (eds), 389.

Firth, J. (1974) *Reminisences of an Orkney Parish together with Old Words, Riddles and Proverbs (1920)*. Stromness, W. R. Rendall.

Flodin, L. (1989) *Kammakeriet i Trondheim ca. 1000–1600*, Trondheim, Riksantikvaren Meddelselser 14.

Forster, A. K. (2004) Shetland and the trade of steatite goods in the North Atlantic region during the Viking and Early Medieval period: an investigation into trade and exchange networks in the Norse North Atlantic and the extent to which steatite goods manufactured in Shetland were included in such networks. Unpublished PhD thesis, University of Bradford.

Forster, A. K. (2005) Steatite, Resource Control and the Orkney Earldom. In O. Owen (ed.), *The World of Orkneyinga Saga, The Broad-Cloth Viking Trip*, 55–74. Kirkwall, The Orcadian.

Forster, A. K. (2006) An early Viking steatite assemblage from Norwick, Unst, Shetland. Unpublished report for GUARD Archaeology, Glasgow.

Forster, A. K. (2010) Steatite. In S. J. Dockrill *et al.*, 258–303.

Forster, A. K. (2014) Steatite finds from Hriesheimar. Unpublished report submitted to Fornleifastofnun Íslands.

Forster, A. and Jones, R. (2017) Homeland to Home; Using Soapstone to Map Migration and Settlement in the North Atlantic. In G. Hansen and P. Storemyr, *Soapstone in the North, Quarries, Products and People 7000 BC – AD 1700*, Bergen, UBAS 9, 225–48.

Francis, R. J., Bond, J. M. and Thompson, J. B. (2010) Charcoal from the Pictish and Viking phases of Structures 6 and 11 at Old Scatness. In S. J. Dockrill *et al.*, 196–7.

Fraser, J. (1923) Antiquities of Sandwick Parish. *Proceedings of the Orkney Antiquarian Society* 2, 24.

French, C. A. I. (1991) Barnhouse excavations (1989), soil micromorphological analyses. Unpublished report, University of Cambridge.

French, C. A. I. (1994) The micromorphological analysis of the buried soil. In J. Downes (ed.), Excavation of a Bronze Age cairn at Mousland, Stromness, Orkney. *Proceedings of the Society of Antiquaries of Scotland* 124, 141–54.

French, D. H. (1971) An Experiment in Water Sieving. *Anatolian Studies* 21, 59–64.

Fuglesang, S. H. (1980) *Some Aspects of the Ringerike Style*, Medieval Scandinavia Supplements 1. Odense, Odense University Press.

Fuglesang, S. H. (1991) The axe-head from Mammen and the Mammen style. In M. Iversen (ed.), *Mammen: Grav, Kunst og Samfund i Vikingetid* (Jysk Arkæologisk Selskabs Skrifter XXVIII; Højberg), 83–108.

Gaffney, C. and Gater, J. (2003) *Revealing the Buried Past, Geophysics for Archaeologists*. Stroud, Tempus.

Gale, R. and Cutler, D. (2000) *Plants in Archaeology. Identification Manual of Artefacts of Plant Origin from Europe and the Mediterranean*. Otley and Westbury, Royal Botanic Gardens, Kew.

Galloway, P. (1976) Notes on the description of bone and antler combs. *Medieval Archaeology* 20, 154–6.

Garson, J. G. (1884) On the osteology of the ancient inhabitants of the Orkney Islands. *Journal of the Anthropological Institute of Great Britain and Ireland* 13, 54–86.

Gé, T., Courty, M.-A., Matthews, W. and Wattez, J. (1993) Sedimentary formation processes of occupation surfaces. In P. Goldberg, D. T. Nash and M. D. Petraglia (eds), *Formation Processes in Archaeological Context*. Madison, Prehistory Press, 149–63.

Gibbons, B. (1991) *The Lomond Guide to Seashore Life of Britain and Europe*. London, New Holland.

Gilbertson, D. D., Schwenninner, J.-L., Kemp, R. A. and Rhodes, E. J. (1999) Sand-drift and soil formation along an exposed North Atlantic coastline, 14,000 years of diverse geomorphological, climatic and human impacts. *Journal of Archaeological Science* 26, 439–69.

Gísladóttir, G. and Forster, A. K. (2014) Steatite finds from Sveigakot. Unpublished report submitted to Fornleifastofnun Íslands.

Goodall, I. (1984) Iron Objects. In A. Rogerson and C. Dallas (eds), *Excavations in Thetford 1948–59 and 1973–80*. East Anglian Archaeology 22, 76–106.

Goodall I. H. (2011) *Ironwork in Medieval Britain, An Archaeological Study*. Society for Medieval Archaeology Monograph No 31. Leeds, Maney.

Goodlad, A. (1971) *Shetland Fishing Saga*. Lerwick, Shetland Times.

Gordon, K. (1990) A Norse Viking-Age grave from Cruach Mhor, Islay. *Proceedings of the Society of Antiquaries of Scotland* 120, 151–60.

Gotfredsen, A. B. (2014) Birds in Subsistence and Culture at Viking Age Sites in Denmark. *International Journal of Osteoarchaeology* 24, 365–72.

Gotfredsen, A. B., Primeau, C., Frei, K. and Jorgensen, L. (2014) A ritual site with sacrificial wells from the Viking Age at Trelleborg, Denmark. *Journal of Danish Archaeology* 3, 145–63.

Graham-Campbell, J. A. (1976) The Viking-age silver and gold hoards of Scandinavian character from Scotland. *Proceedings of the Society of Antiquaries of Scotland* 107 (1975–76), 114–35.

Graham-Campbell, J. A. (1980) *Viking Artefacts, A Select Catalogue*. London, British Museum.

Graham-Campbell, J. A. (1983) The Viking-Age silver hoards of the Isle of Man. In C. Fell, P. Foote, J. Graham-Campbell and R. Thomson (eds), *The Viking Age in the Isle of Man*, Viking Society for Northern Research, London, 53–80.

Graham-Campbell, J. (1984) Two Viking-age silver brooch fragments believed to be from the 1858 Skaill (Orkney) hoard. *Proceedings of the Society of the Antiquaries of Scotland* 114, 289–301.

Graham-Campbell, J. (1993) The northern hoards of Viking-age Scotland. In C. E. Batey *et al.* (eds), 173–86.

Graham-Campbell, J. A. (1995) *The Viking-Age Gold and Silver Hoards of Scotland (AD 850–1100)*. Edinburgh, National Museums of Scotland.

Graham-Campbell, J. A. and Batey, C. E. (1998) *Vikings in Scotland. An Archaeological Survey*. Edinburgh, Edinburgh University Press.

Graham-Campbell, J. A. and Paterson, C. (forthcoming) *The Pagan Norse Graves of Scotland*. Edinburgh, Edinburgh University Press.

Graham-Campbell, J. (2011a) *The Cuerdale Hoard and related Viking-Age Gold and Silver from Britain and Ireland in the British Museum*. London, British Museum.

Graham-Campbell, J. (2011b) 'The serpent's bed': gold and silver in Viking Age Iceland – and beyond. In S. Simundsson (ed.), *Viking Settlements and Viking Society: Papers from the Proceedings of the Sixteenth Viking Congress*. Reykjavík, National Museum of Iceland, 103–31.

Graham-Campbell, J. and Sheehan, J. (2009) Viking age gold and silver from Irish crannogs and other watery places. *Journal of Irish Archaeology* 18, 77–93.

Grant, A. (1982) The use of tooth wear as a guide to the age of domestic ungulates. In B. Wilson, C. Grigson and S. Payne (eds), *Ageing and Sexing Animal Bones from Archaeological Sites*, 91–108. Oxford, British Archaeological Reports British Series 108.

Gratuze, B., Foy, D., Lancelot, J. and Tereygeol, F. (2003) Les 'lissoirs' carolingiens en verre au plomb: mise en évidence de la valorisation des scories issues du traitement des galènes argentifères de Melle (Deux Sèvres). In D. Foy et M.-D. Nenna (eds), *Echanges et commerce du verre dans le monde antique*. Monique Mergoil, Montagnac (Monographies Instrumentum 21), 101–7.

Gratuze, B., Guerrot, C., Foy, D., Bayley, J., Arles, A. and Téreygeol, F. (2014) Melle: mise en evidence de l'utilisation des scories vitreuses issues de la chaîne opératoire de production de l'argent comme matière première de l'industrie verrière, in *Du monde franc aux califats omeyyade et Abbasside: extraction et produits des mines d'argent de Melle et de Jabali*. Bochum, Deutschen Bergbau-Museums, 211–30.

Gregory, R. A. (2001) Excavations by the late G. D. B. Jones and C. M. Daniels along the Moray Firth Littoral. *Proceedings of the Society of Antiquaries of Scotland* 131, 177–222.

Grieg, S. (1940) Viking antiquities in Scotland. In H. Shetelig (ed.), *Viking Antiquities in Great Britain and Ireland*, Part II. Oslo, Aschehoug.

Griffiths, D. (2006) Birsay and Skaill, Orkney, landscape survey 2003–4. In R. E. Jones and L. Sharpe (eds), *Going Over Old Ground, Perspectives on Archaeological, Geophysical and Geochemical Survey in Scotland*. Oxford, British Archaeological Reports, British Series 416, Archaeopress, 213–24.

Griffiths, D. (2010) *Vikings of the Irish Sea; Conflict and Assimilation AD 790–1050*. Stroud, Tempus.

Griffiths, D. (2013) The Context of the 1858 Skaill Hoard. In A. Reynolds and L. Webster (eds), *Early Medieval Art and Archaeology in the Northern World, Studies in Honour of James Graham-Campbell*. Leiden/Boston, Brill, 501–25.

Griffiths, D. (2015) Status and Identity in Norse Settlements, A Case Study from Orkney. In J. H. Barrett and S.-J. Gibbon (eds), 219–36.

Griffiths, D. and Ashmore, P. (eds) (2011) *Aeolian Archaeology, The Archaeology of Sand Landscapes in Scotland*, Scottish Archaeological Internet Report 48, Edinburgh, Society of Antiquaries of Scotland. Available online at: http://archaeologydataservice.ac.uk/archives/view/sair/contents.cfm?vol=48 (accessed 7/2/18).

Griffiths, D. and Harrison J. (2011) Interpreting power and status in the landscape of Viking Orkney. In S. Simundsson (ed.), *Viking Settlements and Viking Society: Papers from the Proceedings of the Sixteenth Viking Congress*. Reykjavík, National Museum of Iceland, 132–46.

Griffiths, D., Philpott, R. A. and Egan, G. (2007) *Meols, The Archaeology of the North Wirral Coast. Discoveries and observations in the 19th and 20th centuries, with a catalogue of collections*. Oxford, Oxford University School of Archaeology Monograph 68.

Grigson, C. (1982) Sex and age determination of some bones and teeth of domestic cattle, a review of the literature. In B. Wilson, C. Grigson and S. Payne (eds), *Ageing and Sexing Animal Bones from Archaeological Sites*. Oxford, British Archaeological Reports British Series 108, 7–24.

Guðmundsdóttir Beck, S. (2011) Part One – The micromorphology of the Gásir trading booths. In S. Guðmundsdóttir Beck and M. Hayeur Smith (eds), *Gásir Post-Excavation Reports*, Vol. 3. Fornleifastofnun Íslands, Reykjavik, 1–44, i-xix.

Guido, M. (ed. Welch, M.) (1999) *The Glass Beads of Anglo-Saxon England c. AD 400–700. A preliminary visual classification of the more definitive and diagnostic types*. Woodbridge, Report of the Society of Antiquaries of London, No. 58, Boydell.

Guttmann, E. B. (2001) Continuity and Change in Arable Land Management in the Northern Isles, Evidence from Anthropogenic Soil. Unpublished PhD Thesis, University of Stirling.

Guttmann, E. B., Simpson, I. A., and Dockrill, S. J. (2003) Joined-up Archaeology at Old Scatness, Shetland, Thin Section Analysis of the site and hinterland. *Environmental Archaeology* 8, 17–31.

Guttmann, E. B., Simpson, I. A., Davidson, D. A. and Dockrill, S. J. (2006) The management of arable land from prehistory to the present, Case studies from the Northern Isles of Scotland. *Geoarchaeology* 27, 61–92.

Hall, D. W. (no date) The Pottery. In J. Barrett, Excavations at Roberts Haven, Caithness. Unpublished manuscript, University of Cambridge.

Hall, D. W., Blackmore, L., Haggarty, G., Chenery, S., Gallagher, D., Batey, C. E. and Barrett, J. H. (2012) Interpreting the Ceramics and Glass. In J. H. Barrett (ed.), 255–74.

Hall, D. W. and Chenery, S. (2005) New evidence for early connections between Scotland and Denmark? The chemical analysis of medieval greyware pottery from Scotland. *Tayside and Fife Archaeological J Volume* 11, 54–69.

Hall, D. W., Haggarty, G. and Jones, R. (2017) The pottery. In C. Ellis, Monks, Priests and Farmers: A Community Research Excavation at Baliscate, Isle of Mull. *Scottish Archaeological Internet Reports* 68, 56–61. Available online at: http://doi.org/10.9750/issn.2056–7421.2017.68 (accessed 9/12/17).

Halstead, P. H. (1985) A study of mandibular teeth from Romano-British contexts at Maxey. In F. Pryor (ed.), *Archaeology and environment in the Lower Welland Valley. Vol. 1*. East Anglian Archaeology 27, 219–24.

Halstead, P. H. (1998) Mortality models and milking: problems of optimality, uniformitariaism and equifinality reconsidered. *Anthropozoologica* 27, 3–20.

Halstead, P., Collis, P. and Isaakidou, V. (2002) Sorting the sheep from the goats, morphological distinctions between the mandibles and mandibular teeth of adult *ovis* and *capra. Journal of Archaeological Science* 29, 545–53.

Halstead, P. and Collins, P. (no date) Identification manual for postcranial skeleton of European domestic fauna and red deer. Unpublished manuscript, University of Sheffield.

Hamilton, J. R. C. (1956) *Excavations at Jarlshof, Shetland*. Edinburgh, HMSO.

Hamilton, J. R. C. (1958) *Excavations at Clickhimin, Shetland*. Edinburgh, HMSO.

Hamlet, L. E. and Simpson, I. (no date) Belmont, thin section micromorphology. Unpublished manuscript, Viking Unst Project (summarised in Turner *et al.* 2013, 210).

Hansen, G. (2005) *Bergen c.800–1170, the Emergence of a Town*. The Bryggen Papers, Main Series No. 6. Bergen, Fagbokforlaget.

Harland, J. (2012) Animal husbandry, The mammal bone. In J. H. Barrett (ed.), 135–54.

Harland, J., Bennett, R. A., Andrews, J. I., O'Connor, T. and Barrett, J. H. (2012) Fowling, the bird bone. In J. H. Barrett (ed.), 155–60.

Harrison, J. (2013) Building mounds, longhouses, coastal mounds and cultural connections, Norway and the Northern Isles, c. AD 800–1200. *Medieval Archaeology* 57, 35–59.

Harrison, S. and Ó Floinn, R. (2014) *Viking Graves and Grave-Goods in Ireland*. Medieval Dublin Excavations 1962–81. Ser B, 11. Dublin, National Museum of Ireland.

Haslam, R. and Tibbett, M. (2004) Sampling and Analyzing Metals in Soils for Archaeological Prospection, A Critique. *Geoarchaeology* 19, 731–51.

Havernick, T. E. (1968) Perlen und Glasbruchstücke als Amulette. *Jahrbuch Römisch Germanisches Zentralmuseum*, Mainz, 15, 120–33.

Hebsgaard, M., Gilbert, M., Arneborg, J., Heyn, P., Allentoft, M., Bunce, M., Munch, K., Schweger, C. and Willerslev, E. (2009) 'The Farm Beneath the Sand' – an archaeological case study on ancient 'dirt' DNA, *Antiquity* 83(320), 430–44.

Heald, A. (2002) Metalworking objects and debris. In M. Cook, Excavations of an Early Historic settlement within a multi-period landscape at Dolphington, South Lanarkshire. *Scottish Archaeological Journal* 24(1), 61–83 (70–71).

Heald, A., McDonnell, G. and Mack, I. (2011) The ironworking debris. In Cressey and Anderson, 20–4.

Hedges, J. W. (1983) Trial excavations on Pictish and Viking settlements at Saevar Howe, Birsay, Orkney. *Glasgow Archaeological Journal* 10, 73–124.

Hill, P. (1997) *Whithorn and St Ninian. The excavation of a monastic town, 1984–91*. Stroud, The Whithorn Trust, Sutton.

Hines, J., Lane, A. and Redknap, M. (eds) (2007) *Land, Sea and Home, Settlement in the Viking Period*. Leeds, Society for Medieval Archaeology Monograph 20, Maney.

Hinton, M. P. (1991) Weed Associates of recently grown *Avena strigosa* Schreber from Shetland, Scotland. *Circaea* 8(1), 49–54.

Holden, T. G. (1998) *The Archaeology of Scottish Thatch*. Edinburgh, Technical Advice Note 13, Historic Scotland.

Hughes, M. J. (2002–3) Analysis by inductively-coupled plasma atomic emission analysis (ICP-AES) of imported northern French pottery, including a sherd found at the Althea Library, Padstow; Appendix 3, The Pottery. In P. Manning and P. Stead, Excavation of an Early Christian cemetery at Althea Library, Padstow. *Cornish Archaeology* 41–2, 80–106.

Hunter, J. R. (1986) *Rescue Excavations on the Brough of Birsay 1974–82*. Edinburgh, Society of Antiquaries of Scotland Monograph Ser 4.

Hunter, J. R., Bond, J. M. and Smith, A. N. (1995) Some aspects of early Viking settlement in Orkney. In C. E. Batey *et al.* (eds), 272–84.

Hunter, J. R., Bond, J. M. and Smith, A. N. (2007) *Excavations at Pool, Sanday, a Multi-period Settlement from Neolithic to Late Norse Times*, Investigations in Sanday, Orkney 1. Kirkwall, The Orcadian, in association with Historic Scotland.

Irvine, J. M. (2009) *The Breckness Estate, A History of its Lairds, Tenants and Farms, and Skaill House*. Private publication, Ashtead.

Irvine, J. M. (2013) Late Norse High-Status Sites around the Bay of Skaill. *Northern Studies* 44, 36–59.

Irvine, J. W. (1987) *The Dunrossness Story*. Lerwick.

James, H. F. (1999) Excavations of a medieval cemetery at Skaill House, and a cist in the Bay of Skaill, Sandwick, Orkney. *Proceedings of the Society of Antiquaries of Scotland* 129, 753–77.

Jansson, I. (1970) Wikingersschmuck und Münzdatierung. Bemerkungen zu einer Neuerscheinung. *Tor* 13 (1969), 26–64

Jennbert, K. (2011) *Animals and Humans, Recurrent symbiosis in archaeology and Old Norse Religion*. Lund, Nordic Academic Press.

Ježek, M. (2013) Touchstones of archaeology. *Journal of Anthropological Archaeology* 32, 713–31.

Ježek, M. (2014) Touchstones from early medieval burials in Tuna in Alsike. *Journal of Archaeological Science* 42, 422–9.

Jo Ben (possibly John Bellenden) (1529) *Descriptio Insularum Orchadiarum*, reprinted in G. Barry (1808).

Johansen, O.-S., Kristiansen, K. and Munch, G. S. (2003) Soapstone artefacts and whetstones. In G. S. Munch, O.-S. Johansen, and E. Roesdahl (eds), *Borg in Lofoten, A Chieftain's Farm in North Norway*. Trondheim, Tapir Academic Press, 141–58.

Jones, A. K. G. (no date) The fish remains from excavations at Skara Brae, Orkney. Unpublished document, Archive: National Museum of Scotland.

Jones, A. K. G. (1991) The fish remains from excavations at Freswick Links, Caithness. Unpublished D.Phil. thesis, University of York.

Jones, A. K. G., Morris, C. D. and Rackham, D. J. (1995) The fish material. In C. D. Morris *et al.* (eds), 154–91.

Jones, E. P., Skirnisson, K., McGovern, T. H., Gilbert, M. T. P., Willerslev, E. and Searle, J. B. (2012) Fellow travellers, a concordance of colonization patterns between mice and men in the North Atlantic region. *BMC Evolutionary Biology* 2012, 12, 35. Available online at: http://www.biomedcentral.com/1471–2148/12/35 (accessed 2/4/17).

Jones, G. G. (2006) Tooth eruption and wear observed in live sheep from Butser Hill, the Cotswold Farm Park and five farms in the Pentland Hills, UK. In D. Ruscillo (ed.), *Recent Advances in Ageing and Sexing Animal Bones*, 155–78. Oxford, Oxbow Books.

Jones, R., Challands, A., French, C., Card, N., Downes, J. and Richards, C. (2010) Exploring the location and function of a Late Neolithic house at Crossiecrown, Orkney by geophysical, geochemical and soil micromorphological methods. *Archaeological Prospection* 17, 29–47.

Jones, S. (1997) *The Archaeology of Ethnicity*. London, Routledge.

Kaland, S. H. H. (1980) *Westness, Rousay, Viking period graveyard foundations. Discovery and Excavation in Scotland for 1980*, 25.

Kars, H. (1983) Early medieval Dorestad, an archaeopetrological study. Part V, the whetstones and touchstones. *Berichten ROB*, 32, 1–37.

Keatinge, T. H. and Dickson, J. H. (1979) Mid-Flandrian changes in vegetation on Orkney. *New Phytologist* 82, 585–612.

Kershaw, J. (2013) *Viking Identities, Scandinavian Jewellery in England*. Oxford, Oxford University Press.

Kilbride, C., Poole, J. and Hutchings, T. R. (2006) A comparison of Cu, Pb, As, Cd, Zn, Fe, Ni and Mn determined by acid extraction/ICP–OES and ex situ field portable X-ray fluorescence analyses. *Environmental Pollution* 143, 16–23.

Kirpichnikov, A. N. (2004) A Viking Period workshop in Staraya Ladoga, excavated in 1997. *Fornvännen* 99, 183–96.

Koch, U. (1977) *Das Gräberfeld von Schretzheim*. Berlin, Germanische Serie A, Denkmäler der Völkwanderungszeit.

Kosmanowska-Ceranowicz, B. (1999) Naturwisenschaftliche Forschungen uber Bernstein in Polen. In B. Kosmanowska-Ceranowicz and H. Paner (eds), *Investigations into Amber. Proceedings of the International Interdisciplinary Symposium, Baltic Amber and other Fossil resins*. Gdańsk 2–6 September 1997, 9–19. Gdańsk, Polish Academy of Sciences.

Lamb, H. R. (1982) *Climate, History and the Modern World*. London, Methuen.

Lamb, R. (1993) Carolingian Orkney and its transformation. In C. E. Batey *et al.*, 260–71.

Lamb, R. (1997) Historical background to the Norse settlement. In S. Buteux (ed.), 13–16.

Lane, A. and Campbell, E. (2000) *Excavations at Dunadd, an early Dalriadic capital,* Cardiff Studies in Archaeology. Oxford, Oxbow Books.

Lang, J. T. (1988) *Viking-Age Decorated Wood – a study of its ornament and style,* Medieval Dublin Excavations 1962–81. Dublin, Ser.B, vol. 1, Royal Irish Academy.

Layard, N. F. (1907) Anglo-Saxon cemetery, Hadleigh Road, Ipswich. *Suffolk Institute of Archaeology and Natural History,* Vol XIII pt 1, 1–19.

Leach, B. F. (1986) A method for analysis of Pacific island fishbone assemblages and an associated data base management system. *Journal of Archaeological Science* 13(2), 147–59.

Lewis, H. (2012) *Investigating Ancient Tillage: An Experimental and Soil Micromorphological Study.* Oxford, Archaeopress.

Lowe, C. (1993) *St Boniface Church, Orkney, coastal erosion and archaeological assessment.* Stroud, Sutton/Historic Scotland.

Low, G. (1773) (published 1776) Extract of a letter from the Reverend George Low, to Mr Paton of Edinburgh, communicated by Mr Gough, read at the Society of Antiquaries, March 12, 1773 (Stromness, Nov 27, 1772). *Archaeologia* III, 276–8.

Lucquin, A., Colonese, A. C., Farrell, T. F. G. and Craig, O. E. (2016). Utilising phytanic acid diastereomers for the characterisation of archaeological lipid residues in pottery samples. *Tetrahedron Letters,* 57(6), 703–7.

Lysaght, A. M. (1974) Note on a grave excavated by Joseph Banks and George Low at Skaill in 1772. *Proceedings of the Society of Antiquaries of Scotland* 104, 285–9.

MacGregor, A. (1975) The Broch of Burrian, North Ronaldsay, Orkney. *Proceedings of the Society of Antiquaries of Scotland* 105, 63–118.

MacGregor, A. (1985) *Bone, Antler, Ivory and Horn, The Technology of Skeletal Materials Since the Roman Period.* London, Croom Helm.

MacGregor, A., Mainman, A. J. and Rogers, N. S. H. (1999) *Craft, Industry and Everyday Life, Bone, Antler, Ivory and horn from Finds from Anglo-Scandinavian and Medieval York.* York, The Archaeology of York 17/2, Council for British Archaeology.

MacKie, E. W. (2002) *The roundhouses, brochs and wheelhouses of Atlantic Scotland c. 700BC – AD500, architecture and material culture Part 1 – The Orkney and Shetland Isles.* Oxford, British Archaeological Reports, British Series 342.

Magnell, O. and Iregen, E. (2010) Veitsu hvé blóta skal? The Old Norse blót in the light of osteological evidence from Fröso church, Jämtland, Sweden. *Current Swedish Archaeology* 18, 223–50.

Mainland, I. L. (1994) The animal bone from the 1989 excavations at the Earl's Bu, Orphir, Orkney. *Sheffield Environmental Facility Report 930.* Unpublished report, Dept of Archaeology, University of Sheffield.

Mainland, I., Ascough, P., Griffiths, D. and Batey, C. (2015) They graze on wave and ocean plants. Foddering strategies in island environments, pig, sheep/goat and cattle diet in Viking and Late Norse Orkney (poster paper presented to EAA, Glasgow, 2015).

Mainland, I. and Batey, C. (2019) The nature of the feast: commensality and the politics of consumption in Viking Age and Early Medieval Northern Europe. *World Archaeology.*

Mainland, I. and Halstead, P. (2005) The economics of sheep and goat husbandry in Norse Greenland. *Arctic Anthropology* 43, 103–12.

Mainland, I., Towers, J., Ewens, V., Davis, G., Montgomery, J., Batey, C., Card, N. and Downes, J. (2016) Toiling with teeth, an integrated dental analysis of sheep and cattle dentition in Iron Age and Viking-Late Norse Orkney. *Journal of Archaeological Science Reports* 6, 837–55.

Mainman, A. J. and Rogers, N. S. H. (2000) *Craft, Industry and Everyday Life, Finds from Anglo-Scandinavian York.* York, The Archaeology of York 17/14, Council for British Archaeology.

Margeson, S. (1997) *The Vikings in Norfolk.* Norwich, Norfolk Museums Service.

Martin, S. L. (2014) The Recovery and Analysis of Macrobotanical Remains from Hrisbru. In D. Zori and J. Byock (eds), *Viking Archaeology in Iceland, Mosfell Archaeological Project,* 193–206. Turnhout, Brepols.

Marwick, H. (1952) *Orkney Farm Names.* Kirkwall, W. R. Mackintosh.

Marwick, H. (1970) *The Place-Names of Birsay.* Aberdeen, Aberdeen University Press.

Maté, I. D. (1996) The geology and soils. In C. D. Morris, 13–14.

McCormick, F. (2002) The distribution of meat in a hierarchical society: the Irish evidence, In P. Miracle and N. Milner (eds), *Consuming Passions: Patterns of Consumption.* Cambridge, Cambridge University Press, 25–31.

McDonnell, G. (1986) The classification of Early Ironworking slags. Unpublished PhD thesis, Aston University.

McDonnell, G. (1994) The slag report. In Ballin Smith, B. (ed.), 228–34.

McDonnell, G. (1996) Industrial Waste. In C. D. Morris, 135–6.

McDonnell, G. (1998) Metalworking. In C. Lowe, 143.

McGovern, T. H., Perdikaris, S., Mainland, I., Ascough, P., Ewens, V., Einarsson, A., Sidell, J., Hambrecht, G. and Harrison, R. (2010) The Hofstaðir archaeofauna. In G. Lucas (ed.), *Hofstaðir, A Viking Age Center in Northeastern Iceland,* 168–252. Reykjavik, Institute of Archaeology.

McLaren, D. (2013) The rotary quern stones. In I. Armit and J. McKenzie, *An Inherited Place. Broxmouth hillfort and the south-east Scottish Iron Age,* 309–29. Edinburgh, Society of Antiquaries of Scotland.

McLaren, D. (forthcoming) Ferrous Metalworking. In J. Hunter and K. Colls, *Excavations at Horgabost, Isle of Harris.* Edinburgh, Society of Antiquaries of Scotland.

McLaren, D. and Dungworth, D. (forthcoming) The manufacture of iron at Culduthel, ferrous metalworking debris and iron metallurgy. In C. Hatherley and R. Murray, *Culduthel: An Iron Age Craft Centre and Settlement in North-East Scotland.* Edinburgh, Society of Antiquaries of Scotland.

McLaren, D. and Heald, A. (2006) The vitrified material. In A. Armit, *Anatomy of an Iron Age Roundhouse. The Cnip wheelhouse excavations.* Edinburgh, Society of Antiquaries of Scotland, 155–8.

McLaren, D. and Heald, A. (forthcoming) The vitrified material from Bostadh. In T. Neighbour *et al. Traigh Bostadh,*

Great Bernera, Lewis: Excavations of a 1st Millennium AD settlement. Edinburgh, Society of Antiquaries of Scotland.

McLaren, D. and Hunter, F. (2008) New aspects of rotary querns in Scotland. *Proceedings of the Society of Antiquaries of Scotland* 138, 105–28.

McLaren, D. and Hunter F. (2014) The stone objects [Burland]. In H. Moore and G. Wilson (eds), *Ebbing Shores. Survey and Excavation of coastal archaeology in Shetland, 1995–2008'*, 284–305. Edinburgh, Historic Scotland Archaeology Report 8.

Mejdahl, V. (1979) Thermoluminescence dating: beta-dose attenuation in quartz grains. *Archaeometry* 21, 61–72.

Metcalf, D. M. (1995) The monetary significance of Scottish Viking-age coin hoards, with a short commentary. In J. Graham-Campbell, 16–25.

Middleton, W. D. and Price, T. D. (1996) Identification of activity areas by multi-element characterization of sediments from modern and archaeological house floors using inductively coupled plasma-atomic emission spectroscopy. *Journal of Archaeological Science* 23, 673–87.

Milek, K. (2001) *Archaeological soil survey in Rackwick and Aikerness, Westray, Orkney*, Interim Report. York, University of York.

Milek, K. (2012) Floor formation processes and the interpretation of site activity areas, an ethnoarchaeological study of turf buildings at Thverá, northeast Iceland. *Journal of Anthropological Archaeology* 31, 119–37.

Milek, K., Zori, D., Connors, C., Baier, W., Baker, K. and Byock, J. (2014) Interpreting social space and social status in the Viking Age house at Hrísbrú using integrated geoarchaeological and microrefuse analyses. In D. Zori and J. Byock (eds), *Viking Archaeology in Iceland, Mosfell Archaeological Project*. Turnhout, Brepols, 143–62.

Moore, D. T. (1978) The petrology and archaeology of English honestones. *Journal of Archaeological Science* 5, 61–73.

Moore, H. and Wilson, G. (forthcoming) The excavations at Berst Ness, Knowe of Skea, Orkney. Edinburgh.

Morales, A. and Rosenlund K. (1979) *Fish bone measurements. An Attempt to Standardize the Measuring of Fish Bones from Archaeological Sites.* Copenhagen, Steenstrupia, Zoologisk Museum.

Morris, C. D. (ed.) (1985) Skaill, Sandwick, Orkney, preliminary investigations of a mound-site near Skara Brae. *Glasgow Archaeological Journal* 12, 82–92.

Morris, C. D. (1989) *The Birsay Bay Project, Volume 1, Brough Road Excavations 1976–1982*. Durham, Department of Archaeology Monograph Series 1, University of Durham.

Morris, C. D. (1996) *The Birsay Bay Project, Volume 2, Sites in Birsay Village and on the Brough of Birsay, Orkney*. Durham, Department of Archaeology Monograph Series 2, University of Durham.

Morris, C. D. (forthcoming) *The Birsay Bay Project, Volume 3, The Brough of Birsay, Orkney, Investigations 1957–2007*. Edinburgh, Society of Antiquaries of Scotland.

Morris, C. D. and Rackham, D. J. (eds) (1992) *Norse and Later Settlement and Subsistence in the North Atlantic*. Glasgow, Department of Archaeology Occasional Paper Series No.1.

Morris, C., Batey, C. E. and Rackham, D. J. (1995) *Freswick Links, Caithness. Excavation and survey of a Norse Settlement.* Inverness and New York, NABO/Historic Scotland.

Mortimer, C. (1995) Glass Line Smoothers from 16–22 Coppergate, York. Ancient Monuments Laboratory Report 22/95. London, HBMCE (English Heritage).

Muir, T. (1998) *The Mermaid Bride and Other Orkney Folk Tales*. Kirkwall, Orcadian Press.

Muir, T and Irvine, J. (2014) *George Marwick, the Collected Works of Yesnaby's Master Storyteller.* Kirkwall, The Orcadian.

Mulville, J. (2015) Dealing with Deer, Norse response to Scottish isles cervids. In J. H. Barrett and S.-J. Gibbon (eds), 278–98.

Mulville, J., Bond, J. M. and Craig, O. (2005) The white stuff: milking in the outer Scottish Isles. In J. Mulville, J. and A. K. Outram (eds), *The zooarchaeology of fats, oils, milk and dairying*. Oxford, Oxbow Books, 167–82.

Murphy, C. P. (1986) *Thin section preparation of Soils and Sedmiments*. Berkhamstead, Academic Press.

Murray, A. S., Wintle, A. G., (2000) Luminescence dating of quartz using an improved single-aliquot regenerative-dose protocol. *Radiation Measurements* 32, 57–73.

Mykura, W. (1976) *British Regional Geology, Orkney and Shetland*. Edinburgh, HMSO.

Naysmith, P., Cook, G., Freeman, S., Scott, E. M., Anderson, R., Dunbar, E., Muir, G., Dougans, A., Wilcken, K., Schnabel, C., Russell, N., Ascough, P. and Maden, C. (2010) ^{14}C AMS at SUERC, improving QA data from the 5 MV tandem AMS and 250 kV SSAMS. *Radiocarbon* 52, 263–71.

Neighbour, T. and Burgess, C. (1996) Traigh Bostadh. *Discovery and Excavation in Scotland for 1996*, 113–4.

Nicholson, R. A. (1991) An investigation into variability within archaeologically recovered assemblages of faunal remains, the influence of pre-depositional taphonomic processes. Unpublished D. Phil Thesis, Department of Biology, University of York.

Nicholson, R. A. (1992) Bone survival, the effects of sedimentary abrasion and trampling on fresh and cooked bone. *International Journal of Osteoarchaeology* 2.1, 79–90.

Nicholson, R. A. (1997) Fish bones. In S. Buteux (ed.), 244–46.

Nicholson, R. A. (2004) Iron-Age fishing in the Northern Isles, the evolution of a stored product? In R. A. Housley and G. Coles (eds), *Atlantic Connections and Adaptations. Economies, environments and subsistence in lands bordering the North Atlantic*. Oxford, Oxbow Books, 155–62.

Nicholson, R. A. (2007) The fish remains. In J. R. Hunter *et al.*, 263–79.

Nicholson, R., Barber, R. and Bond, J. M. (2005) New evidence for the introduction of the house mouse and the field mouse to Shetland. *Environmental Archaeology* 10, 143–51.

Nicholson, R. A. and Dockrill, S. G. (1998) *Old Scatness Broch, Shetland, Retrospect and Prospect*. Bradford.

NSA (1845) The New Statistical Account of Scotland, Society for the Benefit of the Sons and Daughters of the Clergy. Edinburgh, Blackwood.

Newkirk, R. (2015) *Flax Feed Industry Guide*, Canadian International Grains Institute Pamphlet. Manitoba, Flax Canada.

Niven, K. J. (2003) Viking-Age hoards in Scotland: a GIS-based investigation of their landscape context and interpretation. Unpublished MSc dissertation, University of York.

O'Connor, S. (1987) The Identification of Osseous and Keratinaceous Materials at York. In K. Starling and D. Watkinson (eds), *Archaeological Bone, Antler and Ivory*, 9–21. London, Occasional Papers No. 5, The United Kingdom Institute for Conservation of Historic and Artistic Works.

Oliver, A. P. H. (2004) *Phillips's Guide to Seashells of the World*. London, Octopus Publishing.

OSA (1795) Old Statistical Account, 1791–99 *The Statistical Account of Scotland, Drawn Up from the Communications of the Ministers of the Different Parishes, Volume 16 (Orkney)*. Edinburgh, John Sinclair.

Ottaway, P. (1992) *Anglo-Scandinavian Ironwork from Coppergate*. The Archaeology of York, The Small Finds 17/6. York, York Archaeological Trust/Council for British Archaeology.

Ottaway, P. with D. Griffiths (2007) Later medieval iron objects, 1050–1100 to 1500–1550. In D. Griffiths *et al.*, 188–213.

Owen, O. A. (1993) Tuquoy, Westray, Orkney. A challenge for the future? In C. E. Batey *et al.* (eds), 318–39.

Owen, O. (2015) Galloway's Viking treasure: the story of a discovery. *British Archaeology* (January/February 2015), 16–23.

Owen, O. and Dalland, M. (1999) *Scar, A Viking Boat Burial on Sanday, Orkney*. Edinburgh, Tuckwell Press/Historic Scotland.

Owen, O. and Lowe, C. (eds) (1999) *Kebister, the four-thousand-year-old story of one Shetland township*. Edinburgh, Society of Antiquaries of Scotland Monograph 14.

Pálsson, H. and Edwards, P. T. (trans.) (1978) *Orkneyinga Saga. The History of the Earls of Orkney*. London, Penguin.

Panter, I. (2000) Amber working tools and techniques. In A. J. Mainman and N. S. H. Rogers (eds), 2501–19.

Papakosta, V., Smittenberg, R. H., Gibbs, K., Jordan, P. and Isaksson, S. (2015) Extraction and derivatization of absorbed lipid residues from very small and very old samples of ceramic potsherds for molecular analysis by gas chromatography–mass spectrometry (GC–MS) and single compound stable carbon isotope analysis by gas chromatography–combustion–isotope ratio mass spectrometry (GC–C–IRMS). *Microchemical Journal, Devoted to the Application of Microtechniques in All Branches of Science*, 123, 196–200.

Parker Pearson, M., Mulville, J., Sharples, N. and Smith, H. (2011) Archaeological Remains on Uists's machair: threats and potential. In D. Griffiths and P. Ashmore (eds), 55–85.

Parker Pearson, M., Sharples, N. and Symonds, J. (2004) *South Uist, Archaeology and History of a Hebridean Island*. Stroud, Tempus.

Parker Pearson, M., Smith, H., Mulville, J. and Brennand, M. (2004) Cille Pheadair, the life and times of a Norse period farmstead, *c.* 1000–1300. In J. Hines *et al.* (eds), 235–54.

Paterson, C. (2017) A tale of two cemeteries: Viking burials at Cumwhitton and Carlisle, Cumbria. In E. Cambridge and J. Hawkes (eds), *Crossing Boundaries: Interdisciplinary Approaches to the Art, Material Culture, Language and Literature of the Early Medieval World*. Oxford, Oxbow Books, 149–59.

Paterson, C. (forthcoming) The Early Medieval Small Finds. In J. Zant, C. Paterson and A. Parsons (eds), *The Early Medieval Cemetery at St Michael's Workington*. Lancaster, Lancaster Imprints.

Payne, S. (1973) Kill-off patterns in sheep and goats, the mandibles from Asvan Kale. *Anatolian Studies* 23, 281–303.

Perdikaris, S. (1996) Scaly heads and tales, Detecting commercialization in early fisheries. *Archaeofauna* 5, 21–33.

Perdikaris, S. (1998) From chiefly provisioning to state capital ventures, the transition from natural to market economy and the commercialization of cod fisheries in medieval arctic Norway. Unpublished PhD thesis, City University of New York.

Perdikaris, S. (1999) From chiefly provisioning to commercial fishery, long-term economic change in Arctic Norway. *World Archaeology* 30(3), 388–402.

Peterkin, A. (1820) *Rentals of the Ancient Earldom and Bishoprick of Orkney, with some other documents, collected by A. Peterkin*. Edinburgh.

Petersen, J. (1919) *De Norske Vikingesverd. En typologisk-kronologisk studie over vikingetidens vaaben*, Skrifter Utgitt av det Norske Videnskaps-Akademi i Oslo 1, Jacob Dybwad, Oslo.

Petersen, J. (1951) *Vikingetidens redskaper*. Skrifter Utgitt av det Norske Videnskaps-Akademi i Oslo 2, Jacob Dybwad, Oslo.

Petrie, G. (1868) Notice of ruins of ancient dwellings at Skara Brae, Bay of Skaill, in the parish of Sandwick, Orkney, recently excavated. *Proceedings of the Society of Antiquaries of Scotland* 7, 201–19.

Petrie, G. (1872) Notice of the Brochs or Round Towers of Orkney. *Archaeologia Scotica* V (published 1890), 71–94.

Photos-Jones, E. (2008) Metallurgical waste analysis. In R. Coleman and E. Photos-Jones, Early Medieval settlement and ironworking in Dornoch, Sutherland, excavations at The Meadows Business Park. *Scottish Archaeological Internet Reports* 28, 13–15.

Photos-Jones, E., Ballin Smith, B., Hall, A. J. and Jones, R. E. (2007) On the intent to make cramp, an interpretation of vitreous seaweed cremation 'waste' from prehistoric burial sites in Orkney, Scotland. *Oxford Journal of Archaeology* 26(1), 1–23.

Porter, D. (1997) Small Finds. In S. Buteux (ed.), 96–132.

Prescott, J. R. and Hutton, J. T. (1994) Cosmic ray contributions to dose rates for luminescence and ESR dating: large depths and long-term time variations. *Radiation Measurements* 23, 497–500.

Provoost, S., Jones, M. L. M. and Edmondson, S. E. (2011) Changes in landscape and vegetation of coastal dunes in northwest Europe, a review. *Journal of Coastal Conservation* 15, 207–26.

Rackham, D. J. (1989) Domestic and wild mammals. In C. D. Morris, 232–47.

Rackham, D. J. (1996) General discussion. In C. D. Morris, 186–91.

Rackham, D. J., Spencer, P. J. and Cavanagh, L. M. (1989) Environmental Survey. In C. D. Morris, 44–53.

Rackham, D. J. and Young, R. (1989) Overall Assessment. In C. D. Morris, 102–3.

Ravoire, F. (2014a) Le mobilier ceramique de la premiere phase d'occupation (premiere moitie du XIIe siecle). In J.-Y. Dufour (ed.), *Le Château de Roissy-En-France (*Val D'Oise), ArchéoEnv, 58–60.

Ravoire, F. (2014b) Le mobilier ceramique de la maison seigneuriale et de sa basse-cour dans la premiere moitie du XIIIe siecle. In J.-Y. Dufour (ed.), *Le Château de Roissy-En-France (Val D'Oise)*, ArchéoEnv, 119–25.

Reed, D. (1989) Geology of Birsay Bay. In C. D. Morris (ed.), *The Birsay Bay Project Volume* 1, 1–5.

RCAHMS/RCAMS (1946) *Twelfth Report with an Inventory of the Ancient Monuments of Orkney and Shetland.* Edinburgh, HMSO, 3 vols.

Reimer, P. J., Bard, E., Bayliss, A., Beck, J. W., Blackwell, P. G., Bronk Ramsey, C., Buck, C. E., Cheng, H., Edwards, R. L., Friedrich, M., Grootes, P. M., Guilderson, T. P., Haflidason, H., Hajdas, I., Hatté, C., Heaton, T. J., Hoffmann, D. L., Hogg, A. G., Hughen, K. A., Kaiser, K. F., Kromer, B., Manning, S. W., Niu, M., Reimer, R. W., Richards, D. A., Scott, E. M., Southon, J. R., Staff, R. A., Turney, C. S. M., van der Plicht, J. (2013) IntCal13 and Marine13 radiocarbon age calibration curves 0–50,000 years cal BP. *Radiocarbon* 55, 1869–1887.

Resi, H. G. (1990) *Die Wetz- und Schliefsteine aus Haithabu*, Berichte über die Ausgrabungen in Haithabu 28, L. Wackholtz, Neümunster.

Resi, H. G. (2008) Whetstones and grindstones used in everyday life at Kaupang. In H. Askvik and H. G. Resi, *Whestones and grindstones in the settlement area. The 1956–1974 excavations. Kaupang-funnene*, vol. 3, C Norske Oldfunn, vol. 29. Oslo, Universitets Oldsaksamling.

Resi, H. G. (2011) Whetstones, grindstones, touchstones and smoothers. In D. Skre, *Things from the Town, Artefacts and Inhabitants in Viking Age Kaupang*. Kaupang Excavation Project Publication Series, Volume 3, 373–93. Aarhus, Aarhus University Press.

Rhodes, E. J. and Schwenninger, J.-L. (2007) Dose rates and radioisotope concentrations in the concrete calibration blocks at Oxford. *Ancient TL* 25, 5–8.

Richards, C. (2002) Vestra Fiold, Orkney (Sandwick Parish), Neolithic quarry;?chambered cairn. *Discovery and Excavation in Scotland 3*, 88.

Richardson, C. (1993) The Borre Style in the British Isles and Ireland – a reassessment. Unpublished M.Litt Thesis, University of Newcastle upon Tyne.

Riddler, I. (1990) Saxon Handled Combs from London. *Transactions of the London and Middlesex Archaeological Society* 41, 9–20.

Ritchie, A. (1977) Excavation of Pictish and Viking-age farmsteads at Buckquoy, Orkney. *Proceedings of the Society of Antiquaries of Scotland* 108, 174–227

Ritchie, A. (1993) *Viking Scotland*. London, Batsford/Historic Scotland.

Ritchie, A. (1995) *Prehistoric Orkney*. London, Batsford.

Ritchie, W. (1966) The post-glacial rise in sea level and coastal changes in the Uists. *Transactions of the Institute of British Geographers* 39, 79–86.

Ritchie, W. (1979) Machair chronology and development in the Uists and adjacent islands. *Proceedings of the Royal Society of Edinburgh* B77, 107–22.

Ritchie, W. and Whittington, G. (1994) Non-synchronous aeolian sand movements in the Uists, the evidence of the intertidal organic and sand deposits at Cladach Mór, North Uist. *Scottish Geographical Magazine* 110, 40–6.

Roesdahl, E., Graham-Campbell, J., Connor, P. and Pearson K. (eds) (1981) *The Vikings in England and their Danish Homeland*. London, Anglo-Danish Viking Project.

Rogers, N. S. H. (1993) *Anglian and other finds from Fishergate*. York, The Archaeology of York 17/9, Council for British Archaeology.

Rogers, N. S. H., Batey, C. E., Holmes, N. M. McQ and Barrett, J. H. (2012) The Metal Finds and their Implications. In J. H. Barrett (ed.), 245–53.

Russell, N. (2011) Marine Radiocarbon Reservoir Effects (MRE) in Archaeology, Temporal and Spatial Changes through the Holocene within the UK Coastal Environment. Unpublished PhD Thesis, University of Glasgow.

Rygh, O. (1885) *Norske Oldsager*. Oslo, Cammermeyer.

Salem, M, Nasser, R. A., Zeidler, A., Elansary, H. O., Aref, I. M., Böhm, M., Ali, H. M. and Ahmed, A. I. (2015) Methylated Fatty Acids from Heartwood and Bark of Pinus sylvestris, Abies alba, Picea abies, and Larix decidua: Effect of Strong Acid Treatment, *BioResources* 10(4), 7715–24.

Searle, J. B., Jones, I. and Gunduz, I. *et al.* (2009) Of mice and (Viking?) men, phylogeography of British and Irish house mice. *Proceedings of the Royal Society* Series B 276, 201–7.

Schmidt, E. (1972) *Atlas of Animal Bones for Prehistorians, Archaeologists and Quaternary Geologists.* Amsterdam, Elsevier.

Schulting, R., Budd, C., Sheridan, A. and Griffiths D. (forthcoming) ^{14}C dating of human remains from Skara Brae. In D. V. Clarke (ed.) *Skara Brae*. Edinburgh, National Museums of Scotland.

Schweingruber, F. H. (1990) *Anatomy of European Woods.* Berne and Stuttgart, Paul Haupt Publishers.

Scott, E. M. (2003) The Third International Radiocarbon Intercomparison (TIRI) and the Fourth International Radiocarbon Intercomparison (FIRI) 1990–2002, results, analysis, and conclusions. *Radiocarbon*, 45, 135–408.

Scott, G. R. and Jolie, R. B. (2008) Tooth-tool use and yarn production in Norse Greenland. *Alaska Journal of Anthropology* 6, no. 1 and 2, 253–64.

Scott, W. and Palmer, R. (1987) *The Flowering Plants and Ferns of the Shetland Islands.* Lerwick, The Shetland Times.

Serjeantson, D. (1988) Archaeological and ethnographic evidence for seabird exploitation in Scotland. *Archaeozoologia* 2, 209–24.

Serjeantson, D. (2001) The great auk and the gannet, a prehistoric perspective on the extinction of the great auk. *International Journal of Osteoarchaeology* 11, 43–55.

Serjeantson, D. (2007) The bird bones. In J. Hunter *et al.* (eds), 279–85.

Sharman, P. M. (1999) The Steatite. In O. Owen and C. Lowe (eds), 168–78.

Sharples, N. (1998) *Scalloway, A Broch, Late Iron Age Settlement and Medieval Cemetery in Shetland.* Oxford, Oxbow Monograph 82, Oxbow Books.

Sharples, N. (2005) *Excavations at Mound 3, Bornais, South Uist,* Cardiff Studies in Archaeology. Oxford, Oxbow Books.

Shetelig, H. (1945) The Viking graves in Great Britain and Ireland. *Acta Archaeologica* 16, 1–55.

Shetelig, H. (1954) The Viking graves. In H. Shetelig (ed.), *Viking Antiquities in Great Britain and Ireland,* Part VI, 65–111. Oslo, Aschehoug.

Shetland Sheep Society (2018) http://www.shetland-sheep.org.uk/index.php (accessed 5/4/18).

Shillito, L.-M., Bull, I. D., Matthews, W., Almond, M. J., Williams, J. M. and Evershed, R. P. (2011) Biomolecular and micromorphological analysis of suspected faecal deposits at Neolithic Çatalhöyük, Turkey. *Journal of Archaeological Science,* 38(8), 1869–1877.

Simms, M. J. (2000) The sub-basaltic surface in northeast Ireland and its significance for interpreting the Tertiary history of the region. *Proceedings of the Geologists' Association* 111, 321–36.

Simpson, I. A. (1997) Relict properties of anthropogenic deep top soils as indicators of infield management in Marwick, West Mainland, Orkney. *Journal of Archaeological Science* 24, 365–80.

Simpson, I. A., Barrett, J. H. and Milek, K. B. (2005) Interpreting the Viking Age to Medieval period transition in Norse Orkney through cultural soil and sediment analyses. *Geoarchaeology* 20, 355–77.

Simpson, I. A., van Bergen, P. F., Perret, V., Elhmmali, M. M., Roberts, D. J. and Evershed, R. P. (1999) Lipid biomarkers of manuring practice in relict anthropologenic soils. *The Holocene* 9, 223–9.

Simpson, I. A., Bol, R., Bull, I. D., Evershed, R. P., Petzke, K.-J. and Dockrill, S. J. (1999) Interpreting early land management through compound specific stable isotope analyses of archaeological soils. *Rapid Communications in Mass Spectrometry* 13, 1315–9.

Simpson, I. A., Dockrill, S. J., Bull, I. D. and Evershed, R. P. (1998) Early anthropogenic soil formation at Tofts Ness, Sanday, Orkney. *Journal of Archaeological Science* 25, 729–46.

Small, A., Thomas, C. and Wilson, D. M. (1973) *St. Ninian's Isle and its Treasure.* Oxford, Oxford University Press.

Smirnova, L. (2005) *Comb-making in Medieval Novgorod (950–1450), An Industry in Transition.* Oxford, British Archaeological Reports, International Series 1369, Archaeopress.

Smith, A. N. (2007a) Copper Alloy Objects. In J. R. Hunter (ed.), 433–9.

Smith, A. N. (2007b) Worked bone. In J. R. Hunter (ed.), 459–514.

Smith, A. N. with Buttler, S. and Weber, B. (1999) Steatite, vessels, bakestones and other objects. In B. E. Crawford and B. Ballin Smith (eds), 129–43.

Smith, A. N. and Forster, A. K. (2007) Steatite. In J. R. Hunter (ed.), 412–32.

Smith, H. and Mulville, J. (2004) Resources Management in the Outer Hebrides, An assessment of the faunal and floral evidence from archaeological investigations. In R. A. Housley and G. Coles (eds), *Atlantic Connections and Adaptation, Economics, environments and subsistence in the North Atlantic,* Symposia for the Association of Environmental Archaeology 21. Oxford, Oxbow Books, 48–64.

Smith, H. (2005) Plants. In N. Sharples (ed.), 189.

Smith, R. (2004) The Antler Comb Making Debris from Bornais, South Uist. Unpublished report for Cardiff University.

Soils Survey of Scotland (1981) *1:50,000 Soil Maps of Orkney, Orkney Mainland.* Aberdeen, MacAulay Institute for Soil Research.

Solberg, B. (1985) Norwegian spear-heads from the Merovingian and Viking periods. Unpublished Dr. Philos. Thesis, University of Bergen.

Spencer, P. J. (1975) Habitat change in coastal sand-dune areas: the molluscan evidence. In J. G. Evans, S. Limbrey and H. Cleeve (eds), *The Effects of Man on the Landscape: the Highland Zone,* 96–103. London, Research Report 11, Council for British Archaeology.

Stolpe, H. and Arne, T. A. J. (1927) *La Nécropole de Vendel,* Kungl. Stockholm, Vitterhets Historie och Antikvitetsakademien Monografiserien 17.

Stuiver, M. and Reimer, P. J. (1986) A computer program for radiocarbon age calibration. *Radiocarbon,* 28 (1986), 1022–30.

Spearman, R. M. (1995) Industrial residue. In C. D. Morris *et al.* (eds), 132–4.

Spearman, R. M. (1997) The smithy and metalworking debris from Mills Mount. In S. Driscoll and P. Yeoman, *Excavations within Edinburgh Castle in 1988–91,* Society of Antiquaries of Scotland, Edinburgh, 164–8.

Stace, C. (1997) *New Flora of the British Isles.* Cambridge, Cambridge University Press, 2nd Edition.

Stapleton, C. P. and Bowman S. G. E. (2005) An examination of cramp from Barnhouse and Mouseland, Mainland, Orkney. In C. Richards (ed.), *Dwelling amongst the monuments. The Neolithic village at Barnhouse, Maeshowe passage grave and surrounding monuments at Stenness, Orkney.* Cambridge, McDonald Institute Monographs, 381–4.

Starley, D. (2000) Metalworking debris. In K. Buxton and C. Howard-Davis (eds), *Bremetenacum, Excavations at Roman Ribchester 1980, 1989–1990,* 337–47. Lancaster, Lancaster Imprints Ser No. 9.

Stead, I. M. and Rigby, V. (1986) *Baldock. The Excavation of a Roman and pre-Roman Settlement, 1968–72.* London, Britannia Monograph Series 7.

Steele, K. and Wright, D. (2013) *Naked Barley for Healthy and Sustainable Food,* Leaflet, Henfaes Research Centre, Bangor University. Bangor, Welsh Assembly Government and HGCA.

Stevenson, R. B. K. (1966) *Sylloge of Coins of the British Isles, 6: National Museum of Antiquities of Scotland, Edinburgh. Part I, Anglo-Saxon Coins.* Edinburgh, British Academy.

Stewart, W. B. (1914) Notes on a further excavation of ancient dwellings at Skara, in the parish of Sandwick, Orkney, made during August 1913. With notes on the remains found, by Hon Professor W. Boyd Dawkins. *Proceedings of the Society of Antiquaries of Scotland* 48, 352.

Stuiver, M. and Kra, R. S. (1986) Editorial comment. *Radiocarbon* 28, ii.

Stuiver, M. and Polach, H. A. (1977) Reporting of ^{14}C data. *Radiocarbon* 19, 355–63.

Stuiver, M. and Reimer, P. J. (1993) Extended ^{14}C data base and revised CALIB 3.0 ^{14}C calibration program. *Radiocarbon* 35, 215–30.

Stummann Hansen, S. (2013) Toftanes, A Viking Age Farmstead in the Faroe Islands, Archaeology, Environment and Economy. *Acta Archaeologica*, Volume 9 of Centre of World Archaeology series. Oxford, Wiley-Blackwell.

Suckling, G. (1980) Defects of enamel in sheep resulting from trauma during tooth development. *Journal of Dental Research* 59 (9), 1541–8.

Telldahl, Y. (2012) Skeletal changes in lower limb bones in domestic cattle from Eketorp ringfort on the Öland island in Sweden. *International Journal of Palaeopathology* 2, 208–16.

Tempel, W.-D. (1970) Die Kämme aus Haithabu (Ausgrabungen 1963–64). *Berichte über die Ausgrabungen in Haithabu* 4, 34–45, Neümunster, Wackholtz.

Tempel, W.-D. (1979) Die Kämme aus der frühgeschichtlichen Wurt Elisenhof, *Studien zur Küstenarchäologie Schleswig-Holsteins. Serie A, Elisenhof, Band 3.* Frankfurt, Lang.

Thomas, F. W. L (1852) Account of some of the Celtic antiquities of Orkney, including the Stones of Stenness, tumuli, Picts-houses, etc., with plans. *Archaeologia* 34, 88–136.

Thomas, R. and Johanssen, N. (2011) Articular depressions in domestic cattle phalanges and their archaeological relevance. *International Journal of Palaeopathology* 1, 43–54.

Thomson, W. P. L. (1983) *Kelp Making in Orkney*, Aspects of Orkney 1. Stromness, Orkney Press.

Thomson, W. P. L. (1987) *History of Orkney.* Edinburgh, Mercat Press.

Thomson, W. P. L. (1995a) Orkney farm names, a re-assessment of their chronology. In B. E. Crawford (ed.), *Scandinavian Settlement in Northern Britain*, 42–63. Leicester, Leicester University Press.

Thomson, W. P. L. (1995b) The landscape of medieval Birsay. In B. E. Crawford (ed.), *Northern Isles Connections, Studies Presented to Per Sveaas Andersen*, 47–75. Kirkwall, Orkney Press.

Thomson, W. P. L. (1996) *Lord Henry Sinclair's 1492 Rental of Orkney.* Kirkwall, The Orkney Press.

Thomson, W. P. L. (2001) *The New History of Orkney.* Edinburgh, Mercat Press.

Thomson, W. P. L. (2008) *Orkney, Land and People.* Kirkwall, The Orcadian.

Tucker, F. and Armit, I. (2009) Human Remains from the Iron Age Atlantic Scotland Dating Project, results obtained during 2009. *Discovery and Excavation in Scotland* 10, 214–6.

Turner, V. E., Bond J. M. and Larsen, A.-C. (2013) *Viking Unst.* Lerwick, Shetland Heritage Publications.

Van Doorn, N. L., Hollund, H. and Collins, M. J. (2011) A novel and non-destructive approach for ZooMS analysis, ammonium bicarbonate buffer extraction. *Archaeological and Anthropological Sciences* 3, 281–9.

Veen, M. van der (1989) Charred Grain Assemblages from Roman-Period Corn Driers in Britain. *Archaeological Journal* 146, 302–19.

Vince, A. (2005) Characterisation of La Londe Ware using Chemical Analysis (pdf available at Vince 2010).

Vince, A. (2006) 'Appendix E, Comments on the chemical analysis of medieval whitewares from Wood Quay. In C. McCutcheon (ed.), *Medieval Pottery from Wood Quay, Dublin, The 1974–6 Waterfront Excavations*, Series B 7, 156–62. Dublin, Royal Irish Academy.

Vince, A. (2010) *Medieval Pottery Research Group (2010) Alan Vince Archive* [data-set], York, Archaeology Data Service [distributor] Available online at: http://archaeologydataservice.ac.uk/archives/view/alanvince_eh_2010/ (accessed 5/5/16).

Vince, A. (2011) Characterising French whiteware imports in Britain and Ireland and Northwest Europe. In A. Bocquet-Liénard and B. Fajal (eds), À propo[t]s de l'usage, de la production et de la circulation des terres cuites dans l'Europe du Nord-Ouest autour des XIVe-XVIe siècles, 197–208. Caen, Tables rondes du CRAHAM 5.

Von den Driesch, A. (1976) *A Guide to the Measurement of Animal Bones from Archaeological Sites.* Cambridge MA, Peabody Museum Press.

Von den Driesch, A. and Boessneck, J. (1974) Kritishe Anmerkungen zur Widerristhöhenberechnung aus Längenmassen vor- und frühgeschichtlicher Tieknochen, *Säugetierkundliche Mitteilungen* 22, 325–48.

Von Holstein, I. C., Ashby, S. P., van Doorn, N. L., Sachs, S. M., Buckley, M., Meirai, M., Barnes, I., Brundle, A. and Collins, M. J. (2014) Searching for Scandinavians in pre-Viking Scotland, molecular fingerprinting of early medieval combs. *Journal of Archaeological Science* 41, 1–6.

Wainwright, F. T. (ed.) (1962) *The Northern Isles.* Edinburgh, Nelson.

Walton Rogers, P. (1997) *Textile Production at 16–22 Coppergate.* York, Archaeology of York 17/11, Council for British Archaeology.

Walton Rogers, P. (1999) Textile making equipment. In A. MacGregor *et al.* (eds), 1964–71.

Watt, G. (1820) Notice regarding the submarine remains of a grove of fir-trees in Orkney. *Proceedings of the Edinburgh Philosophical Society*, Article XVIII (3), 100–2.

Watt, W. G. T. (1888) Notice of the discovery of a stone cist with an Iron Age interment at Skaill Bay. *Proceedings of the Society of Antiquaries of. Scotland.* 22, 283–5.

Webster, G. (1953) A Saxon treasure hoard found at Chester. *Antiquaries Journal* 33, 22–32

Welander, R. D. E., Batey, C. and Cowie, T. G. (1987) A Viking burial from Kneep, Uig, Isle of Lewis. *Proceedings of the Society of Antiquaries of Scotland* 117, 149–74.

Wheeler, A. (1978) *Key to the Fishes of Northern Europe.* London, Frederick Warne.

Wheeler, A. and Jones, A. K. G. (1976) Fish remains. In A. Rogerson (ed.), 'Excavations on Fuller's Hill, Great Yarmouth', *East Anglian Archaeology* 2, 208–26.

Wheeler, A. and Jones, A. K. G. (1989) *Fishes.* Cambridge, Cambridge University Press.

Wiberg, T. (1987) Kammer. In E. Schia (ed.), *De Arkeologiske utgravninger i Gamlebyen, Oslo Bind 3, Vol 3*. Oslo, Alvheim and Eide.

Williams, G. (2013) The 'Northern hoards' revisited: hoards and silver economy in the northern Danelaw in the early tenth century. In A. Reynolds and L. Webster (eds), *Early Medieval Art and Archaeology in the Northern World: Studies in Honour of James Graham-Campbell*. Leiden/Boston, Brill, 459–86.

Wilson, B. (1978) Methods and results of bone analysis. In M. Parrington (ed.), *The excavation of an Iron Age settlement, Bronze age ring-ditches and Roman features at Ashville Trading Estate, Abingdon (Oxfordshire) 1974–76*. London, Oxford Archaeological Unit Report 1, Council for British Archaeology Research Report 28, 100–33.

Wilson, C. A., Davidson, D. and Cresser, M. (2008) Multi-element soil analysis, an assessment of its potential as an aid to archaeological interpretation. *Journal of Archaeological Science* 35, 412–24.

Wilson, D. (1851) *The Archæology and Prehistoric Annals of Scotland*. Edinburgh, Sutherland and Knox.

Wilson, D. M. (1973) The Brooches. In A. Small *et al.*, 81–105.

Wilson, D. M. (1974) *The Viking Age in the Isle of Man: The Archaeological Evidence*. Odense, Aarhus University Press..

Wilson, D. M. (2008) *The Vikings in the Isle of Man*. Aarhus, Aarhus University Press.

Wilson, D. M. and Klindt-Jensen, O. (1966) *Viking Art*. London, Allen and Unwin.

Wintle, A. G. and Murray, A. S. (2006) A review of quartz optically stimulated luminescence characteristics and their relevance in single-aliquot regeneration dating protocols. *Radiation Measurements* 41, 369–91.

Wooding, J. E. 2010. The Identification of Bovine Tuberculosis in Zooarchaeological Assemblages. Unpublished PhD Thesis, University of Bradford.

Yalden, D. (1999) *The History of British Mammals*. London, Poyser Ltd.

Young, T. (2005) Slag and related materials. In N. Sharples (ed.), 174–6.

Young, T. (2011) Some preliminary observations on hammerscale and its implications for understanding welding. *Historical Metallurgy* 45(1), 26–41.

Young, T. P. (2012) The slag. In N. Sharples (ed.), *A Late Iron Age farmstead in the Outer Hebrides Excavations at Mound 1, Bornais, South Uist*. Oxford, Oxbow Books, 289–95.

Zohary, D. and Hopf, M. (2000) *Domestication of Plants in the Old World*. Oxford, Oxford University Press, 3rd Edition.

Zori, D., Byock, J., Erlendsson, E., Martin, S., Wake, T. and Edwards, K. J. (2013) Feasting in Viking Age Iceland, sustaining a chiefly political economy in a marginal environment. *Antiquity* 87, 150–65.

Index

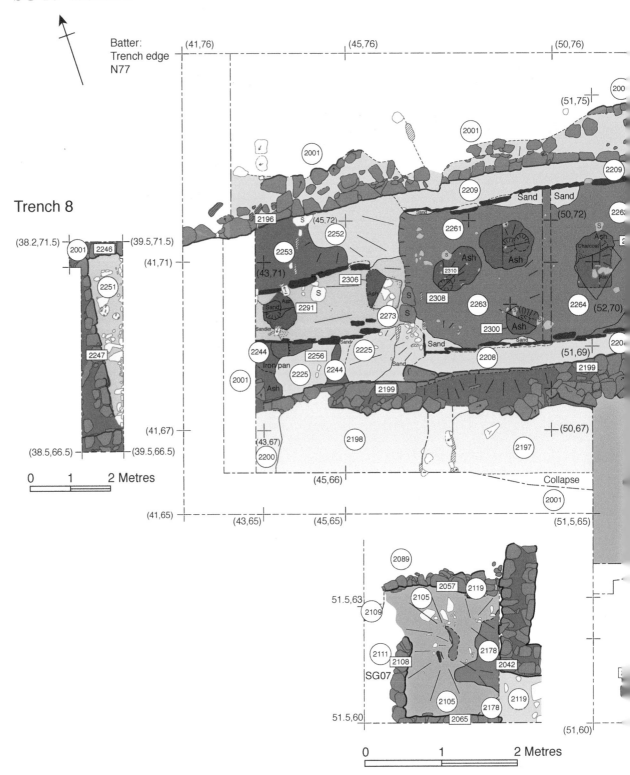

SG 10 Trench 5

Trenches 5 & 8, overall final plan in 2010 (colour code Fig. 4.43)